A Companion to
Arthurian Literature

Blackwell Companions to Literature and Culture

This series offers comprehensive, newly written surveys of key periods and movements and certain major authors, in English literary culture and history. Extensive volumes provide new perspectives and positions on contexts and on canonical and post canonical texts, orientating the beginning student in new fields of study and providing the experienced undergraduate and new graduate with current and new directions, as pioneered and developed by leading scholars in the field.

Published Recently

COMPANION TO

ARTHURIAN LITERATURE

EDITED BY

HELEN FULTON

WILEY-BLACKWELL

A John Wiley & Sons, Ltd., Publication

This paperback edition first published 2012
© 2012 Blackwell Publishing Ltd

Edition history: Blackwell Publishing Ltd (hardback, 2009)

Blackwell Publishing was acquired by John Wiley & Sons in February 2007. Blackwell's publishing program has been merged with Wiley's global Scientific, Technical, and Medical business to form Wiley-Blackwell.

Registered Office
John Wiley & Sons Ltd, The Atrium, Southern Gate, Chichester, West Sussex, PO19 8SQ, UK

Editorial Offices
350 Main Street, Malden, MA 02148-5020, USA
9600 Garsington Road, Oxford, OX4 2DQ, UK
The Atrium, Southern Gate, Chichester, West Sussex, PO19 8SQ, UK

For details of our global editorial offices, for customer services, and for information about how to apply for permission to reuse the copyright material in this book please see our website at www.wiley.com/wiley-blackwell.

The right of Helen Fulton to be identified as the author of the editorial material in this work has been asserted in accordance with the UK Copyright, Designs and Patents Act 1988.

Library of Congress Cataloging-in-Publication Data
A companion to Arthurian literature / edited by Helen Fulton.
    p. cm.—(Blackwell companions to literature and culture ; 58)
  Includes bibliographical references and index.
  ISBN 978-1-4051-5789-6 (cloth) 978-0-4706-7237-2 (pbk.)
1. Arthurian romances—History and criticism.   2. Arthur, King.   I. Fulton, Helen, 1952–
  PN685.C55 2009
  809′.93351—dc22

                              2008030353

A catalogue record for this book is available from the British Library.

Set in 11 on 13 pt Garamond 3 by Toppan Best-set Premedia Limited

1   2012

Contents

List of Illustrations

Notes on Contributors

Elizabeth Archibald is Reader in Medieval Studies at the University of Bristol. She is the co-editor, with A. S. G. Edwards, of *A Companion to Malory* (1996), and has published numerous essays on Arthurian literature; she is currently co-editing, with Ad Putter, *The Cambridge Companion to the Arthurian Legend* (forthcoming 2008). She is also the author of *Apollonius of Tyre* (1991) and *Incest and the Medieval Imagination* (2001).

Susan Aronstein is Professor of English at the University of Wyoming and the author of *Hollywood Knights: Arthurian Cinema and the Politics of Nostalgia* (2005). She has also published articles on medieval French and Welsh Arthurian romances, Arthurian film, and medievalism and popular culture. She and Robert Torry are currently co-writing a book on the films of Steven Spielberg.

Geraldine Barnes has a personal chair in medieval literature at the University of Sydney. Her main research interests are the ethos and development of romance in medieval England and Iceland, the reception of Old French chivalric narrative in Scandinavia, the Norse "discovery" of America as related in the "Vínland sagas," and medieval influences on early modern English travel writing. Her books include *Counsel and Strategy in Middle English Romance* (1993), *Viking America: The First Millennium* (2001), and the edited collection *Travel and Travellers from Bede to Dampier* (2005).

Inga Bryden is Reader in English and Head of Research in the Faculty of Arts at the University of Winchester, UK. She has published on nineteenth-century literature and culture, the Pre-Raphaelites, and the city in literature and visual culture. Her publications include the monograph *Reinventing King Arthur: The Arthurian Legends in Victorian Culture* (2005) and an article on revivalism and fashion in Victorian culture, in a special issue of the international journal *Arthuriana* (2011).

Lesley Coote, from the University of Hull, is the author of *Prophecy and Public Affairs in Later Medieval England* (2000) and has written (and co-written) several articles on this subject. She specializes in teaching literature through film, and runs courses on medieval outlaws, Arthurian and other medieval romance, Augustan satire, and the Hollywood western. Her recent article on Arthurian film for *Studies in Medievalism* was co-written with her late colleague Dr Brian Levy, for whose memorial volume she has produced an article on monstrosity and humor in *Richard Coeur de Lyon*. A committed educationalist and Fellow of the Higher Education Academy, she has produced a "student-friendly" edition of Chaucer's *Canterbury Tales* (2002) and has just completed two pedagogical projects on creative assessment in English Studies and on the use of electronic technology in learning and teaching English.

Roger Dalrymple is Principal Lecturer in Education at Buckinghamshire New University and publishes in both medieval English studies and education studies. He is author of *Language and Piety in Middle English Romance* (2000) and *Middle English: A Guide to Criticism* (2004) and co-editor of the monograph series, *Studies in Medieval Romance*.

Tony Davenport is Emeritus Professor of Medieval Literature in the University of London and Fellow of the English Association. His most recent book is *Medieval Narrative: An Introduction* (2004). He has published essays recently on the Welsh element in Middle English romances, on *Pearl*, and on dreams in Gower's *Confessio Amantis*.

Geraint Evans is a member of the Department of English Language and Literature at Swansea University. His research interests include the history of the book in Britain, literary modernism and the literatures of Wales in the twentieth century. He has published widely on early Welsh printing and on Welsh writing in English and is currently completing a book on David Jones.

Laurie A. Finke is Professor of Women's and Gender Studies at Kenyon College. She is author of *Feminist Theory, Women's Writing* (1992) and *Women's Writing in English: Medieval England* (1999), as well as editor of the *Norton Anthology of Theory and Criticism* (2001). Professor Finke is a long-standing collaborator with Martin B. Shichtman, and they are currently co-authoring *Cinematic Illuminations: The Middle Ages on Film*.

Jeanne Fox-Friedman is a Professor of Art History at New York University. She has published on both medieval and modern visual interpretations of the Arthurian legend. Her scholarly investigations include such diverse subjects as the Romanesque art of northern Italy, medieval women artists, and nineteenth-century children's book illustration.

Helen Fulton is Professor of Medieval Literature in the Centre for Medieval Studies at the University of York. Her main research areas are the interface between medieval Welsh and English literatures, multilingual manuscripts in Wales, political and prophetic poetry, and medieval representations of urban space. Recent books include edited collections, *Medieval Celtic Literature and Society* (2005) and *Urban Culture in Medieval Wales* (2011).

Joan Tasker Grimbert is Professor of French and former Chair of Modern Languages and Literatures at Catholic University (Washington, D.C.). Treasurer of the International Arthurian Society, she has published six books, primarily on Arthurian romance, including *"Yvain" dans le miroir: une Poétique de l'ambiguïté dans le "Chevalier au lion" de Chrétien de Troyes* (1988), *Tristan and Isolde: A Casebook* (1995; 2002), *A Companion to Chrétien de Troyes*, with Norris J. Lacy (2005), and *Chrétien de Troyes in Prose: The Burgundian "Erec" and "Cligés"*, with Carol J. Chase (2011).

Andrew Hadfield is Professor of English at the University of Sussex. He is the author of numerous works on English Renaissance literature, including *Shakespeare and Republicanism* (2005, paperback 2008), and *Literature, Travel and Colonial Writing in the English Renaissance, 1545–1625* (1998, paperback, 2007). He is the editor of the *Cambridge Companion to Spenser* (2001) and, with Abe Stoll, *The Faerie Queene, Book Six and The Mutabilitie Cantos* (2007).

Will Hasty is Professor of German Studies, Chair of the Department of Germanic and Slavic Studies, and Co-director of the Center for Medieval and Early Modern Studies at the University of Florida. He has published extensively on court literature of the twelfth and thirteenth centuries, with particular focus on Germany and the romances of Hartmann von Aue, Wolfram von Eschenbach, and Gottfried von Strassburg. His books include *Adventures in Interpretation: The Work of Hartman von Aue and their Critical Reception* (1995) and the edited collection *A Companion to Gottfried von Strassburg's Tristan* (2003).

Nickolas Haydock is professor of English at the University of Puerto Rico, Mayagüez. He has written two books, *Movie Medievalism: The Imaginary Middle Ages* (2008) and *Situational Poetics in Robert Henryson's "Testament of Cresseid"* (2011). He has also edited (with E. L. Risden) *Hollywood in the Holy Land: Essays on Film Depictions of the Crusades and Christian-Muslim Clashes* (2009). Current book projects include *The American Middle Ages: Vikings and Saracens in Literature and Film* for Boydell and Brewer and a co-authored book (with E. L. Risden) on *Beowulf* and Viking films.

Nicholas Higham is Professor Emeritus in the Department of History at the University of Manchester. His research interests center on the insular early Middle Ages in the areas primarily of history and archaeology, and the landscape history of medieval England, with a particular focus on the northwest. Recent monographs include *King Arthur: Myth-Making and History* (2002), *A Frontier Landscape: The North West in the Middle Ages* (2004), and *{Re}Reading Bede: The Ecclesiastical History in Context* (2006), and he is also a frequent contributor to a variety of academic and popular journals.

Karen Jankulak is Lecturer in Medieval History and Director of the MA in Arthurian Studies at the University of Wales Trinity Saint David. Her research interests are in the connections between Ireland, Wales, Cornwall, and Brittany, especially as shown in the cults of saints and the Arthurian legends. She has recently published the monograph *Geoffrey of Monmouth* in the Writers of Wales series for the University of Wales Press (2010).

Edward Donald Kennedy is Professor of English and Comparative Literature at the University of North Carolina at Chapel Hill. He is the author of *Chronicles and Other Historical Writing* (vol. 8 of *A Manual of the Writings in Middle English*, ed. A. E. Hartung [1989]) and editor of *King Arthur: A Casebook* (1996, 2002). He edited *Studies in Philology* for twelve years and has written over one hundred articles and reviews, primarily on Arthurian subjects. He is subject editor for English and Scottish chronicles for the *Encyclopedia of the Medieval Chronicle* (2010).

Roberta L. Krueger is Burgess Professor of French at Hamilton College. She is the author of *Women Readers and the Ideology of Gender in Old French Verse Romance* (1993) and editor of *The Cambridge Companion to Medieval Romance* (2000). She participated in the TEAM translation of the *Lancelot–Grail* Cycle (1992–6) and has written numerous articles on medieval French romance, as well as on late medieval conduct literature, including the *Ménagier de Paris*, the *Enseignements* of the Chevalier de la Tour Landry, and the didactic work of Christine de Pizan. Her current research examines the intersection of conduct literature and courtly narrative in medieval France.

Robert Paul Lamb received his doctorate in American Civilization from Harvard University and is professor of English at Purdue University. The co-editor of Blackwell's *A Companion to American Fiction, 1865–1914* (2005; paperback 2009), he has authored *James G. Birney and the Road to Abolitionism* (1994), *Art Matters: Hemingway, Craft, and the Creation of the Modern Short Story* (2010; paperback 2011), and *Reading the Hemingway Short Story: The Return and Value of Craft Criticism* (forthcoming), as well as several dozen journal articles. In 2008 he was named the Indiana Professor of the Year by the Carnegie Foundation for the Advancement of Teaching.

Alan Lane is Senior Lecturer in the School of History and Archaeology, Cardiff University. He is a specialist in the study of the settlements and artifacts of the post-Roman Celtic West and North. His excavations and publications include the early medieval settlement of Longbury Bank, the Brecon royal crannog site of Llangorse, and Dunadd, the royal capital of early Dál Riata.

Carolyne Larrington teaches medieval English at St John's College, Oxford. She has recently written *King Arthur's Enchantresses* (2006), about Morgan le Fay and other Arthurian enchantresses, and she is currently working on some Old Norse versions of Arthurian texts.

Ceridwen Lloyd-Morgan retired in 2006 as Head of Manuscripts and Visual Images in the National Library of Wales, Aberystwyth. She is Honorary Research Fellow in the School of Welsh, Cardiff University, and a Member of the Centre for Medieval Studies, Bangor University.

Alan Lupack is the author of *The Oxford Guide to Arthurian Literature and Legend* (2005) and co-author of *King Arthur in America* (1999). He has edited medieval and post-medieval Arthurian texts, serves as the Associate Editor of the TEAMS Middle English Texts series, and is creator and General Editor of the electronic database *The Camelot Project* at the University of Rochester.

Andrew Lynch teaches in English and Cultural Studies at the University of Western Australia. His publications include *Malory's Book of Arms* (1997) and articles on Malory. He also writes on the medieval tradition of war and peace, on modern medievalism, and on Australian literature. He is co-editor of *Parergon*.

Julia Marvin is Associate Professor in the Program of Liberal Studies, the Great Books program of the University of Notre Dame, and a fellow of Notre Dame's Medieval Institute. She studies medieval historical writing and literature and is editor and translator of *The Oldest Anglo-Norman Prose "Brut" Chronicle* (2006).

Lister M. Matheson is Professor of Medieval Studies in the Department of English at Michigan State University. His publications include *Popular and Practical Science of Medieval England* (gen. ed., 1994), *The Prose Brut: The Development of a Middle English Chronicle* (1998), and *Death and Dissent: Two Middle English Chronicles* (1999). He has been an Associate Editor of the *Middle English Dictionary* and has also authored many book chapters and articles on a wide variety of topics in Middle English language and literature, including historical writings and fifteenth-century manuscripts and dialects.

David Matthews is senior lecturer in Middle English literature and culture at the University of Manchester. He is the author of *Writing to the King: Nation, Kingship and Literature in England, 1250–1350* (2010) and co-editor of *Reading the Medieval in Early Modern England* (2007).

Joseph Falaky Nagy is a Professor in the Department of English at the University of California, Los Angeles. He has written books and articles on medieval Celtic literatures, including *The Wisdom of the Outlaw: The Boyhood Deeds of Finn in Gaelic Narrative Tradition* (1985) and *Conversing with Angels and Ancients: Literary Myths of Medieval Ireland* (1997).

Ad Putter is Professor of Medieval English Literature at the University of Bristol. He has published widely on Arthurian literature and the Middle English popular romances. He is co-editor (with Jane Gilbert) of *The Spirit of Medieval English Popular Romance* (2000). His latest book (with Judith Jefferson and Myra Stokes) is *Studies in the Metre of Alliterative Verse* (2007).

Raluca L. Radulescu is Lecturer in Medieval Literature and Director of the Centre for Medieval Studies at Bangor University, UK. She has published a monograph, *The Gentry Context for Malory's Morte Darthur* (2003), and several articles on Arthurian literature, and co-edited several collections of essays, one of them on Malory (2005). Her other publications, and current research, focus on historical writing and popular romance.

Jan Shaw is Lecturer in English Language and Early English Literature at the University of Sydney. Her research interests are primarily in feminist approaches to Middle English texts and their reconfigurations in contemporary fantasy. She also has a minor research interest in feminist approaches to the language of leadership. Her current research project considers religion in fantasy literature.

Martin B. Shichtman is Professor of English Language and Literature at Eastern Michigan University. He is co-editor of *Culture and the King: The Social Implications of the Arthurian Legend* (1994) and author of more than 20 articles on medieval literature, contemporary critical theory, and film. In a collaboration that has spanned twenty years, Professor Shichtman and Laurie A. Finke have written *King Arthur and the Myth of History* (2004) and co-edited a number of essay collections, including *Medieval Texts and Contemporary Readers* (1987).

Tom Shippey has now retired from the Walter J. Ong Chair of Humanities at Saint Louis University. His most recent works are *Roots and Branches: Selected Papers on Tolkien* (2007), and the edited collection *The Shadow-walkers: Jacob Grimm's Mythology of the Monstrous* (2005). Until recently he also edited the journal *Studies in Medievalism.*

Juliette Wood is Associate Lecturer in the School of Welsh, Cardiff University, and also a Director of the Folklore Society at the Warburg Institute, London. She specializes in medieval folklore and Celtic tradition and is interested in the modern revivals of magic and Celticism. In addition to television and radio work on folklore topics, she has just completed a book on the legends of the Holy Grail.

Jonathan M. Wooding is Reader in Church History in the School of Theology, Religious Studies and Islamic Studies at the University of Wales Trinity Saint David. His research interests range across the medieval histories of Britain, Ireland and Scandinavia. His publications include *Communication and Commerce along the Western Sealanes* (1996) and the edited volumes *The Otherworld Voyage in Early Irish Literature* (2000), *Ireland and Wales in the Middle Ages*, with Karen Jankulak (2007), and *Adomnán of Iona: Theologian, Lawmaker, Peacemaker* (2010).

Introduction: Theories and Debates

Helen Fulton

Since the name and shape of Arthur began to emerge in manuscripts of the twelfth century, the set of legends and characters associated with him, along with the persona of Arthur himself, have been in a constant state of reproduction, reinvention, and, to anticipate Laurie Finke and Martin Shichtman's concept in chapter 32, remediation.

If the essays in this volume teach us one thing, it is that there is no "original" Arthur and no originary or authentic Arthurian legend. There are, however, ideas – of leadership, kingship, empire, nation, social identity, religion, power – which, in order to be represented, require corporeal form and have, at various times and in different combinations, realized themselves through Arthurian characters. This volume, then, is not simply about Arthur or the characters associated with him. It is about representation and the processes of signification, the ways in which meaningful uses can be made of characters and legends embodying cultural beliefs and ideologies.

Drawing on the postmodern theory of Jean Baudrillard, it is possible to interpret Arthur as a simulacrum – that is, as a copy which has no original. The textual Arthurs that survive are reformatted copies of earlier ideas of Arthur, referring always to each other but never to an originary Arthur, since such a person cannot be identified or retrieved. The weight of this constant reinvention and copying causes lacunae in the legend, periods of time when the Arthurian legend falls out of fashion, when the baggage attached to the multiple Arthurs becomes too unwieldy for yet another reinterpretation. These are the moments when negative views of Arthur are inserted into the tradition, such as the Latin saints' lives mentioned by Nicholas Higham (chapter 2) or the satires and parodies popular in the eighteenth and nineteenth centuries, as discussed by Alan Lupack (chapter 23) and David Matthews (chapter 24).

From the variety of Arthurian representations discussed in this volume, amid the whirl of floating signifiers and unstable meanings it is possible to isolate some central issues and debates that provide moments of coherence and stability. From the vantage point of these platforms, we can see that Arthurian literature of all ages and in all forms is effectively a site of ideological struggle, a place where competing viewpoints engage in complex dialectics, interrogating contemporary concerns. However far in the past the literature is situated, it inevitably inscribes within itself the anxieties of the present. It is those moments of "the present in the past," explicitly identified by most of the authors in this volume, that help us to read Arthurian texts as coherent and meaningful documents.

The Question of Historicity

In a recent review for the *Times Higher Education Supplement*, Jonathan Powell wrote: "Scholarship, especially where the evidential base is limited, comes in two kinds: the constructive kind, which extrapolates the whole statue of Hercules from his foot, and the demolitionist kind, which asserts that all we really have is the foot and our own imagination" (January 4, 2008: 21). On the face of it, this seems an appropriate summation of the history of Arthurian scholarship, preoccupied as it has been with the big question of whether "Arthur" existed as a historical person. While some scholars, such as archaeologist Leslie Alcock, promoted a "constructivist" approach, reconstructing an authentic Arthur and his historical context from small amounts of surviving evidence, others, including David Dumville, have gone for the "demolitionist" approach, and in the first chapter of this volume Alan Lane charts the debate between these methodologies.

From a more theoretical perspective, however, the binary opposition of the two approaches collapses into a single act of imagination, which can be both constructive and iconoclastic. In the digital age, for example, film uses imagination not to demolish but to create a "real" – because fully realized – Arthur. This collapse of a binary opposition applies to the big question of Arthur's historicity as well, still a question to which people return, though – as many of the chapters in this volume assert or imply – it is a question unlikely ever to be answered definitively.

In part this is because it is the wrong question to ask. Was Arthur a historical person or not? This apparently simple binary elides a number of ideological issues now comprehensively interrogated by poststructuralist and postmodern theory. The first issue is to do with individual identity and the extent to which it is stable, distinctive, and retrievable. A "real" Arthur implies that all individuals possess an intrinsic authenticity, an absolute meaning, which pre-exists the social formation and can be retrieved in exactly the same form at any point in time. Yet identity itself is plural, unstable, and adaptive to different situations. If we find it hard to identify "the real me" from the plurality of our social selves, how can we identify "the real Arthur"?

The second issue is that of representation. What connection might there be between a living, breathing "historical" Arthur and the many textual representations of Arthur that still survive? In literature, history, and iconography – all the material covered in this volume, in fact – there are plural Arthurs, constructed in many different forms and identities. Even when a "real" Arthur has been detected in the historical or archaeological evidence (as a Romano-British chieftain, for example, as Tom Shippey describes in chapter 30), this version has no greater claim to authenticity or "reality" than any other of the textual versions.

This problem of multiple versions is connected with a third ideological viewpoint, which is the privileging of "history" over other forms of textual representation. The main reason why there has been a constant search for the "real" Arthur is because his name appears in some early documents, particularly the *Annales Cambriae*, which, despite recognized difficulties of authorship and date, are regarded as part of the historical record of early medieval Britain. The first two chapters in this volume, by Alan Lane and Nicholas Higham, deal admirably with the pitfalls and difficulties posed by this empirical evidence as a means of reconstructing a historical Arthur. The question has been whether the Arthur named in these chronicles refers to a "real" Arthur or to an already legendary figure from fiction. But this is the wrong question, because it sets up a false binary. What we should be assessing is the function of these chronicles as acts of imaginative reconstruction, something which Karen Jankulak and Jonathan Wooding attempt in chapter 5, in relation to the early historical context.

The big Arthurian question of historicity, then, is an example of "the present in the past": it reveals more about twentieth-century preoccupations with identity, empiricism, historicity, celebrity, and authenticity than it does about the figure of Arthur, a floating signifier, empty of meaning until attached to a particular context in a specific period of time. Many film versions of Arthur have attempted to authenticate him by locating him in an identified historical period, whether the Dark Ages or the Middle Ages, and Nickolas Haydock gives an astute analysis of this historicizing impulse in his chapter on the film *King Arthur* (chapter 35). It is only with the rise of fantasy texts, written and digital, that a postmodern Arthur begins to emerge, one whose historicity and "reality" are less important than the qualities and cultural beliefs attached to him. Jan Shaw's well-theorized chapter on the ideologies of Marion Zimmer Bradley's novel *The Mists of Avalon* (chapter 31) and Susan Aronstein's illuminating analysis of a number of Arthurian films in relation to contemporary political concerns (chapter 33) are exemplary studies of the post-historical Arthur.

Chronicle, Romance, Fantasy

Relatively unconcerned about questions of historicity, literary scholars have traditionally focused on the kinds of texts in which Arthur appears as a literary character. These can be grouped together under the generic headings of chronicle, romance, and fantasy, which can be regarded as types of discourse rather than as separate genres. Malory's *Morte Darthur* contains examples of all three discursive styles but is conventionally described as a "romance." I have suggested (in chapter 6) that the dominant mode of Welsh Arthurian material is fantasy, though the discourses of chronicle and romance are also found in Welsh.

The chronicle style claims for itself the empirical status of written history and therefore a high "truth value" compared to either romance or fantasy. A major reason for the long debate about Arthur's historicity is that his story first "went global," as it were, via the medium of Geoffrey of Monmouth's twelfth-century chronicle, *Historia Regum Britanniae*. Despite the misgivings about Geoffrey's truth value, voiced in his own time and again in the modern period (as described by Lister Matheson in chapter 4 and Alan Lupack in chapter 23), Arthur's placement in a purportedly historical chronicle endowed him with the status, however mythologized, of a historical figure, a populist reading that has outlasted all the scholarly attempts at "demolition."

Yet we should not underestimate the impact of Geoffrey's chronicle as the main conduit of Arthurian literature throughout the Middle Ages and beyond. I have argued in chapter 3 that the basic framework of the Arthurian legend was put into place by Geoffrey and transmitted through multiple versions of the text in a variety of translations. As a consequence of the rich transmission history of Geoffrey's *Historia*, writers as various as Chrétien de Troyes, Malory, and Shakespeare were influenced by the very different versions that were available in their own times. As Julia Marvin shows in chapter 15, the development of the *Brut* tradition based on Geoffrey's British history was central to the self-fashioning of English identity after the Norman conquest. We can add that this Galfridian version of English nationhood based on a British (rather than a Norman) past persisted right through the Renaissance and formed the bedrock of Shakespearean history and Tudor prestige. The political appeal of Galfridian chronicle is manifold: its authority is derived from the privileging of history as a form of documentary record, it foregrounds absolute kingship, and it invented a specifically British tradition of epic heroism located in its monarchy.

The historiographical tradition of Arthur begun by Geoffrey of Monmouth was equally salient for the Welsh, Cornish, and Scottish nations overshadowed by English rule. For the Welsh, Geoffrey's account of British history authoritatively established the sovereignty of the British (ancestors of the Welsh) before the coming of the Saxons, a right to rule over the whole Island of Britain, which was claimed by successive generations of Welsh poets right up until the triumph of Henry VII, the first Tudor king, in 1485. To the Welsh, then, it was particularly important that Arthur was a "real" king, one of a line of legitimate British kings displaced by the Saxons. Juliette Wood has shown (in chapter 7) that Cornwall and Scotland made their own claims to the "original" Arthur and that, intriguingly, Scottish chronicles interpreted Geoffrey's account of Arthur's rule in a negative light, criticizing Arthur's dubious birth and supporting Mordred as the legitimate ruler of Britain.

Largely thanks to Geoffrey of Monmouth, the British Arthurian tradition was essentially a chronicle tradition, based in history, however loosely defined, and concerned with the politics of kingship and the building of nationhood. The more familiar Arthurian world of Lancelot and Guinevere, tournaments, knightly adventure, and the Grail quest was the world imagined by French writers, inspired in part by the work of Geoffrey but also by tales told by singers and storytellers who amalgamated themes from Britain, Brittany, and France. In a rich and wide-ranging account of the

Tristan romance (chapter 10), Joan Tasker Grimbert traces the dissemination of the "matter of Britain" – Arthurian tales, many of Breton origin – throughout France, Italy, and Spain, showing how the assimilation of history and fantasy worked to create a far-reaching tradition of popular romance in Europe, one which fed back into medieval English literature in productive and powerful ways.

In the creation of Arthurian romance, the twelfth-century French poet Chrétien de Troyes plays as significant a role as Geoffrey of Monmouth did in the formation of the chronicle tradition. Elizabeth Archibald suggests (chapter 21) that the love affair between Lancelot and Guinevere, unknown in the chronicle tradition, was invented by Chrétien, whose narrative poem *Le Chevalier de la Charrette* ("The Knight of the Cart") records Lancelot's first appearance in literature. Similarly, as Edward Donald Kennedy has shown in his detailed and scholarly piece on the Grail story (chapter 14), the first Grail quest was composed by Chrétien, with later additions by Robert de Boron, which became part of the great French Vulgate Cycle in prose, source of much of Malory's *Morte Darthur*. Roberta L. Krueger's lucid chapter on Chrétien (chapter 11), tracing some of his sources and outlining his innovations, clearly sets out the extent of Chrétien's contribution to modern notions of Arthurian romance. His impact on medieval writers was just as significant, with imitations and analogues of his work found in Wales, in the so-called "Welsh romances" discussed by Ceridwen Lloyd-Morgan in chapter 9; in Germany, where, as Will Hasty argues in chapter 12, Arthurian romance had a particular political significance; and in Scandinavia, whose appropriation of Arthurian romance has been the subject of modern scholarly debate, as outlined by Geraldine Barnes in chapter 13. Ireland, which had its own Arthurian tradition cognate with that of Wales though extending much further into the Middle Ages and beyond, is notable for its relative lack of interest in the French Arthurian tradition; as Joseph Falaky Nagy tells us in chapter 8, the earliest Arthurian romance translated into Irish dates from the fifteenth century and is likely to have had an English source.

The French tradition of Arthurian romance is responsible, virtually single-handedly, for the popularity of Arthurian themes in medieval English literature. Yet the English Arthurian texts are not slavish copies of Chrétien or of the Vulgate Cycle but rather local interpretations of popular texts which circulated in oral versions as well as (or instead of) written versions. The English language was emerging as a literary language only in the fourteenth century, and many of the French Arthurian texts would have been enjoyed in French by noble families living in England. But a growing audience for courtly texts in English also resulted in new Arthurian works such as the Alliterative *Morte Arthure*, part of the *Brut* tradition, and the Stanzaic *Morte Arthur*, based on the Vulgate *Mort Artu*, elegaic works about the death of Arthur which seemed to voice English concerns about the decline of kingship at the end of the fourteenth century.

At the same time, popular versions of Arthurian romance were circulating in English as part of an oral tradition of English-language culture, alongside more courtly inventions addressed to local nobilities and wealthy urban merchants. As Ad

Putter describes in chapter 16, the English romance of *Sir Percyvell of Gales* is clearly related to Chrétien's *Conte du Graal* but based on a memory of it rather than a written text. *Sir Launfal* is one of a number of texts in English based on the French *lais* by Marie de France, which had a wide circulation in France and England. The cycle of stories associated with Tristan and Isolde, found widely dispersed throughout Europe in written texts, oral variants, and artistic representations (the latter described by Jeanne Fox-Friedman in chapter 26), also had a representative in Middle English, *Sir Tristrem*. Tony Davenport points out in chapter 19 that the English version, a simplified retelling of a French original, has its own particular angle, which is to make the story into the kind of hero-tale familiar to English audiences. Most English romances, with their origins in Anglo-Norman and French narratives, are characterized by an emphasis on the courtly hero who performs deeds of arms and makes conquests in love, heroes such as Bevis of Hamtoun, Havelok, and Guy of Warwick. In this framework, the English Tristrem, like Sir Launfal and Sir Percyvell, is portrayed as less of a lover and more of a knightly hero.

This emphasis on the individual hero overcoming obstacles to win a noble reputation is particularly demonstrated in the set of English Gawain romances that formed a considerable part of the corpus of Arthurian works in Middle English. Roger Dalrymple lists some of these poems in chapter 18 and identifies a variety of ways in which Gawain is depicted, from warrior knight to flawed hero to paragon of courtly virtue. It is in this latter role that he is the subject of one of the most famous texts in Middle English, the fourteenth-century romance *Sir Gawain and the Green Knight*. Apart from its accomplished language and style, making it a clearly literary composition, designed to be read aloud rather than recited or sung from memory, *Sir Gawain* is distinguished by its originality. Carolyne Larrington observes in her finely drawn analysis of the poem (chapter 17) that there is no known source and the anonymous author has combined traditional Arthurian motifs with new themes to create a unique text.

The Arthurian romance tradition, then, in both French and English, shares some basic objectives with the romance genre in total, which celebrates the ideals of knighthood rather than kingship, the value of knights in peace as well as in war, and the contribution of the nobility to the maintenance of the Christian empire during and after the Crusades. Though the romances often describe the love between knight and noblewoman, secular love is consistently subordinated to spiritual commitment. In Arthurian romance, knights and king have specific identities that can be used to further the ideological goals of the genre. The Arthurian knights set for themselves the highest standards of religious virtue, and judge each other according to these ideals. Arthur himself, as the product of an all-too-secular liaison, is placed in the background as a symbol of kingship which is implicitly inadequate for the power it enjoys, needing the support of the knights to achieve any kind of success or redemption.

A feature of romance as a type of discourse is the prominence of magic and supernatural motifs, which are used to make implicit moral judgments on the behavior of specific characters. This is the element of "fantasy" which characterizes Arthurian literature from its earliest beginnings in Welsh legend, when the Arthur of *Culhwch ac Olwen* ("Culhwch and Olwen") is served by warriors who can speak the languages of animals or turn themselves into birds or make themselves invisible. In the French tradition of Arthurian romance, the fantasy element is either minimized, as in the secular poems of Chrétien de Troyes, which aim for something approaching realism, or directed toward a specifically Christian and mystical agenda, as in the Vulgate *Queste del Saint Graal*, where monks and hermits interpret supernatural events. The "magic naturalism" of the early Welsh texts (which I have described briefly in chapter 6), replicated in much of the Vulgate Cycle, where events simply unfold without obvious authorial mediation, is balanced by the "magic realism" of clearly authored texts such as those of Chrétien, where the narrative voice has greater power to determine the action than any supernatural force.

The return of fantasy in modern fiction and film, through the modes of both realism and magic realism, has reinvigorated the Arthurian legend. T. H. White's *The Once and Future King*, the harbinger of the new fashion for Arthurian fantasy, shows what the naturalistic violence — almost a "cartoon" violence — of the medieval Arthurian legend looks like when viewed from a realist perspective as actual violence. As Andrew Hadfield argues (chapter 28), it is not a pretty sight, reinforcing White's pacifist agenda and his pessimism about the power of the state and state-sanctioned violence during and after World War II. In a chapter on Marion Zimmer Bradley's *The Mists of Avalon* (chapter 31), Jan Shaw connects the mode of fantasy with a feminist politics which needs to find a space beyond the real world in order to represent female agency. Contemporary Arthurian films that make use of special effects to achieve both realistic and supernatural events, such as Eric Rohmer's *Perceval le Gallois* (discussed by Lesley Coote in chapter 34), blur the boundaries between the two, making anything seem possible and therefore reinstalling a medieval viewpoint. At the same time, fantasy in modern fiction and film is often an expression of nostalgia for an imagined past when science had not yet destroyed the endless possibilities of mythic belief.

The medieval discourses of chronicle, romance, and fantasy unite most evidently, as I have suggested, in Malory's *Morte Darthur*. Andrew Lynch points out (chapter 20) that Malory drew attention to the historicity of his account of Arthur's life and achievements, constantly stressing his reliance on authorized sources, whether chronicle or romance. In Elizabeth Archibald's discussion of Malory (chapter 21), she suggests that the love affair between Lancelot and Guinevere, a staple element of the French Arthurian tradition but less prominent in English literature before Malory, provides an important means of illustrating aspects of Lancelot's nobility and prowess. The fantasy element is most pronounced in Malory's account of the Grail quest, where, as Raluca Radulescu argues (chapter 22), Malory uses Lancelot as the penitent sinner who acts as witness to supernatural and mystical events. We can perhaps infer from the explicitly Christian nature of these events in the Grail quest that other supernatural events throughout the whole *Morte* have a similarly Christian origin and significance, unless otherwise attributed.

The Politics of Arthur in the Modern World

In the transition from the medieval to the modern era, the Arthurian legend became a site of competing ideologies which charted the development of modern attitudes toward what was perceived as medieval. The immediate post-medieval period, the sixteenth and seventeenth centuries, rejected medieval literature as part of a worldview that was seen as superstitious, unscientific, and, in the wake of the Reformation, altogether too Catholic in its religious beliefs. As Alan Lupack shows (in chapter 23), the historicity of Arthur was endorsed as part of royal politics in the sixteenth century. While the Tudor kings relied on Geoffrey of Monmouth's account of British history to authenticate their claims to the throne, and Henry VII named his first son Arthur, the medieval tradition of Arthurian romance undermined Arthur's historical presence in the royal genealogy. The high culture of courtly and noble society and the increasingly liberated urban culture of the growing towns and cities competed to appropriate Arthur as a symbol of their particular values. Dismissed as old-fashioned, Arthurian romance was reimagined through the courtly discourses of heroic epic (as in Spenser's *Faerie Queene*) and court masque, while taking on a growing presence in popular culture. Throughout the seventeenth and eighteenth centuries, Arthurian characters and themes became increasingly embedded in urban culture, through popular drama and romance, ballads and almanacs, satires and parodies.

The restoration of Arthur as a politically significant symbol coincided with the rise of empire in the eighteenth and nineteenth centuries. National history based on unbroken lines of power and a ruling class legitimized by common values were foundational aspects of empire, and both could be reinforced by analogy with the Arthurian world. David Matthews emphasizes, in chapter 24, the importance of the reappearance of Malory's *Morte Darthur* in two new editions of 1816 after nearly two centuries out of print. Not only did Malory's work provide a locus for political and imperial concerns, but it stimulated an antiquarian interest in other medieval texts. A peculiarly nineteenth-century version of medievalism, derived largely from Malory and other English romances and slanted toward the Romantic values of anti-industrialism, Celticity, and the natural world, was used to support ideals of a new chivalry practiced by the same aristocratic class that ran the empire. Tennyson was the chief poet of the new chivalry, as the Pre-Raphaelites were its artists. Inga Bryden comments (in chapter 25) on the link between Arthurian romance, British history, and nostalgia for a coherent and fully realized past which could be used to explain the present, in particular the perceived cultural and racial superiority of Englishness which lay at the heart of imperialism.

The imperial Arthur survived into the twentieth century, as Tom Shippey recounts in chapter 30, with a return to the argument – more in hope than belief – that Arthur had been a "real" historical character. But the tension at the heart of the Malorian version of Arthur, the glory of the Round Table and its terrible destruction, was taken seriously by early-twentieth-century writers who tried to reconcile, as Shippey argues, an imperialism which harked back to Geoffrey of Monmouth and the reality of the "fall of empire" manifested all too clearly in World Wars I and II. T. H. White's series of novels, published under the single title *The Once and Future King*, is perhaps the most overtly political work of the post-imperial Arthurian tradition, with references to fascism, the Irish Republican Army, and the dangers of nationalism. As Andrew Hadfield points out (chapter 28), White uses the Arthurian world to exemplify high ideals that ultimately fail to counteract the abuse of power and what he sees as an innate human drive towards violence. More indirect but just as politically charged are the modernist Arthurian texts by Welsh writers described by Geraint Evans in chapter 29. In a genuinely post-imperial and post-colonial movement, these texts reclaim Arthur for the Welsh as a symbol of autonomy and sovereignty, refashioning him as a key element in Welsh, rather than English, national identity.

The theme of national and cultural identities is particularly pronounced in American versions of Arthurian material, in both novel and film. Key ideas are those of heroism in a barbaric society (the opening up of the American West), the uses of the past to explain the present (the collision between old and new worlds), and the quest for the Grail (the "American dream"). Robert Paul Lamb, in his illuminating chapter on Mark Twain (chapter 27), contextualizes Twain's vision of the Arthurian past in a late-nineteenth-century American present when myths of white cultural supremacy and an unproblematic model of (white) masculinity were stretched to breaking point. Like imperial Britain in the nineteenth century, America looked back to the medieval past as a glowing reminder of the values that now seemed to be under threat from capitalism, industrialization, and a cultural heterogeneity represented by colonialism in Britain and by immigration in America.

More recently, in the twentieth century, film adaptations of the Arthurian legends have used aspects of "round table" medievalism to explore contemporary concerns and concepts of utopia. Drawing on earlier studies of "cinema Arthuriana," Susan Aronstein outlines (in chapter 33) a taxonomy of different kinds of American Arthurian film, locating them in particular cultural contexts, including the Depression, Cold War nervousness, and the "war on terror." Both Aronstein and Lamb emphasize the importance of American myths about its place in the world – particularly its self-belief as a nation destined to lead – as a fertile ground for the reception and appropriation of Arthurian legends. While America's technological superiority and staunch democratic principles enable the "Connecticut Yankee" (appearing in a range of guises from Twain's hero through to SpongeBob SquarePants) to outsmart medieval feudalism, fears of a social chaos never far beneath the surface of national greatness are articulated through Arthurian chronicles of heroic rescue, decline and renewal, and the defeat of forces of darkness by the positive power of community and nationhood. In the mythic context of America as a democratic utopia, the Grail is referenced as a symbol of a pluralistic and unifying faith in eternal unchanging values.

Remediations of Arthur

Returning to Finke and Shichtman's application of the concept of remediation, it is clear from their chapter (chapter 32) that with the digital age we are seeing new possibilities for multimodal versions of the Arthurian legends, in audiovisual and written texts, in theatre and musicals, in merchandizing and accessories. Finke and Shichtman argue that the media themselves shape the texts in particular ways — form determines content — with key ideas and characters translated into the discourses of new media. They use the example of the Round Table, a logical impossibility in T. H. White's *Once and Future King*, which becomes a cumbersome stage prop in the stage musical *Camelot* only to be realized as a vast symbolic presence in Joshua Logan's film of *Camelot*, built to fit Hollywood conventions and the new technology of Cinemascope. Here is a perfect example of hyperreality: a table too large to fit into any space smaller than a Hollywood soundstage is convincingly passed off as the "real" Round Table, dwarfing its knights and speaking more about technology than about chivalric values.

In a sense this whole volume is about remediation, the translation of Arthurian legends from one medium into another with each version shaped by the discourses, technologies, and ideologies of its own context, and by those of earlier forms. This returns me to the point where I began: just as there is no "original" Arthur, so there is no original legend. The legends of Arthur and Merlin which were appropriate to the Welsh tradition — concerned with the loss of British sovereignty under the Saxons — were remediated by Geoffrey of Monmouth into the prestige discourses of chronicle and national history, claiming a truth value that was more a product of those discourses than of empirical fact. In the Middle Ages, Breton and French storytellers had their own myths of nobility through which to interpret the matter of Britain, while the hegemonic discourses of imperialism, in both Britain and America, appropriated and reconfigured the Arthurian legends throughout the modern age.

Now, in the digital age, computer graphics are translating narrative into special effects, creating hyperreal Arthurian knights whose digitally enhanced capabilities turn myths of superhuman powers into realities. Yet the development of the Arthurian legend is not always linear; it is sometimes circular, returning to pre-existing templates remediated through new technologies. In the hyperreality of digital performance, we can trace a return to the magic naturalism of medieval myth, a postmodern refusal of authorial mediation, which leaves the Arthur of the *King Arthur* computer game staring back empty-eyed toward the equally unknowable Arthur of *Culhwch ac Olwen*.

A NOTE ON SPELLING AND TRANSLATIONS

In the course of editing this book, I have necessarily had to negotiate many different spellings of the principal Arthurian characters, particularly Lancelot, Guinevere,

Merlin, Tristan and Isolde. Rather than impose a single spelling throughout, I have tried to follow the forms used by different texts and authors as they are cited. This means that the spelling of names is not consistent throughout the book, and is often not consistent within a chapter, as authors range over a number of different texts, each using a different spelling. Readers can be assured that all spellings used in this book are attested in one text or another.

All texts in languages other than English have been translated. Unless otherwise specified, all translations are the authors' own.

Part I
The Arthur of History

1
The End of Roman Britain and the Coming of the Saxons: An Archaeological Context for Arthur?

Alan Lane

The last time an archaeologist seriously engaged with the matter of Arthur was in 1971 with the publication of Leslie Alcock's book *Arthur's Britain*. Subtitled *History and Archaeology AD 367–634*, this was a rigorous academic attempt to put the historical evidence for Arthur alongside the archaeology for the period in which he might have existed. It was written in the context of the late Professor Alcock's excavations between 1966 and 1973 at Cadbury Castle, Somerset, where he had investigated the major Iron Age hill fort identified by Leland as the alleged site of Camelot (Alcock 1972). Alcock's work was a detailed account of the archaeology, framed by a critical discussion of the early historical evidence for the period and the few sparse "early" references to Arthur. Aimed at both students and an interested public, it ranged over both Anglo-Saxon and Celtic evidence throughout the British Isles.

Arthur's Britain offered an analysis of the supposed Arthurian evidence but was perhaps unfortunate in coinciding with an upsurge in Arthurian iconoclasm whereby most historians decided Arthur was either a myth or at best unknowable. Alcock concluded that one reference – that to Arthur in the *Annales Cambriae* ("Welsh Annals") for 537, "The battle of Camlann, in which Arthur and Medraut fell" – was "the irreducible minimum of historical fact" and that this assured us "that Arthur was an authentic person" (Alcock 1971: 88). However, in 1977 David Dumville published a trenchant review paper in the journal *History*, which rejected the claim that any of the references to Arthur, including those in the Welsh annals, were contemporary and concluded: "This is not the stuff of which history can be made. The fact of the matter is that there is no historical evidence about Arthur; we must reject him from our histories and, above all, from the titles of our books" (1977: 188).

This view that there is no reliable historical evidence for Arthur is one held by all serious historians of the period. Thus in 1991 Thomas Charles-Edwards' discussion of the ninth-century *Historia Brittonum* concluded that: "At this stage of the enquiry, one can only say there may well have been an historical Arthur," but "the historian can as yet say nothing of value about him" (1991: 29). The skepticism of historians about Arthur was matched by a general rejection of the fifth- and sixth-century historical sources for Britain as a whole. Previous credibility given to Bede and the *Anglo-Saxon Chronicle* has now been replaced by a conclusion that little historical material pre-600 can be relied upon, and Dumville's view that a "historical horizon" of credibility begins sometime in the mid- to late sixth century for some Irish, English, and British sources seems to be widely accepted (1977: 189–92; Yorke 1993; see also chapter 2, this volume).

But if historians cannot agree on evidence for a historical Arthur, what can archaeology say? Since Dumville's 1977 paper, no serious archaeologist has tried to combine archaeology and Arthur. There is of course an archaeology of Arthurian folklore and fakes – the numerous Arthur's Stones (often megalithic tombs, such as Arthur's Stone on the Gower peninsula in south Wales); other Arthurian place names in the landscape (Higham 2002: figs 16 and 18); and fakes ranging from the twelfth-century "discovery" of Arthur's body at Glastonbury (Barber 1972: 59–65) to the more recent claims often expressed on the internet and in popular books (Higham 2002: 34–5) as well as in otherwise reputable daily newspapers (see for example the *Sunday Telegraph* newspaper of October 16, 1994). Indeed, Oliver Padel has argued that the earliest references to Arthur in the ninth century indicate that he was already a mythical figure attached to dramatic features of the landscape and that, by analogy with the Fionn cycle in Ireland, no historical Arthur ever existed (1994).

However, if we wanted to portray an archaeological context for a notional Arthur, where and when would that be? Barber has pointed to four genuine historical figures called Arthur who appear in reliable sources. These are all associated with Irish/Scottish colonies and show that the name was current in Dál Riata and Dyfed in the later sixth and seventh centuries. Barber suggests that Arthur, son of Áedán mac Gabráin, the late-sixth-century king of Dál Riata who was killed fighting the Picts in the 590s, may be the original historical figure to whom subsequent legends were attached (1972: 29–38). However, the attachment of Arthur's name to the battle of Badon and the battle list in the *Historia Brittonum*, together with his prominence in later British/Welsh sources, has led to him being regarded as a British hero associated with the native resistance to the Germanic conquest of southern and eastern Britain which gave rise to the creation of the Anglo-Saxon kingdoms of England.

As to date, Arthur's absence from British genealogies and reliable historical sources before the ninth or tenth centuries means that most attempts to place him historically have to push him back to the later fifth or earlier sixth century. After about 550 the historical silence about Arthur becomes more damning. In 500 British political units would probably still have ruled much of Britain from the Forth–Clyde line in Scotland south to the English Channel, though the extent of Anglo-Saxon territorial control is not historically documented at this period. Consequently the archaeological context for a notional British Arthur might be thought to be the post-Roman British kingdoms of the fifth and sixth centuries between Edinburgh in the north and Cornwall in the southwest. This chapter, then, will look at some current debates on the fifth- and sixth-century history and archaeology of the British kingdoms.

Gildas and the History of Britain in the Fifth and Sixth Centuries

Opinions about the nature of fifth-century and early sixth-century Britain have varied since Alcock wrote in 1971. In 400 Britain was still part of the Roman Empire, which, though politically divided between a western emperor in Ravenna and an eastern emperor in Constantinople, still stretched from Hadrian's Wall in the north to an eastern frontier in modern Turkey and Syria. By 476, with the deposition of the last western emperor, successor Germanic barbarian kingdoms were increasingly coming to dominate the whole of the Western Empire (Cameron et al. 2000). The fate of the British provinces is not well documented after 400. If the late-sixth-century Byzantine historian Zosimus is to be believed, the British rebelled against Roman rule and laws, but the exigencies of the sources are such that no secure narrative of fifth-century Britain is possible.

Historians are much more wary now of using either Bede's *Historia Ecclesiastica* (eighth century) or the *Anglo-Saxon Chronicle* to date the *adventus Saxonum* (Sims-Williams 1983). However, in contrast to Alcock's view, it is now recognized that Gildas's *De excidio Britanniae* ("Concerning the ruin of Britain," hereafter abbreviated to *DEB*) is the only real source for much of fifth-century and early sixth-century British history. Whereas Alcock was rather scathing about Gildas, revisionist views now place him firmly as the key source from which the entire traditional account of the English conquest derives (Dumville 1977; Lapidge & Dumville 1984). The difficulty with Gildas is of course the absence of names and dates which would allow us to calibrate his narrative against continental sources. As is well known, after the death of Magnus Maximus in 388 Gildas probably names only one independently dated person – Agitius (Aetius), who was consul for the third time in 446–52. However, attempts to date the fifth-century sequence of events in *DEB* are less convincing and the contradiction between Gildas's sequence and that in Bede has led to several distinct versions of fifth-century history being posited by modern scholars (Sims-Williams 1983; Higham 1994).

Gildas is conventionally dated to the early sixth century, with *DEB* written in the mid-sixth century. Higham has tried to push him back into the fifth century (1994: 118–45) and although this has not been met with general assent, scholars such as Wood seem to allow an early date (1984: 23). Gildas describes a long series of disasters for the Britons after 388: attacks and threats of attack from Pictish and Irish raiders, the rise of kings and civil wars, the invitation of Saxon mercenaries to fight the Picts and Irish, the rebellion of the Saxon federates and the wholesale destruction that ensues. Following all this, an apparently long process of warfare ensues until a British resistance led by Ambrosius Aurelianus has some success (Sims-Williams 1983). The battle of Badon is cited by Gildas as a major British victory, although one which leaves much of the former Roman provinces of Britain in Germanic hands. One difficulty in interpreting Gildas is that the areas where he describes, and denounces, surviving British kingdoms and the "tyrants" who rule them seem limited to the extreme south and west of Britain. This has led Higham to posit Germanic control either directly or as overlords over most of lowland England by the mid- or late fifth century (1994: 190–93).

The Archaeology of Britain in the Fifth and Sixth Centuries

The degree of survival of Roman material culture and the nature of fifth-century British material culture are still contested issues. On the basis of archaeological evidence, it is undeniable that the most obvious features of Roman archaeology – mass coinage, mass-produced pottery and other goods, villas, walled towns, masonry buildings, mosaics, hypocausts, sculpture – had ceased to be significant features of Britain in the sixth century. Our problem of course is the poverty of evidence for the continuation of Romano-British material culture after the late fourth century. Unlike some parts of the Western Empire, the evidence for the continuation of Roman technology in Britain is poor (Esmonde Cleary 1989). Opinion on the speed of change in Britain – how quickly Roman technology and lifestyle was lost, and why – has therefore been a long-term matter of debate, with two central positions emerging. On the one hand, some scholars have seen the disappearance of Roman culture from Britain as swift, catastrophic, and violent (Faulkner 2000). Gildas is one of the sources of this interpretation. On the other hand, an argument has been made for substantial continuities in material culture well into the fifth, sixth, and seventh centuries, ironically, perhaps, also using Gildas as evidence (Dark 1994, 2000).

This difference of opinion is of course linked to theories about the date, scale, and speed of Germanic takeover and the thorny issue of British survival in lowland England. In recent years this debate has focused on what is sometimes called the "late antiquity" paradigm. This is an influential historical view which emphasizes the cultural continuities in Europe from the third to the eighth centuries – the period of "late antiquity" – and downplays both the significance of the "fall" of the Western Empire and the warfare and displacement that may have accompanied it (Ward-Perkins 2005). Until recently, this paradigm had relatively little influence in Britain since it was difficult to see pagan Anglo-Saxon England having much late-antique flavor, while the Celtic west was visualized as comprising heroic, rather than "barbarian," societies (Alcock 1971). However, in recent years the concept of a late-antique culture of continuity has been applied to the Celtic west of Britain, in particular in the work of Ken Dark (2000: 15).

The interest in the concept of late antiquity, with its implication of continuity and relative stability, has cross-fertilized with other theoretical ideas current in British academia, in particular the rejection of invasion and migration as significant forces for change in the historical and archaeological record. The rejection of the "invasion hypothesis," which dominated older British archaeological interpretations, can be seen particularly in prehistoric studies from the 1960s onwards. Initially, invasions or settlements by Anglo-Saxons, Vikings, and perhaps Irish immigrants were accepted as significant, alongside a dominant pattern of endogenous change, since these could be supported by historical sources, and, at least in the Anglo-Saxon case, by substantial archaeological evidence of burials and settlements (Clark 1966). However, historical skepticism about the reliability of early sources, coupled with a desire by archaeologists to write "history-free" interpretations, led to the downgrading of even these few remaining invasions (Harke 1998). Continuity and population survival became *de rigueur* and the impression was given that violence or population displacement were not convincing explanations of cultural change and could be rejected except perhaps for small-scale elite replacement.

The hitching of the Celtic west to the "late antique" bandwagon may, however, be a step too far, especially at a time when its general applicability to the Western Empire, at least in its more extreme pacifist manifestations, is being questioned. Ward-Perkins' recent book on *The Fall of Rome* (2005) makes a strong case for understanding how dramatic and painful the collapse of the Western Empire was for many who experienced it. Likewise Peter Heather's *Fall of the Roman Empire* cites evidence for the destructiveness of barbarian armies and the massive decline in productivity caused by warfare (2005). The completeness of the disappearance of Roman material culture in Britain should not be underestimated. It is arguable that by 500, and probably a lot earlier, there were no towns, villas, coinage, wheel-made pottery, or other mass-produced goods. Virtually all the physical manifestations of Roman material culture had gone (Esmonde Cleary 1989; Wickham 2005: 306–12). No one built a mortared masonry structure, tiled a roof, threw a pot on a fast wheel, or fired a pottery kiln from sometime in the fifth century until the seventh century.

Views about the speed of material collapse in Britain and its explanation vary. Some Romanists see decline having set in substantially in the fourth century and the break from the Western Empire in 406–10 merely finishes off a weakened elite superstructure. Esmonde Cleary suggested that decline on Roman sites could be traced through the later fourth century and that collapse followed within a few decades in the fifth (1989). A similar pattern is traced by Faulkner, who argues that the Roman state was parasitic, and that speedy collapse was inherent in its internal social contradictions. He argues vehemently against the "late antique" paradigm and suggests that "overall the Romanised settlement pattern and associated material culture had collapsed to almost nothing by the late fourth and early fifth century" (2004: 10). In his view, "all the archaeological indicators of *Romanitas* reached zero or close to zero in the fifth century. This is true of settlements, structures and artefacts" (2002: 74); and he went on to reiterate his position that there was a "clear material culture gap separating the final collapse of Romanised settlements and assemblages in c. AD 375/425, and the emergence of distinctive Early Dark Age ones from c. AD 450/75 onwards" (2004: 10).

The alternative view regarding late antiquity was put by Dark: "Rather than being the area of the former Roman West in which Late Roman culture was most entirely swept away in the fifth century, ... quite the opposite would seem to be true. It ... was the only part of the West in which the descendants of Roman citizens lived under their own rule, with their own Romano-Christian culture and in recognisably late-Roman political units, into the sixth century" (Dark 2000: 230). At its most extreme, claims Dark, the argument could be made that Roman Britain's last province did not fall until the thirteenth century when Edward I finally conquered north Wales (Dark 1994: 256).

One does not need to take Faulkner's "Life of Brian" view of what the Romans ever did for us to accept that there is little convincing evidence of Roman culture surviving in Britain to be taken over by the Anglo-Saxons in the middle and later decades of the fifth century. Though attempts have been made to demonstrate town and villa life in the fifth century, the new Anglo-Saxon society dominating lowland England seems to be markedly different and technologically quite apart. In spite of various claims no one has yet shown Roman technology and forms continuing beyond the fifth century.

The problem of Faulkner's view of speedy total collapse, and Dark's alternative of a substantial late-antique survival, is how to date and interpret late fourth- and early fifth-century deposits. Faulkner's dating of decline is dependent on coin and pottery dates. If late fourth-century coins and pottery continue in use unchanged then his theory of speedy collapse must be extended into the fifth century. Various attempts have been made in the past to show continuation of Roman material culture well into the fifth century (Frere 1987). Hines has argued that though a few Anglo-Saxon items turn up on the latest deposits of Roman sites, by and large the English set up new sites and new types of site even if some agrarian continuity is likely (1990). The apparent absence of widespread landscape change has been a key argument for the continuity theorists. While there can be no doubt that many Late Roman sites were abandoned, and some areas show evidence of much less intense agriculture and some forest regeneration, much of the landscape continued to be exploited in one way or another. Most scholars, however, would agree that there is a substantial population decline between the fourth century and the seventh or eighth century, though this apparent reduction in settlement density must be partly attributed to the loss of visibility of the material culture.

We thus have two alternative views: speedy collapse of Roman material culture in Britain, and perhaps population collapse; alternatively, many Roman sites may have continued in use with archaic Roman finds. There remains the possibility of Roman culture surviving in British territories outside the areas of early Anglo-Saxon settlement, which will be discussed below, but the problem of recognizing and identifying the British and their culture in the fifth century is a real one. For some areas we have virtually no evidence of settlement sites and buildings and for much of the fifth century the picture of the "Dark Ages" is truly dark.

Germanic Settlement

The date of Germanic settlement, its scale, and its social and political impact are likewise contested. Some linguists have argued that the apparent massive dominance of English place names and the absence of significant linguistic borrowing from Brittonic require large-scale migration by Germanic populations (Gelling 1993). Although some Celtic names and words are recognizable in England and English names denoting British speakers exist, their numbers are still small. English appears to have totally dominated the landscape as far west as the Welsh and Cornish borders before the late pre-Norman period. Historians and archaeologists such as Higham (1992: 189–208) and Hodges (1989: 65–7) have argued that this linguistic supremacy can be explained by an "elite dominance" model and thus is compatible with minimal English settlement in Britain. However, other Anglo-Saxon specialists argue for a substantial Germanic migration without subscribing to oversimplistic arguments about language and numbers (Harke 2003), while some linguists have restated the case for large numbers and/or widespread violence with some vigor (e.g. Padel 2007).

Some aspects of this debate on the scale of Germanic immigration are due to new evidence and reconsideration of old evidence, but academic fashions and modern social trends play their role too. When Alcock wrote in 1971, a number of scholars were arguing for a significant Germanic settlement in Britain pre-400 when it was still under Roman control. The evidence for this was primarily provided by J. N. L. Myres' suggested dating of pagan Anglo-Saxon funerary urns to the fourth century or even earlier (1986). Coupled with the evidence of belt buckles and the idea that the fourth-century term "Saxon Shore" (describing late third-century fortifications on both sides of the English Channel) might indicate an area of Saxon settlement, a theory of peaceful Germanic settlement in Britain was advanced which would then allow for gradual acculturation of the native population. The evidence for this theory was strongly challenged by Anglo-Saxon specialists in the 1980s though it took some time to penetrate through to more popular books (Hills 1979). Current opinion suggests that securely dated Anglo-Saxon graves begin in the period around 420–40, with most evidence coming after 450 (Hines 1990). A few brooches may be of earlier date, bracketed 380–420 on continental dating, but there are no secure deposition contexts before 420. The absence of stratified Germanic material occurring together with Late Roman finds tends to imply that Roman material culture had largely collapsed before significant Anglo-Saxon settlement had taken place. That is not to say that there may not have been people of Germanic origin in Britain before 400, but the current archaeological evidence suggests that, with rare exceptions, they were not signaling a separate identity any more than the numerous other groups who had been included within the empire.

So if we were to take c. 450 to 550 as the rough period in which we would wish to position Arthur, what can we say about the nature of that society? Anglo-Saxon graves are found through much of midland and eastern Britain (Hines 2003: map 5). Although some of these cemeteries are near Roman towns there is little to suggest that the towns are still functioning. The nature of the population of Anglo-Saxon England is obviously a consideration. The likelihood that the Anglo-Saxon kingdoms were populated in large part by descendants of the Romano-British is still vigorously debated, though it is extremely difficult to demonstrate from evidence as opposed to *a priori* assumptions (Harke 2003; Hills 2003: 57–71). If we exclude from our remit those areas of Anglo-Saxon settlement defined by graves, we still have a substantial part of Britain that can be regarded as British in the fifth and sixth centuries. For our purposes, the distribution of "Anglo-Saxon" burial sites is probably the best guide to the nature of the population, though the gaps within the distribution may conceal surviving British populations (Dark 2000). However, the speed of Germanic takeover of the British provinces is difficult to evaluate from the sparse historical sources, and Anglo-Saxon political control may be much wider and earlier than core zones of Germanic burial (Higham 2002: 68–9, fig. 7).

Towns

The fate of Roman towns has been central to discussions of continuity and the nature of post-Roman society. Debates about the possible continuation of Roman towns have oscillated over the past fifty years, with opinion mainly shifting between speedy abandonment, gradual decay, and continuing low-level urban activity until Anglo-Saxon takeover in the seventh century. Biddle put an influential case for continuing "central place" functions at a number of sites, with Winchester claimed as demonstrating British/English continuity (1976: 103–12). Wacher's concept of limited non-urban occupation of former Roman towns, that is, "life in towns" rather than an economically salient "town life," has had some support (1995: 408–21). However, subsequent analysis of the evidence has led to the general view that towns did not survive the Roman withdrawal, and the beginnings of proto-urban use in England is now generally dated to the seventh century (Palliser 2000).

A key site for the discussion of urban life in the British west is the Roman town of Wroxeter (in the modern county of Shropshire), the *civitas* capital of the British tribe of the Cornovii in the West Midlands. Since the 1960s, Wroxeter has been cited as a classic excavation demonstrating major building activity post-400 in a Roman town and indeed the continuing existence of urban life well into the sixth or even seventh century (White & Barker 1998: 118–36). Perhaps inevitably, one popular book on Arthur claims he was king of Wroxeter (Phillips & Keatman 1992: 160–161). In many ways this site is central to the late antiquity model and to arguments for the continuation of *Romanitas* in western Britain (Dark 2000). White and Barker's claim was that significant building activity continued in the town as late as the seventh century with several phases of building after 400, including a massive two-story structure in a Romanized style (Dark 2000: fig 26). This was not, he argued, an isolated building but part of continued use of the town generally.

The difficulty with White and Barker's proposal is that there is virtually no material culture at Wroxeter to associate with this fifth-, sixth-, and early seventh-century urbanism unless of course fourth-century artifacts were still in use in successive centuries. Most students have accepted the Wroxeter model and indeed considerable effort has been expended trying to replicate it elsewhere, with only occasional public skepticism being voiced (e.g. Gelling 1992: 23; Ward-Perkins 1996: 9–10). However, the recent publication by Fulford of an important review of the Baths Basilica excavations in Wroxeter casts doubt on the evidence of major building activity as an indication of continuous town use. Instead, he puts a serious case that the rubble spreads attributed to large post-Roman timber-framed buildings are evidence of Late Saxon stone-robbing for church building (2002: 643–5). Fulford does suggest that the evidence of less elaborate buildings may be genuine and comparable to the late structures he postulates at Silchester (in the modern county of Hampshire, near Reading). Some post-Roman activity at Wroxeter is demonstrated by the Cunorix stone, whose Latin inscription seems to indicate a high-ranking Irish figure on the site in the fifth or sixth century (Sims-Williams 2002: 25–6), and the finding of a stray bronze coin of Valentinian III (c. 430–35) has recently been confirmed (Abdy & Williams 2006: 31). However, the absence of the kind of British finds which occur at sites such as Cadbury Congresbury, in Somerset, or New Pieces, Powys, a small site only sixteen miles west of Wroxeter; and the absence of Anglo-Saxon imports, which occur on other British sites of late fifth- and sixth-century date, would seem to rule out significant activity at Wroxeter (Campbell 2000: table 1).

The Celtic West

There are, however, some parts of the "Celtic west" where we can with confidence claim later fifth- and sixth-century activity because examples of imported Mediterranean ceramics have been identified at a number of sites. This material has been studied in increasing detail since the 1930s when it was first recognized in England and Ireland but it is only in the past few decades that its chronology has been firmly established (Campbell 1996; 2007).

Late fifth century color-coated fine wares from the Aegean and North Africa, Phocaean Red Slip ware and African Red Slip ware (PRS and ARS respectively, both formerly referred to as A ware), can be quite closely dated in the Mediterranean. These can be used to date the arrival in Britain of amphorae (B ware), which are in themselves less closely datable. If correctly dated, these three types of pottery seem to have reached Britain in a fairly narrow time zone from c. 475 to 525 (Campbell 2007: 26). Following this or perhaps overlapping with it, small quantities of gray color-coated pottery, *sigille paleochretienne grise* (D ware), arrived from western France, probably dating to the mid-sixth century. Subsequently we find E ware, again from western

France, not closely dated in its presumed continental source area but seemingly of late sixth- to late seventh-century date, in Britain and Ireland (Campbell 2007: 46). Substantial quantities of imported glass, again largely of western French origin, seem to occur in the same period, perhaps mid-sixth to late-seventh century (Campbell 2000; 2007). Campbell has suggested that two distinct phases of importation are recognizable, allowing us two clear chronological horizons of 475–550 and 550–650, with only a few imports of pottery or glass recognizable after the end of the seventh century (2007: 125–39).

The Mediterranean imports identify sites that were in use around AD 500. These lie most densely in a zone centered on Cornwall, west Devon, Somerset, and south Wales, with occasional outliers in north Wales, Ireland, and southern Scotland. Such imports seem to be absent from the English west and north. With some exceptions they allow us to identify enclosed and defended sites that are likely to be those belonging to the kind of British military aristocracy glimpsed in Gildas's denunciations. The key sites are still those reported by Alcock in 1971 and here I only have space to mention briefly the most important in the southern core zone.

Tintagel

Tintagel, a dramatic cliff-girt coastal promontory sited on the north Cornish coast, has figured in Arthurian discussion since Geoffrey of Monmouth located Arthur's conception there. It has also been central to debates about the post-Roman imported pottery since the 1930s. Initially interpreted as a monastery and virtually viewed as the beachhead for desert monasticism in the Celtic west, it was convincingly reinterpreted as a defended secular site in the 1970s (Burrow 1973). It is now generally regarded as the primary royal site of the kings of Dumnonia (whose name survives in the modern Devon). Its importance and remembered symbolism may be indicated by the presence of a medieval castle of the mid-thirteenth century built on top of it as well as a possible footprint inauguration carving. Defended by a deep rock-cut ditch and bank as well as its natural defenses, it is a naturally impressive site. By far the largest quantities of Mediterranean imports in Britain have been found here in spite of quite limited excavation. There is no doubt, then, that this was an important site in the fifth and sixth centuries, but the precise nature of its function and use is the subject of continuing debate: suggestions include an *entrepot* for Mediterranean merchants, a Byzantine diplomatic outpost, a defended royal citadel, an occasional summer residence, or even a town (Dark 2000: 153–6).

Tintagel has no E ware and seems to have lost its importance by the time these western French imports reach the area, though radiocarbon dates may show some continued use. Stone foundations for more than one hundred buildings were traced on the summit area and slope terraces after a grass fire removed surface cover, but we do not know how many were in occupation at any one time (Harry & Morris 1997: fig. 2). Some of the more obvious rectangular structures are thought to be medieval and belong to the thirteenth-century castle phase. Nevertheless, recent excavations on one of the terraces have confirmed the presence of irregular square and sub-rectangular stone footings, possibly for turf-walled structures (Harry & Morris 1997: 121–5). Very little of the site has seen modern excavation but the suggestion that it had substantial numbers of rather temporary-looking structures seems to have widespread agreement. Dark, however, envisages more substantial structures and an internal organization that he compares to a Roman "small town" (2000: 156). There is no doubt that Tintagel is an important site though the limited modern excavation inhibits secure interpretation. That it is the major royal site of the Dumnonian kings seems probable though we cannot currently identify any other high-status structures or artifacts to associate with the richness of its ceramic material.

Cadbury Castle

Cadbury Castle (variously South Cadbury or Cadbury Camelot), dug by Leslie Alcock in the 1960s, is a major multi-walled Iron Age hill fort, occupied in the late fifth century and early sixth century. The apparent re-defense of the entire eight-hectare enclosure makes it the biggest of the definite post-Roman hill forts. The use of timber-laced stonework is comparable to sites found in north Britain though Alcock was inclined to see some Roman military experience in the apparent gateway tower.

Unfortunately the finds and structural evidence for the site are limited as the interior had been heavily plowed, removing the stratigraphy and presenting a 3,000-year palimpsest of pits, postholes, gullies, and other structural features for interpretation. From these postholes Alcock suggested a large rectangular summit hall dated by the presence of PRS, ARS, and amphorae. There is no doubt about the presence of a structure and the associated pottery concentration, but doubt must persist about the precise form of the building. Round houses also occur on the site but could be of Iron Age date. There is no way of knowing how much of the site was in use or the likely population involved. The site has no evidence of E ware and it is thought to have been abandoned in the sixth century, perhaps due to Anglo-Saxon encroachment (Alcock 1995). Although the Arthurian association of the site cannot be shown to be earlier than the fifteenth century, this was clearly an important site c. 500, though given the small scale of excavation and poor preservation little more can currently be said.

Dinas Powys

The location of the bulk of Mediterranean finds on both sides of the "Severn Sea" suggests links across the Bristol Channel and Severn estuary between Wales, Somerset, and Dumnonia. The short distance and intervisibility of the Welsh and Somerset coasts allow the possibility of significant political linkages – the sea facilitates as well as separates pre-modern contact – and it is generally thought that Tintagel may have had primacy in the distribution of the wine and oil that the imported amphorae are thought to have contained.

As in Dumnonia, the putative high-status sites in Wales are hill forts. Dinas Powys, a small inland promontory site near Cardiff in south Wales, remains the richest and best-explored site in Wales nearly fifty years after it was excavated (Alcock 1963). Alcock's proposed chronological sequence, which envisaged the triple multi-vallation (outer defensive walling) as belonging to the Norman period, has been disputed by Campbell and Dark, and it seems clear that the whole defensive sequence should be placed in the fifth to seventh centuries (Edwards & Lane 1988: 58–61; Campbell 2007: 96–7, figs 67 and 68). This means that the initial rather weak single rampart enclosure was replaced in the sixth or seventh century by massive triple ramparts. The enclosure is quite small – roughly 0.2 hectares – but the input of labor and the seriousness of the defenses cannot be doubted. The large assemblage of pottery, glass, metalwork, metalworking debris, bonework, and stone implements gives us some idea of what might be expected on a reasonably rich site with good preservation. The evidence of fine metalworking in copper alloy, silver, and gold is particularly important. The animal-bone assemblages suggest that food was supplied from neighboring settlements. The house structural evidence is poor and Campbell rejects Alcock's hypothetical stone buildings, arguing instead for timber structures within the outlines of the drip gullies. The presence of E ware takes us into the seventh century, by which time Tintagel may have lost its trading dominance and all the Somerset sites, save Carhampton on the north coast, have been cut off from the later sixth- to seventh-century trading network.

Western and Northern England

Few advances have been made in identifying British sites beyond the core import zone described above, though various sites have been postulated without secure artifactual sequences. The ceramic imports are strangely missing in the western English zone north from Somerset as far as the modern Scottish border, as if there were a political boundary on the Severn blocking the Mediterranean trade. Early to mid-fifth-century activity in York – described as "grandee feasting" in a declining post-imperial twilight (Roskams 1996) – or possible evidence of activity on Hadrian's Wall could both provide a context for our Arthurian search but it is only in southern Scotland that we again meet the Mediterranean dating and accompanying finds which allow secure dating of c. 500, as at the Strathclyde royal citadel of Dumbarton (Alcock & Alcock 1990).

Conclusion

The archaeological interpretation of fifth-century Britain remains highly contentious. Only limited areas of the British west have well-dated sites and finds, as we have demonstrated at Cadbury, Tintagel, and Dinas Powys, and some areas of England have virtually no evidence until securely dated Anglo-Saxon material appears much later. Most of the western British sites have been known since the early 1970s. New discoveries do occur, particularly of the later E ware phase of importation in Ireland and Scotland, but it is striking how few new discoveries of the earlier imports have been made. This may be partly because they are largely confined to enclosed and defended sites, which are less likely to be excavated by rescue archaeology (mandatory excavations preceding planned building development).

The distribution of the Mediterranean imports remains firmly rooted in Dumnonia and Wales and shows no sign of occurring in the Roman towns of central and western England. Whether this means these sites were genuinely abandoned, as Gildas says, or some other economic/social/ethnic explanation should be preferred remains to be seen. But the imports do allow us to identify some fifth- and sixth-century sites and assemblages.

What social context does this give us for a hypothetical British "Arthur"? Faulkner posits a period of fifth-century anarchy or revolution followed c. 500 by the rise of exploitative chieftains or self-styled kings (Gildas's "tyrants") in their hill forts (2004). Alternatively, Dark envisages a gradually declining *Romanitas* in a successful late-antique Romano-Christian West (2000: 227–30). Unfortunately, much of the evidence remains vague and open to very different interpretations.

We can say, then, that the archaeological picture presented by Leslie Alcock in 1971 has been modified but the account of Dumnonia/Wales/Somerset remains stubbornly close to how it is presented in *Arthur's Britain*. No modern scholar would seek to place Camelot at Cadbury rather than in the pages of Chrétien de Troyes. Nor would anyone claim we can show that a historical figure called Arthur had any association with the fifth- and sixth-century hill fort sites of the British west. Only with the unlikely discovery of new historical sources proving that King Arthur was located in a specific place and time could archaeology tell us anything about him. Until that happens archaeologists will follow Dumville and keep him from their reconstructions – if not their chapter titles.

References and Further Reading

Abdy, R. & Williams, G. (2006). A catalogue of hoards and single finds from the British Isles, c AD 410–675. In B. Cook & G. Williams (eds), *Coinage and history in the North Sea world, c. AD 500–1200: Essays in honour of Marion Archibald*. Leiden: Brill, pp. 11–73.

Alcock, L. (1963). *Dinas Powys*. Cardiff: University of Wales Press.

Alcock, L. (1971). *Arthur's Britain: History and archaeology AD 367–634*. London: Allen Lane.

Alcock, L. (1972). *"By South Cadbury is that Camelot . . .": The excavation of Cadbury Castle 1966–1970*. London: Thames & Hudson.

Alcock, L. (1995). *Cadbury Castle, Somerset: The early medieval archaeology*. Cardiff: University of Wales Press.

Alcock, L. & Alcock, E. A. (1990). Reconnaissance excavations on Early Historic fortifications and other royal sites in Scotland, 1974–84: 4, Excavations at Alt Clut, Clyde Rock, Strathclyde, 1974–75. *Proceedings of the Society of Antiquaries of Scotland*, 120, 95–149.

Barber, R. (1972). *The figure of Arthur*. London: Longman.

Biddle, M. (1976). Towns. In D. M. Wilson (ed.), *The archaeology of Anglo-Saxon England*. London: Methuen, pp. 99–150.

Burrow, I. (1973). Tintagel: Some problems. *Scottish Archaeological Forum*, 5, 99–103.

Cameron, A., Ward-Perkins, B., & Whitby, M. (eds) (2000). *The Cambridge ancient history*, vol. 14: *Late antiquity: Empire and successors, AD 425–600*. Cambridge: Cambridge University Press.

Campbell, E. (1996). The archaeological evidence for external contacts: Imports, trade, and economy in Celtic Britain AD 400–800. In K. Dark (ed.), *External contacts and the economy of Late Roman and post-Roman Britain*. Woodbridge: Boydell & Brewer, pp. 83–96.

Campbell, E. (2000). A review of glass vessels in western Britain and Ireland AD 400–800. In J. Price (ed.), *Glass in Britain and Ireland, AD 350–1100*. London: British Museum, pp. 33–46.

Campbell, E. (2007). *Continental and Mediterranean imports to Atlantic Britain and Ireland, AD 400–800*. York: CBA Research Report 157.

Charles-Edwards, T. M. (1991). The Arthur of history. In R. Bromwich, A. O. H. Jarman, & B. F. Roberts (eds), *The Arthur of the Welsh*. Cardiff: University of Wales Press, pp. 15–32.

Clark, G. (1966). The invasion hypothesis in British archaeology. *Antiquity*, 40, 172–89.

Dark, K. R. (1994). *Civitas to kingdom: British political continuity, 300–800*. Leicester: Leicester University Press.

Dark, K. R. (2000). *Britain and the end of the Roman Empire*. Stroud: Tempus.

Dumville, D. N. (1977). Sub-Roman Britain: History and legend. *History*, 62, 173–92.

Edwards, N. & Lane, A. (eds) (1988). *Early medieval settlements in Wales*. Bangor: Research Centre Wales, University College of North Wales; Cardiff: Department of Archaeology, University College Cardiff.

Esmonde Cleary, A. S. (1989). *The ending of Roman Britain*. London: B. T. Batsford.

Faulkner, N. (2000). *The decline and fall of Roman Britain*. Stroud: Tempus.

Faulkner, N. (2002). The debate about the end: A review of evidence and methods. *Archaeological Journal*, 159, 59–76.

Faulkner, N. (2004). The case for the Dark Ages. In R. Collins & J. Gerrard (eds), *Debating late antiquity in Britain AD 300–700*. Oxford: British Archaeological Reports, pp. 5–12.

Frere, S. S. (1987). *Britannia: A history of Roman Britain*, 3rd edn. London: Routledge & Kegan Paul.

Fulford, M. (2002). Wroxeter: Legionary fortress, baths, and the "great rebuilding" of c. AD 450–550. *Journal of Roman Archaeology*, 15(2), 639–45.

Gelling, M. (1992). *The West Midlands in the Early Middle Ages*. Leicester: Leicester University Press.

Gelling, M. (1993). Why aren't we speaking Welsh? *Anglo-Saxon Studies*, 6, 51–6.

Harke, H. (1998). Archaeologists and migrations: A problem of attitude. *Current Anthropology*, 39, 19–45.

Harke, H. (2003). Population replacement or acculturation? An archaeological perspective on population and migration in post-Roman Britain. In H. Tristram (ed.), *The Celtic Englishes III*. Heidelberg: Universitätsverlag C. Winter, pp. 13–28.

Harry, R. & Morris, C. (1997). Excavations in the lower terrace, site C, Tintagel Island, 1990–94. *Antiquaries Journal*, 77, 1–143.

Heather, P. (2005). *The fall of the Roman Empire*. London: Macmillan.

Higham, N. J. (1992). *Rome, Britain and the Anglo-Saxons*. London: Seaby.

Higham, N. J. (1994). *The English conquest: Gildas and Britain in the fifth century*. Manchester: Manchester University Press.

Higham, N. J. (2002). *King Arthur: Myth-making and history*. London: Routledge.

Hills, C. (1979). The archaeology of Anglo-Saxon England in the pagan period: A review. *Anglo-Saxon England*, 8, 297–329.

Hills, C. (2003). *Origins of the English*. London: Duckworth.

Hines, J. (1990). Philology, archaeology and the *Adventus Saxonum vel Anglorum*. In A. Bammesberger & A. Wollman (eds), *Britain 400–600: Language and history*. Heidelberg: Universitätsverlag C. Winter, pp. 17–36.

Hines, J. (2003). Society, community, identity. In T. Charles-Edwards (ed.), *After Rome: The short Oxford history of the British Isles*. Oxford: Oxford University Press, pp. 61–103.

Hodges, R. (1989). *The Anglo-Saxon achievement: Archaeology and the beginnings of English society.* London: Duckworth.

Lapidge, M. & Dumville, D. N. (eds) (1984). *Gildas: New approaches.* Woodbridge: Boydell.

Myres, J. N. L. (1986). *The English settlements.* Oxford: Clarendon Press.

Padel, O. J. (1994). The nature of Arthur. *Cambrian Medieval Celtic Studies,* 27, 1–31.

Padel, O. J. (2007). Place-names and the Saxon conquest of Devon and Cornwall. In N. Higham (ed.), *Britons in Anglo-Saxon England.* Woodbridge: Boydell, pp. 215–30.

Palliser, D. M. (2000). The origins of British towns. In D. M. Palliser (ed.), *The Cambridge urban history of Britain,* vol. 1: *600–1540.* Cambridge: Cambridge University Press, pp. 17–24.

Phillips, G. & Keatman, M. (1992). *King Arthur: The true story.* London: Century.

Roskams, S. (1996). Urban transition in early medieval Britain: The case of York. In N. Christie & S. T. Loseby (eds), *Towns in transition: Urban evolution in late antiquity and the early Middle Ages.* Aldershot: Scolar Press, pp. 262–88.

Sims-Williams, P. (1983). Gildas and the Anglo-Saxons. *Cambridge Medieval Celtic Studies,* 6, 1–30.

Sims-Williams, P. (2002). The five languages of Wales in the pre-Norman inscriptions. *Cambrian Medieval Celtic Studies,* 44, 1–36.

Wacher, J. (1995). *Towns of Roman Britain,* 2nd edn. London: B. T. Batsford.

Ward-Perkins, B. (1996). Urban continuity. In N. Christie & S. T. Loseby (eds), *Towns in transition: Urban evolution in late antiquity and the early Middle Ages.* Aldershot: Scolar Press, pp. 4–17.

Ward-Perkins, B. (2005). *The fall of Rome and the end of civilization.* Oxford: Oxford University Press.

White, R. H. & Barker, P. (1998). *Wroxeter: The life and death of a Roman city.* Stroud: Tempus.

Wickham, C. (2005). *Framing the Early Middle Ages: Europe and the Mediterranean 400–800.* Oxford: Oxford University Press.

Wood, I. (1984). The end of Roman Britain: Continental evidence and parallels. In M. Lapidge & D. N. Dumville (eds), *Gildas: New approaches.* Woodbridge: Boydell, pp. 1–25.

Yorke, B. (1993). Fact or fiction? The written evidence for the fifth and sixth centuries. *Anglo-Saxon Studies in Archaeology and History,* 6, 45–50.

2

Early Latin Sources: Fragments of a Pseudo-Historical Arthur

N. J. Higham

Arthur emerges for the first time in an insular context as a pseudo-historical character in a series of Latin works written in Wales and Brittany in the ninth, tenth, eleventh, and early twelfth centuries (Jackson 1959; Jones 1964; Bromwich 1975/6). These works were of several different kinds, including a synthetic pseudo-history (the *Historia Brittonum*, "History of the Britons"), a chronicle (the *Annales Cambriae*, "Welsh Annals"), a set of genealogies written in southwest Wales in the tenth century, and several hagiographies.

Despite the variety of genre, all derived from a comparatively restricted group of monks and/or clerics, each of whom was arguably conversant with earlier "Arthurian" references; to this extent, these several texts spread across more than three hundred years can be viewed as a single interrelated group, produced within a single tradition by clerics who shared a common culture and sense of ethnicity, but differed regarding their immediate political and dynastic contexts. They will here be explored in chronological order, to show how the several Arthurs variously featured in these works developed sequentially across the period, each drawing to some extent at least on what had gone before.

The *Historia Brittonum*

The most complex of these works was also the earliest. The popularity of the *Historia Brittonum* throughout the Middle Ages means that it is today extremely difficult to establish the original text, but it is generally acknowledged that the earliest surviving manuscript, British Library, Harley MS 3859 of c. 1100, should be preferred (Dumville 1977/8). The *Historia Brittonum* is dated internally to the fourth regnal year (829/30) of Merfyn Frych, king of Gwynedd (Dumville 1986), and, again on internal evidence, was arguably written by a clerk with personal experience of the southern March and southeast Wales, but under the patronage of Merfyn, in Gwynedd and perhaps at court. The text is best treated as anonymous, although it is often ascribed to one Ninnius or Nennius (Dumville 1972–4; Field 1996). The author seems to have been attempting to write a narrative history on the basis of a small number of pre-existing texts (Dumville 1986, 1994; Charles-Edwards 1991), such as a lost *Life of Germanus* (see *Historia Brittonum*, ch. 47). Some sources, this included, were arguably very recent at the time of writing: the Anglian genealogies in the *Historia*, for example, refer to Offa of Mercia's son, Ecgfrith (ch. 60), who reigned in 796. We should be hesitant, therefore, in ascribing any particular antiquity to the author's sources and cautious about judging it as historically accurate as regards the depiction of the fifth and sixth centuries. There is much legend and myth included, which must once again tell against its historicity. The author was arguably less interested in what had actually happened than in shaping the past for the specific needs of his contemporary audience, writing as a political polemicist rather than a historian.

The immediate political circumstances probably played an important part, therefore, in determining the underlying message of this work. Across the late eighth and early ninth centuries, successive Mercian kings had sought to impose themselves on Wales, but Mercian hegemony was undermined and then shattered as a consequence of a prolonged succession dispute across the 820s. This led to the defeat of King Beornwulf by Egbert of Wessex in 825, then his death at the hands of the East Angles, leaving Egbert to assert West Saxon superiority across England. The *Anglo-Saxon Chronicle* claims Egbert as the eighth "Ruler of Britain" in succession to the seven named by Bede (*Historia Ecclesiastica* II, 5), and recalls that the Mercians, Northumbrians, and Welsh all submitted to him in 828.

This, then, provides the immediate context for composition. The West Saxons do not appear in the *Historia Brittonum*, reflecting perhaps the danger attached to comment thereon, but the Mercians are generally denigrated. The author found space in the recent collapse of Mercian power for a new nationalistic rhetoric, coupled with condemnation of the "Saxons" (as the English are termed) variously as *fallax* ("treacherous"; ch. 45), *in mente interim vulpicino more* ("in mind and custom like the fox," i.e. "cunning," as opposed to heroic; ch. 46) and *genus ambronum* ("a people of savages"; ch. 63). Central to the work is its reinterpretation of the "Loss of Britain" as told firstly by Gildas in *De Excidio Britanniae* ("Concerning the Ruin of Britain," hereafter abbreviated to *DEB*) and then Bede (c. 673–735) in the *Historia Ecclesiastica* ("Ecclesiastical History," hereafter abbreviated to *HE*). Gildas had portrayed the Britons as if militarily inept latter-day Israelites experiencing divine punishment for their numerous sins, and the Saxons as if Old Testament Assyrians and Babylonians, so as a scourge of his people inflicted upon them by a vengeful God (Higham 1994). Two centuries later Bede developed Gildas's positioning of the Britons to portray them as "opposed by the power of God and man alike" (*HE*, V, 23), out of communion with Rome, and following deviant practices (*HE*, II, 2), with the heroic and martial English by implication now his chosen people within Britain. In the window of opportunity offered by Mercia's eclipse in the 820s, our author sought to reconnect the Britons with God and with the heroic deeds to be expected of a great nation, lacing his narrative with virtuous clerics and brave warriors. This was the more necessary, perhaps, since Merfyn was not apparently himself a king's son and launched his claim for the throne from outside, arguably from the Isle of Man (Sims-Williams 1994), so had a need to bolster his own legitimacy with nationalistic rhetoric. The *Historia Brittonum* reads as one element in just such a political project.

The author therefore refocused the wickedness that led to the Anglo-Saxon settlement on Vortigern alone. His sins are balanced by the excellence of bishop Germanus (an amalgam of the Gaulish bishop of Auxerre with that presumably British St Garman remembered in the place name Llanarmon-yn-Iâl) and of his own reputed son, the hero Vortimer. Central to this narrative in a ninth-century context is the prophecy that was explained to Vortigern by the boy Emrys, interpreting the struggle between two dragons on a cloth floating in an underground lake (ch. 42), perhaps derived from a foundation story attached to Dinas Emrys (Dumville 1986). The fighting between these dragons, one red, one white, representing the Britons and Saxons respectively, provides a prophetic insight into the future of the struggle for control of Britain which Vortigern had unleashed: three unsuccessful attempts to drive out the Saxons would leave the Britons temporarily the weaker, but they would ultimately triumph and expel their enemies.

In the very next chapter, Vortimer's victories against the Saxons represent as the first attempt, Arthur's triumphs follow in chapter 56, then Urien's in chapter 63. The period of the red dragon's weakness seems a fitting metaphor for the state of Wales in the immediate past. Thereafter, by implication, the ultimate triumph of the Britons was imminent, so Merfyn was being invited to take upon himself the role of national hero under divine protection. That he was sufficiently freckled to attract the by-name "Frych" may even mean that Merfyn's hair was exceptionally red, in which case the red dragon becomes a metaphor for the king himself. Whether or not, this account of the "Loss of Britain" is a highly contemporary one, designed to position the king of the day as the ultimate savior of his people (Higham 2002).

It is in this context that we should read Arthur's part in this retelling of the past (ch. 56). Arthur enters at the close of an extended treatment of Patrick, the British missionary to the Irish (chs 50–55). Our author had apparently found in Gildas the association of the proud British tyrant responsible for inviting in the Saxons (here Vortigern) and the Egyptian pharaoh of Exodus fame, and he developed this by representing Patrick as a British type of Moses, drawing on Irish hagiographical works associated with Armagh (Bieler 1979). Just as Moses ushered in the warrior figure of Joshua, so is the British Moses depicted in the *Historia Brittonum* succeeded by a God-beloved war leader, namely Arthur. There are enough connections to suggest that the author was conscious of this model (Higham 2002): Joshua is termed *dux belli* ("leader in battle") in the opening lines of the Book of Judges, while our author introduces Arthur as *dux bellorum* ("leader in battles"); Joshua was responsible for organizing the Israelites in twelve tribes, signaled their formation by picking up twelve stones from the Jordan, and fought battles across the first twelve chapters of the Book of Joshua, while Arthur fought twelve battles. Arthur's portrayal in chapter 56 was therefore arguably intended to invoke biblical parallels and this has affected his representation. The core passage is necessarily the listing of his battles:

> The first battle was in the mouth of the river which is called *Glein*. The second, and third, and fourth, and fifth [were] on another river, which is called *Dubglas*, and it is in the region of *Linnuis*. The sixth battle [was] on a river which is called *Bassas*. The seventh battle was in the wood of Caledonia, that is called *Cat Coit Celidon*. The eighth battle [was] in the castle of *Guinnion*, in which Arthur carried the image of Saint Mary the perpetual virgin on his shoulders, and on that day the pagans were put to flight and a great slaughter was upon them through the power of our Lord Jesus Christ and the power of Saint Mary his holy virgin mother. The ninth battle was fought in the city of the Legions. The tenth battle was waged on the bank of the river called *Tribruit*. The eleventh battle occurred on the mountain which is called *Agned*. The twelfth battle was on the mountain of Badon, in which there fell in one day nine hundred and sixty men from one charge [of] Arthur; and no-one slew them except him alone, and in all battles he was the victor.

It has long been suggested that this list could have been based upon a Welsh vernacular battle-catalogue poem (Chadwick & Chadwick 1932), of a type surviving about several early British figures. Certainly the types of battle-site used are comparable but this is arguably to take a far too positivist view of this ninth-century text. In practice, the list looks to be synthetic: it has apparently been concocted by taking battles previously reported in literature of various kinds (including Gildas's *DEB* and Bede's *HE*) and reallocating them. It must be relevant that the author abandoned the self-imposed task of naming every battle, instead allocating all of numbers two to five to the banks of the same river. This looks like an attempt to reach the preferred overall number of twelve despite a poverty of examples, which highlights the significance to this author of the biblical parallel and undermines the possibility that his list is historically accurate. The very breadth of his geography also seems improbable; the sites, to the extent that they can be identified (Crawford 1935; Jackson 1945), seem to be scattered across the old Roman diocese and even beyond (i.e. Caledonia). The author's biblical metaphor encourages us rather to explore this passage through different lenses. The Virgin Mary has a surprisingly large role herein; the author perhaps had a particular affection for this saint or was attached to a church with that dedication. Arthur is supported by a warrior-figure of Christ in his slaughter of the pagan hosts; that the names Joshua and Jesus were synonymous in Hebrew was widely recognized in the Middle Ages. Via this parallel, by direct association with both Christ and Mary, and by biblical number, Arthur is himself here portrayed as a type of the warrior Christ.

It is in his description of Arthur's final battle, the name of which derives from Gildas, that the author betrays the likeliest origin of his Arthur, for any warrior who single-handedly slew 960 of the enemy in a single charge was necessarily mythic or legendary rather than historical. This has connections with other occurrences of Arthur in this work, within the listing of "marvels" which make up chapter 73, two of which deserve our attention here:

> There is another wonder in the region which is called Builth. There is a pile of stones there and one stone positioned on top of the heap has the footprint of a dog on it. When he hunted the boar *Troynt*, *Cabal*, who was the hound of Arthur the warrior, made an imprint on the stone, and Arthur afterwards collected up the heap of stones under the stone in which was the footprint, and it is called *Carn Cabal*. And men come and they carry the stone in their hands for the space of a day and a night, and on the next day it has returned to the top of the pile.

This story is located in the upper Wye valley, where Carn Gafallt, meaning "horse's cairn," still identifies a prominent hill. It relates to the story of the hunting of the great boar *Turch Trwyth*, which is a feature of the central medieval Welsh vernacular story *Culhwch and Olwen* (Bromwich & Evans 1992). But what is significant from our viewpoint is the sense herein of a wild type of Arthur, a huntsman figure of the high country associated with a great hound named "horse," who has become associated with a hill name via a local etymological story. This is a folkloric Arthur, therefore, rather than a historical one.

A second "Arthurian" marvel follows:

> There is another miracle in the region which is called Ergyng [Archenfield]. There is there a grave next to a spring, which is called *Llygad Amr*, and the name of the man who is buried in the tumulus is called *Amr*; he was a son of the warrior Arthur, and he himself killed him in that very place and buried him. And men come to measure the grave, which is sometimes six feet long, sometimes nine, sometimes twelve, sometimes fifteen. Whatever length you measure on one occasion, you do not repeat that measure, and I have tried myself.

Again, this recalls a wild warrior Arthur linked to the site via a local etymological story which has apparently come into existence following the personification of the old river name. That the author had himself first-hand knowledge of this site is self-evident. These Arthurian place-name stories were arguably the immediate source of his historicization in chapter 56 of the *Historia Brittonum*. A folkloric Arthur, therefore, seems to precede the warrior Arthur of the *Historia* (Padel 1994) and may even have been localized in the southern marches in Welsh territory, in Builth and Archenfield, where the author had earlier come across them. That said, the spellings of Arthur's name from the ninth century onwards suggest that its origin was Latin rather than Old Welsh, so the name at least does seem to have derived ultimately from Roman Britain, perhaps from some such figure as the Lucius Artorius Castus who served there in the later second century (Malone 1925).

Whatever his ultimate origin, the "historical" Arthur is very much a product of the *Historia Brittonum*. The construction of a warrior Arthur leading the soldiers of British kings in a victorious holy war against the pagan intruder provided a fundamental impetus to the rise and rise of Arthurian legend. Such a text should, however, be read with great caution and with close attention both to the overall context in which its author was writing and to the particular role of Arthur within a text which was obedient to imperatives deriving from current cultural and dynastic politics rather than historical veracity.

The *Annales Cambriae*

The *Historia Brittonum* proved popular and was quickly accessible in other parts of Wales. The historicized Arthur next appears in a set of annals written in Dyfed, probably at St David's, in the mid-950s, known as the *Annales Cambriae*. Again, the original is lost and the earliest version available is a copy in British Library, Harley MS 3859 of c. 1100. These annals were structured so as to encompass a paschal cycle of 532 years plus one, from c. 444 to 977, but there are no entries against the final 23 years, which may imply that it was written as a single exercise approximately contemporary with the final entry.

The basic structure of this chronicle divides into three sections (Hughes 1973): early material deriving from a lost Irish chronicle of the Clonmacnoise group (Grabowski & Dumville 1984); early-seventh- to late-eighth-century material largely derived from northern Britain; and later material from a set of annals kept locally from the 790s onwards. Arthur appears in two entries in the earliest section but the immediate context of tenth-century authorship influenced the way that he was characterized, so we will focus first on how the early sixth century was being represented in the mid-950s.

The *Annales* were written following the death in 950 of Hywel Dda, herein termed *rex Brittonum* ("king of the Britons"). From a starting point in Deheubarth (Dyfed and Ceredigion), Hywel obtained control of Gwynedd and Powys following the defeat of his cousin Idwal of Gwynedd by the English in 942 and seems to have ruled virtually all Wales as an ally of King Eadred of England, on occasion attending his court. At Hywel's death, his throne passed to his sons, initially Rhodri (died 954, the last event in these annals) and finally Owain (died 988), but Idwal's sons re-secured the northern kingdoms and waged war against Deheubarth, defeating their cousins at Carno in 951. Rhodri's death only four years after his father's was followed by his brother Edwin's perhaps only a year later. Owain's sole reign therefore began in the heat of a dynastic and military crisis. In that context, Welsh nationalistic rhetoric was the preserve of his opponents and hope of his survival arguably lay to some extent at least in the hope of an English reimposition of peace, such as seems to have occurred in 955 when the two warring kings both attended the English court and signed one of King Eadred's last surviving grants. It is perhaps therefore unsurprising that there is a marked lack of anti-English rhetoric in the *Annales*, and Arthur appears in a very different guise to his appearance in the *Historia Brittonum*.

This invites, of course, the question, where did this author acquire his Arthurian material? As already stated, the early section of this chronicle derives primarily from an Irish original, which explains the presence within it of several Irish religious figures, plus Patrick and Gildas, who appear frequently in Irish annals. Up to AD 600, there are only seven further "British" entries, of which only the first three need concern us here:

> [516]   The battle of Badon, in which Arthur carried the cross of our Lord Jesus Christ for three days and three nights on his shoulders and the Britons were the victors.
>
> [537]   The *gweith* [battle of] Camlann, in which Arthur and Medraut fell, and there was a great mortality [i.e. plague] in Britain and in Ireland.
>
> [547]   The great mortality [i.e. plague] in which died Maelgwyn, king of Gwynedd.

The fame of both Badon and Maelgwyn derive ultimately from knowledge of Gildas's *DEB* although the author of the *Annales* shows no obvious sign of having actually read that text himself; rather, his information arguably came from the *Historia Brittonum*. Detailed attention to the Arthurian entries reveals the recurrence of language from the *Historia* to be so frequent as to make it reasonably certain that the author was plagiarizing heavily. The *Annales* entries for 516 and 537 are based primarily on *Historia Brittonum* chapter 56, with additional borrowings of specific words or phrases from elsewhere (Higham 2002). Taking the two entries together, of the 31 Latin words used only 5 are on this count original, of which one is a personal name and another a place name.

The author of the *Annales* found in the *Historia Brittonum* a depiction of Britain post-Vortigern enjoying a "golden age" characterized by the extraordinary achievements of Patrick followed by the God-given victories of the heroic Arthur; but glorification of the deeds of Cunedda in that work (*Historia Brittonum* chs 14, 62), who evicted the Irish from Wales, defined this "golden age" in narrowly "British" terms. The monastery of St David's was in close communication with Ireland and the author of the *Annales* was heavily reliant on an Irish chronicle in this section. Additionally, he was writing in a political context hostile to the nationalistic stance taken by the court of Gwynedd, and for a dynasty conscious of its own Irish ancestry; thus in his own work he extended commemoration of this glorious epoch by reference to Irish material concerning both Irish and British Christian heroes. This positioning also affected his commemoration of Arthur, who appears here in a noticeably un-martial guise, stripped of his role as a great warrior. The Badon entry is arguably much influenced by the description of Arthur's eighth battle in the *Historia Brittonum*, which had Arthur carrying the image of Mary. The substitution in the *Annales* of Christ's cross invokes the parallel of Simon the Cyrenian, who in Luke 23:26 carried Christ's cross before his crucifixion; the phrase therein, *crucem portare post Iesum*, "carrying the cross after Jesus," may very well have been the source of our author's *portavit crucem Domini nostri Jhesu Christi*, "he carried the cross of our Lord Jesus Christ." We have here, therefore, a writer who interpreted Arthur's presence in history according to the context in which he was himself writing. He had come across Arthur as a Joshua-like martial figure beloved of God in the *Historia Brittonum*, but rethought that characterization radically in favor of a far more saintly figure, an Arthur as Christ-helper, wrapped around with a much less martial and more Christian imagery.

This impression is confirmed by the second entry. Once again, although a battle is named, Arthur is not explicitly a martial figure. Instead, it is his death that is noted, alongside that of one other named individual, Medraut. The arrival of plague in the same year implies that the author was presenting Arthur's death as something for which the Lord had punished the Britons and Irish, which perhaps reinforces the Christ-like qualities of Arthur in this text. Camlann is un-located and the historicity of its association with Arthur is now beyond recall.

The author's selection of dates for these entries has been much debated. Clearly the Arthurian events are unlikely to have been present in the Irish chronicle on which this section was based; indeed, even the plague that concludes the second entry does not occur in Irish texts, although later plague episodes do. Patrick's death in 457, which will have been in the author's Irish source, presumably dictated that Arthur should belong to the subsequent period, but 516 does look very late given that Arthur follows Patrick without intermission in the *Historia Brittonum*. Despite arguments to the contrary, the author of the *Annales* does not seem to have had available to him any Welsh annals even close to contemporary with this time frame, so we should suppose that his dating of the Arthur entries was deductive at best. One suggestion (Wiseman 2000) is that he was aware of Bede's *Chronica Majora* ("Greater Chronicle," written c. 725), which locates the British victory at Badon in the period 474–91, then added the 44 years which are associated with the battle by both Gildas (*DEB*, XXVI, 1) and Bede (*HE*, I, 16), giving a time frame for Arthur of 518–35, which equates quite closely with the Arthurian entries here in 516 and 537. There are difficulties with this reasoning, however, given that neither Gildas nor Bede mentions Arthur, and Bede, in his *Historia Ecclesiastica* at least, placed the battle 44 years after the Anglo-Saxon arrival in Britain. An alternative would be to suggest that the author of the *Annales* was aware of Maelgwyn's approximate dates, allowed sufficient time for the numerous battles leading up to Badon to have occurred after Patrick's death, and then made sure to have concluded his Arthurian entries prior to introducing Maelgwyn.

How precisely the author came to these dates is unknowable but these entries are unlikely to reflect a pre-existing and reliably dated Arthurian account that was independent of the *Historia Brittonum*. Despite the fact that the *Annales Cambriae* have often been viewed as a separate source capable of confirming the historicity of Arthur as first introduced into the *Historia Brittonum* (Alcock 1971), this is to take too positivist a reading of the text, which should instead be viewed as a reinterpretation of that same Arthur for different purposes and in different political circumstances.

Genealogy

It is when the collection of tenth-century Welsh genealogies is introduced that fresh light is thrown on the perspective adopted by the author of the *Annales Cambriae*.

These occur earliest in the same manuscript, British Library, Harley MS 3859, as the other materials so far reviewed. Since Owain heads both the first and second genealogies, being his paternal and maternal lineages respectively, they were arguably written in this form within his reign (c. 954–88). Given their political value as demonstrations of Owain's claims to kingship, it is arguable, at least, that the genealogies, like the *Annales*, were written in the first critical year or so of his rule, in the context of internecine war with his cousins.

Owain's maternal ancestor thirteen generations removed was named *Arthur map Petr* ("Arthur son of Peter"). The name does not appear to have been added at this time, since it also occurs in an earlier version of the same genealogy. The presence of this genealogical Arthur was presumably well known to clerks in the service of the court, including the author of the *Annales Cambriae*, so it seems reasonable to assume that the Arthur of the annals was being reinterpreted in part on the assumption that he was an ancestor of the present king, and therefore thoroughly "owned" by the local political elite in the mid-tenth century. The Arthur of the *Historia Brittonum* was thus recruited by the author of the *Annales* and reinterpreted as a noticeably un-martial and almost saintly hero on the assumption that he was a local figure capable of offering support to the native lineage.

This court pedigree offers further important insights to the contemporary regime and attitudes detectable in the *Annales Cambriae*. Entries at the center of this genealogy include several Irish names, which reflect the widely held assumption that there were Irish kings in Dyfed in the fifth and sixth centuries. Their inclusion in this pedigree necessarily associated the present regime with that Irish presence and distinguished it from its principal rivals in Gwynedd, where the expulsion of Irish colonists was viewed as one of their great political achievements of the period. This concurs, therefore, with that sense of a Cambro-Irish "golden age" of Christianity in the opening section of the *Annales*, including the second Arthurian entry. It also concurs with later perceptions of St David as having been eager to conduct missionary work in Ireland, and the local belief in Dyfed that Patrick derived from that neighborhood.

It may also be relevant that the court pedigree betrays a comparatively recent development, around the time of Owain's rule, with the purpose of promoting claims on Owain's behalf. From the Irish group of names, the genealogy was extended a further fourteen generations back, via Magnus Maximus, widely regarded as the last Roman emperor to have ruled Britain (*Historia Brittonum*, ch. 29), to Constantine the Great and Helen, "who left Britain to seek the cross of Christ even to Jerusalem and then bore it to Constantinople and it is there even now today." This additional mention of *crux Christi* ("the cross of Christ") recalls the first Arthurian entry in the *Annales*, which may of course even have been written by the same clerk.

Owain's maternal pedigree may shed fresh light, therefore, on some of the thinking behind the Arthurian entries in the *Annales Cambriae*. Such maternal pedigrees are extremely rare; that this one was considered sufficiently valuable to have been copied out implies that it had political value. Owain was a descendant of the native lineage of Dyfed only via his mother, and it was this that distinguished him from his cousins in Gwynedd, with whom he shared descent from Merfyn Frych. In its existing form as copied into Harley MS 3859, this genealogy reveals that Arthur was understood locally as a member of the native dynasty and a direct antecedent of the present king, whose rule this pedigree was designed to sustain. And this lineage was also extended backward to include Constantine and Helen, used here to invest in the political legitimacy and religious rectitude of Owain's kingship in the present. Again, therefore, we are confronted by a writer whose principal purposes lay more in present politics than in accurate revelation of the past.

Hagiographies

The final category of "Arthurian" texts to be introduced here is the group of Welsh and Breton saints' lives in which Arthur has at least a walk-on part. The bulk of these have survived in the manuscript British Library, Cotton Vespasian A.xiv, of c. 1200 in an Anglo-Norman hand, all of which derive from Wales. These include the *Vita Sancti Cadoci* ("Life of St Cadog") by Lifris son of Herwald (Herwald was bishop of southeast Wales, 1056–1104), almost certainly written at Llancarfan, Glamorgan, late in the eleventh century; the *Vita Prima Sancti Carantoci* ("First Life of St Carannog"), perhaps written at Llangrannog in Ceredigion around 1100; and the *Vita Sancti Iltuti* ("Life of St Illtud"), written at the monastery of Llanilltud Fawr, Llantwit Major, Glamorgan, no earlier than the mid-twelfth century. Excepting the last, these should be read as defensive works written in the immediate context of Norman penetration into Wales and the irruption, into what had been a comparatively closed cultural community, of Anglo-Norman barons and the clergy and monks in their patronage, with little immediate interest in or sympathy for traditional local saints (Tatlock 1939).

Arthur features in the prologue of the *Vita Sancti Cadoci*, in a scene reminiscent of his appearances in the *mirabilia* of the *Historia Brittonum* (ch. 73). Arthur, Cai, and Bedwyr, *tres heroes strenui* ("three lively heroes"), are seated on a hilltop playing dice and witnessing the flight of King Glywys with the maiden Gwladus, pursued by her father. Arthur lusts after the maiden and proposes to secure her but is restrained by his companions and persuaded to adopt a more responsible role, determining who is in the right and then succoring the fleeing king and throwing back his enemies. This is, therefore, the king whom Tatlock termed "the silly and unstable Arthur" (1939: 352), a figure of the wild, frontier hill-country, but at the same time capable of action as a protective figure to uphold rights to land and lordship. Given that the pursuing forces had supposedly already slain two hundred of Glywys's men, this is also the heroic warrior Arthur, the one whose personal achievements at Mount Badon were recorded in *Historia Brittonum* chapter 56. The episode in the *Vita* leads directly to the marriage of Glywys and Gwladus, which produced Cadog as their first-born son, whose procreation is, therefore, depicted as a direct consequence of Arthur's intervention. Thus the wild Arthur is here serving Almighty God for his own purposes, albeit apparently unbeknown to Arthur himself at the time. He is far from the fundamentally Christian figure of the *Annales Cambriae* and far closer to the warrior and folkloric hero as embraced by the author of the *Historia Brittonum* in chapter 73.

Arthur re-emerges thereafter in chapter 22 of the *Vita* as *rex illustrissimus Brittannie* ("the most illustrious king of Britain"), characterized as a vengeful lord. Cadog's difficulties in negotiating terms between Arthur and his enemy, largely due to Arthur's unwillingness to settle his feud, leads eventually to a miracle, in the face of which Arthur is converted to a suppliant, asking forgiveness of the saint as spokesman for the Lord. Cadog obviously gains moral status and authority from this exchange, in which Arthur might be read as a metaphor for unbridled lordly power. His role in the following two chapters is more honorable: he is termed *herous fortissimos* ("most brave hero") and portrayed as Cadog's patron and protector. Their opponents are the north Welsh, here portrayed as raiders and robbers. Once again, therefore, we have a sense of a local Arthur, claimed as a protector figure by a particular community to be invoked versus incursion from outside, which has significance in present circumstances. Arthur is portrayed as the archetypal figure of secular power, whose proper activity is to attend to God's business and to provide protection to his principal representatives (in the immediate context, the monks of Llancarfan, near Barry in south Wales). All goes well when he performs this role effectively but Arthur faces humiliation when his appetites are unbridled.

This Arthur was clearly founded on pre-existing characterizations of several kinds, the very fluidity of which allowed him to perform a variety of roles within a single work, to the ultimate benefit of the author's contemporary agenda. Arthur was, of course, portrayed here as a king, but that was surely the natural interpretation of his prominence in other texts: in the *Historia Brittonum*, wherein he was "the leader in battle" of the "forces of the kings of the Britons," in his entries in the *Annales Cambriae*, and in a royal genealogy. All three of the Welsh hagiographies are southern works, the authors of which are likely to have been familiar with Arthur's commemoration as an antecedent of the kings of Deheubarth, and they may well have also known folkloric stories featuring Arthur emanating from the same region as had already produced the Arthurian *mirabilia* in the *Historia Brittonum*.

Arthur's appearance in the *Vita Prima Sancti Carantoci* (ch. 4) is not dissimilar in kind. Here he is depicted as joint-ruler of Ceredigion and protector of the land versus a terrible monster (something of a St George role), which he is unable to locate. When the saint reforms the monster and gives it protection, Arthur proves respectful of the new situation and leaves them in peace. Here, therefore, Arthur is representative of proper secular authority in harmony with the cult site and honoring its special status close to God.

In the *Vita Sancti Illtuti* (ch. 2), Arthur is one of several figures depicted in glowing terms in such a way as to lend his prestige to Illtud. So, *audiens, interea, miles magnificus*

Arthurii regis consobrini magnificentiam, cupivit visitare tanti victoris curiam ("the magnificent soldier [i.e. Illtud], hearing of the magnificence of his cousin, King Arthur,
desired to visit the court of so great a victor"). Illtud gained credit from the association and the author apparently intended that his value should be enhanced by that
attached to the great ruler who welcomed him, but this vision of Arthur as presiding
monarch perhaps derives from Geoffrey of Monmouths's portrayal, which probably
preceded this work by several decades.

One further work deserves our attention, which was written in Brittany rather than
Wales. This is the *Legenda Sancti Goeznovii* ("Life of St Goeznovius"), which survives
in a fifteenth-century manuscript but was putatively written by William, chaplain to
a bishop Eudo of Leon in 1019. That said, this date seems far too early for Norman-
named clergy to be in post in western Brittany and this Eudo is otherwise unknown.
The dating is therefore probably apocryphal and the origin somewhat later. The early
chapters offer a "historical" introduction to the life of Goeznovius, which refers to
several legends familiar from the *Historia Brittonum* (including the story of Brutus),
but adding others which occur in Geoffrey of Monmouth, then attempts a brief narrative of the foundation of Brittany and its churches (ch. 2), leading up to the disasters
of Vortigern's reign and their aftermath in chapter 3:

> In the due process of time, the usurper king Vortigern, to guarantee the defence of his
> kingdom of greater Britain which he held unjustly, called in warlike men from parts of
> Saxony and made them his allies in the kingdom. These, who were pagans and devilish
> men, lusting by their very nature to shed blood, brought great evils down upon the
> Britons. Their pride was for a while held back by the great Arthur, king of the Britons,
> by whom they were cleared from the greater part of the island and forced into subjec-
> tion. After many victories which he achieved gloriously in British and Gaulish parts,
> however, that same Arthur was summoned at last from human deeds; the way was open
> for the Saxons to return to the island, and they greatly oppressed the Britons, sacked
> the churches and persecuted the saints.

The primary source for this was arguably the *Historia Brittonum*, the basic story having
however been rewritten for a Breton audience. There is therefore a new focus on the
Britons on the Continent, and Arthur's wars are said to have included Gaul. This has
obvious connections with Geoffrey of Monmouth's later depiction of Arthur as a king
active across western Europe but it need derive from nothing more than a reading of
Historia Brittonum chapter 56 in the expectation that some at least of the battles – most
of which this author will have been no better able to locate than we are – might have
been fought in continental Europe. The modern association, particularly by Geoffrey
Ashe (2003), of Arthur with the sixth-century figure Riothamus, a British war leader
known to have been operative in the Loire valley, has very little to commend it; this
William is most unlikely to have made this connection for himself and even if he had
it would not provide us with any evidence regarding Arthur's historicity, so late is
this text.

Conclusion

These several texts provide us, therefore, with the early development of Arthur within Latin works written by authors operative in Wales and, in one instance, Brittany. An early ninth-century Welsh writer who was himself familiar with folkloric stories featuring Arthur local to the southern March developed him as a pseudo-historical figure within a framework influenced by his reading of the Bible, as part of a repositioning of Gwynedd's king as British leader in the late 820s. This historicized Arthur was then recaptured for a southern Welsh agenda for the *Annales Cambriae*, apparently written in the knowledge that Arthur was locally considered an antecedent of the present king of Deheubarth via his maternal line from the kings of Dyfed. This author reimagined him as a Christ-helper, whose death signaled the end of a golden age that characterized early British and Irish history.

Arthur's kingship was implicit in these works, although never actually stated. Later clerics utilized him as an iconic figure to represent secular lordship, drawing to an extent on these same texts but also at times on the type of folkloric Arthur first revealed in the *mirabilia* of the *Historia Brittonum*. By the early eleventh century, his place in the story of the loss of Britain had been consolidated and he appeared even in a Breton Latin text, which featured an Arthur extracted from the *Historia Brittonum* as part of the general historical backdrop to his own particular saint's life, but reoriented to his own local audience. Arthur emerges as a highly adaptable figure, capable of being recast in a variety of guises to fulfill the differing needs of writers producing works at different times, for very divergent audiences. Biblical parallels were apparently significant for some authors, imagining him as a British type of Joshua and the warrior Christ, but others opted for a much more down-to-earth, secular figure of dubious moral positioning, so as to cast a particular saint in a better light. Arthur's heroic credentials coupled with his very fluidity were, perhaps, his greatest strengths and the source of his appeal to a wide range of authors and their audiences, with different facets capable of combination in myriad ways that would emerge across the next half-century in the world of Anglo-Welsh/Norman authorship.

Primary Sources

Bromwich, R. & Evans, D. S. (1992). *Culhwch and Olwen: An edition and study of the oldest Arthurian text*. Cardiff: University of Wales Press.

Thorpe, L. (trans.) (1966). *Geoffrey of Monmouth: History of the kings of Britain*. Harmondsworth: Penguin.

References and Further Reading

Alcock, L. (1971). *Arthur's Britain: History and archaeology AD 367–634*. Harmondsworth: Penguin.

Ashe, G. (1995). The origins of the Arthurian legend. *Arthuriana*, 5(3), 1–24.

Ashe, G. (2003). *The discovery of King Arthur*. Stroud: Sutton.

Bieler, L., with a contribution from Kelly, F. (1979). *The patrician texts in the Book of Armagh*. Dublin: Dublin Institute for Advanced Studies.

Bromwich, R. (1975/6). Concepts of Arthur. *Studia Celtica*, 10/11, 163–81.

Chadwick, H. M. & Chadwick, N. K. (1932). *The growth of literature*, vol. I. Cambridge: Cambridge University Press.

Chambers, E. K. (1927). *Arthur of Britain*. London: Sidgwick & Jackson.

Charles-Edwards, T. M. (1991). The Arthur of history. In R. Bromwich, A. O. H. Jarman, & B. F. Roberts (eds), *The Arthur of the Welsh*. Cardiff: University of Wales Press, pp. 15–32.

Crawford, O. G. S. (1935). Arthur and his battles. *Antiquity*, 9, 277–91.

Dumville, D. N. (1972–4). The Corpus Christi "Nennius." *Bulletin of the Board of Celtic Studies*, 25, 369–80.

Dumville, D. N. (1975/6). "Nennius" and the *Historia Brittonum*. *Studia Celtica*, 10/11, 78–95.

Dumville, D. N. (1977/8). The Welsh Latin Annals. *Studia Celtica*, 12/13, 461–7.

Dumville, D. N. (1986). The historical value of the *Historia Brittonum*. *Arthurian Literature*, 6, 1–26.

Dumville, D. N. (1994). *Historia Brittonum*: An insular history from the Carolingian age. In A. Scharer & G. Scheibelreiter (eds), *Historiographie im frühen Mittelalter*. Vienna: R. Oldenbourg.

Field, P. J. C. (1996). Nennius and his history. *Studia Celtica*, 30, 159–65.

Grabowski, K. & Dumville, D. (1984). *Chronicles and annals of Medieval Ireland and Wales: The Clonmacnoise group*. Woodbridge: Boydell.

Higham, N. J. (1994). *The English conquest: Gildas and Britain in the fifth century*. Manchester: Manchester University Press.

Higham, N. J. (2002). *King Arthur: Myth-making and history*. London: Routledge.

Hughes, K. (1973). The Welsh Latin chronicles: *Annales Cambriae* and related texts. *Proceedings of the British Academy*, 59, 233–58.

Jackson, K. H. (1945). Once again Arthur's battles. *Modern Philology*, 43, 44–57.

Jackson, K. H. (1959). The Arthur of history. In R. S. Loomis (ed.), *Arthurian literature in the Middle Ages*. Oxford: Clarendon Press, pp. 1–11.

Jones, T. (1964). The early evolution of the legend of Arthur. *Nottingham Medieval Studies*, 8, 3–21.

Malone, K. (1925). Artorius. *Modern Philology*, 22(4), 367–74.

Padel, O. J. (1994). The nature of Arthur. *Cambrian Medieval Celtic Studies*, 27, 1–31.

Sims-Williams, P. (1994). Historical need and literary narrative: A caveat from ninth-century Wales. *Welsh History Review*, 17, 1–40.

Tatlock, J. S. P. (1939). The dates of the Arthurian saints' legends. *Speculum*, 14(3), 345–65.

Wiseman, H. (2000). The derivation of the date of the Badon entry in the *Annales Cambriae* from Bede and Gildas. *Parergon*, n.s., 17(2), 1–10.

3

History and Myth: Geoffrey of Monmouth's *Historia Regum Britanniae*

Helen Fulton

In his twelfth-century history of the kings of Britain before the rule of the Saxons, Geoffrey of Monmouth created our earliest surviving biography of King Arthur: not just "a" biography but "the" biography, the one which set the pattern for all successive accounts of Arthur's life. Though Geoffrey's reputation as a historian waxed and waned throughout the centuries, his account of the milestones of Arthur's life – Arthur's conception through Merlin's magic, his succession to the kingship and early victories against the Saxons, his marriage to Guinevere, his conquest of Europe, his defeat of the emperor of Rome, Mordred's treachery, and the deaths of Arthur and Mordred at Camlan – was never substantially revised. Even the character of Gawain, Arthur's nephew, and the removal of the wounded Arthur to Avalon, both staple features of later Arthurian stories, appear first in Geoffrey's account. The evidence of the Modena sculpture, showing named Arthurian characters and dated to c. 1120–30 (see chapter 26), indicates that there were popular versions of Arthurian stories circulating orally (and possibly in written form) before Geoffrey's time (Loomis 1928), and additions were certainly made, particularly by French romance writers such as Chrétien de Troyes, who probably invented the character of Lancelot (see chapter 11). Nevertheless, the essential outlines of the biography were put in place by Geoffrey and have remained up until the present day largely as he set them out. Almost without exception, what was known about Arthur in the Middle Ages was what Geoffrey had authorized.

Little is known of Geoffrey's life apart from what he tells us in his writings together with a few references in ecclesiastical documents. He was a secular cleric who probably came from Monmouth, on the Welsh border: he refers to himself as "Galfridus Monumotensis" ("Geoffrey of Monmouth," *HRB* book 11), while sometimes signing his name or being referred to by others as "Gaufridus Artur" (Geoffrey Arthur), suggesting a nickname derived from his well-known interest in Arthur (Padel 1984: 2). Geoffrey did his clerical training at Oxford, possibly under the supervision of Walter, archdeacon of Oxford, whose name appears with Geoffrey's on a number of charters

(Thorpe 1966: 12). Geoffrey may well have been a canon at the college of St George, under the leadership of Walter, and probably taught at the college for the greater part of his career. An appointment to higher office in the church was a long time coming, and arrived only after the college of St George was closed in 1148. At last, in 1152, Geoffrey was ordained in London as a priest and awarded the bishopric of St Asaph in north Wales, though he almost certainly remained in London until his death in about 1155.

During his long career as a cleric in Oxford, Geoffrey wrote a number of works dedicated to influential patrons in the hope of securing a clerical appointment. His earliest work was probably the *Prophetiae Merlini*, "Prophecies of Merlin," dedicated to Alexander, bishop of Lincoln, a work which was already in circulation when Geoffrey wrote the *Historia Regum Britanniae*. Geoffrey clearly envisaged the Prophecies as a central part of the *Historia* and simply reissued the Prophecies as book 7 of the *Historia*, where they function as an elliptical commentary on the "historical" events described in the *Historia*, and on contemporary events of Geoffrey's own day, particularly the civil war between Stephen and Matilda and the rebellious uprisings of the Welsh and Scots (Dalton 2005). As a genre legitimized by religious and biblical tradition, the Prophecies provided an additional voice, beyond that of Geoffrey the historian, validating the genealogical connection between the Norman kings and their British ancestors (Ingledew 1994).

The *Historia* was written about 1138, though some scholars argue for an earlier date of about 1136 (Thorpe 1966: 9; Roberts 1991: 98). Dedicated to Robert, Earl of Gloucester, the illegitimate son of Henry I, it claims to be a history of the British people from the foundation of the island by Brutus, great-grandson of Aeneas of Troy, to the final conquest of the island by the Saxons in the seventh century. According to Geoffrey's account, the Saxons occupied Britain more or less by default, following civil war and a major plague that decimated the British population. Cadwallader, the last king of Britain, acknowledged that the British deserved to lose their island and were rightfully punished by God for their sins. Just as he is about to return to Britain from his exile in Brittany, an angelic vision warns him that God did not wish the Britons to rule in Britain any longer, not until Merlin's prophecy of a triumphant return of the heirs of the British kings was fulfilled (*HRB* book 12). Cadwallader retreats to a holy life in Rome and the Saxons continue their colonization of the island, occasionally harassed by a last degenerate rump of British survivors known as the "Welsh." Geoffrey makes no secret of his opinion that the Welsh represent a mere shadow of their ancestors, the great British kings who founded an imperial line stretching forth beyond the Saxons to the glorious regime of the Norman kings.

Late in his life, about 1150, Geoffrey wrote another major work, the *Vita Merlini* ("Life of Merlin"), a long poem purporting to be a biography of Merlin the prophet, the character more or less invented by Geoffrey for the *Historia*. His account of Merlin in the *Vita*, however, draws on British legends from the north of Britain to create a rather different character from the one depicted in the *Historia* (see chapter 6). Though

Geoffrey attempts to smooth over the discrepancies by saying he is continuing the story he started in the *Historia*, where Merlin was a young man, and is giving an account of the prophet's later life, he cannot rationalize away the central problem that the two Merlins belong to two different centuries – the late fifth century in the *Historia*, where Merlin is a contemporary of Vortigern, and the late sixth century in the *Vita*, where Merlin is said to have gone mad at the battle of Arfderydd in northern Britain, dated to 573 in the *Annales Cambriae* ("Welsh Annals"). If, as Oliver Padel argues, the *Vita* represents Geoffrey's second attempt at securing an ecclesiastical appointment, he achieved success by embellishing his previous account of Merlin in the *Historia* with British legends about Lailoken, the "wild man" of the north, conflating the two to create a fully formed biography of Merlin (Padel 2006).

The *Historia* as History

The status of Geoffrey's account as "history," in the sense of factual truth, was called into question within decades of the *Historia*'s appearance. William of Newburgh and Gerald of Wales, both writing in the last two decades of the twelfth century, were early skeptics (see chapter 4), while Renaissance historians such as Raphael Holinshed and Polydore Vergil, who were attempting to develop a rigorous historiographical methodology which broke with the credulity and superstition of the medieval past, dismissed Geoffrey's work as inaccurate and quite possibly fanciful (see chapter 23). There is no documentary evidence for characters such as Brutus or Belinus, nor for a British invasion of Gaul or confrontation with Rome, not to mention a host of other supernatural and clearly fictional details which form the bedrock of the *Historia*, interspersed with cunningly inserted references to actual historical figures and places. Despite its evidently fictional nature, the shape of Geoffrey's life of Arthur was constantly refreshed and redrawn, often by Geoffrey's sternest critics as well as by his supporters, and even the rise of robustly empirical methodologies in the twentieth century has not completely laid to rest the Galfridian biography of Arthur as a historical character.

There remains, in fact, a residual desire to associate Arthur, whether fictional or not, with a specific and "real" historical period. The early twentieth-century historian R. G. Collingwood felt that "through the mist of legend" it might be possible "to descry something which at least may have happened" (Collingwood & Myres 1936: 324; see also chapter 30, this volume). Geoffrey Ashe suggested that a historical figure called Riothamus, called "King of the Britons" in a number of manuscripts, might have been the model for Geoffrey's Arthur (Ashe 1985). Modern film-makers attempt to (re)construct an "authentic" historical past in which to locate Arthur, implying that even if Arthur himself may prove to be fictional, there was a historical context, pre-dating Saxon rule and similar to that described by Geoffrey, in which he may have been active. Geoffrey's achievement, in effect, was to create a "myth" of Arthur, both in the sense of "legendary account" and in the Barthesian sense (from the theory of Roland Barthes) of a deeply connotative set of meanings that are passed off as natural and denotative.

Geoffrey's work is a "history" in the classical Latin sense of *historia*, that is, a chronological account of the deeds of great men whose military and political achievements deserve to be commemorated. He declares this as his project in the opening words to the *Historia*:

> While my mind was often pondering many things in many ways, my thoughts turned to the history of the kings of Britain, and I was surprised that, among the references to them in the fine works of Gildas and Bede, I had found nothing concerning the kings who lived here before Christ's Incarnation, and nothing about Arthur and the many others who succeeded after it, even though their deeds are worthy of eternal praise and are proclaimed by many people as if they had been entertainingly and memorably written down. (*HRB* prologue; Reeve & Wright 2007: 4)

The writing of history in the Middle Ages conformed not to the modern historiographical project of recording documentary evidence of names and dates, but to a specifically medieval impulse to create history as a series of narratives, linked sets of anecdotes ranging from the heroic and martial to the local and supernatural. This is the structure of Geoffrey's *Historia* and of the histories of other twelfth-century writers such as William of Malmesbury and Gerald of Wales (Tatlock 1950; Hanning 1966). So appealing are some of Geoffrey's narratives that they were taken up by later writers: Shakespeare's plays *Cymbeline* and *King Lear* are both based on stories that originally appeared in the *Historia* and were then reworked by Renaissance historians as part of the legendary history of Britain.

The main features of medieval historiography can be summarized as the juxtaposition of events paratactically, without causative links; the lack of a sense of anachronism; and a disregard for evidence (Burke 1969). For a modern historian, these are serious failures indeed. In the medieval context, however, they simply reveal a different set of priorities and ideologies, an alternative epistemology. The paratactic style of historiography, where events occur sequentially like beads on a string, with no clear set of preceding causes, is inevitably a function of the standard practice of keeping historical records in the form of year-by-year chronicles and annals. This way of thinking about events, as a series of occurrences linked only by their time frame, was central to all medieval prose narratives, not just histories but stories, fables, and romances as well. According to Nancy Partner, "vernacular narratives . . . were the natural contemporary models for history" (Partner 1977: 196), but it is just as likely that historical narratives, fixed firmly in chronology, exerted a significant influence on the structure of secular narratives.

Another significant model for medieval historiography was that of religious writing, starting with the Bible itself. Just as the events of the Old Testament were interpreted as prefigurings, often allegorical in nature, of later events occurring in the New Testament, so for medieval writers events long in the past seemed to anticipate and correspond to more recent happenings. The past could be used to interpret the present. Thus Geoffrey is preoccupied with explaining the origins of things – nations, towns, conquests, the line of kings – as a means of representing present circumstances as the inevitable, and therefore natural, outcome of what had gone before. For the island of Britain, Geoffrey constructs a genealogy that goes back to the ancient city of Troy. According to the ninth-century *Historia Brittonum*, the eponymous founder of Britain was Brutus, great-grandson of Aeneas, and Geoffrey creates a prophecy for him, spoken by the goddess Diana, which prefigures a great line of imperial kings:

> "Brutus, to the west, beyond the kingdoms of Gaul, lies an island of the ocean, sur-rounded by the sea; an island of the ocean, where giants once lived, but now it is deserted and waiting for your people. Sail to it; it will be your home for ever. It will furnish your children with a new Troy. From your descendants will arise kings, who will be masters of the whole world." (*HRB* book 1; Reeve & Wright 2007: 20)

Britain, then, is figured as the homeland of a new line of kings and a new empire. When Brutus arrives at his "island in the ocean," he establishes a capital city on the banks of the Thames and names it Troia Nova, "new Troy."

Geoffrey's method of seeking the origins of the present in the past worked very successfully to create an authentic British history for the Norman kings of his own time (Knight 1983). His "devotion to origins" underpinned the "genealogical impera-tive on the part of aristocrats and monarchs to invent a legitimating past" (Ingledew 1994: 680). Not only were the Normans represented as the natural successors to an illustrious line of foundational British kings, but they were clearly positioned as the heirs of Arthur, whose military leadership and imperial ambitions prefigured those of the Normans themselves. Geoffrey makes this quite explicit in his description of Arthur's conquest of Gaul:

> After nine years had passed, in which he secured the surrender of all the Gallic provinces, Arthur returned to Paris and held court there, summoning clergy and laymen to confirm the rule of peace and law in the kingdom. He presented Estrusia, now called Normandy, to his butler Bedwerus, the province of Anjou to his steward Kaius, and many other regions to noble men of his retinue. (*HRB* book 9; Reeve & Wright 2007: 208)

The myth of Arthur, then, supports the myth of Norman legitimacy in Britain. Care-fully distinguished from the usurping and treacherous Saxons, the Normans are posi-tioned by Geoffrey as the true heirs of Arthur's Britain – and his empire.

Nevertheless, Geoffrey's reference at the end of the *Historia* to Merlin's prophecy to Arthur (whom he never in fact meets during the *Historia*) seems to offer a subtle reminder that the Prophecies predict the return of British sovereignty. This can be read as a warning to the contemporary Norman leadership, whose authority was under threat in the period when the *Historia* appeared, that unless it regained decisive control it faced the loss of the kingdom, either to foreign invaders, which is how the British lost control in the first place, or through the triumphant return of British rule, represented by Breton, Cornish, and Welsh descendants of Brutus (Dalton 2005). Criticisms of Geoffrey's work by William of Newburgh and Gerald of Wales can therefore be interpreted as political ripostes to Geoffrey's veiled hints of a British return. The bones of Arthur were supposedly "discovered" in a grave at the monastery of Glastonbury about 1190, as reported by Gerald of Wales (in two of his works, *De Principis Instructione*, "On the Instruction of Princes," c. 1193, and *Speculum Ecclesiae*, "Mirror of the Church," c. 1217), who claimed to have been present at the exhumation. Though the discovery may well have been part of a ploy by the Glastonbury monks to attract financial support, it had the additional effect of proving not only that Arthur had been a "real" person but that, far from planning a return from the Isle of Avalon, he was indisputably dead. Since the figure of Arthur had long been regarded by Norman conservatives as a politically dangerous messianic symbol who incited the remaining British peoples (mainly in Wales and Cornwall) to rebellion, the discovery of his bones was a convenient sign which discredited Geoffrey's hints of a British return to power and enabled the Norman monarchy to appropriate Arthur as an early ancestor of their own royal line (Crick 1999).

Manuscripts and Sources

There is little doubt that Geoffrey's *Historia* was one of the most popular texts of its time. It survives in approximately 215 Latin manuscripts copied between the twelfth and eighteenth centuries, which can be divided into three main versions: the First Variant, Second Variant, and Vulgate (or standard) text (Crick 1991). There is no sense in which any of these texts are the "original" as written by Geoffrey; as with most examples of handwritten texts, medieval or modern, constant revisions by the author and copyists disrupt the concept of an "original" text, an artificial concept that has been produced largely by print culture. As well as this long history of Latin manuscript versions of the *Historia*, it was also translated into most of the major vernacular languages of the Middle Ages: firstly into Norman French (or Anglo-Norman) by Wace in his *Roman de Brut*, c. 1155, which was itself translated into Middle English by Layamon in the late twelfth or early thirteenth century (see chapter 4); and then into Middle Welsh during the thirteenth century (Reis 1968; Roberts 1976, 1991).

Geoffrey clearly drew on a range of sources for the *Historia*, though not all of them are known. He names Gildas and Bede in his opening dedication (to Robert, Earl of Gloucester), and has obviously copied or adapted large sections of the *Historia Brittonum*, without acknowledgment. For his rhetorical style and his method of writing history he was indebted mainly to classical and late-antique models, including the work of Virgil (particularly the *Aeneid* and the *Georgics*), Augustine of Hippo, and the *De Rerum Natura* of Lucretius (Curley 1994; Ingledew 1994). He refers to illustrious Latin writers such as Cicero, Livy, Lucan, and Juvenal as a means of conferring authority upon his own text, and was familiar with King Alfred's translation of law codes into English (Thorpe 1966: 18). The Old Testament, with its ideology of the Promised Land and the origins of a people, is also influential on the work, reflecting Geoffrey's clerical background and the significance of biblical motifs as part of the fabric of medieval literary allusion.

What appears to be Geoffrey's most significant source is, however, irretrievable. In the Prologue, Geoffrey refers to "a very old book":

> I frequently thought the matter over in this way until Walter, archdeacon of Oxford, a man skilled in the rhetorical arts and in foreign histories, brought me a very old book in the British tongue (*quendam Britannici sermonis librum uetustissimum*) which set out in excellent style a continuous narrative of all their deeds from the first king of the Britons, Brutus, down to Cadualadrus, son of Caduallo. Though I have never gathered showy words from the gardens of others, I was persuaded by his request to translate the book into Latin in a rustic style, reliant on my own reed pipe; had I larded my pages with bombastic terms, I would tire my readers with the need to linger over understanding my words rather than following my narrative. (*HRB* prologue; Reeve & Wright 2007: 4)

Walter, the "archdeacon of Oxford," certainly existed: he was the Provost of the small college of Augustinian canons, St George's, in Oxford, where Geoffrey spent the larger part of his career, and his name appears on a number of charters and documents, sometimes as a co-signatory with Geoffrey himself (Thorpe 1966: 12). Of the "very old book in the British tongue" there is, however, no trace whatsoever. Geoffrey claims that his *Historia* is simply his own humble translation of that book, though this is almost certainly a conventional way of conferring authority and historical authenticity on work that is largely his own. In the Arthurian section he says that he found the story of the battle of Camlan, between Arthur and Mordred, in the "British book" and that he heard an oral account of it from Walter of Oxford (*HRB* book 11), suggesting that the story circulated in both oral and written forms. A reference to Camlan, where "Arthur and Medraut" were killed, occurs in the *Annales Cambriae*, to which Geoffrey almost certainly had access.

Assuming that the "very old book" did exist – and scholars are by no means convinced of this – it cannot have been the sole or even major source of the *Historia*, which draws on a much wider range of materials, both Latin and vernacular, and reveals in its structure and style the creative genius of Geoffrey himself. One theory is that the "very old book" represented a collection of popular Welsh legends, of the kind preserved in the late-medieval Triads, which may have given Geoffrey some ideas about early Welsh history before the coming of the Saxons. Since he clearly had access to a copy of the *Historia Brittonum*, which contains an account of the "Cities and Marvels of Britain," it is likely that he also had access to similar British material such as the *Annales Cambriae* and the medieval Welsh royal genealogies. Geoffrey knew about Owain son of Urien (*Hiwenus filius Uriani*), for example, British princes whose names appear in early Welsh praise poetry and genealogies, and he may have got the idea of the battle of Camlan from the *Annales Cambriae*. He also associates Arthur specifically with Cornwall, perhaps drawing on earlier Welsh material which establishes this connection: in the early Welsh prose tale, *Culhwch ac Olwen*, for example, which may pre-date the *Historia*, Arthur's court is located at Kelliwig in Cornwall (Padel 1984). It is also possible that some of the Welsh translations of the *Historia*, appearing in the thirteenth century, may in fact preserve some of the same British sources that Geoffrey drew on (Thorpe 1966: 15).

Geoffrey's reference to the book being "in the British tongue" is also slightly misleading. Most modern scholars assume that this means "Welsh." In the twelfth century, however, *Britannia* referred both to the island of Britain and to Armorica, or modern Brittany. In his history of the founding of Brittany, conquered from the Gaulish Armorici by Maximianus, king of the Britons, Geoffrey describes how it was colonized by British settlers from the southwest and refers to it as *regnum Armoricum, quod nunc Britannia dicitur* ("the kingdom of Armorica, which is now called Brittany," *HRB* book 5). In the epilogue attached to some manuscripts of the *Historia*, Geoffrey says that Walter of Oxford brought the ancient British book with him *ex Britannia*. Since Walter already resided in Britain, it seems more likely that "Britannia" here means Brittany and not Britain. If the "very old book" came from Brittany it could have contained legendary and chronicle material relating to both Brittany and the southwest of Britain, and the "British tongue" in which it was written may have been exactly that, an old form of the British language, "common Brittonic," which was the ancestor of Welsh, Breton, and Cornish.

The Arthurian Section of the *Historia*

Geoffrey begins his account of Arthur's kingship at the opening of book 9, where he describes Arthur's coronation, by popular consent, following the death of his father Uther Pendragon. In the previous book, we are told the circumstances of Arthur's conception: through the magic of Merlin, Uther, king of the Britons, assumes the appearance of Gorlois, Duke of Cornwall, in order to spend the night with Gorlois's wife Ygerna. Arthur is the product of this supernatural liaison, establishing his credentials as an extraordinary hero. Uther and Gorlois are at war and Gorlois is killed in battle, leaving Ygerna free to be claimed by Uther. They live together, producing a second child, Anna, until Uther, falling ill, is finally poisoned by Saxon enemies, just as Merlin had predicted.

Arthur's succession to the crown is strongly legitimated by Geoffrey. Not only is Arthur the rightful heir of Uther but his nomination is supported by all the British leaders and he is crowned by Dubricius, the Archbishop of Caerlleon, a fictitious office but one which carries a certain authority for the purposes of establishing Arthur as a fully endorsed king. Arthur arrives on the throne in the nick of time. Hearing of Uther's death, Saxon hordes pour into the country and overrun the north of Britain. Acting decisively and boldly, determined to demonstrate his claim to the whole island, the young King Arthur (Geoffrey tells us he was 15 years old) lays siege to the city of York. With the help of his cousin, the king of Brittany, Arthur masses a huge army and routs the Saxons in a series of battles (taken from the battle-list in the *Historia Brittonum*), culminating in the battle of Badon Hill in which Arthur carries a shield bearing the image of Mary and wins a decisive victory against the Saxons.

Throughout this lengthy account of the way in which Arthur restores peace to the island of Britain, Geoffrey continually emphasizes Arthur's excellence as a king. Not only is he fearless in battle, he is a skilled tactician and leader who issues orders to his allies and delivers stirring speeches to his men. He grants safe passage to the remaining Saxons to return to their own lands, having divested them of their treasure and exacted a tribute, but is unremitting in his vengeance when the Saxons defy him and re-invade Britain. He fights in the name of God, always reassuring himself that he is waging a "just war," sanctioned by God because he is in the right, and supported by the Archbishop Dubricius, who confirms the justice of Arthur's mission. Above all, Arthur is no tyrant: he constantly seeks, and listens to, the advice of his counselors, retreating from battle or making truces on their advice. Even in peacetime, Arthur knows how to behave. Having restored royal control in Britain, Arthur marries a noble woman, Guinevere, raised in Cornwall but of Roman descent, as a fitting partner and matriarch of the royal line. He expands his retinue to include distinguished knights from many kingdoms, developing a code of courtly dress and behavior that sets the model for noble men throughout the world.

The next section of Arthur's career concerns his conquest of Europe. Norway, Denmark, and Gaul fall to the Arthurian armies; siege warfare, the dominant military technology of Geoffrey's own day and the staple tactic of the crusading armies, is described in convincing detail. Arthur is the exact opposite of the *roi fainéant*, "do-nothing king," of later French romance, being constantly in motion, constantly in the thick of every battle. Geoffrey's assured pacing of the narrative, from the broad sweep of Arthur's sea crossings to the blow-by-blow account of the duel between Arthur and Frollo, the Gaulish tribune, conveys something of the breakneck speed with which Arthur effortlessly extends his rule across great stretches of the Continent. Having secured Gaul, Arthur turns politician and delegates power to his allies, doling out the Gaulish provinces (including Normandy, as cited above) to his own men and to local noblemen who supported him, thereby ensuring their loyalty once his armies leave.

Another period of peace ensues, and Geoffrey inserts here a portrait of royal pageantry and celebration, a set-piece description that displays Geoffrey's powers of rhetoric to full effect. Arthur decides (with the agreement of his courtiers) to hold a state coronation at Caerlleon, inviting world leaders to pay homage to him and confirm their continuing peace treaties. Geoffrey begins the account of this illustrious event with a brief but rhetorically correct description of the city of Caerlleon, using conventional formulae found in urban eulogies. References to the site of the city, to its access by water, its churches, its wealth, and its educated inhabitants are standard topics of urban eulogy, found in descriptions of the great European and crusader cities such as Rome and Jerusalem. It is clearly a mark of Geoffrey's fondness for Caerlleon, a very small town in southeast Wales, that he sets it on a par with the great cities of the world.

Following the urban eulogy there is a long list of the guests who attend the coronation, including regional and international kings, archbishops, earls, and other dignitaries. Again, this is a conventional narrative device, designed to emphasize the full extent of the king's power by itemizing all those who pay homage to him or who are ready to fight in his armies. Similar lists are found in vernacular romance, such as the guest list at the wedding of Erec and Enide in Chrétien de Troyes's romance, and there are what appear to be parodies of the device in the Welsh tales of *Breuddwyd Rhonabwy* ("The Dream of Rhonabwy") and *Culhwch ac Olwen*, where the list of Arthur's allies is so long, and so eccentric, that it becomes ridiculous. Here, however, Geoffrey's purpose is entirely serious, and he follows the list with a detailed account of the ceremonial, the feasting, and the entertainments, claiming that Britain under Arthur's rule had become the epitome of courtly brilliance and sophistication. The celebration continues for four days, and on the final day Arthur distributes land grants to those who have served him faithfully, a testament to Arthur's generosity and political acumen.

The spirit of festival celebration and well-being conjured up in this section forms a dramatic contrast to the next scene, in which a delegation from the Roman emperor, Lucius Hiberius, presents Arthur with a letter accusing him of being a tyrant who has wrested Gaul away from the empire and who now refuses to pay tribute. Cador, the duke of Cornwall, comments that it is about time the knights went out to battle again, since their life of ease in the court, playing games and flirting with women, is making cowards of them, a familiar topic from French romance. Arthur delivers a rhetorically charged speech to his allies, following the lines of Ciceronian argument to put a persuasive case for invading Rome. He refers to his royal ancestors, including Belinus, Constantine, and Maximianus, who all held Rome when they were kings of the Britons, and uses them as precedents for supporting his own claims to Rome. The motif of genealogy is explicit here: Arthur belongs to a royal line of legitimate rulers who have a right not only to Britain but to Rome itself. Arthur's appeal to his men is answered in equally sonorous terms by Hoel, king of Armorica, and Auguselus, king of Albany (Scotland), both of whom support Arthur's call to arms as an act of vengeance against the Roman Empire for its former enslavement of Britain.

Geoffrey's description of the mustering of Arthur's huge army alludes, no doubt deliberately, to the mounting of a crusade. The First Crusade of 1099 had resulted in the re-conquest of Jerusalem from the Jewish and Muslim occupiers and the establishment of the Kingdom of Jerusalem, a western outpost in the Holy Land. During the period when Geoffrey was writing the *Historia*, Muslim forces were beginning to reunite, and with the recapture of Edessa by Muslims in 1144 a second crusade was called in 1147. Geoffrey's account of Arthur's attack on Rome models a political and ideological conflict between West and East: while Arthur's armies are drawn from Western Europe, the Roman emperor Lucius, at the opening to book 10, calls on the "Kings of the Orient" to send troops to assist him. An exotic roll-call follows: Greeks,

Africans, Parthians, Medes, Egyptians, Babylonians – all the representatives of the eastern empire come to the aid of Rome against the forces of the West, led by Britain. Under Arthur's leadership, Britain is positioned as the scourge of Rome, equal to the combined power of the East.

As Arthur embarks for Rome with his army, Geoffrey inserts, almost as an afterthought, the crucial information that Arthur hands over the defense of Britain to his nephew Mordred (*Modredus*) and to his queen, Guinevere. In Geoffrey's construction of the Arthurian genealogy, Mordred is the son of Arthur's sister Anna and her husband King Loth. The theme of Arthur's incestuous paternity of Mordred, first found in the French Vulgate Cycle of prose tales, is not part of Geoffrey's scheme; in accordance with his model of historiography, events have few explicit causes but simply unfold with an almost biblical or prophetic inevitability. But it was Geoffrey who first portrayed Mordred as the traitor who seized Arthur's kingdom and his wife, causing the final tragedy of Camlan in which they are both fatally wounded.

With the kind of narrative skill we have already observed, Geoffrey keeps postponing the major battle between Arthur and Lucius, setting up a sense of anticipation and impending drama which carries us through a complex series of military tactics. On the way to battle, Arthur is sidetracked into a single combat with a fierce giant whom he kills on the top of Mont-Saint-Michel in Brittany, an episode which demonstrates yet again Arthur's courage and skill as a warrior. In an unusual piece of authorial commentary, Geoffrey tells us that Arthur decides to fight the giant single-handedly in order to inspire his men, but there is a symbolic meaning here too, with Arthur enacting the liberation of a nation subdued beneath a tyrannical power.

A number of Arthur's men, including his nephew Gawain, brother of Mordred, engage in a series of preliminary skirmishes with Lucius's forces, and we see here the beginnings of the characterization of Gawain as rash, defiant, and hot-headed, a personality profile which reappears in the French romance tradition, though less often in the English tradition, where Gawain is more typically represented as the exemplar of courtly behavior and practice (see chapter 18). After some detailed descriptions of various military maneuvers, Geoffrey at last comes to the point: Lucius and Arthur prepare to do battle at Autun. In the wake of a number of reversals and losses, Lucius is nervous and indecisive; by contrast, Arthur is clear-headed, strategic, and completely in control of his large and diverse forces. Geoffrey gives a very specific description of Arthur's tactics, relying heavily on military jargon and technical terms, commenting on the formation of infantry battalions, cavalry reserves, left and right wings, and the disposal of divisions.

When Arthur has positioned all his troops and generals where he wants them, he delivers a powerful battle-speech, reminding the soldiers of their previous successes against the Danes, Norwegians, Gauls, and Romans, the strength of their current position, waiting in ambush for the Roman forces, and the promise of great rewards when they capture Rome itself. Geoffrey matches this speech with one delivered by

Lucius to the opposing army, reminding them of the past glory of their ancestors whose battles on behalf of the Republic paved the way for the triumphs of the Empire. But Lucius's speech rings hollow, revealing his indecision and lack of strategy compared to Arthur. He more or less asks his army to expose themselves to almost certain death before Arthur's front lines, in the vain hope of breaking through Arthur's first assault.

The battle begins, and because Geoffrey has spent so long setting up the armies and naming the various generals we feel the impact of the terrible losses that soon begin to mount up. Bedwerus the butler and Kaius the steward are early casualties, and Geoffrey is soon reeling off the names of the dead on both sides, while keeping us abreast of tactical movements as divisions retreat or move forward, falter or rally. As Gawain engages in single combat with Lucius, Arthur suddenly appears in the throng like an avenging warrior, swinging his sword Caliburn, spurring his men on with insults to the enemy, and mowing down the opposition with mighty strokes. Just as Arthur had hoped when fighting the giant of Mont-Saint-Michel, his courage and ferocity inspire his men. The infantry regroups and charges at the Romans as the cavalry attacks from another angle. After furious fighting on both sides, with the loss of thousands of men, Lucius is killed by an unknown hand and the Britons are the victors.

In Geoffrey's account of the aftermath of the battle, he makes it clear that the Romans have brought this disaster on themselves. On behalf of all of Britain, Arthur has taken revenge on the Romans for their oppression of the island when it was part of the empire and their continued demands for unwarranted tribute. In his attitude to Rome, Geoffrey is not merely harking back to perceived injustices in the days of the Roman Empire but is commenting on the power of Rome in his own day, as the center of a revived imperial state which included most of France, Italy, and Germany. Significantly, Arthur never gets to Rome or fulfills his plan to capture it. On his way there, he hears of Mordred's treachery, his seizure of the crown, and adulterous relationship with Guinevere, and is forced to return to Britain to reclaim his kingdom.

To compound his wickedness, Mordred has enlisted the help of the Saxons, along with the Scots, Picts, and Irish, all the traditional enemies of the Britons. As Arthur lands in Britain with his troops, Gawain is killed in battle, and Arthur marches on to Winchester in pursuit of Mordred. A siege and then open battle bring about huge losses among Mordred's army and he flees to Cornwall, pursued once more by Arthur. Finally the two armies meet at Camlan, which Geoffrey locates in Cornwall, the region he most frequently associates with Arthur as the land of his birth. We are given an abbreviated account of military tactics and a mere summary, in indirect speech, of Arthur's rallying cry to his troops. This time, Geoffrey does not want to prolong the moment of battle because the end is so near and utterly inescapable. First Mordred is killed, though not explicitly by Arthur, followed by a list of the fallen on both sides. At the very end of book 11, almost as an afterthought, we are told that Arthur was mortally wounded and carried off to Avalon. His heir is his cousin Constantine, son of the Duke of Cornwall; the year, so Geoffrey tells us, was 542.

The Myth of Arthur

In this Arthurian section of the *Historia*, Geoffrey creates a hero for his own day, a warrior king who is wise and generous and who is sufficiently skilled in both war and politics to maintain a peaceful kingdom and an empire beyond his own shores. Arthur is represented as the true product of prophecy; as a secular messiah, his coming is predicted by Merlin as the "boar of Cornwall" who will repel the foreigners (the Saxons), command the forests of Gaul, and strike fear into the House of Romulus (Rome).

At the level of denotation, the meaning of Arthur as a benchmark for the Norman kings is very clear. But a plurality of connotative and symbolic meanings surrounds the figure of Arthur, in keeping with the medieval predilection for allegory, both religious and secular. He is a symbol of imperial power, nationhood, the realization of God's will on earth, and the importance of genealogy in legitimating kingship. These are the myths that Arthur embodies, the ideologies that define Geoffrey's view of his own historical moment. Yet even while Geoffrey is confirming these myths through his account of Arthur's exploits, his story undermines them and reveals their internal contradictions. Imperial power is built on human sacrifice; the myth of nation depends on an elision of competing rights and needs; the will of God is not self-evident but is mediated through the church, which has its own agendas. Genealogy, the basis of Geoffrey's entire account of the line of British kings, cannot claim any superior status as a determiner of the distribution of power when families can cause their own destruction, like Mordred and Arthur, who is left without a direct heir.

The central myth of the *Historia Regum Britanniae* is the legitimacy of the Norman regime in Britain, achieved by conquest and then normalized by Geoffrey, who created a foundational myth which justified the Norman conquest as a natural progression dictated by history, genealogy, and the will of God. Arthur is the validating ancestor of the Normans, and a reminder that if the Normans depart from the standards of kingship set by Arthur, their own regime will be imperiled. The story of Arthur, invented by Geoffrey of Monmouth from the pieces of old legends, creates a myth of imperial kingship that, like every version of the Arthurian story since then, contains within it the seeds of its own destruction.

PRIMARY SOURCES

Reeve, M. (ed.) & Wright, N. (trans.) (2007). *Geoffrey of Monmouth: History of the kings of Britain.* Cambridge: Boydell.

Thorpe, L. (trans.) (1966). *Geoffrey of Monmouth: History of the kings of Britain.* Harmondsworth: Penguin.

REFERENCES AND FURTHER READING

Ashe, G. (1985). *The discovery of King Arthur*. London: Doubleday.

Brooke, C. N. L. (1976). Geoffrey of Monmouth as a historian. In C. N. L. Brooke, D. Luscombe, G. Martin, & D. Owen (eds), *Church and government in the Middle Ages*. Cambridge: Cambridge University Press, pp. 77–91.

Burke, P. (1969). *The Renaissance sense of the past*. London: Arnold.

Collingwood, R. G. & Myres, J. N. L. (1936). *Roman Britain and the English settlements*. Oxford: Clarendon Press.

Crick, J. (1991). *The* Historia Regum Britannie *of Geoffrey of Monmouth, vol. 4: Dissemination and reception in the later Middle Ages*. Cambridge: Brewer.

Crick, J. (1992). Geoffrey of Monmouth: Prophecy and history. *Journal of Medieval History*, 18, 357–71.

Crick, J. (1999). The British past and the Welsh future: Gerald of Wales, Geoffrey of Monmouth and Arthur of Britain. *Celtica*, 23, 60–75.

Curley, M. (1994). *Geoffrey of Monmouth*. New York: Twayne.

Dalton, P. (2005). The topical concerns of Geoffrey of Monmouth's *Historia Regum Britannie*: History, prophecy, peacemaking, and English identity in the twelfth century. *Journal of British Studies*, 44, 688–712.

Echard, S. (1998). *Arthurian narrative in the Latin tradition*. Cambridge: Cambridge University Press.

Gransden, A. (1974). *Historical writing in England, vol. 1: c. 500 to c. 1307*. London: Routledge & Kegan Paul.

Hanning, R. W. (1966). *The vision of history in early Britain: From Gildas to Geoffrey of Monmouth*. New York: Columbia University Press.

Ingledew, F. (1994). The Book of Troy and the genealogical construction of history: The case of

Geoffrey of Monmouth's *Historia Regum Britanniae. Speculum*, 69, 665–704.

Knight, S. T. (1983). *Arthurian literature and society*. London: Macmillan.

Loomis, R. S. (1928). Geoffrey of Monmouth and Arthurian origins. *Speculum*, 3, 16–33.

Otter, M. (1996). *Inventiones: Fiction and referentiality in twelfth-century English historical writing*. Chapel Hill, NC: University of North Carolina Press.

Padel, O. J. (1984). Geoffrey of Monmouth and Cornwall. *Cambridge Medieval Celtic Studies*, 8, 1–27.

Padel, O. J. (2006). Geoffrey of Monmouth and the development of the Merlin legend. *Cambrian Medieval Celtic Studies*, 51, 37–65.

Partner, N. F. (1977). *Serious entertainments: The writing of history in twelfth-century England*. Chicago, IL: University of Chicago Press.

Reis, E. (1968). The Welsh versions of Geoffrey of Monmouth's *Historia. Welsh History Review*, 4, 97–127.

Roberts, B. F. (1976). Geoffrey of Monmouth and Welsh historical tradition. *Nottingham Medieval Studies*, 20, 29–40.

Roberts, B. F. (1991). Geoffrey of Monmouth, *Historia Regum Britanniae* and *Brut y Brenhinedd*. In R. Bromwich, A. O. H. Jarman, & B. F. Roberts (eds), *The Arthur of the Welsh*. Cardiff: University of Wales Press, pp. 97–116.

Tatlock, J. S. P. (1950). *The legendary history of Britain*. Berkeley, CA: University of California Press.

Tolhurst, F. (2006). *Geoffrey of Monmouth as feminist historian, mythmaker and mythographer*. Basingstoke: Palgrave Macmillan.

Wood, J. (2005). Where does Britain end? The reception of Geoffrey of Monmouth in Scotland and Wales. In R. Purdie & N. Royan (eds), *The Scots and medieval Arthurian legend*. Cambridge: Brewer, pp. 9–24.

4

The Chronicle Tradition

Lister M. Matheson

After the appearance and rapid initial dissemination of Geoffrey of Monmouth's *Historia Regum Britanniae* ("History of the Kings of Britain"), full-scale chronicles of British/English history written in England between the twelfth and sixteenth centuries almost invariably included an extensive narrative of the reign of King Arthur (Fletcher 1906/66; Matheson 1990). Such accounts were either directly or ultimately based on Geoffrey's work, though often with additions and modifications arising from the spread of Arthurian materials in other genres such as the romance, or reflecting changes in contemporary political conditions and literary or propagandist agendas.

By their nature, the various chronicles of England had a *prima facie* claim and even an inherent generic obligation to historical "truth," and the chronicle writers are often scrupulous in asserting the authenticity of their narratives (cf. Moll 2003; Given-Wilson 2004). Self-justification probably served two purposes: it reassured readers and, perhaps more importantly, warned would-be chroniclers, potential rivals, of the accuracy and definitive nature of the work in hand. The chronicles, therefore, served, or purported to serve, as the "received" or "official" history of King Arthur and his reign, a historical context within which readers could then view Arthurian romances and other quasi-historical tales.

When considering the chronicle accounts of Arthur, we should keep in mind that he and his reign formed part of a larger narrative that is often designated "the legendary history of Britain" by modern historians but that was regarded as a truly historical part of a seamless whole by the original chroniclers and their readers. Arthur was the descendant of Brutus, the eponymous founder of Britain, who was in turn the successor of Albina, daughter of the king of Syria and eponymous founder of Albion, and fits easily within the pantheon of such semi-mythological figures (MacDougall 1982; Ingledew 1994; Drukker 2003).

The major chronicles available in medieval England that include the reign of Arthur are listed and discussed below. It should be borne in mind that much of English society was multilingual, and chronicles were written in Latin,

Anglo-Norman, English, and Welsh (though not, apparently, in demographically challenged Cornish). Even though readers became increasingly monolingual, using English as their sole or first language, educated authors remained fluent or proficient in several languages and were thus subject to multiple influences. Not all chronicles were equally well known in their times, however, and the level of post-medieval antiquarian and modern scholarly interest in a particular work is not necessarily an absolute indicator of its medieval authority. The following list of chronicles that include the reign of King Arthur is chronological by date of original composition; it includes for each work the approximate numbers of surviving manuscripts and the dates of their copying, thus indicating potential or apparent influence and allowing a sense of whether the work and its narrative remained "contemporary."

Geoffrey of Monmouth's seminal *Historia Regum Britanniae* first appeared around 1138; it underlies the entire chronicle tradition of King Arthur and is treated at length in chapter 3. The amount of narrative space (about one fifth of the entire work) that Geoffrey accorded to Arthur demonstrated and established his centrality in the scheme of English history. The *Historia* survives in over two hundred manuscripts (including several written on the Continent), and this enormous number testifies to the work's importance throughout the Middle Ages; around fifty belong to the twelfth century, the rest being spread over the following three hundred and more years. The misgivings of the few early doubters, such as Gerald of Wales and William of Newburgh, of Geoffrey's veracity were buried under this avalanche of texts, and it is not until Ranulph Higden's limited criticisms of Geoffrey in the early to mid-fourteenth century (see below) that any serious doubts tentatively entered the mainstream chronicle tradition. Most of the manuscripts of the *Historia* were copied in and owned by religious houses, but its influence soon extended beyond monastic walls into secular literary culture.

There were some early skeptics of Geoffrey's detailed and fully fledged account of King Arthur and his reign, but they were few and far between, and (apart from Ranulph Higden's much later *Polychronicon*) their works were of limited circulation and influence. In any case, with one exception, the skeptics questioned the Galfridian narrative in detail rather than *in toto*. The exception is William of Newburgh, who prefaced his *Historia Rerum Anglicarum* ("History of English Affairs," covering the period 1066 to 1198) with a powerful general attack on Geoffrey of Monmouth's integrity and veracity, especially in his account of Arthur and his exploits since they are not recounted by earlier domestic and foreign historians. However, William's outright dismissal of Geoffrey's Arthur did not gain general acceptance, perhaps partly because William's *Historia* began in 1066 and did not offer a substitute history for earlier times. No less a critic than Giraldus Cambrensis, who clearly despised the *Historia Regum Britanniae* and its success, accepted Arthur and felt no compunction about appropriating parts of Geoffrey's work when he felt like it. But even among Geoffrey's earliest adherents there was some uneasiness about Arthur's Continental conquests. Thus Alfred of Beverley, whose *Annales* (Brutus to 1129) are compiled primarily from Geoffrey of Monmouth and Simeon of Durham, wondered why Arthur and his war against the Romans in France are unrecorded by Roman, Frankish, Greek, or Oriental historians. Thereafter, however, this nascent suspicion about the Roman war episode, uncorroborated as it is by independent foreign chronicles, lay dormant until Higden's *Polychronicon*, the first version of which was written in the 1320s.

The earliest vernacular chronicle response to Geoffrey of Monmouth's *Historia* for which there is evidence was a metrical retelling in Anglo-Norman by Geffrei Gaimar, commissioned by Custance Fitz Gilbert and written in the 1140s in Hampshire and Lincolnshire. Gaimar's chronicle consisted of two parts, the first of which was a history of the Britons drawn from Geoffrey of Monmouth, while the second was a history of the English (*L'estoire des Engleis*). The first part, which included the reign of Arthur, has, however, been lost, for later copyists replaced this section by a metrical work composed by the Norman poet Wace, a Jerseyman by birth who worked for much of his life in Caen in Normandy.

Completed in 1155, Master [Robert] Wace's *Geste des Bretons* (or *Roman de Brut*, as it became known) was a free and skilful adaptation of Geoffrey's *Historia* that retained in the main the historical substance of the latter but added many minor details and corrections drawn from outside sources and traditions. Wace's *Brut* owed much to the verse form (octosyllabic couplets), vivid style, and chivalric characterization of the French metrical romances. The work enjoyed a steady readership, surviving in a respectable 24 complete and fragmentary manuscripts, the latest of which date to the fourteenth century, around the time that English-language works were beginning to dominate the secular literary scene. Wace's *Brut* also became a major conduit mediating between Geoffrey's *Historia* and many of the later vernacular chronicles.

To Layamon, an obscure secular parish priest in Ernley, Worcestershire, goes the literary-historical distinction of being the first chronicler to write in English since the final, tenacious continuators of the *Anglo-Saxon Chronicle*. His *Brut* was a remarkable achievement, written around the turn of the twelfth and thirteenth centuries, without any recent literary antecedents as guides. Layamon's immediate primary source for the historical material of his chronicle was a variant version of Wace's *Roman de Brut*, very freely adapted and extended to more than double the length of the earlier work, with the Arthurian section being expanded to around half the entire poem. Layamon synthesized new and old, very successfully blending elements of Wace's French-romance-influenced style with older native English elements. His additions and changes alter considerably the tone of Wace's work, changing it into an old-fashioned warrior epic rather than a chivalric tale. Layamon's choice of an English diction that may have been rather archaic at the end of the twelfth century was perhaps prompted by a politico-cultural agenda that sought to champion the native language and promote an English historiography (Tiller 2007).

Layamon's *Brut* must have had a very limited circulation and its influence cannot be detected in any subsequent chronicle. Only two manuscripts have survived, though textual comparison shows that at least one more must have once existed. (Indeed, we are lucky that even these two copies survived the fire of 1731 in Sir Robert Cotton's library.) The earlier manuscript dates to the first quarter of the thirteenth century, while the second was written some fifty years later. The compiler of the second text seems to have realized the potential market shortcomings of Layamon's *Brut*, for he revises and shortens its narrative, modernizes the diction, and reduces the alliteration. Despite his efforts, however, Layamon's *Brut* remained, as I have characterized it elsewhere, "a mighty backwater" in the development of the chronicle tradition (Matheson 1990: 251).

Indeed, chronologically the next major chronicle to be compiled was the Anglo-Norman Prose *Brut*, which differed diametrically from Layamon's *Brut* in language, medium, and style. The importance of the Prose *Brut* and its major versions can easily be obscured by the ordering of works and arrangement of genres in modern literary histories and anthologies, where the work is treated monolithically in one place alone. Accordingly, I have chosen in the remainder of this chapter to discuss the individual major versions of the Prose *Brut* at their chronological places in order to suggest the market competition among various contemporary chronicles.

The earliest version of the Anglo-Norman Prose *Brut*, a substantial work that ended with the death of Henry III in 1272, was composed and compiled around the end of the thirteenth century and thus pre-dates the major Middle English verse chronicles that were written after Layamon's. It has been tentatively suggested that Margaret Longespée, wife of Henry de Lacy, Earl of Lincoln, might have been the patroness behind the original composition (Marvin 2006: 44–7). The early narrative is largely based on Wace's *Roman de Brut* (up to King Oswy, with details from the next), Gaimar's *Estoire des Engleis* (to around the Norman Conquest), and then a Latin work similar to a chronicle associated with the monastery of Barlings in Lincolnshire. The writer supplemented these sources with material and details taken from other monastic and secular sources.

As the choice of language and the suggested identity of the patroness of the original work suggest, the intended audience was the French-speaking aristocracy and higher gentry of England in the late thirteenth century. Over the course of the next two hundred years several revisions and augmentations and many copies of the Anglo-Norman *Brut* would be produced, though relatively few manuscripts containing only its original form to 1272 have survived. It would not, therefore, have been immediately obvious to contemporary writers that this was the work that would eventually dominate the chronicle field in the fourteenth and especially fifteenth centuries. Accordingly, prospective authors of potentially competitor chronicles were not discouraged from their work.

The Middle English *Metrical Chronicle* linked with the name of Robert of Gloucester survives in two recensions, though only the continuation to 1270 in the first recension can be confidently ascribed to a writer, probably a monk, named "Robert." The association with Gloucester is inferential, though dialect evidence shows that the original work was indeed composed in southwest England. The first, longer version was compiled around 1300, while the second, shorter version was produced within the following quarter century. Both recensions of the *Metrical Chronicle* are similar in content up to the death of Henry I in 1135 and thus generally agree in their Arthurian section.

The section to 1135 is ultimately based on Geoffrey of Monmouth's *Historia*, as far as it goes, supplemented by other historical and oral materials and clarified in details. The influence of the French Arthurian romances colors the chronicler's characterization of Arthur, his knights, and Merlin.

Despite his superficially "popular" rhyming couplets, the chronicler's asseverations that he is writing for a "lewd" (that is, unlettered or, at least, non-Latinate) audience should be taken primarily as a standard, self-deprecatory, rhetorical flourish justifying or excusing his use of the English rather than the Latin language. The chronicle's length and the quality of its surviving manuscripts suggest that it did not circulate any lower in the social scale than gentry owners. Nevertheless, the number of surviving full and fragmentary texts (sixteen, ranging from the fourteenth to the sixteenth centuries) shows that the *Metrical Chronicle* had a healthy continuing circulation among wealthy members of the book-owning classes.

Peter (Peres de) Langtoft, a canon of the Augustinian priory of Bridlington in Yorkshire, wrote his Anglo-Norman verse *Chronicle* soon after 1307, in which year the final recension of the work ends. The first part of his narrative, and thus the Arthurian section, is a fairly close adaptation of Geoffrey's *Historia*, shortened, paraphrased, and supplemented by a few conscious authorial additions, changes, and interpretations. Langtoft's choice of language demonstrates the persistent strength of that insular dialectal version of French used by those less fortunate worthies who were not conversant with "Frenssh of Paris" as a perceived language of cultivation and literature in fourteenth-century England. The number of surviving manuscripts (at least fifteen, with two further untraced ones) attests to a healthy circulation of Langtoft's *Chronicle* among its targeted audience.

The anonymous *Short English Metrical Chronicle*, which was first composed at some point between 1312 and 1330, seems to have been deliberately designed to reach an audience lower down the social scale than that for Robert of Gloucester's chronicle. It is included here because of its scope (Brutus to, originally, the death in 1312 of Piers Gaveston, with later continuations) rather than its length, which is suitable for oral performance or, perhaps, teaching purposes. The style and tone are reminiscent of those of contemporary English metrical romances such as *King Horn* and *Havelok the Dane*. The ultimate source for the early period is Geoffrey's *Historia*, but the narrative of Arthur's reign is proportionately much briefer compared to the accounts found in the longer chronicles of Britain/England. The seven surviving texts, two of which are fifteenth century, seem to represent five different recensions of the work that vary considerably in their factual details concerning Arthur.

Ranulph Higden, a monk of the Benedictine abbey of St Werburgh's, Chester, completed in the late 1320s the now lost first version of his *Polychronicon*, a vast, encyclopedic universal chronicle from the Creation to the author's own day (first to 1327, and eventually to 1340, with brief entries to 1352). Higden continued to work on his text until his death around 1362/3, producing a series of revised and expanded versions. It is worth noting that the texts of the different versions of the *Polychronicon* show that Higden's thoughts on Arthur and the Roman war evolved during his revisions, becoming more skeptical about Geoffrey's account of King Arthur's Continental war against the Romans. Thus, in the so-called intermediate (or AB) version, surviving in almost seventy copies, the best known both then and now, Higden quotes with approval William of Malmesbury's distrust of extravagant tales concerning Arthur and then launches into a powerful attack on Geoffrey's account of the Roman war. As Higden notes, such an event does not occur in the Roman, French, Saxon, or (as the earlier CD version adds) British chronicles; furthermore, Geoffrey's characters are unhistorical and his chronology is quite wrong. Even Geoffrey, says Higden, wondered about the absence of Arthur from the works of Bede and Gildas, but Higden finds it a greater wonder that Geoffrey should praise so highly a character whom ancient, veracious, and famous historians mention hardly at all. However, Higden then proceeds to temper his criticisms by noting that it is natural for every nation to exaggerate the fame of its particular national heroes.

Higden's work survives in over 120 fourteenth- and fifteenth-century manuscripts and was clearly an influential historical force. Copies were owned by monasteries, friaries, priories, cathedrals, collegiate churches, colleges, hospitals, parish churches, some individual clerics, and a few laymen. Continuations were written, mainly in religious houses, and the work was freely mined for information by later chroniclers.

The massive Middle English verse chronicle sometimes attributed to Thomas Castleford was written in Yorkshire sometime between 1327 (when the narrative ends) and 1350. Judging from his interests in warlike matters, the author may have been a knight rather than a cleric. The Arthurian section is based primarily on Geoffrey's *Historia*, with details added from earlier chronicles and local Yorkshire tradition. The single extant manuscript was copied in the first quarter of the fifteenth century, and there must, therefore, have been at least one earlier text. Nevertheless, the work's circulation was probably very limited and restricted by length and language to a northern gentry audience.

Working some thirty years after Peter Langtoft, Robert Mannyng of Brunne, Lincolnshire, was well aware of the earlier writer's work, which he used as the basis for the later part of his chronicle, written in English and finished in 1338. For the earlier part, however, including the reign of Arthur, Mannyng turned to Wace's *Brut*, which he considered fuller, as the source for his narrative, with only the occasional detail borrowed from Langtoft. Mannyng, either a canon or lay brother of the Gilbertine house at Sempringham, declares that he writes in plain Middle English for an unsophisticated, lay (rather than learned) audience whose language is limited to that native tongue. Such assertions cannot, of course, be taken at simple face value. Manuscripts of the length of Mannyng's *Chronicle* were not cheap, and only three (one of which is a fragment) survive, copied at the end of the fourteenth and in the first half of the fifteenth centuries.

By the middle of the fourteenth century, the basic Anglo-Norman Prose *Brut* to 1272 received a further boost to its vitality in the form of two redactions that added independent continuations to the year 1332/3. The great majority of the around fifty manuscripts of the Anglo-Norman work belong to these so-called Short and Long Versions and were copied at various points throughout the fourteenth and fifteenth centuries.

The currency of Anglo-Norman as a literary language manifests itself again in the *Scalacronica*, a long prose chronicle of universal, British, and English history to 1363 written by Sir Thomas Gray, a Northumbrian knight who was constable of Norham Castle. Gray was captured in 1355 by the Scots and imprisoned in Edinburgh Castle, where he had ready access to a wide range of Latin, French, and English chronicles that formed the basis for the work that he began while incarcerated. His situation and circumstances are remarkably similar to those in which a later "knight-prisoner," Sir Thomas Malory, composed his *Morte Darthur*. Gray's account of King Arthur and his reign was heavily dependent on his sources, which included the *Brut* and the *Polychronicon*, supplemented by snippets of local tradition and details from the romances. Although it may not have been apparent at the time to Gray or his contemporaries, these two works among his various sources were in the process of achieving a market dominance and share that are perhaps responsible for the survival of the *Scalacronica* in only a single manuscript.

Although chronicles written in the Anglo-Norman and Latin languages continued to be copied, and indeed composed (especially in the latter language, in monastic settings), in the late fourteenth and fifteenth centuries, social and cultural changes ensured the steady reassertion of English as the primary language of literature during this time span. Gray's *Scalacronica* was perhaps the last major Anglo-Norman chronicle to treat Arthur's reign, and its readership was clearly very limited. On the other hand, the Anglo-Norman *Brut* and the Latin *Polychronicon* greatly extended their audiences through translations into English in the late fourteenth century. Both translations were made in southwest England, which seems to have been a center of literary activity in late medieval times. The Long Version of the Anglo-Norman *Brut*, ending in 1333 with the English victory over the Scots at the battle of Halidon Hill, was anonymously translated into English, probably in Herefordshire and perhaps as early as around 1380. John Trevisa, vicar of Berkeley in Gloucestershire, completed his English translation of Higden's Latin *Polychronicon* in 1387, his work having been undertaken at the request of Thomas, Lord Berkeley.

The first form of the Middle English *Brut* is witnessed by perhaps ten manuscripts, the earliest of which date to around 1400; a couple of texts that originally ended in 1333 received subsequent continuations beyond that year to make them more up-to-date. The English translation is faithful to the Anglo-Norman and thus contains much the same narrative content for the reign of Arthur (for convenient texts, see Böddeker 1874; Brie 1906; Marvin 2006), and the intended audience seems to have been a gentry one, similar to that of the Anglo-Norman work. The mere fact of translation, however, opened the way for a widening of ownership and readership.

Similarly, John Trevisa's translation of the massive *Polychronicon* (with a continuation to 1360), which survives in fourteen full manuscripts and as excerpts in a number more, strengthened the already considerable influence of Higden's work in religious and scholarly circles and increased its accessibility to and ownership (if not actual readership) by members of the lay community. Trevisa was not slavish and unthinking in his work, for he inserted new material and comments on sources, carefully labeled as his own. Thus he summarily dismissed William of Malmesbury's views on Arthur (quoted approvingly by Higden) and added a vigorous defense of the historicity of Arthur after his translation of Higden's doubts about the veracity of Geoffrey of Monmouth's extended account of Arthur's Roman war (for which, see above), though he did concede that over-praise of one's national heroes is a common occurrence. It is, however, important to note that not all texts of Trevisa's Middle English work included his rejoinder, and thus a number of readers, including William Caxton (see further below), would have been confronted with Higden's unmediated skepticism only.

Both the Latin and English versions of the *Polychronicon* enjoyed a healthy circulation in the late fourteenth and fifteenth centuries, especially considering the length of the work and the density of its contents. Its popularity, however, as a vehicle for a standard historical account of King Arthur was surpassed by that of the Middle English Prose *Brut*, almost all of whose 180 manuscripts belong to the fifteenth century. The original translation was first augmented by a continuation to 1377 and then by one to 1419. The so-called "Common Version" to 1419, a highly successful stage in the evolution of the text, was joined by "Extended" and "Abbreviated" versions, by derivative groups of texts, including a substantial one that ended in 1430, and by many minor groups of reworked texts and individual, highly engaged reworkings. Many additions to the basic text to 1419 took their material from the civic chronicles of London, reflecting an expansion of readership into the increasingly important merchant class of late medieval England. Working individually and in small groups, a number of professional scribes specialized in producing *Brut* manuscripts, confident of a ready market that did not rely on specific commissions. In the fifteenth century the Middle English Prose *Brut* must have been the standard history of England for owners and readers (not always the same) of the work, and thus the standard, received, and authoritative historical account of the Arthurian period. As literacy and book ownership increased and wealth and social importance diversified, copies of the *Brut* were owned across a wide spectrum of literate society: gentry and merchants, and their families, including a number of women; male and female religious houses; Oxford and Cambridge colleges; and secular priests and clerks.

Nevertheless, undeterred by such strong competition, two major Middle English chronicles that include the Arthurian period survive from the mid-fifteenth century, each compiled for different purposes and targeted at very specific (and different) audiences. The northerner John Hardyng's verse *Chronicle* survives in two versions. The first, Lancastrian, version (Brutus to 1437), completed by 1457, was intended for presentation to King Henry VI and appears in a unique manuscript, while the second, Yorkist, revised version, completed by 1464, was intended for Richard Duke of York, and, after the duke's death in 1460, was presented to his son Edward, by then king of England. Among Hardyng's impressive array of sources was at least one version of the Middle English Prose *Brut*, from which he may have taken some details for his Arthurian section. Hardyng notably introduces the history and quest for the Grail, and his chronicle was later one of the sources used by Sir Thomas Malory. In accordance with book ownership trends in general, copies of Hardyng's *Chronicle* (the second version) were soon acquired by gentry and London merchant owners further down the social scale than the originally intended recipient, and such circulation was reinforced by the appearance in print of this version of the chronicle in 1543.

However, John Capgrave, prior of the Augustinian friary at Lynn in Norfolk and prior provincial of his order, makes only the briefest of mentions of Arthur and his reign in his *Abbreuiacion of Cronicles* (Creation to 1417, perhaps left incomplete at the author's death in 1464). Capgrave's universal chronicle belongs to the annalistic, monastic tradition of chronicle writing and is primarily based on the works of Thomas Walsingham, though the Arthurian notices are drawn from Martinus Polonus's *Chronicon Pontificum et Imperatorum* ("Chronicle of Popes and Emperors"). The very restricted circulation and apparently non-existent influence of the *Abbreuiacion of Cronicles* is reflected by the two surviving manuscripts, both of which are closely connected to Capgrave himself, as an autograph or as a copy of an autograph.

On the other hand, the status of the English translations of the Prose *Brut* and the *Polychronicon* as standard accounts of the Arthurian period was consolidated and expanded yet further for late-fifteenth-century and later readers by William Caxton's decisions to publish them as, respectively, the first and second printed histories to appear in England. Both works must have entailed considerable investments of time, materials, and money for the printer, and it is highly unlikely that he published them without knowing that there would be a ready audience for them. Caxton's first edition of the *Brut* appeared in 1480 under the title *The Chronicles of England*, followed by an almost duplicate (except for spelling and punctuation) second edition in 1482. He used a Common Version text that ended in 1419 as the basis of his edition, adding a continuation to 1461 that was probably compiled by the printer himself. The Arthurian section was, therefore, textually identical to that found in the major manuscript tradition that Caxton had chosen to use.

The situation was, however, different in Caxton's edition of John Trevisa's translation of the *Polychronicon* (with a continuation to 1461), which was published around the same time (between July 2 and November 20, 1482) as the second, reset edition of *The Chronicles of England* (October 8, 1482). Unfortunately, the manuscript on which Caxton based his edition contained Ranulph Higden's attack on Geoffrey of Monmouth's account of Arthur's Continental war against the Romans but omitted Trevisa's sharp dismissal of William of Malmesbury and vigorous rebuttal of Higden (see above). On the other hand, *The Chronicles of England* contained a lengthy account of the Roman war, while the inadvertent omission in the *Polychronicon* edition created an apparent, awkward inconsistency between the two printed works. I would argue that Caxton attempted to compensate for the omission in his prologue to his edition of Malory's *Morte Darthur* (Matheson 1990: 264–65) and that the Roman war narrative in his *Chronicles of England* underlay his major revision of the corresponding book in Malory's work. By such editorial interventions, Caxton brought into closer factual agreement the accounts of Arthur's reign in two of his major publications.

Soon after Caxton's second edition of *The Chronicles of England*, perhaps in 1483, the Schoolmaster-Printer of St Albans published a version of Caxton's text that was much augmented by material taken from Werner Rolewinck's *Fasciculus temporum*, a popular compilation of historical facts, which was the source of numerous interpolations throughout the text on popes and foreign rulers. Of the ten subsequent early printed editions to 1528, two followed Caxton's simpler form while eight preferred the supplemented St Albans version. After Caxton's *editio princeps* there were two further editions of the *Polychronicon* by 1527, but of the other major chronicles written before 1500 that recounted the reign of Arthur, only the second version of John Hardyng's was printed, twice in 1543 by Richard Grafton.

Despite the continuing popularity of printed editions of *The Chronicles of England* in the first part of the sixteenth century, there were also signs that its standard historical account of King Arthur was coming under increasing challenge as "chroniclers" slowly succumbed to more recognizably modern "historians," who attempted to compare and evaluate their sources critically. Robert Fabyan's *New Chronicles of England and France* is an early example of a new humanist-influenced approach to historiography. Fabyan was a citizen of London, a draper who had served as alderman and sheriff. He completed his *New Chronicles* (Creation to 1485) in 1504, and the work, with a short continuation to 1509, was published posthumously in 1516. While Fabyan's earlier British and English history drew heavily upon the *Brut* (or the printed *Chronicles of England*) and he accepted the existence of Arthur, like Higden he questioned Geoffrey of Monmouth and rejected the Roman war. Fabyan's work was used by Polydore Vergil, an Italian humanist historian whose Latin *Anglica Historia* only found a publisher at Basel in 1534, despite having been commissioned by Henry VII and dedicated to Henry VIII. Vergil's incredulity about Geoffrey of Monmouth's veracity attracted the patriotic, xenophobic, and religious ire of English writers and probably retarded skepticism on the part of English writers concerning Arthur (Carley 1984). But what Thomas Nashe called in 1592 "our English Chronicles . . . rustie brasse, and worme-eaten bookes" increasingly became the heavily annotated province of critical antiquarian and historical writers like Edward Hall, John Stow, and Raphael Holinshed, through whom such material as was judged to be correct was mediated to a general public. Thus by the mid-seventeenth century, John Milton could confidently speak in his *History of Britain* of the "unlikelihoods of Arthur's Reign and great Atchievements" and characterize the king as "more renown'd in Songs and Romances, than in true stories" (see chapter 23).

Nevertheless, during their heyday in the fourteenth and fifteenth centuries, the chronicles provided English people in general with authentic histories of King Arthur. In particular, the many manuscripts of the Prose *Brut* and printed copies of the multiple editions of *The Chronicles of England* suggest that the account of Arthur related in these two associated works formed the standard, "true" narrative of his life and reign. It is in the context of these historical works that we should consider more self-consciously literary Arthurian narratives such as romances and, indeed, Thomas Malory's *Morte Darthur* and William Caxton's printed edition thereof. The medieval and early modern English chronicle accounts are not monolithic – there are differences between works and even within sub-versions of the same work (and, unsurprisingly, nationalistic Scottish chroniclers take a disparaging view of Arthur and his legitimacy). Such variation and adaptation testify to continued, lively interest in the figure and actions of England's greatest king.

PRIMARY SOURCES

Arnold, I. (ed.) (1938–40). *Le roman de Brut de Wace*, 2 vols. Paris: Société des anciens textes français.

Babington, C. & Lumby, J. R. (eds) (1865–86). *Polychronicon Ranulphi Higden monachi Cestrensis; together with the English translations of John Trevisa and of an unknown writer of the fifteenth century*, 9 vols. Rolls Series. London: Longman.

Barron, W. R. J. & Weinberg, S. C. (eds trans) (2001). *Layamon's Arthur: The Arthurian section of Layamon's Brut (lines 9229–14297)*, rev. edn. Exeter: University of Exeter Press.

Bell, A. (ed.) (1960). *L'Estoire des Engleis: By Geffrei Gaimar*. Oxford: Blackwell.

Böddeker, K. (1874). Die Geschichte des Königs Arthur. *Archiv*, 52, 1–32.

Brie, F. W. D. (ed.) (1906, 1908). *The Brut; or, the Chronicles of England*, 2 vols, o.s. 131, 136. London: Early English Text Society.

The Chronicles of England (1480). Westminster: William Caxton. 2nd edn 1482.

The Chronicles of England (?1483). St Albans: Schoolmaster-Printer.

Eckhardt, C. D. (ed.) (1996). *Castleford's Chronicle, or, The Boke of Brut*, 2 vols. EETS vols 305, 306. Oxford: Oxford University Press.

Ellis, H. (ed.) (1811). *The new chronicles of England and France, in two parts; by Robert Fabyan. Named by himself The concordance of histories. Reprinted from Pynson's edition of 1516. The first part collated with the editions of 1533, 1542, and 1559; and the second with a manuscript of the author's own time, as well as the subsequent editions: including the different continuations*. London: F. C. & J. Rivington.

Ellis, H. (ed.) (1812). *The chronicle of Iohn Hardyng. Containing an account of public transactions from the earliest period of English history to the beginning of* the reign of King Edward the Fourth. Together with the continuation by Richard Grafton, to the thirty fourth year of King Henry the Eighth. London: F. C. & J. Rivington.

Ellis, H. (ed.) (1846). *Polydore Vergil's English History, Vol. I., containing the first eight books, comprising the period prior to the Norman Conquest*. Camden Society vol. 46. London: J. B. Nichols & Son.

Hearne, T. (ed.) (1716). *{Alfred of Beverley.} Aluredi Beverlacensis Annales, sive historia de gestis regum Britanniæ, libris IX*. Oxford: e Theatro sheldoniano.

Howlett, R. (ed.) (1884–9). *William of Newburgh. Historia rerum Anglicarum*, vols 1 and 2 of *Chronicles of the Reigns of Stephen, Henry II and Richard I*, 4 vols. Rolls Series 82. London: Longman.

Lucas, P. J. (ed.) (1983). *John Capgrave's Abbreuiacion of cronicles*. EETS vol. 285. Oxford: Oxford University Press.

Marvin, J. (ed. trans.) (2006). *The oldest Anglo-Norman Prose Brut chronicle: An edition and translation*. Woodbridge: Boydell.

Mason, E. (trans.) (1976). *Geste des Bretons. Arthurian Chronicles {by} Wace and Layamon*. London: Dent. Repr. Toronto: University of Toronto Press, 1996.

Milton, J. (1991). *The history of Britain* (ed. G. Parry). Stamford, CA: Paul Watkins (facsimile edn).

Nashe, T. (1966). *Pierce Penilesse, his Supplication to the Divell, 1592* (ed. G. B. Harrison). Elizabethan and Jacobean Quartos vol. 11. New York: Barnes & Noble.

Spisak, J. W. & Matthews, W. (eds) (1983). *Caxton's Malory*. Berkeley, CA: University of California Press.

Stevenson, J. (ed.) (1836). *Scalacronica: by Sir Thomas Gray of Heton, knight. A chronical of England and Scotland from A.D. MLXVI to A.D. MCCCLXII.* Edinburgh: Maitland Club.

Stevenson, J. (trans.) (1996). *The History of William of Newburgh.* Lampeter: Llanerch.

Sullens, I. (ed.) (1996). *Robert Mannyng. The Chronicle.* Binghamton, NY: Medieval & Renaissance Texts & Studies.

Walsh, P. G. & Kennedy, M. J. (eds trans) (1988). *William of Newburgh. The history of English affairs: Book 1.* Warminster: Aris.

Wright, T. (ed.) (1866–68). *The chronicle of Pierre de Langtoft, in French verse from the earliest period to the death of King Edward I,* 2 vols. Rolls Series 47. London: Longmans, Green, Reader, & Dyer.

Wright, W. A. (ed.) (1887). *The Metrical Chronicle of Robert of Gloucester,* 2 vols. Rolls Series 86. London: Eyre & Spottiswoode.

Zettl, E. (ed.) (1935). *An anonymous short English metrical chronicle.* EETS o.s. vol. 196. London: Oxford University Press.

REFERENCES AND FURTHER READING

Carley, J. (1984). Polydore Vergil and John Leland on King Arthur: The battle of the books. *Interpretations,* 15, 86–100.

Drukker, T. (2003). Thirty-three murderous sisters: A pre-Trojan foundation myth in the Middle English Prose Brut chronicle. *Review of English Studies,* 54, 449–62.

Fletcher, R. H. (1966). *The Arthurian material in the chronicles.* New York: Franklin (original work published 1906).

Given-Wilson, C. (2004). *Chronicles: The writing of history in medieval England.* London: Hambledon.

Ingledew, F. (1994). The Book of Troy and the genealogical construction of history: The case of Geoffrey of Monmouth's *Historia Regum Britanniae. Speculum,* 69, 665–704.

MacDougall, H. A. (1982). *Racial myth in English history: Trojans, Teutons, and Anglo-Saxons.* Montreal: Harvest House.

Marx, W. & Radulescu, R. L. (eds) (2006). Readers and writers of the Prose *Brut. Trivium,* 36 (special issue).

Matheson, L. M. (1990). King Arthur and the medieval English chronicles. In V. M. Lagorio & M. L. Day (eds), *King Arthur through the ages,* vol. 1. New York: Garland, pp. 248–74.

Matheson, L. M. (1998). *The Prose Brut: The development of a Middle English chronicle.* Tempe, AZ: Medieval & Renaissance Texts & Studies.

Moll, R. J. (2003). *Before Malory: Reading Arthur in later medieval England.* Toronto: University of Toronto Press.

Summerfield, T. (1998). *The matter of kings' lives: The design of past and present in the early fourteenth-century verse chronicles by Pierre de Langtoft and Robert Mannyng.* Amsterdam: Rodopi.

Tiller, K. J. (2007). *Layamon's Brut and the Anglo-Norman vision of history.* Cardiff: University of Wales Press.

Part II
Celtic Origins of the Arthurian Legend

5

The Historical Context: Wales and England 800–1200

Karen Jankulak and Jonathan M. Wooding

Insofar as the Arthurian legend is historical, it is the history of the fifth and sixth centuries interpreted in terms of the cultural nationalism of later centuries. Britain at the close of the first millennium was an island of several different cultural and linguistic communities – some of long duration in Britain, some of quite recent arrival. Between them they spoke at least five languages: British (Welsh, Cornish, and related dialects), Old English (Anglo-Saxon), Irish (Gaelic), Latin, and Old Norse. The development among these nations of an expansive, often multicultural, vision of their own identities provided the context in which the Arthurian legend began to develop into the form we know today.

The "matter of Britain," which gave rise to "pseudo-" or "synthetic" histories of British cultural identity as well as to poems and stories for performance in the setting of rulers' courts, was in part a product of the rich relationship between the Irish, Welsh, and English during the eighth to tenth centuries. Already in the ninth century Welsh and English rulers such as Merfyn Frych of Gwynedd and Alfred the Great can be seen as the patrons of learned men of international origin, active in their royal courts. By the beginning of the second millennium the reformed monastic orders on the Continent had begun to find patrons in both Anglo-Saxon England and Celtic Britain. The appearance of the Normans in this environment, as well as the Bretons who followed in their train, fueled what was already a dynamic court and church culture interested in the "British" past, an interest which found its greatest advocate in Geoffrey of Monmouth.

Britain at the Opening of the Ninth Century

At the beginning of the ninth century the kingdoms of the Anglo-Saxons occupied much the same area as modern-day England. Celtic British populations, speaking the ancestor of the modern Welsh and Cornish languages, occupied the west, the southwest, and parts of the northwest of the island of Britain, though all of these groups were under pressure from Anglo-Saxon expansion. In the far north, the Irish (Gaelic)-speaking "Scots" were expanding to become the dominant political group, taking over what had been the kingdom of the Picts. Britain in 800 had just begun to experience the terror of raiding by Vikings from Scandinavia.

The Anglo-Saxon kingdoms were numerous, but from the seventh century tended to be dominated by a "heptarchy" of larger kingdoms, made up of the East Angles, East Saxons, Kentish, Mercians, Northumbrians, South Saxons, and West Saxons. These kingdoms were ruled by kings generally of established royal family, but still according to the pattern of kingship they had brought with them from their origins in Scandinavia and Germany. This style of kingship was, however, gradually changing. Bede pointedly describes seven Anglo-Saxon kings as holders of *imperium*, denoting an overkingship of a number of Anglo-Saxon kingdoms; the *Anglo-Saxon Chronicle* translates Bede's list and uses the term *bretwalda*, a title clearly denoting overkingship (Bede, *Historia Ecclesiastica* II.5; Swanton 2000: 60–1). This drift toward overkingship is seen generally in Europe at this time; in neighboring Francia, which enjoyed close links to Anglo-Saxon England, Charlemagne was crowned emperor in 800. The rise of the *imperium* concept could be interpreted in moral terms as political evolution, imitation, or opportunism – even necessary consolidation in the face of threat. Whether such a development was inevitable is arguable. Circumstances, in any event, fuelled it. The sack of Lindisfarne in Northumbria in 793 was followed by further raids, probably by Norwegian Vikings, upon the northeast, while Danish forces raided seasonally in southern England from 835 onward. In the 870s raids upon East Anglia, resulting in the martyrdom of King (later Saint) Edmund, and the capture of York, were the prelude to the establishment of more permanent Scandinavian kingdoms in Britain.

Events in Wales at the same period are only dimly known on account of the very limited documentary evidence. The earliest sources are the *Annales Cambriae* ("Welsh Annals") and their vernacular (Welsh) continuation, the *Brut y Tywysogion* ("Chronicle of the Princes"). These year-by-year chronicles are based at some point on contemporary records, but much of their early material is retrospectively compiled from unknown sources and is of varying degrees of authority (see chapter 2). A handful of early sources supplement this material: some charters imperfectly preserved from Llandaff, some notes in the *Vita Sancti Cadoci* ("Life of St Cadoc"), references in the *Vita Ælfredi regis* ("Life of King Alfred") by the Welshman Asser (d. 909), and genealogies of the princes.

In Wales we have evidence of early kingdoms in the northwest (Gwynedd) and southwest (Dyfed), described by Gildas as early as the sixth century. Other kingdoms whose names are known from later date are entities whose early history is more debatable. Brycheiniog, Ceredigion, Powys, and Glywysing all feature in events around the eighth and ninth centuries and their existence is assumed in the formation of the polities into which they were later absorbed. These include the expanded polity of Gwynedd in the ninth century (Gwynedd, Ceredigion, Powys), and the southern kingdoms of Deheubarth (Dyfed, Brycheiniog, Ceredigion, Powys) and Morgannwg (Glywysing), which emerged in the tenth and eleventh centuries.

England and Wales in the Ninth to Eleventh Centuries

In the late 700s the Welsh Annals record successive conflicts between King Offa of Mercia (r. 757–96) and the Welsh. In 777 or 778 is recorded "the devastation of the southern Britons by Offa," and again in the summer of 783 or 784. At the Battle of Rhuddlan in 796 or 797 Offa died along with King Maredudd of Dyfed (Morris 1980: 47, 88). The annals record the death of Caradog of Gwynedd at the hands of the Saxons the following year. Offa's death was coincident with the first Viking raids, which may have put off further attempts at Anglo-Saxon expansion into Wales.

Around the time of these conflicts we begin to see the emergence of ambitious rulers whose courts had familial and intellectual links beyond Wales. The father of Merfyn Frych (d. 844), Gwriad, is commemorated on an inscription (*crux Guriat*, "the cross of Gwriad") at Maughold in the Isle of Man, implying relations that took his interests beyond the local context (Kermode 1907: 122–3). Merfyn is shown as a king already with pretensions to overkingship when he is described in the famous Bamberg cryptogram as "glorious king of the Britons." The cryptogram itself is evidence for the presence of Irish scholars in Gwynedd, a presence that serves to give a context to education and literary ideas at the royal court (Mac Cana 2007: 29). This relationship – logical in terms of the proximity of Anglesey to Ireland – also provides a context for the presence in the *Historia Brittonum* (chs 13–14) of material later found in Irish pseudo-historical narratives (Morris 1980: 61, 201; Carey 1993: 2–3, 8–9).

Rhodri Mawr (d. 878), the son of Merfyn Frych and Nest of Powys, was the figure who oversaw the rise to dominance of Gwynedd in the ninth century. His inheritance of both Gwynedd (844) and Powys (855), and his marriage to Angharad of Ceredigion, saw Rhodri, on the death of Angharad's brother Gwgon (872), gain control of the greater part of Wales. Rhodri's son Anarawd raided in south Wales, inspiring the kings of Dyfed and Brycheiniog to build relationships with the ascendant Alfred the Great (r. 871–99) of Wessex.

The rise of Wessex under Alfred was in many ways a consequence of the Viking settlements, which all but extinguished the power of Northumbria, Mercia, and Essex. The exceptional qualities of Alfred himself came to the fore in this changed political environment. Alfred wielded centralized power in an unprecedented program of defenses (as shown by the Burghal Hideage), which saw off the Viking threat to Wessex, and effectively set in motion the transformation of numerous kingdoms into the nascent kingdom of England. Moreover, Alfred presided over a program of writing and translation, reflecting his own tastes – some of the translations are by his own hand – but also echoing a trend at the Carolingian court, which Alfred had visited in his youth. At some date, perhaps in 885, Asser, a member of the episcopal family at Menevia (St David's), traveled to England to be bishop of Sherborne under the patronage of Alfred. Asser's *Vita Ælfredi regis* has as its models the "Lives" of the saints and Einhard's "Life of Charlemagne" (Keynes & Lapidge 1983: 94–6).

As well as illustrating the dialogue between England and Wales under Alfred, Asser provides a snapshot of Welsh learning in the ninth century and its sources (Lapidge 2003). Early in the same century Irish scholars had been active at the court of Gwynedd. We have no specific evidence that Menevia was also in contact with Irish scholarship at the same time, although it is reasonable to believe that it was. In the eleventh century a bishop of St David's, Sulien, studied in both Ireland and Scotland (Lapidge 1973/4). Wales, far from being a backwater, was a route of cultural exchange into Britain. The southwest had its place in these relations as well, especially under the West Saxon king Athelstan, at whose court Frankish rulers as well as Breton nobility and churchmen sought refuge from Viking raids.

What is striking in the tenth and eleventh centuries is the extent to which the ruling families, now very much of shared ancestry, formed polities that increasingly came to reflect the bonds of ancestry and marriage. The marriage of Hywel ap Cadell (Hywel Dda, "Hywel the Good," d. 949/50) to Elen of Dyfed probably helped to legitimize the royal family of Gwynedd's claim to rule both Gwynedd and Dyfed. The later tenth and eleventh centuries saw control of Gwynedd and Dyfed (the latter in the eleventh century being merged with the southeastern kingdoms to form the larger polity known as Deheubarth) fluctuate with the fortunes of descendants of these two, now interlinked, dynasties. The longest reigning ruler of Gwynedd in this period, Gruffudd ap Llywelyn of Gwynedd (r. 1039–63), was the son of Llywelyn ap Seisyll, who had married into the Dyfed line but who won control of Gwynedd (1018) and Deheubarth (1022) by force. On Llywelyn's death Iago ab Idwal, a member of the Gwynedd line, assumed power in Gwynedd, but on his death (perhaps at the hand of his own troops) in 1039, Gruffudd assumed power. Iago's son Cynan was exiled to Dublin, whence his son Gruffudd ap Cynan (d. 1137) would return in 1075 and 1081 to fight the Normans, as a Latin *Life* tells us (Russell 2005: 60–1, 68–9). Gruffudd ap Llywelyn died in 1063, in a campaign led by Harold and Tostig – though the Irish *Annals of Ulster* names "a son of Iago" (Cynan?) as the actual slayer. His death brought an end to an unprecedented achievement: almost the whole of Wales was united under his rule, and he himself was a force to be reckoned with in English affairs. This wide-ranging power would not be wielded by any subsequent Welsh ruler.

English kingship across the same period was similarly a matter of increasingly complex aristocratic intermarriage. King Aethelred ("the Unready," r. 979–1016), of the West Saxon royal lineage, lived against the backdrop of increased Danish expansion in England. After over a decade of debilitating Viking raids, Sveinn Forkbeard invaded in 1013 and his son Cnut (r. 1016–35) assumed the throne in 1016, ruling England for the next nineteen years. Cnut married the widow of Aethelred, Emma (herself the daughter of Richard I, Duke of Normandy); Cnut's son Harthacnut (r. 1040–42) was thus the half-brother of Edward the Confessor, Aethelred's son with Emma. Edward, who had been raised in exile in Normandy since 1013, assumed the throne in 1042. When Edward died in 1066, William the Conqueror claimed his throne based on their close relationship. The simultaneous attempt to take the throne by Harald Hardrada of Norway in 1066 also had its basis in a dynastic claim, in this case via the Danish ruling house. By the eleventh century the Danes were no longer foreigners, but simply one of several dynastic groups in the British Isles, a fact exemplified by the abovementioned Gruffudd ap Cynan, who was the great-grandson of the Danish ruler Sygtrygg of Dublin. The enlistment by Gruffudd of Danish forces was therefore not a matter of making an alliance with outsiders. From the tenth century onward, the past was called upon to shore up ideologies of kingship that no longer had simple roots in local culture. Rulers had to make choices as to what to identify with in their now often multi-ethnic ancestries.

The literary proponents of political actions were similarly obliged to work in a multi-ethnic context. In the tenth century the writer of the poem *Armes Prydein Fawr* ("The Great Prophecy of Britain") called upon his Irish Sea neighbors, including "the heathens of Dublin," to unite under the banner of St David. David was ethnically Welsh, but his spiritual leadership was claimed to extend in this case to the entirety of the Irish Sea basin, at least in the perhaps highly theoretical world invoked by the poem (Isaac 2007: 177). In the eleventh century the learning of Sulien and his sons Rhygyfarch and Ieuan at Llanbadarn Fawr was similarly deployed against incoming Norman propagandists. Sulien, as noted above, was educated abroad, but was also the product of a continuous tradition of learning in his diocese. The genre of heroic biography, as we have seen, was already in use in Menevia in the time of Asser. The use of this genre by Rhygyfarch ap Sulien to set a historical figure against Norman claims over the Welsh church represents the promotion of David not as leader of a separate Welsh church but of the churches of Britain as a whole.

The culture of this church was one organized around *clas* communities or "mother churches" (also partly paralleled in the English *mynsters*), essentially colleges of secular canons (Blair 2005: 3–5). The courts of British kings, apart from being in contact with each other, were also increasingly engaged with ecclesiastical reform in Europe. Under Edgar (r. 959–75) England had begun to embrace the Benedictine reform. In England and Wales the Augustinian canons and reformed Benedictine orders found patronage beyond the territory conquered by the Normans. These institutions, replacing the older, often now maligned, "mother churches" were parts of international orders that fed new ideas of literary education into Britain. Rhygyfarch and his contemporaries show that the native tradition was well able to appropriate and turn its own past to new political ends (as did the composer of the Book of Llandaff; see Davies 2003: 63–75), but the incoming orders soon also took on this role, promoting the cults of local saints and taking a clear interest in native tradition. The decline of the literary center of Llanbadarn Fawr, for example, was offset by the literary work of the nearby Cistercian house at Strata Florida, where the source of *Brut y Tywysogion* was written in the Middle Ages.

The Coming of the Normans

Rhygyfarch's assertion of the claim of St David's to archiepiscopal primacy over Britain can be interpreted as a proactive defense of Welsh sovereignty (Wooding 2007: 17). In visions such as Rhygyfarch's, however, the claim was couched in terms of ownership of *Britain*, through resort to a past – Arthurian or otherwise – when Britain was one nation. In this Rhygyfarch echoed one of the most powerful themes of medieval Welsh historians or pseudo-historians: that a unified sovereign Britain had existed in the past, was interrupted by the Anglo-Saxons, and should rightfully exist again in the future. This claim formed the basis of Geoffrey of Monmouth's account of British origins and early history, partly because it is inherent in his main source, *Historia Brittonum*, but also, clearly, because it suited Geoffrey's purpose. It is an interesting question as to what extent Geoffrey was typical of early Anglo-Norman and Cambro-Norman historians in his enthusiasm for this particularly British argument (Roberts 1976: 29–40). Later Cambro-Norman historians, such as Gerald of Wales, certainly had some sympathy with it, however much they might doubt Geoffrey's historical veracity (Crick 1999: 60–75). However, twelfth-century Anglo-Norman historians, such as William of Malmesbury and William of Newburgh, were often overtly hostile to the notion of a "British" history.

The Normans took control in 1066. Harold Godwinsson, appointed king by the English nobles on the death of Edward the Confessor, defeated the claim of Harald Hardrada at Stamford Bridge on September 25, having marched from London to the Humber in four days, only to die in defeat at Hastings on 14 October. The kingship of England was of disproportionate value to the Norman dukes on account of their ducal inferiority to the king of France. The claim of William to the English throne, often represented as a usurpation, was valid enough in Continental, if not in British, terms. But few claims in the eleventh century were valid without strength of conviction in backing them up. Propaganda such as the Bayeux Tapestry (which potentially enjoyed a wider audience than most texts), whatever the exact interpretation of its narrative, demonstrates the value the Normans placed upon projecting their own vision of history. That the craftspersons who created the Tapestry may well have been English is not surprising in view of the now international quality of kingship and patronage of media. The Norman takeover was characterized by a systematic suppression of local resistance, which extended to attacks on the allies of the Anglo-Saxon monarchy in Gwynedd and Dyfed. Initial gains in Gwynedd were swiftly recouped by its princes so that Gwynedd remained a stronghold of a native ruling line until the death of its last prince in the late thirteenth century. Elsewhere the Norman and at times Breton barons made slower but more lasting gains, in particular in the southeast and along the south coast, with the mountainous center, however, remaining chiefly the preserve of native Welsh princes.

The Normans have been portrayed as consummate manipulators of identity and media: they began as Scandinavian settlers in Normandy in the early tenth century, but only one and a half centuries later arrived in Britain as culturally French rulers (Davis 1976). The great database of Domesday shows an impressive command of information. The range of pseudo-historical works that appeared under their patronage implies an imaginative investment in cultural history. In view of their common Scandinavian origins, the deliberate exclusion of the Anglo-Saxon past from these histories is ironic. The pseudo-histories of the *Brut* genre presented the Normans with a seemingly valid claim to a unified Britain from the distant past, and with a sacral kingship – two things that were manifestly not the legacy that William had acquired. The Normans adopted this mythology, but its origins were in British tradition.

Though one might imagine that Wales would be a mediator of Celtic material under the Normans, it is important to note the large proportion of Bretons, who clearly shared with the Welsh a common pool of pseudo-historical material, among the incoming Norman nobility. The Breton origins of many of these nobles is obscured by their nominal affiliation to Norman towns and estates (Davis 1976: 105–6). Norman links with neighboring Brittany may have given access to the matter of Britain in Breton sources. Our greatest figure in this respect, Geoffrey of Monmouth, may have had both Breton and Welsh affiliation.

Geoffrey began his work in the reign of Henry I (r. 1100–35), who was the second son of William I to hold the throne after William II ("Rufus," r. 1087–1100). The Arthurian narrative of Geoffrey's history has been interpreted partly as an allegory of Henry's campaign against his brother Robert for control of Normandy. Notwithstanding the validity of this identification, this may not have been the only cause of the adoption of Arthur into Norman mythology. Henry II's (r. 1154–89) son Geoffrey, Duke of Brittany, gave the name Arthur to his son, who was for a time the heir of Richard I. The birth-year of this Arthur (1187) is adjacent to the identification (1190) of the legendary Arthur's grave at Glastonbury. The two events have been seen as linked, but may simply speak to a wider enthusiasm for the Arthurian legend in Britain and Brittany at the time. At least one literary appearance of Arthur was in a more ambiguous role. Etienne of Rouen's pro-Angevin chronicle *Draco Normannicus* mocks the idea of an Arthurian return in his account of Henry II's crushing of a rebellion in Brittany in 1167–8: in it one of the Breton rebels, Roland de Dinan, writes to King Arthur, who rules in the Antipodes, asking for help. Arthur writes to Henry, advising him to read Geoffrey of Monmouth and threatening a return. Henry's reaction, according to Etienne, is a curious mixture of ridicule and compliance (Echard 1998: 85–93).

A feature of the Norman court in the reigns of Henry I and II is the degree of education of both monarchs – both were learned in Latin and law. Henry II's wife Eleanor of Aquitaine (d. 1204) was educated in Europe's most cultivated court and was proficient in Latin and music. Eleanor herself is often cited as a key figure in the literary patronage of Arthurian material on the Continent, but specific evidence of such patronage relates not to Eleanor but to Marie de Champagne, her daughter by her first husband (Aurell 2007: 376–81).

"Native" and Norman Cultures

In Wales the advent of the Normans left the kingdoms of Gwynedd, Powys, and Deheubarth still commanding parts of the coast and most of the impenetrable interior. The princes, while often termed "native," were native in the sense only of being independent of the English crown, while still intermarried with Norman families and in material terms often indistinguishable from their Norman neighbors. A journey across a watershed in Powys or Ceredigion takes one past native and Norman mottes, castles, and monastic foundations that are barely distinguishable in cultural terms. The landscape was not one of simple boundaries: a prince such as Rhys ap Gruffudd (the Lord Rhys, ruler of Deheubarth 1155–97) was buried not in his own territory with his family at Strata Florida, but at St David's, under the Norman bishop Peter de Leia.

The pretensions of the princes and their courts were fueled in part by a desire to participate in the Continental court culture of their Norman neighbors. The princes, as much as the Normans, were patrons of powerful new monastic orders, in particular Cistercians, but also others, including Premonstratensians, Augustinians, and Tironians. While some of these new monastic houses were Anglo-Norman in origin and in orientation, many were founded or patronized by the native Welsh princes as well, the Lord Rhys being particularly notable in such patronage. Strata Florida, for example, was in origin a Norman foundation, but was soon afterwards taken over by Rhys, and subsequently occupied a central position in symbolic gestures of Welsh rulership: not only were several Welsh princes buried there, but it was the venue, in 1238, for the assembly that Llywelyn ap Iorwerth (Llywelyn Fawr, "Llywelyn the Great," d. 1240) called of "all the princes of Wales" (according to *Brut y Tywysogion*) in order to swear fealty to his son Dafydd. Moreover, Strata Florida took over from the older, unreformed church of Llanbadarn Fawr as one of the key places at which manuscripts were copied and historical records kept, including *Brut y Tywysogion* and the Hendregadredd manuscript of court poetry. The growth of Cistercian houses in terms of wealth, literary activity and political influence and activity is one of the key aspects of Norman-era Wales. The Augustinians and Cistercians, regardless of patronage, evinced a general interest in the Celtic past, a pattern also seen in Ireland (Carville 1982). The oldest manuscript entirely in Welsh, *Llyfr Du Caerfyrddin* ("Black Book of Carmarthen," c. 1225–50), is linked to the Norman-sponsored Augustinian priory of St John the Evangelist and Teulyddog in Carmarthen.

In terms of literary and historical activity, we should perhaps differentiate between what we have in written form and what we believe to have been performed but not recorded, at least at the time, with the former originating from churches, probably monasteries, and the latter taking place as far as we know at the prince's court. We should, however, be wary of hard and fast distinctions between the two categories, and keep in mind that we base our conclusions on what survives in written form, in both Latin and Welsh. There was ready availability of literate education and a continuation of the learned clerical culture that had existed in the *clas* system. In the early years of the Norman period the *clas* of Llanbadarn Fawr (mentioned above) produced an impressive range of written (often illustrated) Latin texts – these are the earliest manuscripts that can be attributed to an identifiable Welsh scriptorium (Huws 2000: 10). Some manuscripts strongly suggest Norman interest in Britain's Celtic past – again, these are ecclesiastical productions (Davies 1981). A figure such as Giraldus Cambrensis (Gerald of Wales) straddled both worlds; of mixed Norman and Welsh ancestry, and at home in both traditions, he asserted the primacy of St David's as a Norman candidate – ultimately unsuccessful – for the episcopacy.

   The role of religious houses in the transmission of tradition was central, but increasingly less exclusive as the Middle Ages drew to a close. From the later twelfth century we find evidence of non-monastic scribes, and by the fifteenth century we find evidence of professional lay scribes (Pryce 1993: 18). Nevertheless, most of our earliest manuscripts in Welsh, which date from the thirteenth century, were probably composed in monastic scriptoria. Among these are manuscripts of Welsh laws, known collectively (and anachronistically) as the Laws of Hywel Dda. These laws are of particular importance to any discussion of the development of medieval Welsh Arthurian material in that they, along with several mentions in medieval Welsh prose tales (chiefly the tale *Math uab Mathonwy*), supply our evidence for what must have been the most important (not to say the only) forum for the composition and performance of literary and historical works, which include almost all our Welsh Arthurian texts: the prince's court.

The Poets and the Princes

We know from Gildas's *De Excidio Britanniae* ("Concerning the Ruin of Britain") that post-Roman Britain had multiple kingdoms supplying numerous rulers. His famous denunciation of one of these, Maelgwn of Gwynedd, includes his bitter complaint that Maelgwn entertained himself with the help of poets singing his praises – the implication is that Maelgwn validated his behavior with respect to the pronouncements of the poets (Winterbottom 1978: 34, 103). It is telling, moreover, that even Gildas, who lamented so insistently the loss of Roman ecclesiastical culture, not only observed the flattering of these rulers by their poets but may have shared in the larger literary culture which they represented (Sims-Williams 1984). We have a number of examples of this type of poem in praise of rulers, arguably from the later sixth and seventh centuries. Then, in the twelfth and thirteenth centuries, we have an explosion of a genre of poetry so intimately concerned with praise of princes (although not limited to this subject matter) that the 35 or so poets concerned acquire the classification *Beirdd y Tywysogion* ("Poets of the Princes"). Despite an apparent hiatus in the writing down of texts between these very early and later poets, there is a very strong case for seeing a continuity of activity (Koch 2005: 30).

The prince's court, *llys*, was the venue of social, literary, military, and governmental business (Davies 1991: 253–4). There would have been a large number of courts, either fixed or itinerant. The three largest kingdoms, Gwynedd, Powys, and Deheubarth, had "chief courts" at Aberffro, Mathrafal, and Dinefwr, respectively, but there would have been many smaller courts as well. Huw Pryce lists 111 individual rulers who produced Latin *acta*, operating in nine main polities, themselves often split into smaller entities (Pryce 2005) – this of course does not include those rulers who did not produce such records. Several great courts stand out: one, often retrospectively described as the first *eisteddfod*, was held in 1176 by the Lord Rhys at his court at Cardigan with competitions between poets and musicians. *Brut y Tywysogion* grandly claimed that it had been "proclaimed a year before it was held throughout Wales and England and Scotland and Ireland and many other lands" (Jones 1955: 166–7). The Welsh laws throw up two interesting suggestions as regards poets at courts: the first is that one type of poet, the *pencerdd*, practiced his craft in one or more kingdoms (and certainly at multiple courts); the second is that there were different types of literary entertainment going on at the court, some specifically viewed as secondary to the main business and pointedly described as of interest to the queen (Jenkins 2000: 150, 159–60). The former, which is reinforced by the evidence of praise poetry of individual poets addressed to different, often widespread, rulers, provides a powerful context for the development of a multiplicity of versions of essentially the same cultural artifacts. The latter, coupled with the evidence of storytelling provided by the tale *Math uab Mathonwy* (Davies 2007), suggests that we can perhaps extend what we know about praise poetry to other genres, including prose, albeit somewhat speculatively.

The historical background to the Arthurian legend in the ninth through thirteenth centuries is thus one of a literate Celtic tradition, only traceable from limited sources but clearly with a considerable historical and pseudo-historical interest, finding its place in an emerging court culture. By the end of the first millennium, after centuries of exchange between English, Welsh, and Scandinavians, court culture in Britain and Ireland was already international and multi-ethnic in flavor. The advent of first the reformed religious orders and then the Normans brought further ideas of history into this environment, and drew upon the matter of Britain from both their new conquests in Wales and their earlier connections in Brittany.

PRIMARY SOURCES

Davies, S. (trans.) (2007). *The Mabinogion*. Oxford: Oxford University Press.

Jones, T. (ed.) (1955). *Brut y Tywygosyon or The Chronicle of the Princes. Red Book of Hergest Version*. Cardiff: University of Wales Press.

Keynes, S. & Lapidge, M. (trans) (1983). *Alfred the Great. Asser's Life of King Alfred and other contemporary sources*. Harmondsworth: Penguin.

Morris, J. (ed. trans.) (1980). *Nennius: British History and the Welsh Annals*. Chichester: Phillimore.

Swanton, M. (ed. trans.) (2000). *The Anglo-Saxon chronicles*. London: Phoenix.

Winterbottom, M. (ed. trans.) (1978). *Gildas: The Ruin of Britain and other documents*. London: Phillimore.

REFERENCES AND FURTHER READING

Aurell, M. (2007). Henry II and the Arthurian legend. In C. Harper-Bill & N. Vincent (eds), *Henry II: New interpretations*. Woodbridge: Boydell, pp. 362–94.

Blair, J. (2005). *The church in Anglo-Saxon society*. Oxford: Oxford University Press.

Carey, J. (1993). *A new introduction to Lebor Gabála Érenn*. London: Irish Texts Society.

Carville, G. (1982). *The occupation of Celtic sites in Ireland by the canons regular of St Augustine and the Cistercians*. Kalamazoo, MA: Cistercian Studies.

Crick, J. (1999). The British past and the Welsh future: Gerald of Wales, Geoffrey of Monmouth and Arthur of Britain. *Celtica*, 23, 60–75.

Davies, J. R. (2003). *The Book of Llandaf and the Norman church in Wales*. Woodbridge: Boydell.

Davies, R. R (1991). *The age of conquest: Wales 1063–1415*. Oxford: Oxford University Press.

Davies, W. (1981). Property rights and property claims in Welsh *vitae* of the eleventh century. In E. Patlagean & P. Riché (eds), *Hagiographie, cultures et sociétés IVe–XIIe siècles*. Paris: Études Augustiniennes, pp. 515–33.

Davies, W. (1982). *Wales in the early Middle Ages*. Leicester: Leicester University Press.

Davis, R. H. C. (1976). *The Normans and their myth*. London: Thames & Hudson.

Echard, S. (1998). *Arthurian narrative in the Latin tradition*. Cambridge: Cambridge University Press.

Huws, D. (2000). *Medieval Welsh manuscripts*. Aberystwyth: National Library of Wales & University of Wales Press.

Isaac, G. R. (2007). *Armes Prydein Fawr* and St David. In J. W. Evans & J. M. Wooding (eds), *St David of Wales: Cult, church and nation*. Woodbridge: Boydell, pp. 161–81.

Jenkins, D. (2000). *Bardd teulu* and *pencerdd*. In T. M. Charles-Edwards, M. E. Owen, & P. Russell (eds), *The Welsh king and his court*. Cardiff: University of Wales Press, pp. 142–66.

Kermode, P. (1907). *Manx crosses*. London: Bemrose.

Koch, J. (2005). Why was Welsh literature first written down? In H. Fulton (ed.), *Medieval Celtic literature and society*. Dublin: Four Courts Press, pp. 15–31.

Lapidge, M. (1973/4). The Welsh-Latin poetry of Sulien's family. *Studia Celtica*, 8/9, 68–106.

Lapidge, M. (2003). Asser's reading. In T. Reuter (ed.), *Alfred the Great*. Aldershot: Ashgate, pp. 27–48.

Lloyd, J. E. (1911). *History of Wales*, 3rd edn. London: Longman.

Mac Cana, P. (2007). Ireland and Wales in the Middle Ages: An overview. In K. Jankulak & J. M. Wooding (eds), *Ireland and Wales in the Middle Ages*. Dublin: Four Courts Press, pp. 17–45.

Pryce, H. (1993). *Native law and the church in medieval Wales*. Oxford: Clarendon Press.

Pryce, H. (ed.) (2005). *The acts of the Welsh rulers 1120–1283*. Cardiff: University of Wales Press.

Roberts, B. F. (1976). Geoffrey of Monmouth and Welsh historical tradition. *Nottingham Medieval Studies*, 20, 29–40.

Russell, P. (2005). *Vita Griffini Filii Conani. The medieval Latin Life of Gruffudd ap Cynan*. Cardiff: University of Wales Press.

Sims-Williams, P. (1984). Gildas and vernacular poetry. In M. Lapidge & D. N. Dumville (eds), *Gildas: New approaches*. Woodbridge: Boydell, pp. 169–90.

Wooding, J. M. (2007). The figure of David. In J. W. Evans & J. M. Wooding (eds), *St David of Wales: Cult, church and nation*. Woodbridge: Boydell, pp. 1–19.

6
Arthur and Merlin in Early Welsh Literature: Fantasy and Magic Naturalism

Helen Fulton

If the historical tradition of Arthur can be found in Latin chronicles, and the romance tradition owes its origins to French court poets, where then does the Welsh Arthur reside? For many scholars, the Arthur who appears in medieval Welsh literature is the most authentic because he is the oldest of the vernacular Arthurs, perhaps even as old as Gildas's account of the fifth-century struggle between British and Saxons, and certainly pre-dating Geoffrey of Monmouth's *Historia Regum Britanniae*.

Yet the Welsh Arthur is hardly a seamless or coherent character, acting consistently from one story to the next like modern cultural inventions such as Sherlock Holmes or Superman. There are plural Arthurs in Welsh, representing various ideals of leadership and political identity for different kinds of audiences. In chapter 2, Nicholas Higham distinguished between a "historical" and a "folkloric" Arthur in the early Latin chronicle tradition. In the early Welsh literary tradition, Arthur appears in both these guises and others besides, particularly as a supernatural figure who exerts control over otherworldly forces. The dominant mode of the Welsh Arthurian tradition, then, is neither chronicle nor romance, but fantasy, expressed through a narrative style that I am calling "magic naturalism."

Arthur as Warrior-Hero

Pre-existing traces of the "historical" Arthur of the chronicles appear in Welsh literature from around the ninth century (though the manuscript evidence begins in the twelfth). The surviving fragments of this vernacular tradition, both oral and written, which lies behind the Latin texts of the *Historia Brittonum* (ninth century) and Geoffrey of Monmouth's *Historia Regum Britanniae* (c. 1138), reveal the outlines of a hero-king, identifiably British as distinct from either Saxon or Norman. This is the role that comes closest to the construct of the "historical" Arthur, the one which so appealed to Geoffrey and his adapters, where Arthur is the British battle-leader uniting his people against the Saxon foe. The main texts in which Arthur appears in this role, albeit fleetingly, are:

- *Y Gododdin*, "The Gododdin" (Jarman 1988; Koch 1997).
- Eulogy to Gereint (Jarman 1982: 48).
- Dialogue between Gwyddneu Garanhir and Gwyn ap Nudd (Jarman 1982: 71–3).
- *Marwnad Cynddylan*, "Elegy to Cynddylan" (Williams 1935: 50–52; Rowland 1990: 174–9).
- References in twelfth-century court poetry (Padel 2000: 51–61).
- *Breuddwyd Rhonabwy*, "The Dream of Rhonabwy" (Richards 1972; Davies 2007).

The heroic elegy known as *Y Gododdin*, surviving in a single manuscript of the thirteenth century, the Book of Aneirin, comprises a long series of stanzas each of which commemorates a single fallen warrior of the men of Gododdin. This was one of a number of British territories located in the "old north" (that is, what is now northern England and southern Scotland), centered around modern Edinburgh. The poem constructs a historical period of the mid- to late sixth century and was probably composed in that period or shortly afterwards, either in the north, from where it was transmitted to Wales, or in Wales itself, which still had close linguistic and cultural connections with the British north. Unusually for an early secular text, the poem has a named author, Aneirin, one of several Welsh poets mentioned by the ninth-century *Historia Brittonum* as having been active at the time of the Saxon king Ida and the Welsh prince Maelgwn Gwynedd, that is, in the late sixth century (Morris 1980: 37; Huws 1989).

The poem seems to be referring to a disastrous battle at Catraeth (modern Catterick in Yorkshire), which brought the men of Gododdin and their allies against men from Bernicia and Deira, areas further to the south populated mainly by invading Saxons (Dumville 1972; Roberts 1972; Charles-Edwards 1978). The most recent editor of the poem, John Koch, suggests a date of composition around 570, and makes the point that the enemies named in the poem may not have been exclusively Saxons but probably included other British tribes who, for reasons of political and military expediency, chose to ally themselves with the Saxons against the northern Britons (Koch 1997: xiii–xliii). The nationalistic model of Arthur as a British leader against Saxon usurpers was from the beginning, then, a useful but reductive literary fiction.

Arthur's name is mentioned once in the poem, in a stanza typical of the general style and purpose of the whole sequence. Most of the hundred-odd stanzas are each devoted to a single hero, who is ceremoniously named after the incantation of a number of assertions verifying his heroic qualities (Fulton 1994). The poem, composed to be recited, thus functions as the oral equivalent of a modern-day war memorial displaying the roll call of names of the fallen soldiers. In a stanza celebrating the hero Gwawrddur, whose name literally means "steel-lord," we hear of his exploits in the battle of Catraeth:

> Ef guant tratrigant echassaf
> ef ladhei a [pher]uet ac eithaf
> oid guiu e mlaen llu llarahaf
> godolei o heit meirch e gayaf
> gochore brein du ar uur
> caer ceni bei ef arthur
> rug ciuin uerthi ig disur
> ig kynnor guernor guaur[dur].
>   (Williams 1938: 49)

> He struck down more than three hundred of the warriors,
> he killed both middle and outer [ranks].
> The most generous one belonged at the forefront of a host,
> he would give horses from his herd in winter,
> he would feed black ravens on a rampart
> of a fortress, though he was not Arthur.
> Among the strong ones in battle,
> at the front, an alder-wood rampart, was Gwawrddur.

The stanza seems to be saying that although Gwawrddur displayed all the virtues of the warrior nobility, fighting bravely and ferociously, sharing generously, protecting his men like a stout wooden rampart, still he was not Arthur. Arthur is being held up as the archetype of the best warrior in the world, one whom others strove to emulate but could never equal.

The significance of this brief Arthurian allusion lies partly in its early date and partly in its context of a decisive battle between British and (mainly) Saxons, in which the British were devastatingly defeated. If the poem was first composed shortly after the battle of Catraeth which it commemorates, that is, around 570 AD, it would not be far away, less than a century, from the historical context associated with the "authentic" Arthur, the Romano-British leader fighting against the incoming Saxons. However, the surviving text of the *Gododdin* preserves at least two strata of material, an older layer of "original" stanzas and a later layer of additional stanzas, which may include the Gwawrddur stanza quoted above. The language and orthography of the whole text have been dated to about the ninth century, which means that the reference to Arthur is at least that old, and may be as old as the late sixth or early seventh century if (as John Koch believes) it was part of the original poem (Koch 1997: 147).

The appearance of Arthur's name in the *Gododdin* has been used to support the view that the "real" Arthur probably came from the "old north," but there are a number of warriors named in the poem who are known to have lived in other areas of Britain. The point about the army of the Gododdin is that the men were not all from the territorial region of Gododdin itself but were drawn from many British-held parts of the country, forming a powerful union in defense of the northern lands (Jarman 1988: xxviii–xl; Rowland 1995). What the Gwawrddur stanza appears to tell us, then, is that of all the British warriors throughout British-held lands, Arthur was the mightiest, and that by the ninth century at least his name was synonymous with the heroic endeavors of the British to fight for their sovereignty against the Saxons.

This same construct of the heroic battle-leader is found in the eulogy to Gereint, a chieftain of the Dumnonians in southwest Britain and possibly the same person as the historical Cornish king Geraint who ruled in the early eighth century. There is a reference to Gereint in the *Gododdin*, perhaps signifying the same ruler (Williams 1938: stanza 85; Koch 1997: 124–5), and his name was later drawn into the Continental tradition of Arthurian romance, where he appears in the Welsh prose romance of *Gereint ac Enid* ("Geraint and Enid"), corresponding to the French *Erec et Enide* of Chrétien de Troyes (see chapter 9). Though the eulogy to Gereint constructs a historical context of late sixth- or early seventh-century Britain, the poem itself was probably composed at a later date, perhaps the tenth or eleventh century, when the dynasties of Wales and Cornwall were still suffering the effects of Saxon pressure on their borders (Charles-Edwards 1991: 15). The poem is one of a number found in the Black Book of Carmarthen, a manuscript collection dated to the second half of the thirteenth century (Jarman 1982).

In a series of 26 stanzas, the poet celebrates the battle triumphs of Gereint and his men against their enemies, primarily the Saxons. Using the conventional formula of the eyewitness account ("I saw . . ."), the poet lists a number of battle locations where the British fought (not always victoriously), including Llongborth (perhaps to be identified with Langport in Somerset), where Arthur was present:

> En llogborth y gueleis e giminad.
> guir igrid a guaed am iad.
> rac gereint vaur mab y tad.
>
> En llogporth gueleis e gottoev.
> a guir ny gilint rac gvaev.
> ac yved gvin o guydir gloev.
>
> En llogporth y gueleis e arwev
> guir a guyar in diuev.
> a gvydi gaur garv atnev.
>
> En llogporth y gueleis e. y arthur
> guir deur kymynint a dur.
> ameraudur llywiaudir llawur.
>
> (Jarman 1982: 48)
>
> At Llongborth I saw the cutting down
> of men trembling, blood round their heads,
> before Gereint the great, his father's son.

> At Llongborth I saw spurs
> and men who would not flee from spears,
> and wine being drunk from bright glass.
>
> At Llongborth I saw weapons
> of men, and blood flowing,
> and after the shouting, a bitter burial.
>
> At Llongborth I saw with Arthur
> brave men who slashed with steel,
> emperor, leader of action.

The poem evokes the same heroic virtues as the *Gododdin*, fierceness in battle, a willingness to fight to the death, generosity in peacetime. Arthur's name is again invoked as that of a warrior-hero who takes the lead in any conflict between the British and their enemies, regardless of location. It seems that Arthur was as well known in the southwest as in the north, appearing at the head of a super-force to support British princes wherever there was conflict (Padel 1984). Significantly, Arthur is here referred to as *ameraudur*, "emperor," a borrowing from Latin *imperator*, perhaps a dim echo of the Romano-British princes who ruled Britain in Gildas's time. Certainly the epithet, however anachronistic, indicates a recognition of Arthur's status as superior to that of local rulers such as Gereint, suggesting a construction of Arthur as overlord and protector of all the British territories.

In these early heroic references, Arthur has a symbolic as well as a historical function. Not only does he validate Welsh territorial claims stretching back into an ancient past which pre-dates the arrival of the Saxons in Britain, he personifies the sovereignty of British rule. The mythic belief in a pre-existing autonomous British rule over the whole island of Britain, a political sovereignty that was cruelly and unrightfully usurped by the Saxons, formed the bedrock of much Welsh literature right through the Middle Ages. During the successive invasions and settlements of the Anglo-Saxons and later the Normans, the latter into the very heartlands of Wales itself, Arthur was used to support an insistent claim by Welsh court poets that there had once been a unified British kingdom, and that the Welsh rulers now praised by the poets were the natural successors to this Arthurian sovereignty. When poets lamented the loss of British rule, Arthur's name was associated with heroic accounts of British resistance to the Saxons as a symbol of the ancient political autonomy of the British people.

The mythic importance to the Welsh of this heroic construct of Arthur as the archetypal leader of the British against the Saxons is indicated by a later satire of Arthur in this very role. The prose tale *Breuddwyd Rhonabwy*, "The Dream of Rhonabwy," composed in the late twelfth or early thirteenth century, satirizes not only the literary construct of Arthur as a great British king, as found in Geoffrey of Monmouth's *Historia* and in Welsh and French romance, but also contemporary Welsh leaders such as Llywelyn ap Iorwerth, ruler of Powys and Gwynedd, who attempted to emulate the power of the great feudal kings of England and France (Richards 1972;

Slotkin 1989; Lloyd-Morgan 1991). In this dream-vision story – itself a satire of the Continental genre of dream-visions – the Welsh soldier Rhonabwy is shown a vision of Arthur and his men about to confront a huge army of Saxons. Immobilized by the number of troops and horses surrounding him, and by the rich splendors of his material wealth, Arthur has all the outward trappings of power but is unable to act – he is literally the *roi fainéant*, the "do-nothing king" of French romance. Instead of using his resources to defeat the Saxons, Arthur passively sends his youngest servant to negotiate with the enemy before the two armies drift away without a spear being raised. It is as if the storyteller is suggesting, through the metaphorical structure of the dream-vision, that it is time for Wales to put away one particularly recurrent dream, the old vision of British supremacy against the Saxons, symbolized by the figure of Arthur. At a time when the rulers of Gwynedd were trying to equalize their relationship with the English crown and were marrying into the English royal family – Llywelyn ap Iorwerth was married to Joan, illegitimate daughter of King John – the Arthurian fantasy had passed its prime as a focus for Welsh hopes of political power in Britain.

Arthur in Welsh Popular Tradition

The Latin *mirabilia* or marvels of the *Historia Brittonum* (see chapter 2) provide evidence of a rich local tradition of Arthurian folklore and legend in Wales, a tradition which also emerges in some vernacular survivals. Most of these references to Arthur as a popular figure of legend are found in the thirteenth-century manuscript known as *Llyfr Taliesin*, the Book of Taliesin, a compilation of Welsh texts dating largely from the pre-Norman period (Evans 1910, 1915; Haycock 2006, 2007).

There are four references to Arthur in poems from the Book of Taliesin, which allude to a folk-tale version of the historical poet Taliesin and which invoke the powers of bardic enchantment, inspiration, and shape-shifting. This coupling of Arthur and the folk-tale Taliesin enables them to alibi each other as "genuine" characters from the sixth century. In "Cat Godeu" ("The Battle of the Trees"), the poet describes a battle fought by a variety of trees and shrubs – alders, willows, ash, blackthorns, and many others, perhaps making allegorical or symbolic use of these names to hint at more human armies (Bromwich 1978: 207–8; Haycock 2007: 167–73). Characters from legend are invoked, such as Math and Gwydion from the fourth branch of the *Mabinogi* (the collection of medieval Welsh prose tales), while explicitly Christian references hint at the coming of Judgment Day. Toward the end of the poem, the poet calls on druids to prophesy to Arthur, instating Arthur as a great king who should receive such prophecies because he alone can act on them.

In "Cadeir Teyrnon" ("Teyrnon's Seat"), the poet celebrates the achievements of a fellow bard, Teyrnon, who sings of Arthur's exploits in battle, indicating that tales of Arthur's deeds are a familiar and appropriate topic for bardic song. In a third poem, a *marwnad*, or elegy, to Uthyr Ben, a prototype of Uther Pendragon (Bromwich 1978:

520–23; Haycock 2007: 503–4), the poet extols his own powers of bardic excellence and battle ferocity, claiming that "Arthur has a [mere] ninth of my valour" (Haycock 2007: 505). Lastly, in a poem combining religious celebration with further declamations of skill and shape-shifting, the poet lists the horses belonging to heroes such as Caradawg, Gwawrddur, Taliesin, and Arthur.

Slightly later than the references in the Book of Taliesin is a dialogue poem dated to the mid-twelfth century but found only in manuscripts of the fourteenth century and later. This is the poem known as *Ymddiddan Arthur a'r Eryr* ("Dialogue of Arthur and the Eagle"), in which Arthur, over a series of about fifty *englynion* (stanzas in the *englyn* meter), converses with his nephew Eliwlad, who has been transformed into an eagle (Haycock 1994: 297–312; Coe & Young 1995: 103). As with Nennius and other Latin writers, native folk traditions have been co-opted by a clerical writer in the interests of spiritual advice and encouragement: when Arthur, who is presented as a ruler of Cornwall, asks if he can free the eagle from its enchantment, he receives some Christian instruction regarding the power of God and the need for resignation to the fate laid down for each of us:

ARTHUR:	Yr Eryr, nefaw[l] dyghet,
	Or ny chaffaf y welet,
	Beth a wna Crist yr a'e kret?
YR ERYR:	Arthur, wydua llewenydd,
	Wyt lluossawc argletryd:
	Ty hun Dydbrawt a'e gwybyd.
	(Haycock 1994: 307)
ARTHUR:	Eagle, heavenly my fate,
	if I cannot see him,
	what will Christ do for those who believe in him?
THE EAGLE:	Arthur, throne of joy,
	you are a lord of many troops:
	you will know it yourself on the Day of Judgment.

In its form, the poem resembles the conventional clerical genre of the instructional dialogue for lay audiences, with Arthur as the worldly ruler who defines himself through material status, and the Eagle as the contemplative soul who has forsaken the things of the world. Arthur is here a long way from his heroic British persona, representing instead a local semi-pagan chieftain who needs to be taught the superior power and jurisdiction of the church, a role he also occupies in some of the twelfth-century Latin saints' lives, such as those of Cadog and Padarn (Roberts 1991a; Coe & Young 1995; Padel 2000).

The most significant evidence that the character of Arthur was absorbed into the native Welsh folk tradition is that of the Triads. Found in a number of manuscripts from the thirteenth to sixteenth centuries, the Triads are lists of story titles and topics grouped into threes by theme (Bromwich 1969, 1978). Many of the names recorded in the Triads are known from other surviving literary material, either in Welsh or in Latin, while other names are not preserved outside the Triads themselves. They therefore provide a unique record of the story materials of early Wales used by poets and storytellers, dating back at least to the twelfth century. A number of the later Triads, and perhaps some of the earlier ones, suggest connections with Geoffrey of Monmouth's *Historia* (Padel 2000: 84) though any influence could have been in both directions, from the early Triads to Geoffrey and from Geoffrey back to the later Triads.

Arthur is mentioned in a number of the earlier Triads as a prominent member of pre-Saxon British society. In Triad 12 he appears as one of the "Three Frivolous Bards of the Isle of Britain," along with Cadwallawn son of Cadfan and Rahawd son of Morgant, both of whom are known from other stories as part of the traditional British ruling class. In another Triad (20), Arthur is listed as one of the "Three Red Ravagers of the Isle of Britain," along with Rhun son of Beli and Morgant Mwynfawr. Again, these are names associated with pre-Saxon Britain, and Arthur's name has been attached to them as part of the same cultural context.

The process by which Arthur became drawn into an existing set of folk-tale names and traditions which defined, for medieval Welsh storytellers and their listeners, an idealized period of British political sovereignty is shown most clearly in those Triads where Arthur's name is added as a fourth item in a pre-existing Triad. In Triad 2, for example, his name is appended in some of the manuscripts to a group of three. This extended Triad was cited by a twelfth-century poet, Prydydd y Moch (Padel 2000: 86) and was therefore known at that time:

> Tri Hael Enys Prydein:
>   Nud Hael mab Senyllt,
>   Mordaf Hael mab Seruan,
>   Ryderch Hael mab Tudwal Tutclyt.
> (Ac Arthur ehun oedd haelach no'r tri.)

> Three Generous Men of the Island of Britain:
>   Nudd the Generous, son of Senyllt,
>   Mordaf the Generous, son of Serwan,
>   Rhydderch the Generous, son of Tudwal Tudglyd.
> (And Arthur himself was more generous than those three.)
>   (Bromwich 1978)

In Triad 80 there is an allusion to Arthur's wife, Gwenhwyfar:

> Teir Aniweir Wreic Ynys Prydein. Teir merchet Kulvanawyt Prydein:
>   Essyllt (F)yngwen, (gordderch Trystan);
>   a Phenarwan, (gwreic Owein mab Urien);
>   a Bun, gwreic Flamdwyn.
> Ac un oed aniweirach nor teir hynny: Gwenhwyfar gwreic Arthur,
> kanys gwell gwr y gwnai hi gyweilyd idaw no neb.

Three Faithless Wives of the Island of Britain. Three Daughters of
Culfanawyd of Britain:
    Essyllt Fair-Hair (Tristan's mistress),
    and Penarwan (wife of Owain son of Urien),
    and Bun, wife of Fflamddwyn.
And one was more faithless than those three: Gwenhwyfar, Arthur's
wife, since she shamed a better man than any.

(Bromwich 1978)

This Triad refers to three of the best-known characters of the later Arthurian romances, Tristan and Esyllt (the Welsh form of Iseult or Isolde), and Owain son of Urien, the sixth-century hero of Taliesin's praise poetry, who reappears in the twelfth-century Welsh romance, *Owein, Iarlles y Ffynnawn* ("Owain, or The Lady of the Fountain"), and whose French counterpart is Yvain in *Le Chevalier au Lion* ("The Knight with the Lion"), composed by Chrétien de Troyes. To these names were added, in fifteenth-century manuscripts, those of Arthur and Gwenhwyfar, quite obviously later attachments to a pre-existing group of stories. The theme of Guinevere's adultery with Lancelot was a French development (possibly invented by Chrétien himself – see chapter 21) and there are no other early native references to the Welsh Gwenhwyfar as a faithless wife. Geoffrey of Monmouth referred to Guinevere as the lover of Mordred, and it may be this episode that is alluded to in the Triad. Whether it refers to Geoffrey or to the French tradition, the additional element in Triad 80 cannot be earlier than the twelfth century.

There are other references in the Triads that show influence from Geoffrey and post-Geoffrey traditions, including mentions of Medraut, or Mordred. In the native Welsh tradition, Medraut is known either as the man who fell with Arthur at the battle of Camlan, or as a heroic warrior (Padel 2000: 113). The expanded story of his treacherous usurpation of Arthur's lordship of Britain, which precipitated the fateful battle of Camlan (as summarized in Triad 51), has been drawn from a version of Geoffrey's *Historia*.

In most of the Triad references, Arthur is identified as one of a number of prominent British chieftains in the pre-Saxon period, but there are several Triads (for example, 37R) in which his name edges out others as the chief lord of the whole of Britain, one of the unbroken line of British rulers whose traditional rights over Britain formed the basis of Welsh complaints about Saxon tyranny. This Arthurian persona, as the sovereign ruler of Britain, was perhaps inserted into the Triads post-Geoffrey of Monmouth, since Geoffrey's history positioned Arthur very explicitly in a chronological context. In any event, the evidence of the Triads suggests that the early heroic persona of Arthur as a symbol of British sovereignty was reinforced by storytellers from about the twelfth century and that their creation of Arthur in this role both assisted, and was assisted by, Geoffrey's historical account of the kings of Britain. The Triads therefore share with Geoffrey of Monmouth a view of Arthur as part of a chronological list of the great kings of Britain before the coming of the Saxons.

Fantasy and Magic Naturalism

Perhaps the most authentically "Welsh" construct of Arthur is that which presents him as a supernatural hero associated with the Otherworld. The fantasy element found in many of the Welsh Arthurian allusions was reconfigured by Continental adapters such as Chrétien de Troyes, who were developing a more mimetic mode of narrative with a strongly Christian foundation. Nevertheless, the fantasy references to Arthur invariably position him as the head of an illustrious and superhuman warband, which provided an appealing model for the warrior knights of French romance. The tension between a powerful political leader who is often off-stage and an entrepreneurial retinue which actually engages with social issues – the standard framework of Continental Arthurian romance – is foreshadowed by the Welsh fantasy stories which feature Arthur and his warband.

The primary evidence for the fantasy version of Arthur in early Welsh tradition can be summarized as follows:

- "Englynion y Beddau," "Stanzas of the Graves," in the Black Book of Carmarthen (Jarman 1982: 36–44, 1983)
- "Pa Gur" (literally "what man?"), a dialogue poem between Arthur and the gate-keeper of a fortress – also found in the Black Book of Carmarthen (Jarman 1982: 66–8; Sims-Williams 1991).
- "Preiddeu Annwn," "The Spoils of Annwn," in the Book of Taliesin (Haycock 1983/4, 2007).
- *Culhwch ac Olwen*, "Culhwch and Olwen" (Davies 2007).

The last three of these appear to be interconnected, sharing some of the same characters and events with each other and with the Triads, and presumably drawing on a common set of traditions clustering around the name of Arthur, or to which Arthur's name was attracted. The complex and opaque poem "Preiddeu Annwn," "The Spoils of Annwn," describes a journey by Arthur and his warband, aboard his ship Prydwen, to Annwn, the Otherworld, to retrieve the cauldron of the chief of Annwn. On the voyage, the warband visits a number of strange fortresses and meets with some kind of disaster from which only seven survive. Borrowing from the heroic tradition of the eyewitness account of battle, here spoken by the legendary Taliesin, the poem alludes to many of the legends and tales found in the Triads and in the Four Branches of the *Mabinogi*, grouping these references around the figure of Arthur as the leader of a fearless warband.

The story of Arthur's quest for the cauldron, as well as elements from the "Pa gur" dialogue poem, are reactivated in what is perhaps the most significant Arthurian text of the early Middle Ages, the prose tale *Culhwch ac Olwen*, "Culhwch and Olwen" (Jones 1972; Knight 1983). Combining conventional European folk-tale motifs with native Welsh Otherworld traditions, the tale is a long saga of the warband's accomplishments, presided over at ceremonial moments by Arthur himself. Though the tale is found in fairly late manuscripts of the fourteenth century, along with other native prose material, including the Four Branches of the *Mabinogi* and the Welsh tales of *Owein, Peredur,* and *Gereint,* the language and content of *Culhwch ac Olwen* place it earlier than the other stories in the collection, in the late eleventh or early twelfth century. It is usually assumed to pre-date Geoffrey of Monmouth's *Historia,* and although it is not a direct source for that work, the two texts seem to be drawing on a similar stock of Welsh story materials, including the Triads.

The basic structure of the tale is a version of the common folk-tale motif "Six Go through the World," in which a hero, wishing to marry the daughter of a powerful man, enlists the help of six magically gifted companions in order to fulfill a list of impossible tasks. Culhwch, the young hero, is the victim of a curse: he must marry Olwen, daughter of the grim giant Ysbaddaden, or he will not marry at all. Ysbaddaden lays out a long series of fantastical and impossible tasks which Culhwch must complete before Olwen will be given to him. Fortunately, as Arthur's cousin, Culhwch is able to call on the almost limitless resources of the great king, including six companions with magic powers, to complete a token number of the tasks before the giant is killed and Culhwch is able to marry Olwen.

Distributed through this basic plot structure are a great variety of myths and legends, native and European, incorporated into the tasks that Culhwch must complete. The story of Arthur's flight to the Otherworld to retrieve the cauldron of the chief of Annwn, elliptically described in the poem "Preiddeu Annwn," "The Spoils of Annwn," is here given narrative motivation through the giant's request for the cauldron belonging to Diwrnach the Irishman. Arthur and his men therefore invade Ireland (a convenient physical manifestation of the abstract Otherworld) and bring back the cauldron of plenty, which will provide endless food for the guests at Olwen's wedding feast. Mabon son of Modron and Gwyn ap Nudd, mythical figures known from the Triads and other native material, are both released by Arthur's men from their imprisonments so that they can take part in the hunt for the great boar, Twrch Trwyth. The hunt itself, involving Arthur and all his armies, from Britain and the Continent, and a mobile campaign from Britain to Ireland and back to Britain, where the boar is finally driven out to sea at Cornwall, is one of the great set pieces of the tale, combining the supernatural power of the boar, a key icon of Celtic mythology, with the construction of Arthur as the head of an army mighty enough to destroy a fifth part of Ireland.

As well as this native material, expressing Welsh concerns such as the rivalry between Wales and Ireland, there are a number of story motifs belonging to the wider pool of international folklore, including the "Oldest Animals" motif, in which the oldest, and therefore wisest, member of various animal types is asked for advice (Fulton 2004); and the "Grateful Animals" motif, in which animals (or in this case insects, the ants) that have been saved or protected by the hero reciprocate by helping him with one of his tasks (Jackson 1958). Underlying the whole tale are themes relating to tribal societies in general, particularly those of fertility and reproduction and the tribal need to replace itself with a steady supply of both warriors and farmers (Knight 1983). The release of Mabon son of Modron (literally "Son son of Mother"), the curse laid on Culhwch that he will not marry (or produce legitimate heirs) unless he marries Olwen, the portrait of Olwen as the personification of fertile virginity (white flowers spring up wherever she walks), the seasonal battle between Gwyn ap Nudd and Gwythyr for possession of the maiden Creiddylad, the inevitability of the giant's death before Culhwch can marry Olwen – all these events in the tale are expressions of a profound engagement with the mysteries and critical importance of symbolic and actual reproduction.

In all the narrative richness of the tale, Arthur fades in and out, sometimes a major actor, sometimes delegating the tasks to his men. He is represented as a powerful overlord, greeted by Culhwch as "chief lord of the Island of Britain," leader of massive armies, controller of vast resources of manpower and technology. Responsibility for helping Culhwch is delegated to the six companions, including Cei and Bedwyr (Kay and Bedivere of later French romance), Cynddylig the Guide, and Gwrhyr Interpreter of Tongues, each of whom has magical powers. Arthur's prestige derives not only from his status, but also from his command of an illustrious and super-skilled band of men. This foregrounding of the warband is signaled early in the tale by the huge and over-determined list of Arthur's men, including not only his personal retinue but all those who owe him allegiance, wherever they live. This immense roll call of hundreds of names, one of the most outstanding features of the tale, is not simply conventional, though parallels can be found in other Irish and Welsh sources; it also draws attention to the size and scope of Arthur's resources. In this hyperbolic and perhaps comic way, not unlike the exaggerations of *Breuddwyd Rhonabwy*, "The Dream of Rhonabwy," Arthur is constructed as the powerful sovereign of many territories, like the Norman kings of the eleventh and twelfth centuries.

When Arthur does take part in the completion of the tasks, his role is both practical and symbolic. It is he who leads the troops on the two expeditions to Ireland, for the cauldron of Diwrnach and the hunt for Twrch Trwyth, because only he commands the necessary armies. At the end of the tale, Arthur is the only one who can kill the Black Witch when four of his men have failed, indicating his absolute power over forces of evil. While his men have only a single supernatural gift each, Arthur has gifts that are both physical and mental: he can slice a witch in half with a single throw of his knife; he can explain how Twrch Trwyth used to be a king but was transformed into a pig; he knows where to find the cauldron of plenty. His superior physical skills match his superior knowledge. The evidence of the Triads reminds us of the supernatural powers attributed to Arthur by medieval storytellers: as one of the Red Ravagers of the Island of Britain, for example (Triad 20W), he lays waste the ground wherever he walks for seven years.

Besides its many striking features and its undoubted originality, perhaps one of the most characteristic aspects of the tale of *Culhwch ac Olwen* is its narrative mode.

With a plot that moves without explanation and with limited causality from one event to another, and which incorporates magic and supernatural events into the day-to-day running of a court, again without comment, the narrative style is typical of Welsh and Irish prose tales but less common in Continental or English medieval texts. The style is what I am calling "magic naturalism," in that it shares with the modern mode of "magic realism" (manifested in the work of writers such as Gabriel García Márquez) a seamless alternation between possible and impossible events, but it is entirely naturalistic rather than realistic. In other words, in early Welsh tales there is no narrative voice guiding us through the text, as there is in the works of more realist writers such as Chrétien de Troyes or even in the anonymous *Sir Gawain and the Green Knight*. Events appear to unfold without any particular motivation or causality but are simply juxtaposed as if in a natural order. No evaluations or judgments are offered; the reader or listener is obliged to apply their own discrimination and to rank the worth and priority of events and characters as they see fit. In this mode of magic naturalism, where moral judgments are never made, the moral center of the story is not the narrator, or the Christian system of values, but simply the hero – Arthur in the case of *Culhwch ac Olwen*. This is the true meaning of his power: he is not only politically pre-eminent, as the tale demonstrates, but is implicitly positioned, by the style of the narrative, as the natural center of moral authority.

The Three Merlins

The popular concept of Merlin as the tutor, protector, and adviser to Arthur, and the misguided lover of the treacherous Viviane, is one of three incarnations of the character of Merlin, who as a literary invention is as plural and unstable as Arthur himself. This version of Merlin belongs to thirteenth-century French accounts of the Arthurian legend, from where it was adapted by Malory in the fifteenth century to provide a coherent narrative of Merlin's part in Arthur's conception, birth, and education as a king.

Before the twelfth century, and specifically before Geoffrey of Monmouth wrote his *Historia Regum Britanniae*, the figure of Merlin, known by his Welsh name of Myrddin, formed a minor part of the legendary literature of Wales. Like many other characters from this literature, including Tristan, Cei, Owain, and others, Myrddin was originally unconnected with Arthur. He was drawn into his orbit only when Geoffrey of Monmouth made a connection between them in his *Historia Regum Britanniae*. Most of the early Myrddin literature is found in the same manuscripts as the early Arthurian references, particularly the Book of Taliesin, the Red Book of Hergest, and the Black Book of Carmarthen (Jarman 1991: 118–20), where he is represented as a poet and prophet like Taliesin. In an early (c. 1100) dialogue poem from the Black Book of Carmarthen, *Ymddiddan Myrddin a Thaliesin*, "Dialogue of Myrddin and Taliesin," the two legendary poet-prophets discuss a sixth-century battle between the men of Dyfed and the army of Maelgwn, probably Maelgwn Gwynedd, prince of the northern Welsh province of Gwynedd, who died c. 547. In this poem Myrddin seems more familiar with the traditional heroes of Dyfed, in the south, while Taliesin aligns himself with the men of the north. Myrddin speaks as a prophet in this dialogue and forewarns of a battle at Arfderydd, in the north of Britain, but there is no reference to his taking part in the battle.

A later poem, *Cyfoesi Myrddin a Gwenddydd ei Chwaer* (Red Book of Hergest, c. 1400) explicitly associates Myrddin with the battle of Arfderydd. This is a battle known about from other sources, particularly the *Annales Cambriae* ("Welsh Annals"), which date the battle to 573, and a series of poems in the Black Book of Carmarthen, supposedly narrated by Myrddin himself, although there is no clear indication of this in the manuscript. A twelfth-century Latin Life of St Kentigern, by Joceline of Furness, tells the story of a "wild man of the woods" who was driven mad after the battle of Arfderydd and took up residence in the Forest of Celyddon (Caledonia), but the wild man was said to be a prophet called Lailoken. At some stage, the Welsh prophet Myrddin became associated with the "wild man" legend concerning the battle of Arfderydd, and this Myrddin legend found expression in Welsh poems such as the *Cyfoesi*. It is possible, as Oliver Padel has suggested, that Geoffrey of Monmouth was the writer who conflated the Welsh Myrddin with the "wild man" legend in order to create a new biography for Merlin in his *Vita Merlini*, "Life of Merlin" (Padel 2006). Certainly, the absence of Myrddin from the Welsh Triads indicates that he was not a major figure of Welsh legend before the twelfth century.

The version of Myrddin as "wild man" is associated with the north of Britain: historical kings of the northern provinces, including Rhydderch Hael, Morgant Fawr, and Urien of Rheged, all active in the sixth to seventh centuries, appear in the Welsh poems, while Arfderydd, the site of the battle which drove Myrddin into madness and exile, is associated with the old north, possibly near Carlisle. Even in this early, and admittedly obscure, tradition of Myrddin in the Welsh manuscript record, he appears in two slightly different guises, as the "wild man of the woods" associated with the north and as a poet-prophet of Wales, located in the south. This latter persona is supported by the place name Caerfyrddin, the Welsh form of the city of Carmarthen in southwest Wales. Etymologically derived from *caer*, "fort," and *moridunon*, "sea-fort," the name was interpreted as "the fortress of Myrddin," by analogy with other place names formed on a similar model of *caer* followed by a personal name. On the assumption that a person called Myrddin was the founder of the city, a legend about him had to be fashioned, and this legend would plausibly have involved powers of prophecy (Jarman 1991: 138). The tenth-century prophetic poem *Armes Prydein*, "The Prophecy of Britain," found in the Book of Taliesin, refers to Myrddin as a prophet, "dysgogan Myrddin," "Myrddin foretells" (Williams 1972: line 17), indicating that he was already established in that role. There is even a reference to Myrddin in *Y Gododdin*, a faint suggestion that he was known as a poet-prophet, though the reference is found only in the later text of the poem, dated to the ninth century (Koch 1997: ciii, 159; Jarman 1988: 30). Later Welsh court poets, composing to twelfth-century princes, referred to Myrddin as a historical poet and prophet living at the same time as the sixth-century poet Taliesin (Bromwich 1978: 471).

It is these two Welsh legendary figures, the "wild man" and the prophetic founder of Caerfyrddin, that Geoffrey of Monmouth embraced and made very much his own. Not only did Geoffrey change Myrddin's name to the Latin form Merlinus, he also brought Merlin for the first time into the orbit of Arthur. Geoffrey's first interest in Merlin was as a prophet, and his *Prophetiae Merlini*, "Prophecies of Merlin," supposedly translated by Geoffrey from Welsh sources, was in circulation several years before the publication of his *Historia Regum Britanniae* (Roberts 1991b: 97). In the *Historia*, Merlin is configured as a boy-wizard, who reveals the fighting dragons undermining the foundations of Vortigern's new fortress. The story of the dragons was borrowed by Geoffrey from the ninth-century *Historia Brittonum*, itself a significant source of early Arthurian legend. In the *Historia Brittonum*, the boy's name is Ambrosius and he comes from Glywysing (Glamorgan); Geoffrey renames him Merlin – sometimes referring to him as Merlin Ambrosius – and locates him in Carmarthen (Caerfyrddin), evidently drawing on local place-name legends in which a legendary Myrddin was the founder of the city. The incorporation of the *Prophetiae Merlini* into the larger *Historia* was a deliberate editorial act that established Merlin's credentials as a sage and prophet, in line with popular Welsh legends about Myrddin.

Some years after the publication of the *Historia Regum Britanniae*, Geoffrey composed a long Latin poem called the *Vita Merlini*, dated to about 1150 (Jarman 1991: 132). No doubt capitalizing on what was evidently a popular topic, and drawing on material similar to that found in the Arfderydd poems in the Black Book of Carmarthen, Geoffrey developed an entire life story for Merlin, based on the genre of the saint's life. In what may have been Geoffrey's own invented idea, the Merlin of the *Vita* is represented as the "wild man" of Welsh poetic fame rather than the fearless young prophet who featured in the *Historia* (Padel 2006). Many of the names and events found in early Welsh poetry – Rodarchus (Rhydderch), Telgesinus (Taliesin), the forest of Calidon (Celyddon) – are brought together in a more or less coherent narrative of Merlin's life, which includes his madness in battle, exile in the forest, and the additional (and original) sub-plot of Arthur as a wounded king waiting to return as a leader of the British people. Though Geoffrey claimed that the Merlin of the *Historia* and of the *Vita* were one and the same person, represented at different stages of his life, readers were more skeptical. In his *Itinerarium Kambriae*, "Journey through Wales" (II.8), Gerald of Wales makes a firm distinction between the two characters, whom he calls Merlin Ambrosius (found in Welsh texts as Myrddin Emrys) and Merlin Celidonius or Merlin Silvester (whose Welsh equivalent is Myrddin Wyllt, "Wild Merlin") (Thorpe 1978: 192). In the only one of the Triads in which Merlin is associated with Arthur (Triad 87), he appears as two of the three "skilful bards" at Arthur's court: Myrddin son of Morfryn and Myrddin Emrys, along with the third poet, Taliesin.

In Geoffrey's *Vita Merlini*, Merlin has a wife, Guendoloena, from whom he endured long separations and infidelity before choosing to spend his remaining days with a group of exiles in the forest. Here are the seeds of Merlin's transformation into the figure of French romance, the visionary who could not prevent his own madness and betrayal in love. Transmitted from Geoffrey's *Historia* via Wace's Anglo-Norman translation, the Merlin of romance first emerges in about 1200 in Robert de Boron's Old French poem, *Merlin*, where he is drawn into the religious associations of the Grail. The prose continuations, in the Vulgate Cycle and the *Suite du Merlin*, establish Merlin in his third and final persona as the wizard and sage who masterminds Arthur's conception, birth, and rise to power, only to succumb to the treachery of Viviane. While French courtly audiences looked for realism and answers to questions about their own lives within a deeply spiritual context, Geoffrey was following the earlier Welsh tradition of fantasy and magic naturalism, locating both Arthur and Merlin in a supernatural world whose power was greater and more unpredictable than that of any leader or prophet.

PRIMARY SOURCES

Bromwich, R. (ed.) (1978). *Trioedd Ynys Prydein* [The Triads of the Island of Britain], 2nd edn. Cardiff: University of Wales Press.

Coe, J. B. & Young, S. (1995). *The Celtic sources for the Arthurian legend*. Felinfach: Llanerch.

Davies, S. (trans.) (2007). *The Mabinogion*. Oxford: Oxford University Press.

Evans, J. G. (1910). *Facsimile and text of the Book of Taliesin*. Llanbedrog.

Evans, J. G. (1915). *Poems from the Book of Taliesin*. Llanbedrog.

Ford, P. (1977). *The Mabinogi and other medieval Welsh tales*. Berkeley, CA: University of California Press.

Haycock, M. (ed.) (1994). *Blodeugerdd Barddas o Ganu Crefyddol Cynnar* [The Barddas anthology of early religious poetry]. Abertawe: Barddas.

Haycock, M. (ed. trans.) (2007). *Legendary poems from the Book of Taliesin*. Aberystwyth: CMCS.

Huws, D. (1989). *Llyfr Aneirin. Ffacsimile* [Book of Aneirin. Facsimile]. Aberystwyth: National Library of Wales.

Jarman, A. O. H. (ed. trans.) (1982). *Llyfr Du Caerfyrddin. The Black Book of Carmarthen*. Cardiff: University of Wales Press.

Jarman, A. O. H. (ed. trans.) (1988). *Aneirin: Y Gododdin. Britain's oldest heroic poem*. Llandysul: Gomer.

Koch, J. (1997). *The Gododdin of Aneirin: Text and context from dark-age north Britain*. Cardiff: University of Wales Press.

Morris, J. (ed. trans.) (1980). *Nennius: British history and the Welsh annals*. Chichester: Phillimore.

Richards, M. (ed.) (1972). *Breudwyt Ronabwy* [The dream of Rhonabwy]. Cardiff: University of Wales Press.

Rowland, J. (1990). *Early Welsh saga poetry: A study and edition of the Englynion*. Woodbridge: Brewer.

Thorpe, L. (trans.) (1978). *Gerald of Wales. The journey through Wales/The description of Wales*. Harmondsworth: Penguin.

Williams, I. (ed.) (1935). *Canu Llywarch Hen* [The poetry of Llywarch Hen]. Cardiff: University of Wales Press.

Williams, I. (ed.) (1938). *Canu Aneirin* [The poetry of Aneirin]. Cardiff: University of Wales Press.

Williams, I. (ed.) (1968). *The poems of Taliesin* (trans. J. E. Caerwyn Williams). Dublin: Dublin Institute for Advanced Studies.

Williams, I. (ed.) (1972). *Armes Prydein, The Prophecy of Britain* (trans. R. Bromwich). Dublin: Dublin Institute for Advanced Studies.

References and Further Reading

Ashe, G. (2006). *Merlin: The prophet and his history.* Stroud: Sutton.

Bromwich, R. (1969). *Trioedd Ynys Prydein in Welsh literature and scholarship.* Cardiff: University of Wales Press.

Chadwick, H. M. & Chadwick, N. K. (1932). Merlin in the works of Geoffrey of Monmouth. In H. M. & N. K. Chadwick (eds), *The growth of literature,* vol. I. Cambridge: Cambridge University Press, pp. 123–32.

Chadwick, N. K. (1976). *The British heroic age.* Cardiff: University of Wales Press.

Charles-Edwards, T. M. (1978). The authenticity of the *Gododdin:* An historian's view. In R. Bromwich & R. B. Jones (eds), *Astudiaethau ar yr Hengerdd: Studies in old Welsh poetry.* Cardiff: University of Wales Press, pp. 44–71.

Charles-Edwards, T. M. (1991). The Arthur of history. In R. Bromwich, A. O. H. Jarman, & B. F. Roberts (eds), *The Arthur of the Welsh.* Cardiff: University of Wales Press, pp. 15–32.

Dumville, D. (1972). Early Welsh poetry: Problems of historicity. In B. F. Roberts (ed.), *Early Welsh poetry: Studies in the Book of Aneirin.* Cardiff: University of Wales Press.

Fulton, H. (1994). Cultural heroism in the old north of Britain: The evidence of Aneirin's *Gododdin.* In L. S. Davidson, S. N. Mukherjee, & Z. Zlatar et al. (eds), *The epic in history.* Sydney: Sydney Association for Studies in Society & Culture, pp. 18–39.

Fulton, H. (2004). George Borrow and the Oldest Animals in *Wild Wales. Transactions of the Honourable Society of Cymmrodorion,* 10, 23–40.

Haycock, M. (1983/4). *Preiddeu Annwn* and the figure of Taliesin. *Studia Celtica,* 18/19, 52–78.

Haycock, M. (1988). Llyfr Taliesin [The Book of Taliesin]. *Journal of the National Library of Wales,* 25, 357–86.

Haycock, M. (2006). *Taliesin a Brwydr y Coed* [Taliesin and the Battle of the Trees]. Aberystwyth: Canolfan Uwchefrydiau Cymreig a Cheltaidd.

Higham, N. J. (1992). *Rome, Britain and the Anglo-Saxons.* London: Seaby.

Jackson, K. H. (1958). *The international popular tale and early Welsh tradition.* Cardiff: University of Wales Press.

Jarman, A. O. H. (1976). *The legend of Merlin.* Cardiff: University of Wales Press.

Jarman, A. O. H. (1981). *The Cynfeirdd: Early Welsh poets and poetry.* Cardiff: University of Wales Press.

Jarman, A. O. H. (1983). The Arthurian allusions in the Black Book of Carmarthen. In P. B. Grout, R. A. Lodge, C. E. Pickford, & E. K. C. Varty (eds), *The legend of Arthur in the Middle Ages.* Cambridge: Brewer, pp. 99–112.

Jarman, A. O. H. (1991). The Merlin legend and the Welsh tradition of prophecy. In R. Bromwich, A. O. H. Jarman, & B. F. Roberts (eds), *The Arthur of the Welsh.* Cardiff: University of Wales Press, pp. 117–45.

Jones, G. (1972). *Kings, beasts and heroes.* Oxford: Oxford University Press.

Knight, S. T. (1983). *Arthurian literature and society.* London: Macmillan.

Lloyd-Morgan, C. (1991). *Breuddwyd Rhonabwy* and later Arthurian literature. In R. Bromwich, A. O. H. Jarman, & B. F. Roberts (eds), *The Arthur of the Welsh.* Cardiff: University of Wales Press, pp. 183–208.

Padel, O. J. (1984). Geoffrey of Monmouth and Cornwall. *Cambrian Medieval Celtic Studies,* 8, 1–28.

Padel, O. J. (1994). The nature of Arthur. *Cambrian Medieval Celtic Studies,* 27, 1–31.

Padel, O. J. (2000). *Arthur in medieval Welsh literature.* Cardiff: University of Wales Press.

Padel, O. J. (2006). Geoffrey of Monmouth and the development of the Merlin legend. *Cambrian Medieval Celtic Studies,* 51, 37–65.

Roberts, B. F. (ed.) (1972). *Early Welsh poetry: Studies in the Book of Aneirin.* Cardiff: University of Wales Press.

Roberts, B. F. (1991a). *Culhwch ac Olwen,* the Triads, saints' lives. In R. Bromwich, A. O. H. Jarman, & B. F. Roberts (eds), *The Arthur of the Welsh.* Cardiff: University of Wales Press, pp. 73–95.

Roberts, B. F. (1991b). Geoffrey of Monmouth, *Historia Regum Britanniae* and *Brut y Brenhinedd.* In R. Bromwich, A. O. H. Jarman, & B. F. Roberts (eds), *The Arthur of the Welsh.* Cardiff: University of Wales Press, pp. 97–116.

Rowland, J. (1985). The prose setting of the early Welsh *englynion chwedlonol*. *Ériu*, 36, 29–43.

Rowland, J. (1995). Warfare and horses in the *Gododdin* and the problem of Catraeth. *Cambrian Medieval Celtic Studies*, 30, 13–40.

Sims-Williams, P. (1991). The early Welsh Arthurian poems. In R. Bromwich, A. O. H. Jarman, & B. F. Roberts (eds), *The Arthur of the Welsh*. Cardiff: University of Wales Press, pp. 33–71.

Slotkin, E. (1989). The fabula, story and text of *Breuddwyd Rhonabwy*. *Cambrian Medieval Celtic Studies*, 18, 89–112.

7

The Arthurian Legend in Scotland and Cornwall

Juliette Wood

Ever since Geoffrey of Monmouth wrote his history of the British kings, the identity of King Arthur has been a subject for speculation. Many solutions have been proposed, but the essential problems remain the same. Prominent among them is whether the considerable body of material centered on this figure is rooted in history or whether it is derived from mythical Celtic traditions. Two areas with strong Celtic links, Scotland and Cornwall, both claim him, either as an important traditional figure or as a historical "native son." Neither region has a body of Arthurian material comparable to other areas such as Wales or France. Nevertheless, both Scotland and Cornwall have made substantial contributions to the development of the complex traditions associated with Arthur.

Both areas are integrated into Geoffrey of Monmouth's view of British history, in which the island of Britain was presented as an ancient unity. The story of Brutus's three sons in Geoffrey of Monmouth's *Historia Regum Britanniae* – Locrinus, the founder of England (Welsh *Lloegr*); Kamber, the founder of Wales (Cambria); and Albanactus, the founder of Scotland (Alba) – together with Brutus's ally Corineus, founder of Cornwall, provided a unifying myth for defining Britain's role in the context of politics and culture that spanned a period from the twelfth to the seventeenth centuries. During the same period, Geoffrey's image of Arthur as king of Britain served to articulate regional relationships and to define concepts of identity and difference within the parameters of a British world. In addition to material in Geoffrey, references in chronicles, place-name lore, ballads, folk tales, and literary texts from Scotland and Cornwall present differing perspectives on Arthur as a historical or traditional figure. As a supposedly historical ruler of Britain in medieval sources such as chronicles, the figure of Arthur had political implications for medieval and early modern British politics. By contrast, present-day concerns with Arthur's historical origins are more focused on modern ethnic and spiritual identities. Today, the figure of Arthur functions in both Scotland and Cornwall as a symbol of regional identity.

Geoffrey's work was, at least in part, a response to new literary developments on the Continent, and to the growing power of the Anglo-Normans during the twelfth century. Arthur's role, with its powerful emotional and political possibilities, was central to this largely mythic history. Not all of Geoffrey's contemporaries accepted his historical framework, and some made the point, as relevant today as it was then, that no validation for Arthur exists outside Geoffrey's work or his known sources (Keeler 1946). Nevertheless, the importance of Geoffrey's Arthur as a pseudo-historical myth went unchallenged for many years, even among the historians who questioned its accuracy. The critique of Geoffrey's historical model mounted by Tudor historians and those writing in the wake of the Reformation did not by any means obliterate Arthurian tradition, but it did change the direction of the argument. When scholars engaged once again with questions about Arthur's historicity at the beginning of the twentieth century, they were looking for a different figure, one whose origin was linked to a specific region and a specific historical context. Contemporary Scottish and Cornish visions of Arthur give primacy to traditions that place him in a local context, but they nevertheless retain the main elements of the Arthurian narrative, namely the unifying power of a charismatic leader and its legacy, which gives meaning to and sustains a national enclave.

Early references to Arthur in British literature led to a search for a real figure who could be localized geographically as well as historically. Wales and England, as well as Scotland and Cornwall, claimed the historical Arthur. Frequently these claims for an "original" Arthur depended on overly literal interpretations of early historical references, folklore, and archaeological sites. The earliest accounts were considered the most accurate because they, apparently, lacked later embellishments. Interpreting folklore and textual material created even more confusion. Here too the emphasis fell on the oldest strata. Hypothetical reconstructions of original versions were used to interpret resemblances between older and more recent material as "folk" memories of distant history (Wood 1998). By the 1950s some scholars were looking to archaeology to complete the cultural context of the Arthurian world. Far from providing the expected historical proof for references to Arthur, archaeology appears to complicate the argument even further (see chapter 1). The matter is as yet unresolved, and the search for Arthur continues (Dumville 1977; Padel 1994; Higham 2002; Green 2007).

Scottish Chronicles and Arthurian Tradition

Medieval and early modern Scottish chroniclers were aware of Arthur both as a figure in romance and as a folk hero, but the most important aspect of Arthur in these sources revolved around notions of kingship and national sovereignty. Although the dominant image of Arthur in Scottish chronicles is that of a historical king embedded in Geoffrey's myth of British unity, the attitude to him is ambiguous, even at times hostile (Boardman 2002; Royan 2002; Wood 2005). In the eyes of a number of the

Scottish chroniclers, Modred, as the legitimate son of the Scottish lord Loth and Anna (Arthur's sister or close relative), had the stronger claim to the throne. Arthur, on the other hand, was conceived out of wedlock, and only legitimized later. Edward I's claim to Scotland, based on Geoffrey's *Historia Regum Britanniae*, highlighted the problem of Arthur's legitimacy in relation to Scottish sovereignty, and these claims were the subject of a detailed refutation by the Scot Baldred Bisset in 1301 (Keeler 1946: 51–4, 130). John of Fordun's *Chronica Gentis Scotorum*, "Chronicle of the Scottish People" (c. 1385), the earliest Scottish chronicle to consider Arthur's position in history, was conscious of Edward's Scottish ambitions. Fordun attempted to refocus Geoffrey's myth in the context of an independent Scotland, by acknowledging that, despite his illegitimate birth, Arthur as a mature king was preferable to the underage rightful heirs. In the mid-fifteenth century, Walter Bower's *Scotichronicon* expanded John of Fordun's work and reflected further developments in Scottish attitudes to Geoffrey's depiction of Arthur. Anna's sons, Modred and Gawain, remain the rightful heirs, and Bower emphasized Arthur's illegitimate parentage, a product of the "wizard Merlin's unlawful arts" (*inaudite arte merlini vatis*). In his *Originall Chronicl* written in Older Scots (c. 1412), Andrew of Wyntoun claimed that he had a specific source that allowed him to side-step the controversies about Geoffrey. In Wyntoun's account, Modred is closer to the treacherous figure of romance (Wood 2005).

The *Annales Cambriae* ("Welsh Annals") state only that Modred and Arthur were killed in the battle of Camlann, while medieval Welsh poetry depicted Modred (or Medrawt) as a rather courteous figure. In Geoffrey's account, he opposes the rightful king, thereby transforming Arthur into an exemplum of a hero brought down by treachery. The very different relationship between Arthur and Modred in Scottish chronicles is therefore interesting. While Scottish sources accept that Arthur was chosen because the legitimate heir, Modred, was too young, the observation that Arthur was conceived out of wedlock sticks to him. In a mid-fifteenth century chronicle, the *Scottis Originale*, Arthur is characterized as "that tyrant," "son of adultery," and "hurisone" (literally "whore's son") whose birth was further contaminated with hints of supernatural and diabolic intervention from the "devilry of Merlin." Although John Mair, writing at the beginning of the sixteenth century, exonerates Ygerne's role in this, the attitude prevalent in the Scottish chronicles frequently undermines Arthur's heroic status (Alexander 1975; Wood 2005).

Another interesting feature of the Scottish chronicles is the tension between Geoffrey's Arthur as sovereign and a more literary and traditional image of Arthur as a pattern for heroic or courtly life. This tension between the dynastic figure and the heroic king of romance literature varies from chronicle to chronicle and is reflected in other Scottish works as well (Purdie & Royan 2005: 1–8). *The Spectacle of Luf* treats Guinevere's infidelity with Modred, but there is no mention that the latter had any right to the throne. Equally interesting is *The Roit or Quheill of Tyme*, which denies Arthur's claim to the throne, but retains his character as heroic leader. It notes "fabillis" ("fables") written about him, but claims that these gave him "no domination of Scotland" (Alexander 1975: 21–2).

The skepticism of later Scottish commentators such as Hector Boece, John Mair, John Bellenden, John Stewart, John Leslie, and John Buchanan further undermined the credibility of a historical Arthur (see chapter 23). However, Geoffrey's Arthurian myth was still an important presence even in these sources. Although Merlin is treated as a mere necromancer, he is still asked to prophesy whether "the crown of Britain should be recovered again to the Britones." In depicting the Arthurian world, both Boece's original Latin text and its Scots translations emphasize that the alliance between the Britons and the Scots is one between equals. Political expediency remains the basis for Arthur's claim to kingship, but the Britons break their promise and give the crown to Constantine, son of Cador of Cornwall. In this context of eventual treachery, Modred's battle on the banks of the Humber has some justification, at least in retrospect. Afterwards, Guanora (Guinevere) is captured and remains a prisoner for the rest of her life. The ambiguity felt toward Arthur is clear, but, on the whole, Geoffrey's narrative itself is not questioned until much later, in, for example, the work of John Buchanan. None of these sources attempts to relocate Arthur as a Scottish-born king. Indeed it makes more sense for the cause of Scottish independence to keep a ruler of illegitimate birth outside the Scottish dynastic line, and the idea that the Arthurian legend originated in Scotland is much later.

If Arthur's position as a historical king is ambiguous in Scottish material, so too was the alleged discovery of the king's grave at Glastonbury in 1190 and the legends about his eventual return. Geoffrey is ambiguous on the matter of Arthur's return, but it became an important aspect of the Arthurian legend elsewhere. Walter Bower noted that Arthur was going to "come again to restore the scattered and fugitive Britons to their rights" (*superventurus est dispersos et profugos Britones ad propria restaurare*). The appearance of such references in Scottish chronicles may reflect the growing popularity of the "matter of Britain" in sophisticated circles in medieval Scotland, as elsewhere in Europe. In the *Historia Majoris Britannie*, "History of Greater Britain" (1521), John Mair expresses his doubts that Arthur will return, but he quotes *Hic jacet Arthurus Rex magnus rex futurus* ("Here lies Arthur, the great and future king") all the same (Kelly 1979: 437–8; Boardman 2002; Wood 2005: 10–16). Another area in which British heritage was a factor in the Scottish use of Arthurian material concerned the dynastic claims of the Campbells of Argyll, which incorporated Arthurian references into their genealogical lore and bardic poetry as a counterbalance to the Gaelic, ultimately Irish, claims of other clans (Gillies 1976–8: 280–83, 1982: 66–7).

An important dimension of Geoffrey's vision of Arthur was the assumption that unity brought stability under a legitimate king. In Scotland, there was a greater concern with the obligations of the good ruler and with Scottish sovereignty and independence. Concern for the latter helps explain the ambiguous and sometimes contradictory attitudes to Arthur in Scottish chronicles. The figure of Arthur gave coherence to a genealogical narrative that started with Brutus and gave legitimacy to rulers by creating an ancestry with an unbroken continuity. While Geoffrey's vision could provide a basis for inclusion and alliance, it could also, by contrast, form the basis for exclusion and a unique independence. Arthur is the point at which Scottish chronicles can claim an independent genealogical coherence because of Arthur's illegitimacy. The questionable legitimacy of Arthur's claim to sovereignty compared to that of Modred and Gawain, his sister's (or alternatively aunt's) children by the Scottish king Loth, is a consistent feature of the Scottish chronicle material, although the chronicles never reject the figure of Arthur outright. However, later Scottish historians writing in a humanist tradition remain critical of the unorthodox nature of Arthur's birth story, although the tone is more pro-Scot and anti-Geoffrey, rather than anti-Arthur (Kelly 1979). If ever Geoffrey's vision approached reality for Scotland, it should have been when James VI of Scotland became James I of England and Ireland in 1603. An envoy from Venice to the English court observed: "It is said that the king disposed to abandon the titles of England and Scotland and to call himself King of Great Britain . . . like that famous and ancient king Arthur" (Morrill 1996: 20–21).

Folk Tradition and the Figure of Arthur

The use of folklore in works such as chronicles reveals a great deal about cultural attitudes and about the interpretations writers wish to convey (Wood 1998). Insofar as it is possible to talk about an original Arthur, he seems to have been a hero of legend without a clear genealogy or location (Padel 1994; Green 2007). One of the many contentious aspects of sources such as Geoffrey of Monmouth's work or the Arthurian romances is the degree to which popular beliefs and oral tradition about a legendary hero contributed to the creation of a symbol of medieval kingship and courtly virtue. Geoffrey seems to have favored elements that allowed him to present Arthur as historical and realistic. He did, however, incorporate traditions about giants, such as the giant of Mont-Saint-Michel, whom Arthur has to defeat. Encounters between heroes and giants are frequently localized at unusual landscape features, and heroes themselves are often depicted as gigantic, larger than life figures (Padel 1991; Grooms 1993: 79–110). The location of the narratives and the confrontations between giant and hero follow a traditional legendary pattern, but the relation between traditional and learned lore is never simple. Here as elsewhere Geoffrey may be drawing on and at the same time reinforcing tradition. In the medieval Welsh prose tale *Culhwch and Olwen*, the clearest expression of Arthur as a heroic figure before his transformation via the material in Geoffrey of Monmouth, the king and his men must perform a series of tasks set by a giant. One of these tasks involves killing another giant in order to gain control of his possessions. Another Welsh medieval tale, *Breuddwyd Rhonabwy*, depicts Arthur and his men as the gigantic heroes of old looking askance at the littleness of modern men. The giants provide a validation for Arthur's greatness, either as a measure for his own stature or by providing suitable opposition. It seems likely that Geoffrey shared this perspective of Arthur with traditions already well established in traditional lore, and, given the biblical sanction for giant figures, may have considered them suitable for his vision of history.

Geoffrey continues the theme of giant-slayer in his characterization of Corineus, the eponymous founder of Cornwall, although he also gives an alternative meaning for the name as *cornu*, "horn," because of its geographical location. Corineus, the leader of an exiled group of Trojans, defeats giants as if they were "mere boys." He chooses Cornwall as his domain because it has more giants than any other place in Britain, and his crowning achievement is the defeat of Gogmagog in a wrestling match, which concludes with an onomastic tag popular in Celtic stories, namely that Corineus threw the giant's body off a cliff still called the Giant's Leap.

In the *Scotorum Historia*, "History of the Scots," compiled by Hector Boece (1527) and translated later into Older Scots by John Bellenden as the *Chronicles of Scotland*, the Irish hero Finn MacCool is depicted as a giant, and the narratives attached to him are compared to tales of Arthur. Boece and his translators contrast the "gestes [deeds] of Arthur" favorably with the "vulgar" traditions about Finn MacCool. It is easy to over-interpret such references, but Finn and Arthur as leaders of warrior bands have much in common, and both are endowed with gigantic stature (Nagy 1985). A series of Welsh tales gathered in the early seventeenth century with the specific purpose of defending Geoffrey's history against the attacks of men like Hector Boece also characterized Arthur as a giant or a trickster/giant-slayer. These narratives are examples of a common story type in which a clever hero outwits a supernatural being. Arthur's character in these tales is unlike either the courtly hero of the romances or the dynastic figure of the chronicles. These traditional tales raise the possibility that the characterization of giants in folklore provided a positive view of Arthur in sources dating from before Geoffrey and continuing into the seventeenth century.

By contrast, Boece seems to incorporate traditional material in other contexts as a way of undermining the credibility of Geoffrey's Arthur. For example, he lists Merlin's prophecies concerning Arthur, but follows them with a series of possession tales whose tone is skeptical. Another interesting reference to possible folk traditions is the odd tradition that Guinevere was captured by the Picts after Arthur's death and held prisoner for the remainder of her life. Her tombstone, actually a carved Pictish stone at Meigle in Scotland depicting the biblical story of Daniel in the lion's den, causes infertility and is, according to Boece, avoided by all women except nuns. There is a commonplace and long-running legend about sites that promote fertility, or cause unexpected, and presumably unwanted, pregnancy. The rather snide reference to nuns wishing to avoid pregnancy is an interesting bit of anti-clerical propaganda, perhaps reflecting Boece's humanist stance, but he may very well have known a version of this legend which he adapted. Whatever his actual intentions, this slight narrative serves as a reminder of just how complex and multilayered the Arthurian tradition had become by this time (Wood 2005).

Prophecy is another area in which popular and learned traditions overlap. The Scottish chronicle writers John of Fordun and Walter Bower were familiar with Galfridean prophecy. Although Bower links Arthur's birth with Merlin's dark arts, he credits him as the source of a tradition that the eagles of Loch Lomond flocked together to prophesy. He even tries his hand at prophetic poetry when he paraphrases a version of a "hope of Britain" prophecy. He takes a distinctively Scottish stance, saying, "Yet the Welsh say they can never recover their rights in full without the help of the ally long ago, the people of Scotland." In addition, he mentions the prophecies of the eagle and prophecies addressed to Cadwaladr and to Arthur (Griffiths 1937: 197–8; Wood 2005).

The Arthurian heritage as laid out in Geoffrey's work provided an image of the past that could be applied to contemporary affairs and to more general notions of identity. Scottish interpretations rejected the notion that Arthur conquered Scotland, but, as descendants of the sons of Brutus, they could see themselves as inheritors of Arthur's kingdom. By contrast, Welsh and Cornish interpretations stressed the fact that they, and not the English, were the original Britons and the true heirs to Arthur's kingdom. Although writing much earlier than Boece, John of Cornwall's commentary on the *Prophetiae Merlini*, a work which expanded as well as commented on Geoffrey, was conscious of the role of Cornish history and tradition in the achievement of Geoffrey's British vision. For example, John of Cornwall expands Geoffrey's prophetic phrase that the Cornish shall kill six brothers. This "prophetic" reference is linked to an act of anti-Norman rebellion in Cornwall in the early part of the twelfth century in which Cornishmen killed six Norman brothers, apparently in revenge for the death of one of their kinsmen (Curley 1982; Padel 1984; Hale et al. 2000: 42–8).

The Arthur of Romance

Other images of Arthur, such as his standing as a romance figure and his function within folk narrative tradition, also influenced both Scottish and Cornish sources, and the attempts to balance these different and complex images can be very revealing. John of Fordun denied the romance account that made Modred a child of incest, probably in an attempt to preserve the basis for Scottish independence, but Arthur functioned as a heroic standard in other Scottish sources (Alexander 1975; Purdie & Royan 2005: 9–20).

Arthurian romance influenced Gaelic audiences, in both Ireland and Scotland, in the early modern period just as it did most other European literatures, and its effect was felt in the storytelling tradition. It is generally accepted that the surviving oral heroic-romantic tales are descended from literary romances. Gaelic texts dating from the fourteenth to seventeenth centuries, and found in paper manuscripts from the seventeenth to nineteenth centuries, revised earlier material but were open to wider literary influences such as the Continental Arthurian tradition. This mingling of Gaelic, French, and English cultures in post-Norman Ireland provided the context for the inclusion of Arthurian material into native Gaelic literature (Bruford 1969: 69–164; Gillies 1982: 63). Gaelic Arthurian folk tales comprise a small element within this enormous storytelling corpus, but these heroic-romantic tales constitute a distinctive sub-set, and several are set in the court of Artair MacIuthair (Arthur son of Uther) or concern Arthurian characters. These include tales like Sir Uallabh

O'Còrn and the Knight of the Red Shield, the latter known in Nova Scotia, as well as ballads with Arthurian affinities such as *Am Bròn Brinn* ("The Sweet Sorrow") or *Laoidh an Bhruit* ("Lay of the Mantle"), a form of the chastity test. The narrative of *An tAmadán Mor* ("Lay of the Great Fool") with its links to the Perceval story exists in ballad, tale, and early modern romance versions, and attests to the influence of Arthurian themes in the early modern tradition. In addition, some of the elements of the Arthur and Gorlagros romance are related to Gaelic versions of the "Werewolf" tale (Kittredge 1903).

It is more difficult to determine whether these tales are the result of the popularity of Arthurian literature or a shared Celtic heritage. The international context of many tale motifs makes it difficult to decide whether Gaelic tradition influenced Arthurian literature or vice versa. Names like Arthur son of Uther (Artair Mac Iuthair or Ioghair, or Uir) and the generally late date of most of the Scottish Gaelic texts seem to reflect Geoffrey's Arthurian world and the influence of Arthurian romance. On the other hand, the lack of a strong chivalric element suggests connections with Gaelic heroic tradition (Gillies 1981: 65–6, 1982: 48–50, 52–60). The precise proportions of literary romance, international folklore, and specifically Gaelic tradition have been contested (Henderson 1912; Chadwick 1953; Loomis 1955–9; Bruford 1969; Gillies 1981, 1982; Gowans 1992a,b, 1998).

Only two Scots Arthurian romances survive, *Gologros and Gawaine* (Purdie 2005) and *Lancelot of the Laik* (Archibald 2005), both dating from the fifteenth century and written in Older Scots. One of the protagonists, Gawain of Lothian or Orkney, is actually a Scottish knight in the parallel world of Arthurian tradition, as is, by implication, his brother Modred. Malory's *Morte Darthur* presents an interesting external perspective on the Scottish figures of Arthurian tradition. His account stresses the role of Gawain and his Scottish-born relatives in the entrapment of Guinevere and thus makes them more central to the fall of Arthur (Rushton 2005: 109). The Scottish romance of *Lancelot of the Laik*, although based on a French source, does foreground the notion of what makes a good king, thus reflecting themes attached to the treatment of Arthur in Scottish chronicles (Archibald 2005). Similar themes of sovereignty and good governance are found in the romance of *Gologros and Gawaine*, as well as a tantalizing link with the "Werewolf" transformation tales of wider Gaelic tradition (Purdie 2005).

Cornwall

No medieval romances written in Cornish survive, but the *drolls*, traditional Cornish tales, were an important genre for preserving Cornish tradition in a wider context than just the Arthurian legend. Although they are late, they do contain some references to Arthurian lore (Hunt 1881; Pearce 1974). Drama was also an important Cornish literary and popular genre, and a recently discovered Middle Cornish play from the second half of the sixteenth century, *Bewnans Ke*, "The life of St Kea," contains a substantial Arthurian section (Thomas & Williams 2007). Despite the lacunae in the text, the dramatic action can be reconstructed from a seventeenth-century summary of a lost Latin life of St Kea. In both the Latin life and the Cornish play, the saint returns from Brittany to avert a potential civil war between Arthur and his nephew Modred, caused by the latter's abduction of Guinevere. The arrival of a Saxon army, however, causes that saint to abandon his hopeless task and return to Brittany. On his way back, he passes through Winchester, where he persuades Queen Guinevere to enter a nunnery. This section is ultimately dependent on Geoffrey of Monmouth, rather than oral traditions, and follows his version of events. Although the Arthur section is based on Geoffrey, the Cornish were aware of how their own history and traditions could be interpreted as a fulfillment of Geoffrey's vision, and this would certainly have influenced how the text was received and interpreted. The Cornish glosses in John of Cornwall's commentary on Merlin's prophecies may be making such connections (Curley 1982; Padel 1984).

The Tristan romance material provides perhaps the strongest connection between the Arthurian legend and Cornwall. The two only became associated in the twelfth century, and ultimately the Tristan and Isolde material was absorbed into a wider Arthurian framework. The background of the Tristan romance lies in Cornish folklore, not history, but several important motifs are localized in Cornwall and reflect pre-Geoffrey Cornish legends (Padel 1981, 1991; Thomas 1993, 2002). In addition, at least one of the romance writers, Béroul, who composed a *Roman de Tristan* in the middle of the twelfth century, seems to have had local knowledge of the region (Padel 1981).

One of the most significant motifs in the Tristan romance is the castle at Tintagel (see chapter 1). Tintagel as an Arthurian site was not firmly established in local Cornish lore until the nineteenth century. However, archaeological investigations have revealed that it was an important Dark Age site (c. 450–600), although later abandoned. The name Tintagel ("fort of the narrow neck") describes its location and, as it could not have been occupied all year round, may also give a clue to its function as a defensive site. Geoffrey undoubtedly introduced it into international legend when he used it as the site of Arthur's birth, and he might have been adapting existing legends about Tintagel as a stronghold of the Cornish rulers. Although the site had been abandoned from the seventh century onward, a ditch and rampart from an earlier structure might have been visible in Geoffrey's time and could have provided a context for the localization of geographical traditions. The popularity of Geoffrey's narrative probably influenced the newly created Duke of Cornwall to build a castle at the famous site in about 1230 (Padel 1991; Thomas 1993). It is not clear whether Tintagel was linked specifically with Arthur prior to Geoffrey, but it certainly appears as an Arthurian site in the Tristan legends.

When legends about Tintagel first appeared in Geoffrey of Monmouth's history and the Tristan romances, it was depicted as some kind of royal residence associated either with King Gorlois, the husband of Arthur's mother Igerne, or with King Mark, the overking in the Tristan legend. What lies behind these traditions is not by any means clear. Despite Geoffrey setting Arthur's birth at Tintagel, it was not prominent in subsequent medieval Arthurian romances. The Tristan romances associate the site with King Mark, and Cornish legends about Tintagel may have provided a source for both Geoffrey and the Tristan stories, although Cornish derivation of the Tristan story is not the same as claiming Cornish origin for it (Padel 1981: 70–74). King Mark is linked firmly to Cornwall via the Tristan legend, but other traditions connected with Mark are localized in areas where, presumably, such tales were current. For example, the legend that he had horse's ears, instead of human ones, explains his name Mark, i.e. Welsh *march*, "horse," and is found outside Cornwall. In this context he seems to be less the romance king and more a pan-Brittonic figure of legend, like Arthur, and therefore typical of a character whose origin lies in folklore rather than history (Padel 1981). The French writer Béroul claimed local knowledge of Cornish matters in his Tristan romance. He mentioned several narrative motifs – Tristan's leap, and the story about King Mark's horse's ears, as well as the existence of Isolde's robe at St Samson's chapel (Padel 1981: 63–5, 77) – that may depend on Cornish folk-tale material known at least as early as the tenth century.

In Geoffrey's myth of British origins, Corineus, the founder of Cornwall, appeared as an ally to Brutus's sons. As a result Cornwall did not figure in arguments about political precedence based on Geoffrey as it did in Scotland, or Wales and England for that matter. That is not to say that Cornwall did not play an important role in the development of Arthurian tradition. Cornish rulers are inserted into the line of Brutus at several points. Arthur is born and dies there, and his wife is raised there. It was still predominantly Cornish speaking when Geoffrey composed his history, but its prominence in *Historia Regum Britanniae* is out of proportion to its position in either the earlier Brittonic or contemporary Norman world. Geoffrey sets Arthur's court at Caerleon, but sources outside Geoffrey and probably pre-dating his influential work consistently locate one of Arthur's courts, Kelliwic (i.e. "forest grove"), in Cornwall, even though no specific place can be identified with it (Padel 1984, 1991).

Geoffrey's claim that Tintagel was the site of Arthur's birth ensures its importance in the world of Arthurian legend, even after post-Tudor historiography challenged Geoffrey of Monmouth's view of history. By the seventeenth century, historical speculation on Cornish origins began to look elsewhere, and only in the nineteenth century was the figure of Arthur revived as a way of defining the origins, continuity, and differences associated with Cornish identity. Since then Arthur has become, in Cornwall as elsewhere, an expression for cultural legitimacy, but one which focuses less on Geoffrey's myth of British sovereignty as a means to validate political power and more on the question of where the elements of the legend originated and in particular on the historical reality of the figure of Arthur himself. Not surprisingly, it is the link established between Tintagel and the Arthurian legend by Geoffrey and subsequently reinforced by nineteenth-century writers that has formed the basis for locating a historical Arthur in Cornwall. This, together with other references to southwest Britain, has created an impression of a "King in the West" whose historical reality could be demonstrated by piecing together references in literature, early historical sources, archaeology, and folklore (Dunning 1988). Arthur's association with Cornwall has enhanced the sense of regional difference and has become a symbol of Cornish resistance to absorption into an anglicized culture (Hale 2000: 21; Saunders 2000: 24, 29).

Cornwall is the context for a tradition about the survival of Arthur that is substantially different from that found elsewhere. The epitaph of the grave so conveniently discovered at Glastonbury at the end of the twelfth century claimed Arthur as the future king, and this tradition was incorporated into romances, most famously that of Malory, and mentioned in some Scottish chronicles. However, the local Cornish folk belief seems to have been that Arthur changed into a bird, specifically a Cornish chough, a type of crow with red legs. The chough legend first appeared in late sixteenth-century Spanish sources. As so often with Arthurian motifs, the earliest record occurs somewhat after the flowering of Arthurian literature. It is, however, well documented in the folklore of southwest Britain and was noted by Hunt (1881: 308–9).

Place Names, Personal Names, and the Oldest Strata of Arthurian Legends

A small group of people named Arthur appeared in western Scotland during the sixth to seventh centuries, and it has been suggested that these names commemorate an earlier historical figure, the much-sought Arthur of history. Too often a priori considerations of the importance of Arthur distort such considerations (Bromwich 1963, 1975/6: 178–9; Padel 1994: 24; Green 2007) but the quest for a historical Arthur surfaces still in popular writing. Names containing the element *art(h)* meaning "bear" illustrate a fundamental problem that arises when folklore and history are invoked to support the existence of a historical Arthur. The discovery of a stone with a sixth-century(?) inscription *PATER COLIAVI FICIT ARTOGNOV* ("Artognou, father of a [?]descendant of Coll, made this") at Tintagel ignited the controversy yet again as to whether a historical Arthur could have been associated with this Cornish site. The element *art(h)* is fairly common in Gaulish, Irish, and British personal and place names, but there is no special link between any of these names and the name Arthur. An early inscription attached to the most emotionally evocative site in Cornwall is another instance of an *arth* name in which the desire for a context that would support a historical Arthur has been at variance with the more sober reservations expressed by archaeologists and scholars (Green 2007).

Several place-name legends that could be, and indeed have been, interpreted as native lore relating to early strata of the Arthurian legend are located in Lowland Scotland. For example there is a reference to Arthur's Bower at Carlisle in the 1170s (Padel 1991). These have been cited in attempts to locate Arthur as a Brittonic hero originating in Scotland, although both Dumbarton (Dun Breatann) and Dunbuck (Dun Buic) are given as locations for Arthur's court in the Scottish Gaelic sources (Gillies 1982: 69). Gaelic ballads continued to use Arthurian references from the seventeenth century onward, but changing fashions in historiography ultimately undermined Arthur's political significance in Scotland (Gillies 1982: 74–5). The evidence of place names in areas where Brittonic languages had been spoken does indicate that elements of the Arthurian legend were known, and some of these clearly pre-date Geoffrey of Monmouth (Padel 1994; Boardman 2002: 55–7). This evidence is especially intriguing when the place name is linked to an onomastic or etiological tale, and, while examination of such tales does not lead to a historical Arthur, they clarify some aspects of the traditional background.

On their journey across southwest Britain in 1113, which was actually recorded later in 1145, canons from Laon in northern France were shown several local Arthurian sites in the *terra arturi*, "land of Arthur," most likely the area including Dartmoor in Devon and Bodmin Moor in Cornwall. Such local lore is extremely common as a way of giving meaning and significance to landscape. This Arthur is associated with remote uninhabited places and is very different from the courtly king and dynastic figure of romance and chronicle. A comparable local landscape tradition comes from Scotland as a list of *mirabilia* compiled by Lambert of Omer in 1120. This list cites a structure in Pictland known as "Arthur's Palace" supposedly decorated with his noble deeds, and this may be identical to a site known a century later as "Arthur's Oven" (Padel 1994: 4–6). The Arthur of folklore, if such a concept can be established as valid, is not fixed in any particular place. He is typically linked to local sites and, where narratives are attached to these sites, acts as a gigantic hero or a trickster figure. He is a figure of legend rather than history, and if these pre-Galfridian references represent the earliest strata of his legend, then the later historical king is even more likely to be a legendary one.

Given the Cornish context for Geoffrey's Arthurian history, it is hardly surprising that Cornish antiquarians found evidence of Arthur in their local environment. Antiquarian writers from the Tudor period onward located the battle of Camlan on the river Camel on the basis of similar sounding names. In his *Survey of Cornwall* (1602), the Cornish antiquary Richard Carew took it as accepted fact. An inscription on a commemorative stone nearby was interpreted as Arthur's grave, although in fact the inscription does not mention Arthur. Attempts to concretize Arthurian events in Cornish geography have been an influential means of historicizing Arthur in that region. Béroul's twelfth-century Tristan romance places Mark's residence at Lancien (modern Lantyan), but the location has since shifted to a nearby hill fort, Castle Dore. The existence of a stone inscribed to "Drustanus son of Cunomorus" led to a series of excavations in the 1930s which attempted to link it to the Tristan legend, but the supposed folklore here is the result of relatively modern archaeology.

Identifying Arthurian sites with similar-sounding modern names is still a popular technique in forging links between a fictional Arthurian world and modern Cornwall, but too often the links between places named in Arthurian sources and their modern locations are not supported by tradition. Domelioc, where Gorlois was killed, can be identified with Domellick in Cornwall, but there is no evidence either in folk tradition or archaeology to indicate why. Folklore and archaeology remain important criteria for the authentication of Arthurian material because of their seeming modernity as disciplines for investigation of the past. But folklore is a most elusive arena for Arthurian sources, especially when it is perceived as a conservator of ancient lore. Too often it is used to bridge gaps in historical evidence or to supply a narrative for an archaeological site, and this overlooks the fact that it is a dynamic process (Loomis 1958). The best conclusion that can be drawn from folklore is that it preserves a pan-Brittonic figure of local wonder tales, and the "historical" Arthur is a secondary development (Padel 1994: 30–31).

Conclusion

The Arthurian tradition in Scotland and Cornwall, like so much about the whole corpus, is rich and varied and not easily reduced to neat categories. Scottish chronicles, and to some extent the genealogical sources, present Arthur in the context of sovereignty and kingship. He is frequently an ambiguous figure used to comment on the nature of kingship itself. Only much later does he become a symbol of Scottish or Cornish resistance against cultural erosion, and a focus for regional and ethnic identity.

The eighteenth-century Cornish antiquarian William Borlase summed up the perennial appeal of Arthurian tradition: "whatever is great, and the use and author unknown, is attributed to Arthur" (Padel 1994). Although the emergence of a British nation, which unified the "ancient kingdoms" in the post-Tudor period, actually undermined the individual identities of Scotland and Cornwall, the figure of Arthur continued to address both the changing political worlds of medieval Britain and modern views of the meaning of nationhood. The idea of Arthur as a historical figure emerged from a legendary hero who was not associated with any particular region. However, the "Cornish" Arthur and the "Scottish" Arthur continue to influence modern debates on Arthur as history. Visions of Arthur embody present-day wishes for spiritual and cultural wholeness projected backward onto a romanticized pre-Roman world. The legendary Arthur, rooted in traditional tales and popularized by Geoffrey of Monmouth, continues to be a focus for identity, whether based on loyalty to a legitimate ruler or a region, or on language and geography.

PRIMARY SOURCES

Gowans, L. (ed.) (1992a). *Am Bròn Binn: An Arthurian ballad in Scottish Gaelic*. Eastbourne: Linda Gowans.

Gowans, L. (ed. trans.) (1998). *Sir Uallabh O Còrn: A Hebridean tale of Sir Gawain. Scottish Gaelic Studies*, 18, 23–55.

Hunt, R. (ed.) (1881). *Popular romances of the west of England*, 3rd edn. London: Chatto & Windus.

Thomas, G. C. & Williams, N. G. (eds trans) (2007). *Bewnans Ke. The Life of St Kea: A critical edition with translation*. Exeter: University of Exeter Press, in association with the National Library of Wales.

REFERENCES AND FURTHER READING

Alexander, F. (1975). Late medieval Scottish attitudes to the figure of King Arthur: A reassessment. *Anglia*, 93, 28–34.

Archibald, E. (2005). *Lancelot of the Laik*: Sources, genre, reception. In R. Purdie & N. Royan (eds), *The Scots and medieval Arthurian legend*. Cambridge: Brewer, pp. 71–82.

Boardman, S. (2002). Late medieval Scotland and the matter of Britain. In E. J. Cowan & R. J. Finlay (eds), *Scottish history: The power of the past*. Edinburgh: Edinburgh University Press, pp. 47–72.

Bromwich, R. (1963). Scotland and the earliest Arthurian tradition. *Bulletin Bibliographique de la Société Internationale Arthurienne*, 15, 85–95.

Bromwich, R. (1975/6). Concepts of Arthur. *Studia Celtica*, 10/11, 163–81.

Bruford, A. (1969). *Gaelic folktales and mediaeval romances: A study of the early modern Irish "romantic tales" and their oral derivatives*. Dublin: Folklore of Ireland Society.

Chadwick, N. K. (1953). The lost literature of Celtic Scotland: Caw of Pritdin and Arthur of Britain. *Scottish Gaelic Studies*, 7(2), 115–83.

Curley, M. J. (1982). A new edition of John of Cornwall's *Prophetia Merlini*. *Speculum*, 57, 217–49.

Dumville, D. N. (1977). Sub-Roman Britain: History and legend. *History*, 62, 173–92.

Dunning, R. W. (1988). *Arthur: The King in the West*. Gloucester: Sutton.

Higham, N. J. (2002). *King Arthur: Myth-making and history*. London: Routledge.

Gillies, W. (1976–8). Some aspects of Campbell history. *Transactions of the Gaelic Society of Inverness*, 50, 256–95.

Gillies, W. (1981). Arthur in Gaelic tradition, part I. Folktales and ballads. *Cambridge Medieval Celtic Studies*, 2, 47–72.

Gillies, W. (1982). Arthur in Gaelic tradition, part II: Romances and learned lore. *Cambridge Medieval Celtic Studies*, 3, 41–75.

Gowans, L. (1992b). Arthurian survivals in Scottish Gaelic. In K. Busby (ed.), *The Arthurian yearbook 2*. New York: Garland, pp. 27–76.

Green, T. (2007). *Concepts of Arthur: The making of a legend*. Stroud: Tempus.

Griffiths, M. E. (1937). *Early vaticination in Welsh with English parallels*. Cardiff: University of Wales Press.

Grooms, C. (1993). *The giants of Wales*. Lampeter: Edwin Mellen Press.

Hale, A. (2000). King Arthur and modern Cornwall. In A. Hale, A. Kent, & T. Saunders (eds), *Inside Merlin's cave: A Cornish Arthurian reader, 1000–2000*. London: Francis Boutle, pp. 20–27.

Hale, A., Kent, A., & Saunders, T. (eds) (2000). *Inside Merlin's cave: A Cornish Arthurian reader, 1000–2000*. London: Francis Boutle.

Henderson, G. (1912). Arthurian motifs in Gadhelic literature. In O. Bergin & C. Marstrander (eds), *Miscellany presented to Kuno Meyer*. Halle: Max Niemeyer, pp. 18–33.

Keeler, L. (1946). *Geoffrey of Monmouth and the Late Latin chroniclers, 1300–1500*. Berkeley, CA: University of California Press.

Kelly, S. (1979). The Arthurian material in the *Scotichronicon* of Walter Bower. *Anglia*, 97, 431–8.

Kittredge, G. L. (1903). *Arthur and Gorlagon*. Boston, MA: Ginn.

Loomis, R. S. (1955–9). Scotland and the Arthurian legend. *Proceedings of the Society of Antiquaries of Scotland*, 79, 1–21.

Loomis, R. S. (1958). Arthurian tradition and folklore. *Folklore*, 69, 1–25.

Mapstone, S. & Wood, J. (eds) (1998). *The rose and the thistle: Essays on the culture of late medieval and renaissance Scotland*. East Linton: Tuckwell.

Morrill, J. (1996). Preface: The British problem, c. 1534–1707. In B. Bradshaw & J. Morrill (eds), *The British problem, c. 1534–1707: State formation in the Atlantic archipelago*. Basingstoke: Macmillan, pp. 1–39.

Nagy, J. F. (1985). *The wisdom of the outlaw*. Berkeley, CA: University of California Press.

Padel, O. J. (1981). Cornish background of the Tristan stories. *Cambrian Medieval Celtic Studies*, 1, 53–82.

Padel, O. J. (1984). Geoffrey of Monmouth and Cornwall. *Cambrian Medieval Celtic Studies*, 8, 1–27.

Padel, O. J. (1991). Some southwestern sites with Arthurian associations. In R. Bromwich, A. O. H. Jarman, & B. F. Roberts (eds), *The Arthur of the Welsh*. Cardiff: University of Wales Press, pp. 229–47.

Padel, O. J. (1994). The nature of Arthur. *Cambrian Medieval Celtic Studies*, 27, 1–31.

Pearce, S. M. (1974). The Cornish elements of the Arthurian tradition. *Folklore*, 85, 145–63.

Purdie, R. (2005). The search for Scottishness in *Gologros and Gawane*. In R. Purdie & N. Royan (eds), *The Scots and medieval Arthurian legend*. Cambridge: Brewer, pp. 95–108.

Purdie, R. & Royan, N. (eds) (2005). *The Scots and medieval Arthurian legend*. Cambridge: Brewer.

Roberts, B. F. (1991). Geoffrey of Monmouth, *Historia Regum Britanniae* and *Brut y Brenhinedd*. In R. Bromwich, A. O. H. Jarman, & B. F. Roberts (eds), *The Arthur of the Welsh*. Cardiff: University of Wales Press, pp. 97–116.

Royan, N. (2002). "Na les vailyeant than ony uthir princis of Britaine": Representations of Arthur in Scotland 1480–1540. *Scottish Studies Review*, 2(1), 9–20.

Rushton, C. J. (2005). "Of an uncouthe stede": The Scottish knight in Middle English. In R. Purdie & N. Royan (eds), *The Scots and medieval Arthurian legend*. Cambridge: Brewer, pp. 109–20.

Saunders, T. (2000). King Arthur and ideology. In A. Hale, A. Kent, & T. Saunders (eds), *Inside Merlin's cave: A Cornish Arthurian reader, 1000–2000*. London: Francis Boutle, pp. 27–34.

Thomas, C. (1993). *Tintagel: Arthur and archaeology*. London: Batsford and English Heritage.

Thomas, C. (2002). Cornish archaeology at the millennium. *Cornish Studies*, 10, 80–89.

Wood, J. (1998). Folkloric patterns in Scottish chronicles. In S. Mapstone & J. Wood (eds), *The rose and the thistle: Essays on the culture of late medieval and renaissance Scotland*. East Linton: Tuckwell, pp. 116–35.

Wood, J. (2005). Where does Britain end? The reception of Geoffrey of Monmouth in Scotland and Wales. In R. Purdie & N. Royan (eds), *The Scots and medieval Arthurian legend*. Cambridge: Brewer, pp. 9–24.

Wormald, J. (1996). James VI, James I and the identity of Britain. In B. Bradshaw & J. Morrill (eds), *The British problem, c. 1534–1707: State formation in the Atlantic archipelago*. Basingstoke: Macmillan, pp. 148–71.

8

Arthur and the Irish

Joseph Falaky Nagy

In the prose genre of late-medieval/early-modern Irish literature known in scholarly parlance as the romantic tale (*scéal rómánsaíochta*), Arthur looms large. Of the approximately sixty examples of the genre that have survived, five (the earliest stemming from the fifteenth century) involve Arthur and/or Arthurian characters (particularly Gawain, but also including a daughter of Arthur!), and none of the stories they tell can be traced back to any extant sources outside of Ireland. "No other body of foreign heroes had this sort of success," declared Alan Bruford in his description and inventory of the romantic tale (1969: 11).

Yet, as noted by William Gillies in his survey of the Arthurian waifs and strays to be found in the folk tales, folk songs, and local legends of Scotland (Gillies 1981, 1982: 68–70; Gowans 1992), only a few traces of these seemingly indigenous Arthurian tales survived into the Irish and Scottish Gaelic oral storytelling tradition, which probably incubated the genre as a whole, and which, as recorded in the past two hundred years, proved in the main very hospitable to the narrative material of the romantic tales, especially in those cases where the protagonists are "native" characters. Still, given the close connections between manuscripts and oral performance that obtained in Ireland from the beginnings of Irish literature down to the nineteenth century, it is likely that this corpus of Irish Arthurian story was part of the popular mainstream of storytelling, not limited to a literary or antiquarian backwater. In fact, one of these Arthurian tales (*Eachtra an Mhadra Mhaoil*, "Adventure of the Cropped Dog") is witnessed in over three dozen manuscripts, surely a sign of the story's popularity. (The Irish word *eachtra*, cognate with Latin *extra* and used in earlier literature to designate tales of travel into the Otherworld, comes to be used in the genre of the romantic tale to convey the sense of "adventure".)

Before the era of the romantic tale, the earliest references in medieval Irish literature to an "Arthur" who might be the same as the famous Arthur of Britain cluster around the death of a legendary scion of the royal dynasty of the Dál nAraidi, a people of eastern Ulster. Mongán mac Fiachna, the fosterling of the wizardly seafarer Manannán mac Lir (who sired him in the guise of Fiachna), is said in these sources (including annals) to have been slain in the early seventh century by an "Artú(i)r son of Bicóir" from Britain, with a "dragon stone from the sea" (*ail dracoin din muir*; Nutt & Meyer 1895: 1.29, 1.84, 1.137–9; Mac Mathúna 1985: 43; Dooley 2004: 18; White 2006: 40, 58). In light of the fact that Mongán's conception tale (preserved in a text as early as the seventh or eighth century) stands as the closest Celtic analogue to the account of Arthur's deception-laden origins given by Geoffrey of Monmouth centuries later (Mac Cana 1972: 128–9), it is tempting to speculate that an Irish author familiar with both narrative traditions thought it would be fitting to have Mongán's life come to an end at the hands of a figure that he construed as his British counterpart – or that the tradition the author was following was linking together figures who in other respects as well appear to be cognate reflections of a Celtic mythological type. Another "Artúr" mentioned in early Irish sources (where the name is hardly common) is the son of Áedán mac Gabráin, the sixth-century king of the Dál Riata, another eastern Ulster tribe, which also established itself in Argyll and set the foundation of what was to become the kingdom of Scotland. In Adomnán's famous Latin life of St Columba (written in the late seventh century), the Irish saint and contemporary of Áedán, who became best known for his work of establishing churches and monasteries in Scotland, predicts the death of this Arthur (bk. 1, ch. 9; Sharpe 1995: 119–20). That the latter figure was also blended into the tradition concerning the death of Mongán may be deduced from the detail that his slayer came from Dál Riata territory (Kintyre, in Argyll; see Stokes 1896: 178). Remarkably, as early as the fifteenth century, the poets and genealogists of the Campbell clan, dominant in this southern part of the Scottish Highlands, were asserting a family connection between the Campbells and Arthur of Britain (Draak 1956: 238–40; Gillies 1982: 60, n. 70, 66–8; Gillies 1999).

In the same early cycle of stories about the mysterious Mongán cited above, in one of the most extraordinary references to reincarnation to be found anywhere in Celtic literatures (Nagy 1997: 303–7), we learn that he was a rebirth of the Irish hero Finn mac Cumaill, around whom is centered the so-called Fenian or Ossianic tradition of story and song, and whose long-lived fame was still attested in the repertoires of Irish and Scottish storytellers of the last century. The connection between Mongán and Arthur would be even stronger, then, if we accept the Dutch Celticist A. G. van Hamel's unjustly overlooked thesis (anticipated in Nutt & Meyer 1895: 2.22–5) that Arthur the *dux bellorum* and Finn the leader of Ireland's premier *fian*, "hunting and warring band," are matching cognate manifestations of what he dubbed the Celtic "exemplary hero"(1934: 219–33). A socializing leader of fellow heroes, this figure protects society against hostile, often supernatural, invasion and goes on forays into the Otherworld, from which he emerges with treasures to share and stories to tell. The hero-leader as profiled by van Hamel is also devoted to hunting, particularly of boars, and takes an interest in the development of young heroes in the making. The Arthur of *Culhwch ac Olwen* certainly fits this description, as does the Finn nostalgically presented in the twelfth- or thirteenth-century Irish prosimetric omnibus text

Acallam na Senórach, "Dialogue of the Old Ones" (Stokes 1900; Dooley & Roe 1999).

An Irish translation of the ninth-century *Historia Brittonum* including the *Mirabilia* was produced in the eleventh century, but in this version the Arthurian material is handled perfunctorily, even carelessly (Dooley 2004: 10–15). There is, however, an Arthur who figures in the *Acallam* mentioned above, one of the most important surviving repositories of medieval Fenian tradition (Stokes 1900: 5–9). Son of the king of the Britons, this Arthur is a rogue member of Finn's *fian*, who in the course of a hunt steals Finn's dogs and takes them back with him to Britain. Finn dispatches a party of his men to recover his dogs, a quest on which they are successful. (Artúr is found hunting in the vicinity of Sliabh Lodáin meic Lír – surely this refers to Lothian, the district around Edinburgh, which may well have its own Arthurian associations; Gillies 1981: 58, n. 36). In addition to the hounds and a chastened Arthur, Finn's men also return with some British horses that become the progenitors of the horses used by the members of the *fian*. Like the reference to a lost Irish story known as *Aígidecht Artúir*, "The hosting of Arthur," in a tale list no later than the twelfth century (Mac Cana 1980: 47), the story of this wayward Arthur in the *Acallam* affirms the impression, also to be gleaned from the references to Irish heroes as members of Arthur's retinue in *Culhwch ac Olwen*, of lively communication, exchange, and even rivalry operating between Irish and Welsh literary culture (Dooley 2004: 20–23; Bernhardt-House 2007).

The Normans along with their Breton and Welsh allies established a foothold in Ireland in 1169, and there are signs of increased influence from and interest in Anglo-Norman and Continental literature in post-twelfth-century Irish literature. There is no evidence, however, that a translation of Geoffrey of Monmouth's *Historia Regum Britanniae* into Irish was ever attempted. Furthermore, "Arthurian references in Classical bardic verse are rare and late" (Gillies 1982: 66) – a telling statement, given the importance and quantity of this genre in late medieval Irish literature. One of those rare references comes relatively early in the bardic record (fourteenth century), but the mention occurs only in passing, as part of a mildly invidious comparison between Irish and foreign paradigms of nobility (Dooley 1993). In this poem, for the first time in the Irish literary record, an Artúr is designated as a king – but the word used is the Irish one (*rí*) as opposed to the English borrowing *cing*, discussed below.

The actual production of "native" Arthurian literature seems to have started in Ireland in the fifteenth century, perhaps inspired by the *Lorgaireacht an tSoidhigh Naomhtha*, "Quest of the Holy Grail" (Falconer 1953). This is the editor Sheila Falconer's choice of title. *Lorgaireacht* was picked from among the various Irish words used to translate *queste* in the text, which, as it has survived in three manuscripts, is fragmentary and without a beginning. According to Falconer, this is (for the Middle Ages) a relatively straightforward translation into Irish of what seems to have been in turn a straightforward pre-Malory English translation of the Vulgate *Queste*, now lost (1953: xix–xxxi). The only one of the many translations of foreign romance literature produced in medieval Ireland that is based on an Arthurian text, the

Lorgaireacht is dated as early as the middle of the fifteenth century (Falconer 1953: xxxii). Arthur is *Cing Artúr*, Galahad is *Sir Galafas*, and Lancelot is *Sir Lámsalóid*. The borrowings *cing* and *sir*, also commonly used in the indigenous Arthurian tales, are among the formidable arguments for positing an English original for the *Lorgaireacht*. For the concept of "grail" the translator resorted to an Irish word for "vessel" (*soidheach*), hence the "McGuffin" of the story is referred to as the *Soidheach Naomhtha*, "Holy Vessel."

The text's general fidelity to its ultimate source notwithstanding, there are some twists that distinguish it from the *Queste*. In a telling switch, Percival (*Persaual*) and his savage ways are French, not Welsh. Guinevere (*Genebra*) is the daughter of the king of the Romans. Merlin is *Merling*, possibly under the influence of the name of the popular Leinster saint Moling, who in native tradition is associated with a figure some scholars have considered an Irish "reflex" of Merlin, the madman Suibne (Falconer 1953: xiv–xv, xxvi; Nagy 1996). Moreover, promise and prophecy (concerning the Grail, Galahad, and other key story elements) play a noticeably larger role here than they do in the *Queste* (Falconer 1953: xvi, n. 3; 294, n. on l. 120). Here and elsewhere in Irish Arthuriana, Gawain is B(h)albhuaidh (misinterpreted as Galahad in Macalister 1998), a form of the name suggestively closer to the original Welsh *Gwalchmei* than its Latin or French derivatives (Gillies 1982: 60–61). In sum, the *Lorgaireacht* constitutes evidence for literary communication between Ireland and England on matters Arthurian. If this link could be extended back into the fourteenth century, and viewed as not simply one-way, then what some scholars have seen as the possibly "Irish" features of *Sir Gawain and the Green Knight* (Jacobs 2000) would be indeed more explicable.

Already witnessed in a manuscript from 1517 (Bruford 1969: 260) is the earliest surviving homegrown Arthurian tale, the "Adventure of the Cropped Dog," mentioned above (Macalister 1998: 2–72). While the key motif in the story, that of the hero-turned-wolf (or dog), is familiar from mainstream European romance tradition – as in *Guillaume de Palerne*, translated into Irish as *Eachtra Uilliam* (C. O'Rahilly 1949) – it may well have originally entered into that mainstream from Celtic tradition. And here again, as in the *Acallam* episode discussed above, Arthur and a "human" dog are brought together in the story line: the most important of the hunting dogs stolen from Finn by Artúr in that episode is Bran, Finn's metamorphosed cousin (Bernhardt-House 2007: 18–20). Although Arthur and Gawain (Balbhuaidh) feature prominently in the *Eachtra*, they are in some respects out of character, or more in an "Irish" character. As Bernadette Smelik has pointed out, at the opening of the story, Arthur, the *Rí an Domhain*, "King of the World" (Macalister 1998: 2), a designation not uncommon in the world of the romantic tale (Bruford 1969: 22), is a victim not of any yen for adventure but a *geis*, "interdiction," an Irish term/concept that permeates native literature (Smelik 1999: 147–8), according to which he must hunt on the Plain of Wonders in the Dangerous Forest for seven years, a condition that leaves him and his companions vulnerable to near-fatal attack by the magician-warrior *Ridire an Lóchrainn*, "Knight of the Light" (*ridire*, a common Irish rendering of "knight" in these tales, is a borrowing from English "rider," while *lóchrann* or *lócharn* is a borrowing from Latin *lucerna*).

Left bound, helpless, and inordinately thirsty, Arthur turns to his beloved foster son Balbhuaidh, the only one of the king's company not overwhelmed by the Knight of the Light, to find him some water. This Gawain, however, is not the urbane adult knight commonly encountered in Arthurian story but a beardless youth, who asks to be knighted before he fulfills his lord's request, since it would not be fitting for Arthur to be served by anyone below the rank of knight. Smelik points out (1999: 148–52) that the immature Balbhuaidh of the *Eachtra* is more reminiscent of the equally beardless Irish hero Cú Chulainn, the sister's son of the king of Ulster, who precociously wins his heroic spurs and proves his loyalty and usefulness to the king and the other adult heroes of the province, all of whom are in effect his foster fathers, in the eighth–ninth-century section of the text *Táin Bó Cúailnge*, "Cattle Raid of Cúailnge" (recension 1), known as the *Macgnímrada*, "Boyhood Deeds (of Cú Chulainn)" (C. O'Rahilly 1976: 13–26). Also worth noting is the parallel between Balbhuaidh's quest and the Irish type scene of the hero obtaining water or nourishment for his king incapacitated on the battlefield, on display in the *Macgnímrada* (C. O'Rahilly 1976: 16) and in another Irish saga of the late first millennium AD, the *Togail Bruidne Da Derga*, "Destruction of Da Derga's Hostel" (Knott 1936: 43–4).

Balbhuaidh not only fetches water for Arthur but returns in the company of the Madra Maol, who drives away the Knight of the Light (his half-brother) when he reappears in an attempt to finish off Arthur and his men. The enchanted dog-hero then leads Balbhuaidh on a chase after the Knight, a multi-episode pursuit that constitutes the rest of the story and climaxes in the reconciliation of the brothers and the restoring of the Madra Maol to his human form, and to his rightful throne in India. The dog-hero in effect takes over the pre-eminent role in the story that at the beginning of the *Eachtra* would appear to be assigned to Balbhuaidh. Given the patterning after the *Macgnímrada* with which the tale seems to begin, and given that Cú Chulainn is the consummate dog-like hero (*cú* meaning "dog"), it is perhaps fitting for an actual dog-hero to take over the job begun by Balbhuaidh.

There may be one more Irish Arthurian production surviving from the fifteenth century. Among the contents of British Library MS Egerton 1781, an Irish manuscript written in 1484–7, a list (added in the sixteenth century) includes a tale titled *Sgél Isguide Léithe*, "The Story of Iosgaid Liath" ("Gray Hollow-at the-Back-of-the-Knee," or simply "Gray Leg" or "Gray Thigh"). The part of the manuscript containing this tale is lost, but it has been convincingly argued that the *Sgél* is the same as the Arthurian tale *Céilidhe Iosgaide Léithe*, "The Visit of Iosgaid Liath," witnessed only in two considerably later manuscripts (Draak 1956). As is the case with all of these Irish Arthurian tales, the prosimetric *Céilidhe* is written in Classical Modern Irish, the literary standard developed in the late Middle Ages and used down to the nineteenth century. Hence there is nothing in the language of *Céilidhe* that would preclude its composition in the fifteenth century.

Perhaps the most imaginative of the native Arthurian narratives, the *Céilidhe* (Mac an tSaoi 1946: 42–70), like the *Eachtra*, is not as interested in the Arthurian characters or milieu as in a remarkable enchanted, and enchanting, creature of unmistakable Irish make who, coming from afar, creates profound displacement within the Arthurian ensemble and wreaks havoc with our Arthurian expectations. "Gray Hollow" is a supernatural female who in the shape of a deer lures one of Arthur's knights, the son of the king of Gascony, to her home, where she seduces him. She is later discovered by the knight's wife, who invites her rival to the court. Arthur and his knights all fall in love with the beautiful stranger, and so the Gascon prince's wife and the other jealous spouses attempt to discomfit her by revealing her secret: a tuft of persistent gray hair on the back of her leg. Iosgaid Liath, however, has the last laugh: she lifts her skirt to reveal smooth legs, while the women of Arthur's court, ordered to reveal their own legs, are found to sport the accursed tuft themselves. The otherworldly female then reveals her name (Ailleann) and her somewhat surprising identity as the daughter of the king of the Picts. Condemning her rivals to a life of spinsterhood, Ailleann invites the men of the court to abandon their current wives and come with her to a realm where they will find new ones. A fresh set of wives is indeed provided there for Arthur and his knights, but before this adventure is concluded, they undergo an ordeal arranged by Ailleann: a deer hunt that turns into a massacre of the Arthurian hunting party when they are attacked by savage cats, mares, and bitches. In desperate straits, similar to those in which they find themselves at the beginning of the *Eachtra*, Arthur and Gawain remain as the only survivors. When Gawain is about to strike an attacking dog, Ailleann tells him to desist, since the dog is his bride. She and the other new wives (her fellow murderous beasts) are then returned to their human forms by Ailleann, who also revives Arthur's men, and the happy couples enjoy wedded bliss back in the court of Arthur: *Rí an Domhain .i[d est]. Cing Artúir*, "the King of the World, that is, King Arthur" (Mac an tSaoi 1946: 70).

Perhaps the most conspicuously Irish element in the story is its rather villainous heroine. A supernatural female who confronts the hunter hero in the shape of a deer, who has something hideously ugly about her, who is deeply resented by her female colleagues, and who leads the way to an Otherworld wholly populated by women, Ailleann clearly has much in common with the goddess-like embodiment of sovereignty frequently encountered in medieval Irish tales and classical bardic poetry. Cited by the editor of the *Céilidhe* as a likely reference to this tale (Mac an tSaoi 1946: xi), a poetic *aisling* or "vision" by Tadhg Dall Ó hUiginn (seventeenth century) interrogates a female allegorical representation of Ireland concerning her visits to the courts of various legendary Irish kings, asking whether it was she who visited the *Bórd Cruinn*, "Round Table," of *Cing iongantach Artúr*, "wondrous King Arthur" (Knott 1922: 269).

The embarrassment of the women of Arthur's court perhaps derives from the story (well attested in Continental literature) of the chastity test undergone by the wives of Arthur and his knights, who for the most part fail miserably, but the story also exists in a native Fenian form (Gillies 1981: 64–6), and may be Celtic in origin.

Besides, the wives in the *Céilidhe* are more than embarrassed, since they suffer a death-like punishment of loneliness and privation. Their fate echoes the even more brutal treatment meted out in a Fenian tale to the womenfolk of Finn's *fian* by the aged *fian* member Garaid mac Morna, who in revenge for a trick played upon him locks them in a house and burns them to death (Gwynn 1904). Similarly, Cú Chulainn kills the Ulsterwomen *en masse* after they abuse his foster son's wife (Marstrander 1911). In both of these heroic cycles, this act of genocide signals an impending *Götterdämmerung* and the dangerous dynamics that will ultimately bring down the heroic house of cards, but in the *Céilidhe*, where, after all, the women are not actually slain and their husbands are not at all unhappy about leaving them, there is more the sense of a heroic cycle being renewed and refreshed, courtesy of Ailleann's remarkably disruptive visit.

Preserved in manuscripts of the seventeenth and eighteenth centuries is the third of our five surviving Irish Arthurian tales, the prosimetric *Eachtra Mhacaoimh an Iolair*, "Adventure of the Eagle Boy" (Macalister 1998: 74–196). "Eagle Boy" is the irresistible translation offered by R. A. S. Macalister, but since *macaomh*, as Bruford points out, conveys in the romantic tales a sense similar to that of archaic English "childe" (1969: 24), a translation such as "The Noble Youth of the Eagle" might be more accurate. This is another story, like the *Eachtra an Mhadra*, that centers on a character dispossessed of his right to the throne whom Arthur happens to meet. The Eagle Boy, however, unlike the Cropped Dog, develops a close relationship with Arthur, into whose lap he is dropped by an eagle that comes to the rescue in response to the prayer of the boy's mother, who fears that her newborn child will be put to death by his evil uncle. Arthur has the unknown youth raised as if he were the king's son. But when he learns that he is no son to Arthur, the foundling requests knighthood of Arthur, who is sad to see him go, and sets out to find his true patrimony. Along the way, he finds his true love and slays the evil husband of a damsel in distress, who subsequently becomes Arthur's wife. Eagle Boy finds his homeland (Sorcha, a country familiar from the geography of the romantic tales), is reunited with his family, confronts and slays his evil uncle, fetches his beloved from her home in India, and becomes the rightful king of Sorcha.

Perhaps the most notable feature of the otherwise unremarkable *Eachtra Mhacaoimh* is a colophon copied along with it into one of the eighteenth-century manuscripts that preserve the text. It is written by a Brian Ó Corcráin, who claims (in Irish) to have "got the bones of this story from a gentleman who said that he himself had heard it told in French." The subsequent passage in the note has been interpreted in two different ways: Ó Corcráin either claims to have composed the Irish text himself, "inserting these little poems to complement it," or says that, upon Ó Corcráin's expression of interest, the narrator of the story wrote it down for him and added the verse (Breatnach 2004). The colophon concludes, "Until now the story itself has never been available in Irish." Whether it was Ó Corcráin or his unidentified source who wrote the version of the story we know as the *Eachtra Mhacaoimh*, and whether this is the Brian Ó Corcráin who was a cleric in Co. Fermanagh in the fifteenth century,

or the poet of the same name who worked in the early seventeenth century, are important questions, albeit impossible to answer definitively unless more information comes
to light. There are, however, details that unambiguously and instructively stand out
in the colophon: the fascinating metaphor of French "bones" fleshed out in the Irish
language; the understanding of this narrative repertoire as not just written but heard;
and Ó Corcráin's proud assumption of responsibility for having nativized the story (a
process that includes telling it prosimetrically), or for having brought about the production of an original native story out of foreign elements.

Even more such Arthurian "bones" may lie within the Irish Arthurian tale that is
best known among scholars of Arthurian literature (Gowans 2003), the *Eachtra an
Amadáin Mhóir* "Adventure of the Big Fool" (Ó Rabhartaigh & Hyde 1927; as we
shall see, *amadán* has a range of meanings beyond "fool"). It is the story's obvious
kinship with the Perceval romance that has attracted considerable attention to this
text, preserved in three eighteenth-century manuscripts (Bruford 1969: 251), with
the final episode attested in narrative verse form as well (Gillies 1981: 66–72). The
Eachtra, however, is no translation of Chrétien de Troyes or one of his epigones, nor
is the *amadán*, "fool," simply an Irish counterpart to Perceval. At many points in the
story, the *Eachtra* seems almost like a burlesque of what late medieval Irish tradition
managed to absorb of the enormous body of Arthurian lore concerning Perceval and
the quest for the Grail – except that in the *Eachtra*, the Grail is nowhere in sight.
The *amadán*, like Perceval, is alienated from his patrimony, but his family includes
Arthur, and the alienation threatens Arthur's kingship itself. The *amadán* is actually
Arthur's nephew, raised in secret and away from knighthood and weaponry, lest he
lose his life in trying to take revenge on Arthur for having slain the *amadán*'s brothers, who were trying to put their father on the throne. When the Fool does finally
stumble upon Arthur's court, all he wants is really to be a court fool, and Arthur
cynically manipulates him and his desire. Among his picaresque adventures, which
lead the hero far from Arthur's court, making the Arthurian connection almost neg-
ligible, the Fool encounters a monstrous one-eyed cat who reveals the Fool's family
background to him (shades of Perceval's hermit and Kundry!), and also reveals his
own background as a member of the *Tuatha Dé Danann* (literally, "tribes of the
goddess Danu"), the pre-Christian Irish pantheon fondly remembered and utilized for
various plotting purposes in the romantic tales. In another episode, reminiscent of the
genre of *fabliau* rather than romance, the *amadán*'s first act of intercourse is described
as a matter of "making a fool" of a woman. The joke is perhaps an allusion to the
distinctly feminine connotations of Irish *am(m)ait*, "sorceress, supernatural female,
foolish woman" (T. O'Rahilly 1942: 149–52), the word from which the hero's designation *amadán* derives. And the conclusion that sexual identity is at issue in this story
becomes inescapable with the story's final episode, in which the Fool spends a good
deal of time missing his legs, of which he has been magically deprived, and depending
on a woman to help him move around in search of a remedy.

A consideration of the wild array of motifs in the *Eachtra an Amadáin Mhóir*, many
of which are familiar to readers of Arthurian literature as through a glass darkly,

compels us to ask the question: is it possible that at least in some cases in these tales the resemblances are not the result of Irish exposure to English and French romances but evidence for the Celtic roots shared between traditional Irish narrative and the ensemble of motifs and story patterns operating in Continental Arthurian tradition? Tracing those motifs/patterns back to Celtic sources, to cultural exchange between the Irish and the Welsh in pre-Norman Britain, or to Irish influence entering Arthurian tradition via the Norman connection is now out of scholarly fashion, but there is still much to be said for viewing medieval Irish literature as a narratological "parallel universe" for Arthurian tradition.

The only surviving Irish Arthurian tale that focuses on the exploits of a figure who is not introduced to Arthur in the course of the story but is presented from the beginning as a member of the court and/or Arthur's family paradoxically features two main protagonists whose names hardly sound Arthurian: this is the *Eachtra Mhelóra agus Orlando*, "Adventure of Melóra and Orlando" (Mac an tSaoi 1946: 1–41; Draak 1948). Melóra is Arthur's daughter (in her own way as powerful a figure as Iosgaid Liath/ Ailleann), who falls in love at the beginning of the story with the hero Orlando, new in her father's court. While the young couple are not quite said to have been enamored of each other before they met – an Irish motif that actually may be of international provenance (Maier 2006) – their love and subsequent tribulations have been prophesied to each of them individually. The wicked Sir Mádor and Merlin (said to be Arthur's *draoi*, "druid, wizard") conspire to imprison Orlando, whose disappearance greatly distresses Melóra. She wheedles the truth from Sir Mádor and sets forth disguised as a knight to obtain the magical items (including the spear of Longinus) needed to rescue her beloved from his rock-bound imprisonment. Of course, this Irish sister to Ariosto's Bradamante (who has been cited as a possible source; Draak 1948: 10–11), Lenore, and any number of other women warriors in popular traditions worldwide, succeeds in her mission, and brings her father, the *Rí an Domháin*, and the entire court with her to witness her performance of the rescue of Orlando, who needs the application of some magical pig oil in order to recover his human shape. He and the others then learn much to their surprise that Orlando's rescuer, the hero of the story, is Arthur's own daughter, through whose intercession Mádor and Merlin are spared from the royally mandated punishment of death, and whose request to marry Orlando is granted by her father.

In sum, the Irish Arthurian tales demonstrate both the openness of Irish literary tradition to outside sources, which are eagerly embraced and exploited, and also the persistence of native traditional models and motifs. The genre of the *scéal rómánsaíochta* in general, and the *scéal artúraíochta* in particular, not only provided exotic, eye-catching entertainment but also an unmistakable cultural statement. Perhaps the closest analogue to the medieval romantic tale in the modern world is "Bollywood," the world of mass-produced popular Indian cinema as it has grown to gargantuan proportions and complexity during the twentieth century, in the course of India's establishing itself as an independent nation. From a superficial perspective, all Bollywood films, like all romantic tales, are profoundly derivative productions. If you have seen/heard/read one, you have seen/heard/read them all. And yet, each example of the genre presents its own often remarkable variation on a theme: namely, the simultaneous acceptance of foreign narratives, media, and values as fair game for narrative purposes, and the fiercely possessive attempt on the part of storytellers and their audiences to make these imports unmistakably the native culture's own – to show who are the *real* "Kings of the World."

PRIMARY SOURCES

Dooley, A. & Roe, H. (trans) (1999). *The tales of the elders of Ireland: Acallam na Senórach*. Oxford: Oxford University Press.

Draak, M. (ed.) (1948). Orlando agus Melora. *Béaloideas*, 16, 3–48.

Draak, M. (ed.) (1956). Sgél Isgaide Léithe. *Celtica*, 3, 232–40.

Falconer, S. (ed. trans.) (1953). *Lorgaireacht an tSoidhigh Naomhtha. An Early Modern Irish translation of the Quest of the Holy Grail*. Dublin: Dublin Institute for Advanced Studies.

Gowans, L. (ed.) (1992). *Am Bròn Binn: An Arthurian ballad in Scottish Gaelic*. Eastbourne: Linda Gowans.

Gwynn, E. J. (ed. trans.) (1904). The burning of Finn's house. *Ériu*, 1, 13–37.

Knott, E. (ed. trans.) (1922, 1926). *The bardic poems of Tadhg Dall Ó Huiginn*, 2 vols. London: Irish Texts Society.

Knott, E. (ed.) (1936). *Togail Bruidne Da Derga*. Dublin: Stationery Office.

Mac an tSaoi, M. (ed.) (1946). *Dhá sgéal Artúraíochta mar atá* Eachtra Mhelóra agus Orlando *agus* Céilidhe Iosgaide Léithe. Dublin: Dublin Institute for Advanced Studies.

Macalister, R. A. S. (ed. trans.) (1998). *Two Arthurian romances*. Dublin: Irish Texts Society (originally published 1908).

Mac Cana, P. (1972). Mongán mac Fiachna and *Immram Brain. Ériu*, 23, 102–42.

Mac Cana, P. (1980). *The learned tales of medieval Ireland*. Dublin: Dublin Institute for Advanced Studies.

Mac Mathúna, S. (ed. trans.) (1985). *Immram Brain: Bran's journey to the land of women*. Tübingen: Max Niemeyer.

Marstrander, C. (ed. trans.) (1911). The deaths of Lugaid and Derbforgaill. *Ériu*, 6, 201–18.

O'Rahilly, C. (ed. trans.) (1949). *Eachtra Uilliam: An Irish version of William of Palerne*. Dublin: Dublin Institute for Advanced Studies.

O'Rahilly, C. (ed. trans.) (1976). *Táin Bó Cúailnge, recension I*. Dublin: Dublin Institute for Advanced Studies.

Sharpe, R. (trans.) (1995). *Adomnán of Iona, Life of St Columba*. Harmondsworth: Penguin.

Stokes, W. (ed. trans.) (1896). The annals of Tigernach: Third fragment. *Revue Celtique*, 17, 119–263.

Stokes, W. (ed.) (1900). *Acallamh na Senórach*. Leipzig: S. Hirzel.

White, N. (ed. trans.) (2006). *Compert Mongáin and three other early Mongán tales*. Maynooth: National University of Ireland.

REFERENCES AND FURTHER READING

Bernhardt-House, P. (2007). Horses, hounds, and high kings: A shared Arthurian tradition across the Irish Sea? In J. F. Nagy (ed.), *Myth in Celtic literatures*, CSANA yearbook 6. Dublin: Four Courts Press, pp. 11–21.

Breatnach, C. (2004). Brian Ó Corcráin and *Eachtra Mhacaoimh an Iolair. Éigse*, 34, 44–8.

Bruford, A. (1969). *Gaelic folktales and mediaeval romances: A study of the early modern Irish "romantic tales" and their oral derivatives*. Dublin: Folklore of Ireland Society.

Dooley, A. (1993). Arthur in Ireland: The earliest citation in native Irish literature. In J. P. Carley & F. Riddy (eds), *Arthurian literature*, vol. XII. Cambridge: Brewer, pp. 165–72.

Dooley, A. (2004). Arthur of the Irish: A viable concept? In C. Lloyd-Morgan (ed.), *Arthurian literature*, vol. XXI: *Celtic Arthurian material*. Cambridge: Brewer, pp. 9–28.

Gillies, W. (1981). Arthur in Gaelic tradition, part I: Folktales and ballads. *Cambridge Medieval Celtic Studies*, 2, 47–72.

Gillies, W. (1982). Arthur in Gaelic tradition, part II: Romances and learned lore. *Cambridge Medieval Celtic Studies*, 3, 41–75.

Gillies, W. (1987). Heroes and ancestors. In B. Almqvist, S. Ó Catháin, & P. Ó Héalaí (eds), *The heroic process: Form, function and fantasy in folk epic*. Dun Laoghaire: Glendale, pp. 57–73.

Gillies, W. (1999). The "British" genealogy of the Campbells. *Celtica*, 23, 82–95.

Gowans, L. (2003). The *Eachtra an Amadáin Mhóir* as a response to the *Perceval* of Chrétien de Troyes. In K. Busby & R. Dalrymple (eds), *Arthurian literature*, vol. XIX: *Comedy in Arthurian literature*. Cambridge: Brewer, pp. 199–230.

Hamel, A. G. van (1934). Aspects of Celtic mythology. *Proceedings of the British Academy*, 20, 207–48.

Hartnett, C. P. (1973). Irish Arthurian literature, 2 vols. PhD thesis, University of Michigan, Ann Arbor.

Jacobs, N. (2000). *Fled Bricrenn* and *Sir Gawain and the Green Knight*. In P. Ó Riain (ed.), *Fled Bricrenn: Reassessments*. London: Irish Texts Society, pp. 40–55.

Maier, B. (2006). At first sight: Notes on a poem by Donald John MacDonald. *Scottish Gaelic Studies*, 22, 221–9.

Nagy, J. F. (1996). *A new introduction to* Buile Suibhne (*The Frenzy of Suibhne*). Dublin: Irish Texts Society.

Nagy, J. F. (1997). *Conversing with angels and ancients: Literary myths of medieval Ireland*. Ithaca, NY: Cornell University Press.

Nutt, A. & Meyer, K. (1895). *The voyage of Bran son of Febal to the land of the living*, 2 vols. London: David Nutt.

Ó Corcráin, B. (1912). *Eachtra Mhacaoimh an Iolair* (ed. I. de Teiltiún & S. Laoide). Dublin: Hodges Figgis.

Ó Rabhartaigh, T. & Hyde, D. (eds) (1927). An t-Amadán Mór. *Lia Fáil*, 2, 191–228.

O'Rahilly, T. F. (1942). Notes, mainly etymological. *Ériu*, 13, 144–219.

Smelik, B. (1999). *Eachtra an Mhadra Mhaoil*: Ein richtiger Artusroman? In E. Poppe & H. L. C. Tristram (eds), *Übersetzung, Adaptation und Akkulturation im insularen Mittelalter*. Münster: Nodus, pp. 145–59.

9
Migrating Narratives: *Peredur*, *Owain*, and *Geraint*

Ceridwen Lloyd-Morgan

The Middle Welsh prose tales of *Peredur*, *Owain*, and *Geraint* have been the subject of constant debate since the first half of the nineteenth century. When Lady Charlotte Guest published her pioneering and influential translation of Welsh narratives that would henceforth be inaccurately but conveniently known collectively as *The Mabinogion*, she gave priority to the Arthurian texts. *Owain* and *Peredur* appeared in her first volume, published in 1838, and *Geraint*, accompanied by *Culhwch and Olwen* and *The Dream of Rhonabwy*, in the second, in 1840.

Lady Charlotte had been determined to see her work published before that of the Breton scholar Théodore Hersart de la Villemarqué, whose French translation, *Romans des Anciens Bretons*, appeared in 1842. For the first time, these Arthurian narratives became widely accessible to an international audience and the subject of constant debate. Much of the discussion over the past century and a half has focused on the relationship of *Peredur*, *Owain*, and *Geraint* to three French analogues. Both Lady Charlotte Guest and Villemarqué had observed that the three Welsh narratives were paralleled by three Old French romances in verse, composed in the 1170s and 1180s by Chrétien de Troyes, namely *Le Roman de Perceval* or *Le Conte del Graal*, *Yvain* or *Le Chevalier du Lion*, and *Erec et Enide*. Lady Charlotte had further underlined this connection by including as an appendix to her version of *Owain* a transcript of Chrétien's *Yvain*, which Villemarqué had provided for her from Paris, Bibliothèque Nationale, MS fr. 12560 (*olim* Bibliothèque du roy, no. 1891). As the original texts of both the French romances and the Welsh tales gradually became available, scholars attempted to establish their relative chronology and their precise relationship. Much of that long-standing debate, especially until the later decades of the twentieth century, was motivated by emotion and by preconceived ideas. Many French scholars, convinced of the genius of Chrétien de Troyes, could not entertain the possibility that his work could be beholden to apparently less sophisticated Welsh texts and insisted that the Welsh tales were simply incompetent translations, while some Welsh scholars, and Celtophiles outside Wales, insisted that the Welsh tales preserved the narratives in an older and perhaps "original" form. Fortunately, the development of new forms of criticism, more information about the wider literary context and traditions of textual transmission, and advances in linguistic research have all helped to move the debate on.

The Manuscript History

The evident parallels between *Peredur*, *Owain*, and *Geraint*, and Chrétien's romances, coupled with their grouping in translations from Lady Charlotte's *Mabinogion* onward, has fed an assumption that these three texts form a group. That assumption was further encouraged by the misleading modern practice of referring to them as "the three romances," as Brynley Roberts has stressed:

> The name "the three romances" began life as a useful label for three Welsh stories felt to be different from the other *Mabinogion*. But about 1960 the usage changes, and instead of being a description of three stories it begins to denote a group with its own unity. . . . The similarities between the three romances are emphasized to such a degree that they are assumed to be the work of a single author called "the author", "the romancier", "one of the greatest writers of Middle Welsh prose". (Roberts 1992: 142–3)

In fact there is no evidence whatsoever that the three were seen as a group in the Middle Ages. This is evident from their manuscript tradition. Each tale has its own, individual textual history, even though all three were included in the two most important Welsh manuscript compendia: the White Book of Rhydderch (Aberystwyth, National Library of Wales [NLW], Peniarth MSS 4 and 5), compiled in Ceredigion in the mid-fourteenth century, and the Red Book of Hergest (Oxford, Jesus College MS 111, in the Bodleian Library), produced in Glamorgan between 1382 and c. 1400. The other Middle Welsh tales now included in the so-called *Mabinogion* group were also copied in these important manuscripts, with the exception of *Breuddwyd Rhonabwy* ("The Dream of Rhonabwy"), which is preserved only in the Red Book and may never have been in the White Book. As Table 9.1 shows, the order of the tales in each compendium is different.

In neither manuscript are *Peredur*, *Owain*, and *Geraint* presented as a group, in contrast to the compilers' treatment of the *Four Branches of the Mabinogi*, despite the latter not being labeled as a group in the manuscripts. As far as our three tales are concerned, the only consistent element in the order is that *Geraint* is in both cases paired with *Culhwch*.

If *Peredur*, *Owain*, and *Geraint* were not perceived as a closely related group in the Middle Ages, neither were they referred to as *romances* (Lloyd-Morgan 2004: 44–8). The texts themselves have no formal titles, consistently applied, and employ other descriptive terms. *Ystorya* (<Latin *historia*) is that favored in *Peredur* in both the White Book and Red Book: *megys y dyweit yr ystorya* ("according to the story," Goetinck 1976:

Table 9.1 The order of tales in the White Book and the Red Book

White Book	Red Book
Pedair Cainc y Mabinogi ("The Four Branches of the Mabinogi")	*Breuddwyd Rhonabwy* ("The Dream of Rhonabwy")
Peredur	[other texts]
Breuddwyd Macsen ("The Dream of Maxen")	*Owain*
Lludd a Llefelys ("Lludd and Llefelys")	*Peredur*
Owain	*Breuddwyd Macsen*
[other texts]	*Lludd a Llefelys*
Geraint	*Pedair Cainc y Mabinogi*
Culhwch ac Olwen ("Culhwch and Olwen")	*Geraint*
	Culhwch ac Olwen

56.15; Davies 2007: 94.8–9); *ac ny dyweit yr istorya am Walchmei hwy no hynny, yn y gyfeir honno* ("but the story says no more than that about Gwalchmei on the matter," Goetinck 1976: 61.11–13; Davies 2007: 97.1–2). Here *ystorya* may refer not to the current text as presented by a particular redactor, however, but to the source (possibly a written source?) that lay behind his text. In a similar way, *li estoires* or *li contes* is often used in Old French romances as an authority formula. In NLW, Peniarth MS 7 another term, *kynnyd*, is used at the end of *Peredur*: *Ac y velly y tervyna kynnyd paredur ap Efrawc* ("and so ends the *kynnyd* of Peredur ab Efrawg" [my translation], Goetinck 1976: 181). *Kynnyd* (Mod.W. *cynydd*) can mean "progress" but also a "reign following conquest," which would be appropriate here, where the text closes with Peredur's 14-year reign with the empress of Constantinople. *Ystorya* is also found in a rubric preceding the Red Book copy of *Geraint* (col. 769): *llyma mal y treythir o ystorya gereint uab erbin* ("This is what is told of the story of Gereint fab Erbin" [my translation]). Again, this could refer to the source, or to the story behind the written text, rather than to the present narrative text. In the case of *Owain*, the Red Book text (col. 655) once more provides a descriptive phrase, this time as a colophon referring to the preceding narrative: *ar chwedyl hwn a elwir chwedyl iarlles y ffynnawn* ("And this tale is called the Tale of the Lady of the Well," cf. Thomson 1968: 30; Davies 2007: 138). Here *chwedyl* seems to have much the same semantic field as *ystorya* in *Peredur*.

"Romance" was not used as a label for these tales before the Romantic period (the use of Welsh *rhamant* to mean a narrative text was coined by the eccentric scholar Edward Williams ("Iolo Morgannwg") in the late eighteenth century). Its modern usage was driven by the Guest translation and by debates about the relationship between these three texts and their French analogues. Yet that relationship, if it was ever perceived by their redactors and (even less likely) their audiences, was evidently irrelevant to the scribes of the White Book and Red Book, and indeed to the scribes of the other manuscript witnesses of each, and should not, therefore, be allowed to influence unduly our readings of the Welsh texts today.

No surviving vernacular Welsh manuscript can be dated prior to the mid-thirteenth century, though there is ample evidence that the tradition of copying vernacular literature goes back at least as far as the ninth century, and many texts copied in the thirteenth and fourteenth centuries are far older than their earliest written witnesses. Based on current dating (Huws 2000a: 57–60), the earliest known copy of any of our three tales is a late-thirteenth-century fragment of *Geraint* in NLW, Peniarth MS 6, part iii, followed by an incomplete copy of *Peredur* in NLW, Peniarth MS 7, again late thirteenth century, possibly even pre-dating the Edwardian conquest of Wales in 1282 (Huws 2000b: 5). A second fragment of *Geraint* in NLW, Peniarth MS 6, part iv, dates from the early fourteenth century, and a fragment of *Peredur* in NLW, Peniarth MS 14, part ii, was copied sometime during the first half of that century. The only medieval copy of *Owain* apart from the White Book and Red Book is found in Oxford, Jesus College MS 20, copied around the turn of the fourteenth and fifteenth centuries and therefore roughly contemporary with the Red Book. As is so often the case in Wales, the manuscripts give no indication of the date of the texts they preserve, neither do they contain any explicit information concerning their geographical origins. The question of the date and origin of the texts must therefore depend on other criteria, to which we shall return.

Although it is now generally agreed that the three corresponding verse romances by Chrétien de Troyes were important sources for the three Welsh texts, the latter are not translations and they are far shorter than the French romances. They are, perforce, prose works, since poetry was not then a narrative genre in Welsh. However, the precise relationship between the Welsh and the French narratives is different in each case, and can vary from one Welsh copy to another. Variation between the medieval manuscript versions of the Welsh texts is most limited in *Geraint* and *Owain*. Although an analysis of variant readings sets the White Book apart from the Red Book and the two fragments of *Geraint* preserved in Peniarth MS 6, in his edition Thomson argues that these reflect two lines of transmission descended from the same original version. He concludes that, "nothing here impairs the fundamental unity of the textual tradition" (Thomson 1997: xviii). In the case of *Owain*, neither the Red Book version nor that in Jesus College MS 20 is dependent on the earlier White Book version; the Red Book and Jesus College MS 20 copies are independent of each other. Nonetheless, Thomson again concluded that the variations were sufficiently minor that all three "separately descend from a common original," albeit perhaps "at several removes in some cases" (Thomson 1968: xvi). The implication is that in the case of these two tales the surviving medieval manuscript witnesses all descend ultimately from a single adaptation of each French romance into Welsh.

The case of *Peredur* is quite different, for the surviving medieval copies display a remarkable degree of textual instability. The White Book of Rhydderch and the Red Book of Hergest preserve a long version, which in the past was often characterized as a "complete" version. This conclusion, based on the uncertain premise that greater length, coupled with a narrative conclusion more acceptable to modern readers, made for a "better" text, may also have been partly conditioned by the prestige afforded to these manuscripts as the two most important medieval Welsh compendia. We do not know how the narrative in Peniarth MS 14 was concluded, for the fragment breaks off in mid-sentence during Peredur's visit to his second uncle, but the Peniarth MS 7 copy, in contrast to the "long" versions, brings the narrative to an apparently deliberate close at the end of a sequence of adventures not found in Chrétien, ending with Peredur's joint 14-year reign with the empress of Constantinople. In the "long" versions the story then returns to Arthur's court and the visit of the Black Maiden before pursuing the adventures to a conclusion in the castle that corresponds to Chrétien's Grail castle.

New research on the linguistic, stylistic, and manuscript evidence has led to increasing consensus that the "short" version in Peniarth MS 7 is earlier than the "long" one and that the final sequences of adventures, from the Black Maiden's visit onward, may have been added later, after the "short version" had been in circulation for a while. It is now believed that Peniarth 7, the earliest extant witness, was produced in Gwynedd, and that Peniarth 14, the next oldest, is also from north Wales, but it is not possible to identify a more specific area (Huws 2000b: 2–7). The manuscript evidence is consistent with linguistic evidence. The earliest *written* evidence, as Peter Wynn Thomas concludes, points to a redaction of *Peredur* – a short version similar to that found in Peniarth MS 7 – being made in north Wales by about 1275 (Thomas 2000: 41–2). A second redaction appears to have been made, again in north Wales, before about 1350, by which time a northern copy of it had traveled further south, where the text evolved still further. Both the scribe of the White Book version, in Ceredigion, and that of the Red Book version, in Glamorgan, had access to other versions, probably locally produced. The far-reaching implications of this evidence will be considered later.

Welsh and French Traditions

Many detailed comparisons of *Geraint*, *Owain*, and *Peredur* with Chrétien's *Erec*, *Yvain*, and *Perceval* have been made (see Thomson 1968, 1997; Goetinck 1975) and need not be repeated in detail here. Of the three, *Geraint* is arguably the closest to the corresponding French text, *Erec*. At times following Chrétien's text almost line by line, it preserves equivalents of most episodes found in the French. Yet the Welsh version does not always follow exactly the same order of events, omits some incidents and adds others, and overall there is considerable variation in narrative details.

Owain follows Chrétien's *Yvain* in its broad outlines but seems further away from the French text than the versions in German, English, and Scandinavian languages that have survived from the Middle Ages (Thomson 1968: xxvii–xxviii). The Welsh tale falls into the usual main sections: in the first, Cynon (corresponding to Calogrenant in *Yvain*) tells of his adventurous journey to the magic spring; the next follows

Owain's journey to the same destination, culminating in his killing of the knight who defended the spring, and his marriage to the new widow; the third relates how Arthur and his men go in search of Owain and bring him back to court, betraying his promise to his lady, which leads to a period in the wilderness before he is eventually reintegrated into human society and into Arthur's court, along with his lady. This is followed by a coda, in which Owain rescues 24 women from captivity at the hands of the Du Traws. This additional adventure corresponds to the *Pesme Aventure* episode in *Yvain*, where the hero releases 300 maidens kept in slave labor by the king of the Island of Maidens, although in the French romance this takes place before the hero is finally reunited with his lady.

Comparative readings of both *Geraint* and *Owain* suggest that the main source of the medieval Welsh texts was the corresponding romance by Chrétien. Where the Welsh versions depart from the French original, the changes do not significantly change the narrative outcome: episodes may be substantially altered but their consequences do not generally change the main thrust of the narrative. *Peredur*, on the other hand, presents a far more complex model of composition in terms of its sources, for Chrétien's *Perceval* is not the only French text to which it is related. The opening sequence, recounting the family background and boyhood of Peredur, follows the *Bliocadran* prequel far more closely than it does Chrétien's account in his *Perceval* (Lloyd-Morgan 2000: 121–2). The sequence of episodes of the Magic Chessboard, the killing of the stag, and the combat with the "black man" (Goetinck 1976: 66.21–69.14; Davies 2007: 100–101) is not represented in *Perceval* but follows closely two later, post-Chrétien romances, the *Deuxième Continuation* (Roach 1971: 42–72) and the *Didot Perceval* (Roach 1941: 165–76; see Lloyd-Morgan 2000: 122–4). The precise chronology of these two French texts is uncertain, but one was probably influenced by the other. Either could have been the source of this section of *Peredur*, though of the two, the *Didot Perceval* seems the closer to *Peredur*. Similarly, the description of the tree, half burning, half in green leaf (Goetinck 1976: 48.6–8), might possibly have been inspired by another episode in the *Deuxième Continuation* (Roach 1971: lines 32,071–89), where Perceval, on his return journey to the Grail castle, sees a tree full of candles burning like stars, a motif also found in *Durmart le Gallois*, although that text may in turn be derived from the *Deuxième Continuation* (Lloyd-Morgan 2000: 124–5).

Peredur also contains a sequence of adventures (Goetinck 1976: 35.24–42.18; Davies 2007: 82–6) not attested in any known French romance, nor indeed in any other source. This begins with his first meeting with Angharad Law Eurawg at Arthur's court. He declares his love for her, swears he will not utter a word to any Christian until she reciprocates her feelings, and then embarks on a journey where he proves his worth as a knight in various adventures. Eventually, after fighting incognito with Cai and others, he is reintegrated into the Arthurian court and wins Angharad. It is generally agreed that this section derives from native Welsh tradition. Some of the adventures it recounts, such as the serpent and the ring, do indeed bear all the hallmarks of a traditional tale, whereas the final episode, where Peredur, unrecognized by Arthur and his entourage, jousts with Cai and other knights, could have been composed on the pattern of similar episodes in French romance, where the theme of the *Bel Inconnu* (the "Fair Unknown") is a standard feature.

The inclusion of the Angharad Law Eurawg sequence points to redactors familiar with the indigenous traditions of storytelling as well as having the skills necessary for adapting written French sources into Welsh, not to mention being in a position to gain access not only to one but possibly three French romances. Sioned Davies has amply demonstrated that Middle Welsh prose tales provide a bridge between orality and literacy (Davies 1995, 1998); whether the texts as we know them derive partly or chiefly from oral tradition or draw on pre-existing written sources, their redactors were aware of the requirements of both media. Moreover, the medieval practice of reading aloud from a written text, perhaps with a strong performative element, to a non-literate audience, ensured constant contact between the two modes of transmission. In these circumstances cross-fertilization would be common if not inevitable and the narrative could continue to evolve.

This appears to have been the case with *Peredur*. The manuscript evidence indicates that more than one Welsh version was produced, for there are at least two independent adaptations of the French Perceval narrative into Welsh at different times and in different places. This would not be a unique case in Middle Welsh, as witness, for example, the two distinct versions of *Ystorya Adaf*, one being a translation from a Latin original, made before the second half of the thirteenth century, the other from c. 1400 and based on an Anglo-Norman version (Rowles 2006). The first version of *Peredur* contained only the first sequences of adventures. Whether this was because the first redactor's copy of his French material was itself incomplete or whether it was a deliberate choice is impossible to tell, but the colophon appears to bring the narrative to a definitive close. The modern tendency to view the longer version as more "complete" in some sense is surely an inappropriate, anachronistic response, as the careful copying of the shorter version shows that it was thought worthy of preservation.

The manuscript witnesses of *Peredur* point to constant evolution of the tale, whose textual instability derives not only from two separate redactions from French sources, but also from its transmission in both written and oral contexts. The model of the single author or redactor in full command and control of his material, which, once written, remains in a stable written form, seems singularly inappropriate here. Instead we should envisage a more mixed pattern of written and oral versions circulating in parallel, subject to constant evolution, undergoing a continual process of collective editing. Manuscript versions might be copied and recopied with changes introduced deliberately, perhaps in response to performed presentations of oral and/or written versions, and the shorter redaction of *Peredur* attested in Peniarth MS 7 might well reflect a telling that included only certain episodes rather than all of those represented in the longer Welsh versions. At least one of our three Arthurian tales continued to circulate in oral tradition as late as the mid-nineteenth century, for the author and antiquary "Glasynys" (Owen Wynne Jones, 1828–70) recorded in 1860 how he had heard an octogenarian woman in Merionethshire tell the story of *Owain*, which she had used to hear her grandfather telling at his fireside (cf. Davies 2003: 329).

The survival of seven late medieval and early modern manuscripts of *Owain* again demonstrates the parallel evolution of written and oral versions of the tale. NLW, Peniarth MS 120 (late seventeenth/early eighteenth century) and NLW, Llanstephan MS 148 (c. 1697) are direct copies of earlier witnesses (Oxford, Jesus College MS 20 and the Red Book of Hergest, respectively), and three others – NLW, Llanstephan MS 171 (1574) (of which NLW MS 2034B, formerly Panton MS 68, is a copy), NLW MS 13075B, formerly Llanover MS B 17 (1585–90), and NLW, Cwrtmawr MS 20 (mid-eighteenth century) – testify to a continuing written tradition, with minor changes, such as linguistic modernizing, being introduced at each stage. As Thomson notes, three of the later manuscripts do not contain any of the episodes featuring the lion, except for that of the Du Traws, where the lion is in any case mentioned only briefly at the beginning in the three main, early copies (Thomson 1968: x). This raises the possibility that there once existed a shorter early version of *Owain* as of *Peredur*. If so, does the longer redaction represent a second redaction, based more closely on Chrétien's *Yvain* than the first putative version? But if the longer redaction, with the lion adventures, were the earlier, would a subsequent storyteller or redactor of a written version have gone to the trouble of carefully excising all references to the lion? If he did do so, was the longer version, exemplified in the earlier manuscripts of *Owain*, produced earlier, and did it derive from a different copy of *Yvain*? At present we can only speculate. Yet another late manuscript of *Owain*, NLW, Llanstephan MS 58, written during the first half of the seventeenth century by the antiquarian George William Gruffydd of Penybenglog in Pembrokeshire, was dismissed by Thomson as "a very free retelling of the story, with relatively little value for textual purposes" (Thomson 1968: x). More recently, however, Sioned Davies has shown that this manuscript is significant for preserving a version almost certainly derived from oral tradition (Davies 2003).

In view of the evident fluidity of the textual tradition, no one manuscript version should be regarded as representing a standard or "best" version of each narrative. Moreover, each version is valuable in reflecting the process by which French material was incorporated into the canon of medieval Welsh literature and came to be preserved in important compendia. Whether the first redactors to transfer the French narratives into Welsh preserved the main outline of Chrétien's narrative, as in the case of *Geraint*, whether they drew on other material in French and/or Welsh, as happened with *Peredur*, and whether redactors of the shorter versions of *Peredur* and *Owain* chose not to include all the episodes or whether the source they used was already shorter, none of them can be described as translators as such. In each case the French material has been adapted to the traditions of Welsh *cyfarwyddyd* (storytelling) and presumably to the requirements of the target audience.

Changes were introduced at different levels within the tales, and affect narrative content, themes, atmosphere, narrative techniques, and style. Even at first sight it is obvious that the Welsh texts are far shorter than their French counterparts.

Abridgement is characteristic of a number of other Welsh adaptations or translations of French narratives, though rarely is the difference in length so striking as in these examples. Whereas close, avowed translations such as *Y Seint Greal* (c. 1400), which is based on *La Queste del Saint Graal* and *Perlesvaus*, appear from their length and their style to be more appropriate for private reading, *Geraint, Owain*, and *Peredur* fall naturally into distinct episodes or sections of suitable length for oral delivery to an audience (Davies 1995, 1998). The first section of *Owain*, in which Cynon recounts his adventures to members of the court, provides a reminder that stories are essentially to be told (or read) aloud to others, and his story within a story follows narrative patterns and style reminiscent of oral storytelling and familiar from earlier tales such as *Culhwch* and the *Four Branches* (Hunt 1973; Davies 1995). Many of the narrative techniques in all three tales, as Sioned Davies has amply demonstrated, derive from their dual inheritance as written texts incorporating material that had evolved within the native traditions and as texts that lent themselves for oral presentation, and the style of each, despite having its own character, is still close to that of earlier, native tales.

Other major differences between *Geraint, Owain*, and *Peredur* on the one hand and the corresponding romances of Chrétien de Troyes on the other include a far greater emphasis on action than on ideas. This may be partly a reflex of the general abridgement of the Welsh narratives in comparison with the French, but it may reflect not only the particular taste of a target audience, but also a different function for narrative in Wales. The structure of the Welsh tales, stripped of Chrétien's *conjointure* and *sen*, is looser, more paratactic, especially in *Peredur*, with its mixture of sources. The French romances reflect a society where Christian observance is an integral part of society, structuring daily life and the calendar of events, but in the Welsh texts references to Christian institutions are far more limited and tend to remain on the surface of the narrative structure. For all the references to churches and Christian feast days in *Geraint*, the marriage of the hero and Enid, like that of Branwen and Matholwch, is conducted without priest or church: *Ac Arthur a uu rodyat ar y uorwyn y Ereint, a'r rwym a wneit yna rwg deudyn a wnaythpwyd y rwg Gereint a'r uorwyn* ("Arthur gave the maiden to Geraint, and the bond that was made at that time between a couple was made between Geraint and the maiden," Thomson 1997: lines 529–31; Davies 2007: 153). The complete absence of any reference in *Peredur* to the Grail as such, despite the presence of obvious parallels to the Grail castle and Grail procession in Chrétien's *Perceval* and its continuations by other authors, may perhaps reflect Welsh unease with spiritual elements in prose narratives still cast in a largely traditional mould. (It is noteworthy that the term *grail* is not borrowed into Welsh before the translation of *La Queste del Saint Graal* and *Perlesvaus* around 1400.) Not only is the Christian observance embedded in the French romances largely discarded in the Welsh tales, the Welsh and French texts have very different value systems, reflecting native social structures and institutions, as Helen Roberts has shown (Roberts 2004; cf. Thomson 1997: lxii–lxiii). Roberts also stresses that the firm localization of events in *Geraint* in southeast Wales, in the Forest of Dean, Caerllion, and Cardiff, and with reference to the rivers Severn and Usk, contrasts sharply with the more insubstantial geography of Chrétien's romances.

The Welsh redactors had little difficulty in substituting Welsh equivalents for major characters, where an exact match could often be found (e.g. Gwenhwyfar/ Guinevere, Owain/Yvain, Gwalchmei/Gauvain), or failing that an appropriate native alternative, such as Cynon for Calogrenant. An individual given only an epithet in the French may acquire a suitable, traditional equivalent in Welsh: the king of the Island of Maidens in *Yvain*, for instance, becomes the sinister-sounding Du Traws in *Owain*. Persons and adventures not found in the French romances may be introduced, as in the sequence of adventures in *Peredur* motivated by Angharad Law Eurawg and apparently of native Welsh origin. In *Geraint* the redactor adopts various strategies: he chooses Welsh forms of the main characters' names, but in some cases borrows directly from Chrétien's *Erec* (Gwiffret Petit and Limwris), and also adds some Welsh names (Owain fab Nudd, Gryn, Ryfuerys) which are not found elsewhere, while others are shared with *Culhwch* (Thomson 1997: 99).

Of these last, about a dozen are not found in any Middle Welsh source other than *Geraint* and *Culhwch*. Four names occur in *Breuddwyd Rhonabwy* as well as in *Culhwch* and *Geraint*, and one in *Geraint* and *Breuddwyd Rhonabwy* alone. *Breuddwyd Rhonabwy*, which seems to parody the Arthurian world, probably post-dates *Geraint* and may have drawn those proper names from it. A few others reflect traditions preserved in the *Historia Brittonum* and *Mirabilia* attributed to Nennius and may therefore belong to the earliest strata of Welsh Arthurian tradition. Since the *Mirabilia* testify to these traditions being embedded in southeast Wales (Roberts 1991: 89–92), this is at least consistent with the localization of events in *Geraint* in that region. The degree of Normanization of society, strikingly more so than in *Peredur*, would again suggest a southeastern origin. Similarly, the fragment of *Geraint* in the early-fourteenth-century Peniarth MS 6, part iv, seems to have links with the southeast, for the same hand occurs in a number of other Welsh manuscripts, most notably Peniarth 2 (The Book of Taliesin), which Marged Haycock has convincingly linked with eastern Glamorgan or its borders with Monmouthshire (Haycock 1988). At the same time, the evidence of the shared proper names, especially those not found elsewhere, is indicative of a connection between the earlier history of *Geraint* and that of *Culhwch*. The long list naming those in Geraint's escort (Thomson 1997: lines 601–8, and p. 99) is so reminiscent of *Culhwch* as to raise the possibility of borrowing. Since there can be little doubt that *Culhwch*, with its more archaic language and fewer loanwords, antedates *Geraint* (Thomson 1997: lxxv–lxxvi), it is not impossible that the redactor of *Geraint* had been influenced by *Culhwch*. The consistent association of these two texts in both the White Book and the Red Book again points to a shared history at some stage in the development of these two texts.

But *Geraint*'s textual history appears to have links too with the content of the mid-thirteenth century Black Book of Carmarthen (NLW, Peniarth MS 1). This, the earliest surviving Welsh vernacular manuscript, contains an important early poem to *Gereint fil' Erbin*, in which the hero is already associated with Arthur. Scholars have suggested it was composed before 1100 and derives from narrative traditions connected with the lineage of kings from the southwest (Jarman 1982: lix–lx). The dialogue with the porter at the fort of Wrnach Gawr in *Culhwch ac Olwen* (Davies 2007: 201) apparently draws on the dialogue poem *Pa Gur?* ("What man is the porter?") in the Black Book. The scarce and archaic adverb *nu*, "now", found in *Geraint*, but not in either *Owain* or *Peredur*, is attested in *Culhwch* and in the Black Book and the Book of Taliesin, whose scribe also produced the copy of *Geraint* in Peniarth 6, part iv, as we have seen. Rachel Bromwich and Simon Evans suggested that both the Black Book and *Culhwch ac Olwen* originated in Carmarthen, perhaps at the Augustinian priory there (Bromwich & Evans 1992: lxxxiii, cf. Huws 2000a: 72). However, the tradition linking the Black Book with Carmarthen is not attested before the sixteenth century, and R. Geraint Gruffydd has argued that it may have been produced elsewhere, perhaps further west, at Whitland (Gruffydd 1969; Jarman 1982: li). Be that as it may, it is not impossible that a first redaction of *Geraint*, the ancestor of the texts preserved in fragmentary form in the two parts of Peniarth MS 6, should have been produced in southeast Wales, in the very region where early Norman penetration would tend to facilitate access to French manuscripts, or, indeed, to the public reading of French narratives such as Chrétien's romances, bearing in mind the vignette in the *Pesme Aventure* section of *Yvain* of a young girl reading a romance aloud to her presumably non-literate parents. But a later version of *Geraint*, closer to that which we now have in the White Book and Red Book, could have been produced in the southwest, in the same milieu as the Black Book, whether that were at Carmarthen or Whitland.

Date and Provenance

Since *Peredur*, *Geraint*, and *Owain* all derive to a greater or lesser extent from the corresponding romances by Chrétien de Troyes, it has often been assumed that all three emerge from a single milieu and even that they were the work of the same redactor or author. Their very different textual histories indicate, however, that this is highly unlikely, if not impossible. The earliest versions of *Geraint* could be from the southeast, but it was in northwest Wales that the first written copies of *Peredur* were probably produced. Although, as Thomson observes, *Geraint*, *Owain*, and *Peredur* "share a substantial common vocabulary" (Thomson 1997: xxiv), the fact that this is "held in common with the Four Branches also" simply reflects the profound importance for the redactors of those tales of firmly embedding their French-derived material into the native storytelling tradition where the tales could take their place next to the *Four Branches* or *Culhwch*. In fact, as Thomson again notes, "the vocabulary common to all three . . . is as low as 317 items," while there are 134 which are common to *Peredur* and *Geraint* but not found in *Owain*.

There is insufficient evidence to provide any firm or precise dates for the redactions of the Welsh tales, or for establishing beyond doubt their relative chronology. *Peredur*, however, must post-date not only Chrétien's *Perceval* (1181–90) but also the continuations on which the longer Welsh redactions draw: *Bliocadran*, *Didot Perceval*, and the *Deuxième Continuation*, all of which appear to belong to the first quarter of the thirteenth century. The first redaction of *Peredur* might therefore have been made as early as the second quarter of that century, but the uncertainties surrounding the dates of the French continuations, and the loss of the opening section of Peniarth 7, which might or might not have drawn on the *Bliocadran*, make it difficult to push the date further back. In the case of the earliest redactions of *Geraint* and *Owain*, where Chrétien appears to be the only French source, a slightly earlier date might be possible, but the second or third decade of the thirteenth century might still be a reasonable guess at present. This would mean they slightly pre-dated *Ystorya Bown de Hamtwn*, the Welsh version of the Anglo-Norman *Geste de Boeve de Haumtone*, and thus belong to what we might characterize as the first wave of adaptations of secular French narratives into Welsh.

Various periods of composition have been proposed on the basis of supposed correlations between narrative elements and certain historical events or circumstances, and links suggested between them and the reigns of specific rulers. The court of Llywelyn ap Iorwerth (1173–1240) in Gwynedd has been proposed as an important center for literary production, including for prose tales such as the *Four Branches of the Mabinogi*. His marriage in 1205 to Joan, illegitimate daughter of King John of England, would undoubtedly have strengthened the use of Anglo-Norman and perhaps facilitated circulation of French romances in that milieu. The earliest redaction of *Peredur* might have originated in Gwynedd, but the earliest evidence of *Geraint* appears to point to the southeast, and there is no clear indication of *Owain*'s geographical origins. Even where there would seem to be grounds for linking one of our tales with a milieu such as that of Llywelyn ap Iorwerth's court, it must be stressed that this would apply only to one version, which may have differed to a greater or lesser extent from the texts preserved in the manuscripts. Moreover, were a tale in any way to reflect ideas, concerns, or circumstances from such a specific time and place, it is a moot point whether later audiences would identify or react to these in the same way as the original audience. It is hard to believe that in the mid-fourteenth century, when *Geraint*, *Owain*, and *Peredur* were set down in the White Book, Rhydderch and his circle would read these narratives in the same way as those who had originally received them. Major changes had occurred in Welsh life since the Edwardian conquest of 1282, and Rhydderch himself, as a deputy justiciar, belonged to the new world of compromise and collaboration with the English crown, while still being immersed in traditional Welsh learning and culture. Like Hopcyn ap Thomas, the Glamorganshire patron of the Red Book some decades later, Rhydderch must have had an interest in narratives derived from French literature, for the White Book contains not only the oldest native prose tales but also Welsh versions of *chansons de geste* such as the *Chanson de Roland* and *Pèlerinage de Charlemagne*, as well as *Ystorya Bown de Hamtwn*. There is every reason to believe that both patrons were literate, and that manuscripts produced for them were intended at least partly for private reading rather than purely for reading aloud to the household as earlier manuscripts may have been.

Although we have so little firm evidence of the circumstances in which our three Arthurian tales were produced, they are undoubtedly part of an increasing trend toward borrowing from French sources. Wales had never been an island of undiluted Celtic culture, but the Norman and Edwardian conquests brought the Welsh into ever-closer contact with French and Anglo-Norman literature. From the thirteenth to fifteenth century the fashion for French narratives continued unabated and it is striking that the only new, secular prose tales to appear in Welsh from the late fourteenth century onward are translations or adaptations of foreign texts. Whereas later translations such as *Y Seint Greal* follow the source texts quite closely, may even allude to their status as translations from French, and were probably produced for private reading, *Geraint*, *Owain*, and *Peredur*, while they draw their narratives from French romance, cast them into a different form in accord with the traditions of native storytelling which derived from oral performance. With their fluid textual tradition, the three Welsh tales reflect a collaborative process of composition and editorial change over time, of continuous interaction between written and oral versions. Responding to an increasing interest in fashionable French literature, these texts provide a bridge not only between the old and the new, native and foreign, but also exemplify the gradual shift from orality to written culture, from public performance to private reading.

Primary Sources

Bromwich, R. & Evans, D. S. (eds) (1992). *Culhwch ac Olwen: An edition and study of the oldest Arthurian text*. Cardiff: University of Wales Press.

Davies, S. (trans.) (2007). *The Mabinogion*. Oxford: Oxford University Press.

Goetinck, G. W. (ed.) (1976). *Historia Peredur vab Efrawc*. Cardiff: University of Wales Press.

Jarman, A. O. H. (ed.) (1982). *Llyfr Du Caerfyrddin*. Cardiff: University of Wales Press.

Roach, W. (ed.) (1941). *The Didot Perceval according to the manuscripts of Modena and Paris*.

Philadelphia, PA: University of Pennsylvania Press.

Roach, W. (ed.) (1971). *Continuations of the Perceval*, vol. IV. Philadelphia, PA: American Philosophical Society.

Thomson, R. L. (ed.) (1968). *Owein or Chwedyl Iarlles y Ffynnawn*. Dublin: Dublin Institute for Advanced Studies.

Thomson, R. L. (ed.) (1997). *Ystorya Gereint uab Erbin*. Dublin: Dublin Institute for Advanced Studies.

References and Further Reading

Bromwich, R., Jarman, A. O. H., & Roberts, B. F. (eds) (1991). *The Arthur of the Welsh*. Cardiff: University of Wales Press.

Charles-Edwards, T. M. (2001). The textual tradition of medieval Welsh prose tales and the problem of dating. In B. Maier, S. Zimmer, & C. Batke (eds), *150 Jahre Mabinogion – Deutsch-Walisische Kulturbeziehungen*. Tübingen: Max Niemeyer, pp. 23–39.

Davies, S. (1995). *Crefft y Cyfarwydd*. Cardiff: University of Wales Press.

Davies, S. (1998). Written text as performance: The implications for Middle Welsh prose narratives. In H. Pryce (ed.), *Literacy in Medieval Celtic societies*. Cardiff: University of Wales Press, pp. 133–48.

Davies, S. (2003). O Gaer Llion i Benybenglog: testun Llanstephan 58 o "Iarlles y Ffynnon." In

I. Daniel, M. Haycock, D. Johnston, & J. Rowland (eds), *Cyfoeth y Testun. Ysgrifau ar lenyddiaeth Gymraeg yr Oesoedd Canol*. Cardiff: University of Wales Press, pp. 326–48.

Davies, S. & Thomas, P. W. (eds) (2000). *Canhwyll Marchogyon. Cyd-destunoli Peredur*. Cardiff: University of Wales Press.

Goetinck, G. W. (1975). *Peredur: A study of Welsh tradition in the Grail legends*. Cardiff: University of Wales Press.

Gruffydd, R. G. (1969). "Cyntefin Ceinaf Amser" o Lyfr Du Caerfyrddin. *Ysgrifau Beirniadol*, 4, 12–26.

Haycock, M. (1988). Llyfr Taliesin [The Book of Taliesin]. *Journal of the National Library of Wales*, 25, 357–86.

Hunt, T. (1973). The art of *Iarlles y Ffynnawn* and the European *Volksmärchen. Studia Celtica*, 8/9, 107–20.

Huws, D. (2000a). *Medieval Welsh manuscripts*. Cardiff: University of Wales Press.

Huws, D. (2000b). Y pedair llawysgrif ganoloesol. In S. Davies & P. W. Thomas (eds), *Canhwyll Marchogyon. Cyd-destunoli Peredur*. Cardiff: University of Wales Press, pp. 1–9.

Lloyd-Morgan, C. (2000). Y cyd-destun Ewropeaidd. In S. Davies & P. W. Thomas (eds), *Canhwyll Marchogyon. Cyd-destunoli Peredur*. Cardiff: University of Wales Press, pp. 113–27.

Lloyd-Morgan, C. (2004). Medieval Welsh tales or romances: Problems of genre and terminology. *Cambridge Medieval Celtic Studies*, 47, 41–58.

Roberts, B. F. (1991). *Culhwch ac Olwen*, the Triads, saints' lives. In R. Bromwich, A. O. H. Jarman, & B. F. Roberts (eds), *The Arthur of the Welsh*. Cardiff: University of Wales Press, pp. 73–95.

Roberts, B. F. (1992). *Studies on Middle Welsh literature*. Lampeter: Edwin Mellen Press.

Roberts, H. (2004). Court and *cyuoeth*: Chrétien de Troyes' *Erec et Enide* and the Middle Welsh *Gereint*. In C. Lloyd-Morgan (ed.), *Arthurian literature*, vol. XXI: *Celtic Arthurian material*. Cambridge: Brewer, pp. 53–72.

Rowles, S. (2006). *Ystorya Adaf*: golwg ar un o ffynonellau cyfieithwyr y chwedlau crefyddol. *Llên Cymru*, 29, 44–63.

Thomas, P. W. (2000). Cydberthynas y pedair fersiwn ganoloesol. In S. Davies & P. Thomas (eds), *Canhwyll Marchogyon. Cyd-destunoli Peredur*. Cardiff: University of Wales Press, pp. 10–43.

Part III
Continental Arthurian Traditions

10

The "Matter of Britain" on the Continent and the Legend of Tristan and Iseult in France, Italy, and Spain

Joan Tasker Grimbert

In the preface to his epic, *La Chanson de Saisnes*, Jehan Bodel (d. 1210) distinguishes among the three principal matters, that of France (*chansons de geste*), Rome (romances of antiquity), and Britain (Breton or Arthurian romances), denigrating the latter as *vain et plaisant* ("frivolous and pleasant"). Yet by this time the "matter of Britain" was gaining an enthusiastic audience in France, where it had taken hold in the twelfth century and flourished, spreading quickly to Germany, Scandinavia, and the Italian and Iberian peninsulas before re-crossing the Channel back to England, greatly enriched. Although it was originally addressed to courtly, aristocratic circles, from the thirteenth century on it filtered down to the lower echelons of society, especially as the urban classes gained prominence. The appearance of print editions only broadened its readership and increased its popularity.

The matter of Britain is first exemplified on the Continent by the Arthurian romances of Chrétien de Troyes and the Old French verse romances of Tristan and Iseult. These works captured the imagination by their appealing blend of "historical" elements (inherited from Geoffrey of Monmouth and Wace) and fantastic motifs and themes, most drawn from Celtic legends. Love and chivalry were prominent, and the audience was invited to reflect on the heroes' attempts to reconcile conflicting personal and professional demands. The great prose romances of the thirteenth century – the Vulgate and Post-Vulgate Cycles and the Prose *Tristan* – developed these predominantly secular themes, but the religious motifs first introduced by Chrétien's *Conte du Graal* added a whole new dimension.

Since the matter of Britain on the Continent – a vast subject – is the focus of several different contributors in this volume, we will limit the scope of this chapter to the evolution of the legend of Tristan and Iseult in a few areas that had close linguistic and cultural ties: Occitania and France, Italy, and Spain and Portugal. We shall be able to appreciate the tremendous impact of an important component of the Arthurian legend and the complex network of influences involved in its transmission. It is, of course, somewhat anachronistic to refer to these regions as if they were modern nations, especially since frontiers were, in the Middle Ages, extremely permeable, and the knowledge of French very widespread. Keith Busby has spoken recently of a "medieval Francophonia," arguing that patterns of manuscript production in different regions of present-day France, Belgium, England, and Italy put into question the very concept of "medieval French literature" (2002: 4). The diffusion of the Tristan legend in southern Europe suggests that this "medieval Francophonia" encompassed parts of the Iberian Peninsula as well.

The story of Tristan and Iseult was originally separate from the Arthurian tradition. Although Arthur appears briefly in the verse *Tristan*s, it is only in the Prose *Tristan*, where Tristan actually joins the Round Table, that the two legends intersect fruitfully, even though Chrétien had already drawn on the Tristan legend to depict the adulterous passion of Cligés and Fenice and of Lancelot and Guenevere.

France and Occitania

We owe to lyric poets living in Occitania (southern France) the earliest Continental allusions to the legend. Of all the Arthurian characters, Tristan and Iseult are cited most in the poetry of the troubadours and of their northern French counterparts, the *trouvères*. Poets used them as emblematic figures, standards by which to measure, in hyperbolic terms, their own virtues, celebrating Tristan's prowess, Iseult's beauty, their love ardor, and the daring ruses employed to meet secretly. Most allusions are brief – one or two lines – but in *Non chant per auzel*, Raimbaut d'Aurenga's poet-lover extends over three strophes the story of how Iseult gave Tristan the "gift" of her virginity and cleverly managed to conceal it from her husband. This allusion, conceived as an exemplary lesson for the poet's beloved, underscores how the love of Tristan and Iseult, made reciprocal by the potion, differed from the *fin' amor* that the typical troubadour celebrated as he labored to seduce his – often recalcitrant – Lady.

The precise sources of the legend are unknown. Scholars have found analogues in the tales of the Celts, and certain motifs may have been borrowed from Hellenic, Persian, and Arabic sources. But the story that has fired the imagination of artists from the Middle Ages onward stems from the versions composed in Europe in the late twelfth and early thirteenth centuries. These texts derive from two "traditions" identified by Joseph Bédier, who also believed in the existence of a non-extant "archetype." The so-called *version commune* (common or primitive version) is thought to preserve an earlier state of the legend; it is represented in French by Béroul (between 1150 and 1190) and in German, in a slightly different strand, by Eilhart von Oberg (between 1170 and 1190). The so-called *version courtoise* (courtly version) incorporates features doubtless influenced by court culture. The Old French verse *Tristan* composed by Thomas de Bretagne (c. 1170–75) formed the basis for the poems in Middle High German by Gottfried von Strassburg (c. 1210) and in Old Norse by Friar Róbert (1226).[1]

Since we do not know the exact sources used by these poets, and because they and later writers emphasized different elements, a rough sketch of the legend (based on the early *Tristan* poems) will serve as a frame of reference for subsequent discussion, both in this chapter and in later ones.

Born to King Rivalin of Lyonesse and Blancheflor, sister of King Mark of Cornwall, Tristan is orphaned early on and raised by his tutor Governal, who becomes his trusted companion. Endowed with both martial and courtly skills (hunting, music), he wins his uncle's heart on arriving at his court. When the Irish champion Morholt (the Irish queen's brother) comes to demand the annual tribute, Tristan defeats him, inflicting a fatal blow to the head, where a piece of his sword lodges. Ailing from a poisonous wound received in that fight, Tristan sets himself adrift in an open boat with his harp and arrives by chance in Ireland. Disguised as a minstrel, he is cured by the Queen and Princess Iseult before returning to Cornwall, where Mark's affection for him causes the jealous barons to urge their lord to marry. Volunteering for the bridequest, Tristan returns to Ireland and slays the dragon ravaging the land. Poisoned by the flames emanating from its mouth, he is nursed back to health by Iseult. Though outraged to discover the telltale notch in his sword, Iseult is persuaded not to kill him. As the dragon-slayer, Tristan obtains permission to take the princess back to Cornwall for Mark, and the two set out with Iseult's confidante, Brangain, to whom the Queen has entrusted a love potion for the bridal couple.

On board the ship, Tristan and Iseult mistakenly drink the potion and consummate their ill-fated love. In Cornwall, they lead a double life, meeting secretly while trying to thwart attempts by the evil dwarf Frocin and the felonious barons to prove their treachery to Mark, whose affection for the couple blinds him to their disloyalty. In one famous episode, Mark is persuaded to spy on them by hiding in a tree in his orchard, but the lovers spot his reflection in the water and manage to dispel his doubts. Eventually they are caught, and Tristan is condemned to death, while Iseult is turned over to a leper colony. They escape and flee to the Morois forest, where they lead an existence whose harshness is mitigated only by their mutual passion. At one point, Mark learns of their whereabouts, but upon finding them asleep fully clothed and separated by Tristan's sword, he again persuades himself of their innocence and allows them to return to court. The hermit Ogrin urges them to repent of their sin, but they believe themselves innocent. Although in some versions the lovers' desire to return to court is set off by the abatement of the potion's effects after three or four years, their real incentive is to reclaim their rightful roles in society. While Mark is happy to take back his wife, the barons persuade him to exile Tristan and to make Iseult swear her innocence, an ordeal at which King Arthur is present and from which she emerges unscathed thanks to a clever oath that respects the letter, if not the spirit, of the law.

Tristan spends time at Arthur's court, where he increases his prowess immeasurably and earns the affection of the knights, who accompany him to Tintagel and demonstrate solidarity when Mark attempts to trap Tristan by placing sharp blades around Iseult's bed. After leaving Arthur's court, Tristan finds a new home in Brittany, entering the service of Duke Hoël, whose son, Kaherdin, becomes his companion. He eventually marries Hoël's daughter, Iseult of the White Hands; temporarily bewitched by her name and beauty (and his lust), he feels remorse on his wedding night and is unable to consummate the union. Following this abortive attempt to replace Iseult the Blonde, he has statues of her and Brangain erected in a cave and visits periodically. The Queen languishes in Cornwall where with no news from Tristan she is pestered by Cariado, a suitor who reports on Tristan's marriage. She also quarrels with Brangain, who reproaches her for her faithlessness and threatens to denounce her. Tristan makes several return visits to Cornwall disguised variously as leper, pilgrim, and fool. Back in Brittany, he is fatally wounded by a poisoned spear. All remedies failing, he sends Kaherdin to fetch the Queen, instructing him to hoist, on the return trip, a white sail if she is aboard, a black sail if she is not. His eavesdropping wife, apprised at last of his relationship and also of this code, informs Tristan that the white sail on the returning ship is black. Tristan, thinking his lover has ceased to care for him, expires on the spot, as does the Queen when she arrives to find him dead. In some versions, a repentant Mark, upon learning of the potion, buries them side by side in Tintagel. From their tombs spring two vines that intertwine.

The extant portion of Béroul's poem, a 4,485-line fragment composed in octosyllabic couplets and preserved in a single manuscript, recounts the middle part of the legend, from the orchard rendezvous to Tristan's banishment. This tryst, immortalized by so many medieval artists, establishes the lovers' unrepentant talent for verbal and visual duplicity and Marc's touching gullibility. These same qualities repeatedly surge to the fore in cyclical fashion as Marc's barons strive relentlessly to catch the lovers in a compromising situation that will prove their guilt. But Tristran[2] – and especially Yseut – are more than a match for their enemies who, though they are in the right, apparently do not even have God on their side, no doubt because they are motivated by spite and jealousy. One of the most astonishing illustrations of the lovers' ruse is the "ambiguous oath" that Yseut pronounces near the Mal Pas swamp in the presence of King Artus, called to witness the ordeal. Having arranged to have Tristran, disguised as a leper, carry her across the swamp on his shoulders, she can swear honestly that she has never had any man between her thighs except her lord Marc . . . and the leper.

As Yseut tells Ogrin, she and Tristran believe themselves innocent because of the love potion, yet they continue to meet and scheme even after the drink's effects wear off. The surprisingly upbeat tone of the poem stems in part from the lovers' mischievous delight in their ability to exploit language and appearances to achieve their subversive ends and partly from the narrator's overt espousal of their cause. But although the "epic" narrator applauds the lovers' successive victories and their enemies' every defeat, Béroul himself may not have entirely approved of this unorthodox situation, especially since Marc is, on the whole, an extremely sympathetic cuckold, and the lovers reveal no qualms about betraying him and violating the most sacred social and religious ties. Even when the potion's effects wane, the lovers regret not their disloyalty to Marc but rather their inability to fulfill their rightful roles in society. Béroul invites us to read between the lines of a work that, while entertaining and even comical on the surface, is deeply troubling in its implications.

Thomas's poem, composed about the same time as Béroul's, is very different in tone. It may have been composed for the Plantagenet court, and indeed Artus is depicted as King of England. The various fragments (totaling 3,298 octosyllabic lines) are preserved in ten different manuscripts and represent about a quarter of the original. Judging from the outline to be gleaned from Róbert and Gottfried, both of whom cite this poem as their source, it was Thomas who expanded the love story of the hero's parents to anticipate that of Tristran and Ysolt. Except for a recently discovered fragment describing the potion scene, the extant pieces recount the last third of the romance, starting with the lovers' adieu as Tristran goes into exile and ending with their deaths. The episodes in between focus on the acute alienation felt by both Tristran and Ysolt – his various attempts to replace her (marriage, cave of lovers); Ysolt's quarrel with her confidante; Tristran's frequent trips back to Cornwall; and the combat in which he receives a fatal wound through the loins.

By a curious coincidence, the extant portions of Thomas's poem take up the story just before Gottfried's poem breaks off, and early scholars, failing to note the difference in tone between the two works, believed that Thomas was depicting an ennobling love. However, it is clear that the account of the legend furnished by Thomas, undoubtedly a cleric, is bleak in the extreme. His narrator analyzes the impossible situation of the lovers and their respective spouses: all lack the power (*poeir*) to realize their heart's desire (*voleir*), as Tristran too acknowledges in the famous monologue that nevertheless ends with his resolution to wed, a decision that only accentuates his dilemma and multiplies the misery of all concerned.

Roughly contemporary with the poems of Béroul and Thomas are a few episodic texts that recount variously Tristan's return visits to Cornwall. In the *Folie Tristan de Berne* (574 lines) and the *Folie Tristan d'Oxford* (998 lines), named after the location of the library where each is housed, Tristan's disguise as a fool enables him to speak freely – and even crudely – to Marc and Yseut as he provides distorted accounts of his past history with the Queen. The particular events he relates in each poem link the Berne *Folie* to the *version commune* and the Oxford *Folie* to the *version courtoise*.

Another twelfth-century piece was contributed by Marie de France in *Chevrefoil*, the shortest of her famous *lais* (a mere 118 lines), which neatly encapsulates the lovers' plight. Tristram, unable to endure his exile, learns that the Queen will be traveling to Tintagel for Pentecost. Upon spotting her in the procession, he signals his presence by tossing in her path a hazel branch engraved with his name (or a message) signifying that their situation is analogous to that of the honeysuckle entwining the hazel, for they cannot long endure when separated. The visit ends on a joyful note as the Queen expresses the hope of a reconciliation between Tristram and Marc. Tristan also visits Yseut in a short text (1,524 lines) inserted into the Fourth Continuation of *Perceval* and called *Tristan Menestrel* because after drawing Arthur's knights to Marc's court, he disguises himself as a minstrel in order to win a night of love with the Queen.

The romances of Chrétien de Troyes (Lacy & Grimbert 2005) were composed during the same late-twelfth-century period as the early Tristan poems, but at least one romance, *Cligés*, reveals in its structure, themes, and rhetoric prior knowledge of Thomas's poem, although nothing is known of his poem "del roi Marc et d'Iseut la blonde" cited in the prologue of *Cligés*. Chrétien's romances themselves had a tremendous impact, particularly on the great prose romances of the following century known as the Vulgate and Post-Vulgate Cycles. Chrétien also influenced over twenty twelfth- and thirteenth-century Arthurian verse romances (Schmolke-Hasselmann 1998; Kelly 2006).

Starting in the thirteenth century, the romance that had the greatest impact on the diffusion of the Tristan legend in France, Italy, and Spain was *Le Livre (ou le roman) du bon chevalier Tristan de Leonois*, commonly known as the Prose *Tristan*, composed in the second and third quarters of the thirteenth century and attributed – no doubt falsely – to Luce del Gast and Hélie de Boron. Transmitted in two basic versions, it was extremely popular and is extant in more than eighty manuscripts and fragments and in eight printed editions dating from 1489 to 1533. The long version is sometimes called the "cyclical version" because a portion of the Vulgate is interpolated into certain manuscripts. The authors were clearly familiar with the *Lancelot–Grail* (Vulgate) Cycle especially the *Lancelot–Queste–Mort Artu*, for they set Tristan's prowess on a level with that of Lancelot and Galahad and grafted his story onto the scheme provided by the Prose *Lancelot* (see chapter 14).

The Prose *Tristan* extends the hero's story both backward and forward in time. It begins with an account of Tristan's ancestors and relates his sojourn with Governal at the court of King Pharamont of Gaul, where he has two love affairs. After he arrives at Marc's court, his story follows the verse narratives up to his marriage in Brittany, after which he returns to Cornwall before Marc banishes him for good. But his fate is no longer that of an alienated individual spending a lonely exile pining away for his beloved. He becomes a knight-errant and gains such a sterling reputation measuring himself against Artus's best knights that he is invited to occupy, aptly, Morholt's vacant seat at the Round Table. At this point, the influence of the *Lancelot–Grail* becomes preponderant as Tristan is integrated into the Arthurian orbit and will even participate in the Grail quest.

The authors of the Prose *Tristan* dilute strikingly the subversive force of the original love story. First, they set up a stark opposition between the virtuous Artus and his brave knights and a thoroughly villainous King Marc and the cowardly Cornish. Second, they multiply the number of characters who fall in love with – and sometimes even die for – Tristan and Yselt, including the Gaulish princess Belide, Tristan's brother-in-law Kaherdin, and the Saracen Palamedes (a newly invented character). In fact, as is appropriate in a romance where love and chivalry are so intimately linked, Tristan's amorous interest in Yselt is first aroused at a tournament where Palamedes, a rival knight, hopes to win her through a love-inspired display of prowess. Third, the decision to place the Cornish lovers in a space contiguous with that of the Arthurian kingdom at its height inevitably invites comparison with their Logrian counterparts, Lancelot and Genevre. And, just as in the Prose *Lancelot* the eponymous hero is celebrated as Artus's greatest champion, Tristan is endowed here with an analogous social function, thereby muting the subversive impact of his adulterous affair. Finally, the primary love intrigue is virtually dwarfed by the maze of adventures that occupy both Tristan and his fellow knights: "The reader is swept along by a succession of interlacing episodes, repeated motifs, echoes and correspondences, reminiscent of the self-generating narrative of the serialized novel" (Baumgartner 2006: 329; see also her landmark 1975 study).

The changes that the Prose *Tristan* wrought in the legend suggested a distinctively different ending consonant with the new emphasis on chivalry and destined to become the dominant model in all the countries where this romance was imported. Only one manuscript of the Prose *Tristan* features the traditional death scene; in all the others, Tristan is treacherously slain by Marc with a poisonous lance as he listens to Yselt perform a lay, and Yselt expires in her lover's ardent embrace. Tristan, who would have preferred to die in battle, pleads that his arms be presented to Artus and Lancelot.

The popularity of the Prose *Tristan* in France generated interest in stories about Tristan's father Meliadus and his descendants. *Palamedes*, a kind of prequel, is a collection of tales about Meliadus's generation, including the fathers of Palamedes, Artus, and Erec. Its two parts were often considered independent texts and were published separately in the sixteenth century as *Meliadus de Leonnoys* and *Guiron le Courtois*. Rustichello (Rusticiano) da Pisa composed the first version of *Palamedes* as part of his *Roman du Roi Artus* or *Compilation* (c. 1272). It was included as well in the Arthurian compilations of Jehan Vaillant de Poitiers (c. 1391) and Michot Gonnot (1470). The Prose *Tristan* also spawned a kind of dynastic continuation in the early fifteenth century called *Ysaÿe le Triste*, which was published in 1522. It recounts the serio-comic adventures of the lovers' son, Ysaÿe, and grandson, Marc, who set about to restore harmony in the Arthurian realm by eliminating the evil forces and customs. Two other Tristan romances were published subsequently, Pierre Sala's *Tristan* (1525–9) and Jean Maugin's *Premier Livre du nouveau Tristan de Leonnois, chevalier de la Table Ronde et d'Yseulte Princesse d'Yrlande, Royne de Cornouaille* (1554), which was to be followed by a second book that never materialized.

Italy

In Italy, Tristan was by far the most beloved and widely cited of all Arthurian characters. As was the case in France, lyric poets early on used the celebrated lovers as yardsticks to measure their own experience. Henricus of Settimello made the first reference in a Latin poem (1193) where he compared his own sorrows to Tristano's greater ones. But the first phase of courtly lyric poetry centered around the court of Frederick II of Sicily (1220–50), where poets enjoyed close ties with the troubadours and, like them, celebrated Tristano's consummate strength and courage, Isotta's superlative beauty, and the enduring force of their love. Shortly afterwards, the great master of rhetoric Brunetto Latini, writing in France (and in French), included an elaborate description of Isotta in the section on rhetoric in his *Li Livres dou Trésor* (1266).

The most famous Italian poets had conflicting attitudes toward the Arthurian legend. In his *De Vulgari Eloquentia* (1303–4) Dante cited Arthur as evidence of the pre-eminence of French, but in his *Divina Comedia* (between 1308 and 1321), his allusions to Arthurian literature are pejorative. The best known is his presentation of the sinful passion of two contemporaries from Rimini, Paolo and Francesca (*Inferno* V), who lament that they fell in love while reading the Prose *Lancelot*. Although there is no explicit mention of Tristano and Isotta here, some scholars (e.g. Gardner, Hoffman) believe their story is woven into that of Paolo and Francesca, who, as Dante knew, were slain by Paolo's brother, just as Tristano was slain by his uncle. In any case, Tristano, though not Isotta, figures at the end of Canto V in the list of famous characters undone by love. A bit later, Petrarca, speaking contemptuously of "popular" literature in his *Trionfo d'Amore*, groups the Logrian and Cornish lovers with the couple from Rimini who lament having been subjugated by love. Similarly, Boccaccio, in his *Amorosa Visione*, includes them in his Arthurian cavalcade and in the pageant of lovers, but his later allusions to Arthurian figures tend to be cynical or licentious (Gardner 1930: 136–41, 228–32).

Another type of Italian poetry is represented by the *Cantari* (mid-thirteenth to late fifteenth centuries), popular narrative poems composed in *ottava rima*, which draw on both oral and written sources. Three are Tristan-related: Tristano's combat with Lancilotto at the Merlin stone, the lovers' deaths, and Lancilotto's vendetta against Marco. In the so-called *Cantare dei cantari* (c. 1380–1420), the poet lists the subjects in his repertory, which includes the whole course of sacred and profane history, with nine stanzas devoted to Arthurian subjects (Gardner 1930: 265–72).

The Prose *Tristan* was the basis for all the Italian romances. French was understood by educated speakers, and about twenty percent of the extant manuscripts of the Prose *Tristan* were actually copied in Italy. The earliest prose romance written by an Italian was the above-mentioned romance composed in French by Rustichello da Pisa, the late thirteenth-century *Compilation*, whose two parts were translated into Italian as *Girone il Cortese* and *Il gran re Meliadus*. The romances composed in Italian were all based on the same unorthodox non-extant redaction of the Prose *Tristan*. The earliest (late thirteenth century), *Tristano Riccardiano*, is a Tuscan–Umbrian adaptation of elements from the Prose *Tristan* combined with new episodes. Nearly half of the extant romance concerns Tristano's marriage and his adventures in Brittany. The *Tristano Veneto* and the *Tristano Corsiniano* are both translations of the Prose *Tristan* in the

Venetian dialect. The *Tristano Panciaticchiano* is much more eclectic, an "Arthurian medley" made up of five disparate sections (Gardner 1930: 114).

But the undoubted masterpiece of this group is the *Tavola Ritonda* (Tuscan dialect, second quarter of the fourteenth century), which integrates into an innovative framework elements borrowed from Thomas's *Tristan*, the Prose *Tristan*, *Palamedes*, Robert de Boron's *Merlin*, the Vulgate *Queste* and *Mort Artu*, and a source it shares with the *Tristano Riccardiano*. (See Delcorno Branca's masterful 1968 study, which includes an episode-by-episode chart comparing this romance with its various sources.) The *Tavola*, extant in ten manuscripts of the fourteenth and fifteenth centuries, was obviously very popular. Like Malory, the author plainly wished to provide a *summa* of the Arthurian cycle. After announcing his intention to speak of both the Old and New Tables, he soon dispenses with this grand plan and focuses on the "Tavola Nuovo" – Artù's fellowship – before cutting in short order to a comparison of Tristano and Lancilotto. Stating that he will begin with Tristano, who was "the source and foundation of all chivalry," he will set out his noble lineage and birth, his perfect love and his cruel death, and the very great vengeance taken on his behalf. Although this outline sounds like the Prose *Tristan*, the emphasis is markedly different in the *Tavola*, which drastically reduces the number of chivalric adventures and is clearly designed to refocus attention on Tristano and Isotta's love, portrayed as both overpowering and exemplary.

Tristano is compared to Lancilotto throughout, as in the Prose *Tristan*, where they are both exemplary knights and lovers. But in the *Tavola* they also share family ties: Tristano's mother is Artù's niece and the cousin of Lancilotto's father; his father, Meliadus, is Marco's brother. The marriage of Tristano's parents was negotiated by Lancilotto, of a generation older than Tristano, whose birth occurs at the moment that the Logrian lovers consummate their love. Lancilotto and Ginevara will eventually be surpassed both in beauty and in the quality of their love. Although the author celebrates Lancilotto, Tristano, and Galeotto (Galehaut) as the most noble knights, he laments that they were neither secret nor wise in their loves; however, he states that Tristano was excused by the potion. The author celebrates the pre-eminence of Tristano and Isotta as lovers because they were initially joined in a "loyal love" and only succumbed to adultery upon drinking the potion, whereas Lancilotto and Ginevara's love, conceived when they set eyes on one another, was a case of *willful excess*, which was precisely what undermined Arthurian ideals and spelled the destruction of the Round Table. In the Arthurian hierarchy, Galasso (Galahad) owed his greatness to God's grace, but Tristano was the best secular knight because he had "a heart in love," the cornerstone of all chivalry (Grimbert 2005).

Tristano and Isotta's deaths confirm their superiority as the ending adapted from the Prose *Tristan* takes on unmistakably christological overtones. Tristano, dying at 33, expresses remorse for his preoccupation with worldly matters but hopes Christ's precious blood will redeem his sin. The lovers believe they will be forgiven, a likelihood underscored by the pope's offer of indulgences to all who pray for their souls.

Particularly striking is the description of the allegorization of the vine that roots in the lovers' hearts: it "invites an ecstatic exegesis that blends Dionysian celebration with eucharistic devotion, recreating Tristan as the patron of a new communion of lovers who will drink the wine transubstantiated from his body and blood" (Hoffman 1990: 177). Following Tristano's death, the Arthurian realm sinks into gloom, and after carrying out their high vendetta against Marco, the knights give in to such excess that the Round Table self-destructs. After its destruction, it is said that Carlo Magno rode into Logres and, upon seeing the statues of Artù's greatest knights that had been erected after the tournament at Verzeppe, proclaimed that Artù deserved his death, for with five such noble knights, he should have had all Christians and Saracens under his sway.

This intersection of the matter of Britain with that of France, which was to characterize Italian epic during the Renaissance, is seen in the Franco-Italian epic, *Entrée d'Espagne* (before 1320), where epic heroes are endowed with the amorous and chivalric sensibility of Arthurian knights even while the Breton fables are pronounced inferior, as in Nicola da Casola's *Attila* (after 1350). The conflation of the Arthurian and Carolingian cycles naturally anticipates Boiardo's *Orlando Innamorato* and Ariosto's *Orlando Furioso* (Gardner 1930: 218–20).

Unlike France, which had a relatively stable monarchy, the situation in Italy was quite volatile, especially after Frederick II's death in 1250. The rise of the city-states (communes) in central and northern Italy may well have influenced the ideology of the Tristan romances. For example, the character of Dinadan, who serves in the Prose *Tristan* (where he was first introduced) as a critic of both chivalric and amorous ideals, is endowed in the *Tavola* with a wider range of attitudes and types of discourse that embrace the bourgeois sensibility. It is possible that the author uses Dinadano's moralizing gloss of Arthurian ideals to verbalize his own criticism (Kleinhenz 1975), but the celebration of Tristano throughout the romance, and especially the ecstatic description at the end, suggests that he was as enamored of the Cornish lovers as many of his compatriots seem to have been.

Spain and Portugal

The diffusion of the matter of Britain in Iberia spans an unusually long period, from the early twelfth century to the sixteenth. In Castile and Léon, Arthurian names were known as early as the 1130s, even before Geoffrey of Monmouth composed his *Historia*. Moreover, a sculpted image on a column from the old Romanesque façade of the cathedral at Santiago de Compostela that shows an ailing Tristan lying in an open boat holding a notched sword upright pre-dates all the extant French verse poems and points to a very early penetration of the legend (Sharrer 1996: 407–8). If the Arthurian legend's appeal endured well into the Renaissance, it is because chivalry was held in high esteem in Spain, where the *Reconquista* justified the existence of a class that assured national survival and defense of the faith (Hall 1983: 85).

A number of historical factors favored the diffusion of the matter of Britain on the Iberian Peninsula. The earliest version of the only Occitan Arthurian romance, *Jaufré* (c. 1170), was written at the court of Alfonso II of Aragon, whose successor, Pedro II (1196–1213), was often compared to Arthur. More importantly, in 1170, Alfonso VIII of Castile married Eleanor of England, the daughter of two great patrons of Arthurian literature, Henry II and Eleanor of Aquitaine (whose grandfather, Guillaume IX, was the first troubadour). In 1254, his great-granddaughter, Leonor of Castile, sister of Alfonso X (Brunetto Latini's patron), married Edward I, who was the great-grandson of Henry II and Eleanor. Edward was also the patron of Rustichello's *Compilation*, which, as we recall, was written in French by an Italian; it would be translated into Castilian about 1293 (Entwistle 1925: 33–4, 50–52).

One point of entry of the Tristan legend into Spain was Catalonia, thanks to the close linguistic and cultural ties between Occitania and the Catalan troubadours, one of whom, Giraut de Cabrera, was the first to cite Tristan, in a poem composed around 1170. But it was the hybrid Galician-Portuguese language, used by the court lyric poets in the western two-thirds of the peninsula from 1150 to 1300, that formed the real bridge between Occitania and Iberia. Although Alfonso X alluded to Tristán, Artus, and Merlin in his Galician-Portuguese poems, the legend was not widely known in Castile until the mid-fourteenth century. The *Cancioneiro de Baena*, which collects the lyrics of Castilian poets of the late fourteenth and early fifteenth centuries, includes many references to Iseo's beauty and Tristán's passion and musical skills (Hall 1983: 77).

The earliest substantial Tristan works were five anonymous Galician-Portuguese troubadour narrative lyrics, or *romances*, the *Cancioneiro de Lisboa* or *Lais de Bretanha* (late thirteenth to early fourteenth century). Especially prized was the widely glossed ballad, *Herido está don Tristán*, recounting the death of the lovers at Marco's court on the model of the prose romances, "a masterpiece of poignancy and compression" (Lida de Malkiel 1959: 413).

The Hispanic *Tristan* romances are all related to the French Prose *Tristan*, most to the same non-extant version from which the Italian romances were generated. There are several small fourteenth-century fragments (one to four folios): two Catalan, two Castilian, and one Galician-Portuguese. A much more substantial Castilian and Aragonese manuscript (131 folios), *El Cuento de Tristán de Leonís*, dates from the late fourteenth or early fifteenth century. Two sixteenth-century imprints complete the picture. The first, *El Libro del esforçado cauallero don Tristán de Leonis y de sus grandes fechos en armas*, appeared in 1501 and was re-edited several times. A sequel dates from 1534, *Corónica nuevamente emendata y añadida del buen cavallero don Tristán de Leonís y del rei don Tristán de Leonís el joven su hijo*. Just as the Prose *Tristan* had extended the legend backward to include the hero's ancestors, this sequel, like *Ysaÿe le Triste*, extends it forward to recount the adventures of his offspring, Tristán and Yseo. It was to be translated into Italian as *I due Tristani* (Venice, 1555).

The Castilian *Tristan*s rework the Prose *Tristan* by refocusing attention on the primitive legend. They omit almost all the adventures in which Tristán does not participate, inverting the order of some, and adding others, and they eliminate both the genealogical "prologue" and the post-mortem "epilogue." Moreover, unlike in the Prose *Tristan*, there is no disproportion between the episodes comprising the traditional material (up to Tristán's marriage) and those originally designed to integrate the lovers' story into the Arthurian cyclical romances. The author of the *Libro* devotes the same number of chapters to Tristán the lover as to Tristán the knight, clearly conceiving of the story as a love tragedy: Tristán was destined to be the greatest knight, but another fate intervened – that of being the most *enamorado* – and enamored, tragically, of his uncle's wife (Cuesta Torre 1994: 49, 205–7, 217–18).

The *Libro* tones down the irony and humor of the *Cuento* by presenting the protagonists in a serious, uncritical manner. It also eliminates or refines incidents involving disreputable characters and – more importantly for our purposes – glosses over the moral implications of the lovers' adultery by removing references to their sinfulness. In this, it was clearly influenced by the "sentimental romance" genre, which emerged in the second half of the fifteenth century; indeed, it incorporates seven lengthy passages from Juan de Flores's *Grimalte y Gradissa* (Hall 1983: 84; Sharrer 1996: 415–17).[3] Of course, these modifications could not totally disguise Lanzarote's and Tristán's disloyalty toward their respective monarchs, nor could they mask their adultery. The popular imitation of Arthurian romance, *Amadís de Gaula* (1508), would eschew such difficulties by creating two protagonists who are exemplary in every way. Amadís and Oriana fall in love at first sight, *sans* philter. They have no other lovers, and their passion, though secret, is not adulterous (Cuesta Torre 1994: 217–18, 224–5).

The sequel to the *Libro*, the *Corónica*, reflects even more than its predecessor the new pro-matrimonial ideology. In the first part, the author revises the *materia antigua* by adding several new chapters to set the scene for the birth of the lovers' offspring and by changing their ardent passion into a love that is quasi "matrimonial" as Yseo becomes the perfect spouse and mother. The second part, which is totally new, relates the adventures of their children, Tristán and Yseo, after the parents' death. Tristán will accede to the thrones of Cornwall and Leonís, marry the infanta María, and arrange the marriage of his own sister with his brother-in-law, King Juan of Spain (Cuesta Torre 2002). Thus, an "expurgated" version of the Tristan legend, much removed in spirit from the original French poems, became securely anchored in Spain.

Iberia's main contribution to the diffusion of the matter of Britain on the Continent was actually the influence it had on Hispanic romances that contain brief allusions to Arthurian characters (such as the Catalan *Tirant lo Blanch* [1460] by Joanot Martorell and Martí Joan de Galba) and on works that simply imitate Arthurian romance, borrowing familiar themes and motifs and fusing them with the indigenous genre of the sentimental romance, as does *Amadís de Gaula*. The first four books of the *Amadís*, which had antecedents in either Castilian or Portuguese, were initially published in 1508, by Garci Rodríguez de Montalvo, who claimed to have amended the first three books and authored the fourth. Hugely popular, it generated dozens of sequels and translations throughout the sixteenth century, not only in Castilian, but also in French, Italian, English, German, Dutch, and even Hebrew.

In 1605, Miguel de Cervantes published the first part of his *Don Quijote*, considered by many as the first "modern" novel. In this work, destined to become the most influential of the Spanish Golden Age, Cervantes cited as sources both *Orlando Furioso* and *Tirant lo Blanch*, and although he mentions Tristán only once in passing, there are curious similarities with the 1534 Tristán romance (Cuesta Torre 1994: 229–30). Don Quijote was obsessed with chivalric romance, but Cervantes was as critical as he was enamored of it. Surely, there is no better proof of the impact of the matter of Britain on the Continent than the universal appeal of works like *Amadís de Gaula* and *Don Quijote*, which were shaped by Arthurian romance.

In this brief survey, we have observed how, in areas that enjoyed close ties, the legend of Tristan and Iseult retained its charm throughout the Middle Ages, undergoing various reincarnations. Beginning in France and Occitania in the twelfth century as a subversive tale whose protagonists blithely violated the most sacred social and religious ties, its impact was somewhat diluted in thirteenth-century France as Tristan, henceforth a knight of the Round Table, became engaged in dozens of adventures. In fourteenth-century Italy, where the lovers were either condemned or exalted, their story, brought decisively to the fore, regained much of its primitive force. Finally, Renaissance Spain was to see the lovers properly integrated into a pro-matrimonial society as loyal spouses and parents.

NOTES

1 On the early French *Tristan* poems, see Grimbert (1995: xv–xxxiii) and Hunt and Bromily (2006).

2 The names of the lovers – and of other Arthurian characters – vary. I adopt in my discussion of each work the most prevalent form.

3 Sharrer notes the influence of *Grimalte y Gradissa* on a late medieval epistolary exchange, *Carta enviada por Hiseo la Brunda a Tristán de Leonís*, especially in Tristán's response to Iseo's complaint about his marriage, expanded from her letter in the Prose *Tristan* (416).

PRIMARY SOURCES

France

Curtis, R. L. (ed.) (1963–85). *Le Roman de Tristan en prose*, 3 vols. I, Munich: Max Hueber (1963); II, Leiden: Brill (1976); III, Cambridge: Brewer (1985).

Curtis, R. L. (trans.) (1994). *Romance of Tristan*. Oxford: Oxford University Press.

Giacchetti, A. (ed.) (1989). *Ysaÿe le triste: roman arthurien du moyen âge tardif.* Rouen-Maromme: Qualigraphie.

Lacy, N. J. (ed.) (1998). *Early French Tristan poems*, vols I & II. Cambridge: Brewer.

Ménard, P. (gen. ed.) (1987–97). *Le Roman de Tristan en prose*, 9 vols. Geneva: Droz.

Pickford, C. E. (ed.) (1977). *Guyron le Courtoys*. London: Scolar Press.

Pickford, C. E. (ed.) (1980). *Meliadus de Leonnoys*. London: Scolar Press.

Italy

Allaire, G. (ed. trans.) (2002). *Il Tristano panciatichiano*. London: Brewer.

Bertoni, G. (ed.) (1937). *Cantari di Tristano*. Modena: Società tipografica modenese.

Cigni, F. (ed.) (1994). *Il romanzo arturiano di Rustichello da Pisa.* Pisa: Cassa di risparmio di Pisa, Pacini.

Donadello, A. (ed.) (1994). *Il libro di messer Tristano ("Tristano Veneto").* Venice: Marsilio.

Galasso, M. (ed.) (1937). *Il Tristano corsiniano.* Cassino: Casa Editrice "Le Fonti."

Heijkant, M.-J. (ed.) (1991). *Il Tristano Riccardiano.* Parma: Pratiche.

Heijkant, M.-J. (ed.) (1998). *La Tavola Ritonda.* Milan: Lumi.

Shaver, A. (trans.) (1983). *Tristan and the Round Table: A translation of "La Tavola Ritonda."* Binghamton, NY: Medieval & Renaissance Texts & Studies.

Spain

Cuesta Torre, M. L. (ed.) (1997). *Tristán de Leonís y el rey don Tristán el joven, su hijo, 1534.* México: Universidad Nacional Autónoma de México, Instituto de Investigaciones Filológicas.

Cuesta Torre, M. L. (1999). *Tristán de Leonís, 1501.* Alcála de Henares: Centro de Estudios Cervantinos.

Wright, R. (ed. trans.) (1987). *Spanish ballads.* Warminster: Aris & Philipps.

References and Further Reading

Baumgartner, E. (1975). *Le Tristan en prose: essai d'interprétation d'un roman médiéval.* Geneva: Droz.

Baumgartner, E. (2006). The Prose *Tristan.* In G. S. Burgess & K. Pratt (eds), *The Arthur of the French.* Cardiff: University of Wales Press, pp. 325–41.

Bédier, J. (1902–5). *Le Roman de Tristan par Thomas,* 2 vols. Paris: Firmin Didot.

Branca, D. (1968). *I Romanzi italiani di Tristano e la Tavola Ritonda.* Florence: Olschki.

Burgess, G. S. & Pratt, K. (eds) (2006). *The Arthur of the French.* Cardiff: University of Wales Press.

Busby, K. (2002). *Codex and context: Reading Old French verse narrative in manuscript,* 2 vols. Amsterdam: Rodopi.

Cuesta Torre, M. L. (1994). *Aventuras amorosas y caballerescas en las novelas de Tristán.* Léon: Universidad, Secretaria de Publicaciones.

Cuesta Torre, M. L. (2002). El rey don Tristán de Leonís el Joven [1534]. *Edad de Oro,* 21, 305–34.

Entwistle, W. J. (1925). *The Arthurian legend in the literatures of the Spanish Peninsula.* London: Dent.

Gardner, E. G. (1930). *The Arthurian legend in Italian literature.* London: Dent.

Grimbert, J. T. (ed.) (1995). *Tristan and Isolde: A casebook.* New York: Garland. Repr. London: Routledge, 2002.

Grimbert, J. T. (2005). Changing the equation: The impact of Tristan-love on Arthur's court. In N. J. Lacy (ed.), *The fortunes of King Arthur.* Cambridge: Brewer, pp. 104–15.

Hall, J. B. (1983). A process of adaptation: The Spanish versions of the romance of Tristan. In A. H. Diverres, R. A. Lodge, & P. B. Grout (eds), *The legend of Arthur in the Middle Ages: Studies presented to A. H. Diverres.* Cambridge: Brewer, pp. 76–85.

Hoffman, D. L. (1990). The Arthurian tradition in Italy. In V. M. Lagorio & M. L. Day (eds), *King Arthur through the ages,* vol. 1. New York: Garland, pp. 170–88.

Hunt, T. & Bromily, G. (2006). The Tristan legend in Old French verse. In G. S. Burgess & K. Pratt (eds.), *The Arthur of the French.* Cardiff: University of Wales Press, pp. 112–34.

Kelly, D. (ed.) & Contributors (2006). Arthurian verse romance in the twelfth and thirteenth centuries. In G. S. Burgess & K. Pratt (eds.), *The Arthur of the French.* Cardiff: University of Wales Press, pp. 393–460.

Kleinhenz, C. (1975). Tristan in Italy: The death or rebirth of a legend. *Studies in Medieval Culture,* 5, 145–58.

Kleinhenz, C. (1996). Italian Arthurian literature. In N. J. Lacy (ed.), *The new Arthurian encyclopedia.* New York: Garland, pp. 245–7.

Lacy, N. J. (ed.) (1996a). *Medieval Arthurian literature: A guide to recent research*. New York: Garland.

Lacy, N. J. (ed.) (1996b). *The new Arthurian encyclopedia*. New York: Garland.

Lacy, N. J. (ed.) (2006). *A history of Arthurian scholarship*. Cambridge: Brewer.

Lacy, N. J. & Grimbert, J. T. (eds) (2005). *A companion to Chrétien de Troyes*. Cambridge: Brewer.

Lida de Malkiel, M. R. (1959). Arthurian literature in Spain and Portugal. In R. S. Loomis (ed.), *Arthurian literature in the Middle Ages*. Oxford: Clarendon Press, pp. 406–29.

Schmolke-Hasselmann, B. (1998). *The evolution of Arthurian romance: The verse tradition from Chrétien to Froissart* (trans. M. & R. Middleton). Cambridge: Cambridge University Press.

Seidenspinner-Núñez, D. (1996). Tristan in Spain and Portugal. In N. J. Lacy (ed.), *The new Arthurian encyclopedia*. New York: Garland, pp. 471–3.

Sharrer, H. L. (1996). Spain and Portugal. In N. J. Lacy (ed.), *Medieval Arthurian literature: A guide to recent research*. New York: Garland, pp. 401–49.

11
Chrétien de Troyes and the Invention of Arthurian Courtly Fiction

Roberta L. Krueger

Legends about King Arthur circulated widely in oral tales and written texts before the mid-twelfth century, as previous chapters have shown. But it was not until after around 1160 that the Arthurian court with its retinue of well-known characters – among them Arthur, Guenevere, Gawain, Kay, Yvain, Lancelot, and Perceval – became a regular feature of European fiction. Although it is impossible to know what the course of literary history would have been without him, the northern French author Chrétien de Troyes, composer of the first full-blown Arthurian romances, shaped courtly narrative in a way that inspired continuators, translators, and a host of direct and indirect successors to spin chivalric tales about Arthur's court throughout the European Middle Ages and beyond.

The Author and his Works

Chrétien de Troyes composed five Arthurian romances: *Erec et Enide*, *Cligès*, *Le Chevalier au Lion* (*Yvain*), *Le Chevalier de la Charrette* (*Lancelot*), and *Le Conte du Graal* (*Perceval*) (see the editions in the bibliography, which have translations into modern French). The romances' precise chronology remains debatable. *Erec et Enide* was certainly the first of the series and *Perceval*, which remains unfinished, the last. Chrétien probably flourished in the 1160s–80s and died before 1191.

All that we know about Chrétien must be been gleaned from the romances themselves. The author identifies himself as "Crestïens de Troyes" or, more frequently, as "Crestïens" at some point in each romance. In the Prologue to *Erec*, Chrétien vaunts that he will do better than popular storytellers who destroy their material; his own work, which he describes as a *bele conjointure* drawn from a *conte d'aventure*, will last in memory as long as *crestïantez* (Christianity) (9–26). Chrétien could not have known how successful his works would be, of course, but the opening words of his first romance, *Erec et Enide*, reveal great literary ambition.

In the Prologue to *Cligès*, Chrétien explains that in addition to *Erec et Enide* he has composed stories about the Tristan legend and has translated several of Ovid's works. The only extant text from this list besides *Erec* is *Philomena*, which was later compiled in a fourteenth-century translation of the *Ovide moralisé*. By asserting his mastery of Latin classics, Chrétien places himself squarely in the tradition of *translatio studii*, the translation or carrying forth of classical learning from Greece to Rome and then to France and England. Chrétien's linguistic and rhetorical skills identify him as a well-read cleric who participated in the flowering of vernacular culture during what is known as the twelfth-century "renaissance."

Chrétien dedicates *Le Chevalier de la Charrette* (*Lancelot*) to *ma dame de Champagne*, the countess Marie, daughter of Eleanor of Aquitaine, who married Henry the Liberal of Champagne in 1159. Marie's grandfather, William of Aquitaine, was well known as a troubadour poet. Although Chrétien's claim that Marie was largely responsible for the *matiere et sens* of his romance may be something of a flattering exaggeration (see lines 24–9), it leaves little doubt that Chrétien found himself in the midst of heady ideas about love and chivalry that circulated at the court of Champagne, inspired in part by troubadour lyrics. Chrétien appears to have abandoned *Lancelot* near the end, since another clerk, Godefroy de Leigni, announces that he has completed the story according to Chrétien's instructions (7102–10). Some critics have suggested that by concluding in this manner, Chrétien expressed his disapproval of Lancelot and Guenevere's adultery, the subject that Marie may have "commanded."

There is no doubt that Chrétien claims pride of authorship for *Yvain*; his name is inscribed prominently in the Epilogue: "Del chevalier al lion fine/Crestïens son romant issi" (6,804–5). Because of references within *Yvain* to events in *Lancelot*, Chrétien probably wrote *Le Chevalier au Lion* and *Le Chevalier de la Charrette* at roughly the same time, possibly as companion romances.

In the Prologue to *Perceval*, we learn that Chrétien composed his last romance for Philip of Flanders. Like Marie of Champagne, Philip belonged to a powerful family and was an important patron of the arts. Philip served for a short time as counselor to young King Philip Augustus and was briefly engaged to Marie (McCash 2005). Chrétien's association with such prominent patrons suggests that his talents were recognized during his lifetime. Chrétien probably died while writing *Perceval*, since the romance trails off in the midst of Gauvain's adventures. By praising Philip's virtue and piety and citing biblical parables in this last prologue, Chrétien elevates his final romance to a higher spiritual dimension. The author portrait that emerges from Chrétien's prologues and epilogues is that of a self-conscious literary craftsman who draws upon a diverse range of learned and popular sources and acknowledges the support of prominent patrons with his own distinctive flair.

Chrétien and his Sources

Chrétien's path-breaking works emerged within a literary climate ripe for innovation. By the 1150s and 1160s, the vogue for works *en romanz* – in the Old French vernacular – was well established. The so-called *romans d'antiquité*, which were translated from Latin sources and included the *Roman de Thèbes* (1150), the *Roman d'Enéas* (1155), and Benoît de Sainte-Maure's *Roman de Troie* (1165), circulated at King Henry and Queen Eleanor's court in England and at elite courts in northern France. These works added a number of fictional features not in their "historical" sources: amplified descriptions of architectural structures such as tombs; extended portraits of heroes and, especially, heroines; and lengthy monologues exploring emotional states in depth.

When Chrétien's characters digress on Love, they often do so with a rhetorical flourish inspired by Ovid, whose works Chrétien translated and whose amorous discourse he imitates and sometimes parodies. Chrétien was also well versed in lyrics of the troubadours and Northern French *trouvères*; two such poems in Chrétien's voice have survived.

But above all, the first Arthurian romancer drew copiously from the *matière de Bretagne* (matter of Britain), the body of Breton lore and Celtic myth that circulated widely in oral tales (Duggan 2001: 183–270). Chrétien's narrator refers frequently to the Tristan legend, and the author had obviously heard tales about Arthur and his knights. Chrétien may have known a few early written Arthurian sources, in particular Wace's *Roman de Brut*, a French translation of Geoffrey of Monmouth's *Historia Regum Brittaniae* written for the Plantagenet court in 1155 (see chapter 4). Wace's image of Arthur as an ideal ruler undermined by internal tensions at home might have inspired Chrétien in a general way. Yet Chrétien's imaginative blend of elements drawn from classical, popular, and vernacular sources was distinctly his own creation.

Chrétien composed his five romances in rhyming octosyllabic couplets to be read aloud or performed in a court setting, perhaps accompanied by gestures and dramatic inflections (Vitz 1999: 86–227). Narratorial interventions in nearly every scene convey a speaker's presence before an audience, undoubtedly comprised of knights and ladies – as fictional scenes of oral storytelling and reading aloud from a book depicted in *Yvain* suggest. No manuscripts of Chrétien's works survive from his lifetime. But forty manuscripts dated from the beginning of the thirteenth century to the middle of the fourteenth century preserve his works, which constitutes a particularly rich tradition (Busby et al. 1993). Most codices compile one or more of Chrétien's romances with other courtly narratives, often complementary Arthurian fictions (Walters 1985). Chrétien's original Arthurian tales fell out of favor in the late Middle Ages, as more contemporary retellings flourished, but critical interest since the nineteenth century has been unabated.

Erec et Enide: The First Arthurian Romance

Erec et Enide establishes Arthur's court as the center of courtly values and the scene of social crisis. Chrétien, as we have seen, sought to surpass other storytellers by creating *une moult bele conjointure* ("a very beautiful composition"). As it highlights the exploits of an individual knight who undergoes moral transformations while displaying remarkable feats of arms, the romance explores tensions between a monarch's desire for traditional community and the knights' aggressive competition, as well as the conflict between pleasure and duty. In *Erec et Enide*, Chrétien inaugurates romance as a forum for debate about social issues.

Like all of Chrétien's works, *Erec* has a clearly delineated structure. This romance can be divided into two parts, which treat first the hero's initiation as knight and then a crisis in his marriage. The story begins on Easter day at Arthur's court in Cardigan, where the courtiers ponder a dilemma. How can King Arthur uphold the custom of the White Stag, in which the hunter who kills the stag may kiss the most beautiful lady present, without creating dissension among his knights about which maiden of the court should be chosen? By the conclusion of the first part, Erec has proven his chivalric valor, punished a discourteous knight, fallen in love with the most beautiful lady, and has rescued Arthur's court from its predicament. All the requirements for a harmonious conclusion seem to have been fulfilled.

But *Erec et Enide* does not end at this easy resting point. In the second part of the romance (roughly two thirds of the narrative), Chrétien explores the conflict between Erec's love for his new bride, now identified as Enide, and his responsibilities as a knight. The young husband is so smitten with love that he forsakes chivalry for the pleasures of the marriage bed; the once-valiant Erec becomes an example of *recreantise*, lazy knighthood, causing tongues to wag about such "shame and sorrow." Without explaining his motives, and to the consternation of his family and townspeople, Erec orders Enide to don her finest gown and fetch her best palfrey and then departs with her for unknown territories. The husband's sole instructions to his wife impose an interdiction that she consistently breaks: if she sees anything remarkable, he orders her never to speak unless spoken to first (2768–71). During the course of their adventures, Enide repeatedly intervenes and speaks up first to protect her husband. When Erec is considered dead after a brutal battle and an evil count tries to force Enide's hand in marriage, her defiant words waken Erec, who valiantly rushes to defend her and slay the count. With this proof of Enide's virtue, Erec pardons Enide and vows to be "at her commandment" forever after.

But before the romance celebrates the couple's reconciliation, Chrétien explores another version of the marriage crisis dramatized within a mysterious castle where a malevolent custom prevails. A possessive lady, whom we see reclining in bed, has persuaded her husband, Maboagrain, to remain at her side and slay any knight approaching the grisly orchard – decorated with stakes displaying the heads of defeated knights – where they have long been enclosed. Erec defeats Maboagrain and his victory unleashes the "Joy of the Court," a festive three-day celebration. The romance concludes with a splendid coronation after the death of Erec's father. Erec dons a magnificent robe, woven by fairies, that depicts the quadrivium of the liberal arts: geometry, music, arithmetic, and astronomy.

Chrétien's first romance thus weaves together an intricate tale that celebrates the highest expression of civilized life at court: chivalry in the service of king and kin; mutual understanding in marriage; aesthetic beauty; and moral education. In some ways, *Erec et Enide* presents Chrétien's most "harmonious" vision of society, as the narrative seems to tie up all the nagging problems it has encountered along the way. Yet even in this first romance, Chrétien invites the audience's reflection. As Erec stands up to tell his story at Arthur's court, the narrator asks if his listeners think he will tell them *why* Erec left with Enide in this first place. He will not do so, he says, because they already know *le voir* (the truth), explained earlier (6467–74). Such an intervention prompts readers to wonder precisely what that "truth" might be and so invites them to reflect on the romance's themes – the relationship between prowess and love, between social duties and private desires, between men and women. In *Erec et Enide*, Chrétien places moral analysis at the core of Arthurian romance.

Cligès: Carrying Romance from Britain to Byzantium and Beyond

Cligès seems an unlikely source for later Arthurian fictions. Much of the action takes place outside Arthur's domain, in Germany and in Constantinople, seat of the Byzantine Empire. The protagonists, of mixed genealogy, are not stock Arthurian figures. Although Cligès boasts Arthurian lineage through his mother, who is Gauvain's sister, his father hails from Greece. Cligès's beloved *amie* and future wife is German, daughter of the emperor. The romance's central drama involves not a threat to Arthur's realm, but rather a crisis of succession in the eastern Christian empire, where the throne has been usurped by Cligès's uncle. Rather than evoke the marvels of the distant Breton past, *Cligès* alludes, more than Chrétien's other romances, to the contemporary political climate, notably to the strained relationship between western Christendom and the eastern Byzantine world, which was both Christian and distinctly "other" in the wake of the Second Crusade (Kinoshita 1996). Chrétien also engages more overtly in literary parody and Ovidian love casuistry than in his other romances.

Yet for all these reasons, *Cligès* helps to define as distinctly as any of Chrétien's works the protean shapes and imaginative potential of future Arthurian romances. The prologue, as we have seen, embraces the practice of *translatio*, the transference of learning from ancient Greece to Rome and Britain. By telling the story of Greek knights at Arthur's court, Chrétien portrays that court as a dynamic social group that absorbs new energies, shifts locations, and exports its ethos to the very limits of the western world, from Wales to Constantinople.

Like *Erec*, *Cligès* has a bipartite structure. It first recounts the tale of the Greek knight, Alexander, heir to the throne of Constantinople, and then that of his son, Cligès. Sent by his father to Arthur's court to become a knight, Alexander displays largesse and performs feats of valor involving ruse and subterfuge for the Breton king. The focus of the second part shifts to Constantinople, scene of conflict and deception. Cligès's uncle, Alis, has usurped the throne but agrees not to marry so that Cligès may eventually inherit the kingdom. When Alis's barons pressure him to become betrothed to Fénice, the German emperor's daughter, Cligès becomes smitten with his uncle's intended bride – a situation that recalls Tristan's love for his uncle's fiancée and eventual wife, Iseut. Chrétien's characters self-consciously and ingeniously recast the tragic *Tristan* plot (Haidu 1968). Fénice asserts that she will not share her body with two men, as Iseut had done (3100–108), and enlists the aid of a magician, Thessala, to create a potion quite unlike the legendary *beivre* that seals the Breton lovers' fate. Here it is the husband who drinks the potion, which makes him falsely imagine that he possesses his wife. In fact, he never touches her, and Fénice remains a virgin until her eventual union with Cligès.

Long sections of the romance are devoted to military exploits in which Cligès defends Fénice on his uncle's behalf against contenders for her hand and later proves his valor – as his father had – at Arthur's court. In these scenes, Chrétien creates chivalric *tours de force* that will become the stock-in-trade of Arthurian romance – the lover who spurs on her flagging knight in battle; the knight who fights his peers incognito. Fénice's plan to sleep with only one man, strikingly different from Iseut's sexual duplicity, involves an elaborate plot that nearly fails. With Thessala's aid, Fénice stages a mock death. Three physicians from Salerno who doubt that Fénice is really dead beat her mercilessly; she endures a martyr's suffering. If some critics see Chrétien taking the high ground by denouncing the lovers in the Tristan legend, others have pointed out that Fénice's and Cligès's solution hardly seems more ethically sound (Grimbert 2005). In a scene that recasts King Mark's discovery of his wife lying beside Tristan, the lovers are discovered enlaced in each other's arms. Alis realizes that he has been duped. Just as Cligès prepares to mobilize the Arthurian world in his defense, his uncle conveniently dies, leaving throne and empress to their rightful heir and partner. Chrétien ends *Cligès* with an ironic explanation that keeps his readers guessing about the romance's moral vision: because of Fénice's deceitful *traïson* (treachery), all future emperors of Constantinople safeguard their wives by locking them up under the protection of eunuchs.

Combining Ovidian love talk, Arthurian chivalry, and the ingenuity of an oriental tale, Chrétien has created a rich literary tapestry in *Cligès*. Transposing his intrigue throughout England, the Continent, and the Byzantine world, Chrétien exhibits the remarkable elasticity of Arthurian fiction. *Cligès* exemplifies the capacity of romance to explore and to create new dimensions – geographical, magical, psychological, ethical, and aesthetic – and to blend them together with surprising twists.

Le Chevalier de la Charrette (Lancelot): The Queen's Lover

At first glance, *Le Chevalier de la Charrette* and *Le Chevalier au Lion*, which may have been written simultaneously, seem poised as diametrical opposites. *Yvain* explores marriage and *Lancelot* adultery; *Yvain* concludes in apparent harmony, and *Lancelot* ends without resolution of its moral crisis. Yet if we viewed these romances as complementary visions of the same troubled courtly universe, we can see that each explores chivalry's potential to restore and to destroy the social order.

The *Lancelot* narrator invites our questions from the start. In the opening lines, the narrator professes to be entirely devoted (*come cil qui est suens antiers*) to his patroness, *ma dame de Champagne*, the countess Marie. Although he claims not to flatter her, he offers praise nonetheless and credits her with providing the *commandement* and the *matiere et sens* for the ensuing work. For Gaston Paris, writing in 1883 in a now-classic article, the *sens* (the meaning or topic) that Marie imposed on Chrétien was the story of Lancelot and Guenevere's *amour courtois*, an adulterous passion that both ennobles and debases the knight (Paris 1883). According to Paris and some others, Chrétien composed this story of adultery reluctantly. Recent critics have tended to read the narrator's ambiguous statements as a clever strategy designed precisely to highlight interpretative problems in the ensuing romance, where questions about Lancelot's identity recur (Bruckner 1986). Should we praise Lancelot as the perfect knight, mock him as a love-struck fool, or blame him as a shameless sinner?

The romance opens at Arthur's court where an evil knight, later identified as Meleagant, son of King Bademagu, menaces King Arthur, who is sadly resigned to his threats. Meleagant challenges a knight to defend the queen's safe passage in exchange for all the prisoners he holds in Gorre. After Kay the Seneschal impulsively requests – and is granted – a rash boon, Arthur reluctantly permits him to escort Guenevere and protect her from Meleagant's advances. Shortly after Arthur's knights realize that Guenevere has been abducted, they encounter an unknown knight riding through the forest on an exhausted horse. The knight accepts the closest horse, rather than the best, offered by Gauvain, who follows him through a series of adventures. Soon Gauvain witnesses the mysterious knight, horseless once again, as he pauses before a cart of the sort used to parade criminals through town. Hesitating for the space of two steps, while Love and Reason debate within his heart, the knight mounts the cart of shame and asks the dwarf who drives it to take him to the queen. Is the mysterious knight's willingness to ride the cart evidence of his selfless love or a sign of his scandalous shame? With this problematic gesture, the quest of the Knight of the Cart begins.

The episodes recounting the knight's journey to the queen seem calculated to heighten the mystery behind this enigmatic, anonymous figure. The knight fights against a flaming lance in a forbidden bed, grazing his skin in the process. He is so overcome with passion as he glimpses the queen from a balcony that he nearly falls and kills himself. He chooses to take the hardest path, that of the Sword Bridge, leaving Gauvain to follow the way of the Water Bridge. He falls so deeply into thought of his lady that he does not hear a knight who forbids him to cross a ford; afterwards, he handily defeats the knight in combat. Perhaps strangest of all is the episode of the "Immodest Damsel," in which the knight accepts hospitality in exchange for agreeing to sleep with his hostess (932–1280). He enters her chamber only to discover that she has staged a mock-rape, forcing him to defend her against her would-be attackers, who are in reality armed men of her own retinue. The Knight of the Cart fights valiantly, but refuses to be seduced by the damsel, who finally lets him sleep by himself and declares him the best knight she has ever known.

Le Chevalier de la Charrette hints at the sexual violence lurking beneath knightly conduct, but stops short of dramatizing it fully. In subsequent scenes during the knight's quest, he is alternately mocked as a shameful coward or praised as the best knight of all: he raises his own tombstone in the Cemetery of the Future, thus fulfilling a prophecy that he will liberate the prisoners of Gorre; crosses through the perilous Stone Passage; conquers a knight who shames him publicly for riding in a cart, and then engages in a lengthy internal monologue between Pity and Generosity over whether to spare the knight or present his head to an aggrieved maiden (Meleagant's sister, as we will learn). Finally, the knight crosses the Sword Bridge on bleeding arms and knees to reach King Bademagu and Guenevere, who observe his suffering from the other side of the river. At a critical moment, as Lancelot fights Meleagant in the presence of Bademagu and Guenevere – almost exactly midway through the narrative – a damsel asks Guenevere who this knight might be and she pronounces his name – Lancelot of the Lake – for the first time in the romance (3660). Lancelot first fights badly as he strains to keep Guenevere in view, but then fights valiantly by positioning Meleagant between himself and the queen. Fearing for his son's life, King Bademagu suspends the combat for one year.

As in other romances where Chrétien delays resolution to explore deeper tensions, the narrative now takes a surprising turn. Guenevere refuses to see the knight who has pursued her so valiantly, and Lancelot leaves in confusion. A painful period of separation ensues, during which the lovers experience mutual fears that the other has died, harbor thoughts of death, or attempt suicide: love is portrayed as abjection. But reconciliation and pardon follow. Guenevere explains that she refused Lancelot because he hesitated slightly before riding in the cart; the knight begs and receives her forgiveness (4484–97) and the promise of a tryst. That night, Lancelot boldly bends the iron bars of Guenevere's bedroom windows. He enters her chamber with bleeding hands, and the lovers at last consummate their passion. The bed's bloody sheets cause Meleagant to blame not Lancelot but Kay for having slept with the queen.

Delay, suspension, and deception mark the last third of the romance. Lancelot defends Guenevere against Meleagant; Bademagu once again puts off the final combat. In a series of false steps, Lancelot is imprisoned in a tower, Gauvain nearly drowns under the Water Bridge, and Guenevere is lured under false pretences back to Arthur's court. The final episodes of the romance explore Lancelot's bonds to a number of women who seek to serve him or constrain him. Lancelot twice fights at his worst at

Guenevere's command before he emerges victorious at the tournament of Noauz. He returns to his tower prison, but is freed by Meleagant's sister. As we learn in the epilogue, Chrétien has charged another clerk, Godefroy de Leigni, with the task of composing the last episodes, which seem more perfunctory than Chrétien's sections. Lancelot finally defeats Meleagant, beneath the gaze of Guenevere, King Arthur, and the other courtiers. The evil scourge has been vanquished, but the victor remains an adulterer and a traitor to his king. The romance explores Lancelot and Guenevere's transgression no further. *Lancelot*'s problematic conclusion, penned by another clerk, begs for elaboration.

Le Chevalier de la Charrette is a milestone in European literary history. It presents Lancelot and Guenevere as adulterous lovers for the first time. It serves as the direct source for a large segment of the thirteenth-century *Lancelot–Grail* Cycle, which sets Chrétien's verse into prose within a much larger context that links Arthurian and Christian history (Lacy 1992–6: vol. 3; see also chapter 14). With Lancelot, Chrétien has created an enigmatic character whose forbidden passion fuels great prowess, who acts as both criminal and savior, and whose devotion to the queen and treasonous actions toward the king foreshadow glory and destruction in the Arthurian realm – all themes that the monumental Vulgate prose romances and their avatars will explore in depth.

Yvain or the Knight of the Lion: Protecting the Fountain

Many critics view *Yvain* as Chrétien's most aesthetically accomplished and morally satisfying romance. Some view it also as highly ironic and paradoxical. Like Chrétien's previous romances, the story follows the exploits of a knight who excels in chivalric prowess and faces challenges in love. *Yvain* demonstrates more programmatically than Chrétien's earlier romances that the individual knight bears responsibility to a greater social world, which includes courtly peers, his wife and countrymen, and the dispossessed, particularly helpless women. At the same time, the romance masterfully displays Chrétien's skills as ironic commentator on the ideals of love and chivalry.

After extolling Arthur and his court as the incarnation of chivalric values and refined behavior in the romance's opening lines (1–17), Chrétien portrays the feast of Pentecost at Carduel as a disorderly event. Arthur has been detained by the queen in bed; Kay mocks Calogrenant, who alone rises to his feet to greet the queen; the courtiers squabble. At Guenevere's insistence, Calogrenant reluctantly recounts a tale not of honor but of shame – his defeat by a fierce red knight at the fountain of Brocéliande, where Calogrenant poured water on a stone to provoke a terrible storm. When Yvain immediately avows to avenge his cousin's dishonor, Kay derides the chivalric gesture, and Yvain chastises Kay for his *mauvaise langue* ("bad language"). In *Yvain*'s opening scene, Chrétien promotes Arthur's court as a Golden Age of chivalry even as he critically observes tensions within the ranks.

Undaunted by Kay's mockery, Yvain sets off alone for Brocéliande. Like Calogrenant did before him, he encounters a vavasour, a beautiful maiden, and a grotesque rustic, and provokes a terrible storm at the fountain. But Yvain conquers Esclados the Red and follows the dying knight to his castle. There, Yvain falls in love with his victim's wife at first sight. A shrewd and quick-thinking maiden whom Yvain has previously befriended offers moral and tactical support. Lunete's clever verbal manipulations convince the wary Laudine to marry the man who has killed her husband, for who would better protect her fountain than the knight who has conquered its guardian? As the fountain's new defender, Yvain defeats Kay, who provokes another storm when Arthur and his knights appear in Brocéliande. The first part of *Yvain* then concludes in a burst of joyous festivity that reaffirms courtly values. Yvain has proved his valor, avenged the disgrace of his cousin, shamed the discourteous seneschal, and married a beautiful noblewoman whose domain he vows to protect.

Yet, as in *Erec*, Chrétien's romance moves beyond an initial harmonious resolution to explore deeper amorous and chivalric tensions. After Gauvain warns Yvain of the dangers of spending too much time with his wife, Yvain requests leave from Laudine, who stipulates that he must return within one year. The knight overstays his term, thus betraying his wife and endangering all those who depend upon the fountain. After being publicly reprimanded for his broken promise, Yvain goes mad and lives like a savage beast in the forest. The rest of the romance explores Yvain's gradual return to humanity, his defense of helpless women, and his ultimate reconciliation with Laudine. Assisting his moral rehabilitation is a lion, whose life Yvain has saved by slaying a menacing serpent – even as he sliced off a bit of the lion's tail (3376–85). The grateful lion remains his constant companion, providing a boost of strength and comic interest at crucial moments. For some critics, the lion symbolizes Yvain's new moral stature; for others, the civilized beast embodies the complexity of chivalric identity in Chrétien's ironic fiction.

The final section of the romance is carefully constructed around interlacing adventures that portray Yvain's expiation of the wrong he has done against his wife and others. Still alienated from his wife and socially marginalized, Yvain must complete his rehabilitation as a knight by continuing to fight on behalf of defenseless women. In the two final, interlaced episodes, as he prepares to defend the younger sister of Noire Espine, who has been wrongly disinherited by her sister, championed by Gauvain, Yvain comes upon three hundred abused, enslaved silkworkers, whom he eventually liberates, at the Castle of Pesme Aventure. The Pesme Aventure scene, the penultimate episode in the romance, works as a kind of *mise en abyme*, or metacommentary, of the romance itself. Reclining on a silk coverlet, the castle's lord and lady listen to their daughter read aloud from a romance. By juxtaposing the leisured readers of romance with the impoverished young women who toil to produce the beautiful articles they enjoy, Chrétien breaks down the divide between fantasy fiction and the "real" world and thus invites his own readers to ponder the ethical dimension of their aesthetic pleasures.

In the final battle, waged on behalf of the sisters of Noire Espine, Gauvain and Yvain fight fiercely, neither realizing that he opposes his companion. Chrétien examines the paradox of two knights who both love and hate each other simultaneously. When Yvain and Gauvain finally recognize each other, both vie to grant the other victory. King Arthur cleverly tricks the older sister into admitting that she has wrongly disinherited her younger sister, who receives her rightful share. Meanwhile, still seeking his wife's pardon, Yvain returns to the Fountain of Brocéliande, where he provokes another storm so that Laudine will be forced to acquiesce. Lunete convinces Laudine that the Knight of the Lion offers the best hope of protection. When she discovers that she has agreed to take back Yvain, Laudine accuses Lunete of having tricked her but remains true to her word, for fear of perjuring herself.

In the end, the narrator assures us that Yvain and Laudine love and cherish each other, much to Lunete's satisfaction. Yet attentive readers cannot forget that the couple's peace has been forged by sleight of hand. Although one could argue that Yvain has earned Laudine's hand by continually championing the cause of defenseless women, neither Laudine nor Yvain voices this ethical principle. Readers must construct for themselves the *sens* of Yvain's moral rehabilitation. As in the companion romance, *Lancelot*, Chrétien's narrative constructs paradoxical situations and creates ambiguous symbols – the cart, the lion – so that readers may question characters' motivations and their social responsibilities.

Le Conte du Graal: Perceval's Education and the Grail

Even in its unfinished state, *Le Conte du Graal* or *Perceval* is Chrétien's longest and most ambitious romance. As he did in *Cligès* and, to a lesser extent, in *Yvain* and *Lancelot*, Chrétien conjoins the stories of two knights – in this case, Perceval and Gauvain. Their adventures in *Le Conte du Graal* form an interlacing narrative structure that will become a prominent feature of later prose romances. By portraying his hero's encounter with the sacred vessel as an enigma, Chrétien's version inspires numerous retellings and creates the Grail as the quintessentially elusive object of chivalric quest.

Chrétien traces Perceval's evolution from a naive country lad into a newly minted knight whose quest leads him to discover unexpected social and spiritual obligations. Gauvain's story depicts Arthur's most valued knight defending himself against charges arising from a troublesome, violent past. The topics that have become Chrétien's hallmarks – chivalric responsibilities and the relationship between men and women at court – are set within a spiritual dimension that is more pronounced than in any of his earlier works. *Perceval* portrays its protagonists' exploits as enigmatic quests whose deepest meanings both characters and readers must struggle to understand.

The story begins in springtime in the Deserted Forest, when a naive young Welshman introduced as the "son of the widow" (*veuve dame*) is dazzled by the appearance of five armed knights whom he first mistakes for devils and then angels. The youth's desire to become a knight deeply distresses his mother: she has lost two sons to chivalry, and her husband was fatally maimed in the thigh. Seeing that she cannot dissuade her last son from leaving, the mother offers essential instructions about social behavior. The over-eager lad observes his mother fall into a faint as he rides away.

Perceval's progress from self-absorbed country bumpkin to socially responsible and spiritually aware knight includes comic missteps, heroic feats, an amorous encounter, missed opportunities, and lessons learned. In his first adventure beyond home, the lad clumsily misapplies his mother's lessons by forcing a kiss upon a maiden who will later be punished by her jealous lover. He proves his valor at Arthur's court by defeating the Red Knight, but only after being taunted by Kay. Perceval then receives lessons in chivalry from Gornement de Goore and valiantly defends the Castle of Beaurepaire for the beautiful maiden Blanchefleur, with whom he falls in love.

After saving Blanchefleur and the denizens of Beaurepaire, the youth wonders at last what has become of his mother and sets off to find her. An attempt to explain the knight's next adventure risks flattening a narrative constructed to convey mystery and wonder; the reader, like Perceval, does not fully understand the significance of events until later in the narrative. Perceval happens upon two men, one of them wounded, who fish from a boat and direct him to a nearby castle. There the maimed king, unable to rise, receives Perceval and bestows a sword upon him. As they speak, the youth witnesses a mysterious procession: a squire passes bearing a bleeding lance, a maiden carries a dazzling vessel (the Grail), and another maiden processes with a silver bowl. As they pass before him, Perceval follows Gornemont's instructions not to talk too much. He refrains from asking questions about what he has seen throughout dinner. By the next morning, the castle is empty and it is too late.

The Welsh knight learns only belatedly that he is somehow implicated in the events he witnessed and that he should have asked questions about what transpired. The next day, he meets a disconsolate maiden weeping over a dead knight, who informs Perceval – as he now identifies himself for the first time in the romance – that his host was the Fisher King, who had been maimed in his thigh. (The resonance with Perceval's father's wound is striking.) The maiden, who is his cousin, laments that Perceval has failed to ask questions about the Grail; had he done so, the king would have been cured. His silence, she explains, arose from his sin toward his mother, who died of sorrow for her son.

After the weeping damsel departs, Perceval continues to fight valiantly, seemingly confronting the consequences of his presumptuous behavior. At the end of this long narrative sequence, Perceval is reunited with the Arthurian court, having proved his prowess, fought for women in distress, and demonstrated his courtly refinement. As in Chrétien's other romances, however, this harmonious resolution is only temporary, prelude to a deeper exploration of social and psychological forces. Perceval must complete his spiritual education. A Hideous Damsel appears at Arthur's court to remind the knight about his failure at the Grail castle: not only will the Fisher King remain an invalid as a result, but women will become widows and orphans and the land will

remain barren. Haunted by his failure to inquire about the Grail and by his unkind-
ness to his mother, Perceval must return to the Grail castle, to learn the mystery of
its relationship to him.

The narrative here bifurcates to follow the path of Gauvain, whose adventures both
contrast with and run parallel to those of Perceval. Gauvain, too, is haunted by his
past, but he is more directly responsible for deeds that are more violent. He defends
himself against a murder charge, champions a sweet young maiden in a tournament,
and dallies with the daughter of a lord whom he has slain, whose son has offered him
hospitality. Gauvain's adventures in *Le Conte du Graal*, which tell a darker tale of
mature knighthood, occupy nearly as much as space as those of Perceval.

The romance then returns to Perceval, whose pursuit of chivalry has removed him
from the path to spiritual truth. A group of penitent pilgrims remind him of Christ's
story, from Virgin birth to the Christ's passion. Weeping and on his knees, Perceval
confesses to a hermit: he has forgotten God, pursued evil, and failed to inquire about
the Lance and the Grail when he saw them. The hermit explains that it was Perceval's
sin in abandoning his mother that caused him to hold his tongue; had his mother not
prayed for her son, he would have died.

Perceval learns that the *riche roi* ("rich king") served by the Grail is the hermit's
brother, and brother of Perceval's mother, which means that both the hermit and the
Grail king are Perceval's uncles. The Fisher King is the king's son and thus Perceval's
cousin. The Grail is a "holy vessel" that carries a "host" which has sustained the Grail
king for twelve years. Although Chrétien eventually links the Grail to Eucharistic
practice, he neither explicitly identifies the Grail as the vessel that collected Christ's
blood, nor connects the lance to Longinus's sword, as later romancers will do (Mahoney
2000: 16–18). Chrétien's Grail functions primarily as the catalyst for Perceval's spiritual quest rather than as a relic embodying Christian history.

Imposing penance upon Perceval, the hermit provides him with a set of religious
teachings, his third set of instructions. Perceval's confession and repentance on Good
Friday mirror Christ's own suffering. The sinner takes communion on Sunday, a day
of spiritual renewal. Chrétien's incomplete romance thus recounts the knight's evolution from a naive simpleton, impetuous and rude; to an accomplished knight, who
protects Blanchefleur and avenges the laughing damsel; and finally to a penitent
Christian knight. Yet Perceval's integration of his social, chivalric, and spiritual selves
remains an open question. The final episodes of Chrétien's romance once again follow
Gauvain's adventures, which focus on worldly rather than spiritual matters. The
unfinished *Le Conte du Graal* breaks off in the midst of Gauvain's pursuit of several
intersecting chivalric engagements and his encounter with his mother, grandmother,
and sister, to whom he has yet to reveal his identity.

Perceval extends and embellishes a pattern that Chrétien's earlier romances have
developed: the bifurcation and branching out of multiple stories; the suspension of
explanations; the mix of the familiar and the marvelous. By highlighting family
secrets and moral failure, by intermingling heroic predestination with imminent
destruction, and by raising more questions than answers about the enigmatic Grail,

Chrétien's *Conte du Graal* inspired future romancers to pursue Arthurian fiction along diverse and mysterious paths (Groos & Lacy 2002).

Chrétien's Legacy

Chrétien's impact on future courtly narratives was immense (Lacy et al. 1987–8). His romances were copied in collections of Arthuriana throughout the thirteenth and fourteenth centuries. In addition to inspiring four continuations of *Perceval* and the *Lancelot–Grail* Cycle, Chrétien's romances also influenced dozens of thirteenth-century verse romances, among them romances that explored the character of Gauvain, whose reputation became increasingly problematic (Schmolke-Hasselmann 1998; Busby 1980). Chrétien's work further inspired translations and adaptations in English, German, Dutch, Norse, Welsh, and Swedish, including Wolfram von Eschenbach's *Parzival* and the anonymous northern English *Yvain and Gawain*. In France, the popularity of Chrétien's original verse narratives faded in the wake of the Vulgate Cycle's enormous popularity and the rise of other forms, such as the *Roman de la Rose* or the so-called *romans réalistes*. His work did not disappear completely, however. There were late renderings of *Cligès* and *Erec* into prose for the fifteenth-century Burgundian court and sixteenth-century prose renderings of *Le Conte du Graal* and *Le Chevalier au Lion*. Among twentieth-century adaptations, Eric Rohmer's *Perceval le Gallois* (1978) enacts a brilliant cinematic interpretation of Chrétien's text, displaying sensitivity to many details of Chrétien's intrigue in their medieval context as it evokes the romance's underlying spiritual mystery.

But Chrétien's legacy encompasses far more than those works for which his romances were a direct source. Chrétien's rhetorical art and his subtle irony established Arthurian fiction as a sophisticated medium for reflection about social identity and chivalric ethics. In five remarkably diverse, distinctive romances, Chrétien created a vast imaginative space encompassing history and fiction, the marvelous and the real, love casuistry and violent combat, hidden pasts and ominous or glorious futures, Celtic legends and Christian teachings, proverbs and wordplay, comedy and wisdom, east and west, enterprising women and callous or courageous knights, adulterers and wise men, the bleeding lance, the broken sword, and the Grail. Chrétien's Old French romances constitute a major cornerstone – or, perhaps more appropriately, a marvelously regenerating fountain – for future Arthurian fictions.

PRIMARY SOURCES

Baumgartner, E. (ed.) (2000). *Pyramus et Thisbé, Narcisse, Philomena: trois contes du XIIe siècle français imités d'Ovide*. Paris: Gallimard.

Chrétien de Troyes (1994). *Chrétien de Troyes: Romans, suivis des "Chansons", avec, en appendice,* "Philomena." La Pocothèque. Paris: Librairie Générale Française.

Fritz, J.-M. (ed. trans.) (1992). *Chrétien de Troyes. Erec et Enide*. Paris: Librairie Générale Française.

Hult, D. F. (ed. trans.) (1994). *Chrétien de Troyes.*
Le Chevalier au Lyon ou Le Roman d'Yvain. Paris:
Librairie Générale Française.

Méla, C. (ed. trans.) (1990). *Chrétien de Troyes. Le*
Conte du Graal ou Le Roman de Perceval. Paris:
Librairie Générale Française.

Méla, C. (ed.) (1992). *Chrétien de Troyes. Le Cheva-*
lier de la Charrette ou Le Roman de Lancelot. Paris:
Librairie Générale Française.

Méla, C. & Collet, O. (eds trans) (1994). *Chrétien de*
Troyes. Cligès. Paris: Librairie Générale Française.

Staines, D. (trans.) (1990). *The complete romances of*
Chrétien de Troyes. Bloomington, IN: Indiana
University Press.

References and Further Reading

Bruckner, M. (1986). An interpreter's dilemma:
Why are there so many interpretations of Chrétien's *Chevalier de la Charrette? Romance Philology*,
40, 159–80.

Busby, K. (1980). *Gauvain in Old French literature*,
2nd edn. Amsterdam: Rodopi.

Busby, K., Nixon, T., Stones, A., & Walters, L.
(eds) (1993). *Les Manuscrits de Chrétien de Troyes*
[The manuscripts of Chrétien de Troyes], 2 vols.
Amsterdam: Rodopi.

Duggan, J. J. (2001). *The romances of Chrétien*
de Troyes. New Haven, CT: Yale University
Press.

Grimbert, J. T. (2005). *Cligès* and the *chansons*: A
slave to love. In N. J. Lacy & J. T. Grimbert
(eds), *A companion to Chrétien de Troyes.* Cambridge: Brewer, pp. 120–36.

Groos, A. & Lacy, N. J. (eds) (2002). *Perceval/Par-*
zival: A casebook. London: Routledge.

Haidu, P. (1968). *Aesthetic distance in Chrétien de*
Troyes: Irony and comedy in Cligès *and* Perceval.
Geneva: Droz.

Kelly, D. (1976). *Chrétien de Troyes: An analytic*
bibliography. London: Grant & Cutler.

Kelly, D. (2002). *Chrétien de Troyes: An analytic*
bibliography. Supplement 1. Woodbridge: Boydell
& Brewer.

Kinoshita, S. (1996). The poetics of *trans-*
latio: French–Byzantine relations in Chrétien
de Troyes's *Cligès. Exemplaria*, 8(2), 315–
54.

Krueger, R. L. (1983). *Women readers and the ideol-*
ogy of gender in Old French verse romance. Cambridge: Cambridge University Press.

Lacy, N. J. (gen. ed.) (1992–6). *Lancelot–Grail: The*
Old French Arthurian Vulgate and Post-Vulgate in
translation, 5 vols. New York: Garland.

Lacy, N. J. & Grimbert, J. T. (eds) (2005). *A com-*
panion to Chrétien de Troyes. Cambridge: Brewer.

Lacy, N. J., Kelly, D., & Busby, K. (eds) (1987–8).
The legacy of Chrétien de Troyes, 2 vols. Amsterdam: Rodopi.

Mahoney, D. (2000). Introduction and comparative table of medieval texts. In D. Mahoney
(ed.), *The Grail: A casebook.* New York: Garland,
pp. 1–102.

McCash, J. H. (2005). Chrétien's patrons. In N. J.
Lacy & J. T. Grimbert (eds), *A companion to*
Chrétien de Troyes. Cambridge: Brewer, pp.
15–25.

Paris, G. (1883). Études sur les romans de la Table
Ronde: Lancelot du Lac, II: *Le Conte de la Char-*
rette. Romania, 12, 459–534.

Schmolke-Hasselmann, B. (1998). *The evolution of*
Arthurian romance: The verse tradition from Chré-
tien to Froissart (trans. M. & R. Middleton).
Cambridge: Cambridge University Press.

Vitz, E. B. (1999). *Orality and performance in early*
French romance. Woodbridge: Brewer.

Walters, L. (1985). Le rôle du scribe dans
l'organisation des manuscrits de Chrétien de
Troyes. *Romania*, 106, 303–25.

12

The Allure of Otherworlds: The Arthurian Romances in Germany

Will Hasty

Arthurian romance took hold in Germany in the latter decades of the twelfth century. The reception seems to have been primarily a literary and literate one, based on romances produced by French authors, particularly the pioneer Chrétien de Troyes. The German reception was doubtless facilitated by the presence along and to the west of the Rhine of powerful noble families – such as the imperial Hohenstaufen – who were in a position to continue the cultivation of the stories of Arthur as a literary tradition. There are indications that Arthurian romance was produced early on in both Dutch and German, and romances continued to be produced in both these languages into the thirteenth century. At the same time, Arthurian narratives continued to be disseminated to the east, eventually leading to works in non-Germanic languages such as Czech (for a general overview of the dissemination of the Arthurian narratives in Dutch- and German-speaking regions, and from Germany to the east, see the introduction by Jackson and Ranawake [2000]; on the Czech reception in the kingdom of Bohemia, see Thomas [2000]).

If the origins of Arthurian romance involved initial translations from Celtic languages such as Welsh and Breton into French, continuing developments in Dutch and German increase the color of the linguistic kaleidoscope. Once it took hold of German-speaking regions, Arthurian romance did not let go. It continued to be cultivated intensively and on a wide scale for several centuries, before being supplanted by different literary forms, themes, and topics shortly before the turbulent times of the Reformation, only to be brought back to the forefront of literary, artistic, and political developments of the nineteenth century. German Romanticism in its various manifestations made uses of Arthurian romance that can be understood as specific modern elaborations of possibilities for development that were intrinsic in the Arthurian narrative materials from the beginning (this is to say, German Romantic authors and artists did, in their own way, what the medieval authors did, according to the argument to be advanced in this chapter, which was to develop the creative potential inherent in the Arthurian narrative materials).

The initial German reception and elaboration of Arthurian romance occurred during a time traditionally designated as the *Stauferzeit*, the time of the reign of the Hohenstaufen emperors, an age of cultural blossoming and the cultivation of literature in the German vernacular in a Middle High German literary idiom, the relative uniformity of which shows the effort on the part of authors to avoid regional dialect variations. As so often in the history of Germany, particularly during the centuries in which it formed part of the Holy Roman Empire, the overall political and cultural picture was very complex, despite all appearances of cultural unity. An emperor such as Frederick I ("Barbarossa," 1122–90) could try to use the idea of knighthood – during a time when Arthurian romance was becoming the most popular literary articulation of it – to increase his political stature, as at the Whitsun festival at Mainz in 1184, at which his sons were knighted (Fleckenstein 1972), and Barbarossa may have succeeded to some extent in capturing in his person some of the allure of Arthurian royalty and knighthood as depicted in the romances, but a glorious alliance such as this of politics and knighthood remained, at best, a thin veneer, however immediately productive it may have been for the generation of romances. The idea of a chivalric world over which Barbarossa – perhaps in the model of King Arthur – presided was contradicted by the actual political state of affairs in the German kingdom and "Roman" Empire. Barbarossa contended with adversaries on all sides, with questionable lasting success. His continuing disputes with the papacy were a continuation of the investiture controversy, which, although the issue of selecting bishops and investing them with their insignia had already been formally arranged, continued in the form of strained and often hostile relations between emperors and popes, each believing themselves to have a legitimate claim to supreme worldly and spiritual power. Barbarossa's dream of empire placed great importance on the cities of northern Italy, but these regarded him as a foreign aggressor and resisted his attempts to subdue them. Finally, and perhaps most fatefully, Barbarossa had to contend with the unruly German princes. He and his successors conceded numerous rights to them, in exchange for their support of his endeavors south of the Alps, which, combined with his wars against rebellious princes and long absences from Germany, had the overall effect of strengthening the centrifugal tendencies in Germany. Local lords grew more powerful at the expense of imperial authority, a pattern that would become more extreme under Barbarossa's grandson Frederick II (1194–1250).

Emperors, popes, and feudal princes in Germany were all engaged in their own ways in the pursuit and maintenance of power, a power that was articulated in the political rhetoric of the Holy Roman Empire as a supreme one, involving both worldly and spiritual dimensions. It is not surprising in such a broader political situation to find a fascination with Arthurian romance, in which Arthur, along with his knights and court, seemed to be imbued with power. Beyond the court of Arthur are the dangerous yet enticing "otherworlds" of adventure, promising love, fame, and riches, and thus in their own way evocative of power. It is arguably at this broader level of identification, rather than in any more specific propagandistic or political use, that the German nobility engaged and developed the Arthurian narrative material (Jackson

& Ranawake 2000: 4–5). It is telling that none of the romances of the first German authors contain a direct and explicit dedication or homage to a political sovereign. The prologue of Hartmann von Aue's *Iwein* pays a tribute to Arthur himself, rather than to any sovereign of his own time:

> Swer an rehte güete
> wendet sîn gemüete,
> dem volget saelde und êre.
> des gît gewisse lêre
> künec Artûs der guote,
> der mit ritters muote
> nâch lobe kunde strîten.
> (Benecke & Lachmann
> 1968: lines 1–7)

He who turns his mind to true goodness will be attended by happiness and honor. Good King Arthur, who knew how to fight laudably and chivalrously, gives clear proof of this. He lived in such a beautiful way that he wore the crown of honor in his time, and his name does still. (Lawson, in Tobin et al. 2001)

Perhaps due to linguistic, cultural, and political obstacles to a more immediately practical employment of and identification with Arthur and his age, the German poets tap into and develop the marvelous aspects that had been part of the Arthurian narrative materials from the beginning. In a place and time in which the relationships between worldly (secular) and religious (spiritual) aspects of life were complicated, interconnected, and frequently contentious (as in the struggle over investitures), it is not surprising to see the generation of and preoccupation with "otherworlds" that can be construed as specifically literary endeavors to negotiate and give alternative form to these relationships. Otherworlds in the German Arthurian romances might be regarded as fictional constructions – which are made possible by the marvelous and adaptable narrative materials associated with Arthur (as opposed to the "historically" and generically more fixed, and hence less adaptable, narrative materials associated with figures such as Alexander the Great, Aeneas, and others) – which arise in a new creative process that is at least in part responding to the situation of medieval aristocratic people, who need and want to balance their love of worldly wealth, power, and splendor with their desire eventually to experience the bliss of the heavenly afterlife (a bliss they can experience, according to some monastic voices, only by renouncing their worldly involvements). In Germany, the Arthurian romances strive for a balance that may, indeed, only be achievable in the generation of fictional otherworlds ("fictional" because they are alternatives to the officially sanctioned and hence "true" Christian "otherworld" of the heavenly kingdom). These otherworlds can iron out and overcome differences and tensions between worldly and spiritual domains that remain intractable, contentious, and to some degree insoluble outside of (this new fictional) literature.

There is an identifiable movement in the Arthurian romances of Germany in the direction of an otherworld with a quasi-religious significance, the otherworld of the Grail, but this more explicitly (but by no means orthodox) religious otherworld, which becomes supremely important in the German reception and formation of the Arthurian narrative materials, builds upon and flushes out earlier depictions of otherworlds that are more overtly worldly and magical. Magical aspects of German Arthurian otherworlds are able to build on the marvelous component that has formed a significant part of the Latin and Welsh literary transmission of the Arthurian materials. The wondrous elements inserted into the *Annales Cambriae* ("Annals of Wales"), the pseudo-histories, and Welsh tales such as *Culwch and Olwen* seemed both to provide narrative material, and at the same time to extend a poetic license to later authors to experiment with the transmitted material and also to generate entirely new, marvelous figures and places, the veracity of which – in a world still largely shaped by revealed religion with its own quite marvelous characteristics – could not be rejected out of hand.

Already in the first significant Arthurian romance, Hartmann von Aue's *Erec*, there is a clear effort to develop a marvelous otherworld, and the manner in which the poet proceeds shows his creative rendering of a new otherworld to be closely related to the production of fiction (here understood as the creative rendering of an alternative world). In an extensive independent elaboration of a passage in the *Erec et Enide* of Chrétien de Troyes, upon which he is basing himself, Hartmann describes the origins and characteristics of the marvelous horse that is given to Enite shortly before the end of the romance, after her reconciliation with her husband Erec. In an independent elaboration of a passage in his source, Hartmann explains the marvelous characteristics of this horse by saying that it is not from "here" (presumably the real world in which he is narrating his tale). Instead, the dwarf-like king Guivreiz took the marvelous horse from a giant in a fictional place (invented by Hartmann) that, in view of the wondrous creatures inhabiting it, must be viewed as an otherworld. Corresponding to the marvelous aspects of its place of origin are the characteristics of the horse, as well as the horse's saddle and saddle-blanket, upon the description of which Hartmann dwells in a lengthy excursus that exceeds the length of the corresponding text in Chrétien's work twelvefold. Hartmann depicts the marvelous horse as the embodiment of perfect form and grace, and he covers the saddle and saddle-blanket with depictions showing his knowledge of medieval science (specifically the four elements, along with the different kinds of creatures that occupy them) and his knowledge of literary culture (the saddle bears engravings of the love stories of Aeneas and Dido, and Piramus and Thisbe).

An observant member of the audience, attuned to the medieval love of allegory, might have been in a position to suspect that the depiction of this horse, and the otherworld from which it was taken, are actually intended, self-reflectively, to highlight Hartmann's creation of narrative, and the learning that both makes possible and "authorizes" this creative production. Hartmann's creation of the otherworldly horse and its otherworldly origins occurs at an auspicious moment in the narration. While Enite earlier had to trouble herself with the demeaning task of looking after the horses of her husband Erec during an earlier, much more troubled, point in the narrative, here, close to the end of the work, Enite mounts a "horse" that Hartmann has crafted in a manner that is consistent with and elaborates upon the marvelous elements inherent in the Arthurian narrative materials, and that at the same time demonstrates Hartmann's poetic ability and creativity. The otherworldly horse thus constructed lifts Enite up, places her atop the world in a position of prestige and honor, and thus provides a moment of poetic "transcendence," although at this point in the German Arthurian tradition, it is a transcendence that is more strictly secular and magical than religious. In his first Arthurian romance, Hartmann engages his own poetic talent with the allure and power of otherworlds that are inherent in the Arthurian narrative materials in order to achieve, in the case of Enite's restoration to her rightful position of honor, a specifically, and typically literary (and Arthurian), moment of redemption.

Hartmann's final Arthurian romance, *Iwein* (c. 1200), continues the tendency already visible in *Erec* to employ otherworlds in ways that empower the figures who are able to align themselves in different ways with their extraordinary characteristics and powers. In one respect, one could speak of the poet Hartmann empowering himself poetically, albeit in a different way from that in *Erec*. This occurs in the above-cited verses from *Iwein*, and in verses that Hartmann adds later on (independent of his source, Chrétien de Troyes), in which the narrator Hartmann considers the advantages of living during Arthur's ideal age, as opposed to the imperfect age in which he lives, before deciding that he prefers the latter after all:

> ichn wolde dô niht sîn gewesen,
> daz ich nû niht enwaere,
> dâ uns noch mit ir maere
> sô rehte wol wesen sol.
> (Benecke & Lachmann 1968:
> lines 54–57)

I wouldn't want to have lived then and not now, since we can enjoy the story of what those knights did. (Lawson, in Tobin et al. 2001)

Walter Haug argues that Hartmann, in these verses, turns the rhetorical *laudatio temporis acti* on its head. Hartmann states that he would not have wanted to live during the time of Arthur, for then he would not be living in the present (i.e. the time of his literary performance) and thus in a position to convey the story of Arthur to his contemporaries so they can have their beneficial effect. The otherworld in question here is that of King Arthur, and it is justifiably understood as such by virtue of its radical difference from the historical times in which Hartmann is performing his romances. By means of his strategic manipulation of rhetorical tropes, Hartmann positions himself as the one who will bring the otherworld of Arthur, with all of its power and salutary promise, into relation with his own, thus finding another way to empower himself as a poet.

Within Hartmann's narrative, the hero Iwein is also empowered by virtue of his relationship with the otherworld of his initial adventure at the spring and its inhabitants, particularly his wife-to-be, Laudine. The otherworld of Iwein's first adventure is, at first glance, a pleasance, the rhetorically determined rudimentary landscape consisting of a tree and a spring. Scholarly studies have suggested that this place, with all of its marvelous characteristics – particularly the storm that is unleashed when water is poured upon the stone, and the birds that fill the tree and sing more beautifully than ever after the storm has passed – are in all likelihood part of a more archaic story that was already part of the narrative materials as reworked by Chrétien and Hartmann. Hartmann's text takes steps to align the otherworld more closely with the lady Laudine, whose otherworldly beauty captivates Iwein's mind and heart. Iwein's chivalric action, designed primarily to restore his honor after the earlier disparagements of Keie at Arthur's court, may be said to "win" the otherworldly love of Laudine, though it becomes clear that some aspect of this love remains independent of and possibly even contrary to chivalric concerns. When Iwein stays away from his wife too long while adventuring in the company of his Arthurian compatriot Gawein, Laudine formally and publicly withdraws her love from him, causing Iwein to lose his mind, run like a madman into the wilderness, and live for a period of time like a wild beast. This reaction shows the otherworldly love to be much more than a prize won in chivalric action; its allure has made it absolutely essential to Iwein's stability and happiness. The fact that Iwein loses his otherworldly love due to an overemphasis on chivalry is the most overt demonstration that love is not completely reducible to chivalric concerns (i.e. love as a prize of combat), that an essential aspect of it escapes the conventional concerns of Arthur's court, and that in its connection with its otherworldly place of origin, this love remains essentially "other."

Iwein eventually recovers his sanity and chivalric identity, and begins what could be regarded as a quest for his lost otherworldly love. His questing eventually brings him back to the otherworldly realm of his beloved lady, but in the meantime he has become an *other* person, the added dimension of his personality corresponding to the otherworld of which he will definitively take possession. Though, on the surface, he returns to the land of the spring as an invader, resolved to take it by force, or *mit gewalte*, as in his initial adventure there, the successful culmination depends upon his alter ego as the "Knight with the Lion." It was with this appellation, and not his proper name, that Iwein positioned himself to recover his lost otherworld, by virtue of the many adventures following his restoration to sanity, particularly his rescue of the lady-servant Lunete, at the culmination of which Laudine declared her indebtedness to the "Knight with the Lion" and stated that a lady who could be angry with a man like this must be weak in the head. When an unknown invader (who unbeknownst to her is Iwein) enters her kingdom at the end of the romance, Laudine is persuaded by Lunete to call for the aid of the Knight with the Lion (who, also unbeknownst to her, is also Iwein) who had been so helpful to them before. Lunete, who knows the knight's true identity and is eager to orchestrate a reconciliation, brings her lady to agree to swear an oath that she will do all she can to restore the lost favor of the rescuer knight's lady to him, not realizing that she is committing herself with this oath to reconcile *herself* with Iwein.

The supreme goal that is eventually won by the hero's questing is a lady and her love, but the manner in which this lady and her love and the questing for them are depicted contains many of the elements that we will see later on in Wolfram's Grail quest. The otherworldly goal (Laudine's love) is an "existential" one, the achievement of which is essential for the integrity of the hero's identity. The otherworld is replete with marvelous objects (the vessel used to pour water on the stone, magically triggering the storm and subsequent events, might be seen as a prototype of the Grail), and once the hero has been there and experienced its marvels and the beauty of its inhabitants, the need to return is overwhelming and brings about a life change. In both *Erec* and *Iwein*, otherworlds are associated with marvels, magic, love, and power. In these romances, the heroes and the narratives proceed in terms of engagements and accommodations with otherworlds in which the laws of nature and the chivalric world are to some degree suspended. These otherworlds also provided – and perhaps even necessitated – a consideration of their status or "truth value." It is not doubted that the specifics of the horse that is given to Enite to ride and the admirable qualities of the Arthurian world that Hartmann brings to his audience for its betterment are "true," but the marvelous narrative materials produced by authors such as Hartmann in their creative engagement with and elaboration of Arthurian otherworlds is novel enough to require the German authors at least to anticipate the objection that significant parts of their stories are "lies," and who would want to waste one's time with lies? In the excursus on Enite's horse and saddle, Hartmann reinforces the truth value of his otherworldly depictions with appeals to his own education and artistic prowess. Wolfram von Eschenbach, Germany's greatest author of romance, while holding fast to the truth value of his otherworldly Grail kingdom, proceeds in a quite different way.

Wolfram's Grail romance *Parzival* is the most significant poetic achievement in the German language during the Middle Ages. Though the literary production in the German vernacular in the twelfth and thirteenth centuries is vast and multifarious, many of the most significant authors before and after Wolfram seem in some way or another either to be setting the stage for his brilliant literary achievement, or commenting or taking issue with it, which, even when an element of criticism is present, still documents the centrality of Wolfram's *magnum opus* (Jackson & Ranawake 2000: 12). Though it is perhaps, in the first instance, a Grail romance, Wolfram's romance is also a thoroughly Arthurian one. The strong connections to the Arthurian world are maintained by virtue of the integration of Wolfram's second hero, Gawan, whose more strictly worldly adventures are depicted with a dedication and relish that indicate that the Arthurian paragon does not fall far behind the main character Parzival in the heart and mind of the poet.

The adventures of Gawan have been seen as an extension into Wolfram's romance of the more strictly secular concerns of Hartmann's *Erec* and *Iwein*. As in the adventures of Wolfram's predecessor, Gawan's adventures eventually lead him in the direction of an otherworld replete with magical objects and with sorcery. In this case it is the *schastel merveile*, or "castle of marvels," the very name of which highlights its other-worldly character, into which Gawan must enter and in which he must withstand great tests of strength and valor that would kill a lesser man. In contrast to earlier otherworlds (such as the land of the spring in Hartmann's *Iwein*), the castle of marvels is an otherworld on account of a magical spell placed upon it by the sorcerer Clinschor. One of the consequences of this spell is that four queens and four hundred young ladies are being held captive there and are unable to join the Arthurian court where they rightfully belong (presumably in order to contribute to the "joy of the court" that is thematized at the end of *Erec*). Gawan successfully engages with this nefarious magical otherworld and breaks the power of the magic holding the women in their unnaturally isolated position, and much of the remainder of the Gawan plot pertains to the gradual reintegration of these women into Arthur's court (a by-product of which is the setting aside of the trial by combat between Gawan and Gramoflanz, when one of the liberated women, Itonje, turns out to be Gawan's sister and Gramoflanz's lover, thus making the fight between them highly undesirable).

Much like Parzival, Wolfram's second and more strictly Arthurian hero Gawan plays an ultimately redemptive role, liberating the inhabitants of the otherworldly castle of marvels from their suffering and, by breaking the magic spell that has frag-mented normal courtly life by holding significant figures in isolation, he enables the Arthurian court to become healthy and whole. Parzival will achieve a similar goal at the Grail castle, though by virtue of the religious element, never before as clearly and completely articulated in the Arthurian romances, an unprecedented literary and ideological amalgamation of the model of the magical otherworld and the Christian heavenly hereafter is achieved. It is important to recognize that Wolfram reframes his source by rendering and vastly expanding Gawan's adventure at the otherworldly castle of marvels. (The differences between Chrétien's *Perceval* and Wolfram's romance, even where the latter appears to be following the outlines of the story of the former, are vast; the adventures of Gawan just described occur in the extensive concluding section of Wolfram's romance, which has no correspondent in the French poet's work.) Here as elsewhere, it is in the depiction of otherworlds that authors are able to experi-ment with and develop the dynamic narrative potential of the Arthurian narratives.

It is in the sections of Wolfram's romance dealing with Parzival that the narrative possibilities of Arthurian otherworlds achieve their most striking and original devel-opment in the direction of a quasi-Christian domain. In the French source, the spaces connected to the Grail are more explicitly orthodox, as in the episode in which the tearful hero meets and confers with his uncle, at a chapel in the presence of a priest and a cleric. In Wolfram's version, the otherworlds associated with the Grail seem to a much greater degree to have retained aspects of their originally pagan, magical origins. During Parzival's first visit to the Grail court, the Grail appears not as a neutral serving platter (however significant the latent symbolism may be), but rather as a horn of plenty, serving up all the food and drink the Grail community desires. The Grail as cornucopia is one of the significant ways in which Wolfram differs from his French predecessor in rendering the otherworld of the Grail; whether he here follows a lost source, possibly with ultimately Celtic origins, is impossible to say (Loomis 1963). The space of the court does not possess the regularity and simplicity of Chrétien's depiction of the uncle's quasi-eremitic existence, which seems to approximate to conventional religious institutions and rituals. If the Grail was originally a pagan vessel, and its otherworld something that either preceded or was oblivious to Christianity, Chrétien's rendering of it makes it a clearly Christian space which is not really an "otherworld" in the traditional Arthurian sense (i.e. including the worldly, magical element), but rather an Arthurian version of the quite conventional, official "otherworldliness" that is orthodox Christian practice.

By contrast, Wolfram's romance contains no priests, clerics, chapels, or tearful contrition on the part of its hero. In his first confrontation with the Grail, this object appears first and foremost as a marvelous object with wondrous nourishing capacities, and the narrator Wolfram, in the middle of his description of it, shows he is quite aware of the degree to which his creative manipulation – whereby "creative" does not exclude the innovative combination and elaboration of different available sources – probes the limits of believability:

> man sagte mir, diz sag ouch ich
> ûf iwer ieslîches eit,
> daz vorem grâle waere bereit
> (sol ich des iemen triegen,
> sô müezt ir mit mir liegen)
> swâ nâch jener bôt die hant,
> daz er al bereite vant,
> spîse warm, spîse kalt,
> spîse niwe unt dar zuo alt,
> daz zam und daz wilde.
> esn wurde nie kein bilde,
> beginnet maneger sprechen.
> der wil sich übel rechen:
> wan der grâl was der saelden fruht,
> der werlde süeze ein sölh genuht,
> er wac vil nâc gelîche
> als man saget von himelrîche.
> (Lachmann 1965: 238,
> lines 8–24)

Now I have been told and I am telling you on the oath of each single one of you – so that if I am deceiving anyone you must all be lying with me – that whatever one stretched out one's hand for in the presence of the Grail, it was waiting, one found it all ready and to hand – dishes warm, dishes cold, new fangled dishes and old favourites, the meat of beasts both tame and wild . . . "There never was any such thing!" many will be tempted to say. But they would be misled by their ill temper, for the Grail was the very fruit of bliss, a cornucopia of the sweets of this world and such that it scarcely fell short of what they tell us of the Heavenly Kingdom. (Hatto 1980)

In this passage Wolfram's original and unique depiction of the Grail is interwoven with what has been regarded as a literary-theoretical consideration concerning the truth value of his depiction. The highly sensual "worldliness" of Wolfram's Grail – with its appeals to the senses of vision, smell, and taste – is consistent with Wolfram's chivalric and worldly conception of the Grail material more generally. Especially noteworthy here is the relatively simple manner – in comparison to the more complex observations of Hartmann regarding Enite's horse and its provenance – in which the "truth" of Wolfram's original (and fictive) rendering of the Grail is vouchsafed. Wolfram, in contrast to Hartmann and Chrétien before him (see Groos 1995, who distinguishes Wolfram's complex and "carnivalesque" Grail story from the earlier, relatively static "clerical narratives" of Chrétien de Troyes and Hartmann von Aue), forgoes lengthy appeals to clerical learning, in a manner that is consistent with his (probably also fictitious) self-rendering as an unlettered knight (given that it is quite obvious that Wolfram was very learned), as something that might authorize or legitimize his Grail narration.

Instead, Wolfram pursues two different, but related strategies. The first is to commit his audience to the truth of his narration by swearing an oath, not for himself, but on behalf of his audience, so that if Wolfram lies, his entire audience has perjured itself. Perhaps aware that this maneuver is not substantial (or perhaps serious) enough to persuade possible skeptics, he gives a representative voice to one of the skeptics (*esn wurde nie kein bilde* – "there never was any such thing!"), before playing his trump card in the final verses of the cited passage: although a very sensual, worldly object, its truth (and indeed its very nature, as a kind of heaven on earth) is of the same nature as that of the heavenly kingdom, the truth of which no one in his right mind would doubt (Stevens 1999: 108–9). The question of the truth of Wolfram's narrative about the Grail (and by extension his narrative as a whole, which hinges on the Grail) seems to be settled at this point (without a lengthy excursus on his authorial learning and prowess, which was the case with Hartmann, but would be out of character for Wolfram's narrator figure), and the narration of Parzival's fateful visit to the Grail otherworld, his failure to ask the redeeming question, and his subsequent and ultimately successful adventures to recover the Grail he apparently lost, can now be continued.

The Grail is described somewhat differently by Parzival's hermit uncle Trevrizent later in the work. Though its marvelous, sensual characteristics are played down to some degree, and its function as a communication device, whereby divine commandments are transmitted to the Grail community, is stressed, the tone of this episode in Wolfram's romance is starkly different from the equivalent and above-mentioned episode in Chrétien's text involving Perceval, his uncle, a priest, and a cleric. Throughout this episode, as throughout Wolfram's Grail narrative, Wolfram's Grail hero remains proudly and staunchly chivalric. He does not seem to experience the same internal emotional disturbance and contrition, visible externally in the profuse tears the French Grail knight weeps. Parzival continues to advocate the value of chivalric combat in the service of a lady, and for the purpose of winning her love, and it is with these chivalric values that Parzival eventually returns to and takes possession of the Grail and the otherworldly castle and realm in which it is housed.

Like Hartmann and Chrétien before him, though to a much greater degree, Wolfram avails himself of the malleable, dynamic, and formative potential of the Arthurian narrative materials, and in particular those located within or at the thresholds of marvelous otherworlds, in order to render a unique conception of the Grail, and a related conception of the Grail quest, which do not involve a turn away from the chivalric life and the world, but rather their continuation to the point where they are endowed with a quasi-spiritual, religious value. The new "religious" status of knighthood posited by Wolfram is not "orthodox," nor is it a literary rendering modeled on the historical Knights Templar (which is not to say that Wolfram did not borrow isolated aspects from the Templars for his depiction). It is a kind of knighthood that endeavors to preserve the sights, sounds, smells, and tastes of the world, rather than to transcend them. Most of all, it is a kind of knighthood that endeavors to preserve the value of loving women, including the pleasure of erotic love, even as it shows itself in the end to be pleasing to God. The new conception can be deemed a "fiction" to the degree that it forms no part of, nor is based on, orthodox religious beliefs and practice, though we have seen in the case of Wolfram's Grail that the author imagines the truth of his worldly Grail to be, at least, analogous to the bliss of the heavenly afterlife. It might also be deemed a fiction from a more practical perspective, according to which the factual or empirical existence of the Grail and Grail quest cannot ultimately be proven.

However suspect it may remain according to criteria such as these, the "truth" of Wolfram's Grail fiction, which is made possible by an engagement with the not originally, or even necessarily, Christian otherworlds of the Arthurian narrative materials, corresponds to the value of a chivalric life that contains everything that knights in the twelfth and thirteenth centuries desired for themselves: honor, glory, love, and all of life's most vivid sensations, combined with the possibility of ultimately pleasing God and experiencing the bliss of the heavenly afterlife. No pre-existing narrative tradition had allowed the various (and in some ways quite contradictory) elements of such a life to be brought together narratively in this manner. Such a new literary conception first emerges when a poet like Wolfram creatively engages with the formative possibilities of Arthurian otherworlds.

It is because of the ambitious and creative otherworlds at the heart of their romances, and their connection to the literary rendering of new and different (and thus "fictional") secular and religious experiences, that Hartmann von Aue and Wolfram von Eschenbach were long considered, both in the Middle Ages and in modern scholarship, to be the most important German representatives of the Arthurian tradition. In recent years, scholars have focused increasingly on other Arthurian romances produced in Germany that differ, more or less intentionally, from the direction established by Chrétien, Hartmann, and Wolfram. Ulrich von Zatzikhoven's

Lanzelet seems to avail itself of the otherworldly origins of its eponymous hero, who was the son of a water nymph. The allure of this is intensified by his numerous military and amorous successes (in contrast to Chrétien's hero, the German Lanzelet is quite promiscuous), included largely for their inherent entertainment value. Composed in the early thirteenth century, and thus among the first German Arthurian romances, it is quite possible that this differing artistic conception was conceived with the works of Hartmann and Wolfram in mind (see McLelland 2000, 2006: 101, where McLelland states that Ulrich knew Hartmann's romances and may also have been familiar with the early parts of Wolfram's *Parzival*). In Ulrich's conception, there is no attempt to employ the otherworldly element of the Arthurian narrative materials as a means of rendering self-consciously fictional the alternative secular and (quasi-) religious events, figures, and experiences. This is not to say that the marvelous is not derived from multiple sources and artistically arranged, but the artistic conception – one might say the plumbing of the Arthurian otherworlds – eschews the introduction of any radically new alternative artistic, moral, or (quasi-) religious dimension. Similar arguments have been made about other, later Arthurian romances, such as Wirnt von Gravenberg's *Wigalois* (between 1205 and 1235) and Heinrich von dem Türlîn's *Diu Crône* (1220–25), in which the artistic arrangement of the marvelous elements serves more straightforward (conservative) and conventionally dynastic, chivalric, and religious aims, in pointed contrast to the complexity of Wolfram von Eschenbach's otherworldly Grail conception (on the romances of Wirnt and Heinrich, see Thomas 2006).

A related literary development at the fringe of the Arthurian romances, though lacking the strongly chivalric orientation of the latter by virtue of its stricter concentration on the topic of love, was the story of Tristan and Isolde, the most complete courtly version of which was produced by the German poet Gottfried von Strassburg in the second decade of the thirteenth century. Even though the preserved text is substantial, it is nevertheless unfinished, breaking off during the Isolde White Hands section. Gottfried's romance represents a unique achievement, by virtue of its finely crafted verses, its psychologically subtle depiction of emotions and relationships, and its highly provocative conception of the adulterous love of his heroes as a quasi-divine *summum bonum*. One becomes the best and most moral person one can be by experiencing one's love to the fullest, embracing all of its joys and pains without reservation, as Tristan and Isolde do. However different it may be from the romances of Hartmann and Wolfram by virtue of its subject matter, Gottfried's romance still conceives of the savage wilderness (into which the lovers are banished by King Marke in other versions of the Tristan story) as an otherworld of love. Here, the cave of lovers where they take shelter, and where they miraculously sustain themselves in an idyllic countryside with nothing more than stories of love, is modeled on Gothic architecture. This otherworld of love, a spatial rendering of the heroes' bond, is a highly artistic construction and proceeds "fictionally" in a manner analogous to earlier cited examples from Hartmann and Wolfram. Having described the physical characteristics of the cave of lovers in great detail, Gottfried confides in his audience: *ich hân die fossiure erkant / sît mînen eilif jâren ie / und enkam ze Curnewâle nie* (17136–8; "I have known the cave, since I was eleven, and yet I've never been to Cornwall" – my translation). Gottfried crafts an otherworld of love, the truth of which – though it remains beyond any question – is clearly not measurable according to conventional categories of time and space. He thus proceeds in a manner similar to Hartmann and Wolfram before him.

Perhaps by virtue of their distance, geographical and temporal, from British Arthurian origins, and the earliest political uses to which the story of Arthur may have been put (for example by the Plantagenets; see Fletcher 1906/66: 186), German authors and audiences seemed to have been in a position to view the Arthurian materials (and the *matière de Bretagne* generally, so that the Tristan story can be included) as something fundamentally "other." Particularly in the marvelous aspects, which were part of the Arthurian tradition from the earliest sources onward, German authors seemed to have found narrative material, exempt from the conventions and constraints of other genres, that could be developed creatively in new directions. The works of the most famous and influential German poets – Hartmann von Aue, Wolfram von Eschenbach, and Gottfried von Strassburg – show a fascination with otherworlds, a readiness to shape them into alternative ("fictional") realities. In more specific passages, typically situated in narratorial digressions, we also see the beginnings of an awareness on the part of authors (and presumably also their audiences) of the emergence of a new kind of writing that was important and "true" in its own way, even if it was not primarily (or, in the case of a story such as Gottfried's *Tristan*, even remotely) about God, or demonstrable according to other conventional medieval criteria. Arthurian otherworlds, as shaped and elaborated in German Arthurian romances, anticipate, and perhaps help pave the way toward, the literary "supergenre" (to use the Bakhtinian term) that will take hold of Europe not too long afterwards: the novel.

PRIMARY SOURCES

Benecke, G. F. & Lachmann, K. (eds) (1968). *Hartmann von Aue. Iwein*, 7th rev. edn (ed. L. Wolff). Berlin: de Gruyter.

Hahn, K. A. (ed.) (1845). *Ulrich von Zatzikhoven. Lanzelet*. Frankfurt: Brönner. Repr. Berlin: de Gruyter, 1965.

Hatto, A. T. (trans.) (1980). *Wolfram von Eschenbach. Parzival*. Harmondsworth: Penguin.

Kapteyn, J. M. N. (ed.) (1926). *Wigalois. Der Ritter mit dem Rade*. Bonn: Klopp.

Lachmann, K. (ed.) (1965). *Wolfram von Eschenbach. Parzival*. Berlin: de Gruyter.

Leitzmann, A. & Wolff, L. (eds) (1985). *Hartmann von Aue. Erec*, 6th rev. edn (eds C. Cormeau & K. Gärtner). Tübingen: Niemeyer.

Ranke, F. (ed.) (1984). *Gottfried von Strassburg. Tristan* (trans. R. Krohn [modern German]), 2 vols. Stuttgart: Reclam.

Scholl, G. H. F. (ed.) (1852). *Diu Crône von Heinrich von dem Türlîn*. Stuttgart: Bibiothek des Litterarischen Vereins no. 27. Repr. Amsterdam: Rodopi, 1966.

Tobin, F., Vivian, K., & Lawson, R. H. (trans) (2001). *Arthurian romances, tales, and lyric poetry: The complete works of Hartmann von Aue*. University Park, PA: Pennsylvania State University Press.

REFERENCES AND FURTHER READING

Bakhtin, M. (1981). *The dialogic imagination: Four essays by M. M. Bakhtin* (ed. M. Holquist, trans C. Emerson & M. Holquist). Austin, TX: University of Texas Press.

Fleckenstein, J. (1972). Friedrich Barbarossa und das Rittertum. Zur Bedeutung der groß en Mainzer Hoftage von 1184 und 1188. In *Festschrift für Hermann Heimpel*, vol. II. Göttingen: Veröffentlichungen des Max-Planck-Instituts für Geschichte, XXXVI, pp. 1023–41.

Fletcher, R. H. (1966). *The Arthurian material in the chronicles*. New York: Franklin (original work published 1906).

Frasetto, M. (2002). Medieval Germany, history of emperors and empire, c. 750– c. 1350. In F. G. Gentry (ed.), *A companion to Middle High German literature to the 14th century*. Leiden: Brill, pp. 1–25.

Groos, A. (1995). *Romancing the Grail. Genre, science, and quest in Wolfram's "Parzival."* Ithaca, NY: Cornell University Press.

Hasty, W. (ed.) (2006). *German literature of the High Middle Ages*. Rochester, NY: Camden House.

Hasty, W. (2007). Theorizing German romance: The excursus on horse and saddle in Hartmann von Aue's *Erec*. *Seminar*, 43(3), 253–64.

Haug, W. (1985). Programmatische Fiktionalität: Hartmanns von Aue "Iwein" – Prolog. In *Literaturtheorie im Deutschen Mittelalter. Von den Anfängen bis zum Ende des 13. Jahrhunderts. Eine Einführung*. Darmstadt: Wissenschaftliche Buchgesellschaft, pp. 118–30.

Jackson W. H. & Ranawake, S. (eds) (2000). *The Arthur of the Germans: The Arthurian legend in medieval German and Dutch literature*. Cardiff: University of Wales Press.

Loomis, R. S. (1963). *The Grail: From Celtic myth to Christian symbol*. Cardiff: University of Wales Press.

McLelland, N. (2000). *Ulrich von Zatzikhoven's "Lanzelet": Narrative style and entertainment*. Cambridge: Brewer.

McLelland, N. (2006). Ulrich von Zatzikhoven's Lanzelet. In W. Hasty (ed.). *German literature of the High Middle Ages*. Rochester, NY: Camden House, pp. 101–7.

Stevens, A. (1999). Fiction, plot and discourse: Wolfram's *Parzival* and its narrative sources. In W. Hasty (ed.), *A companion to Wolfram's "Parzival."* Columbia, SC: Camden House, pp. 99–123.

Strasser, I. (1993). Fiktion und ihre Vermittlung in Hartmann's "Erec"-Roman. In V. Mertens & F. Wolfzettel (eds) in collaboration with M. Meyer & H.-J. Schiewer, *Fiktionalität im Artusroman: Dritte Tagung der deutschen Sektion der Internationalen Artusgesellschaft*. Tübingen: Niemeyer, pp. 63–83.

Thomas, A. (2000). King Arthur and his Round Table in the culture of medieval Bohemia and in medieval Czech literature. In W. H. Jackson & S. Ranawake (eds), *The Arthur of the Germans: The Arthurian legend in medieval German and Dutch literature*. Cardiff: University of Wales Press, pp. 249–56.

Thomas, N. (2006). Wirnt von Gravenberg's *Wigalois* and Heinrich von dem Türlîn's *Diu Crône*. In W. Hasty (ed.), *German literature of the High Middle Ages*. Rochester, NY: Camden House, pp. 203–14.

13

Scandinavian Versions of Arthurian Romance

Geraldine Barnes

Only with the publication at the end of the twentieth century of bilingual Old Icelandic–English editions has the medieval Scandinavian Arthurian corpus become accessible to audiences beyond Old Norse specialists (Kalinke 1999). Written for the most part in the prose form of the Icelandic sagas, Scandinavian versions of Arthurian romance form a distinctive group among the Old Norse versions of French epic and romance known collectively as the "translated" *riddarasögur* ("sagas of knights"). As tellings of two key branches of the Arthurian legend – Geoffrey of Monmouth's *Historia Regum Britanniae* and three romances by Chrétien de Troyes – these texts constitute a collection ripe for further investigation within the fields of medieval translation, cross-cultural relations, and the reception of Arthurian verse romance. Their period of production coincided with the composition of the Sagas of Icelanders (or "family sagas"), and the possible influence of these two saga modes upon each other remains an under-explored question.

Two significant centers of literary activity – the court of King Hákon Hákonarson ("The Old") of Norway (r. 1217–63) and the monastery of Þingeyrar in northern Iceland – are identifiable as entry points for the Arthurian legend in medieval Scandinavia. Probably via the medium of Angevin Britain (Leach 1921), Hákon initiated the importation and translation of a number of French epics and romances, known collectively to modern scholarship as *riddarasögur*. Among these are translations of Chrétien's *Erec et Enide* (*Erex saga*), *Yvain* (*Ívens saga*), *Le Roman de Perceval* (*Parcevals saga*), other "matter of Britain" material – Thomas's *Tristan* (*Tristrams saga*), *lais* by Marie de France (in the collection known as *Strengleikar*), and the anonymous comic *lai*, *Le mantel mautaillié* (*Möttuls saga*) – and Carolingian *chansons de geste* (*Karlamagnús saga*). Tradition has it that the first of these was *Tristrams saga*, produced in 1226 by an otherwise unidentified translator named in the prologue to the work as "Brother Robert" and, in *Elis saga ok Rósamundu* (from the *chanson de geste*, *Elie de Saint Gille*), as "Abbot Robert." A Swedish poem, *Hærra Ivan*, apparently derived from both *Yvain* and *Ívens saga*, is one of three verse narratives in Swedish from French sources commissioned by Eufemia, wife of the Norwegian king Hákon Magnússon (r. 1299–1319), in the course of securing a dynastic alliance through the marriage of their daughter to Duke Erik, brother of the king of Sweden. The poem *Merlínússpá* ("Prophecy of Merlin") was translated at Þingeyrar by the monk Gunnlaugr Leifsson (d. 1219), who names himself as the author of the work. Gunnlaugr may also have written *Breta sögur* ("Stories of the Britons"), the Norse version of Geoffrey of Monmouth's *Historia Regum Britanniae*.

Surviving manuscripts of five *riddarasögur* name Hákon as their commissioner: *Elis saga ok Rósamundu*, *Ívens saga*, *Möttuls saga*, *Strengleikar*, and *Tristrams saga*. *Erex saga* may have been composed during Hákon Hákonarson's reign, but, with the exception of two fragments from around 1500, this saga is preserved only in manuscripts from the seventeenth century and later. Linguistic, political, and economic ties between Norway and Iceland remained close throughout the two centuries following Iceland's surrender of autonomy to the Norwegian crown in 1262, and most *riddarasögur* are preserved in Icelandic manuscripts from the fourteenth to the seventeenth centuries.

Was there an independent Arthurian tradition in Iceland? Carvings on the church door at Valþjófsstaðir in the east of Iceland, variously assigned to a period between c. 1200 and 1360, with opinion strongly favoring the early thirteenth century, indicate possible familiarity with the lion-knight legend as told in *Yvain* (Harris 1970). Opinion is divided as to whether *Breta sögur* was the work of Gunnlaugr or a Norwegian author, possibly as part of Hákon's translation program (Eysteinsson 1953–5). This saga exists in two versions, the longer, and as yet unpublished, in the fourteenth-century Icelandic manuscript AM 573, and a shorter in the codex *Hauksbók* – which contains a number of historical and learned works – of similar date. *Breta sögur* is not usually considered in discussions of *riddarasögur*, but it has recently been suggested that the composer of the version in AM 573 was operating as a writer of romance (Kalinke 2006). Geoffrey's Arthur, moreover, appears to have been an important influence on the formation of the Norse image of the king.

Trends in Scholarship

Subsequent to the editions and studies of *Erex saga*, *Ívens saga*, and *Parcevals saga* undertaken by the German scholar Eugen Kölbing in the late nineteenth century, scholarship on Scandinavian Arthuriana was scant in the first half of the twentieth, with the notable exception of Henry Goddard Leach's *Angevin Britain and Scandinavia* (1921). Studies of individual texts that appeared in the 1960s and 1970s were devoted in the main to formal comparison of style and content with source material. Vigorous debate, however, over the reliability or otherwise of the extant manuscripts and available editions dominated in the last quarter of the century (see, for example, Kalinke 1981; Barnes 1989): were these faithful transmissions of works composed in thirteenth-century Norway or corrupt redactions by Icelandic scribes – rendered further suspect by nineteenth-century editors – which provided no valid foundation for scholarship? Another point of contention concerned the literary significance of the Arthurian *riddarasögur*: were they and their sources lightweight entertainments or narratives that actively embraced the medieval literary ideal of equal parts of *sentence* and *solas* (Kalinke 1981; Barnes 1989)?

Preoccupation among saga scholars with these matters overshadowed those questions of audience, reception, and ideology of Arthurian romance in the European Middle Ages which were attracting interest among other medievalists in the 1970s and 1980s. Since then, Norse scholarship has revisited the ground pioneered by Leach to investigate the literary circle of Hákon's court, examine the *riddarasögur* within the broader context of medieval European romance and its ideology (Barnes 1987), call for the development of a theory of translation for the *riddarasögur* as rewriting and interpretation rather than imperfect copying (Kjær 1996), and consider the role of audience expectations in the process of *riddarasögur* transmission from thirteenth-century Norway to seventeenth-century Iceland (Glauser 2005).

Scandinavian appropriation of the Arthurian legend was not only a question of the "translation" of individual texts in a new literary form but also of the conventions of a foreign literary culture (Glauser 2005). There was no comparable cultural grid onto which the feudal structures and ethos of twelfth-century courtly romance could be mapped in thirteenth-century Norway or Iceland. The specific historical circumstances of the composition of the two literary modes were very different, too. Chrétien's romances were an aristocratic, not a royal, literature, written during a period when the kings of France sought to extend the bounds of their sovereignty in competition with the princes of Champagne and Flanders, and with Henry II of England. Whereas the image of Arthur in the early *Erec et Enide* may have been intended to flatter Henry II (Over 2005), the romances which Chrétien composed at the courts of Champagne and Flanders (*Le Chevalier de la Charrette* and the *Roman de Perceval*) progressively marginalize the importance of Arthur and treat the monarchy with an irony sometimes bordering on outright disdain.

Although some early-twentieth-century scholars viewed Hákon's program of literary importation as naïve and sycophantic and the king himself as enthralled merely by the surface brilliance of chivalric romance, it is generally agreed that the project was associated with Hákon's desire to expand and upgrade the cultural horizons of his court, to strengthen and raise the status of the Norwegian kingship, to gain the recognition and respect of his European peers, and to propel Norway into the mainstream of international affairs. Hákon had imperial ambitions, too. He regarded himself as the natural lord of Greenland and Iceland, and sought to maintain Norwegian supremacy over the Hebrides, Man, Orkney, and Shetland. After 1250 he tried to exploit the internal weakness of Denmark, with the apparent aim of controlling the Baltic seaway.

Norway and its sphere, or would-be sphere, of influence in the thirteenth century – Orkney, Shetland (Hjaltland), the Hebrides, Denmark, the Faeroes, and Gotland (Iceland and Greenland are notably absent) – are conquered and absorbed into Arthur's empire in the *Historia* and *Breta sögur*. Whereas the rest of Scandinavia is more or less reduced to a list of tributary states, there is an episode in both works in which the Norwegians unsuccessfully oppose Arthur's nominee as king – specifically, in *Breta sögur* (Jónsson 1892–5: 289) because they do not wish to be ruled by a British man. As a group of texts which (re)create the legendary figure of the British king in thirteenth-century Norway, the Arthurian *riddarasögur* may, Susanne Kramarz-Bein has recently speculated (1999: 82), have indirectly revived thoughts of Norwegian claims to the English throne, which dated back to the reign of Magnús the Good (1035–7). With the immediate aim of securing England's neutrality in Norway's long-standing dispute with Scotland over their claims to Orkney and the Hebrides, Hákon had made an unsuccessful bid for a dynastic alliance with Henry III through a marriage between his son, Magnús, and Henry's daughter, Beatrice, but there is no evidence that he himself entertained designs on the English throne.

Why did Hákon commission these translations from the French in the first place? The other major literary undertaking of his reign, and closely associated with Hákon himself, is a *Fürstenspiegel* ("king's mirror"), the *Konungs Skuggsjá* ("King's Mirror"), which subscribes to the notion of the monarch as God's vicar, supreme judge, upholder of order, and possessor of wisdom, understanding, and humility. The work is addressed to princes and to a wider audience, which, to judge by its popularity in Iceland in later centuries, it reached. The question of the influence of its ideas on the *riddarasögur* is a matter of critical debate (see, for example, Kalinke 1981; Barnes 1984; Kramarz-Bein 1999).

Arthur of the Norse

Comparisons with Arthur's career in the *Historia* and Hákon's in *Hákonar saga Hákonarson*, the biography commissioned by his son King Magnús (r. 1263–80), are tempting. Like Arthur, who, according to the *Historia*, was fifteen when he was crowned, Hákon was of illegitimate birth and denied legal claim to the throne according to a Norwegian law of succession, but after gaining substantial support from local assemblies at the age of thirteen, in 1217, he was formally acknowledged as king six years later. Hákon also had significant (and partially realized) imperial ambitions. The *Breta sögur* summation of Arthur's reign calls him the greatest proponent of Christianity of all the kings of Britain: *hann hafi allra Breta konunga merst styrkt kristni a Bretlandi* (Jónsson 1892–95: 295, "he strengthened Christianity in Britain the most of all the kings of Britain"). The eulogy at the end of *Hákonar saga* makes a parallel claim for Hákon: *Hákon konungr lagði meira hug á, at styrkja guðs kristni í Noregi, en engi konungr fyrir honum, síðan var inn heilagi Ólafr konungr* (Jónsson 1957: 461, "King Hákon put more heart into strengthening God's Christianity in Norway than any king before him, since the time of the sainted King Olaf").

The introductory portrait of Arthur in *Breta sögur* combines heroic and chivalric ideals:

Hann var mikill a voxt venn at aliti spekingr at viti avr af fe sterkr harðr ok vapndiarfr glaðr ok goðr vvinvm en grimr vvinvm fastnæmr ok forsiall siðlatr ok sigrsæll vidfrægr ok at ollv vel menntr. (Jónsson 1892–5: 287)

He was tall in stature; handsome in appearance; wise in knowledge; generous with property; courageous and brave; cheerful and good to friends but harsh to enemies; steadfast; famous for his triumphs; and well accomplished in everything.

Chrétien's Arthur comes with the same reputation for courage, victory, and all-round accomplishments, but with a conspicuous lack of immediately demonstrable achievements or action. The thorny question is whether Scandinavian translators and their audiences could decode the irony. Assuming that Geoffrey's Arthur was known in Norway through *Breta sögur* prior to the translation of Chrétien's romances, it must have been difficult to reconcile the latter's *roi fainéant* in *Yvain* and *Le Roman de Perceval* with Geoffrey's dynamic leader. Historical irony comes into play here, in that Hákon's vision for the Norwegian monarchy and his diplomatic maneuverings run counter to the progressive weakening of Arthur in courtly romance. The absence of a Norse version of *Le Chevalier de la Charrette*, for example, suggests that an actively cuckolded Arthur was unacceptable. Traces of Charlemagne adhere to the Norse Arthur (Artús), too. In the opening lines of *Ívens saga*, Artús is said to have been not only king of Rome but also the most popular after Charlemagne "who had lived on this side of the ocean" (Kalinke 1999: II.39). He is also enthroned, another reminder of his royal authority. Lassitude rather than the implied lust of *Yvain* prompts his abrupt departure for the bedroom and the company of Guinevere. Although *Hærra Ivan* shows an interest primarily in the externals of chivalry – social, military, and decorative – its prologue substantially extends the warrior comparison between Arthur and Charlemagne. In *Erex saga*, the hero is introduced with resonances of Charlemagne's *douze peers* as one of Arthur's "twelve wise men and counsellors" (Kalinke 1999: II.223).

Möttuls saga, the story of a chastity test at Arthur's court, opens with an extended portrait of Artús – the longest in Old Norse – in which the image of the heroic leader merges with the archetypal noble knight:

King Arthur was the most renowned ruler with regard to every aspect of valor and all kinds of manliness and chivalry, combined with perfect compassion and most appealing mildness, so that in every respect there was no ruler more renowned or blessed with friends in his day in the world. He was the most valiant man at arms, the most generous with gifts, the gentlest in words, the cleverest in his designs, the most benevolent in mercy, the most polished in good manners, the noblest in all kingly craft, godfearing in his undertakings, gentle to the good, harsh to the wicked, merciful to the needy, hospitable to the companionable, so perfect in his entire authority that neither ill will nor malice was found in him. (Kalinke 1999: II.7)

Critics disagree as to whether this encomium is an attempt to shore up Arthur's dignity (Barnes 1987) or to reinforce an intended ironic contrast with the events which follow (Kalinke 1987: xvi, lix), when a chastity-testing mantle fails to fit all but one of the ladies of Arthur's court, Guinevere included. Contrary to the tendency of the translated *riddarasögur* to reduce their sources, this curiously heavy-handed narrative, which extensively amplifies *Le mantel mautaillié*, might be read as an expression of clerical misogyny rather than as ironic treatment of the Arthurian ideal.

The rituals of chivalry mask the underlying disorder, dissent, and discontent at Camelot in Chrétien's romances (Over 2005). These tensions are eroded in some key scenes in *Ívens saga*, where the Arthurian world presents an image of greater dignity and propriety than it does in *Yvain*. After Arthur's unprecedented departure from the company at the Whitsuntide feast, for example, the quarrel that breaks out among the knights sitting outside his bedroom is absent in both *Ívens saga* and *Hærra Ivan*. Later in *Yvain*, whereas Lunete tells Yvain that he was the only knight who treated her with civility when she was once sent on an errand to the court (Reid 1967: lines 1004–15), in *Ívens saga* she thanks him for having extended her the courtesy to which she considered herself unentitled on that occasion (Kalinke 1999: II.49). Then, exultant after a series of tournament victories, the French Yvain and Gauvain set up their own court outside the town of Chester; since they do not attend his, Arthur is more or less obliged to go to theirs (*Qu'onques a cort de roi ne vindrent, / Einçois vint li rois a lor*, Reid 1967: lines 2690–91, "since they would not go to the court of the king, thus the king came to theirs"), where he sits with his accompanying knights (lines 2685–94) – not, by implication, in the place of honor beside Yvain and Gauvain. The circumstances are rewritten and this snub to royal honor elided from *Ívens saga*, where Artús is said to be in town as the guest at a feast held by the sister of an unnamed earl. When the king hears that Íven and Valven have pitched their tents nearby, he pays them a visit and sits down beside them. It is, moreover, Guinevere's foolishness alone, not a combination of Arthur's folly and her heedlessness (*Cil fu fos et cele musarde*, Reid 1967: l, 3926, "He was a fool and she careless"), that is blamed for her abduction from Kay's care by an unnamed knight.

Perhaps individually inconsequential – and well beyond the scope of this discussion as a potential catalogue of detailed (and textually disputable) direct comparisons – there are sufficient instances of shifts in nuance and resonances of the Galfridian Arthur in the Scandinavian Arthurian corpus to warrant the impression that Norse preconceptions of the king and his court were not attuned to mockery, let alone outright scorn, of the British king.

Saga and Romance: Form and Ideology

In Geoffrey's *Historia*, Arthur's reign is part of a cyclic process of kingly rise and fall, but, intimations of mortality in the *Chevalier de la Charrette* and a progressive diminution of Arthur's power from the high point of *Erec et Enide* to the nadir of *Le Roman de Perceval* aside, Chrétien's Arthurian narratives operate essentially in the present. In their contrasting inclination toward the historical mode, the *riddarasögur* appear to reflect the structural model of the family sagas. In addition to the references to Arthur's past and future career and the retrospective comparison with Charlemagne in *Ívens saga*, *Parcevals saga* and *Erex saga* provide their heroes with completed life histories. In *Parcevals saga*, Parceval returns speedily and without further ado to Blankiflúr (Fr. Blanchefleur) after his instructive Easter sojourn with the hermit, marries her, becomes ruler of her kingdom, and remains undefeated in combat with all other knights (like the Arthur of *Breta sögur* and *Möttuls saga*, he is *sigrsæll*, "blessed with victory"). (Gawain's adventures in *Le Roman de Perceval* are recounted in a separate narrative known as *Valvens þáttr* or "Gawain's Tale," Kalinke 1999: II.185–205.) There is no further reference to the Grail, nor has there previously been any mention of the dire future repercussions of Parceval's failure to ask about the Grail and the bleeding lance. The tableau of Erec's coronation at Arthur's court which brings the narrative to an end in *Erec et Enide* extends to the next generation in *Erex saga*, where Erex and Evida return to their kingdom, rule it with honor and peace, maintain excellent relations with Arthur and his queen, and are succeeded by their sons, who take after their father in valor and knighthood:

> King Erex and Queen Evida take leave of King Arthur and his queen with great friendship, and it lasted as long as they lived. They then rode back to their kingdom and ruled it with honor and glory and in complete peace.
>
> They had two sons; one was named after Evida's father, but the other Ilax after Erex's father. They both became kings and distinguished men, and were like their father in valor and chivalrous deeds, and they inherited the kingdom after their father died.
>
> Here ends the saga of that excellent King Erex and his wife, the beautiful Evida. (Kalinke 1999: II.259)

The elimination of Chrétien's chatty narratorial "I," and the excision and reduction of monologues – particularly as they relate to the "psychological" processes of courtly love – and of descriptions of courtly ritual and pageantry in the Arthurian *riddarasögur* are precisely what might be expected of the application of the conventions of the Sagas of Icelanders to romance narrative. The process amounts to a compositional form of *translatio* in which the rhetorically unfamiliar is recast in familiar mould. The exclusion of the narratorial persona is the most crucial, since it removes the means of the active solicitation of audience complicity in the apprehension of irony, especially as it relates to discrepancies between the ideal of chivalry on the one hand and the conduct of Arthur's knights on the other. The overall effect is the elimination of ethical ambiguity and reduction of the problematic in courtly chivalry, and the promotion of a straightforward, practical code of conduct, which has more in common with the definition of *siðr* ("morality," especially as it applies to professional ethics) in the *Konungs Skuggsjá* than with the often conflicting demands of love and knightly duty in chivalric romance.

The influence of the code of conduct in the Sagas of Icelanders on the *riddarasögur* is an interesting and somewhat under-explored issue. The preservation and defense of personal honor are, for instance, paramount in both saga and chivalric romance. But whereas, for example, the motivation for Erec's quest in *Erec et Enide* is ambiguous, if not entirely obscure, it is clearly propelled in *Erex saga* by considerations of the defense of personal honor. When, in *Ívens saga*, Íven's unnamed bride (Chrétien's Laudine) promises not only that her love will turn to hatred if he fails to return on the day appointed for his return after a furlough from marriage to recoup his fading knightly reputation, but also threatens him with the prospective loss of honor among his peers, she steps outs of the role of courtly lady and into that of the female goader of saga tradition. And whereas Yvain laments the loss of his joy at length when he misses the deadline (Reid 1967: lines 3532–62), the loss of esteem is of equal importance for Íven, who mourns the loss of both his honor and his personal happiness: "I have lost my consolation and joy, and through my own fault brought down my honor and turned my reputation into loss" (Kalinke 1999: II.75).

A substantive difference between the ethos of the Sagas of Icelanders and courtly romance is the ideal of humility, which underlines the chivalric code of service. In the Arthurian *riddarasögur*, humility is not the ritual self-abasement of the courtly lover so much as veneration for the rule of law, the law of God, and secular authority – that is, humility in the sense in which it is defined and propagated in the *Konungs Skuggsjá*. In *Ívens saga*, for example, Íven makes to sit at his lady's feet, not as the gesture of a subservient suitor, as implied in *Yvain* (*Et mes sire Yvains sanblant fist, / Qu'a ses piez seoir se vossist*, Reid 1967: lines 2073–4, "And my lord Yvain acted as if he wished to sit at her feet"), but out of deference to her noble status ("on account of his humility and to acknowledge her noble stature," Kalinke 1999: II.61). In *Parcevals saga* the parting advice which Parceval receives from his mother includes an admonition to "be humble in the presence of persons of importance" (Kalinke 1999: II.111). The exemplum about the lowering of pride implicit in the name of Orgueilleus de la Lande ("Haughty Knight of the Heath"), a knight defeated by Perceval in *Le Roman de Perceval*, becomes ponderously explicit in *Parcevals saga*: "the Haughty Knight became exhausted, and then that haughty man begged for truce and mercy. And then all his haughtiness fell away and against his will he was made humble" (Kalinke 1999: II.159). The priest's parting words to Parceval just before the saga's conclusion add an injunction to be humble to all those in need, as well as to listen to the Mass with humility toward God (Kalinke 1999: II.181). Finally, lack of arrogance is a noteworthy mark of royal virtue in *Erex saga*. Whereas in *Erec et Enide* Arthur is said to be gladdened by the spectacle of the vast number of nobles summoned to Erec's wedding from throughout his empire, Artús is similarly joyful but, at the same time, does not pride himself on his power over his vassals (Kalinke 1999: II.235).

The hero's succession of tutors in *Parcevals saga* instruct him in the practical and ethical fundamentals of social conduct and chivalry. Parceval's mother holds his deceased father up as a model of practice (be godfearing, loyal, eschew foolish pursuits and robbery, be courteous to everyone and especially to women, be merciful in victory, listen to wholesome advice, seek the good, be wise, be humble toward good men, avoid loose women). Her speech (Kalinke 1999: I.111) makes for an interesting comparison with the tradition of women who offer advice in the family sagas (Psaki 2002). Its emphasis on moderation, compassion, kindness, humility, and polite behavior is reminiscent of the advice of father to son in the *Konungs Skuggsjá* (Barnes 1984; Kramarz-Bein 1999) and similar passages elsewhere in the *miroir de princes* tradition. *Parcevals saga* is, in the final analysis, an unambiguous story of instruction, reform, and worldly success – and not only for Parceval himself. After Parceval dispatches Blankiflúr's defeated adversary, Klamadius (Fr. Clamadeus), to Arthur's court, he spends the rest of his days there, implicitly rehabilitated as a model member of the king's household and well accomplished in the standard virtues of Norse chivalry: "courageous in combat, generous with gifts, discreet in counsel, pleasant in speech and proven in valour, renowned and perfect in every way" (Kalinke 1999: II.145).

Madeleine Pelner Cosman (1966) showed how the *enfances* of Tristan, Lancelot, and Perceval in French, English, and German romance have their origin in the *Fürsten-spiegel* ideal. Beneath the layers of moral uncertainty, erotic and spiritual symbolism, narratorial playfulness, and royal–noble tension, Chrétien's romances are stories of young knights who learn how to be rulers through a process of instruction, the acquisition of self-knowledge, and redemption. *Erec et Enide*, in particular, has been interpreted by many critics as a romance about education in kingship (see, for example, Barnes 1987; Over 2005). In the Arthurian *riddarasögur* the elimination or reduction of ethical complexity and chivalric pageantry foregrounds the educative process of chivalric romance. In *Erex saga*, moreover, Artús himself actively assumes the role of princely educator when, with quest fulfilled, Erex returns to the court to learn that his father, King Ilax, has died and gratefully receives good advice from Artús about how to make his new kingdom secure.

From another critical perspective, the apparent absence of irony and the playing down of the rhetoric of "courtly" love in their Old Norse versions reveal subtle seams in Chrétien's narratives concerning the dynamics of rulership. Laudine's relationships with her barons and with Lunete in *Yvain* and Hartmann's *Iwein* have recently been examined in relation to the conventions of the conciliar process among the nobility (Sullivan 2001). The pared-down narrative of *Ívens saga* uncovers a related narrative layer in *Yvain*: a contest between good and bad or inadequate counsel – between an ineffective council of barons on the one hand and salutary counsel by a woman (Lunete) on the other. Consideration of the *riddarasögur* as interpretations rather than as translations of Arthurian romance warrants further examination in the wider arena of the medieval reception of chivalric narrative. In that context, the fifteenth-century Burgundian *mises en prose* of earlier epics and romances discussed below offers an intriguing parallel to the *riddarasögur*, which may reward further investigation.

The Later Middle Ages

Whereas the courtly context of *riddarasögur* composition in thirteenth-century Norway is well documented, little is known about the circumstances of literary production in fourteenth- and fifteenth-century Iceland, although some key *riddarasögur* manuscripts, which contain both translated and indigenous romances, date from this period. It seems reasonable, though, to speculate that the patrons and audiences of romances in Iceland in this period are likely to have included landowners, wealthy merchants, and representatives of the Norwegian kings (Glauser 1983).

The Icelandic manuscript Stockholm Perg 4to:6 (c. 1400) contains three Arthurian *riddarasögur* (*Ívens saga*, *Parcevals saga*, and *Möttuls saga*), three other sagas of probable French origin (*Elis saga*; *Bevers saga*, derived from an unidentified version of *Boeve d'Hamtoun*; and *Flóvents saga*, possibly adapted from a lost *chanson de geste*), and some early indigenous romances, chief among them *Klári saga* (which claims to have a Latin source), *Mírmanns saga*, and *Konráðs saga*. We know nothing of the provenance and early history of this volume, but it might be said to have something of a Christian and educative flavor: the hero and heroine of *Mírmanns saga* retire to a monastery (and the hero converts to Christianity), *Konráðs saga* is about a prince sent to a learned earl for instruction, especially in foreign languages, who must take heed of the wise counsel of a woman before his eventual triumph, and *Flóvents saga* and *Bevers saga* concern militant Christianity. The slightly younger manuscript AM 489 4to (c. 1450), also of unknown provenance, though the hand is from the Western Fiords (Vestfirðr) area of Iceland, contains two translated romances, *Ívens saga*, *Flóres saga ok Blankiflúr* (from *Floire et Blanchefleur*), three indigenous romances, and the "post-classical" family saga (*Bárðar saga*). Foster Blaisdell, editor of the facsimile edition of this manuscript, has suggested that "the volume does make a sort of sense 'as is'," inasmuch as five of its sagas have foreign settings and all have a strong element of the fantastic (Blaisdell 1980: 17).

There are no continuations of *Le Roman de Perceval* or other Arthurian romances in the independent Icelandic romance tradition. The lion-knight motif is popular in a number of indigenous *riddarasögur* (Barnes 1994), but in these sagas it may derive from sources other than *Ívens saga*, such as Latin beast lore and German lion-knight traditions preserved in the thirteenth-century Norse compilation *Þiðreks saga af Bern* (Harris 1970). An Icelandic narrative poem preserved in a manuscript dating from around 1500, the *Skikkju rímur* ("the mantle cantos"), is based on *Möttuls saga* and shows some familiarity with other Arthurian *riddarasögur* (Kalinke 1987: lxxvi–lxxxix). The "Knight of the Cart" motif, possibly derived from Chrétien's *Le Chevalier de la Charrette*, although there is no evidence of direct knowledge of that work in Iceland, appears in the independent fourteenth-century romance *Rémundar saga keisarasonar*. The Tristan story was independently, and possibly parodically, recast in another Icelandic romance of the same period, *Tristrams saga ok Ísoddar*.

In continental Europe, the *riddarasögur* make for interesting comparison with the *mises en prose* of courtly romance and *chansons de geste*, especially with the prose *Erec*, one of two French prose versions of Chrétien's romances (the other is *Cligès*) written for the court of Philip the Good (1396–1467), Duke of Burgundy. Languishing in scholarly neglect until recently, the prose *Erec* – probably written between 1450 and 1460 (Timelli 2000: 9) – has begun to attract critical interest as a significant dem-onstration of the reception and interpretation of Arthurian romance at a ruler-focused court in the later Middle Ages. As in *Erex saga*, one of the most prominent features of the Burgundian *Erec* is its resolution of the ethical ambiguity in Chrétien's *Erec et Enide*. Whereas the pursuit and preservation of honor are the unequivocal moral goals of *Erex saga* (Kalinke 1970), the hero's quest in the prose *Erec* is explicitly a test of Enide's loyalty, to the extent that the work becomes "a sort of manual of wifely conduct" (Lacy 1994: 278). In Jane Taylor's reading, the resolution in the prose *Cligès* and *Erec* of Chrétien's narrative ambiguities constitutes a process of acculturation, whereby "the socio-culturally unfamiliar is recast in familiar terms" (Taylor 1998: 183), such that the prose *Erec* "assimilates the mysterious or the ironic political systems of Arthur's court to a model that would have been comfortably comprehen-sible to a Burgundian audience – a model in which the ruler's choices, the ruler's edicts, are primary and incontrovertible" (Taylor 1998: 190). The Arthur of *Erex saga*, who contemplates his power with humility and takes an active role in counseling the young Erex in kingly strategy, arguably offers an equivalent model of ideal Norse rulership.

In structure, too, the prose *Erec* and *Erex saga* share some striking similarities. Like *Erex saga*, the prose *Erec* is interested neither in courtly internalizing nor descrip-tions of social ritual. Both works adds an episode that showcases the hero as a superbly skilled knight. The additional chapter in *Erex saga* demonstrates his bravery and strength in rescuing a nobleman from a dragon and four knights from a band of robbers, and in the prose *Erec*, a tournament which turns into an exhibition match of Erec's skills is inserted after his coronation. The most striking parallel with *Erex saga*, however, is the addition of a short epilogue in praise of Erec's subsequent exemplary life as ruler, with the beautiful Enide, of his kingdom, and succession by his son. The emphases here are very similar to those of the conclusion to *Erex saga*: a peaceful reign, a brood of progeny, the passing of the royal couple, and a smooth succession:

> Le roi Erec prist hommage et feaulté de sez noblez; et vesqui depuis saintement et glo-rieusement avec sa belle dame la reyne Enide de laquelle il eust pluseurs beaux enfans; et comme ilz fussent venus en eage iceux, le roi Erec et Enide trespasserent en paix de ce ciecle, et furent leurz obsequez fais reveramment a grant pleurz le leurz enfanz, dés-quelz l'aisné filz ful roy; mais non plus n'en fait nostre compte de mencion, si prendrons la fin de ceste presente histoire. (Timelli 2000: 212)

> King Erec received homage and fealty from his nobles and lived piously ever after with his beautiful lady, Queen Enide, by whom he had several fine children; and when these were come of age King Erec and Enide peacefully departed this world, and their obse-quies were made reverently, with deep sorrow, by their children of whom the elder son became king; but our tale makes no more mention of him, and so we take leave of this story.

Parallels between these two works are interesting, and even more so if *Erex saga* was composed in late-fifteenth-century Iceland. Greenland waters were the source for the narwhal tusks which passed for unicorns in the Middle Ages (Plusowski 2004) and both Greenland and Iceland were sources of the highly prized white falcons. Bruges, under the control of the dukes of Burgundy, was a major European trading center and had close links with England, the prominent power in Iceland in the fifteenth century. Philip II, "the Bold" (1342–1404), of Burgundy had ransomed his son from Sultan Bayazid with twelve white falcons in 1396, and Philip the Good's son, Charles the Bold (1433–77), possessed a number of narwhal tusks (Plusowski 2004). The possibility of an Iceland–Burgundy direct cultural connection is tantalizing, but any link beyond coincidence in the prose *Erec* and *Erex saga* must remain, at least for now, in the realm of speculation.

The general pattern of the translation of the Arthurian legend into Old Norse prose is a side-stepping of the ethical ambiguity in twelfth-century romance and a foregrounding of its underlying practical ideals of kingly and knightly conduct. As a collection, the Arthurian *riddarasögur* are governed by an ideology of learning, redemption, and worldly success. Their heroes strive toward an attainable ideal, not an unscalable ladder of spiritual perfection. Overall, the framework of Arthurian exemplarity, which proves to be such a flimsy and rhetorically misleading structure in Chrétien, rests on a more solid foundation in the *riddarasögur*. In their demonstration of the tendency to clarify ambiguity and to operate within a frame of reference and ideology familiar to their audience, the *riddarasögur* can be read as a significant body of medieval interpretations of Arthurian romance. The field is wide open for further study.

Primary Sources

Blaisdell, F. (ed.) (1980). *The Sagas of Ywain and Tristan and other tales: AM 489 4to*, Early Icelandic Manuscripts in Facsimile, vol. 12. Copenhagen: Rosenkilde & Bagger.

Blaisdell, F. & Kalinke, M. (trans) (1977). *Erex Saga and Ívens Saga: The Old Norse versions of Chrétien de Troyes's Erec and Yvain*. Lincoln, NB: University of Nebraska Press.

Glauser, J. (1983). *Isländische Märchensagas: Studien zur Prosaliteratur im spätmittelalterlichen Island*. Basel: Helbing & Lichtenhahn.

Jónsson, F. (ed.) (1892–5). Breta sögur. In *Hauksbók*. Copenhagen: Thiele.

Jónsson, G. (ed.) (1957). Hákonar saga Hákonarsonar. In *Konunga sögur*, vol. III. Reykjavík: Íslendingasaganaútgáfan.

Kalinke, M. (ed.) (1987). *Möttuls saga. With an edition of* Le Lai du cort mantel *by Philip E, Bennett*. Editiones Arnamagnæanæ, ser. B, vol. 30. Copenhagen: Reitzel.

Kalinke, M. (ed.) (1999). *Norse romance*, vol. I: *The Tristan legend*; vol. II: *Knights of the Round Table*; vol. III: *Hærra Ivan* (Arthurian archives, vols III–V). Cambridge: Brewer.

Reid, T. B. W. (ed.) (1967). *Yvain (Le Chevalier au lion): The critical text of Wendelin Foerster with introduction, notes and glossary*. Manchester: Manchester University Press.

Timelli, M. C. (ed.) (2000). *L'Histoire d'Erec en prose: Roman du XVᵉ siècle*. Geneva: Librairie Droz.

REFERENCES AND FURTHER READING

Barnes, G. (1984). Parcevals saga: riddara skuggsjá. *Arkiv för nordisk filologi*, 99, 49–62.

Barnes, G. (1987). Arthurian chivalry in Old Norse. *Arthurian Literature*, 7, 50–102.

Barnes, G. (1989). Some current issues in *riddarasögur* research. *Arkiv för nordisk filologi*, 104, 73–88.

Barnes, G. (1994). The lion-knight legend in Old Norse romance. In X. von Ertzdorff (ed.), *Die Romane von dem Ritter mit dem Löwen*. Amsterdam: Rodopi, pp. 383–99.

Cosman, M. P. (1966). *The education of the hero in Arthurian romance*. Chapel Hill, NC: University of North Carolina Press.

Eysteinsson, J. S. (1953–5). The relationship of *Merlínússpá* and Geoffrey of Monmouth's *Historia*. *Saga-Book*, 14, 95–112.

Glauser, J. (2005). Romance (translated *riddarasögur*). In R. McTurk (ed.), *A companion to Norse–Icelandic literature and culture*. Oxford: Oxford University Press, pp. 372–87.

Harris, R. L. (1970). The lion-knight legend in Iceland and the Valþjófsstaðir door. *Viator*, 1, 126–44.

Kalinke, M. (1970). The structure of the Erex saga. *Scandinavian Studies*, 42, 343–55.

Kalinke, M. (1981). *King Arthur, north-by-northwest: The matière de Bretagne in Old Norse–Icelandic romances*. Bibliotheca Arnamagnæanæ XXXVII. Copenhagen: Reitzel.

Kalinke, M. (2006). The genesis of fiction in the north. In J. McKinnell, D. Ashurst, & D. Kick (eds), *The fantastic in Old Norse/Icelandic literature: Preprint papers of the 13th International Saga Conference*, Durham and York, August 6–12, 2006. Durham: Centre for Medieval & Renaissance Studies, pp. 464–78.

Kjær, J. (1996). La réception scandinave de la littérature courtoise et l'exemple de la *Chanson de Roland/Af Rúnzivals bardaga*: une épopée féodale transformée en roman courtois? *Romania*, 114, 50–59.

Kramarz-Bein, S. (1999). Höfische Unterhaltung und ideologisches Ziel: Das Beispiel der altnorwegischen *Parcevals saga*. In S. T. Andersen (ed.), *Die Aktualität der Saga: Festschrift für Hans Schottmann*. Berlin: Reallexikon der germanischen Altertumskunde: Ergänzungsbände 21, pp. 63–84.

Lacy, N. J. (1994). Motivation and method in the Burgundian Erec. In K. Busby & N. J. Lacy (eds), *Conjunctures: Medieval studies in honor of Douglas Kelly*. Amsterdam: Rodopi, pp. 271–80.

Leach, H. G. (1921). *Angevin Britain and Scandinavia*. Harvard Studies in Comparative Literature, vol. VI. Cambridge, MA: Harvard University Press. Repr. Millwood, NY: Kraus, 1975.

Over, K. L. (2005). *Kingship, conquest, and* patria: *Literary and cultural identities in medieval French and Welsh Arthurian romance*. New York: Routledge.

Plusowski, A. (2004). Narwhals or unicorns? Exotic animals as material culture in medieval Europe. *European Journal of Archaeology*, 7, 291–313.

Psaki, R. (2002). Women's counsel in the *Riddarasögur*. In S. M. Anderson & K. Swenson (eds), *Cold counsel: Women in Old Norse literature and mythology*. New York: Routledge, pp. 201–24.

Sullivan, J. M. (2001). The Lady Lunete: Literary conventions of counsel and the criticism of counsel in Chrétien's *Yvain* and Hartmann's *Iwein*. *Neophilologus*, 85, 335–54.

Taylor, J. H. M. (1998). The significance of the insignificant: Reading reception in the Burgundian *Erec* and *Cligès*. *Fifteenth-Century Studies*, 24, 183–97.

14

The Grail and French Arthurian Romance

Edward Donald Kennedy

[A] squire came forth from a chamber carrying a white lance . . . from whose tip there issued a drop of blood, and this red drop flowed down to the squire's hand. . . . Then two other squires entered holding in their hands candelabra of pure gold, crafted with enamel inlays. . . . A maiden accompanying the two young men was carrying a grail with her two hands . . . The grail . . . was of fine pure gold. Set in the grail were precious stones of many kinds, . . . finer than any others in the world. The grail passed by like the lance; they passed in front of the bed and into another chamber. The young knight watched them pass by but did not dare ask who was served from the grail, for in his heart he always held the wise gentleman's advice. (Kibler & Carroll 1991: 420–21)

Thus Chrétien de Troyes introduces the Grail in his twelfth-century romance *Le Conte du Graal*, written sometime between 1181 and 1190. Later the Grail is further described when Perceval's uncle, a hermit, tells him that, "the rich Fisher King . . . is the son of the king who is served from the grail. And do not imagine he is served pike or lamprey or salmon. A single host that is brought to him in that grail sustains and brings comfort to that holy man – such is the holiness of the grail" (460). From this beginning as a serving dish the Grail developed into an "enduring symbol of aspiration" (Mahoney 2000: 78) of varying significance and appearance in romances of the next few centuries.

Chrétien de Troyes and Robert de Boron

Since Chrétien's romance is incomplete, it is difficult to say what his intentions in writing it were. His source, he claims in the opening lines, was given to him by Philip, Count of Flanders, but like Geoffrey of Monmouth before him, he was probably claiming a source that never existed. While his earlier romances – *Erec et Enide*, *Cligès*, and *Le Chevalier de la Charrette* – are secular, his *Le Chevalier au Lion*, probably written shortly before the *Graal*, indicates a movement toward concern with the moral values of chivalry with its emphasis on helping the weak and on the humility of the hero, Yvain. The *Graal* has been subject to various interpretations, with some thinking that it offers criticism of contemporary chivalry but points ahead to its redemption through the Grail family or, as Cazelles argues (1996), that it shows the failure of traditional chivalric values, criticizes the violence that they cause, and sees no hope of redemption.

Many emphasize the romance's religious content and believe it would have been influenced by contemporary changes in emphasis in the church. In the *Graal* the *naïf* young Welsh knight Perceval has accepted lodging at the castle of the maimed Fisher King, but, having earlier been told it is impolite to ask too many questions, fails to ask the question that would result in the healing of the king. He would spend years trying to correct this mistake. The scene with his hermit/uncle is associated with confession, and the hermit asks Perceval to do penance for the sins that he had unwittingly committed. Chrétien could have been influenced by the new emphasis theologians were placing on confession in the years leading up to the Fourth Lateran Council in 1215 (Ramm 2007: 90–92), and Perceval's quest to find the Grail castle again is an attempt to correct a sin of omission and to try to ease the Fisher King's suffering. As such it is an archetype of the efforts people make to correct mistakes that they have made in life.

Some inspiration for the quest for the Grail castle in which a maimed king lives could have come from the Third Crusade. Chrétien's patron for this romance, Philip, Count of Flanders, left for the crusade in 1190, and the romance is usually dated before then. Helen Adolf (1960) and others, such as Armel Diverres (1990), have suggested that the romance was influenced by descriptions of the Holy Land brought back by travelers to the East, such as the description of the square Grail castle by the sea, which resembles structures in the Holy Land, and by the fact that Jerusalem's King Baldwin IV, who reigned from 1174 to 1185, suffered from leprosy and was thus a maimed king, like the Fisher King. Interest in the East is more explicit in Wolfram von Eschenbach's early thirteenth-century German adaptation of Chrétien's *Graal*, the *Parzival*, and Wolfram had perhaps recognized in Chrétien's romance these allusions.

The Grail's significance varies in different romances, and it is depicted as different objects. Chrétien's Grail is a dish containing a host, presumably representing the body of Christ; yet Chrétien's Grail is not associated with the celebration of the Mass. Scholars' interpretations of the significance of the Grail have ranged from its being a female sexual symbol (accompanied by the spear) to symbols for the Eucharist, the grace of the Holy Spirit, God, and manna from Heaven, to name only some. Much earlier scholarship focused on its origin. Since several medieval versions of the Grail story involve the healing of an impotent king whose kingdom has become a waste land, it has been associated with pagan beliefs that the fertility of a kingdom is related to the fertility of its ruler, a view presented in the early twentieth century in Jessie Weston's *From Ritual to Romance*, which influenced T. S. Eliot's *The Waste Land* and more recently John Boorman's 1981 film *Excalibur* (see chapter 33).

The word "grail" or *graal* in Old French appears to have been derived from the Latin word *gradale*, meaning a wide and somewhat deep serving dish. That is what Chrétien's uncle implies that it is, and the word *graal* is used in the *Roman d'Alexandre* to mean a serving dish (O'Gorman 1991). Since one of the Grail's manifestations is that it provides whatever food and drink one desires, some have associated it with the Celtic platter or cauldron of plenty, which magically provided all kinds of delicacies.[1] Others, however, largely on the importance of the East in Wolfram's version, have argued for an eastern, perhaps Iranian, rather than Celtic, origin. The Grail developed several other identities in the Middle Ages, including an extraterrestrial green stone (in Wolfram von Eschenbach's *Parzival*); a platter carried by two maidens that contains a man's head covered in blood (in the Welsh *Peredur*); and an object that contains the body of Christ (in the thirteenth-century prose *Queste del Saint Graal*).

The concept of the Grail that is most familiar today, however, is the Grail as the cup, sometimes described as a chalice, that Christ used at the Last Supper, and that can be traced to a romance by Robert de Boron, whose influence on the later development of the Grail legend was greater than that of Chrétien. Robert, sometime in the 1190s, is thought to have written at least two French verse romances, the *Joseph of Arimathea* and a *Merlin*, which were later adapted into prose. He is also thought to be the author of at least one more romance, a Grail quest known as the *Perceval* that survives only in a prose redaction. Linda Gowans, however, has recently argued that Robert wrote only the prose version of the *Joseph*, and that the prose *Merlin* and *Perceval* as well as the verse romances were written by later authors (Gowans 2004). Unlike Chrétien's relatively independent romances, these three romances (*Joseph*, *Merlin*, *Perceval*) form a brief cycle or series of works that present the history of Arthur's kingdom from the early story of the Grail until Arthur's death.

Robert transformed the Grail from Chrétien's serving dish containing a wafer to a still more explicitly Christian object. He probably thought of it as a dish rather than a cup since he describes it as a *veissel* rather than a *calice* (Barber 2004: 97). However, since he transformed it from Chrétien's dish containing a wafer to a vessel containing Christ's blood, people began to think of it as a cup, and it is described as such in a later romance, the *Perlesvaus*. Moreover, if references to the Holy Land are implicit in Chrétien's castle with its maimed king, in Robert's *Joseph* the references are explicit. According to Robert, Joseph of Arimathea, who in the Bible provided the tomb for Christ's body, uses a vessel that Christ used at the Last Supper to collect Christ's blood after his body had been removed from the cross. Joseph also establishes a table, corresponding to the table at the Last Supper, at which there is a vacant seat, representing the place of Judas, the *siège périlleux*, in which it is dangerous for anyone to sit except for the chosen knight who will one day find the Grail. The vessel with the Holy Blood in it performs miracles, and although Joseph of Arimathea is destined to spend the rest of his life in the Holy Land, some years after the death of Christ, Joseph's brother-in-law, Bron the Fisher King, takes the Grail to the West, to the vales of Avaron (Avalon), where it will await the arrival of a chosen knight.

In the second romance of this series, the *Merlin*, Arthur's Round Table is described as a table that corresponds to the Grail table and the table at the Last Supper. In the third romance Perceval finds the Grail and is entrusted with keeping it. As Alexandre Micha points out (1980: 28), Perceval, a descendant of the family of Joseph of Arimathea, unites the chivalry of the Round Table with the spirituality of the Grail table and of Christ and his disciples. Robert emphasizes the triumph of Perceval and of Arthurian chivalry in the fulfillment of a quest ordained by God, and this, rather than Arthur's conquest of most of Europe, as in the chronicle tradition begun by Geoffrey of Monmouth, is the most significant event of Arthur's reign.

Robert's influence on the Grail legend was greater than Chrétien's, and it appears even in one of the continuations written for Chrétien's *Graal*. Chrétien's romance is incomplete, and scholars assume that he died while writing it; in the most authoritative of its fifteen manuscripts it ends in mid-sentence at line 9184 (Kibler & Carroll 1991: 521, n. 29). Others wrote four continuations in the late twelfth and early thirteenth centuries, all of which are longer than Chrétien's romance. The First Continuation, varying in length from 9,500 lines to 19,600 lines in different manuscripts, and the Second Continuation, 13,000 lines long, were written in the late twelfth century sometime after 1190. The first focuses on the adventures of Gawain, and although it involves a visit to the Grail castle, where Gawain sees a broken sword which if perfectly mended will reveal the secrets of the Grail castle, it gives no more information about the Grail. The Second Continuation, concerned with the adventures of Perceval, breaks off before the Fisher King explains the significance of the objects at his castle. The third continuation, known as the Menessier Continuation, consists of 10,000 lines written sometime between 1214 and 1227. It begins with the Fisher King explaining that the bleeding lance in the procession is the lance that, according to legend, Longinus had used to pierce the side of Christ at the Crucifixion, and the Grail is the vessel that Joseph of Arimathea used to collect Christ's blood. Thus, although this is a continuation of Chrétien's *Graal*, the author has followed the lead of Robert de Boron and has made the objects of the procession, the bleeding lance and the Grail containing a wafer, into specific Christian objects, both associated with the blood, rather than the body, of Christ.

These three continuations appear in six of the manuscripts of Chrétien's *Graal*, and in two others there is a fourth continuation by Gerbert de Montreuil, written between 1226 and 1230. It tells us nothing more about the nature of the Grail since Gerbert's promised explanation of its secrets is replaced in the manuscripts by Menessier's Third Continuation. Gerbert, however, emphasizes chastity and virginity: Perceval and his love Blanceflor, for example, do not consummate their marriage so that they can be certain of being admitted to Heaven. "Virginity surpasses all," Perceval tells his bride on their wedding day, ". . . and chastity too is of very great worth; and whoever possesses both together will surely win . . . the joy and delight of Paradise" (Bryant 1982: 235). This suggests the influence of still another Grail romance, the thirteenth-century *La Queste del Saint Graal*, discussed below, and also suggests that in the early thirteenth century it too had taken precedence over Chrétien's work.

Perlesvaus

Surviving in ten manuscripts and fragments, the French prose romance *Perlesvaus* (*Le haut livre du graal*), produced in the first decade of the thirteenth century, has been one of the French Grail romances best known to readers of English since Sebastian Evans' translation of it (*The High History of the Holy Grail*) appeared in the popular Everyman's Library series in 1898. It is known too as including in one of its adventures an analogue to *Sir Gawain and the Green Knight* in that Lancelot faces a similar challenge from a red knight. Its first redaction appears to have been produced in England at Glastonbury Abbey, and can therefore be regarded as a Benedictine production.

There are two allusions in it to the abbey: a colophon in two of the manuscripts says that its Latin source was found in the Isle of Avalon in a holy religious house (*une sainte meson de religion*); and at the end of the romance, Lancelot visits Guenevere's tomb at Avalon. Because Glastonbury was surrounded by marshes in the Middle Ages, it seemed to be an island; and although it may have had an association with Avalon from early times, that association became a certainty for many after the monks discovered what were supposedly the bodies of Arthur and Guenevere buried there in 1190. Since the earliest known Continental allusion to the discovery of Arthur's tomb is in a work produced about 1236, and since the *Perlesvaus* is dated earlier than that, it seems most likely that the romance was written at Glastonbury (Nitze & Jenkins 1932-7: 2.71–2). Lancelot's visiting Guenevere's tomb at Avalon would appear to be an allusion to this fairly recent discovery. Moreover, since in Robert de Boron's *Joseph* the Fisher King takes the Grail to Avalon, there would probably have been interest in producing a Grail romance there.

Influenced by Chrétien's *Graal*, its two twelfth-century continuations, and by Robert de Boron's *Joseph*, the Grail in the *Perlesvaus* is that introduced by Robert de Boron: it is "the holy vessel . . . in which the precious blood of the Saviour was gathered on the day when He was crucified to redeem mankind from Hell" (Bryant 1978: 19). Later, it is specifically described as a chalice (61, 195–96), the object that most today associate with the Grail. The *Perlesvaus* has a complex plot and uses the technique of *entrelacement*, the interweaving of a number of plots, which would be used to an even greater extent in the later longer prose romances. It is divided into eleven parts or "branches." At the outset, Arthur has fallen into malaise and 345 of his 370 knights have left the court. He is healed after a journey to St Augustine's Chapel, where he sees a vision of Mary and Christ and learns from a hermit that misfortune has befallen his kingdom because one of his knights (Perlesvaus) had seen the Grail and its Lord but had failed to ask "what was done with it and who was served by it" (27). Branches II–VIII tell of the attempts of Gauvain, Lancelot, and Perlesvaus to find the Grail. Lancelot, in a striking defense of the courtly ideal of loyalty to one's lady, fails in the quest because he refuses to repent of his love for Guenevere ("the sweetest and most beautiful sin that I ever committed," 110). In the ninth branch Perlesvaus makes up for his past mistake by conquering the Grail castle, and Arthur, Gauvain, and Lancelot make pilgrimages to it. While they are gone, Guenevere dies of grief because Sir Keu has slain Arthur's son Lohout. In the tenth branch, Arthur and Gauvain see the Grail during the Mass: it appears in five forms that "should not be revealed" except for the final one, a chalice. In the final branch, Perlesvaus gets vengeance on the enemies of his family and after defeating the Black Hermit sails away to the Isle Pelenteurose and is never heard from again. Thereafter, the Grail castle falls to ruin. The romance seems incomplete at the end after Perlesvaus disappears from the world, but this ending, Kelly argues, indicates that the church and society's struggles against evil will continue until the end of the world (1974: 177).

The *Perlesvaus* concerns the opposition of the New Law to the Old Law, where the New Law is that observed by Christians and the Old is that observed by everyone else. Although in this romance the lands of the Grail family are distinct from those of the Arthurian court, both the Arthurian and Grail societies are allied in their struggles against the Old Law. Lancelot, in spite of his sin with Guenevere, will probably find redemption because of his service on behalf of the New Law. The author of the *Perlesvaus* was undoubtedly influenced by the Crusades. In fact, although the romance apparently originated at Glastonbury, only two of the ten manuscripts were produced in England, and a colophon in a manuscript of a second redaction says that it was written for Jean de Nesle of Bruges, who was a leader of the Fourth Crusade in 1204 (Barber 2004: 46). The romance is concerned with militant Christianity, and the work endorses the violence associated with the Crusades. Perlesvaus has one knight who follows the Old Law, the Sire des Mares, who is drowned by being suspended by his heels and lowered into a vat containing the blood of his decapitated comrades (Bryant 1978: 151–2). Later in the ninth branch Perlesvaus restores peace by killing all who follow the Old Law. As Nigel Bryant observes, this is not a romance about individual knights' quests but one about Arthur's kingdom defending itself against treason and paganism and working to convert all who are not Christian (Bryant 1978: 12). The Christian virtues of compassion and love apply only to those who follow the New Law.

The *Perlesvaus* is innovative in its use of religious symbolism and typology, much of which is the subject of Thomas E. Kelly's book on the romance (1974). Since in this romance Perlesvaus's failure to ask the question resulted in disaster for the world, with all kingdoms being engulfed in war, Perlesvaus's failure, Kelly argues, can be seen as a typological reference to Adam's sin, and the rectification of Perlesvaus's failure may represent Christ's victory over original sin. Hermits appear in the romance to interpret the significance of some of what happens. A hermit explains, for example, that the Black Hermit is Lucifer, and the Coart Chevalier stands for the Old Law. Perlesvaus's victory over the Black Hermit corresponds to Christ's future victory over Satan. The adversaries of the Grail family and the Arthurian court are the evil forces that the church and secular government must continually fight against: treason, apostasy, paganism, and Satan himself (Kelly 1974: 176).

La Queste del Saint Graal and the Vulgate Cycle

The thirteenth-century *Queste del Saint Graal* also makes extensive use of symbolism and allegory and presents monks and hermits who interpret events. Given the similar uses of allegory, the relationship of the *Perlesvaus* and the *Queste* has been the subject of debate. Most now believe that the *Perlesvaus* was written before the *Queste*. The two romances offer different conceptions of Arthur's knights, with the *Perlesvaus* presenting them as defenders of the New Law and the *Queste* as generally sinful men unworthy of finding the Grail. The latter reflects Cistercian interest in reforming the knightly class and bringing them into the service of religion (Barber 2004: 7–8).

In contrast to the *Perlesvaus*, the *Queste* emphasizes patience in working with those outside the faith and God's mercy and grace for the repentant (Pauphilet 1921: 35). The worst sins are pride and lechery; the greatest virtues, humility and chastity. In contrast to Robert de Boron's *Perceval*, where the achievement of the Grail becomes a major success in the history of Arthur's court, in the Vulgate *Queste*, *la chevalerie terrien* ("earthly chivalry") is incompatible with *la chevalerie celestiel* ("celestial chivalry"). While the Grail had originally been taken from the East to the West, the directions respectively associated with Heaven and Earth, at the end of the *Queste* the three Grail knights, Galahad, Perceval, and Bors, withdraw from the Arthurian world and accompany the Grail back to the East. After Galahad looks into the Grail and dies, a hand comes down from Heaven and takes it away. It is never seen again.

The *Queste* is, like Robert de Boron's *Joseph d'Arimathie*, part of a series of interrelated romances. It is one of the prose romances that make up the Vulgate Cycle (also known as the *Lancelot–Grail* Cycle), probably written between 1215 and 1230, according to an outline developed by an "architect" who planned a series of romances to be written by a group of authors (Frappier 1959). The original plan called for the writing of three connected romances, the *Lancelot*, *La Queste del Saint Graal*, and *La Mort le Roi Artu* (*Mort Artu*), telling the story of Lancelot from his birth to his death.

The impetus for the writing of these works appears to have been a non-cyclic prose romance *Lancelot do Lac* written early in the thirteenth century (Kennedy 1980, 1986, 2003). This romance begins with the birth of Lancelot and tells of his being stolen from his mother by the Lady of the Lake and reared in her kingdom until he is old enough to be taken to Arthur's court. Shortly after arriving there, he sees and falls in love with Guenevere. His successful early adventures as a knight are attempts to win her love, and he does so with the help of his friend, Galehot, who arranges for Lancelot and Guenevere to have a meeting, at which they exchange their first kiss. They consummate their relationship (appropriately enough after Arthur has been unfaithful to Guenevere by being duped into getting into bed with a Saxon maiden and then being captured by the Saxons), and it ends with Lancelot having established his reputation as a great knight and his having won the love of Guenevere. So far as the Grail is concerned, it is a quest that Perceval had undertaken sometime in the past.

A romance, however, that ended with lovers committing adultery and getting away with it would have seemed unsatisfactory to some, and the Vulgate Cycle appears to have been created as a response to it. The Vulgate *Lancelot* begins by incorporating the *Lancelot do Lac* as the opening part of the romance, but the author(s) added much more to it, including a prose adaptation of Chrétien de Troyes' romance about Lancelot, *Le Chevalier de la Charrette*, as well as an account of how Lancelot conceived a son Galahad when, under a magic spell at the Grail castle Corbenic, he lay with the daughter of King Pelles, thinking that she was Guenevere. With the Vulgate *Lancelot*, the authors created one of the most popular medieval French romances, surviving in about 97 complete manuscripts and fragments (Trachsler 1996: 557–64). It is also one of the longest, running in its modern edition to eight volumes of text (approximately 2,000 pages) and one of commentary (Micha 1978–82).

The two concluding romances of the Vulgate Cycle, the *Queste* and *Mort Artu*, are relatively short. They circulated at times with the *Lancelot* and at times independently. The *Queste* tells of Lancelot's failure to find the Grail because of his adultery with Guenevere, and the *Mort Artu* recounts the role the adultery played in the destruction of Arthur's kingdom. These two romances thus show the disastrous results of Lancelot's love for Guenevere. Although in the non-cyclic *Lancelot do Lac*, Perceval's Grail quest has occurred in the past, in the Vulgate Cycle the quest has been shifted to the future and takes place after Lancelot and Guenevere have committed adultery. Lancelot's son Galahad replaces Perceval as the Grail hero and is the perfect knight, *li mieldres chevaliers dou monde* ("the best knight in the world," Pauphilet 1923: 12), who inherits his father's virtues and, in finding the Grail, accomplishes what Lancelot might have done had he not sinned with Guenevere. Galahad represented perfection because he fought evil, protected the weak, and was never tempted by women.

Galahad is new to Arthurian romance and was invented for the Vulgate Cycle: the French spelling of the name *Galaad* could suggest a character from Celtic tradition since the French for Wales is Galles, but it also has biblical connotations. It appears to have been suggested by Mount Galaad in the Book of Genesis in the Vulgate Bible (Mount Gilead in the King James Version and Revised Standard Version) where Jacob and Laban make a covenant. In medieval biblical commentaries, the name took on connotations of the great covenant between God and humankind, the sending of Christ into the world, and it thus connoted Christ. A Cistercian commentary on a reference to Mount Galaad in "Song of Songs" says the mountain is "head of the church." The name is a good one since it suggests both Celtic and biblical origins (Pauphilet 1921: 135–41).

The Grail in the *Queste*, as in Robert de Boron and in the *Perlesvaus*, is associated with the celebration of the Mass, but it contains the body of Christ rather than the blood, and on the rare occasions when it is described, it appears to be a dish, once again, rather than a cup. No one other than Galahad clearly sees it, and Pauphilet asks whether it is to be considered not an earthly reality but something immaterial (1921: 23–4). The romance may have been written in part to contribute to a contemporary debate over whether the miracle of transubstantiation occurs after the bread is eaten or only after the wine has been drunk as well; the author, in mentioning only the bread and not the wine and in presenting a popular Eucharistic miracle in which Christ himself is seen emerging from the vessel, is supporting the argument that the miracle occurs after the eating of the bread (Pauphilet 1921: 27–9; on a similar miracle in the *Perlesvaus* see Roach 1939). Although in this romance the Grail is associated with the castle Corbenic in which King Pelles lives, it has no fixed location but can appear anywhere, in, for example, a chapel in the woods or in a boat; and at the beginning of the romance, in a scene reminiscent of Pentecost, it appears in Arthur's hall and floats around the room, surrounded by a nimbus, and the knights, instigated by Gawain, vow to seek it in order to see it more clearly. Étienne Gilson (1925) suggested that in this work the Grail is the symbol of God's grace, and Albert Pauphilet (1921) that it represents humankind's search for God, with most of the knights representing different types – the proud, the murderous, the lecherous – who attempt this search and fall far short of the virtue needed to find God. Possibly written as a rebellion against scholastics' belief that truth rests on reason (Locke 1960: 2–3), the *Queste* is concerned with the irrational longing for something higher and better than ourselves.

In the *Queste*, Lancelot, in contrast to his loyalty to the queen in the *Perlesvaus*, repents of his sin with Guenevere, and although he can never be worthy of finding the Grail, he comes closer than most: he is able to glimpse it in a room in the Grail castle, but when he attempts to enter, he is cast out as unworthy. Yet although Galahad finds the Grail, it is Lancelot with whom most modern readers can identify: he is the good man who tries hard and comes close to achieving his goal, but cannot because of mistakes he has made. In the next romance in the Vulgate Cycle, the *Mort Artu*, Lancelot is able to win redemption after a different type of quest for salvation. There, after doing everything he can in the world, including destroying the wicked sons of Mordred, and after losing his king, his kinsmen, and the woman he loves, he withdraws from the world, becomes a holy man, and when he dies, his soul is welcomed into heaven. Jean Frappier has described Lancelot's quest for salvation as *une longue évolution intérieure* ("a long internal evolution"): in *Mort Artu* he achieves the redemption that was denied him in the *Queste* (Frappier 1972: 229–43).

Although the Vulgate Cycle was originally planned as a series of three romances beginning with Lancelot's birth and ending with his death, two other romances, the *Estoire del Saint Graal* and the *Merlin*, were written as prequels to them. The *Estoire* and *Merlin* are rather long prose adaptations of Robert de Boron's *Joseph d'Arimathie* and *Merlin*. The generally accepted explanation given by Frappier (1959) and more recently Szkilnik (1991a, b) and Elspeth Kennedy (2003), among others, is that these were two later additions, written sometime between 1230 and 1240. Szkilnik sees the *Estoire* as a rewriting of the *Queste* to explain much of what was left unclear in that romance. However, Jean-Paul Ponceau in his recent edition of the *Estoire* argues that it was written between 1220 and 1230 before both the *Queste* and the *Mort Artu* (Ponceau 1997: xii).

Just as the conception of the Grail in the Menessier continuation of Chrétien's *Perceval* was inconsistent with the Grail as Chrétien presented it, the conception of the Grail in the Vulgate *Estoire* is inconsistent with that of the *Queste*: the Grail in the *Estoire* is not a vessel containing the body of Christ but rather the one presented in Robert de Boron's *Joseph* and later in the *Perlesvaus* and the Third (Menessier) Continuation of Chrétien's *Graal*; that is, the vessel used to gather the blood of Christ after his body was taken down from the cross. While Robert de Boron had simply said that Joseph's brother-in-law Bron would take the Grail to the West, to Avalon, in the *Estoire* Joseph, his wife and son Josephés, and other followers go to Britain to establish the Christian faith. As Josephés dies, he entrusts the Grail to a nephew Alain, and it is kept in the castle Corbenic, which the ruler of the Terre Foraine had built to house the Grail.

The *Estoire*, which survives in 52 manuscripts (Trachsler 1996: 564), was important for the influence it had upon the Grail legend. Although the *Perlesvaus* indicates that by the beginning of the thirteenth century someone or some group at Glastonbury was interested in the Grail, and although Robert's *Joseph* had indicated that the Grail would be taken to Avalon, which traditionally was probably associated with Glastonbury, it is nevertheless the *Estoire* that explicitly states that Joseph of Arimathea and his followers brought the Grail to Britain and were missionaries there. This work influenced a monk at Glastonbury Abbey to add interpolations to William of Malmesbury's twelfth-century *De antiquitate Glastonientis ecclesiae* that indicated that Joseph and twelve followers established a church at Glastonbury in apostolic times (Scott 1981: 43–7). The legend was further developed in the 1340s when John of Glastonbury, in his *Cronica sive antiquitates Glastoniensis ecclesie*, wrote that Joseph brought to Glastonbury two vials, one containing the sweat and the other the blood of Christ (Carley 1985: xxx, 52–5). These vials became associated with the Grail, and the belief that Joseph had brought the Grail to Glastonbury became an English legend that lasted into the twentieth century. This story, fostered by the *Estoire*, had political overtones too since its presumed truth gave England claim to occupying a land that had had one of the earliest Christian churches in Europe and thus a claim to precedence among the nations of Europe.

The Vulgate *Merlin* is an account of the early history of Arthur's kingdom. The first part follows Robert's *Merlin* closely, after which there is a continuation, or *suite*, telling of the adventures of Arthur, including his war against the Romans, that was influenced in part by the chronicle version of the Arthurian story begun by Geoffrey of Monmouth and in part by stories about Arthur and his men (such as Arthur's fight with a demonic cat of the Lake of Lausanne) that were either in oral circulation or that were invented by the author. It also provides links to the later Grail quest by mentioning near its conclusion Joseph's having brought to Logres (i.e. England) the Grail, in which he "had caught the blood that flowed from the side of Jesus Christ," and the lance which had pierced his side. "No one knew where they were" and they would not be found until "the best knight in the world came there." Later in the *Merlin* King Pelles predicts that his daughter will give birth to that knight (Lacy 1992–6: 1.352, 359).

The Post-Vulgate *Roman du Graal*

Sometime between 1225 and 1240, two other French prose romances were written that incorporated Grail quests and are intertextually related to the Vulgate Cycle and to one another. One is the *Tristan en prose*; the other, the Post-Vulgate *Roman du Graal* (once known as the Pseudo-Robert de Boron Cycle since some manuscripts incorrectly attribute it to Robert). The *Tristan en prose*, inspired by various twelfth-century verse versions of the story of Tristan and Yseult as well as by the Vulgate Cycle, was one of the most popular romances of the Middle Ages and was the basis for Malory's tale of Tristram (see chapter 19). Surviving in about eighty manuscripts and fragments, there were at least five and possibly six versions of it written between the thirteenth and the end of the fourteenth centuries (Baumgartner 1975: 330; Field 1989).

As Baumgartner points out (1975: 49), in the *Tristan en prose* the Grail quest causes the death of the lovers. The first version of the Prose *Tristan* refers briefly to the opening scene of the Vulgate *Queste* when the Grail appears in Arthur's hall, but then tells of the adventures of Tristan as one of those seeking the Grail. It focuses just on Tristan, the author explains, because the *Queste* had omitted these adventures. While Tristan is away on the quest, Marc enters Arthur's kingdom, captures Yseult, who had fled there with Tristan, and takes her back to Cornwall. Tristan then abandons the quest for the Grail and returns to Cornwall to find her. The prose version ends not with Tristan dying of grief as he does in earlier accounts because he thinks Yseult will not return to heal his wounds but because Mark stabs him in the back with a poisoned spear provided by Morgan le Fay.

Not long after the first version of the Prose *Tristan* was completed, between 1235 and 1240, the Post-Vulgate *Roman du Graal*, an abbreviated version of the Vulgate Cycle, was written (Bogdanow 2003: 50–51). The Post-Vulgate *Roman* focuses more upon Arthur than the Vulgate does and interprets his fall, in part, as a punishment for his having committed the sin of incest with his half-sister and becoming the father of Mordred. Its Grail quest is adapted in part from the Prose *Tristan*, but instead of focusing just on the adventures of Tristan, his exploits are combined with others from the Vulgate *Queste* and with new episodes, either derived from a lost source or invented for this romance. As Bogdanow pointed out (2003), the Grail quest in the Post-Vulgate *Roman* lacks the spiritual interest of the Vulgate version and becomes rather a vehicle for the adventures of Arthur's knights. It ignores the Vulgate *Queste*'s condemnation of earthly chivalry but nevertheless shows the degeneration of knights, particularly Gawain, who, while presented as one of the most unworthy knights in the Vulgate *Queste*, descends even further in this romance into a vengeful murderer who is able to kill Eric only by killing his horse first so that he is unable to defend himself (Bogdanow 1958; Lacy 1992–6: 5.210).

Its different emphasis so far as the Grail is concerned can be demonstrated by its adaptation of the scene in the Vulgate *Queste* in which Lancelot, in the castle of Corbenic, looks into the room in which the Grail is housed. In the *Queste* Lancelot is warned not to enter the room. When he looks in, he sees the vessel surrounded by angels and an aged priest engaged in what appeared to be the consecration of the Mass. Above the priest's outstretched hands are three men, "two of whom were placing the youngest in the hands of the priest who raised him aloft as though he were showing him to the people." What Lancelot sees is the Holy Trinity and the vessel containing the body of Christ. The celebrant, weighed down as he lifts the figure up, looks as if he is about to fall. Lancelot rushes in to help him, but "as he drew near he felt a puff of wind which seemed to him shot through with flame, so hot it was . . . Then he felt himself seized by many hands," and he is thrown out of the room (Matarasso 1969: 262). In the Post-Vulgate *Roman*, Lancelot looks into the room, wanting "to go to the holy table and unveil the Holy Vessel to see what was there." He is warned not to enter but does so anyway, whereupon "he felt many hands, which seized him by the body and arms and hair and pulled him out, and they gave him such a great fall to the ground that he thought he was dying" (Lacy 1992–6: 5.266). The Post-Vulgate version lacks the sacramental nature of the scene in the *Queste*, and the reader does not learn that the vessel contains the body of Christ. Interest is in the adventures of the knights, and the religious significance is muted.

Perceforest

Limitations of space prevent much discussion of the late French romance *Perceforest*. Completed between 1340 and 1344 and rewritten in the mid-fifteenth century, this long romance, which will run to about 7,000 pages when its modern edition is complete, was influenced by the Vulgate *Estoire* and *Queste*, but, like the *Tristan en prose* and Post-Vulgate *Queste*, it shows little interest in the theological concerns of the Vulgate Grail romances. In the final part of the *Perceforest* a chaste knight Gallafur learns the story of Joseph of Arimathea and is healed of leprosy after seeing the Grail. He subsequently becomes the first Christian king of Britain. The author has eliminated much of the *sens mystique* of the *Queste* (Lods 1951, 250–58, 272–3), perhaps because the romance may have been originally written to support fourteenth-century Plantagenet political interests in England, particularly Edward III's desire to control all of Britain (Huot 2007), and the spiritual connotations of the Grail would therefore have been of little interest.

Conclusion

The development of the Grail legend in French romances of the twelfth and thirteenth centuries reveals a shift of emphasis from the religious nature of the Grail to the secular adventures of the knights. Chrétien's *Graal*, with its religious significance, represents his turning away from secular stories like *Erec et Enide* and *Le Chevalier de la Charrette*. His *Graal* suggests influences ranging from theologians' new emphasis on confession and the importance of acknowledging sin to interest in the Third Crusade and the Holy Land. Like the Vulgate *Queste*, it might possibly reflect a desire to present, in reaction to the rationalism of the twelfth-century scholastics, an object that was mysterious and unknowable. Interest in theological issues would continue: in Germany Wolfram von Eschenbach developed the theme of sin and redemption more fully and also made the implicit theme of the interaction between East and West explicit with the final marriage of Parzival's half brother from the East, Feirefiz, with the Grail maiden, Repanse de Schoye. Robert de Boron's *Joseph* presents the Grail as a vessel used by Christ at the Last Supper, and its later rediscovery in the *Perceval* attributed to Robert is presented as the greatest achievement of Arthur's kingdom. There Arthur's knights correspond to Christ's disciples.

After Robert de Boron, the *Perlesvaus* and the Vulgate *Queste* and *Estoire* are the romances most concerned with theological issues. The *Perlesvaus* presents the struggle of the New Law with the Old, but with the cruel fanaticism inspired by the Crusades. The quest for the Grail was central to the Vulgate Cycle, with its emphasis on Lancelot's sin and its effect on him as a knight. The *Queste*, with its rejection of the world, its presentation of individuals' attempts to find God, and its emphasis upon God's grace and redemption, made it a work of interest to readers in France and England for the next four hundred years. Early printed editions of it were available in both countries, and it became widely known to English readers through Malory's close adaptation of it in his *Morte Darthur*, a work published five times in the fifteenth and sixteenth centuries. The French text also had a significant influence on Spenser's *Faerie Queene* (Tuve 1966).

The Vulgate *Estoire*, whether written before or after the *Queste*, explains much that was unclear in the latter, but although it was originally written with much the same spiritual interest as that which motivated the writing of the *Queste*, its presentation of the evangelization of Britain would influence chronicles written at Glastonbury for the greater glory of the abbey, and the legend of Joseph would be changed by English nationalists from a Grail romance to a true story showing that the land they now occupied had been one of the first parts of Europe converted to Christianity. By the time of the *Tristan en prose*, the Post-Vulgate *Roman du Graal*, and the *Perceforest*, the Grail serves only as an excuse for adventures of knights or to support contemporary politics, and its spiritual symbolism has been weakened. This would appear to come from popularization and an attempt to appeal to an audience more interested in secular romances than those with religious themes.

NOTE

1 In the late twelfth-century *Roman de l'Estoire dou Graal*, Robert de Boron fancifully derives the name of the object from the French verb *agreer* (to delight) since it delights those in its presence (Bryant 2001: 36). For discussions of scholarship on the origins of the Grail, see Loomis (1963), Owen (1968), and Barber (2004: 231–55).

Primary Sources

Bogdanow, F. (ed.) (1991–2001). *La Version Post-Vulgate de la Queste del Saint Graal et de la Mort Artu*, 4 vols. Paris: Picard.

Briel, H. de (trans.) (1972). *La première continuation du Roman de Perceval*. Paris: Klincksieck.

Bryant, N. (trans.) (1978). *The high book of the Grail: A translation of the thirteenth-century romance of Perlesvaus*. Cambridge: Brewer.

Bryant, N. (trans.) (1982). *Perceval: The story of the Grail*. Cambridge: Brewer.

Bryant, N. (trans.) (2001). *Merlin and the Grail: Joseph of Arimathea, Merlin, Perceval: The trilogy of Arthurian romances attributed to Robert de Boron*. Cambridge: Brewer.

Cable, J. (trans.) (1971). *The death of King Arthur*. Harmondsworth: Penguin.

Carley, J. P. (ed.) (1985). *The chronicle of Glastonbury Abbey: An edition, translation, and study of John of Glastonbury's "Cronica, sive, Antiquitates Glastoniensis Ecclesie"* (trans. D. Townsend). Woodbridge: Boydell.

Chênerie, M.-L. (trans.) (1990–97). *Le Roman de Tristan en prose*, 9 vols. Toulouse: Editions universitaires du Sud. (Translation of Ménard edition into modern French.)

Corley, C. (trans.) (1989). *Lancelot of the Lake*. Oxford: Oxford University Press.

Curtis, R. L. (ed.) (1963–85). *Le Roman de Tristan en prose*, 3 vols. I, Munich: Max Hueber (1963); II, Leiden: Brill (1976); III, Cambridge: Brewer (1985). (Edition not complete; see Ménard edition below.)

Evans, S. (trans.) (1898). *The high history of the Holy Grail [Perlesvaus]*. London: Dent. Repr. Cambridge: Clarke, 1969.

Frappier, J. (ed.) (1964). *La Mort le Roi Artu*, 3rd edn. Paris: Droz.

Kennedy, E. (ed.) (1980). *Lancelot do Lac: The non-cyclic Old French prose romance*, 2 vols. Oxford: Clarendon Press.

Kibler, W. W. & Carroll, C. W. (trans) (1991). *Chrétien de Troyes. Arthurian romances*. Harmondsworth: Penguin.

Lacy, N. (gen. ed.) (1992–6). *Lancelot–Grail: The Old French Arthurian Vulgate and Post-Vulgate in translation*, 5 vols. New York: Garland.

Matarasso, P. M. (trans.) (1969). *The quest of the Holy Grail*. Harmondsworth: Penguin.

Ménard, P. (gen. ed.) (1987–97). *Le Roman de Tristan en prose*, 9 vols. Geneva: Droz.

Micha, A. (ed.) (1978–82). *Lancelot: Roman en prose du 13e siècle*, 9 vols. Geneva, Droz.

Micha, A. (ed.) (1979). *Merlin: Roman du XIIIe siècle*. Geneva: Droz.

Micha, A. (trans.) (1995). *Robert de Boron. Le Roman de l'histoire du Graal*. Paris: Champion.

Mosès, F. (trans.) (1991). *Lancelot du Lac*, 2 vols. Paris. (Modern French translation of the non-cyclic version.)

Nitze, W. A. (ed.) (1927). *Robert de Boron. Le Roman de l'Estoire dou Graal*. Paris, Champion.

Nitze, W. A. & Jenkins, T. A. (eds) (1932–7). *Le haut livre du graal: Perlesvaus*, 2 vols. Chicago, IL: University of Chicago Press.

Paris, G. & Ulrich, J. (eds) (1886). *Merlin: Roman en prose du XIIIe siècle*, 2 vols. Paris: Didot.

Pauphilet, A. (ed.) (1923). *La Queste del Saint Graal*. Paris: Champion.

Ponceau, J.-P. (ed.) (1997). *L'Estoire del Saint Graal*, 2 vols. Paris: Champion.

Roach, W. (ed.) (1941). *The Didot Perceval according to the manuscripts of Modena and Paris*. Philadelphia, PA: University of Pennsylvania Press.

Roach, W. (ed.) (1949–83). *The continuations of the Old French Perceval of Chrétien de Troyes*, 5 vols. Philadelphia, PA: University of Pennsylvania Press.

Roach, W. (ed.) (1956). *Chrétien de Troyes. Le Roman de Perceval ou le Conte du Graal*. Geneva: Droz.

Roussineau, G. (ed.) (1996). *La Suite du Roman de Merlin*, 2 vols. Geneva: Droz.

Scott, J. (ed.) (1981). *The early history of Glastonbury: An edition, translation, and study of William of Malmesbury's "De antiquitate Glastonie ecclesie."* Woodbridge: Boydell.

Skeels, D. (trans.) (1966). *The romance of Perceval in prose: A translation of the Didot Perceval*. Seattle, WA: University of Washington Press.

Sommer, H. O. (ed.) (1908–16). *The Vulgate version of the Arthurian romances*, 8 vols. Washington, DC: Carnegie Institution.

Taylor, J. H. M. & Roussineau, G. (eds) (1979–2007). *Le Roman de Perceforest*, 4 parts in 9 vols. Geneva: Droz.

Williams, M. (ed.) (1922–5). *Gerbert de Montreuil. La Continuation de Perceval*, 2 vols. Paris: Champion.

References and Further Reading

Adolf, H. (1960). *Visio pacis: Holy City and Holy Grail.* University Park, PA: Pennsylvania State University Press.

Barber, R. (2004). *The Holy Grail: Imagination and belief.* Cambridge, MA: Harvard University Press.

Baumgartner, E. (1975). *Le Tristan en prose: essai d'interprétation d'un roman médiéval.* Geneva: Droz.

Bogdanow, F. (1958). The character of Gauvain in the thirteenth-century prose romances. *Medium Ævum*, 27, 154–61.

Bogdanow, F. (1966). *The romance of the Grail.* Manchester: Manchester University Press.

Bogdanow, F. (2003). The Vulgate Cycle and the Post-Vulgate *Roman du Graal.* In C. Dover (ed.), *A companion to the Lancelot–Grail Cycle.* Cambridge: Brewer, pp. 33–51.

Bruce, J. D. (1923). *The evolution of Arthurian romance,* 2 vols. Baltimore, MD: Johns Hopkins University Press.

Busby, K. (1983). A new fragment of the *Perlesvaus. Zeitschrift für Romanische Philologie*, 99, 1–12.

Carley, J. P. (1992). A fragment of the *Perlesvaus* at Wells Cathedral Library. *Zeitschrift für Romanische Philologie*, 108, 35–61.

Carley, J. P. (1994). A grave event: Henry V, Glastonbury Abbey, and Joseph of Arimathea's burial. In M. Shichtman & J. P. Carley (eds), *Culture and the king.* Albany, NY: State University of New York Press.

Carley, J. P. (ed.) (2001). *Glastonbury Abbey and the Arthurian tradition.* Cambridge: Brewer.

Cazelles, B. (1996). *The Unholy Grail: A social reading of Chrétien de Troyes's "Conte du Graal."* Stanford, CA: Stanford University Press.

Diverres, A. (1990). The Grail and the Third Crusade: Thoughts on *Le Conte del Graal* by Chrétien de Troyes. *Arthurian Literature*, 10, 13–109.

Dover, C. (ed.) (2003). *A companion to the Lancelot–Grail Cycle.* Cambridge: Brewer.

Field, P. J. C. (1989). The French Prose Tristan: A note on some manuscripts, a list of printed texts, and two correlations with Malory's *Morte Darthur. Bibliographical Bulletin of the International Arthurian Society*, 41, 269–87.

Frappier, J. (1959). The Vulgate Cycle. In R. S. Loomis (ed.), *Arthurian literature in the Middle Ages.* Oxford: Clarendon Press, pp. 295–318.

Frappier, J. (1972). *Étude sur la Mort le Roi Artu*, 3rd edn. Geneva: Droz.

Gilson, É. (1925). La mystique de la grace dans la *Queste del Saint Graal. Romania*, 51, 323–47.

Gowans, L. (2004). What did Robert de Boron really write? In B. Wheeler (ed.), *Arthurian studies in honour of P. J. C. Field.* Cambridge: Brewer, pp. 15–28.

Huot, S. (2007). *Postcolonial fictions in the "Roman de Perceforest": Cultural identities and hybridities.* Cambridge: Brewer.

Kelly, T. E. (1974). *Le haut livre du Graal: "Perlesvaus." A structural study.* Geneva: Droz.

Kennedy, E. (1986). *Lancelot and the Grail: A study of the Prose Lancelot.* Oxford: Clarendon Press.

Kennedy, E. (2003). The making of the Lancelot–Grail Cycle. In C. Dover (ed.), *A Companion to the Lancelot–Grail Cycle.* Cambridge: Brewer, pp. 13–22.

Kennedy, E. D. (2005). Visions of history: Robert de Boron and English Arthurian chroniclers. In N. J. Lacy (ed.), *The fortunes of King Arthur.* Cambridge: Brewer.

Locke, F. W. (1960). *The quest for the Holy Grail: A literary study of a thirteenth-century prose romance.* Stanford, CA: Stanford University Press.

Lods, J. (1951). *Le Roman de Perceforest: Origines – composition – caractères – valeur et influence.* Geneva: Droz.

Loomis, R. S. (ed.) (1959). *Arthurian literature in the Middle Ages.* Oxford: Clarendon Press.

Loomis, R. S. (1963). *The Grail: From Celtic myth to Christian symbol.* New York: Columbia University Press.

Mahoney, D. (ed.) (2000). *The Grail: A casebook.* New York: Garland.

Matarasso, P. (1979). *The redemption of chivalry: A study of the Quête del Saint Graal.* Geneva: Droz.

Micha, A. (1980). *Étude sur le Merlin de Robert de Boron.* Geneva: Droz.

O'Gorman, R. (1991). Grail (graal). In N. J. Lacy (ed.), *The new Arthurian encyclopedia.* New York: Garland.

Owen, D. D. R. (1968). *The evolution of the Grail legend*. Edinburgh: Oliver & Boyd.

Pauphilet, A. (1921). *Étude sur la Queste del Saint Graal*. Paris: Champion. Repr. with a study of the manuscripts as *Études sur la Queste del Saint Graal*, Paris: Champion, 1980.

Ramm, B. (2007). *A discourse for the Holy Grail in Old French romance*. Cambridge: Brewer.

Roach, W. (1938). A new "Perlesvaus" fragment. *Speculum*, 13, 216–20.

Roach, W. (1939). Eucharistic tradition in the *Perlesvaus*. *Zeitschrift für Romanische Philologie*, 59, 10–56.

Szkilnik, M. (1991a). *L'archipel du Graal: étude de l'Estoire del Saint Graal*. Geneva: Droz.

Szkilnik, M. (1991b). *L'Estoire del Saint Graal*: réécrire la Queste. In W. Van Hoecke, G. Tournoy, & W. Verbeke (eds), *Arthurus Rex*. Leuven: Leuven University Press, pp. 294–305.

Trachsler, R. (1996). *Clôtures du cycle Arthurien: Étude et textes*. Geneva: Droz.

Tuve, R. (1966). *Allegorical imagery: Some medieval books and their posterity*. Princeton, NJ: Princeton University Press.

Vinaver, E. (1959). The Prose *Tristan*. In R. S. Loomis (ed.), *Arthurian literature in the Middle Ages*. Oxford: Clarendon Press, pp. 339–47.

Weston, J. L. (1920). *From ritual to romance*. Cambridge: Cambridge University Press.

Part IV
Arthur in Medieval English Literature

15

The English *Brut* Tradition

Julia Marvin

Simply descriptive as it may appear, the title of this part of this volume – "Arthur in Medieval English Literature" – poses a number of questions. What is "English"? What is "literature"? The limitations of modern assumptions about and answers to such questions have of course had their effects everywhere in the study of the past and its artifacts: in modern Arthurian studies until the end of the twentieth century, they had the effect of rendering the *Brut* tradition nearly invisible.

Not long ago English medieval drama was still characterized as "pre-Shakespearean," as if it did little more than pave the way for the real thing yet to come. In this sense, Thomas Malory is the Shakespeare of the Arthurian matter of England. Particularly in the wake of Victorian medievalism, Malory's solemn and leisurely retelling of Arthurian stories, in accessible yet appealingly archaic language, became something of a received version: prior Arthurian works, with a few exceptions, tended to be relegated to the status of source or analogue, the chronicle of wasted time that prefigured and made possible Malory's beautiful fifteenth-century fantasy.

Most of the medieval English audience for Arthurian matter would have been perplexed at this state of affairs. Their Arthurian world was far from the romance world of Lancelot and Guinevere, with its tournaments, adventure, magic, lovesickness, and the Grail quest; their Arthur was a figure of history, and their Arthurian tradition was first and foremost the *Brut* tradition.

Geoffrey of Monmouth: Enter Brutus

What constitutes this neglected tradition? The term *Brut* derives from the name of Brutus, a close descendant of Aeneas, who after exile from Italy arrives at an unknown island, exterminates the race of giants inhabiting it, and names the place "Britannia" after himself: this is the British foundation story given full form by Geoffrey of Monmouth in his Latin *Historia Regum Britanniae*, composed in the 1130s. Working from several known sources, such as Bede and Gildas, claiming to be using "a certain very ancient book written in the English language" (*quendam Britannici sermonis librum uetustissimum*) lent by a Walter of Oxford, and almost certainly drawing extensively on his own imagination, Geoffrey provided a king-by-king account of the British from their glorious Trojan origins to their ruination at the hands of invading Saxons (Thorpe 1966: 51; Wright 1985: 1). Their last king, Cadwallader, flees in exile, just as their founder Brutus had come. In between comes the story of the great British warrior king Arthur, not only capable of driving out the Saxons but on the verge of conquering Rome itself when he is undone by the treachery of his kinsman and regent Mordred. Arthur's life takes up about a fifth of the entire text: it is the heart of Geoffrey's work and the root from which all subsequent Arthurian literature springs (see chapter 3).

The *Historia Regum Britanniae* was immediately both popular and controversial, dismissed as a pack of lies by other twelfth-century Latin historiographers such as William of Newburgh and Gerald of Wales but eagerly embraced by English and Continental audiences: over 200 manuscripts of Geoffrey's history survive, and it was still being copied in the fifteenth century (Crick 1989). Small wonder, really. Geoffrey offered his readers an exciting and instructive British past, a narrative allegedly grounded in an ancient, authentic source, the alternative to which was acknowledgment of near-total ignorance of what had happened in England before the Saxons came.

Within a few years, Geoffrey Gaimar was composing a now-lost French Galfridian (i.e. in the tradition of Geoffrey of Monmouth) history of the Britons, and by the 1150s Wace, a cleric from Jersey seeking, and sometimes finding, the patronage of Henry II and Eleanor of Aquitaine, was putting the *Historia* into French verse in his *Roman de Brut*. The vernacular *Brut* tradition took hold.

A *Brut*, then, is a narrative based in, though not necessarily sedulously imitative of or limited to, the Galfridian version of British history: contemporary book lists and wills show that this was a widely used term for such works in both Latin and vernacular languages (Matheson 1998: 9–10; Marvin 2006: 3–4). Flourishing in Anglo-Norman French, Middle English, Welsh, and Latin, the *Brut*, or "chronicle," tradition was to become not only the dominant Arthurian tradition but the dominant historiographic tradition of late-medieval England and Wales. The Prose *Brut* chronicle, which began with an Anglo-Norman Galfridian account of Britain, carried the narrative up to the death of Henry III in 1272, and then, with continuations and translations, into the fifteenth century. With some 250 surviving manuscripts in a number of languages, the Prose *Brut* was the most popular secular vernacular work of the late Middle Ages in England (Matheson 1999: 1–8; Marvin 2006: 1–15). It was the first published Arthurian work in England and the first published history of England: William Caxton printed it as the *Chronicles of England* in 1480, five years before his edition of Malory. It went through thirteen different editions in the early days of print (Matheson 1999: xxxiii–xxxvi). Its matter persisted in later histories such as Holinshed's *Chronicles*, and it influenced works up to Spenser's *Faerie Queene* and beyond.

The life of Arthur is by far the longest section of the Anglo-Norman Oldest Version of the Prose *Brut*, and although the episode became relatively less prominent in the Middle English *Brut*s, with their lengthy fourteenth- and fifteenth-century continuations, annotations in manuscripts suggest that Arthur still continued to command readers' attention. The Prose *Brut* may safely be considered the most widespread Arthurian work of the English Middle Ages.

Wace

To understand the modern obscurity of the *Brut* tradition, given its contemporary popularity, it is necessary to return to the questions of the beginning of this chapter: what is "English"? What is "literature"?

The case of Wace gives a sense of the complexities of defining medieval "Englishness." Born in the Channel Islands, Wace spent much of his life in Caen, Normandy, and his surviving works are composed in what is known as Anglo-Norman French, also called "French of England," or, more accurately but less commonly, "Anglo-French" – that is, the dialect of French descended from the language of the invaders of 1066, in spoken use for some generations after the Conquest, and in written use for some centuries, growing ever more distinct from Continental French in its spelling, vocabulary, and word forms. It survived longest as Law French, which was still spoken in the English courts at the time of Henry VIII, as is known from continuing complaints about its use.

Wace, then, neither lived in England nor wrote in English: why should his work be considered English? Because in his day English culture was not limited to the English language, and the realm of the kings of England was not limited to the British Isles. William the Conqueror was Duke of Normandy before he won the crown of England, and generations of his descendants spent much of their lives seeking to defend and expand their Continental holdings in Normandy and beyond. They themselves might be brought up on the Continent, speaking French, the children of French-speaking mothers, and in their dynastic alliances married to French-speaking women. It is telling that Henry I, son of William the Conqueror, had his heart buried in Rouen, France, and his body in England. It is often suggested that Henry's great-grandson Richard Lionheart spoke no English at all, and he spent almost none of his reign in England. Even after the loss of Normandy and the other catastrophes of John's reign, the kings of England continued to press their Continental claims, and Edward III (not to mention James I) still styled himself King of France.

To oversimplify greatly: Latin was the language of affairs of church and state. English had flourished as a written language before the Conquest but had fallen off thereafter. The Celtic languages continued to thrive in their own milieus. But French was the spoken vernacular of status among the baronial classes of the realm, a written vernacular valuable to those literate in Latin and invaluable to those who were not. A wide corpus of Anglo-Norman writing survives, imaginative, edifying, and practical – everything from tales of adventure, devotional manuals, and saints' lives to chess manuals and recipe books (Dean 1999).

Over time, French came to serve more of the written functions that Latin had served, and it became less and less a spoken language in England, as the use of English broadened, and English itself absorbed so vast an amount of French and Latin vocabulary as to become a truly hybrid language. But only toward the end of the thirteenth century did English begin to re-emerge as a significant written language, and only in the second half of the fourteenth century and beyond would it come to prevail. In the 1150s, nothing could have been more natural for a cleric seeking to please the English court than to take Geoffrey's Latin and put it into French. Wace's book evidently found a receptive audience: parts of over thirty manuscripts survive, in England and on the Continent (far more than most Anglo-Norman works). And later writers gladly used Wace as a source.

It is only later notions of language and nation – the sorts of notions that led to the creation of separate departments of English and French in modern universities – that might make Wace seem any less properly English than, say, Geoffrey Chaucer (who is very likely to have written in French as well as English). But those notions have been influential in determining what has entered the scholarly and cultural canon and what has been excluded from it.

French faculties have not always been hospitable places for the study of Anglo-Norman. With its distinctive spelling and vocabulary, and its precocious abandonment of grammatical structures that were to persist longer elsewhere, Anglo-Norman could seem merely bizarre, insular in the worst sense of the word, when measured against the yardstick of Continental dialects, particularly the idealized forms of those dialects generated in the heyday of critical text editing by scholars intent on reconstituting the original, "pure" state of both language and texts that had been "corrupted" through the processes of scribal transmission. As an inferior dialect that by definition could have no "pure" state, Anglo-Norman was uncongenial, and indeed a standing challenge, to such approaches. It was shunted to the margins: the vitality of Anglo-Norman written culture was generally ignored or explained away, as were such historical inconveniences as the fact that the French literary monument, the *Chanson de Roland*, survives only in an Anglo-Norman manuscript.

Anglo-Norman fared no better in faculties of English. In the nineteenth century, as a scientifically oriented university structure took form, rigorous study of the history of the English language and Anglo-Saxon literature was at the academic forefront (and certainly much-needed, too). This was the time of the foundation of the Early English Text Society, meant both to provide scholarly editions of medieval works in English and to generate data for what became the *Oxford English Dictionary*. Its beautifully chosen emblem is the ninth-century Alfred Jewel, a gem with a portrait of Christ, now housed in the Ashmolean Museum at Oxford, perhaps the handle of a pointer meant to help in reading, possibly commissioned by Alfred the Great himself – both a great Anglo-Saxon warrior king and a great patron of learning, who fostered the production of important texts in English. This was the past – pious, heroic, and learned – to be recovered and celebrated.

Anglo-Norman could seem positively tawdry by comparison, a reminder of England's own history as colonized rather than colonizer, and easy to dismiss as an affectation of the aristocratic classes who had neither the education to use Latin nor the earthy authenticity to use English. The single best-known medieval reference to Anglo-Norman is probably Chaucer's slighting account of the pretentious Prioress as a speaker of French "after the scole of Stratford atte Bowe, / For Frenssh of Parys was to hire unknowe" (*General Prologue* 125–6). The Anglo-Norman Text Society was not founded until 1937, and one of the reasons suggested for the production of the *Anglo-Norman Dictionary* was "to avoid the need for printing texts of which the only interest lay in the vocabulary" (Rothwell 1977–92: General Preface, ix). Its emblem is nothing more than a monogram.

The very idea that there could be a large body of works of which the only interest lay in the vocabulary suggests both how interesting the members of the society found vocabulary and what a limited view even they took of the potential value of Anglo-Norman texts. This is by no means to suggest that most or all Anglo-Norman works (any more than most or all works of any given language, time, or place) are works of genius, or works appealing to modern sensibilities. It is to say that the tendency to consider Anglo-Norman only as an unusual linguistic phenomenon, and to balkanize the study of medieval English literary culture along linguistic boundaries, has led to unnecessarily narrow and distorted understandings, and incomplete, oversimplified narratives of development (Busby 1993; Marvin 2004). Nowhere is this more obviously the case than in Arthurian studies, where neglected works offer the opportunity to form a richer and better-grounded idea of medieval Arthurian traditions as contemporary audiences knew and experienced them, and to reach a clearer view of the significance of Arthurian narrative for English self-understanding and self-representation.

With consideration of Wace's form arises the question "What is 'literature'? – another issue on which modern and medieval thinking may differ drastically and confusingly. Why would Wace choose to translate Geoffrey's history in verse rather than prose? In a time in which poetry is not especially popular, and brief, dense, highly subjective lyric poems predominate, it is easy to think of verse as more artful and difficult than prose, and not at all an appropriate medium for narrative or factual information. But in the Middle Ages (and well beyond), prose could be no less artful than verse, and both lyric and narrative verse were admired and widely practiced.

The ultimate origins of western poetry lie in oral performance, with memorization the oldest means of transmission, and written preservation a later development. Established as norms, the conventions of orality persisted long after writing and written transmission became common, and long after the memorized performance of book-length works had in all likelihood lapsed. In the scribal culture of the western Middle Ages, memorization was a valued art and an important part of education, with versification a tremendous help, both for purposes of retaining needed information and for purposes of performance. Especially in earlier periods, verse was a favored form for all kinds of practical and scientific works such as geographies, calendrical works, bestiaries, medical texts, and histories. To write in vernacular verse was not to make matters difficult or obscure, but appealing, accessible, and memorable – and at least in the twelfth century, the form of verse as such did not imply fictionality.

It must also be remembered that medieval reading, especially in the households and institutions that constituted the main audience for vernacular writing, was not necessarily a quiet, private activity. Although annotations show that some readers studied these texts with pen in hand, books were also read aloud in group settings, so that those who did not possess the skill of reading (a skill that not so many people needed in everyday life) were nevertheless a fundamental part of the audience for written works. Medieval narrative manuscripts are often broken up into sections marked with headings and/or large initials, episodic, easy to locate, and of a length to be heard at one sitting: these works were composed at least as much to be heard by listeners as to be seen by readers. They remained aural in practice long after orality of composition had become a literary conceit.

The notion that Wace is composing first and foremost for an audience of listeners is to be taken seriously. Reading aloud may have been one of his own duties as a *clerc lisant* ("reading clerk"), and his own verse is meant to be heard (Le Saux 2005: 3–5). His diction is generally structured around clear parallels and contrasts, both syntactic and sonic. With consonantal and vocalic sound play extending well beyond his rhyme words, Wace's hallmark as a poet is the sheer pleasure he takes (and gives) in the effect of sound itself, one of the elements least translatable into modern English.

The opening lines of the *Roman de Brut*, composed in vigorous octosyllabic couplets, offer a sense of Wace's approach:

> Ki vult oïr e vult saveir
> De rei en rei e d'eir en eir
> Ki cil furent e dunt il vindrent
> Ki Engleterre primes tindrent,
> Quels reis i ad en ordre eü,
> E qui anceis e ki puis fu,
> Maistre Wace l'ad translaté
> Ki en conte la verité.
> (Weiss 1999: lines 1–8)

> Who wishes to hear and wishes to know,
> From king to king and from heir to heir,
> Who they were and whence they came,
> Who first held England,
> What kings there were in order,
> And who was ancient and who later,
> Master Wace has translated it,
> Who tells the truth about it.

The verse of the beginning is as orderly and confident as the account of the kings promises to be. Its parallel phrasing is both propulsive and leisurely. The repetition of *ki* ("who") at the beginnings of lines and the division of the first three lines into grammatically parallel halves joined by *e* ("and") lead up to the climactic full line declaring the subject of who has held England. This is the central theme, and not just the topic, of the entire work, which, like the *Historia* on which it is based, traces the broad rise and fall of the Britons, and not only the narrowly conceived doings of one king after another. What king would hold England, how securely, and on the basis of what claims, were scarcely topics of theoretical historical interest at the time: when Wace presented the *Roman de Brut* to Eleanor of Aquitaine in 1155, her husband Henry II had been on the throne for less than a year, after a period of anarchy and civil war against his predecessor Stephen that had lasted for nearly twenty years. This may suggest why Wace uses the anachronistic name of England rather than Britain in his opening.

After this first sentence, Wace launches immediately into the story of Aeneas's flight from Troy, *si cum li livres le devise* ("as the book relates") (Weiss 1999: line 9). From the start, he combines the weight of written and oral traditions: the knowledge that his audience will gain by hearing comes from a book, which a writer who gives his name and declares his truthfulness has translated, that is, "carried over," from one medium to another – or, in this case, two media, from Geoffrey's Latin into his own French, and from the page to the listener's ear.

The apparent sources of the *Roman*'s authority – the bases on which the audience is to trust it – are complex here. It is striking that Wace does not name his source, or sources: he drew on two different versions of Geoffrey's *Historia*, known as the Vulgate and the First Variant, while non-Galfridian material, including the first known reference to the Round Table, also appears in the *Roman* (Le Saux 2005: 85– 107, 152). By giving his name Wace makes himself the guarantor of the text's reliability, putting himself into personal, individual relationship with his patrons and audience, as well as reminding them just who deserves the credit for the translation: passing reference to "the book" appears to be a sufficient gesture toward his source material.

At first glance this may seem to be a decidedly different approach from that of Geoffrey of Monmouth. In his dedication (absent from the First Variant version), Geoffrey ponders the problem of just how little is known about the ancient British past. He invokes Gildas and Bede, thus demonstrating his credentials as a man familiar with the learned historiographic tradition, but laments the paucity of information on earlier kings whose deeds "were such that they deserve to be praised for all time" (*digna eternitate laudis constarent*). Now, if there are no books about these men, how can it be known that they are praiseworthy? Through oral tradition, in which "these deeds were handed joyfully down . . . just as if they had been committed to writing, by many peoples who had only their memory to rely on" (*gesta eorum . . . a multis populis quasi inscripta iocunde et memoriter predicarent<ur>*) (Thorpe 1966: 51; Wright 1985: 1). It would seem that oral tradition is good – but apparently not quite good enough, since Geoffrey goes on to claim that his book is not an attempt to record the stories that people tell, but nothing more or less than a translation of the ancient British book that has turned up just when needed. Its antiquity and Britishness make it authentic; its written status makes it stable. Like many other medieval writers, Geoffrey disclaims his own originality by claiming only to be translating an older text. How much the disingenuousness of Geoffrey's source-claim is meant to be recognized by the *Historia*'s original audience is a matter of debate. But in the end, Wace's bland invocation of "the book" as his source is only a less-embellished equivalent to Geoffrey's: in both cases, the anonymous source is presented as an authority exactly because it is written – and the book now offered is presented as a wholly adequate manifestation of that source, effectively "the book" itself, beyond which the lucky audience need look no further.

Covering some hundred kings in just under fifteen thousand lines (of which around four thousand are devoted to Arthur), the *Roman*'s episodes are necessarily brief. Wace spends little time describing his characters' exteriority or explaining their interiority. He enjoys and expands scenes of spectacle such as battles and feasts; he may somewhat elaborate moments of direct discourse in Geoffrey's text; he introduces provocative elements such as Gawain's defense of peace and amorousness in response to Cador's delight at the prospect of war against Rome (Weiss 1999: lines 10733–72); he shows signs of being more moralistic and less secular than Geoffrey. And in one possible signal of his own sense of the credible and edifying, he omits Geoffrey's lengthy prophecies of Merlin. But none of this marks a "fictionalization" of Geoffrey's *Historia*. Nor is the *Roman de Brut* a romance masquerading as history. Wace is presenting it as, and manuscript evidence suggests that its earliest audiences took it as, vernacularized history (Le Saux 2005: 85–9).

Layamon: A Landmark Account

Sometime between 1185 and 1216, Layamon, a priest of Areley Kings near Worcester, translated and expanded Wace's *Roman* into English verse, in just over sixteen thousand alliterating long lines that also use internal rhyme. His *Brut* is huge, ambitious, and puzzling to modern scholars. Layamon acknowledges Wace (and is the one to report that Wace gave his *Brut* to Eleanor of Aquitaine). He also says that he used Saint Bede's *Englisca boc* ("English book") and a Latin work by Saints Albin and Augustine, combining the three books into one: if he did, the latter two have left few traces in the text, but the announcement gives the book a broad linguistic, learned, and saintly pedigree (Barron & Weinberg 1995: lines 16–28). The range of suggested dates for the poem is grounded in differing interpretations of contemporary allusions in the text. But the two surviving manuscripts are substantially later – from the second half of the thirteenth century – and very different from each other. And the language of the poem, particularly in the longer manuscript (British Library, London, Cotton Caligula A.ix), is markedly old-fashioned and very challenging to the modern reader (Le Saux 1989: 1–13).

Works that survive in a single manuscript must be accepted, more or less, as they are. When a work survives in many manuscripts, scholars have a fair amount of evidence (sometimes dauntingly much) for choosing among texts or particular readings if they want to try to identify the "original" text or have a "standard" version to discuss. But when there are only two manuscripts, scholars – and editors – can be in a bind. Which to choose? And on what basis? The complications and frustrations of such questions are themselves enough sometimes to discourage scholarship on a given work, if the "real" work is taken to be what the original author intended and wrote (virtually always a theoretical construct, since so few autograph copies survive), rather than the manuscripts that really circulated and do survive, products of the endlessly transformative processes of scribal transmission (Bryan 1999: 3–60).

Fair scholarly consensus has emerged that the two Layamon manuscripts are separately descended from another manuscript or manuscripts, that the Caligula manuscript represents a version of the text probably closer to what Layamon wrote, and that the other manuscript (British Library, London, Cotton Otho C.xiii) modernizes language and abridges content. The significance of these differences and the relative merits of the two versions are much debated. The Caligula manuscript is generally preferred (and is the one that has been translated into modern English), a conclusion perhaps helped by the fact that the Otho manuscript was terribly damaged in the fire that devastated Robert Cotton's manuscript collection in 1731. Of such circumstances is literary history made. The question of the Caligula manuscript's archaism remains vexed as well: if it is purposeful, what is its purpose? To strengthen the work's resemblance to Old English poetry (assuming that Layamon had access to such a thing) and therefore make it seem more "epic" (to use an anachronistic but well-liked term)? To make it seem more like a Galfridian ancient British book and therefore more authentic and authoritative? If the latter, why should Layamon come right out and say, as he does, that he is basing his work on written sources?

Layamon's work is thus hard to date, hard to read, hard to gauge, textually unstable, and hard for modern sensibilities to take, given its enormous length, horrific violence, and harsh vision of the world. To take one example: in Wace, when St Ursula and her retinue of eleven thousand virgins are shipwrecked and captured by wicked pagans, they are simply led off to Cologne and decapitated (Weiss 1999: lines 6073–4). But in the Caligula text, Ursula is not allowed the dignity and chastity of a quick martyrdom: the evil Melga not only rapes her, but when he is finished with her, *he ȝæf heo his hired-monnen sone to makien to heore* ("he then gave her to his followers to use as their whore") (Barron & Weinberg 1995: line 6040). Though the poem's textual issues have drawn the fruitful interest of historians of English language and literature, its matter aside from its Arthurian section has received relatively little critical attention. Recent translations may help remedy that lack. For the time being, it is still the case that Layamon's *Brut*, one of the unquestionable landmarks of English literature and the *Brut* tradition, remains basically unknown to non-specialists.

The Return to Prose

Unlike students of language and literature, political and legal historians of England after the Conquest have never had the luxury of regarding Anglo-Norman as someone else's problem: the legal and documentary record runs the linguistic gamut. The disciplinary boundaries hemming in historians have instead tended to be those of literary form. However natural verse may have seemed as a medium for historical narrative in the twelfth and thirteenth centuries, in the nineteenth century it could seem eminently ignorable, particularly when it was based on what was called Geoffrey's "pseudo-history." Poems might be scavenged for potentially useful information on proper names, folk customs, military tactics, and the like. But narratives by contemporaries, or better still eyewitnesses, were much to be preferred for their immediacy, and failing that, use might be made of learned Latin histories written by demonstrably judicious men, or at least men who made their leanings clear. For the kinds of history being done at that time, popular or "legendary" histories, and those many generations away from their original sources, were not particularly helpful. But the tendency to regard such works as at best irrelevant and at worst bogus led to reification of the components of medieval historical tradition then found valuable, so that one part of the contemporary picture could too easily be taken for the whole thing (see, for instance, the attitudes manifested and works included or not in Gransden 1974, 1982).

Historical poems might find a place in literature departments, though as discussed above Anglo-Norman remains to this day something of an orphan dialect. But what of prose? The next major development in the *Brut* tradition, the one that would ensure the vernacular currency of the Galfridian narrative well into the sixteenth century, was in prose – Anglo-Norman prose, no less. And it was overlooked both by historians as too literary (and too derivative to be of value, except in some of its continuations) and by literary scholars as too historical and literally prosaic, particularly in the canon-forming days when verse alone effectively constituted medieval vernacular literature. Thus we have the phenomenon of the *Brut* tradition becoming least recognized in modern scholarship at the moment of its greatest prominence in medieval culture, with the rise of the Prose *Brut* chronicle at the end of the thirteenth century.

The Oldest Version of the Anglo-Norman Prose *Brut* was in all likelihood composed during the reign of Edward I, probably in the north of England, possibly in Lincolnshire, by a writer comfortable with both Latin and French who had access to a wide range of materials of the kind found in monastic libraries. It shows every sign of having been written for a secular, baronial audience, and it may well have been commissioned by a family such as the Longespées or the de Lacys, who held the patronage of Barlings Abbey, the Latin chronicle of which is related to the Prose *Brut*.

The Prose *Brut* begins conventionally enough, with the flight of Aeneas from Troy. But in one way after another, it departs from prior tradition. Its form in prose may represent a choice to follow trends in Francophone historiography in the thirteenth century, when verse may have begun to acquire associations of fictionality (Spiegel 1993: 55–60; Damian-Grint 1999: 172–207). Its unadorned style may also represent an attempt to make the text as transparent and apparently untouched by human agency as possible. Rather than exaggerating his sources and calling attention to his labor in translating them, the writer of the Prose *Brut* does not mention them at all, and he does not identify himself, although his sources are many and he goes to considerable effort in translating and synthesizing them, as well as transforming them. The chronicle comes off as something like a bible of English history, a plain, authoritative account of what happened, designed for an audience not necessarily inclined to ask how that is known.

The writer bases the first part of his narrative on Wace, but he also appears to have consulted and integrated matter directly from Geoffrey of Monmouth. And when he has finished with them, he keeps the history going, adapting Gaimar's *Estoire des Engleis* (all surviving manuscripts of which accompany texts of Wace), a close analogue of the Praemonstratensian chronicle of Barlings, and a range of other historiographic, hagiographic, and narrative materials, including a life of Edward the Confessor and Havelok material perhaps in both French and English. The result is a concise, complete account linking the kings of England from Brut all the way to Henry III and his son Edward.

No longer is the connection between the ancient and recent past simply analogical, nor is the Prose *Brut* a simple retelling of past stories. Largely by selection and omission (editorial techniques also favored by his vernacular predecessors) rather than outright alteration, the writer of the Prose *Brut* generates both continuous narrative and as close to continuous lineage as he can, melding British, English, and Norman identity, and doing as much as possible to eliminate the grand pattern of rise and fall fundamental to the Galfridian historical vision. He goes further than Geoffrey to minimize the significance of the Roman occupation of Britain (making it an occasion to tell mostly of British repulses of the invaders); he works to present the Norman Conquest as a restoration of true lineage in the face of Harold's usurpation of the throne; most drastically, he eliminates the ruin and exile of the Britons by the Saxons by selective omission and source-switching at the crucial moment. In its quiet way, the Prose *Brut* is a deeply revisionist work.

In general, it offers a far more optimistic vision than its predecessors and analogues, presenting a world in which it is possible for the people of Britain to go from strength to strength. But this optimism is far from grandiose; instead, it is focused on everyday virtues and dilemmas. The Prose *Brut*'s good kings are dutiful men, attentive to the needs of their people and respectful of their baronage. Its greedy and incontinent kings have a way of meeting nasty deaths, devoured by wolves or sea monsters or brought down by misdirected arrows. Its virtues are socially oriented ones. And the horror that it repeatedly represents, its supreme negative exemplum, is the kind of internal conflict, the triumph of fear, greed, and personal ambition, that leads to civil war. The pervasiveness of this concern, and its pertinence as compared, say, to the threat of invasion by pagans, make excellent sense in the context of the end of the thirteenth century, after the vividly remembered catastrophes of the reign of John (whom the Prose *Brut* represents as a monster) and the conclusion, well within living memory, of the Barons' War against Henry III.

The Arthur of the Prose *Brut* is an ideal king for an audience sick at the thought of civil war, longing for order and stability. He drives out invaders, honors and rewards his barons, and turns violence beyond the shores of Britain. Unlike Wace and Layamon, the writer of the Prose *Brut* takes no interest in scenes of battle for their own sake: he limits himself mostly to reporting the results, sometimes with condemnation of dishonorable tactics, and sometimes with a display of sympathy for the suffering of both sides.

A famous moment in Arthur's career as a warrior encapsulates these tendencies. In Geoffrey of Monmouth and in Wace, Arthur's defeat of the giant of Mont-Saint-Michel, who has abducted and killed his kinswoman Eleine, forms a lengthy episode, with an extended, gory fight. The writer of the Prose *Brut* boils the combat down to this: *e vint lendemain al geant e se combatist oue li, e oue grant peine le conquist e loccist* ("and he came the next day to the giant and fought with him, and with great effort he defeated him and killed him"). The part of the story that the writer retains, and even expands, is the sad account by Eleine's nurse of her captivity in the hands of the giant. The nurse rather than Arthur becomes the central figure of the episode, and Arthur's killing of the giant (which may be considered the prototype for scenes of single combat in later Arthurian narratives) redresses the wrong that she, an old and common woman, has suffered (Marvin 2006: 170–73).

This Arthur is not an occasion for escape into a world of fantastic, mystical, or erotic adventure. Rather, he is a means by which the writer can propose an ideal of kingship that addresses the immediate, mundane hopes and fears of the chronicle's audience. His story remains a tragic one, with Mordred's treason a reminder that no king, however just and generous, can wholly safeguard himself against betrayal by his own. The enemy within is as much to be feared as the enemy without; the forces of history are not so much grand and impersonal as grounded in the choices of individuals, so that it becomes the responsibility of king and people alike to exercise self-control and honor in order to have peace.

Other late-medieval vernacular works in the *Brut* tradition survive, among them the Royal *Brut* fragment (part of another Anglo-Norman verse translation of Geoffrey of Monmouth), the Anglo-Norman verse chronicle of Peter Langtoft, the Anglo-Norman *Scalacronica* of Sir Thomas Gray, the Middle English verse chronicles of Robert of Gloucester and Robert Mannyng, and *Castleford's Chronicle*, also in verse (see chapter 4). The only one of such works to have achieved anything like canonical status in English literature is the anonymous Alliterative *Morte Arthure*, which has the advantages of being strictly Arthurian in content, not gargantuan in length (just over four thousand lines), composed in verse, and a known source for Malory.

Chronicle and Romance

When one recalls the sheer popularity of the Prose *Brut*'s Arthurian narrative, promulgated essentially unchanged in later Anglo-Norman versions and the Middle

English translations of the chronicle, it becomes clear that the question of who Arthur was for his medieval audiences is richer and more complex than standard narratives of Arthurian tradition have recognized, with their emphasis on vernacular works of enduring interest and value but relatively little contemporary influence.

In medieval English culture, the *Brut*, or chronicle, tradition, was not peripheral. Rather, marked by both its continuity and its adaptability, it was historiographically central, textually prevalent, and by no means isolated from or opposed to romance tradition. As Ad Putter has argued, the writers of romance were so vividly aware of and indebted to chronicle tradition that they set their tales in the periods of peace following Arthur's conquests, as reported in Geoffrey and his successors (1994). The *Brut* tradition presents its historical Arthur as a different kind of exemplar, addressing different kinds of concerns from those prevalent in romance, a figure no less instructive and clearly of no less interest to contemporary audiences for all that. The chronicle and romance traditions share in their durability and versatility, and in the ways they make Arthurian narrative an opportunity for societal self-examination, celebration, idealism, and the acknowledgment of the limitations of all human endeavor.

As full of violence as both traditions are, and as much as they both value prowess, peace turns out to be a shared dream of both as well: in the *Brut* tradition, it is the goal, however fleetingly achievable, and in the romance tradition, it is the necessary precondition for adventure. Chronicle provided writers and contemporary audiences with the imaginative space to locate and engage with romance: it can do the same for readers today.

Primary Sources

Barron, W. R. J. & Weinberg, S. C. (eds trans) (1995). *Layamon, Brut; or, Hystoria Brutonum.* Harlow: Longman.

Benson, L. D., Pratt, R., & Robinson, F. N. (eds) (1987). *The Riverside Chaucer.* Boston, MA: Houghton Mifflin.

Brie, F. W. D. (ed.) (1906, 1908). *The Brut; or, the Chronicles of England,* 2 vols, o.s. 131, 136. London: Early English Text Society.

Marvin, J. (ed. trans.) (2006). *The oldest Anglo-Norman Prose Brut chronicle: An edition and translation.* Woodbridge: Boydell.

Thorpe, L. (trans.) (1966). *Geoffrey of Monmouth. History of the kings of Britain.* Harmondsworth: Penguin.

Weiss, J. (ed. trans.) (1999). *Wace's Roman de Brut: A history of the British.* Exeter: University of Exeter Press.

Wright, N. (ed.) (1985). *Geoffrey of Monmouth. Historia Regum Britanniae,* vol. I: *Bern, Burgerbibliothek, MS 568.* Cambridge: Brewer.

References and Further Reading

The Anglo-Norman On-Line Hub. At www.anglo-norman.net, accessed March 30, 2008.

Blacker, J. (1994). *The faces of time: Portrayal of the past in Old French and Latin historical narrative of the Anglo-Norman regnum.* Austin, TX: University of Texas Press.

Bryan, E. (1999). *Collaborative meaning in medieval scribal culture: The Otho Layamon.* Ann Arbor, MI: University of Michigan Press.

Busby, K. (1993). "Neither flesh nor fish, nor good red herring": The case of Anglo-Norman literature. In R. T. Pickens (ed.), *Studies in honor of*

Hans-Erich Keller. Kalamazoo, MA: Medieval Institute Publications, pp. 399–417.

Crick, J. (1989). *The* Historia Regum Britanniae *of Geoffrey of Monmouth*, vol. 3: *A summary catalogue of the manuscripts*. Cambridge: Brewer.

Damian-Grint, P. (1999). *The new historians of the twelfth-century renaissance: Inventing vernacular authority*. Woodbridge: Boydell.

Dean, R., with the collaboration of M. B. M. Boulton (1999). *Anglo-Norman literature: A guide to texts and manuscripts*. London: Anglo-Norman Text Society.

Gransden, A. (1974, 1982). *Historical writing in England*, 2 vols. London: Routledge & Kegan Paul.

Hanning, R. W. (1966). *The vision of history in early Britain: From Gildas to Geoffrey of Monmouth*. New York: Columbia University Press.

Kennedy, E. D. (1989). *Chronicles and other historical writing*, Manual of the writings in Middle English, 1050–1500, vol. 8 (ed. A. Hartung). New Haven, CT: Connecticut Academy of Arts & Sciences.

Le Saux, F. H. M. (1989). *Layamon's "Brut": The poem and its sources*. Woodbridge: Brewer.

Le Saux, F. H. M. (2005). *A companion to Wace*. Woodbridge: Brewer.

Marvin, J. (2004). The unassuming reader: F. W. Maitland and the editing of Anglo-Norman. In S. Echard & S. Partridge (eds), *The book unbound: Editing and reading medieval manuscripts and texts*. Toronto: University of Toronto Press, pp. 14–36.

Marx, W. & Radulescu, R. L. (eds) (2006). Readers and writers of the Prose *Brut*. *Trivium*, 36 (special issue).

Matheson, L. M. (1998). *The Prose Brut: The development of a Middle English chronicle*. Tempe, AZ: Medieval & Renaissance Texts & Studies.

Moll, R. J. (2003). *Before Malory: Reading Arthur in later medieval England*. Toronto: University of Toronto Press.

Putter, A. (1994). Finding time for romance: Mediaeval Arthurian literary history. *Medium Aevum*, 63, 1–16.

Rothwell, W. (gen. ed.) (1977–92). *Anglo-Norman dictionary*. London: Modern Humanities Research Association.

Spiegel, G. M. (1993). *Romancing the past: The rise of vernacular prose historiography in thirteenth-century France*. Berkeley. CA: University of California Press.

Tiller, K. J. (2007). *Layamon's Brut and the Anglo-Norman vision of history*. Cardiff: University of Wales Press.

Wickham-Crowley, K. M. (2002). *Writing the future: Layamon's prophetic history*. Cardiff: University of Wales Press.

16

Arthurian Romance in English Popular Tradition: *Sir Percyvell of Gales*, *Sir Cleges*, and *Sir Launfal*

Ad Putter

The relationship between popular and elite art, between oral-traditional and literate productions, is much more involved than our categorizations admit. Poets writing in the highest aristocratic circles, such as Marie de France, who wrote her lays "in honour of you, noble king [Henry II]" (*Lais*, prologue, line 43), and Chrétien de Troyes, patronized by Countess Marie of Champagne and Count Philip of Flanders, were happy to admit that their materials were popular in origin. In *Erec et Enide*, our earliest surviving Arthurian romance, Chrétien tells us that he has taken the story from professional storytellers – who cannot do the story justice, he adds snootily (20–22). Marie de France claims she is telling the stories that lie behind the songs (the *lais* proper) sung by Breton minstrels. Popular songs and tales could be distilled into court poetry, and in their turn the writings of poets like Chrétien de Troyes and Marie de France could become part of the repertoire of professional minstrels who recited stories in the manor hall.

In a society that was only part literate, romances composed by court poets passed easily from the hands of readers to the memories of minstrels, and from oral performance back into script (Bradbury 1994). The three romances studied in this chapter – *Sir Percyvell of Gales*, *Sir Cleges*, and *Sir Launfal* – are excellent illustrations of this traffic between the written and the oral domains, the aristocratic palace and the provincial manor; and although these romances are usually termed "popular," it might be more accurate to call them transitional: semi-literate and semi-courtly.

Sir Percyvell of Gales

Sir Percyvell survives in a unique copy in the fifteenth-century Thornton manuscript (Lincoln Cathedral MS 91), without which our inheritance of medieval romances would have been much the poorer. (The manuscript also contains unique copies of the Alliterative *Morte Arthure* and *Sir Degrevant*, and versions of, among others, *The*

Awntyrs off Arthure and *Sir Eglamour of Artois*.) The story of *Percyvell* is loosely based on Chrétien de Troyes's *Conte du Graal* (c. 1181), the masterpiece he never finished, presumably because death intervened. Yet *Sir Percyvell* is by no means a slavish translation of Chrétien's romance. If the English poet knew it, as seems likely (Fowler 1975; Busby 1978, 1987),[1] he was probably working not from a written text of the poem but from a memory of having read it (or having heard it read). His adaptation is free, and he omits many of the things (e.g. the Grail, the parallel adventures of Gawain) that make the *Conte du Graal* so wonderful and exasperating, creating a shorter and more straightforward story with a very satisfying shape and conclusion. While Chrétien made his story fit "to be told in the royal court" (*Conte du Graal*, line 65), the poet of *Sir Percyvell* turned it into a story fit to be recited by minstrels – apparently with some success, for the anonymous poet of the *Laud Troy Book* (c. 1400) includes "Percyvell" in a catalogue of heroes celebrated by *gestoures* [minstrels] . . . *at mangeres* [banquets] *and grete festes* (39–40). The other names in the list – Bevis, Guy, Tristrem – suggest that the poet was thinking of the English romance rather than Chrétien's French one.

The *Percyvell* poet's choice of verse form is an interesting one. Chrétien wrote in octosyllabic couplets; the English poet preferred the melodic and characteristically insular tail-rhyme stanza. The basic building block of the tail-rhyme stanza (typically a six- or twelve-liner) is a couplet of rhyming lines, rounded off by a shorter tail-line (rhyming with other tail-lines in the same stanza). Students of medieval literature are likely to have encountered the form in Chaucer's parody *Sir Thopas*, which incidentally takes a swipe at *Sir Percyvell of Gales*:

> Hymself drank water of the well
> As did the knight sire Percyvell
>   So worly under wede.   [*worthy under clothes*]
> (*Sir Thopas*, VII, 915–17)

In *Sir Percyvell*, the tail-rhyme format is extended by the use of triplets rather than couplets. To this metrical template the poet added the device of concatenation. One or more words from the last line of the stanza are repeated in the first line of the next. When used well, as in the example below, the device drives the plot on and asserts continuity in the teeth of stanzaic division:

> The childe couthe no better rede,   [*knew no better course of action*]
> Bot down gun he lyghte.   [*he proceeded to dismount*]
>
> Now es Percyvell lyghte
> To unspoyle the Rede Knyghte . . .
> (Mills 1992: 739–42)

In this example, the end of stanza presents an action as having been begun; the opening line of the next stanza presents the same action as having been completed.

Admittedly, this is not the artful kind of concatenation that is on display in such ornate poems as *Pearl* or *Three Dead Kings*, where it is used to divert and enrich significance rather than to advance the story; but it is nevertheless highly effective in keeping the narrative pulse going despite the stops and starts of each stanza.

In terms of the story, too, *Percyvell's* narrative continuity is impressive. As I have noted already, the poet has simplified his source, and the story that remains can be summed up as follows. After Percyvell's father (also called Percyvell) has been treacherously killed by the Red Knight, Percyvell junior and his mother take refuge in the wild forest, where the hero grows up in complete isolation from the civilized world. One Christmas, while out hunting, he encounters a trio of knights (Gawain, Ywain, and Kay); when these identify themselves as knights of the Round Table, Percyvell resolves to leave his mother to become a knight also. Before he leaves her, his mother gives him a ring. On his way to Arthur's court, Percyvell exchanges rings with a damsel. When he arrives at the king's court he kills Arthur's arch-enemy, who happens to be none other than the Red Knight, the slayer of the hero's father. The Red Knight's mother, a witch, is also dispatched and thrown on to the fire where her son is already smoldering. Percyvell liberates Lady Lufamour from a sultan and his army, who have been laying siege to her castle; he is knighted by King Arthur and subsequently becomes king of Lufamour's land. One Christmas, he remembers his old mother and rides off to find her. He meets again the lady with whom he earlier exchanged rings, and rescues her from her cruel and jealous lover (the Black Knight). However, when he asks to have his ring back, he is told it has been given away to a giant. The giant had wanted to present it to a lady he was courting (Percyvell's mother), but on seeing the ring she went mad, believing the giant had killed her son and taken the ring from him; since that moment she has been running wild in the forest. Percyvell slays the giant, wanders into the forest, finds his mother, and heals her. She remarries, and at the very end of the romance he goes off on crusade and dies a good death.

As this simplified summary indicates, the *Conte du Graal* has become a "family romance," and the poet has improved the internal consistency of his story by turning almost all the characters into blood relatives (Veldhoen 1981). For example, Percyvell's mother (Acheflour) is Arthur's sister in this version; the knights that Percyvell meets in the wild forest (anonymous in Chrétien) are Percyvell's cousins; the sultan who harasses Percyvell's wife and the giant who harasses his mother are brothers; the Red Knight who kills Percyvell's father also has a mother (the witch); and Percyvell inherits his name and his chivalric leanings from his father. The most basic category of relationship, that of kinship, helps to create unity of action.

Narrative coherence and progression are further enhanced by means of certain props – the javelin and the ring – that function to materialize relationships and to signpost the direction of the story (Putter 2004: 178–7, 186–8). The javelin is already associated with the hero in Chrétien's *Conte du Graal*, where we meet the young boy throwing javelins around before he meets five fully armed knights. The boy's fondness for throwing javelins signifies at once his innate nobility and his cultural deprivation:

the spears are, as it were, his arms *faute de mieux*. In *Percyvell*, too, the boy loves "shooting" his javelin – *He wolde schote with his spere / Bestes and other gere / As many als he myghte bere* (213–15) – but the poet gives the weapon a neat prehistory. It is the only possession of Percyvell's father that his mother takes with her in her flight from the world of chivalry (though when she gives the spear to him she claims to have found it in the forest):

> Wolde she noght with hir bere   [*carried nothing with her*]
> Bot a lyttil scotte-spere,[2]   [*javelin*]
>   Agayn hir son yode.   [*for when her son could walk*]
>
> And when hir yong son yode,
> Scho bade hym walke in the wodde,
> Tuke hym the scotte-spere gude,
>   And gaffe hym in hande.
>   (Mills 1992: 189–204)

Handed down from father to son, the spear materializes their connection (also affirmed by the name they share), and it is therefore fitting that when young Percyvell kills the Red Knight, his father's killer, he should do so by means of his father's heirloom.

The poet manages to convey these meanings in a characteristically light-hearted and comical vein (Eckhardt 1974). A good example of his humor is the moment when the Red Knight first sets eyes on our unlikely hero, dressed in goat skins and seated on a pregnant mare:

> And forto se hym with sighte,
> He putt his umbrere on highte   [*raised up his visor*]
> To byhalde how he was dyghte   [*dressed*]
>   That so till hym spake.
> He sayde, "Come I to the, appert fole, [*plain fool*]
> I sall caste the in the pole,
> For all the heghe days of Yole,   [*In spite of*]
>   Als ane olde sakke!"
> Than sayd Percyvell the free   [*noble*]
> "Be I fole, or whatte I bee,
> Now sone of that sall wee see,
>   Whose browes schall blakke."
> Of schottyng was the childe slee;   [*cunning*]
> At the knyghte lete he flee:
> Smote hym in at the eghe,
>   And oute at the nakke.
>   (Mills 1992: 676–92)

This is great comedy, enhanced by a technical detail that was not yet available to Chrétien. By the fourteenth century, the helmet had acquired a movable visor, the *umbrere*, which the Red Knight lifts because he cannot quite believe his eyes. The raising of eyebrow and visor becomes his downfall when the javelin hits *for all the heghe days of Yole* (fighting in anger being forbidden on the holy days of Christmas).

The other object that holds the story together is the ring that Percyvell's mother gives to her son as a parting gift:

> His moder gaffe hym a ryng
> And bad he solde agayn it bryng:
> "Sonne, this sall be oure takennyng,   [*token*]
>   For here I sall the byde."
> He tase the ryng and the spere,   [*takes*]
> Stirttes up appon the mere;   [*Leaps up*]
> Fro the moder that hym bere
>   Forthe gan he ryde.
>   (Mills 1992: 425–32)

At the level of realism, the ring does not make much sense. As Maldwyn Mills observes in his editorial note to these lines, "[s]ince the hero is almost fully grown, it might seem unnecessary to provide the mother with a token by which he can be identified" – so unnecessary, indeed, that when Percyvell is finally reunited with his mother, the ring is not even mentioned (Mills 1992: 194). But the ring's usefulness becomes apparent if we focus on its numerous contributions to the plot. First, it foreshadows the ending that lies in store by promising that mother and son will eventually be reunited. Second, it conveniently produces the obstacles and diversions that all narratives require: it is first exchanged with a damsel (who is thereby marked for reappearance), and then given to a giant (who is thereby marked out for death). Last but not least, the ring generates the confusion and potential tragedy that happy endings need to be truly triumphant. Percyvell's mother concludes from the ring that her son is dead and descends into madness; and that, in short, is the disastrous ending from which the poet must deliver us.

And deliver us he does. To mark Percyvell's homecoming, the hero leaves all his cultural acquisitions (horse, arms, and armor) behind:

> His armour he levede therin;
> Toke on hym a gayt skynne
> And to the wodde gan he wyn,   [*go*]
>   Among the holtis hare.   [*grey forests*]
> A sevenyght long hase he soghte;
> His mothir ne fyndis he noghte,
> Of mete ne drynke he ne roghte,   [*he did not care for food nor drink*]
>   So full he was of care.
> Till the nynthe day byfell
> That he come to a welle,
> There he was wonte forto duelle,   [*dwell*]
>   And drynk take hym thare.

When he had dronken that tyde,   [*at that time*]
Forthirmare gan he glyde;
Than was he warre, hym bysyde,   [*then he became aware, beside him*]
        Of the lady so fre.
Bot when scho sawe hym thare
Scho bygan forto dare   [*cower*]
And sone gaffe hym answare,
        That brighte was of ble.   [*complexion*]
Scho bigan to call and cry:
Sayd, "Siche a sone hade I!"
His hert lightened in hye,   [*at once*]
        Blythe forto bee.
Be that he come hir nere,   [*nearer*]
That scho myght hym here
He sayd, "My modir full dere:
        Well byde ye me!"
        (Mills 1992: 2197–224)

The ending returns us to the well where Percyvell drank as a little boy (*He was fosterde in the felle / And dranke water of the welle*, 6–7) and where, many Christmases ago, his mother had promised she would wait for him: *For here I sall the byde* (428). Percyvell's words to her, *Wel byde ye me*, commemorate her promise, which has finally been fulfilled. Although she is obviously deranged and cowers like an animal, she has somehow managed to stick to her word, and is not so far gone that she cannot recognize her son in the man who now stands before her.

The poet, then, has reshaped the story beautifully. The ending mirrors the beginning, and the return to the past is what makes the happy ending so fulfilling (Putter 2004). The past, *Sir Percyvell* consoles us, *can* be recovered in the present: the hero, now knight and king, can return home to find his mother still waiting for him, and the demented wild woman can recover to be the mother and wife she once was.

Sir Cleges

The romance of *Sir Cleges* is a shorter poem (676 lines in the twelve-line tail-rhyme stanza), extant in two fifteenth-century manuscripts: (National Library of Scotland, Edinburgh Advocates 19.1.11) and Ashmole 61 (Oxford MS Bodleian 6922). It was probably composed in the second half of the fourteenth century. The story is of a knight who is ever-generous to squires, minstrels, and poor folk, but who one day finds himself in such penury that he can no longer celebrate Christmas in the lavish and hospitable style to which he and his wife Clarys were accustomed. On Christmas Eve, Cleges falls into a swoon, and hears (or imagines he hears) from every direction the merry sound of minstrels, which powerfully reminds him of his present deprivations. Clarys cheers him up, and the two go to bed. When the bells sound for

Mass, they go to church. Returning home, Cleges goes into the garden and discovers that the cherry tree has borne fruit. Clarys advises him to present the cherries to the king. Cleges sets off with his son in the morning, but their access to the king is barred by three officers in succession (first the porter, then the usher, and finally the steward), who will only let Cleges pass if he gives each of them a third of what the king will give to Cleges. The latter agrees and, when the king offers him a reward, asks for twelve blows. These he proceeds to divide equally between the greedy court officers. The king retires to his parlor, where he is regaled by a minstrel who sings him a story (484). (In the Advocates MS, this *gest* is a heroic tale of Sir Cleges [Treichl 1896].) The minstrel identifies the knight of the cherries as Sir Cleges, who in happier times was the king's favorite knight, and when Sir Cleges explains to the king why he asked for twelve blows, the king laughs heartily and makes Cleges his steward and Cleges's son his squire.

In this summary, *Sir Cleges* may not sound much like an Arthurian romance, nor is it usually considered as such. For example, there is no mention of it in Barron (1999), a standard reference work to Middle English Arthurian writings. And yet there are good reasons why *Sir Cleges* deserves to be considered in this chapter. One of these is the prologue, which places the story in the days of Uther Pendragon:

> Lystyns, lordynges, and ye shall here
> Of ansystores that before us were,
> > Both herdy and wyght.
> In tyme of Uter Pendragon[3]
> Kyng Artour fader of grete renoune,
> > A semly man of syght.
> He had a knyght, hyght Sir Clegys;
> A doughtyere man was non at nedys
> > Of the Ronde Table ryght.
> (Laskaya & Salisbury 1995: lines 1–9)

In the chronicles, the time of Uther Pendragon is synonymous with hardship and turmoil (to be replaced by prosperity and calm during Arthur's golden rule), so it provides an apt backdrop to a story that has Cleges giving generously to *squyeres that traveyled in lond of werre / And wer fallyn in poverté bare* (16–17) before falling into poverty himself. Nor is this the only connection between *Sir Cleges* and the chronicle tradition. When Cleges gives his cherries to the king, the latter presents them to his lady-love:

> The Kyng therfore made a presente
> And send unto a lady gente
> > Was born in Corneweyle.
> She was a lady bryght and schen;   [*resplendent*]
> And after sche was hys awne Quen,
> > Withouten any feyle.
> > > (385–90)

The poet can afford the teasing allusion to an unnamed queen from Cornwall because we all know who she is: Ygerna, husband of Duke Gorlois of Cornwall. According to the chronicle tradition, Uther fell in love with her, slept with her (after being transformed into her husband's likeness by Merlin's magic), and so conceived Arthur. Wace, the translator of Geoffrey of Monmouth's *History of the Kings of Britain*, adds the pertinent detail that Uther wooed her by showering her with gifts: *Par les privez la salout / E ses presens li enveot* ("He greeted her through his close friends and sent her presents," *Brut*, lines 8590–91). Cleges's cherries are imagined as belonging to this precise moment. Cleges sends them to Uther, Uther to Ygerna, and the rest is history.

Sir Cleges connects not only with the tradition of Arthurian chronicle but also with that of popular literature. Its metrical form, the tail-rhyme stanza, and its orientation toward a listening audience, are consistent with minstrel transmission. It is true that its opening address, *Lystyns, lordynges, and ye shall here* (1), is conventional, and so could be aped by bookish authors (compare Chaucer's opening gambit in *Sir Thopas*: *Listeth, lordes, in good entent*); but the argument that apparent signs of minstrelsy in medieval romance must be literary devices, designed to conceal "a more prosaic actuality – that of the lone reader, the clerics using their library, the family book" (Field 1999: 168; see also Taylor 1992: 62) is open to question. One of many problems with this ingenious and literate argument is that it fails to explain why minstrel addresses should be so notoriously unstable in the manuscript tradition. For instance, in the *Seege of Troy*, all the minstrel addresses vary in wording and placement in each of the four manuscripts (Bradbury 1998: 112–13). It really does seem they were adapted to suit the needs of "live" performance. In the light of Bradbury's findings, it is not surprising to find a different opening address in the Advocates manuscript: *Will ye lysten and ye schyll here*.

The possibility that the work was recited by minstrels would also explain the prominence given to minstrels in the tale. Their absence at the Christmas feast is the thing that distresses Cleges the most, and without them the story would not have a happy ending. Cleges's previous generosity to the minstrel profession – a virtue that is pointedly recommended (46–60) – pays off when a minstrel sings his praises to King Uther. This "pay-off" directs us to the paradoxical moral of *Sir Cleges* and the role of minstrels in it: that giving to others is ultimately self-rewarding (as Cleges's gift of the cherries shows), and, conversely, that penny-pinching, as practiced by the three court officials, is self-defeating. Although God is the ultimate guarantor of this "symbolic economy" – intervening with his own *presande* (304) of miraculous cherries when Cleges's generosity threatens to go unrewarded – minstrels are the great merchants of symbolic capital who show us how the system works: if you give handsomely to minstrels, they will spread your good name, and that symbolic capital (honor, reputation) will in the end win you real capital (e.g. lucrative promotion to steward).

Although there is little that is artful in *Sir Cleges*, the writing is effective and often more coherent than at first appears. Consider, for example, the following stanza in which Cleges, returning from Mass, and thanking God for all that he has sent him, discovers that the cherry tree is in fruit:

> As he knelyd oune hys kne
> Underneth a chery tre,
>   Makyng hys praere,
> He rawght a bowghe in hys hond,   *[took hold of]*
> To ryse therby and upstond;
>   No lenger knelyd he ther.
> When the bowghe was in hys hond,
> Gren levys theron he fond
>   And ronde beryes in fere.   *[in a bunch]*
> He seyd, "Dere God in Trinyté,
> What maner beryes may this be,
>   That grow this tyme of yere?"
>   (192–204)

The cherries seem to appear as if in answer to Cleges's prayer, and Cleges's oath, *Dere God in Trinyté*, is at once an expression of surprise and an acknowledgment of the donor. The poet's painstaking orchestration of Cleges's discovery – he kneels to pray, reaches for a bough to lift himself up, stands up, and then feels with his hand the fresh leaves and round berries – seems cumbersome, but what the poet and his audience appreciated (and not all modern readers have) is that the Mass from which Cleges and his wife have just returned is the Midnight Mass.[4] Cleges, in other words, cannot *see* the tree in fruit; he *feels* it when he lifts himself up by a branch. The poet has imaginatively realized the situation and made effective use of the Christmas setting by making the miracle of the growing fruit coincide with the miracle of Christmas: *Thys nyght this fruyt grew* (307).

   Cleges also has something useful to tell us about the primary audience of these "popular romances." In some discussions of this issue (e.g. Bliss 1960: 42), this audience has been imagined as the peasantry, but as Nicola McDonald (2004) has recently pointed out, the tendency to posit the lower or lower-middle classes as the consumers of popular romances is really based on aesthetic prejudice. If these romances have seemed crude and unsophisticated, then that must be because their audiences were so too, i.e. the audience for them was low ranking or at best bourgeois. Although some romance manuscripts (most notably the Auchinleck manuscript) can indeed be connected with an emergent bourgeoisie (Pearsall 1965), the manuscripts of *Sir Cleges* point to a rather different milieu. The Ashmole manuscript (containing romances, saints' lives, and courtesy books) was probably produced for a Leicestershire gentry family (Blanchfield 1991, 1996), while the Advocates manuscript was probably also connected with a provincial landowning family, as the manuscript companions suggest. These include sketches of armorial bearings, and a copy of Hoccleve's *Regiment of Princes* (Guddat-Figge 1976, 119–20). The Thornton manuscript, containing *Sir Percyvell*, indicates a similar milieu: the manuscript is named after its amateur

scribe, Sir Robert Thornton, a Yorkshire gentleman. A more modest gentleman's
anthology containing several romances (*Sir Amadace*, *Avowing of Arthur*, and *Awntyrs
off Arthure*) is the so-called Ireland-Blackburn manuscript, now in the Princeton University Library, Robert Taylor Collection. This mid-fifteenth century manuscript also
contains various memoranda pertaining to the manor of Hale in Lancashire, and was
presumably copied for the entertainment of the Ireland family who held the manor.
Of course, families like the Thorntons, the Sherbrookes and the Irelands were not
aristocratic, but they had standing in the local community, had reputations to maintain, and, especially during the Hundred Years' War, family fortunes to make or break.
It is tempting to see in the poem's setting – a time of war when squires become
impoverished (16–17) and when manors have to be sold to raise cash (93–4) – a reflection of their own anxieties. The rewards given to Cleges's son are also suggestive of
the poet's own day and age:

> The Kyng made hys son squyere
> And gafe hym a colere forte were
>   With a hundryth pownd of rente.
>   (553–5)

This puts us squarely in the period of "bastard feudalism," when great lords distributed liveries and rewards to build up private armies of followers. William Langland
viewed these developments with much alarm in *Piers Plowman* (c. 1385):

> "Y have seyen grete syres in cytees and townes
> Bere beyus of bryghte gold al aboute hire nekkes
> And colers of crafty werk, bothe knyghtes and squieres . . ."
>   (*Piers Plowman*, C Prol. 177–9)

The *Cleges* poet inhabits this militarized world more comfortably. To his thinking,
the best you could wish for your son is that he might join the retinue of a "great sire,"
wear his "collar" (the necklace displaying the lord's motto or arms), and maintain his
cause in return for financial security.

Sir Launfal

The romance of *Sir Launfal* is also never far removed from the real world and its pres-
sures. The poet, who may also have written *Octavian* and *Libeaus Desconus*, gives his
name in the last lines of the romance:

> Thomas Chestre made thys tale
> Of the noble knyght Syr Launfale.
> Good of chyvalrye.
>   (1039–41)[5]

Interestingly, as has been noticed by Burrow (1996), one "Thomas Chester" is mentioned in a list of soldiers (including Geoffrey Chaucer) captured at Rheims and ransomed by King Edward III in 1360 (Crow & Olson 1966: 24). If this Thomas Chestre is indeed our poet, then his social status as given in the official record was that of *armiger* (i.e. man-at-arms). And although some critics detect in *Sir Launfal* a bourgeois tone, such as might appeal to "less sensitive listeners in market-square or inn-yard" (Bliss 1960: 1), the tale associates itself aggressively with the armed classes (Knight 1986: 105), threatened on the one hand by rich "city folk" and on the other by the need to keep up the spending habits associated with genteel persons and *generosi* (the revealing medieval Latin word for gentlemen).

The story has impeccable courtly credentials since it goes back to Marie de France's *Lanval*. Marie's story concerns a foreign knight at Arthur's court who is sadly overlooked by Arthur when the king distributes his gifts. Disconsolate, he wanders off, lies down in a meadow as if to go asleep, and then sees two beautiful maidens who accompany him to their lady. She offers Lanval love and material support, on condition that he does not talk to anyone about her. When Guinevere sees Lanval lost in thoughts about his lady, Guinevere offers her love to him. Lanval repudiates her; Guinevere angrily says he probably likes boys better than women; and Lanval retorts by claiming that he has a lady, and that her meanest maidens are more beautiful than the queen. Guinevere, offended, accuses Lanval of having propositioned her, and he is then accused of treason by Arthur and assumed guilty unless he can establish his innocence within a year's time. Worse still, Lanval's lady has vanished from his life, since he has broken his promise to keep her secret. A year later, just as Lanval is about to be condemned for treason, some maidens appear to announce their lady's arrival. When Lanval's lady comes riding in, he jumps on her palfrey, and he is never heard of again. And that, Marie de France concludes, is the story behind the lay of Lanval which the Bretons sing.

Marie's story was mediated to Thomas Chestre by a fairly faithful Middle English translation (the couplet *Landevale*), but although the inherited story is still easily discernible, Chestre's various additions and changes of emphasis create a very different narrative (Stokes 2000). It seems to have been Lanval's poverty, rather than his sense of alienation from court, that really caught Thomas Chestre's imagination. As in *Sir Cleges*, the main factor behind the hero's poverty is his boundless largesse, but, again as in *Sir Cleges*, reckless spending is not criticized by the poet but wholeheartedly endorsed. Hence, by the end of the story, King Arthur (like his father in *Sir Cleges*) rewards the spendthrift hero by appointing him as steward. Lanval and Cleges are ideally suited to be in charge of royal household expenditure, or so these poets seem to think.

If this thought strikes us as hopelessly quixotic, it is not because Thomas Chestre did not know what it meant to be poor. Poverty in Chestre's world is a condition so shameful and demeaning that Sir Launfal cannot admit it to his peers. When he can no longer afford his upkeep at Arthur's court and is forced to leave, he tells his companions that he has got to go to his father's funeral; and when, after more savage spending, he has to send his squires back to Arthur's court in shabby clothing, they pretend that Launfal is doing fine, their disarray due not to penury but to a "hunting trip" from which they have just returned. Launfal confides his poverty only to the mayor's daughter, who is not in his class but kindly invites him for dinner while her father attends King Arthur's feast (to which poor Launfal has not been invited). Launfal declines her offer, confesses he has not been able to go to church for want of clean clothing, and asks her to lend him a saddle and bridle. As he rides out, he encounters Dame Triamour, who makes him a conspicuously rich man.

The minor role of the bourgeois daughter is an intriguing one. In the real world, an imprudent and impoverished gentleman like Launfal might well have had to settle for a rich merchant's daughter, but in *Sir Launfal*'s world of make-believe the prospect of social compromise is happily banished by the Lady from Fairy Land. The most fitting gift she has for Launfal is a bottomless purse: evidently, the best reward for knights who spend recklessly is to give them the means to perpetuate their disregard of economic realities, including the inconvenient truth that Launfal owes something to the mayor's daughter (who disappears down a narrative black hole).

Sir Launfal, on this reading, is not so much bourgeois as violently *anti*-bourgeois, and this element of challenged class-consciousness is a notable addition to Chestre's version of the story. His partisan sense of class rivalry between downtrodden gentles and upstart townspeople explains why he found the episode involving the mayor (which he may have found in the later lay of *Graelent*) worth adding. When Thomas Chestre's Launfal leaves Arthur's court, he asks for board and lodging from the mayor of Caerleon. When it emerges, however, that Launfal has fallen out of favor in Arthur's court, the mayor suddenly "remembers" that he has offered hospitality to seven knights from Brittany. All he can offer him now is:

> a chamber by my orchardsyde,
> Ther may ye dwelle with joy and pryde,
> Yyf hyt your wyll were.
>
> (124–6)

This "chamber," as both parties very well know, is the garden shed, and accepting this kind offer really amounts to admitting that you have little honor left, that you are the kind of person who could live "with joy and pryde" in a hovel. Launfal has sunk low enough to be obliged to take up the offer; and it looks as if the mayor, who was once Launfal's servant (line 90), has put one over on the knightly classes.

But Thomas Chestre invites these nightmares of social humiliation only in order to exorcise them more fully. Dame Triamour sends cartloads of riches to Sir Launfal's lodgings, and *when the Meyr seygh that rychesse / And Sir Launfales noblenesse*, he opportunistically invites Launfal for dinner. Launfal is now in a position to reply with undisguised contempt:

> "Now y have more gold and fe,
> (That myne frendes han sent me)
>   Than thou and alle thyne!"
> The meyr for schame away yede.
> Launfal yn purpure gan hym schrede...   [*began to dress in purple*]
>   (412–16)

The point is so basic – Launfal's stock is high, the mayor's flat – that it does not need the elaboration that Chestre gives it; but, since it is Chestre's side that has triumphed and his social rivals that have lost, he naturally relishes the victory and the losers' humiliation.

This brings me to Thomas Chestre's third innovation: the emphasis he puts on the sentiment of "pride" (Hirsch 1967). The negative associations of the word (arrogance, haughtiness) are not operative in *Sir Launfal* except in the false accusations of the villains. In Chestre's usage, as in that of many other medieval gentlemen, "pride" is synonymous with what in our own times certain people (teenage gang members, professional football players) call "respect." The disgrace of poverty is keenly felt as a violation of the "respect" to which Launfal *qua* knight is entitled (*He rood wyth lytyll pryde*, 213). If respect and self-respect depend on economic capital, they also require a demonstration of manly prowess. This kind of masculine display behavior, which is completely absent from Marie de France, comes to the fore in Sir Launfal's battle with a giant (Sir Valentine), and Launfal asserts his masculinity to the very end. The differences between Marie de France's ending (faithfully rendered in *Sir Landevale*) and Thomas Chestre's are particularly revealing in this regard. In Marie de France, Lanval leaps on his mistress's palfrey, and seated behind her he vanishes, never to be seen or heard of again. She has delivered him, and he delivers himself to her. In *Sir Launfal*, the squire Gyfre fetches Launfal his "steed" (i.e. his warhorse) so that he can accompany his lady in proper manly fashion. Together they ride to a "joly isle" called Oliroun, and any man who wants to test his mettle can joust with him once a year on a set day.

The comparison with Marie de France highlights how much beauty is sacrificed in Thomas Chestre's version of the story. Gone are the mysterious otherness and separateness of the Otherworld (never even identified as Fairy Land by Marie), the tantalizing correlation of that Otherworld with a private world of daydreams, and the final liberating surrender of the social self for the sake of personal fulfillment. But it is important also to appreciate the coherence of the mentality that thinks these sacrifices are all for the good. Chestre's ethos, in which self-regard is bound up with the respect you are given by others, requires a more assertive hero than Marie's withdrawn stranger, and cannot countenance the "opposition between public and private on which Marie's story turns" (Spearing 1993: 111).

A final point about *Sir Launfal* that needs to be made in this Arthurian companion is Thomas Chestre's hostility to Guinevere, who is the source of all that is evil and petty in this version. It is she (and not Arthur, as it is in *Lanval*) who overlooks the

hero in the cycle of gift giving, but even before she has done anything wrong Thomas
Chestre has put the knife in:

> But syr Launfal lykede her noght,
>> Ne other knyghtes that wer hende;   [*courteous*]
> For the lady bar los of swych word   [*had a reputation*]
> That she hadde lemannys under her lord,   [*lovers*]
>> So fele ther nas noon ende.   [*many*]
>>> (44–8)

In fairness to Guinevere, it should be noted that at this point in the story she has not
yet taken any "lord" in marriage, but for Chestre that is curiously beside the point.
Guinevere's real problem is that her reputation for promiscuity precedes her, and
Chestre's dislike of her is based not so much on her conduct in this story but on her
role in the wider Arthurian tradition. Guinevere, as Chestre knew, did indeed have
lemmanys under her lord, lovers such as Mordred and above all Lancelot, who is mentioned neither in Marie de France's *Lanval* nor in *Sir Landevale*, but makes two cameo
appearances in *Sir Launfal* (15910) to stimulate our memories of the queen's guilty
secrets.

Guinevere's meanness to the hero is matched only by Chestre's meanness to
her. When she refuses to credit Launfal's boast that his lady's servants are more
beautiful than she is, Guinevere stakes her two eyes on her superior beauty: *Yyf
he bryngeth a fayrer thynge / Put out my eeyn gray!* (809–10). When Launfal's lady
arrives, with damsels far prettier than Guinevere, Guinevere has cause to regret
her words:

> Wyth that Dame Tryamour to the quene geth,
> And blew on her swych a breth
>> That never after myght she se.
>>> (1006–8)

Guinevere may not be blind in any other Arthurian work but, according to Chestre,
that is what she deserves: "she gets what she asked for" (Stokes 2000: 5).

The story of Lanval, curialized by Marie de France and gentrified by
Thomas Chestre, continued to enjoy a long and eventful life after the Middle Ages.
The Middle English couplet version was reproduced in a number of early printed
editions to meet the demands of an expanding market of lay folk who could read, and
for those who could not (i.e. the vast majority) the story continued to be recited by
professional entertainers who knew it by heart. The last trace of that oral tradition is
Sir Lambewell from the seventeenth-century Percy Folio (London, British Museum MS
Add. 27979), which contains several Arthurian ballads descended from Middle English
romances. The Percy version of *Landevale* has all the textual peculiarities (e.g. long-
distance repetitions and transfers) that we associate with memorial transmission
(Curnow 2002: 216–37).

As this afterlife suggests, the popular Arthurian romances survived because they were destined for, and adaptable to, a double life in both oral and literate traditions. For that reason, too, it is important not to underrate the audience of the romances that did survive. If popular romances were really stories for peasants we would not be reading them today: their literature was oral, and it has not survived. Even many years later, the chambermaids who, according to Bishop Percy, were using the Percy Folio to stoke the fire, had nothing to lose since they probably could not read the stories and poems in it. Those who could read and write them were the masters of chambermaids, people like the landowning families of Cheshire and Lancashire (with whom some of the pieces in the Percy Folio are closely associated), or men like Sir Humphrey Pitt, Esquire, from Northumberland, who owned the Percy Folio before Bishop Percy made off with it. Well into the seventeenth century, their manor halls housed not only books and writing implements but also minstrels who provided the family with verbal entertainment: in the words of John Aubrey, "every gentleman almost kept a harper in his house; and some of them could versifie" (Fox 2003: 27). It is this environment that fostered the popular Arthurian romances that I have discussed: a place where gentlemen born to arms still stood on their pride, where oral stories passed into writing, and writing into orality.

NOTES

1   An alternative hypothesis is that *Percyvell* goes back to a primitive version of a Perceval legend that underlies the earliest extant versions – Chrétien's *Conte du Graal*, Wolfram von Eschenbach's *Parzival* (c. 1210), and *Peredur* (13th century). This case has been argued by Griffith (1911) and Brown (1918–25). Some errors of fact have been corrected by Putter (2001a).

2   The MS reads *Scottes spere*, evidently an error for *scotte-spere* (cf. Old English *scot-spera*), "javelin."

3   The Ashmole MS and editions based on it read *In tyme of Uter and Pendragon* (Advocates MS: *In the tyme of kynge Uter*). The Ashmole reading is so obviously corrupt that I have emended it.

4   This solves the apparent chronological problem signaled by the TEAMS editors in their note to line 255: "There seems to be an error of chronology. If the miracle occurs on Christmas Day then Cleges's journey to deliver the gift to King Uther takes place on Boxing Day, the day after Christmas" (Laskaya & Salisbury 1995). The miracle occurs at midnight on Christmas Day, and when Cleges and his son leave, *The morne, when it was dey lyght* (241), it is the morning of Christmas Day, not Boxing Day (Putter 2001b).

5   Quotations are from the edition by Bliss (which also contains a text of the couplet version, *Sir Landevale*) but I have modernized spellings.

PRIMARY SOURCES

Benson, L. D., Pratt, R., & Robinson, F. N. (eds) (1987). *The Riverside Chaucer*. Boston, MA: Houghton Mifflin.

Bliss, A. J. (ed.) (1960). *Sir Launfal*. London: Nelson.

Braswell, M. F. (ed.) (1995). *Sir Perceval of Gales and Ywain and Gawain*. TEAMS. Kalamazoo,

MI: Medieval Institute. Available at www.lib. rochester.edu/camelot/teams/percint.htm and www.lib.rochester.edu/camelot/teams/ywnint. htm, accessed June 30, 2008.

Brewer, D. & Owen, A. E. B. (eds) (1975). *The Thornton manuscript (Lincoln Cathedral MS 91)*. London: Scolar Press.

Burgess, G. & Busby, K. (trans) (1992). *The lays of Marie de France*. Harmondsworth: Penguin.

Crow, M. & Olson, C. (eds) (1966). *Chaucer life-records*. Oxford: Oxford University Press.

Hale, C. B. & Furnivall, F. J. (eds) (1867). *Percy folio. Bishop Percy's folio MS*, 2 vols. London: Trübner.

Hardman, P. (ed.) (2000). *The Heege manuscript: A facsimile of National Library of Scotland MS Advocates 19.3.1*. Leeds Texts & Monographs, n. s. 61. Leeds: Leeds University Press.

Kibler, W. W. & Carroll, C. W. (trans) (1991). *Chrétien de Troyes. Arthurian romances*. Harmondsworth: Penguin.

Laskaya, A. & Salisbury, E. (eds) (1995). *Sir Cleges*. In *The Middle English Breton lays*. TEAMS. Kalamazoo, MI: Medieval Institute. Available at www.lib.rochester.edu/camelot/teams/clegint. htm, accessed June 30, 2008.

Lecoy, F. (ed.) (1984). *Chrétien de Troyes. Conte du Graal*, 2 vols. Paris: Champion.

Lods, J. (ed.) (1959). *Marie de France. Lais*. Paris: Champion.

Mills, M. (ed.) (1992). *Ywain and Gawain, Sir Percyvell of Gales, The Anturs of Arther*. London: Dent.

Pearsall, D. (ed.) (1994). *William Langland. Piers Plowman*. Exeter: University of Exeter Press.

Roques, M. (ed.) (1981). *Chrétien de Troyes. Erec et Enide*. Paris: Champion.

Treichl, A. (ed.) (1896). *Sir Cleges*: eine mittelenglische Romanze. *Erlanger Studien*, 22, 345–89.

Weiss, J. (ed. trans.) (1999). *Wace's Roman de Brut: A history of the British*. Exeter: University of Exeter Press.

Wülfing, E. (ed.) (1902–3). *Laud Troy Book*. Early English Text Society, ordinary series, 121, 122. London: Oxford University Press.

References and Further Reading

Barron, W. R. J. (ed.) (1999). *The Arthur of the English: The Arthurian legend in medieval English life and literature*. Cardiff: University of Wales Press.

Blanchfield, L. S. (1991). The romances of Ashmole 61: An idiosyncratic scribe. In M. Mills, J. Fellows, & C. M. Meale (eds), *Romance in medieval England*. Woodbridge: Boydell & Brewer, pp. 65–87.

Blanchfield, L. S. (1996). Rate revisited: The complication of narrative works in MS Ashmole 61. In J. Fellows, R. Field, G. Rogers, & J. Weiss (eds), *Romance reading on the book: Essays in medieval narrative presented to Maldwyn Mills*. Cardiff: University of Wales Press, pp. 208–20.

Bradbury, N. M. (1994). Literacy, orality, and the poetics of Middle English romance. In M. C. Amodio (ed.), with the assistance of S. G. Miller, *Oral poetics in Middle English poetry*. New York: Garland, pp. 39–69.

Bradbury, N. M. (1998). *Writing aloud: Storytelling in late medieval England*. Urbana, IL: University of Illinois Press.

Brown, A. (1918–25). The Grail and the English *Sir Perceval*. *Modern Philology*, 16, 553–68; 17, 361–82; 18, 201–28, 661–73; 22, 79–98, 113–32.

Burrow, J. A. (1996). Romance. In P. Boitani & J. Mann (eds), *The Cambridge Chaucer companion*. Cambridge: Cambridge University Press, pp. 109–24.

Busby, K. (1978). *Sir Perceval of Galles, Le Conte du Graal* and *La Continuation-Gauvain*. *Études Anglaises*, 31, 198–202.

Busby, K. (1987). Chrétien de Troyes English'd. *Neuphilologus*, 71, 696–713.

Curnow, D. J. (2002). Five case studies on the transmission of popular Middle English romances. PhD dissertation, University of Bristol.

Eckhardt, C. D. (1974). Arthurian comedy: The simpleton-hero in *Sir Perceval of Gales*. *Chaucer Review*, 8, 205–20.

Field, R. (1999). Romance in England, 1066–1400. In D. Wallace (ed.), *The Cambridge history of medieval English literature*. Cambridge: Cambridge University Press pp. 152–81.

Fowler, D. C. (1975). *Le Conte du Graal* and *Sir Perceval of Galles. Comparative Literature Studies*, 12, 5–20.

Fox, A. (2003). *Oral and literate culture in early Modern England*. Oxford: Oxford University Press.

Griffith, R. (1911). *Sir Perceval of Galles: A study of the sources of the legend*. Chicago, IL: University of Chicago Press.

Gudat-Figge, G. (1976). *Catalogue of Manuscripts Containing Middle English Romance*. Munich.

Hirsch, J. (1967). Pride as theme in *Sir Launfal*. *Notes and Queries*, 212, 228–91.

Knight, S. (1986). The social function of the Middle English romances. In D. Aers (ed.), *Medieval literature: Criticism, ideology, and history*. New York: St Martin's, pp. 99–122.

McDonald, N. (2004). A polemical introduction. In N. McDonald (ed.), *Pulp fictions of medieval England: Essays in popular romance*. Manchester: Manchester University Press, pp. 1–22.

Pearsall, D. (1965). The development of Middle English romance. *Mediaeval Studies*, 27, 91–116.

Putter, A. (2001a). The text of *Sir Perceval of Gales*. *Medium Aevum*, 70, 191–203.

Putter, A. (2001b). In search of lost time: Missing days in *Sir Cleges* and *Sir Gawain and the Green Knight*. In C. Humphrey & W. M. Ormrod (eds), *Time and the medieval world*. Woodbridge: Boydell & Brewer, pp. 119–36.

Putter, A. (2004). Story line and story shape in *Sir Percyvell of Gales* and Chrétien de Troyes's *Conte du Graal*. In N. McDonald (ed.), *Pulp fictions of medieval England: Essays in popular romance*. Manchester: Manchester University Press, pp. 171–96.

Spearing, A. C. (1993). *The medieval poet as voyeur: Looking and listening in medieval love-narratives*. Cambridge: Cambridge University Press.

Stokes, M. (2000). *Lanval* to *Launfal*: A story becomes popular. In A. Putter & J. Gilbert (eds), *The spirit of medieval romance*. Harlow: Pearson, pp. 56–77.

Taylor, A. (1992). Fragmentation, corruption, and minstrel narration. *Yearbook of English Studies*, 22, 39–62.

Veldhoen, N. G. H. E. (1981). I haffe spedde better þan I wend: Some notes on the Middle English *Sir Perceval of Galles*. *Dutch Quarterly Review*, 11, 279–86.

17

English Chivalry and *Sir Gawain and the Green Knight*

Carolyne Larrington

Sir Gawain and the Green Knight is the most artistically accomplished and most singular Arthurian poem in Middle English. It has no obvious immediate source, either in French or English; although it contains plot elements and motifs found elsewhere in Arthurian romance, its combination of them is unique. Indisputably English in its language, its characterization of its protagonist, and in its frame, *Sir Gawain* relies for much of its literary effect on its audience's knowledge of French Arthurian tradition and of the habitual behavior of the main characters in the Arthurian intertextual universe.

As a romance *Sir Gawain* reproduces the ideology of English chivalry, rooted in a learned understanding of Arthur as the heir of Aeneas and of Brutus, drawn from the Galfridian account of the kingdom's foundation, and the chronicles that depend on it (Moll 2003). Beyond this formulation of its own non-Anglo-Saxon history, the English aristocracy was nevertheless imaginatively integrated into French chivalric practice; the English nobility read and enjoyed French chivalric romance, peppered its speech with courtly French expressions, and employed a largely French lexis in its definition of what constitutes chivalric behavior. English and French traditions thus play out in *Sir Gawain* to construct a uniquely hybridized version of insular romance. Though apparently straightforward in the trajectory of the plot (the action more or less contained within the space of a year, and in three locales), *Sir Gawain* has, by virtue of its "exquisitely clarifying art" (Spearing 1970: 177), its ambiguities, and its hybridity, generated varying and contested interpretations. Most recently a different kind of hybridity, a reading of the poem inflected by post-colonial theory, focusing on its origins in the English–Welsh borderland, has been adumbrated (Ingham 2001; Arner 2006).

Manuscript and Provenance

Sir Gawain is preserved in a single manuscript, British Library Cotton Nero A.x, dating from the late fourteenth century. The manuscript is written in a single hand in the dialect of the south Cheshire–north Staffordshire area; *Sir Gawain* occupies folios 95–128v (see Edwards 1997 for a full discussion of the manuscript). Three other poems in the same dialect precede *Sir Gawain* in the manuscript. All three have religious subjects; the first, *Pearl*, is a dream-vision in which the dreamer encounters his dead daughter and learns some truths about salvation. The other two poems are biblical paraphrases: *Cleanness* (*Purity* in older editions) yokes together biblical stories under the rubric of sexual and ritual purity; *Patience*, directly preceding *Sir Gawain*, retells the story of Jonah. It is now generally accepted that the four poems are the work of a single author. *Sir Gawain* was first edited along with a number of other English Gawain poems in 1839, and again for the Early English Text Society in 1864; this edition was revised several times in the nineteenth century. Tolkien and Gordon's edition first appeared in 1925; all quotations here are taken from Davis's revised second edition of this text (Tolkien & Gordon 1967).

Nothing is known of the author of the four poems, though a number of candidates, patrons, and contexts have been suggested (Andrew 1997). *Sir Gawain* revels in magnificent description and flaunts its knowledge of the technical vocabulary of armor and hunting, suggesting that its clerical author was indeed "a sympathetic and knowledgeable observer of aristocratic life" (Putter 1995: 195). He wrote for an audience for whom chivalric ideology needed no explanation; whether author and audience regarded chivalry as immune from criticism is a different question. Thus the poems, particularly *Pearl* and *Sir Gawain*, demand a courtly context; that the author was a chaplain attached to the household of a great regional magnate is both plausible and attractive (Bennett 1997: 81–90). Although they are recorded in a regional dialect, the poems need not necessarily have been composed in Cheshire. As Jill Mann has argued, the poet may have worked in the London household of a Cheshire noble (Mann 1986). Familiarity with the merchant culture of the metropolis might explain the poem's marked interest in value, price, and bargains (Trigg 1991; Putter 1995: 191–4).

Sir Gawain consists of 101 stanzas of varying numbers of alliterative lines, traditionally divided into four sections or "fitts." Each stanza is linked by a short one- or two-stress "bob" to a rhyming three-stress, four-line stanza (the "wheel"). The bob initiates the rhyming pattern, so that bob and wheel rhyme ABAB; these sections often provide authorial comment on the action of the preceding stanza.

The Plot

The poet introduces his narrative by reminding its audience of the legendary history of Britain; as Geoffrey of Monmouth recounts in the *Historia Regum Britanniae*, the kingdom was first settled by Felix Brutus, the descendant of Aeneas, and thus inherits the civilization of Troy. Since then, Britain has been a land renowned for the marvels that occur there. One such occurrence, *an outtrage awenture of Arthurez wonderez* ("an outstanding adventure of Arthurian wonder," line 29), is the subject of the poem, which the poet will narrate *with lel letteres loken* ("with faithful letters locked together," line 34), usually understood as a reference to the alliterative meter. The action of the poem proper opens at Camelot on New Year's Day; feasting and revelry are in full swing. Arthur maintains the custom, familiar from earlier tradition, of refusing to eat on high feast days until some marvel occurs. As the court chatter, the hall doors swing open and in rides a huge figure, half-man, half-giant. Both he and his horse are bright green. The Green Knight addresses the court brusquely, offering *a Crystemas gomen* ("a Christmas game," line 283). He will give the enormous green axe he carries to any man who will strike him a blow with it, and who will promise to accept a matching blow from him in a year's time. The court is stunned into silence and an embarrassed Arthur steps forward to take up the challenge. He is pre-empted by Gawain, who modestly claims that his life is of little value and undertakes to present himself for the return blow at next New Year. He strikes off the Green Knight's head, but the figure picks it up and announces that Gawain must seek him at his Green Chapel. The headless knight rides off, leaving the court to their feasting.

The second fitt begins with a lyrical description of the passing of the seasons; the poet warns that the end of the year often does not match its beginnings. On All Souls Day (November 2) Gawain arms himself for his adventure. The poet lingers on a description of Gawain's shield; painted red, with an image of the Virgin Mary on the inside, the shield bears a golden pentangle. Gawain's device, we learn, alludes to five different sets of fives: faith in the five wounds of Christ and the five joys of Mary, faultlessness in the use of his five fingers and his five wits, and his adherence to five particular virtues. These are *fraunchyse, felaʒschyp, cortaysye, pité*, and *clannes*, roughly translatable as independence/generosity, sociability, courtesy, compassion/piety, and purity, respectively (lines 652–4). Thus equipped, he sets off in search of the Green Chapel with no very clear idea of where it can be found, journeying through a bleak wintry landscape along the Welsh–English borders.

On Christmas Eve he anxiously prays to the Virgin for a lodging where he can keep the Christmas feast. Immediately he catches sight of a splendid castle; he is warmly welcomed by its inhabitants and their lord. They are delighted to learn that it is Gawain who will be spending Christmas with them. The lord introduces Gawain to his extraordinarily beautiful wife, and to her companion, an ugly, but greatly respected, elderly woman. When the main Christmas feast is over Gawain says he must continue his quest, but his host reveals that the Green Chapel is only half a morning's ride away, and presses his guest to stay until New Year's Day. The lord plans to spend the next three days in hunting; since Gawain is still recovering from the rigors of his journey, the host suggests that he remain in the castle in the company of the women. By way of amusement, the lord proposes that he and Gawain should exchange what they win during the course of the next three days: Gawain will take whatever the lord manages to catch in his hunting, while the lord will receive Gawain's gains – whatever they might be – from the castle. Gawain readily agrees.

On the first morning the lord sets out early in pursuit of deer, while Gawain lies late in bed. He is surprised and abashed when the lady of the castle quietly lets herself into his bedroom and engages in a flirtatious conversation in which she suggests that she sexually desires him. After some deft and (on Gawain's part, defensive) verbal exchanges, the lady kisses Gawain and departs. When the husband returns home with the deer he has caught, he formally awards them to Gawain, who in return gives him the kiss. He refuses, however, to say where he got it, since this was not part of the covenant. The pair agree to play the game again the following day. Once again the lord sets out early, this time in pursuit of a wild boar; once again Gawain is visited by the host's wife in his chamber. Gawain continues politely to resist, but accepts two more kisses, bestowed on the lord at the end of the day in exchange for the captured boar. On the third day Gawain comes nearest to succumbing to the lady's advances, while the lord spends his day in pursuit of a worthless fox. When the lady finally realizes that she cannot break down Gawain's resistance, she persuades him to take a gift from her – a green and gold girdle. When Gawain tries to refuse, mindful of the exchange agreement, she reveals that it is magical. No one can dismember, *tohewe* (line 1853), the man wearing it, she says. In the light of his forthcoming meeting with the Green Knight, Gawain willingly takes the girdle; later he seeks out a priest and makes his confession. When the lord returns, Gawain hurries to give him the three kisses he has received that day, but neglects to pass on the girdle. In return, the lord hands over the fox pelt, the paltry result of his day in the field.

Next morning Gawain puts on his armor and wraps the girdle over his surcoat. Then, in the company of a guide, he sets out for the Green Chapel. The guide gives a frightening account of the ferocity of the figure who haunts the Green Chapel, and advises Gawain to ride away, promising never to reveal that he did not keep the appointment. Gawain proudly refuses and makes his way down a steep hillside to a strange mound, *nobot an olde caue* ("nothing but an old cave," line 2182), identified by the guide as the Green Chapel. When the Green Knight appears, Gawain bends his neck for the blow, but flinches a little as the blade comes down. The Knight checks his stroke and reproves him. Gawain promises to stand firm, and the Knight brings down the axe again, stopping at the last moment when he sees that Gawain is now resolute. At the third attempt the axe nicks Gawain's neck, but does no further injury.

The Green Knight reveals that he and Gawain's recent host are one and the same. Gawain played the Exchange Game faithfully on the first two days, but *lakked a lytel* (line 2366) on the final day by withholding the girdle: that is why he received the nick. Praising Gawain, the Knight makes him a gift of the girdle as a souvenir of his adventure. Gawain is mortified by the uncovering of his deception; although he permits himself an outburst against the perfidiousness of women, he largely castigates himself for his *cowarddyse and couetyse* ("cowardice and covetousness," line 2374). The Knight identifies himself as a certain Bertilak of Hautdesert, and explains that the plot was undertaken at the behest of Morgan le Fay, the elderly woman in the castle. Gawain declines an invitation to celebrate the New Year at Hautdesert, and makes his way back to Camelot, where he receives a joyful welcome. Gawain refuses to understand his safe return as a triumph, continuing to blame himself for his lack of

integrity, his *vntrawþe* (line 2509). The court adopts the green girdle as a sign of
honor. The poem ends with the theme of the opening lines, the founding of Arthur's
kingdom by Brutus after the fall of Troy. In the manuscript in the same scribal hand
follows the legend "HONI SOYT QUI MAL PENCE," close to, but not identical
with, the motto of the Order of the Garter, founded by Edward III probably in 1348
(see Ingledew 2006 for a provocative discussion of the connections between poem and
order).

Critics have often commented on the symmetricality of the plot and structure of
Sir Gawain (see Hanna 1983: 289 for bibliography). The events of the poem, framed
by the Galfridian introduction and conclusion, take place as part of a typical Arthurian
quest; a stranger comes to Camelot offering a challenge and a member of the Round
Table responds. The plot is driven by the Beheading Game, a motif which occurs in
a number of other medieval texts (Brewer 1992). Typically the Beheading Game is a
straightforward test of courage and promise keeping; having beheaded a (usually)
supernatural opponent, the hero simply has to present himself for the return blow in
order to win. What is ingenious about *Sir Gawain*'s use of the motif, and unparalleled
in the analogues, is the modification whereby the outcome of the Beheading Game is
made dependent on two other games, one of which Gawain perceives as a game, and
one which he does not (Spearing 1970: 180–91). So Gawain's injury is caused by his
failure, a minor one according to Bertilak, in the Exchange Game, when he does not
hand over the girdle on the third day. That Bertilak does not behead Gawain is his
reward for coming through the Temptation Game, resisting the lady's sexual advances
during the three encounters in the bedchamber. It is only now, as Spearing comments,
that Gawain, and the audience, realize that the poem's climax is in fact an anticlimax;
the real trial was elsewhere in what seemed to be a mere interlude on Gawain's journey
(1970: 190–91).

English Chivalry – French Romance – British Otherness

As noted, *Sir Gawain* begins by invoking the history of Britain as mediated by
Geoffrey of Monmouth. The first Britons were of Trojan descent, transmitting the
civilization of their lost city, but also, the first stanza makes clear, originating the
complex interweaving of truth and treachery which is the poem's theme. Paradoxically, Aeneas, Brutus's ancestor, who in Troy was *þe tulk þat þe trammes of tresoun þer
wroзt* ("the man who made the machinations of treason there"), manifested a *tricherie*
("treachery") that is somehow *þe trewest on erthe* ("the truest/most patent on earth,"
lines 3–5). The Gawain who steps forward at the New Year's feast to relieve Arthur
of the axe and the challenge of the Green Knight seems to belong to this English
chronicle tradition, in which Arthur's eldest nephew Gawain is also his closest ally
and best knight (Moll 2003). Although sometimes impetuous, he is famed for his
courtesy – mentioned by Chaucer and repeatedly invoked by the lady (Spearing 1970:
202–6) – his prowess and his faithfulness. Gawain is modest too: if he loses his life

in the adventure, that is only a little loss, for, he maintains, *I am þe wakkest . . . and of wyt feblest* ("I am the weakest and feeblest in intelligence"). In fact his only merit is that Arthur is his uncle: *no bounté bot your blod I in my bodé know* ("I know of no goodness in my body besides your blood," lines 354–7).

The detailed catalogue of the pentangle's symbolic values, even if these are quite arbitrarily assigned to the symbol by the author (Heng 1991: 505), describes the five knightly virtues, which define a Europe-wide conception of essential chivalric values. "Loyalty and truth, hardiness, *largesse* and humility will be the principal qualities of character that we ought to expect in him," Maurice Keen writes of the ideal knight (1984: 10). *Fraunchyse*, freedom of action, possessing the virtues necessary for rule (Keen 1984: 149), *pité*, Christian piety and compassion, *felaȝschype*, the keeping of promises sworn in homosocial lateral bonds, the courtly virtue of *courtoisie*, and the apparently clerical value of *clannes*, the eschewing of lechery and adultery for a moderate practice of service to women – the five points of the pentangle epitomize the chivalric–clerical qualities that the knight should possess (on clerical efforts to refine martial masculinity, see Putter 1995: 209–20).

Armored with this understanding of chivalry, and protected by his private devotion to the Virgin, who appears on the inside of his shield, Gawain rides away on his adventure as the finest representative of the Arthurian court. Indeed, the sorrowing courtiers he leaves behind criticize Arthur for allowing him to take Christmas games so seriously, suggesting that it would have been better to promote Gawain, *and haf dyȝt ȝonder dere a duk* ("and have made that beloved man a duke," line 677) than to send him off to certain death. Their criticism raises questions about the poet's view of the Arthurian court, considered further below. Gawain rides away through the land of Logres and on to North Wales, into a border landscape where the hardships of journeying through winter, of sleeping in one's armor among icy rocks *in peryl and playne and plytes ful harde* (line 733), are worse than the opponents, dragons, wild men, bulls, and giants who harass him on his route; their hostility Gawain takes in his stride. It is piety, not feebleness, which makes him pray for shelter at Christmas; when the castle appears so promptly it seems that his prayers have been answered. Gawain's petition concludes with the good English *Cros Kryst me spede!*, but when he catches sight of Hautdesert, he slips into French, *Now bone hostel!* The change of idiom marks a change of inflection in the understanding of chivalry and of Gawain's character, which will dominate the poem's next section.

The people of Hautdesert are already, it seems, familiar with Gawain and his reputation, but the man they expect to encounter is a rather different character from the honorable Englishman we have seen so far. Courtiers nudge each other excitedly: *Now schal we semlych se sleȝtez of þewez / And þe teccheles termes of talkyng noble* ("now we shall see proper practice of knightly conduct / and flawless terms of noble speech," lines 916–17), they murmur. Gawain is *þat fyne fader of nurture* ("the cultured begetter of civilized standards") and those who listen to him will *lerne of luf-talkyng* ("learn about love-talk," lines 919, 927). Yet these are not boorish provincials: all is courtly and luxurious in Hautdesert, competing with Camelot in the lavishness of provision. Even on Christmas Eve, a day of fasting, Gawain is impressed with the number and variety of fish dishes served for supper. In one respect indeed Hautdesert surpasses Camelot, for the lady of the castle is, in Gawain's eyes, *wener pen Wenore* ("lovelier than Guenevere," line 945).

The scene is set then for the kind of adventure which Gawain is prone to facing in French tradition (Spearing 1970: 198–200; Busby 1980). From Chrétien, where Gawain has a certain affinity with the fair sex, to the thirteenth-century romances in which he is a habitual seducer, Gawain is cast as the ladies' knight *par excellence*. Typical is the episode in the *Chevalier à l'épée*, where, even when warned by the young woman with whom he is sharing a Perilous Bed that any sexual approach is likely to prove fatal, Gawain reflects that he would be ridiculed by his fellow knights if he were to spend a chaste night with one so beautiful; when he tries to embrace the girl, he barely escapes serious injury (Busby 1980: 248–57; Brewer 1992: 109–26). The plotters of Hautdesert – Morgan, Bertilak, and his lady – well-versed in French tradition since they spring from it, thus have good reason to think that Gawain can be compromised by sexual temptation; his eagerness to be introduced to the women even in the castle's chapel and the warmth with which he kisses and embraces the younger one can only encourage them in their belief about his vulnerability. As expected, Gawain slips easily into the role of courtier, demonstrating the pentangle virtue of *felazschyp* by humoring his host in his desire to enliven the last days in the castle with the Exchange Game and readily agreeing to remain in the castle with the women rather than participating in the quintessentially masculine aristocratic pastime of hunting.

Gawain thus finds himself in the hands of the women; although he understands the game he plays with the lord, he is not aware that the women are also playing with him. Though his masculinity is compromised by his confinement in "a tracery of spaces coded as feminine" (Heng 1991: 501), this domain offers much to the unabashedly heterosexual Gawain. As in French romance, the castle's intimate female space must be negotiated by the hero if he is to succeed in his quest (Larrington 2006: 62–5). For despite the homosociality of the Exchange Game, including the man-on-man kisses which Gawain delivers to his host as *sauerly and sadly as he hem sette coupe* ("with as much relish and as vigorously as he was able to give them," line 1937), it is the women who teach Gawain most about competing traditions of chivalry and about his role within them (Dinshaw 1994).

On her first visit to Gawain's bedroom, the lady praises his reputation, his "honor" and *hendelayk* ("courtliness," line 1228), and emphasizes his attractiveness to women. Gawain conventionally offers his service as her knight, but otherwise he *ferde with defence* ("he behaves cautiously," line 1282). On her departure though, the lady shocks Gawain by doubting whether he really *is* Gawain, insinuating that the genuine (i.e. French) Gawain could not spend long with a woman without trying to solicit a kiss (line 1293). Alarmed by this challenge to his identity, Gawain accepts her kiss. The tactic is successful enough for the lady to employ it again the next morning, even slipping briefly into the familiar *pou* form in line 1485. Revealing herself to be a keen consumer of French romance, the lady contends that for true knights, *þe tytelet token and tyxt of her werkkez* ("the inscribed title and text of their deeds") is the *lel layk of luf, þe lettrure of armes* ("the faithful game of love, the literature of arms," lines 1513–15). Knightly deeds, she argues, are only the prelude to bringing *blysse into boure* ("joy into the chamber"); what women really want from knights is *trweluf craftes* ("true love's pursuits," line 1527), not just the love-talk which the people of Hautdesert associate with Gawain, but the satisfaction of sexual desire. Gawain ripostes by noting that he would waste his time, were he *to trwluf expoun, / And towche þe temez of text and talez of armez* ("to expound love / And touch on the themes of its text and its tales of fighting," lines 1540–1), since the lady is a hundred times more versed in such matters than he is. On the third day the poet retreats from reporting the conversation verbatim, indicating that although Gawain "is indeed in a highly inflammable state" (Spearing 1970: 194), experiencing *wiȝt . . . wallande joye* ("powerfully surging pleasure," line 1762), he manages to resist the double-bind created by the pentangle nexus of *clannes* and *courtayse*, which would force him either to accept her love or to offend her by a clear rejection. Reflecting on his loyalty to the lord, the next day's beheading test, his awareness of adultery as a sin, and his anxiety lest he offend his hostess, Gawain resists inscription into the romance text his opponent has in mind and successfully deflects the lady's overtures until she abandons her attempted seduction and persuades him to take the girdle.

On New Year's morning, Gawain is once more carrying his shield. Though Mary was mindful of her knight (line 1769) while he jousted metaphorically with the lady, Gawain seems to have forgotten his holy protectress, exchanging his faith in the chivalric values and divine protection depicted on the shield for the dubiously effective talisman of the girdle (Hanna 1983). Yet, armored once more and away from the discomfiting influence of the women, Gawain reverts to the straightforwardly courageous model of knightliness we saw at the poem's outset. Courteously, but distantly *gruchyng*, he rebuffs the guide's suggestion that he fail to keep his appointment; he bravely summons the knight with a loud vocal challenge on reaching the Green Chapel, and even manages a wisecrack as he bends his head to the fatal stroke, pointing out that his head is not replaceable as the Green Knight's is. The shame that Gawain feels when he realizes the extent to which he has been duped is manifested by his extreme physical reaction: *Alle þe blode of his brest blende in his face* ("all the blood in his chest blended in his face," line 2371) (for thoughtful comment on Gawain's emotional state, see Pearsall 1997: 360–62). Although he blames the women for beguiling him, ultimately he realizes, as Bertilak spells out the identity and motivation of Morgan, that the very blood rising in his cheeks, the blood of Arthur, heir of Brutus and Aeneas, of which he is so proud, is also that of his aunt Morgan, who has both deceived and vindicated him. There is more *bounté* in Gawain than Arthur and Morgan's blood, a *bounté* of deeds, not of lineage.

Bertilak's account of himself and his lady confirms the French romance inflections of Hautdesert and its crew of plotters. Bertilak bears a French name, and his history of Morgan, her relationship with Merlin, and her motivation in setting up the adventure – to test the *surquidré* ("prowess") of the Round Table, and, incidentally, to try to frighten Guenevere to death – are certainly intertextually related to, and most probably derive from, the French *Lancelot* (Rigby 1983; Larrington 2006: 60–68). In thirteenth-century French romance, Morgan is interested in testing the boundaries of chivalry and discovering where its values can be compromised, as well as acting as a spokeswoman for feminine desire within the chivalric system (Larrington 2006: 51–73). Morgan's ugliness, described at some length in the poet's bravura comparison of the two women, encourages both Gawain and the audience to underestimate her. But the unregarded old woman is responsible for the complex series of challenges offered not only to Gawain as the representative of the Round Table, but to the very institution of chivalry, reprising her role in the French romances with which *Sir Gawain*'s aristocratic audience would have been familiar.

Though Bertilak is sanguine about Gawain's *cowarddyse and couetyse* (line 2374), as the knight himself defines his failure, Gawain cannot forgive himself so easily. He rehearses his mortification to the court, maintaining that he cannot undo, *vnhap*, his shame, and declaring that he must wear the girdle, the *token of vntrawþe* (line 2509) for the rest of his life. Gawain has learned, but cannot fully accept, that human perfection is not possible (Aers 1997). Morgan's plan to test the reputation of the Round Table has found its representative to be *on þe fautlest freke þat euer on fote ʒede* ("one of the most faultless men who ever walked," line 2363), and thus the adventure may rightly conclude with the rejoicing of the court and its expression of solidarity with Gawain in agreeing to wear the green girdle, which they interpret as a sign of *þe renoun of þe Rounde Table* (line 2519). English chivalry has been tested against the values of French romance. One of the preoccupations of French Arthurian narrative – how to balance public honor-driven behavior, gendered masculine, and private, emotionally inflected courtliness, gendered feminine – has been interrogated and some provisional answers found (Larrington 2006: 51–73). Chronicle and romance, French and English tradition have fused in a hybrid masterpiece. Gawain's victory is qualified, but although the kingdom of Britain itself may have been born out of truth and treachery in the poem's opening stanza, the final stanza leaves little room for doubt that the girdle is *euermore after* a sign of honor, that Brutus was a *bolde burne* ("brave warrior") and that many such adventures have occurred in Britain as related in the *best boke of romaunce* (lines 2520–21, 2524).

For some recent critics (Ingham 2001; Arner 2006) the hybridity of *Sir Gawain* is rather to be understood in terms of post-colonial theory. The argument hinges on the poem's localization to the Welsh–English marches; it is a text which celebrates Angevin cultural and political hegemony at the same time as it expresses anxiety about the alienness and intractability of the Welsh. Ingham resolves the question by suggesting that the otherness of the Green Knight and the creatures of the borderlands, the exoticism of the *contrayez straunge* (line 713) through which Gawain moves on his journey, are subsumed by his arrival at Hautdesert. There the "multiplicity of region and ethnicity" is elided by "the doubleness of gender" (2001: 121). Though the Green Knight seems terrifyingly "other" at Camelot, and, Ingham argues, superior in virility to the "prodigious imbecilities" of Arthur and his youthful court, when it is established that he is simply the puppet of Morgan, Arthur's authority is restored (2001: 124). The "ethnic heterogeneities finally modulate into nothing more than the differences of an extended family" (132), once Morgan is identified as Gawain's aunt.

This rather cozy view of the effacement of ethnic difference by insisting that homo-sociality can resolve the issue and that English sovereignty and the autonomy of English knights are authorized precisely because they are gendered masculine is contested by Arner (2006). She argues that ethnicity does not simply disappear when the poem's focus appears to move to gender, but "rather there is a rearticulation of ethnic difference at the site of gender." Thus the women – both Bertilak's lady and Morgan – remain recognizably Welsh in their hostility; indeed the lady's feigned desire for Gawain masks an insistent colonial fantasy about the subjugated other (Arner 2006: 93).

Ingham banishes Frenchness from *Sir Gawain*, noting only that Felix Brutus founds Britain *fer ouer þe French flod* ("far over the English Channel," line 13), distancing the kingdom's origins from the post-Conquest royal dynasties. Arner makes no reference at all to the poem's French idioms, inflections, and analogues. However, if *Sir Gawain* reflects the hybridity of insular culture in the late fourteenth century, as I have argued here, it is primarily a reflection of hybridized Anglo-French aristocratic culture to which the poem attends, rather than to the fleeting glimpses of a repressed and alienating Welshness.

Critiquing Chivalry

Had *Sir Gawain* not been preserved along with the other poems in Cotton Nero A.x, but simply been transmitted alone, we might well read it as a straightforward secular Arthurian romance, even as the work of a lay author. Given the company it keeps in the manuscript, however, readers have tended to pay particular attention to its religious elements, asking whether *Sir Gawain* in fact constitutes a clerical critique – if a humane one – of the chivalric and courtly values which romance purports to celebrate. There is some evidence for such a reading. Arthur is described as in his first youth, lively and *sumquat childgered*, ("somewhat child-like," line 86), and, the Green Knight asserts, his court are *bot berdlez chylder* ("just beardless children," line 280). Ingham suggests that Arthur's youthfulness would engender anxieties about a boy-king, fears fully justified by Richard II's troubled reign (2001: 126–7). However, as Sheila Fisher notes, Camelot is still a "prelapsarian court" (2000: 79); Gawain and his brother Agravain are Arthur's highest-ranking knights; Lancelot, though present when Gawain departs, is barely mentioned, and the atmosphere in Camelot, in particular the relieved laughter as the Green Knight gallops out of the feast, suggests youthful high spirits rather than childish folly. Nor should the Green Knight's comment be taken literally, since his intention is to insult and challenge the court. The mutterings of the courtiers when Gawain leaves on his quest may be more problematic. Yet their complaint that Gawain is taking a Christmas game too seriously raises questions about their understanding of games, rather than implying carelessness about promise-keeping and personal honor. Most intriguing is the court's reaction on Gawain's return; as Gawain tells his story, blaming himself for his failure, and shows the girdle, *alle þe court als / Laȝen loude þerat* ("all the court too laughed loudly at it," lines 2513–14). For some critics, this is a laughter of incomprehension, a flawed court's failure to care about human imperfection, reflecting the "instability, immaturity, even the naiveté" of Arthur and his court (Ingham 2001: 133). In contrast, Spearing judges that "their reaction is a healthy one" (1970: 230); the laughter reintegrates Gawain back into his community (Aers 1997: 99–101). The multiple possible interpretations of the girdle are critical here; when the court appropriate this "slippery and equivocal" talisman (Hanna 1983, 290) as the badge of a chivalric order, can they totally recuperate the *falssyng* ("false thing") as a sign of honor?

Assessing the poem's final judgment on his hero and on Camelot depends on our construction of its author: whether we see him as a pragmatic man-of-the-world, as the humane author of *Patience*, with his keenly sympathetic eye for human weakness, or whether we read *Sir Gawain* in conjunction with the severe judgmentalism of *Cleanness* and envisage its author as a priest who sets demandingly high standards for his flock. Either interpretation is possible, as well as a range of positions in between. Some critics argue that Gawain becomes compromised by his retention of the girdle, particularly since this apparently leads to an insufficient confession on his final day at the castle (see bibliography in Wasserman & Purdon 2000: 662–3). Yet the language of confession is employed again by both Gawain and the Green Knight at the Green Chapel. Gawain acknowledges that his behavior has been wrong; Bertilak, laughing, observes that *now* Gawain is confessed clean, has admitted his faults, and has had his penance, so that he is now absolved, *polysed*, as if he had never *forfeted syþen þou watz fyrst borne* ("trespassed since you were first born," line 2394).

Is the audience to concur with Bertilak that Gawain has atoned for his sin of *couetyse* in keeping the girdle, and for his *cowarddyse*? Gawain certainly does not think so, but the court agrees with Bertilak. David Aers robustly argues that the finer points of confession do not particularly matter for the *honourmen*, the nobility for whom the poem was composed; the details of sacramental obligation are for the clerics to take care of, not for secular men of action to fret about: "none of this is of much consequence since nothing will change anyway," he concludes (1997: 99). For Aers, the moping Gawain overreacts to the games he has been playing; the court's laughter models the appropriate reaction to the hero's exaggerated self-castigation. Since the poem moves directly from the court's laughter to its future adoption of the girdle as chivalric symbol, we do not discover whether Arthur is successful in comforting Gawain, and whether the unhappy knight comes round to the court's view of his adventure. The poem returns us to the intertextual Arthurian universe, to *þe best boke of romaunce* (line 2521), where the many wonderful exploits of Arthur's court are related, and where, both in chronicle and romance, the courteous and brave Gawain continues in his chivalric career until he meets his end at the hands of his half-brother, loyal to Arthur to the last.

Although Christianity was always an essential element in the ideology of chivalry, as Keen points out, "the virtue of the soldier was not the same as that of the priest" (1984: 178). The other poems in the manuscript provide, as Bennett notes, "work for reflection and discussion . . . *Sir Gawain and the Green Knight* . . . would have prompted a mixed audience to debate . . . the nature and degree of Gawain's fault" (1997: 81). While the girdle may be adopted as a sign of worldly honor, of human imperfection, and the love of life, "the private desire that includes all others within it," as Fisher notes (2000: 87), it is significant that the chivalric–clerical virtues of the pentangle, tested though they are to their limit, are not found wanting.

The Gawain of this poem is perhaps the first Arthurian character who understands, in the Socratean phrase, that the unexamined life is not worth living. Gawain, "a thoroughly self-conscious and articulate hero" (Spearing 1970: 173), has a psychology and an interiority unexampled in earlier Arthurian literature and equaled in his time only by Chaucer's Criseyde. The poet charts Gawain's reactions to the appearance of the castle's two women and points up the gap between his expressions of joy and relief when he learns how close he is to the Green Chapel and his troubled sleep on New Year's Eve. We perceive the lady of the castle through Gawain's eyes, noting that she *behaves*, "ay . . . let," as if she were in love with him; this leaves open the question of whether we and he are interpreting the situation correctly (Putter 1995: 140–48). And we share with him, on first reading of the poem, the appalled, embarrassed rush of blood to the cheeks when it becomes clear how skillfully the poet, Bertilak, and the women have misdirected us (Pearsall 1997: 361–2). This Gawain has, as Putter argues, internalized many of the qualities, including reflectiveness and self-analysis, which the clerical authors of Arthurian romance aimed to inculcate into the community of *honourmen* whom they entertained and instructed.

Sir Gawain and the Green Knight is deeply rooted in the European chivalric romance tradition, yet it finds its expression in an Englishness sprung from British pseudo-history, the north Midlands landscape bordering on the unstable country of Wales, and in a language which welds Old English, Old Norse, and the French phrases of courtliness and chivalry into a supple and vigorous idiom. *Sir Gawain* asserts the primacy of a considered set of chivalric values at the same time as it emphasizes that the exponents of martial masculinity and the pursuit of honor will always need to take account of the pleasures and emotions of the private domain, of that most deeply-rooted instinct in human nature, the desire for self-preservation, and, finally, to recognize the emergence of a new understanding of interiority and self-consciousness on the part of the *Gawain*-poet and in his all-too-human creation.

References and Further Reading

Aers, D. (1997). Christianity for courtly subjects: Reflections on the *Gawain*-poet. In D. Brewer & J. Gibson (eds), *A companion to the Gawain-poet*. Cambridge: Brewer, pp. 91–101.

Andrew, M. (1997). Theories of authorship. In D. Brewer & J. Gibson (eds), *A companion to the Gawain-poet*. Cambridge: Brewer, pp. 23–33.

Arner, L. (2006). The ends of enchantment: Colonialism and *Sir Gawain and the Green Knight*. *Texas Studies in Language and Literature*, 48, 79–101.

Bennett, M. J. (1997). The historical background. In D. Brewer & J. Gibson (eds), *A companion to the Gawain-poet*. Cambridge: Brewer, pp. 71–90.

Brewer, E. (1992). *Sir Gawain and the Green Knight: Sources and analogues*, 2nd edn. Woodbridge: Brewer.

Burrow, J. A. (1971). *Ricardian Poetry: Chaucer, Gower, Langland and the Gawain-Poet*. London: Routledge & Kegan Paul.

Busby, K. (1980). *Gauvain in Old French literature*, 2nd edn. Amsterdam: Rodopi.

Dinshaw, C. (1994). A kiss is just a kiss: Heterosexuality and its consolations in *Sir Gawain and the Green Knight*. *Diacritics*, 24, 205–26.

Edwards, A. S. G. (1997). The manuscript: British Library MS Cotton Nero A.x. In D. Brewer & J. Gibson (eds), *A companion to the Gawain-poet*. Cambridge: Brewer, pp. 197–219.

Fisher, S. (2000). Leaving Morgan aside: Women, history, and revisionism in *Sir Gawain and the Green Knight*. In T. S. Fenster (ed.), *Arthurian women: A casebook*. London: Routledge, pp. 77–95. First published in C. Baswell & W. Sharpe (eds) (1988), *The passing of Arthur: New essays in Arthurian tradition*. New York: Garland, pp. 129–51.

Hanna III, R. (1983). Unlocking what's locked: Gawain's green girdle. *Viator*, 14, 289–302.

Heng, G. (1991). Feminine knots and the other *Sir Gawain and the Green Knight*. *PMLA*, 106, 500–14.

Ingham, P. C. (2001). *Sovereign fantasies: Arthurian romance and the making of Britain*. Philadelphia, PA: University of Pennsylvania Press.

Ingledew, F. (2006). *Sir Gawain and the Green Knight and the Order of the Garter*. Notre Dame, IN: University of Notre Dame Press.

Keen, M. (1984). *Chivalry*. New Haven, CT: Yale University Press.

Larrington, C. (2006). *King Arthur's enchantresses: Morgan and her sisters in Arthurian tradition*. London: Tauris.

Mann, J. (1986). Price and value in *Sir Gawain and the Green Knight*. *Essays in Criticism*, 36, 294–318.

Moll, R. J. (2003). *Before Malory: Reading Arthur in later medieval England*. Toronto: University of Toronto Press.

Pearsall, D. (1997). Courtesy and chivalry in *Sir Gawain and the Green Knight*: The order of shame and the invention of embarrassment. In D. Brewer & J. Gibson (eds), *A companion to the Gawain-poet*. Cambridge: Brewer, pp. 351–62.

Putter, A. (1995). *Sir Gawain and the Green Knight and French Arthurian romance*. Oxford: Oxford University Press.

Rigby, M. (1983). *Sir Gawain and the Green Knight* and the Vulgate *Lancelot*. *Modern Language Review*, 78, 257–66.

Spearing, A. C. (1970). *The Gawain-poet*. Cambridge: Cambridge University Press.

Tolkien, J. R. R. & Gordon, E. V. (eds) (1967). *Sir Gawain and the Green Knight* (rev. ed. N. Davis). Oxford: Oxford University Press.

Trigg, S. (1991). The romance of exchange. *Viator*, 22, 251–66.

Wasserman, J. & Purdon, L. O. (2000). Sir Guido and the green light: Confession in *Sir Gawain and the Green Knight* and *Inferno* XXVII. *Neophilologus*, 84, 647–66.

18
Sir Gawain in Middle English Romance

Roger Dalrymple

When the hero of *Sir Gawain and the Green Knight* is cornered in his bedchamber by an amorous lady, the knight's would-be seducer questions his identity: *Sir, ʒif ʒe be Wawen, wonder me þynkkez* (line 1481). Suggesting that the hero is not responding to her advances as his reputation would lead her to expect, she questions whether this is indeed Sir Gawain of the Round Table with whom she is cloistered at Christmastide. Though her comment is jocular, both the scene and the wider poem play upon the genuine ambivalence that attaches to the figure of Sir Gawain in Middle English romance – for the presentation of the medieval English Gawain can vary considerably according to the particular text we are reading. Of all the Arthurian protagonists, it is the character of Sir Gawain that most strongly reflects the confluence of traditions and cultures that makes up Arthurian legend, with the result that he appears in Middle English romance in contrasting guises.

The figure of Sir Gawain, nephew of King Arthur, looms large in the corpus of English romance: in addition to the celebrated *Sir Gawain and the Green Knight* (c. 1375–1400), he is protagonist of *Sir Gawain and the Carl of Carlisle* (c. 1400), *The Wedding of Sir Gawain and Dame Ragnell* (c. 1450), *The Turk and Gawain* (c. 1500), and *Golagrus and Gawain* (c. 1500), to name but a few. Likewise, he features as a supporting character in a wide range of texts, including *Ywain and Gawain* (c. 1300–50), the alliterative *Awntyrs off Arthure* (c. 1375–1400) and *The Avowing of King Arthur* (c. 1425); and he is central to medieval English treatments of the fall of Camelot and the death of Arthur such as the Alliterative *Morte Arthure* (c. 1360), the Stanzaic *Morte Arthur* (c. 1400) and, the most famous of such treatments, Sir Thomas Malory's *Morte Darthur* (1469–70). Across these varied texts, the presentation of each Arthurian character is necessarily inflected in different ways but the depiction of Gawain ranges particularly widely. One tradition emphasizes his heroic role as Arthur's esteemed nephew, chief retainer, and most cherished warrior, while another shows him in a diminished role, eclipsed by the figure of Sir Lancelot du Lac, the favored knight of French courtly tradition, and sometimes by other Round Table knights.

Elsewhere Gawain is even depicted with moral shortcomings and ascribed a crucial role in the fall of Camelot before, finally, all these conceptions of the Gawain character are overtaken by a tradition in which he is celebrated as the paragon of courtesy and nobility.

To account for these disparate conceptions of the medieval English Gawain, it is important to recall that the hero was germane to Arthurian tradition from a very early stage. Written precedent for so much of the legend is found in Geoffrey of Monmouth's *Historia Regum Britanniae* (c. 1138), but evidence of the centrality of Gawain to the myth is attested from still earlier. A decade prior to Geoffrey's work, William of Malmesbury's *Gesta Regum Anglorum* ("Deeds of the English Kings," c. 1125) alludes to the hero's fabled Pembrokeshire tomb (a monument of suitably exaggerated proportions) while, attesting to Gawain's early European celebrity, a famous carving in the doorway of Modena Cathedral, dated from before 1130, depicts Sir Gawain in company with King Arthur and two other knights (see chapter 26). Indeed, some scholars have traced the figure back into the earliest Celtic origins of Arthurian legend, suggesting that oral tradition celebrated him as a hero in his own right and arguing that the character whom literary tradition comes to know as Sir Gawain of the Round Table takes his origin from a Celtic deity associated with the sun (Weston 1897; Loomis 1927; see also Day 1984). Vestiges of this numinous origin are apparently reflected in the detail, mentioned in a number of Arthurian texts, that Sir Gawain's strength waxes and wanes with the sun, his might being at its greatest when this astral body is at its highest in the sky:

> Then had Sir Gawain such a grace
> . . .
> When he were in any place
> There he sholde batail don,
> His strength sholde wax in such a space,
> From the under-time til noon.
> (Stanzaic *Morte Arthur*, lines 2802–7)

Whatever Gawain's origins, the fact that he was intrinsic to Arthurian legend at such an early stage is highly significant for his depiction in the extant corpus of Middle English romance. As a core character in the legend from the earliest stages, the figure of Sir Gawain would be greatly affected by the successive elaborations and accretions to Arthurian legend that took place over the course of the Middle Ages. As a succession of writers from the twelfth century onward shaped the legend to conform to the changing literary and cultural tastes of their times, the myth was gradually transformed from a predominantly heroic and dynastic narrative to a courtly narrative embodying themes of chivalry and *fin' amor*, and even, in the hands of the compilers of the French Vulgate Cycle of prose Arthurian romance, a sober narrative conveying penitential themes. These changes served to shift the functions and significances ascribed to the different characters: the fortunes of Sir Gawain ebbed and flowed accordingly, accounting for the considerable divergences in his characterization. More so than the figures of Lancelot, Perceval, and Tristrem (who are comparatively late additions to the fraternity of Round Table knights), the figure of Sir Gawain shows the confluence (and on occasion the conflict) between different traditions of Arthurian writing.

The present survey of the medieval English Gawain thus focuses upon the three dominant interpretations of the character emerging from English Arthurian romance. The first is the heroic Gawain – the Celtic figure celebrated in the Geoffrey of Monmouth tradition, whose deep devotion to Arthur is stressed along with his fortitude in battle and his willingness to embrace any challenge in defense of his uncle and king. Within this tradition lie the English texts Layamon's *Brut* (c. 1190), *Arthour and Merlin* (c. 1250–1300), and the Alliterative *Morte Arthure* (c. 1350–1400).

The second interpretation of the character is darker. It emerges from those English romances that are influenced by medieval French Arthurian tradition, where the elevation of courtly values (as in the works of Chrétien de Troyes) and subsequently of penitential values (as in the Vulgate *Queste del Saint Graal* and *Mort Artu*) results in a diminished or ambivalent depiction of Sir Gawain relative to the portrayal of the more courtly Sir Lancelot, Perceval, or Ywain. English romances in this second group include *Ywain and Gawain* (a translation of Chrétien's original), the Stanzaic *Morte Arthur*, and Malory's *Morte Darthur*.

Finally, an idealized and exemplary portrait of Gawain triumphs in medieval popular romance, thanks to an important collection of texts where the hero's exceptional bravery, courtesy, and loyalty enable the vanquishing of monstrous foes, the breaking of spells, and the transformation of loathly ladies into beautiful young brides. This exemplary Gawain is embodied in such romances as *Sir Gawain and the Carl of Carlisle*, *The Turk and Gawain*, and *The Wedding of Sir Gawain and Dame Ragnell*. This chapter will explore these three dominant interpretations of the medieval English Gawain, showing how the figure's late medieval reputation as the flawless flower of courtesy is achieved only after other aspects of his character have been explored, making him one of the more complex figures in the medieval English Arthurian tradition.

The Heroic Gawain of Chronicle Tradition

Geoffrey of Monmouth's foundational treatment of Arthurian legend in his *Historia Regum Britanniae* frames the figure of Gawain, son of King Lot of Orkney, in heroic and martial terms (see chapter 3). In Geoffrey's account of Arthur's Roman wars, Gawain is the king's trusted adviser and retainer, showing strength in battle and violence of temper in a series of climactic combats. One episode in which Gawain's temper is provoked instates a tradition of ascribing to the hero an impetuous nature, but overall the presentation of Arthur's nephew is resoundingly positive, Geoffrey assuring us that "No better knights than Hoel and Gawain have ever been born down the ages" (Thorpe 1966: 254) and the figure dying a hero's death in the final pages of the Arthurian narrative.

This martial and heroic conception of Gawain is perpetuated in English literary tradition, which is informed in turn by the Anglo-Norman translation of Geoffrey by Wace (c. 1155) (see chapter 15). In the early English *Brut* of Layamon, the trusty character of Gawain is lauded at length:

> Wel wel was hit bi-toȝe þat Waweyn was to manne ibore.
> For Woweyn was edmod of eche þeue he was god.
> He was mete-cousti and cniht mid þan beste.
> Alle þe cnihtes þorh him were swiþe ibalded.
>   (Layamon's *Brut*, lines 11604–7)

> It was a very good thing that Gawain had been born among men for he was noble-minded and possessed of each virtue. He was generous and among the very best of knights. Through his presence all the other knights were emboldened.

Also cast within the Geoffrey of Monmouth tradition, the fourteenth-century alliterative poem *Morte Arthure* picks up the chronicler's portrait of a bellicose and headstrong warrior. Consistently affording Sir Gawain epithets of praise (*Sir Wawain the worthy*, line 1302; *Sir Gawain the good*, line 1368), the poet elaborates the scene in which a *flyting* or war of words between Gawain and the Roman Emperor's uncle escalates into physical violence:

> Then greved Sir Gawain at his grete wordes,
> Graithes toward the gome with grouchande herte;
> With his steelen brand he strikes off his heved.
>   (Alliterative *Morte Arthure*, lines 1352–4)

Any suggestion that this capacity for rash action is a flaw in our hero is downplayed in the Alliterative *Morte Arthure* but the notion will prove important elsewhere in other quarters of Arthurian tradition, where Sir Gawain is painted as a more ambivalent figure. In the Alliterative *Morte Arthure*, Arthur regards his nephew as wise in counsel and wholly dependable, a view which is articulated most eloquently in the threnody the king delivers for the fallen Gawain at the close of the work. The threnody captures the key dimensions of the heroic conception of the Gawain character – as Arthur's cherished blood relative, esteemed warrior, and wise counselor:

> Dere cosin of kind in care am I leved,
> For now my worship is went and my war ended!
> Here is the hope of my hele, my happing in armes,
> My herte and my hardiness holly on him lenged!
> My counsel, my comfort, that keeped mine herte!
> Of all knightes the king that under Crist leved!

Thou was worthy to be king, thou I the crown bare!
My wele and my worship of all this world rich
Was wonnen through Sir Gawain and through his wit one!
                (Alliterative *Morte Arthure*, lines 3956–64)

It is as if Sir Gawain epitomized all that Arthur valued in his kingdom and that his death represents in microcosm the loss of the Arthurian realm.

Despite the pseudo-historical claims of the genre, the heroic Gawain of chronicle tradition nevertheless reflects the character's long-standing association with the supernatural. In addition to references connecting Gawain's strength and the sun, these works also permit the intrusion of other magical elements when it comes to the presentation of Sir Gawain. A vivid example occurs in the Alliterative *Morte Arthure* where a scene of hand-to-hand combat between Sir Gawain and his nobly born opponent Sir Priamus leads to both combatants suffering wounds that look sure to prove fatal until, inspired by each other's steadfastness in battle, they reconcile and take recourse to a miraculous healing potion that Priamus carries about him: *Be it frette on his flesh there sinews are entamed, / The freke shall be fish hole within four houres* (Alliterative *Morte Arthure*, lines 2704–9). Critics of the poem have long paid detailed attention to this scene (Matthews 1960), remarking the incongruity of this romance-derived element with its context (it follows immediately after the episode of the Siege of Metz, related in sufficiently naturalistic and technical detail as to evoke genuine fourteenth-century siege warfare). It seems that the association of Sir Gawain with the world of the supernatural in the earliest stages of the legend continued to exert a power in the later tradition, legitimizing such an episode in a poem largely framed within the chronicle tradition of Arthurian legend.

The heroic Gawain of chronicle tradition recurs across medieval English Arthurian literature, and forms the basis for the dominant conception of the character in the later Middle Ages, when Gawain achieves a popular and proverbial status as not only the worthiest but also the most courteous of Arthurian knights. However, before this positive reputation is cemented, a contrasting portrait of the character emerges, introducing a darker dimension to the Celtic hero.

The Fallible Gawain of Chivalric Romance

When the Arthurian legend was elaborated in the twelfth century by Chrétien de Troyes and his followers, a new set of literary and cultural values was brought to bear upon the myth. In place of a primary focus on the Round Table knights as warriors brought together by a Brythonic chieftain, the Arthurian fraternity were now reconceptualized as courtier knights with a primary devotion to notions of truth, honor, and the service of ladies (see chapter 11). This change of emphasis would be epitomized in the figure of Sir Lancelot du Lac – a new right-hand man for Arthur whose virtues were conceived less in the heroic terms of early tribal Britain and more in the localized, refined, and courtly terms of Camelot.

As the Arthurian legend was modulated into this new courtly register, the figure of Gawain (French *Gauvain*) took on new dimensions. In many ways, the character was comfortably assimilated into courtly culture, his heroic stature being translated into prowess in knighthood. At the same time, Gawain became displaced as Arthur's right-hand man by the dominance of Lancelot and his stature implicitly diminished even as Lancelot's was augmented. In romances where the chivalry of Lancelot, Perceval, and other knights is celebrated, Gawain's role is limited to that of supportive or contrastive figure in relation to the protagonist (Busby 1980). We can see an example of this in the Middle English romance *Ywain and Gawain* – the only extant English translation of a Chrétien romance. Among other themes, the poem addresses the conflict that Sir Ywain experiences in balancing his commitment to knighthood with his devotion to his lady. Although Gawain is presented throughout in a favorable light – he is styled *Sir Gawayn, knyght valiant* (line 541) and *Sir Gawayne the curtayse* (line 1420) – he appears as a figure with limited sympathy for Ywain's dilemma, counseling him to pursue deeds of arms and to resist enfeeblement and enervation by languishing with a lover:

> Syr Gawayn did al his mayne
> To pray Sir Ywaine on al manere
> Forto wende with tham infere.
> He said, "Sir, if thou ly at hame,
> Wonderly men wil the blame.
> That knight es no thing to set by
> That leves al his chevalry
> And ligges bekeand in his bed,
> When he haves a lady wed . . ."
> (*Ywain and Gawain*,
> lines 1452–60)

The effect of the episode is to suggest Gawain's superficial response to the plight of the hero: he shows a limited understanding of the complex courtly code which Ywain is trying so delicately to balance. Thus, while the structure and organization of the English *Ywain and Gawain* implies that both heroes are important in the articulation of the poem's themes, Gawain's role is ultimately secondary to that of Ywain, who is the true focus for the poem's exploration of chivalric and amatory concerns.

This tradition of limiting Gawain's function to a supportive or contrastive role is evident in a number of Middle English romances. One example is the early fifteenth-century romance *The Avowynge of King Arthur, Sir Gawan, Sir Kaye, and Sir Bawdewyn of Bretan* (c. 1425). This unusual poem combines traditional romance motifs with a collection of instructive vignettes, of which the hero is not, as we might expect, Sir Gawain but the lesser-known Sir Baldwin. Early in the work, Gawain is praised by King Arthur in terms that emphasize both his heroic qualities and his courtliness:

"Grete God," quod the King,
"Gif Gawan gode endinge,
For he is sekur in alle kynne thinge,
To cowuntur with a knyghte!
Of all playus he berus the prise,
Loos of ther ladies."
(*The Avowing of King Arthur*,
lines 525–30)

Nevertheless, as the poem unfolds, we once again find Gawain in a contrastive relationship to the true protagonist. The romance involves Arthur, Gawain, Kay, and Baldwin all making solemn vows and proceeding to fulfill them in the course of the poem. While the conventional Arthurian knights make the kind of traditional vows appropriate for a medieval romance (Arthur to hunt a wild boar; Gawain to keep a night-long vigil at the *Tarn Wathelan*; and Kay to patrol the forest and confront all challengers), Sir Baldwin makes three pragmatic vows (never to be jealous of his wife, never to deny any man food, never to fear death) which prove to be rooted in experience and hold an instructive function for the poem's audience. The end result is again a diminished role for Gawain, whose vow to keep a vigil at a lake renowned for marvelous happenings ultimately appears redundant next to the pragmatism of Sir Baldwin, whose vows reflect a patent moral purpose.

While in works such as these the character of Sir Gawain is simply downgraded in significance, in those Middle English texts which draw upon the French Vulgate Cycle of Arthurian prose romances the character's very moral integrity is called into question. The latter portions of the Vulgate Cycle are dedicated to chronicling the quest of the Holy Grail (in which the majority of the Arthurian knights signally fail), the affair of Lancelot and Guinevere, and the descent of Arthur's kingdom into the destruction of civil war (see chapter 14). As these religious and anti-worldly themes are given dominance, so the Round Table knights are depicted in a morally ambivalent aspect. The good character of Sir Gawain is a notable casualty of this revised narrative emphasis, since negative attributes are ascribed to him in both of these branches of the Vulgate. In the Grail section, he is cast as morally imperfect, tending to duplicity and underhandedness in his dealings with both knights and noblewomen. Likewise, he shows vengefulness and a destructive instinct toward tribalism in the final section of the cycle, *La Mort le Roi Artu*, where he is apportioned a share of the blame for the fragmentation of Camelot, the eventual death of Arthur, and the dissolution of the Arthurian fellowship. For it is the unrelenting vengeance of Sir Gawain upon Sir Lancelot that allows civil war to foment in Arthur's kingdom and affords Sir Mordred the opportunity to plot his usurpation of the throne. In the French *La Mort le Roi Artu*, this even draws a reproach from Arthur to his esteemed nephew:

"Nephew," said King Arthur, "your wickedness has done me great harm because it has robbed me of you, whom I loved above all men, and also Lancelot, who was so feared that if Mordred had known he was on good terms with me as formerly, he would never have been so bold as to attempt the kind of disloyalty that he has undertaken." (Cable 1971: 193)

While this image of the flawed Gawain is largely confined to French Arthurian tradition, English adaptations of the Vulgate account of Arthur's death necessarily draw upon it. Thus Malory's adaptation of the Grail quest in *Le Morte Darthur*, while going some way to lessen the religious asceticism of the French source, nevertheless retains such chastening moments for Sir Gawain as his reproach by a hermit during the quest: *whan ye were made first knyght ye sholde have takyn you to knyghtly dedys and vertuous lyvyng. And ye have done the contrary, for ye have lyved myschevously many wyntirs* (Vinaver 1971: 535).

Likewise, in verse retellings of the death of Arthur, this depiction of Gawain as a vengeful figure is retained. Mourning for the death of his brother Gareth (who has been unwittingly killed by Lancelot during the battle which follows discovery of Lancelot and Guinevere's affair), Gawain is unable to summon up his nobler instincts and rise above his quest for vengeance. While Lancelot is reluctant to fight his comrade, and even the cuckolded Arthur becomes conciliatory, Gawain repeatedly goads Lancelot and, even when wounded, will not desist from his campaign of vengeance. The rendering of this section in the Stanzaic *Morte Arthur* is particularly stark, bearing all the force of the origins of Sir Gawain as the fearless tribal warrior of heroic tradition:

> "Certes nay!" said Sir Gawain,
> "He hath wrought me wo ynow,
> So traitourly he hath my brethren slain,
> All for your love, sir, that is trouth!
> To Yngland will I not turn again
> Til he be hanged on a bough;
> While me lasteth might or main."
> (Stanzaic *Morte Arthur*, lines 2676–82)

Gawain's vengeance against Lancelot leads ultimately to his sustaining a head wound which will prove the cause of his death when the wound is reopened in battle against the rebels – an image which crystallizes the notion that Gawain ultimately brings his own death upon himself. This he acknowledges in his last letter to Lancelot, here as rendered by Malory: *I woll that all the worlde wyte that I, sir Gawayne, knyght of the Table Rounde, soughte my dethe, and nat thorow thy deservynge, but myne owne sekynge* (Vinaver 1971: 710). The flawed Gawain of French tradition is nevertheless given a degree of posthumous redemption in the Vulgate account of the fall of the Round Table. After his death, Gawain appears in Arthur's prophetic dream and warns the king against confronting Mordred in battle before a period of truce has elapsed. Acting as God's own messenger – *God hathe sente me to you of Hys speciall grace* (Vinaver 1971:

712) – the more favorable image of Sir Gawain as Arthur's dear and trusted counselor is briefly recovered in this last glimpse of the character.

English Arthurian tradition shows a general reluctance to represent the flawed Gawain though a small number of texts do offer a more ambivalent portrait of the figure. Knowledge that Arthurian tradition included a flawed Gawain as well as a peerless one clearly informs such texts as *Sir Gawain and the Green Knight*, where it is important for the audience to be aware that their hero is ultimately fallible. But English tradition did not dwell long on this second interpretation of Sir Gawain of the Round Table. For if the Vulgate view of Sir Gawain threatened to blacken the character of the Celtic hero, the English popular romances of the late Middle Ages emphatically set the record straight.

The Exemplary Gawain of Popular Romance

In strong contrast to ambivalent depictions of the Arthurian hero, the third dominant medieval English interpretation of the character of Sir Gawain is overwhelmingly positive. A group of late romances sharing a similar narrative structure consistently present an exemplary Gawain, the paragon of courtesy and nobility (Machann 1982). In *Golagrus and Gawain*, *Sir Gawain and the Carl of Carlisle*, *The Greene Knight*, *The Turk and Gawain*, *The Marriage of Sir Gawain*, and *The Wedding of Sir Gawain and Dame Ragnell*, the exemplary Gawain is celebrated. The majority of these romances treat the hero's adventures in a brisk and light-hearted register, embodying simple notions of obedience, loyalty, and devotion (see chapter 16). Gawain is presented as a steadfast and unchanging figure – *on that was sekor and sounde* (*Sir Gawain and the Carl of Carlisle*, lines 2–3), *bold and hardye, / And thereto full of curtesye* (*The Greene Knight*, lines 64–5); *that worthy knight* (*The Turk and Gawain*, line 28); *a curteous knight* (*The Marriage of Sir Gawain*, line 25).

While the fallible Gawain of French tradition often played second fiddle to Lancelot and other Round Table knights, here the hero is provided with his own contrastive figure in the person of the argumentative and mean-spirited Sir Kay. A recurrent figure in Arthurian legend, Arthur's seneschal, Kay, has a long reputation in both French and English romance as the crabbed or churlish knight who repeatedly blunders while Gawain distinguishes himself. Sometimes, Kay is joined by other figures to heighten this contrast still further: in *Sir Gawain and the Carl of Carlisle*, Bishop Baldwin also falls short in charity, humility, and courtesy. Alongside Sir Gawain, even this representative of the church is found wanting.

The exemplary Gawain of popular romance has a regional affiliation. Perhaps on account of his origins as the son of King Lot of Orkney, these romances repeatedly place the hero in a northern setting: Scotland, Sunderland, and Carlisle (Purdie & Royan 2005). These settings are presented as wild and full of adventure: the localities of the "Tarn Wadling" (a deep and mysterious lake) and Inglewood Forest recur in the texts, where associations of fairies and the supernatural are attached to them and where Gawain embraces all adventures and challenges that befall him. The hero is never reticent in taking up a quest or championing a just cause. As is the case in *Sir Gawain and the Green Knight*, Gawain accepts many a challenge as surrogate for his king, viewing this as the duty he owes his uncle. His declaration in *The Wedding of Sir Gawain and Dame Ragnell* is representative:

> "For ye ar my king with honour
> And have worshipt me in many a stoure.
> Therfor shalle I not let."
> (*The Wedding of Sir Gawain and
> Dame Ragnell*, lines 348–50)

As Arthur's sister's son, Gawain shares the same noble blood as Arthur and thus can act in his stead; unlike the king, he is a free agent and able to roam beyond the confines of Camelot in pursuing a quest. As it transpires, it is often just as well that it is Gawain who has taken up the quest as his exceptional character makes possible disenchantments of bewitched opponents or transformations of loathly ladies into blushing young brides. Indeed, the implication of several of these texts is that Gawain passes those tests that his Round Table society would fail, showing a restraint, forbearance, and capacity for self-abnegation that other members of the Arthurian fraternity may not evince so readily.

The hero's embrace of each challenge leads to a defining motif of these exemplary Gawain romances: an encounter with a manifestation of the monstrous (be it an ogre or a loathly lady), and reconciliation not by violence but by the exercise of obedience, forbearance, and, above all, courtesy. Gawain's courtesy works a palpable form of magic, effecting disenchantment from spells, shape-shiftings, and conversion to Arthurian knighthood or to Christianity. It repeatedly transpires in these tales that Gawain's adversaries have been compelled to confront him as the result of a spell or rash vow made some years before. Thus when the "loathly lady" of *The Marriage of Sir Gawain* is transformed by Gawain's courtesy into a beautiful young bride, she reveals that her previous shape was conferred upon her by her wicked stepmother:

> Shee witched me, being a faire young lady,
> To the greene forrest to dwell,
> And there I must walke in womans liknesse,
> Most like a feeind of hell.
> (*The Marriage of Sir Gawain*, lines 179–82)

Likewise, the uncharitable host of *Sir Gawain and the Carl of Carlisle* reveals at the end of that tale that Sir Gawain's exceptional display of courtesy and his willingness to obey the Carl even to the point of decapitating him has freed the Carl from his enchanted state and restored his true identity:

> The Carle sayd, "Gawaine, God blese thee!
> For thou hast delivered mee
> From all false witchcraft –

> I am delivred att the last.
> By nigromance thus was I shapen
> Till a knight of the Round Table
> Had with a sword smitten of my head."
> (*The Carle of Carlisle*, lines 401–7)

Finally, in *The Turk and Gawain* this transformation involves a recovery of Christian identity when Sir Gawain's beheading of the Saracen Turk leads to his transformation into Sir Gromer, who immediately displays a fervent Christian piety:

> And when the blood in the bason light,
> He stood up a stalworcht Knight
> That day, I undertake,
> And song "Te Deum Laudamus –
> Worshipp be to our Lord Jesus
> That saved us from all wracke!"
> (*The Turk and Sir Gawain*, lines 289–94)

The popularity of the disenchantment motif in the Gawain romances again shows how the character's early associations with magic and the supernatural were perpetuated throughout English literary tradition. Similarly, some of these beheading games and shape-shiftings also suggest the influence of *Sir Gawain and the Green Knight* upon the later romances. When we glance back at that fourteenth-century poem we find that the motif of disenchantment is afforded a deepened significance. For when Gawain confronts the Green Knight on New Year's Day and learns of his shortcomings, the true disenchantment is less the transformation of the Green Knight into Sir Bertilak than the transformation of Gawain himself from self-assured hero to self-reproaching penitent who returns to Camelot a sadder and wiser man (see chapter 17).

The image of the exemplary Gawain is consolidated and fixed for posterity by these popular romances. Collected together in the Percy Folio manuscript of late medieval poetry, the texts embody the dominant reception of the figure as folk hero and account for his proverbial status in the late Middle Ages as the epitome of courtesy (Whiting 1947). That status is further confirmed by one of the rare Arthurian allusions in the works of Chaucer, where Gawain is invoked as the yardstick by which to measure the courtly protagonist of *The Squire's Tale*:

> . . . Gawayne with his olde curteisye,
> Though he were comen ayeyn out of Fairye,
> Ne koude hym nat amende with a word.
> (*Squire's Tale*, lines 95–7)

The allusion confirms that for all the refinements and adjustments to the character over the course of the Middle Ages, the late-medieval Gawain remains close to his origins as the peerless figure of heroic tradition.

Conclusion

The figure of Sir Gawain thus appears in three dominant guises in Middle English romance: the heroic warrior derived from chronicle tradition, the fallible knight of chivalric tradition, and the exemplary hero of popular romance. While the last of these interpretations of the character predominates, English Arthurian literature is ultimately the richer for these competing characterizations of the figure and it is surely no accident that the most sophisticated Arthurian work of the period, *Sir Gawain and the Green Knight*, actively plays upon this ambivalence in the hero's character. The medieval English Gawain is a complex figure whose many facets reflect the range of influences and traditions that make up Arthurian legend.

PRIMARY SOURCES

Brook, G. L. & Leslie, R. F. (eds) (1978). *Layamon. Brut.* Early English Text Society. Oxford: Oxford University Press.

Cable, J. (trans.) (1971). *The death of King Arthur.* Harmondsworth: Penguin.

Day, M. L. (ed. trans.) (1984). *The rise of Gawain, nephew of Arthur (De ortu Waluuanii nepotis Arturi).* New York: Garland.

Hahn, T. (ed.) (1995). *Sir Gawain: Eleven romances and tales.* TEAMS. Kalamazoo, MI: Medieval Institute.

Kibler, W. W. & Carroll, C. W. (trans.) (1991). *Chrétien de Troyes. Arthurian romances.* Harmondsworth: Penguin.

Sands, D. B. (ed.) (1986). *The wedding of Sir Gawain and Dame Ragnell.* In *Middle English verse romances.* Exeter: Exeter University Press.

Thorpe, L. (trans.) (1966). *Geoffrey of Monmouth. History of the kings of Britain.* Harmondsworth: Penguin.

Vinaver, E. (ed.) (1971). *Malory. Works.* Oxford: Clarendon Press.

REFERENCES AND FURTHER READING

Ackerman, R. W. (1976). Madden's Gawain anthology. In J. B. Bessinger & R. Raymo (eds), *Medieval studies in honor of Lillian Herlands Hornstein.* New York: New York University Press, pp. 1–18.

Barber, R. (1986). *King Arthur: Hero and legend.* Woodbridge: Boydell.

Barron, W. R. J. (ed.) (1999). *The Arthur of the English: The Arthurian legend in medieval English life and literature.* Cardiff: University of Wales Press.

Busby, K. (1980). *Gauvain in Old French literature,* 2nd edn. Amsterdam: Rodopi.

Evans, W. O. (1973). The case for Gawain reopened. *Modern Language Review,* 68, 721–33.

Kittredge, G. L. (1916). *A study of Sir Gawain and the Green Knight.* Cambridge, MA: Harvard University Press.

Loomis, R. S. (1927). *Celtic myth and Arthurian romance.* New York: Columbia University Press.

Loomis, R. S. (ed.) (1959). *Arthurian literature in the Middle Ages.* Oxford: Clarendon Press.

Machann, C. (1982). A structural study of the English Gawain romances. *Neophilologus,* 66, 629–37.

Matthews, W. (1960). *The tragedy of Arthur.* Berkeley, CA: University of California Press.

Newstead, H. (1967). Arthurian legends. In J. B. Severs (ed.), *A manual of the writings in Middle*

English 1050–1500, vol. 1: *Romances*. New Haven, CT: Connecticut Academy of Arts & Sciences, pp. 38–79.

Pearsall, D. (1976). The English romance in the fifteenth century. *Essays and Studies*, n.s. 29, 56–83.

Purdie, R. & Royan, N. (eds.) (2005). *The Scots and medieval Arthurian legend*. Cambridge: Brewer.

Putter, A. (1995). *Sir Gawain and the Green Knight and French Arthurian romance*. Oxford: Oxford University Press.

Rogers, G. (1978). Themes and variations: Studies in some English Gawain poems. PhD dissertation, University of Wales.

Rushton, C. J. (2007). "The lady's man": Gawain as lover in Middle English romance. In A. Hopkins & C. J. Rushton (eds), *The erotic in medieval British literature*. Cambridge: Brewer, pp. 67–81.

Weston, J. L. (1897). *The legend of Sir Gawain: Studies upon its original scope and significance*. London: David Nutt.

Whiting, B. J. (1947). Gawain, his reputation, his courtesy and his appearance in Chaucer's *Squire's Tale*. *Medieval Studies*, 9, 189–234.

19

The Medieval English Tristan

Tony Davenport

The Chertsey Abbey tiles (c. 1270), which show more than thirty scenes from the story of Tristan and Yseult, are part of the ample evidence of the familiarity of the tale in medieval England. In thirteenth- and fourteenth-century texts the central figures appear as proverbial illustrations both of the power of love and of truth and beauty. The company they keep may be that of other traditional pairings of lovers, as in the elegiac *Love-Rune* of Thomas of Hales:

> Hwer is Paris and Heleyne
> þat weren so bryht & feyre on bleo,
> Amadas & Ideyne,
> Tristram, Yseude and alle þeo?
> (lines 65–8)

They may, on the other hand, be in Arthurian company, as in *Cursor Mundi*, when the author, listing the topics that audiences like to hear about, moves on from *Kyng Arthour þat was so rike* and *Wawan, Cai and oþer stabell* to *Tristrem and hys leif Ysote,/ How he for here becom a sote* (Prologue). They head Gower's list of lovers when, in the vision which brings *Confessio Amantis* to its end, he describes among the *sondri routes* which Cupid brings with him the company of *lusty Yowthe* dancing and discoursing:

> of knyhthod and of armes,
> And what it is to ligge in armes
> With love, whanne it is achieved.
> Ther was Tristram, which was believed
> With bele Ysolde, and Lancelot
> Stod with Gunnore, and Galahot
> With his ladi . . .
> (*Confessio Amantis*, bk VIII,
> lines 2497–503)

The particular conjunction of figures suggests Gower's knowledge of the Prose *Tristan* (Hardman et al. 2003: 95).

In the romance *Emaré* the four corners of the magic cloth which comes to represent the power of the heroine's beauty are embroidered with the figures of lovers, Amadas and Ydoine in the first corner:

> In that other corner was dyght
> Trystram and Isowde so bryght,
> That semely wer to se.
> And for they loved hem ryght,
> As full of stones ar they dyght,
> As thykke as they may be . . .
> (*Emaré*, lines 133–8)

The approval indicated by "they loved hem ryght" is there too in Chaucer's comic picture of himself as *trewe Tristram the secounde* in *To Rosemounde*; he cites *bele Isawde* as the most beautiful of women in *The House of Fame* and in the company of Helen in the Prologue to *The Legend of Good Women*. A darker view is suggested by the lovers' appearance with the tragic figures depicted in the temple of Venus in *The Parliament of Fowls*:

> Semyramis, Candace, and Hercules,
> Biblis, Dido, Thisbe, and Piramus,
> Tristram, Isaude, Paris, and Achilles,
> Eleyne, Cleopatre, and Troylus . . .
> (*The Parliament of Fowls*, lines 288–91)

The insertion of the medieval names into the list (derived from Boccaccio) of instances from Virgil, Ovid, and Statius confirms their classic status, but all are compromised by Chaucer's treatment of Venus and her temple, which many interpreters have seen as "a moral allegory, signifying selfish, lustful, illicit, disastrous love" (Brewer 1972: 31). The view that *they loved hem wrong* is explicitly expressed by Gower in the series of ballades written as an appendix to *Confessio Amantis*:

> Open been bothe cronyk and historie
> Of Lancelote and of Tristram also –
> And yhit their foly is in þe memorye
> For ensampil, yheuyng vnto all tho
> That been alyve nat for to lyuen so.
> (*Traitié*, Ballade XV, trans.
> John Quixley, c. 1400)

Gower's theme is adultery: the occurrence here of the name of Tristram harks back to the controversy about the tale which was there from the start.

The two treatments of the story that exist in Middle English, the late thirteenth-
or early fourteenth-century romance *Sir Tristrem* and Malory's long fifth book of *Le
Morte Darthur*, represent contrasting historical stages in the development of the material, as well as different ways of interpreting the events and the characters. *Sir Tristrem*
presents the pre-Arthurianized tale turned into a hero-centered, "whole life" romance.
In Malory's post-Arthurianized telling, the figures of Tristan and Yseult have been
absorbed into the multi-threaded narrative and reduced to parallels for Lancelot and
Guenevere.

   Sir Tristrem survives in a unique but incomplete copy in the well-known Auchinleck manuscript. The text consists of 3,344 lines in eleven-line stanzas, punctuated
by enlarged capitals that divide the poem into 21 portions; one hesitates to call these
sections or fitts, because the division is rhetorical rather than structural, and incon-
sistently used, but it provides one way of describing the long sequence of episodes,
which cover the plot material usually attributed to the *Tristran* of Thomas of Britain,
as it is represented in the translation into Norwegian in Friar Robert's *Saga of Tristram
and Isönd*. In a short prologue "Tomas" is identified as the poem's source and the name
is referred to also in lines 10, 397, 412, and 2787; these references may indicate
knowledge of Thomas of Britain's poem; if so, the mention of Erceldoune in the first
line (as indicated by the preceding catchword), which led Sir Walter Scott and others
to attribute the romance to Thomas the Rhymer, is a confusion with a later northern
tradition of minstrelsy (Cooper 2005). Sections 2–6 (lines 34–759) narrate the love
of Tristrem's parents, his birth and their deaths, his upbringing by Rohaud, abduction
by Norwegian merchants, arrival in England and acceptance at Mark's court. Sections
7–11 (lines 760–1617) cover Tristrem's conquest of Brittany (by which he avenges
his father), his fighting Moraunt on Mark's behalf, his journeys to Ireland, and his
meeting with Ysoude.[1] The central sections (lines 1618–2255) deal with the marriage
of Ysoude to Mark, Ysoude's aborted plan to kill Brengwain, who has taken her place
in the marriage bed, Tristrem's recovery of Ysoude from the Irish harper, and plots,
led by Meriadok, to catch Tristrem and Ysoude together. After the reconciliation
between king and queen when Ysoude has survived trial by ordeal through subterfuge,
Tristrem goes to Wales, and then is exiled with Ysoude to the woods for a year, after
which he is forced to leave again, this time alone, and goes to Spain and Brittany,
where he marries the other Ysoude (section 17, lines 2256–739). In the final sections
(lines 2740–3344), Tristrem in Brittany overcomes the giant Beliagog, has him build
a hall with statues, and returns to England with his brother-in-law, Gauhardin; the
two men are entertained as lovers by Ysoude and Brengwain, who are fending off the
unwelcome attentions of Canados, and at a final tournament they take vengeance on
Meriadok and Canados. Tristrem is wounded on his return to Brittany but the text
breaks off before Tristrem's death.

   In his edition of *Sir Tristrem* (1804) Sir Walter Scott filled the manuscript's gap
with fifteen stanzas of his own, clearly identified, bringing the story to the black sail
and the deaths of the lovers. In one of the first scholarly printed versions of a Middle

English text, with introduction, notes, and glossary, Scott made this tale, unlike many other medieval romances, available to Romantic and Victorian writers, but:

> the narrative probably aroused little interest because of its difficult Northern Middle English, which is complicated by . . . abrupt transitions, and obscure diction; this version scarcely represents the compelling qualities of the traditional love story. (Taylor & Brewer 1983: 29)

The low critical esteem which this indicates had been the usual reaction to *Sir Tristrem* until recently; standard histories of Middle English romance have tended to view the poet's eccentric verse form as akin to Chaucer's *rym dogerel* and the "skeletal" treatment of the plot material as "unworthy of such a subject" (Barron 1987: 154–5). The accusation that the narrative is "skeletal" is a very familiar type of criticism of shorter English versions of rhetorically ample, courtly French romances: the poet of *Sir Tristrem* covers the complex plot material of Thomas's *Tristran*, but in a style closer to ballad, a staccato, short-lined stanza, which reads at times like mere subtitles to the story. So, the conception and birth of Tristrem is conveyed in a single stanza in which Mark's sister visits the wounded knight, Rouland:

> Sche seyd, "Waylaway",
> When hye herd it was so.   *[ie. that Rouland was wounded]*
> To her maistresse sche gan say   *[governess]*
> That hye was boun to go
> To the knight ther he lay.
> Sche swouned and hir was wo.
> So comfort he that may,
> A knave child gat thai two
> So dere;
> And sithen mon cleped him so:
> Tristrem the trewe fere.
>   (lines 100–110)

This sort of poetry clearly will not offer full, formal expression of thought and feeling; one has to adjust to the laconic registration of key events as a rapid strip-cartoon version of the tale. The poet is not without self-consciousness: not only does his prologue identify a source, but also conveys the transitoriness of life and fame which the poem will illustrate, and the voice of the narrator is heard at intervals; selection and direction are apparent, not merely summary.

What some critics have seen in the romance is a redirection of the material into the mould of a hero-centered biography. Signs of this are the inclusion of Tristrem's parents, his birth and upbringing, his training in courtliness, his undertaking as a chosen champion single combats and traditional heroic challenges from dragon and giant, his winning the hand of three princesses in three different countries, and the narrative's covering the whole span of his life. The English version's brevity in some key scenes of the love story can be set beside some detailed accounts of Tristrem's fighting: the duel with Moraunt on an island (lines 1024–89), his killing of the dragon (lines 1442–85), the fight with Urgan in Wales (lines 2322–98), and the vengeance taken on Meriadok and Canados (lines 3246–89). These scenes provide some of the reason why *Sir Tristrem* appears with *Horn Childe*, *Guy of Warwick*, *Bevis of Hampton*, and the like in the Auchinleck manuscript.

Moreover, Tristrem remains the most cultivated of chivalric heroes, distinguished from a killing machine by his skill as a chess-player and harpist, and his artistry in the chase. He loses some of his accomplishments in the English poem, given no opportunity to display fluency in many languages or knowledge of the seven liberal arts which Friar Robert specifies (*Saga*, chapter 17), nor does the medical technology which enables him to fashion and fit a wooden leg to the giant Moldagog after he has chopped off one leg at the knee (*Saga*, chapter 76) survive, except as implied in the passing reference to the giant Beliagog's use of a "stilt" (line 2956). But he keeps those accomplishments which are essential to specific episodes and themes: chess, where he is particularly artful, in the abduction episode, knowledge of the craft of venery as passage into Mark's court, and musicianship as the basis for his intimacy with Ysoude and his later rescue of her from the Irish harpist. Neither does the greater emphasis on Tristrem's heroic exploits ultimately change the unique quality of the story, though it may shift its balance. Ysoude does not enter the narrative until over halfway through the poem, but it is the love relationship that comes to dominate Tristrem's actions. He goes to Wales only because a fight, wherever it is, will be a release from frustration:

> For he ne may Ysoude kisse,
> Fight he sought aywhare.
> (lines 2298–9)

There is a sharp perceptiveness in the English poet's focusing of some scenes, which makes up for brevity. Take, for example, Tristrem's fury when he returns from hunting to find that Mark has been tricked by the Irish harpist into handing over his wife. In Friar Robert's account it is simply the speed with which Tristan goes to the rescue that is stressed but in the English poem we find the most direct confrontation between nephew and uncle. Mark's weakness is ruthlessly exposed:

> Tho was Tristrem in ten
> And chidde with the King:
> "Gifstow glewemen thi Quen?
> Hastow no nother thing?"
> (lines 1849–52)

In place of one night's rest in the forest after Tristrem has rescued Ysoude (*Saga*, chapter 50), *Sir Tristrem* awards them seven nights of joy in the woods before their return to court and Tristrem's laconic reproof to Mark: "Gif minstrels other thing!" (line 1925).

There are many minor differences between *Sir Tristrem* and the *Saga*, as one might expect since there is no direct textual relationship between them: the comparison is interesting, nevertheless, since the same motifs appear in different guises. Only a Scandinavian redactor would seize on the arrival of the Norwegian merchants in England as an opportunity for local color:

> The cargo included much fur-stuff, ermine pelts and beaver pelts, black sable, walrus tusks and bearskin cloaks, goshawks, gray falcons and many white falcons, wax and cowhides, goatskins, dried fish and tar, train oil and sulphur, and all kinds of Norwegian wares. (Schach 1973, chapter 18)

In *Sir Tristrem* the merchants bring only *haukes white and gray / And panes fair yfold* (lines 300–301). If one looks for equivalent local variations in the English romance, the episode in Wales (lines 2293–420), which occurs where in Friar Robert's text Tristram goes to Poland, is suggestive either of a Welsh path of transmission for the material (supported by the Welsh names Morgan and Roland Rhys), or of influence from other romance texts; Wales does not appear often as a venue in romance, and there is a close enough parallel in *Horn Childe* for it to have been thought that one might have been an influence on the other (Mills 1988: 55–6, 69–70). Tristrem, like Horn, becomes the Welsh king's champion; fighting on his behalf achieves part of his vengeance for the death of his father (the giant Urgan being the brother of Morgan) and wins the love of a princess who has to be put aside, since the hero is committed elsewhere. The earlier episode when Rohaud, his clothes reduced to rags by the length of time and distance he has spent seeking Tristrem, has to overcome the hostility of porter and usher in order to gain access to Mark's court (lines 617–49) is a motif introduced by the English poet which may have Welsh connections: the only other English romance where it occurs (in a fuller and more explicitly comic version) is *Sir Cleges*, another of the small group of romances set in Wales.

One of the places where *Sir Tristrem* differs from the *Saga* is the famous scene when Mark hides in a tree to spy on the lovers. Friar Robert gives us striking pictures of the tryst, Isönd enveloped in a white fur cloak, with covered head, approaching the trees through the garden, while Tristram arrives from the opposite direction through the paling fence; at that moment the moon emerges from a cloud, Tristram sees King Markis's shadow and halts in his tracks, afraid that the queen will not realize the danger, but she too sees the king and they both withdraw, leaving Markis uncertain enough to abandon his anger for a time. In *Sir Tristrem* there appears the more complex idea, present in the texts of Béroul, Eilhart, and Gottfried, that the lovers deliberately exploit the situation in order to deceive Mark. There is typically nothing of Friar Robert's visuality, but concentration on dialogue. No sooner has Tristrem seen Mark than he improvises loudly to alert Ysoude: *Thou no aughtest nought here to be!* (line

2108). They then feign a debate in which Tristrem takes up the position of one sinned against, and determined to leave the court:

> "Ysoude, thou art mi fo;
> Thou sinnest, levedi, on me.
> Thou gabbest on me so
> Mi nem nil me not se.
> He threteneth me to slo.
> More menske were it to the
> Better for to do,
> Bi God in Trinité,
> This tide.
> Or Y this lond schal fle
> Into Wales wide."
>
> (lines 2113–23)

Ysoude both defends herself and reproves Tristrem, swearing her faithfulness with careful ambiguity:

> "Men said thou bi me lay,
> Thine em so understode.
> Wende forth in thi way;
> It semes astow were wode,
> To wede.
> Y loved never man with mode
> Bot him that hadde mi maidenhede."
>
> (lines 2128–34)

In comparison to Gottfried's courtly discourse at this point, the English poet's version might well be seen as lacking subtlety, but the dramatic dialogue conveys the tense improvisation of the moment with a more powerful directness, closer in spirit to Béroul. This is often the case in *Sir Tristrem*; setting himself to render the plot material of the Thomas tradition, the poet's chosen idiom creates vivid snapshots of action and feeling.

A significant absence from *Sir Tristrem* is any reference to Arthur and his court. Friar Robert twice uses the Arthurian story as context, even though, as he puts it, "this does not belong to the subject-matter of the story" (*Saga*, chapter 71). The comparison in the English romance is among the several courts where Tristrem has a temporary place: his position at the courts in Ireland and Wales is that of guest, though he performs the deed that would earn him the hand of the king's daughter in both; his position in Brittany is a sequence of half-measures, winning power but handing it to another, marrying the Duke's daughter but never fulfilling the role of husband or loyal vassal; his position at Mark's court seesaws between high position with the promise of future rule and disgrace and exile. The complexity and absence of stable points of reference partly account for the critical view of the poem as "lacking any sustained moral dimension" with no interest in "the ethical problems raised by Thomas in his story" (Barnes 1993: 94; see also Crane 1986: 195; Sweeney 2000: 125–31). It is true that there is neither clear-cut defense nor criticism of Tristrem and Ysoude's adultery, but the poet displays both positive and negative aspects of the central situation in his narrative. The most romantic episode is the idyllic happiness of the lovers' woodland exile (lines 2454–508), in what is described as an ideal place, an ancient house of earth created by giants with a secret entrance, where love is enough to keep them well fed, though Tristrem's hunting skills and the two dogs, Hodain and Petticrew, also supply their table:

> In winter it was hate;
> In somer it was cold.
> Thai hadden a dern gat
> That thai no man told.
> Ne hadde thai no wines wat,
> No ale that was old;
> Ne no gode mete thai at.
> Thai hadden al that thai wold
> With wille.
> For love ich other bihalt,
> Her non might of other fille.
>   (lines 2487–97)

The bliss of this simple life, reminiscent of Boethius' picture of the Golden Age, is enough to explain the emphasis on dogs in this version of the story: Hodain's licking of the dregs of the love potion and his consequent total devotion to the lovers has struck a number of critical readers as an indicator that the poem is meant to be read as parody, with comedy used to expose the dubious morality of the lovers' actions (Lupack 1994: 147–8; Sweeney 2000: 129), but the training of Hodain and Petticrew as hunting dogs (lines 2470–75) makes them a practical part of the self-sufficient family unit; their images accompany Ysoude in the hall of statues. The negative aspects of the adulterous love relationship are expressed not in explicit moral judgment of the lovers as deceivers and breakers of faith, but in registration of Tristrem's sense of injustice and the shilly-shallying of King Mark, who has little judgment of his own. A rare passage of reflection and self-awareness for Tristrem occurs after his marriage:

> Tristrem a wil is inne,
> Has founden in his thought:
> "Mark, min em, hath sinne;
> Wrong he hath ous wrought.
> Icham in sorwe and pine;
> Therto hye hath me brought.

Hir love, Y say, is mine;
The Boke seyt it is nought
With right."
                              (lines 2663–71)

Though this stanza will not satisfy readers who look for the lengthy inner debate which Thomas gave to his Tristran at this point, it expresses a recognition of moral conflict which is consistent with the poet's handling of the material as primarily the hero's story. In the scenes that bring the poem to its incomplete close, bitterness and pain are assuaged, both for Ysoude, whose tart invocation of God, Mary, and St Katherine to curse Canados and her frantic disappointment when Tristrem appears to have deserted her are melted away by seeing him again, and for Tristrem, who enjoys the love of Ysoude one last time (lines 3224–5) and then pays back Meriadok and Canados; revenge and vindication are his, rather than remorse.

Whatever the omissions of *Sir Tristrem*, there is nothing like the same intensity of feeling in the story when its scenes are dispersed among the mixed adventures of the Round Table, as is the case in the Prose *Tristan* and in Malory's *Morte Darthur*. Malory's enormous *Boke of Sir Trystrams de Lyones*, "Book of Sir Tristram", which occupies nearly 200 of the surviving 480 folios of the Winchester manuscript, was based on two books of a three-book version (as yet not precisely identified) of the French Prose *Tristan*. Though he has mentioned Tristram earlier, in the tale of Marhalt and as a noble knight and the lover of Isode, both with a sense of him as an outsider, Malory now goes back to the beginnings of the story. The first book (Vinaver 1971: 229–343) tells of Tristram's birth and upbringing, the killing of Marhalt, visits to Ireland, the love potion, Isode's marriage to King Mark, Tristram's marriage to Isode le Blaunche Mains, Tristram's madness in the forest and his being sent into exile, and his encounters with other knights in separate combats and in tournament, though these episodes are intermingled with the adventures of others. The second book (Vinaver 1971: 343–511) sees Tristram become a member of the Round Table, which completes one narrative sequence, and, within a mesh of adventures involving a large cast of characters, tells of Mark's malicious plots against his nephew, Tristram's rivalry with Palomydes, Mark's imprisonment of Tristram, and the escape of Tristram and Isode to the haven of Joyous Garde, which could be said to complete a second main sequence, bringing the story of Tristram and Isode to a temporary happy ending. *But here ys no rehersall of the thirde booke*, Malory tells us, where presumably the tragic ending would have been reached; instead he moves to *the noble tale of the Sankegreall*.

A changed perspective is clear in the episode of Segwarydes' wife (Wimsatt 1997). Between Tristram's first visit to Ireland (when he has already promised Isode that he will be *all the dayes of my lyff your knyght*, Vinaver 1971: 243) and his second visit (to ask for Isode's hand on Mark's behalf), uncle and nephew become rivals for the beautiful wife of a Cornish earl. King Mark, resenting Tristram's success, ambushes him on the road to her house; they wound each other in the dark, causing Tristram to leave telltale blood stains in the lady's bed. Segwarydes thus discovers the affair, and in the consequent fight is unhorsed by Tristram. Though the situation puts Tristram in a less than flattering light, it does provide cause for Mark's enmity towards him. But it goes further when Bleoberys, kinsman of Lancelot, also falls for this Cornish siren, boldly asks a boon of Mark, claims the lady, and rides off. The potentially comic picture of an ineffectual husband failing to barricade his marriage against three lustful lovers becomes, lengthily in the Prose *Tristan* and in an abridged form in *Le Morte Darthur*, an exercise in weighing the obligations of love and the duties of husband and lover. Should Tristram, as a true courtly lover, have challenged Bleoberys and prevented the abduction, as is the view of a court lady who *rebuked sir Trystrams in the horrybelyst wyse, and called him cowarde knyght*? Or was it, as Tristram says in his defense, his duty to leave it to the husband and conceal his own involvement? The wife, after Tristram and Bleoberys have fought for a time and Bleoberys proposes that they should let her choose between them, opts for Bleoberys, expressing disillusion with Tristram: . . . *untyll that tyme I wente ye had loved me*. Bleoberys takes her back to her husband, for which, surprisingly, Tristram gets some of the credit.

Not only does the representation of Tristram in these scenes as an experienced adulterer undermine an idealized concept of Tristram as hero, but rating him in a tally of courtly points scored gives the story a shallowness which does not compensate for the greater narrative variety and larger cast list in the prose version. It is no surprise, therefore, that the tragic outcome of the story of Tristram and Yseult almost disappears in Malory, being reported only in retrospect, first in the list of knights assembled in the episode of the healing of Sir Urry, where his murder by Mark is linked to the death of Lamorak because both were greatly lamented and were *with treson slayne* (Vinaver 1971: 666), and more fully in a conversation between Launcelot and Bors as to whether Launcelot should rescue Guenevere from being burnt at the stake, and if he were to do so, where would he keep her? When Bors suggests Joyous Garde, citing the three years spent there by Tristram and Isode, Lancelot resists:

> ". . . for by sir Trystram I may have a warnynge; for whan by meanys of tretyse sir Trystram brought again La Beall Isode unto kynge Marke from Joyous Garde, loke ye how shamefully that false traytour kyng Marke slew hym as he sat harpynge afore hys lady, La Beall Isode." (Vinaver 1971: 681)

Such off-stage reporting sets the seal on the evidence that for Malory the story of Tristram is a secondary matter. It is true that the fifth book is the longest and therefore contains the most substantial body of narrative illustration of the chivalric themes that interested Malory and that the "Book of Sir Tristram" invites comparison with the earlier adventures of Lancelot and Gareth, but it is an overlong hotchpotch including more or less self-contained stories with only oblique reference to Tristram ("La Cote Male Tayle," "Alexander the Orphan"), episodes in the career of Lancelot (particularly the story of Lancelot and Elayne and the birth of Galahad), the adventures of Palomydes, also in love with Isode, and most powerfully the melodramatic tale of

Lamorak, lover of Gawain's mother, shamefully ambushed *in a pryvy place* (Vinaver 1971: 428) by Gawain, Aggravaine, Gaheris, and Mordred, and stabbed in the back by Mordred some time after Gaheris had beheaded their mother. Tristram is, as Terence McCarthy put it, "never quite the hero of his own book" (McCarthy 1988: 32). Helen Cooper puts forward the most positive argument for this multiplicity, suggesting that the original story of Tristan and Yseult was too limited to have served Malory's purpose:

> it was essentially a story of private love, with little or no Arthurian reference and no apparent scope for displaying the broad patternings of chivalrous action that Malory required. (Cooper 1996: 183)

The Arthurian version of the story of Tristram is, in broad terms, the restructuring of a love story between a young Cornish hero and an Irish princess, later Queen of Cornwall, who are caught up in a conflict of loyalties, partly determined by magic events outside their control, and involving not only husband, wife, and lover, but the political relationships of Cornwall, Ireland, and Brittany, into a contributory strand in a multiple narrative of Arthur's court and chivalric brotherhood. Tristram is, in a sense, domesticated from his sea-journeys and shifts of setting into the mainly land-locked world of chivalric adventure, a less precise place populated by wandering knights, singly or in groups, looking for temporary lodgings as they move from tournament to private fight, from meetings with friends to challenges from strangers. The main thrust of Malory's treatment of Tristram is of his becoming a knight of the Round Table, earning a place high in the league table of the best knights, second only to Lancelot. The "Book of Sir Tristram" is a series of staged combats for Tristram, among others, by which reputation may be measured. In the course of the book Tristram unhorses or otherwise buffets, bruises, and overwhelms knights (not necessarily named but identified as individuals) on nearly a hundred occasions, together with many others referred to in groups at tournaments (as with *all of Orkeney*); some of these repeat defeats of the same opponent, as with Palomydes, Bleoberys, Ector, and even Arthur (twice). He kills or mortally wounds Marhalt, Earl Grype, Nabone, the Giant Tauleas, Sir Hemysoun (lover of Morgan), Elyas (leader of the Saxons), together with other Saxon knights, twelve knights out of thirty that ambush him and Dynadan, and three other unnamed knights. He is himself unhorsed on occasion by Palomydes (twice), Lamorak, Arthur, and Lancelot, and more than once calls a halt to a combat, so that honors are even between him and Lamorak, Lancelot, and, eventually, Palomydes, whose career is crowned by his accepting baptism. In the various fights Tristram appears in several identities: as king's nephew and champion of Cornwall; in disguise in Ireland as potential winner of the hand of a princess (until his real identity is discovered); as a young, known knight gradually establishing himself on the chivalric ladder of honor; and as an anonymous, errant knight fighting in disguise, as in the tournament at Lonezep, where he twice withdraws from the mêlée only to return newly armed in red or in black to win honor as an unknown. In the first book, where Tristram is climbing the ladder toward joining the Round Table, he is matched against knights of various levels of prowess, so that a sense of his placing in relation to known knights is cumulatively established. In the second book, where his story is more widely scattered, interspersed with illustrations of Mark's villainy (and periods of imprisonment by Mark) and other adventures, such as those of Palomydes, Tristram's chivalric acts are concentrated in the tournaments, particularly at Lonezep, where he fights disguised in the party opposing Arthur, but then changes sides when Arthur needs support, so demonstrating his shift from individual hero to valued member of the brotherhood.

Part of the chivalric normalizing of the tale is the building up of the roles of knights who act as foils to Tristram: Palomydes, his rival in love, and Dynadan. If the self-lacerations of an anguished Palomydes, together with his impulsive inconsistencies, his combination of respect and enmity toward Tristram, provide a more extreme version of Tristram's own intensity, the elements of comic realism in Dynadan's deflating comments on the foolhardy excesses of chivalry offer a measure for Tristram's fearless, at times reckless, conduct.

The result of this recasting of the narrative is the displacement of the other main characters in the original story. Isode, though she remains the motivation for Tristram's greatest acts of endurance and courage, recedes from the forefront of the narrative, once the bare bones of her situation as Mark's wife and Tristram's mistress have been established, and becomes a mainly absent icon of beauty and desirability, nearly always referred to as "La Beale Isode," as if she were a picture, which is how Arthur treats her in leaving the tournament simply to view her. Mark, through whom in some versions of the story the complexity of the morality of the relationships is interestingly explored, is reduced to a cardboard villain representing the opposite of chivalric values. There is no sense here that the king loves his wife and only reluctantly believes ill of her, nor that he values Tristram as his sister's son and heir until court intrigue forces him to recognize his nephew's disruptive disloyalty. From the rivalry over the wife of Segwarydes Mark becomes Tristram's enemy: *aftir that, thoughe there were fayre speche, love was there none* (Vinaver 1971: 246), and even fair speech does not last long. After Tristram has become a member of the Round Table Mark sets out from Cornwall to kill him, and when the two knights he has taken with him refuse to aid him, he immediately kills one, and later gives the other his death wound in an episode which identifies Mark as a murderer and a coward. Later he swears falsely to Arthur that he will keep to the terms of reconciliation forced on him at Camelot, but subsequently tricks and imprisons Tristram, and further plots against his life, despite the fact that he has to swallow his pride and call on the wounded Tristram to rescue Cornwall from successive invasions by Saxons and Saracens.

Such moral simplification is accompanied by ambiguity elsewhere which stems from conflicting attitudes toward adultery in Malory's sources. Insofar as adulterous love is registered as "true love," it is Tristram's marriage that brings explicit condemnation from Lancelot:

Than seyde sir Launcelot, "Fye uppon hym, untrew knyght to his lady! That so noble
a knyght as sir Trystrames is sholde be founde to his fyrst lady and love untrew, that
is the quene of Cornwayle! . . . the love betwene hym and me is done for ever, and I gyff
hym warnyng: from this day forthe I woll be his mortall enemy." (Vinaver 1971:
273)

Knowledge of Lancelot's enmity matters more to Tristram than the possible response
of Isode herself, as seems clear from the letter Tristram sends to Lancelot:

> . . . excusynge hym of the weddynge of Isod le Blaunche Maynes, and seyde, . . . as he
> was a trew knyght, he had never ado fleyshly with Isode le Blaunche Maynys. And
> passynge curteysly and jantely sir Trystrames wrote unto sir Launcelot, ever besechynge
> hym to be hys good frende and unto La Beall Isod of Cornwayle, and that sir Launcelot
> wolde excuse hym if that ever he saw her. (Vinaver 1971: 288)

On the other hand, when, at a later stage of the story, Perceval reproves Mark for his
enmity toward Tristram and points out that Mark could not survive if Tristram were
to make war on him, the standpoint is very different:

> "That is trouthe," seyde kynge Marke, "but I may nat love sir Trystram, bycause he
> lovyth my quene, La Beall Isode."
>   "A, fy for shame!" seyde sir Percivale. "Sey ye never so more! For ar ye nat uncle unto
> sir Trystram? And by youre neveaw ye sholde never thynke that so noble a knyght as
> sir Trystram is, that he wolde do hymselff so grete vylany to holde his uncles wyff.
> Howbehit," seyde sir Percivale, "he may love youre quene synles, because she is called
> one of the fayryst ladyes of the worlde." (Vinaver 1971: 414)

Another theme is Tristram's progress as a young knight from Cornwall who has to
overcome prejudice from the Round Table against outsiders; he gradually wins respect,
earns the commendation of Lancelot and Arthur, and is accepted into the brotherhood,
with a designated chair at the table waiting for him (formerly Marhalt's). This thread
is built up over a number of dramatized encounters. Early in his career Tristram is
challenged as a feeble Cornish knight by Sagramoure and Dodynas le Sauvage, but he
unhorses them both, declaring:

> "Fayre knyghtes, wyll ye ony more? Be there ony bygger knyghtys in the courte of kynge
> Arthure? Hit is to you shame to sey us knyghtes of Cornwayle dishonour, for hit may
> happyn a Cornysh knyght may macche you." (Vinaver 1971: 248)

Later Tristram encounters Kay, who says *yet harde I never that evir good knyght com oute
of Cornwayle* (Vinaver 1971: 299), to which Tristram gives a tart rejoinder, before
finding himself sitting down to supper with Kay, Tor, and Braundiles, who *spake all
the shame by Cornysh knyghtes that coude be seyde*; Tristram says little but next day

unhorses two of them. The theme develops greater complexity when Mark's actions earn more disparagement for the Cornish, and in the persons of nephew and uncle Cornwall is both honored and shamed. The contrast between the courts of Cornwall and Camelot is pointed out several times but the parallel is identified by Isode, when she incautiously and tactlessly uses Palomydes as the messenger to Guenevere:

> ". . . and tell her that I sende her worde that there be within this londe but four lovers, and that is sir Launcelot and dame Gwenyver, and sir Trystrames and quene Isode." (Vinaver 1971: 267)

Tristram is himself manipulated by Morgan le Fay into bearing to Camelot a shield depicting Arthur and Guenevere dominated by Lancelot, with the intention of bringing shame on the court; this brings the first book to an ominous close and suggests that the figure of Tristram, who defeats both Arthur and Uwayne when challenged in the scene that follows and rides off unidentified, is being set up as a warning to Camelot. This theme is, however, not brought to a head; later moral comment is concentrated on the murder of Lamorak, the subject of one of Malory's longest passages of discussion among knights when Tristram, Palomydes, and Dynadan speak with Gareth about the actions of his brothers, foreseeing the split in the Round Table between the kin of Gawain and of Lancelot.

Elsewhere Malory shows awareness of alternative versions of Tristram's story. Of the multiple talents of the French Tristan as the heroic model of all the graces of courtliness, chivalry, and polished education, only his role as huntsman is given specific accolade:

> And every day sir Trystram wolde go ryde an-huntynge, for he was called that tyme the chyeff chacer of the worlde and the noblyst blower of an horne of all maner of mesures. For, as the bookis reporte, of sir Trystram cam all the good termys of venery and of huntynge . . . that all maner jantylmen hath cause to the worldes ende to prayse Sir Trystram and to pray for his soule. AMEN, SAYDE SIR THOMAS MALLEORRE. (Vinaver 1971: 416)

Malory seems here to add a footnote to fill one of the gaps in the Prose *Tristan*'s version of the tale. Even more striking is the inclusion of the episode of Tristram's madness, which opens up a chasm between Malory's normal plodding accounts of men in armor hitting each other and the wild eccentricity of passion. The episodes involving Tristram as a naked fool in the forest, Isode (believing Tristram dead) planning suicide, which is prevented by Mark, who then sets a watch upon her, Tristram's gradual recovery, his return to court recognized only by his dog, and then his banishment from court all belong to the other "heroic" version of the tale, as does at least the beginning of the bitter speech in which Tristram bids farewell, though Malory weakens the effect by letting it lapse into a summary of all his adventures up to that point:

"Grete well kyng Marke and all myne enemyes, and sey to hem I woll com agayne when I may. And sey hym well am I rewarded for the fyghtyng with sir Marhalt, and delyverd all hys contrey frome servayge. And well am I rewarded for the fecchynge and costis of quene Isode oute off Irelonde and the daunger I was in firste and laste . . ." (Vinaver 1971: 310)

However, the intense and tragic aspects of the love story are merely glimpses of the path from which the main course of the narrative has been diverted so that it may follow the high road *towarde Camelot where that kynge Arthure and quene Gwenyvir was, and the moste party of all the knyghtes of the Rounde Table were there also* (Vinaver 1971: 510), which is, more or less, where the lengthy *mélange* of the "Book of Sir Tristram" comes to rest.

It has been argued that the two Tristan texts discussed here may be connected: Malory perhaps knew *Sir Tristrem* and borrowed details as he did from other English romances (Hardman 2004). But to the reader the differences are more striking. *Sir Tristrem* gives an English slant to the story, with more individuality than many Middle English romances: unique in verse form, with some northernisms but in a London manuscript, swift in narrative style with unusual flashes of life, its exact origins and literary placing invite further research. Malory's treatment is more complicated; only a part of his Arthurian explorations, nevertheless in its length and multiplicity of action it provides massive illustration of the practice and ethics of knighthood and in this respect has been seen as "the center of the *Morte Darthur*, the heart of the work" (Mahoney 1979/2002: 253). The fullest representation in English of the "interlace" of French prose romance, the book has many interesting strands not examined here – the use of letters, the elegiac note in the laments of Lamorak, Palomydes, and Tristram, and the manipulation of the story of Tristram to enhance the standing of Lancelot.

NOTE

1   The forms Ysoude, Rohaud, and Gauhardin are to be preferred to the Ysonde, Rohand, and Ganhardin printed by Sir Walter Scott, McNeill (1886), etc.; see Hardman (2005: 87).

PRIMARY SOURCES

Brewer, D. (ed.) (1972). *Geoffrey Chaucer. The Parlement of Foulys*, 2nd edn. Manchester: Manchester University Press.

Lupack, A. (ed.) (1994). *Lancelot of the Laik* and *Sir Tristrem*. TEAMS. Kalamazoo, MI: Medieval Institute.

Mills, M. (ed.) (1988). *Horn Childe and Maiden Rimnild*. Heidelberg: Carl Winter.

McNeill, G. P. (ed.) (1886). *Sir Tristrem*. Edinburgh: Scottish Text Society.

Schach, P. (trans.) (1973). *The saga of Tristram and Isönd*. Lincoln, NB: University of Nebraska.

Vinaver, E. (ed.) (1971). *Malory. Works*. Oxford: Clarendon Press.

References and Further Reading

Barnes, G. (1993). *Counsel and strategy in Middle English romance*. Cambridge: Brewer.

Barron, W. R. J. (1987). *English medieval romance*. London: Longman.

Cooper, H. (1996). The Book of Sir Tristram de Lyones. In E. Archibald & A. S. G. Edwards (eds), *A companion to Malory*. Cambridge: Brewer, pp. 183–201.

Cooper, H. (2005). Thomas of Erceldoune. In C. Saunders (ed.), *Cultural encounters in the romance of medieval England*. Cambridge: Brewer, pp. 171–87.

Crane, S. (1986). *Insular romance*. Berkeley, CA: University of California Press.

Hardman, P. (2004). Malory and Middle English verse romance: The case of *Sir Tristrem*. In B. Wheeler (ed.), *Arthurian studies in honour of P. J. C. Field*. Cambridge: Brewer, pp. 217–22.

Hardman, P. (2005). The true romance of *Tristrem and Ysoude*. In C. Saunders (ed.), *Cultural encounters in the romance of medieval England*. Cambridge: Brewer, pp. 85–99.

Hardman, P., Le Saux, F., Noble, P. S., & Thomas, N. (eds) (2003). *The growth of the Tristan and Iseut legend in Wales, England, France and Germany*. Lampeter: Edwin Mellen Press.

Mahoney, D. B. (2002). Malory's "Tale of Sir Tristram": Source and setting reconsidered. In J. T. Grimbert (ed.), *Tristan and Isolde: A casebook*. New York: Routledge, pp. 223–53. (Original work published in *Medievalia et Humanistica*, n.s., 9 [1979], 175–98.)

McCarthy, T. (1988). *An introduction to Malory*. Cambridge: Brewer.

Saunders, C. (ed.) (2005). *Cultural encounters in the romance of medieval England*. Cambridge: Brewer.

Sweeney, M. (2000). *Magic in medieval romance*. Dublin: Four Courts Press.

Taylor, B. & Brewer, E. (1983). *The return of King Arthur: British and American Arthurian literature since 1800*. Cambridge: Brewer.

Wimsatt, J. I. (1997). Segwarydes' wife and competing perspectives within Malory's *Tale of Sir Tristram*. In T. Hahn & A. Lupack (eds), *Retelling tales: Essays in honor of Russell Peck*. Cambridge: Brewer, pp. 321–40.

Part V

From Medieval to Medievalism

20

Malory's *Morte Darthur* and History

Andrew Lynch

Thomas Malory's *Morte Darthur* was completed sometime in 1469–70. It is the classic English-language version of an Arthurian legend – still a "history" to some – that stretches back into Celtic antiquity (Higham 2002). The surviving early forms of Malory's text are themselves historical landmarks: Caxton's edition of 1485 is probably the best-known early printed book in English; the *Morte*'s single surviving manuscript, rediscovered by a Winchester schoolteacher in 1934, is also famous.

Malory himself stresses the historicity and antiquity of his narrative in many references that locate it in a previous England, under the *most nobelyst kynge of the worlde* (Vinaver 1990: 459). In medieval times, Arthur was a historical figure, celebrated as the "British worthy" in a list of nine Jews, pagans, and Christians that included Joshua, David, Hector, Alexander, and Charlemagne. Geoffrey of Monmouth's twelfth-century prose Latin *Historia Regum Britanniae* ("History of the Kings of Britain") was still taken as true, and was the ultimate source of Malory's story of Arthur's Roman wars. Malory also sometimes refers to his French romance sources, from the Merlin, Lancelot–Grail, and Tristan traditions, as "authorized" documents based on accounts from people closely involved: Merlin dictates early events to Bloyse (37–8); Arthur has all the Grail knights' testimonies made into great chronicles by clerks (1036); Bedivere survives to have Arthur's ending written down (1242). "Romance provides history with . . . the protocol for recording deeds and for making them into books" (Crofts 2006: 39).

The *Morte* was actually a latecomer in the medieval Arthurian tradition, built on the work of many predecessors, but later retellings have given it the status of a foundation text for English readers, a venerable beginning. It is now one of a very few fifteenth-century English narratives still much read. As a result, it has tended to become decontextualized, either ahistorically viewed in isolation from its own times, or else simplistically taken as direct evidence of their socio-political problems. It has also often been misleadingly treated as a moral fable of sin and punishment, in compliance with the cultural work imposed on the story in the Victorian age. The *Morte*'s heroes are fallible men and women – Lancelot himself is an *erthly synfull man* (934) – but Malory remains convinced of their goodness. This is not to say that modern readers cannot see blind spots and contradictions in his evaluation of their actions, but we will not find him condemning Arthur, Lancelot, or Guenevere for wrongdoing, or treating the downfall of Camelot as their just deserts. Malory's God expresses the same generous attitude: he punishes Arthur's incest through the final "day of destiny" with Mordred, yet sends Sir Gawain from heaven to warn Arthur to postpone the battle, *for pyté of you and many mo other **good men** there shall be slayne* (1234, my emphasis). Divine punishment implies no personal shame or loss of good will. The prevalence of sin and need for repentance and mercy were commonplaces in later medieval religious culture. When a character like Lancelot accuses himself of sinfulness, he is doing what he should in a confessional or penitential context: "his self-condemnation issues from and is sanctioned by the world he inhabits" (Riddy 1987: 121).

The Identity of Thomas Malory

During the Victorian and Edwardian age, the medieval past was gradually installed as the basis of British heritage. Arthurianism, with the *Morte* as its main medieval reference point, was central in the process of inventing a new version of the historical origins and cultural inheritance of the present. At the same time, the success of the medieval revival depended on bringing Arthur up to date: Tennyson saw him as "a modern gentleman" (Tennyson 1969: 597). He acknowledged Malory's prestige, but wanted to detach an ideal Arthur and ideal chivalry from the problematic medium and era in which Malory had presented them – "Touched by the adulterous finger of a time / That hovered between war and wantonness, / And crownings and dethronements" (Tennyson 1969: 1756). Tennyson made the Arthur of *Idylls of the King* "modern" in Victorian terms, a spokesman for contemporary bourgeois attitudes, in ways that have later made him seem very old-fashioned. *Idylls of the King* became a dominant influence on how most English-language readers from about 1850 to 1950, longer in some cases, imagined all Arthurian literature, and made it harder for them to think of *Le Morte Darthur* positively as a fifteenth-century text, a work of its own distinctive era. In literary history the fifteenth century was usually understood as a barren, decadent time between Chaucer and the emergence of Wyatt, Surrey, and the Elizabethans. Malory was typecast as a nostalgic idealist, "a practical and righteous fifteenth-century gentleman, who wished to bring back a decadent England to the virtues of 'manhode, curteyse and gentylnesse'" (Chambers 1945: 195). Such judgments credited the *Morte* with a simple distaste for its own times and an equally simple idealization of a past world.

It has largely been left to more recent scholarship to research and reimagine the relationship of *Le Morte Darthur* to its own historical period. An important issue in that process was to find the identity of the writer, Sir Thomas Malory. Evidence in the manuscript reveals him as a "knight-prisoner" who completed his book "between

3 March 1469 and 4 March 1970" (Field 1993: 1). The only known Thomas Malory who was a knight-prisoner at the time is a member of a gentry family from Newbold Revell in Warwickshire, probably born around 1416, who had become a knight by 1441. The life-records of the same Thomas Malory show him dealing in land, taking up lawsuits, electing people to parliament, and becoming a member of parliament himself for Warwickshire in 1445, and possibly for boroughs in Wiltshire in 1449 and Dorset in 1450. All that is typical of an active member of the gentry, but Malory's extensive record of criminal charges, dating from 1443 and skyrocketing in 1450, is unusual, and a shock to readers of the *Morte*. Very serious allegations are recorded against him: robbery, malicious damage, assault, jail breaking, extortion, rape, ambush, and attempted murder (Field 1996).

Malory was never actually tried, and spent substantial periods free on pardon or on bail. But he had been in prison for the best part of eight years before being freed when the Yorkists came to power in 1460. Trouble resurfaced later, and he is now known to have been in Newgate in April 1469. Imprisonment in Newgate rather than in the Tower of London suggests criminal charges, not the detention of a political prisoner, though if Malory had not had political enemies, or had had more friends in power, criminal proceedings against him would not have been so active. He died in March 1471, quite likely in Newgate. His burial in the nearby church of the Greyfriars may be because it was a fashionable London church, or because gentlemen convicts who died in the prison were often buried there (Sutton 2000).

The *Morte* translates and adapts numerous French and English Arthurian sources. It has puzzled some scholars how a prisoner could gain access to them. Possibly Malory had one or more friends or patrons – there is no evidence for this – who brought him books in jail, or he may have received favors from its keeper. Conditions in Newgate were not pleasant – it was a jail for serious offenders – but it is possible that with the assistance of family, friends, and money, and with the favor of the keeper, his life there was bearable and reasonably social. Perhaps he arranged to buy or hire books from the nearby booksellers (Sutton 2000). It is possible that he wrote with an eye to the commercial book market. The Winchester manuscript may be a copy produced for sale; Caxton soon enough came across Malory's work and saw its commercial potential. It has also been conjectured that Malory was trying to restore his moral reputation by writing a notably idealistic work (Wallace 2006). These motives need not be incompatible. What is certain is that to complete *Le Morte Darthur* under such conditions, he was a remarkably energetic and resourceful man, whom even Newgate could not daunt as long as he was well: *For all the whyle a presoner may have hys helth of body, he may endure undir the mercy of God, and in hope of good delyveraunce* (540).

Malory and Politics

A feature of Malory's career is an apparent habit of changing sides, or of finding them change around him. He seems to have been favored by the Duke of Buckingham, who owned the Wiltshire borough where a Thomas Malory was elected in 1449, yet he was charged with leading a gang to ambush and kill Buckingham early in 1450. The Yorkists pardoned Malory in 1462, and he fought for them in 1462–3 at some locations the *Morte* mentions in Arthur's war against Lancelot, but some time after 1464 Malory was imprisoned again and Edward IV specifically excluded him from general pardons made in 1468 and 1470. Perhaps Malory was caught up in the later falling-out between King Edward and his former supporter the Earl of Warwick. It is not possible to work out from the remaining records just what happened, but at any rate he was now perceived as an enemy, not an ally, by those he had previously served. Given the *Morte*'s emphasis on reward for loyal service, Malory's own apparent situation does not match the ideals of his narrative, but may resemble some developments that occur toward its ending, when Lancelot and the knights loyal to him suddenly find themselves turned against Arthur, and former friends and comrades fight against each other. He could have empathized with Lancelot's anguish at loss of *worship* (standing/good reputation) when Arthur banishes him from England: *And that ys to me grete hevynes, for ever I feare aftir my dayes that men shall cronycle uppon me that I was fleamed* [banished] *oute of this land* (1203).

Shortly before Camelot breaks up into hostile factions, Malory highlights Arthur's praise for Gareth, who has changed sides in a tournament to help Lancelot: *methought hit was my worshyp to helpe hym. For I saw hym do so muche dedis of armys, and so many noble knyghtes ayeynste hym* (1114). Gareth does not place winning the tournament for Arthur's side above everything else, and feels able to balance loyalty to a friend in trouble with his overall duty to the king, in a way that Arthur himself appreciates. Malory concludes: *he that was curteyse, trew, and faythefull to hys frynde was **that tyme** cherysshed* (1114, my emphasis). The episode sets out an understanding of knightly service as principled yet flexible, with an emotional bent, and motivated by personal assessments of situations as they emerge, not by sheer utility to one's own faction. As long as a knight is motivated by good will, without unworthy ulterior motives, his actions can be seen as *worshipful*. Toward the end of *Le Morte Darthur*, the most *worshipful* acts are often those that are not profitable from a party point of view. Lancelot's army captures Arthur, but he refuses to take military advantage from that, let alone kill him, as Sir Bors proposes:

> So whan kynge Arthur was on horsebak, he loked on sir Launcelot; than the teerys braste oute of his yen, thynkyng of the grete curtesy that was in sir Launcelot more than in ony other man. (Vinaver 1990: 1192)

Malory is acutely aware of the clash between political demands and personal sympathies, and tends to favor the latter. The real-life climate in which he operated was harsher. Scarcely more than a year after those lines were written, Henry VI, held captive in the Tower of London, was murdered by the Yorkist powers.

The Ethics of Knighthood

If the criminal charges against Malory were justified, then he had a worrying resemblance to some very bad knights in his own book, like Perys de Forest Sauvage:

> "What?" seyde sir Launcelot, "is he a theff and a knyght? And a ravyssher of women? He doth shame unto the Order of Knyghthode, and contrary unto his oth. Hit is pyté that he lyveth." (Vinaver 1990: 269)

The apparent mismatch between the *Morte*'s view of knighthood and its author's career has troubled readers. Yet whatever Malory's other alleged crimes, it would be rash to accuse him of simply being a turncoat or opportunist. Malory distinguishes between *unhappy* knights like Mordred and Aggravain – we might call them "trouble-makers" – who deliberately cause political conflict for their own *prevy* (secret/private) reasons, and those knights who are just drawn into the conflict, even if the latter, like Lancelot and Gawain, contribute to the problem by recklessness or unreasonable revenge. He also distinguishes between those who fight to honor prior allegiances and those who betray their lords out of ingratitude or in the hope of gain. Lancelot's followers are seen as right in telling him to rescue the queen from burning because *hit ys for youre sake* (1172), even though they see the undesirability of opposing so good a king as Arthur. But the narrative is indignant about Mordred's knightly backers *that kynge Arthur had brought up of nought, and gyffyn them londis, that myght nat then say hym a good worde* (1229). Even then, we should remember Gawain's warning that Arthur's "people" will be killed *on bothe partyes* (1234) in the last battle, and that Mordred does his duty in fighting bravely that day (1236). Malory does not tend to treat fights, even this one, as allegories of good versus evil. It has been suggested that he had in mind some aspects of the actual Battle of Towton in 1461: the day-long combat; the fighting on foot; the pillaging of the dead by moonlight; the vast number killed. Deaths at Towton were estimated at 38,000, which as a percentage of the population is the equivalent of 760,000 today (Field 2000).

To the modern outsider, and to an outraged enemy such as Gawain becomes, it would seem that Lancelot is a traitor to Arthur, since he has "held" the queen and fought against the king to keep her from his judgment and control. But Malory clearly does not see things that way. To him, Lancelot has saved Guenevere from an unjust death wished on her by liars and false counselors, and saved Arthur from the shame of allowing it to happen. "Lancelot is in real fact the only character who continues to be loyal to King Arthur throughout the war" (Radulescu 2003: 133). He is allowed an autonomy of action that exceeds the interpretation of loyalty as strict obedience to a lord.

Famously, the *Morte* complains that Mordred's rebellion is an instance of chronic English fickleness: *Lo thus was the olde custom and usayges of thys londe, and men say that we of thys londe have nat yet loste that custom* (1229). We cannot tell if these impolitic comments indicate a sympathy for Henry VI, whom the Yorkists had ousted, and so give a hint of why Malory was imprisoned so long and remained finally unpardoned. Perhaps they are simply an example of general discontent with an unstable political environment in which it had been too hard to fashion a successful knightly career without incurring crippling enmity. Malory's long "Book of Sir Tristram" is much preoccupied with the problems of ill will, "envy" (hatred), and long-term feuding between knights, and how these might be resolved. Some divisions can be healed, as when Tristram and Palomides (a rival for Isode's love) finally reconcile, but the inherited feud between the descendants of King Lot and King Pellinore seems unending, and results in the shocking murder of the good knight Lamerok, Pellinore's son, by Gawain and three of his brothers. The great Tristram himself is murdered, we later learn, by his treacherous uncle, King Mark. In Malory's world there are no guarantees that virtue will be rewarded, not only because of evildoers, but because, as Lancelot laments, *fortune ys so varyaunte, and the wheele so mutable, that there ys no constaunte aby-dynge* (1201). Like most Malorian comments on the political action, this one contains nothing historically specific, but is itself typical of fifteenth-century moralizing.

The *Morte* in its Time

As a translator and adapter, Malory did not invent the most part of his Arthurian plot-line, and it would be a mistake to see *Le Morte Darthur* as a story written to illustrate the politics of his lifetime. There is little agreement that we can identify its personages with actual figures, nor need the story be treated at all as a close commentary on contemporary events. It is a work of imaginative fiction and we must mainly look inside it for the meaning of its "history." As has been said of Chaucer, we must "read the text as if it were its own politics (developed through its specific envisioning of possible social relations)" (Wallace 1997: 3). Malory's vision is generically limited – he sticks closely to the matters of chivalric romance and chronicle (Field 1971) and prefers to deal with the adventures of great aristocrats – yet the narrative is saturated with the discourses, preoccupations, and attitudes of the gentry of its day, an ambitious landowning group of "gentlemen," active in local and central government (Radulescu 2003: 9). They ranked below the "noblemen" (the aristocracy), but had been raised in political importance by the need of monarchs and magnates to secure their help, and had often received knighthoods as a consequence (Radulescu 2003: 10–11).

The gentry were particularly prominent in the reign of Edward IV, when Malory wrote. Edward had promoted many of them in his household and council, and they were themselves collectors of material in "great books" that matched the interests of *Le Morte Darthur* – historical, political, religious, and chivalric (Cherewatuk 2000; Radulescu 2003: 39). Malory was conscious of having produced a "whole book," to be read "from the beginning to the ending" (Radulescu 2003: 45). Caxton, by contrast, seems to have offered Malory's work to the public as a kind of chronicle, reference book, and anthology – *for to passe the tyme thys book shal be plesaunt to rede in, wyth many wonderful hystoryes and adventures* (Spisak 1983: 3). It covers a range of gentry interests from religious observance, battles, tournaments, and love to marriage, genealogy and inheritance, law, hunting, land management, and table manners. It could serve many functions for the reader: a history of Britain's greatest era, a study of great kingship, a record of notable deeds of arms, a model of good conduct and deportment, a story of faithful love, and a work that inculcated religious piety (Riddy 1987; Cherewatuk 2000). These many interests are not confined to separate stories, though the quest of the Holy Grail is certainly the "holiest" of Malory's books, but thematically and discursively intermingled within the whole structure, allowing the modern reader insights into the distinctive way they could mingle in a fifteenth-century mindset. The story of Gareth combines an interest in food and proper ways of eating with a concern for "lineage, blood and wealth" as the basis of good marriage (Cherewatuk 2005: 23). The Fair Maid of Ascolat hopes that her love-pangs for Lancelot – she has unsuccessfully offered to become his wife or mistress – will be counted as part of her suffering in Purgatory (1093), and Malory says that Guenevere had a *good ende* (that is, died in a state of grace), because she was a faithful lover to Lancelot (1120).

Modern readers know the discourse of the fifteenth-century gentry mainly from the *Morte* itself. When one turns to other gentry documents it can be surprising to see similar language applied to mundane matters. Godfrey Greene wrote to Sir William Plumpton in the 1470s that they had been cheated over a promise to provide writs:

> he hath driuen us from morne to euen, & in conclusioun deceyued us, & hath receued vj*s* vj*d*. And I may nott arreast him nor striue with him for the mony, nor for the decept, because the matter is not worshipfull. And so there is none odere meane but dayly to labor him to gett the writts. . . . The labor is great & perillous and the anger is more because of the decept. (Kirby 1996: 50)

Driven, anger, strife, perilous, labor, and *worshipful* are all prominent words in Malory's vocabulary of knightly deeds. Lancelot performs a miraculous healing at the Chapel Perilous and refers to the Holy Grail quest as *the hyghe servyse in whom I dud my dyligente laboure.* His disastrous break with Arthur causes *a great anger and unhap.* Yet the same words could be applied to a *matter* that was *not worshipful;* it is mainly because we associate this language with *Le Morte Darthur* that it now seems lofty. Such "strife" and "laboring," to manipulate patronage, influence the law, exert muscle in the neighborhood, or get money out of debtors, were part of the daily life of the fifteenth-century gentry. Their acquisitive and abrasive transactions suggest a normative connection between the worldview of a gentry family of Malory's time and his main subject matter – war and combat. The language of gentry lawsuits is notably combative. They muster rolls of allies and reckon up enemies; divided into "parties," they aggressively "defend" themselves; they "labor" jurymen and judges; they issue and receive "challenges," which easily become more than metaphor. Law was only another way of seeking advantage, not at all incompatible with private physical force.

In this very competitive climate, defending one's own interests often meant injuring some one else's. Gentry letters about land commonly relate terrorizing of householders and servants, violent raids and battles, and the forced occupation of disputed estates. John Frende wrote to Thomas Stonor around 1462 that he was housebound by the servants of Richard Fortescue, who

> mauneseth me dayly, and put me in suche fere of my lyffe . . . that I dere not go to cherche ne to chepyng [market] . . . hit is worse than ever hit was . . . thay putteth us in utterance daily that we schalbe undowe [destroyed], for ye nel never come to helpe us. (Kingsford: I.56–7)

In 1466 the same Richard Fortescue, with forty others, allegedly kidnapped Frende for four days and held him to ransom for five marks (Kingsford: I.74–5). Malory would hardly have named a person as lowly as Frende in a knightly romance. Yet in its humble way, Frende's situation is like that of the besieged Lyonesse in the tale of Gareth, or of Gawain and the knights that Lancelot rescues from imprisonment by Sir Tarquin. Gentry figures were very familiar with the requirement to help dependants and "well-willers" in trouble, and to deal with "ill-willers," just as they were with occasional demands for assistance by great lords. In these and other respects, *Le Morte Darthur* can be seen as offering a nobler and aggrandized version of the lives and responsibilities of fifteenth-century landed gentlemen. It is not surprising that a prominent gentry figure like Sir John Paston was a collector of Arthurian material, or that Sir Thomas Malory found the story so congenial. As a knight himself, and a "gentleman" who bore "old arms," Malory might have felt drawn to emphasize the inclusive nature of his Round Table knighthood as an "Order," like the Order of the Garter, that included men of different consequence, even the king, on a notionally equal footing. Mador de la Porte tells Arthur that *thoughe ye be oure Kynge, in that degré ye are but a knyght as we ar, and ye ar sworne unto knyghthode als welle as we be* (1050).

Even the nature of Malory's interest in space and place reveals aristocratic and gentry attitudes. Malorian external space is not organized pictorially by "landscape," but by markers of transition from one scene of contact or conflict to the next, so spaces are either sites of fellowship or disputed by "parties." In peacetime, land is a means for monarchs to reward good service by gift, and to establish supporters in strategic places. It is wealth: a magnate speaks of "my lands" as shorthand for the income he receives from them. In wartime, land becomes a spatial roll of "well-willers" and "ill-willers," where one finds support or opposition. It exists as a means of provisioning and enriching one's own side through requisition, and of harming one's opponents' supply through burning and killing. In tournaments – these had been conspicuously promoted in the reign of Edward IV – space becomes a temporary theatre of "worship," and in the most prominent form it is the "field" of battle, where opposing interests are directly arbitrated by force. As a story of how shifts in collectivity and competition affected "worship" and "profit," *Le Morte Darthur* was highly relevant to the landed classes of its own day, despite the grand and sometimes improbable nature of its romance events.

The "Historical" Arthur and the Nature of the Past

This discussion has centered so far on how modern readers might relate Malory's text to the history of his own times. We can also ask how the *Morte* represents the relation of its own times to the "historical" days of King Arthur, which it sketchily places in the fifth century. Critical answers to that question have been complex and stimulating. Catherine Batt remarks that the *Morte*'s readers are both credited with an intuitive understanding of the historical action, and distanced from it as faithless specimens of "nowadays" (Batt 2002). Felicity Riddy emphasizes "fracture, separation and the division of wholeness" in Malory, concluding: "The dispersal of the Round Table has left nothing at the centre, and Arthur's mysterious departing is a departing from himself" (Riddy 1987: 153). Jill Mann argues that the repeated "emotional counterpointing" of "wholeness" and "departing," of longing and distance, is what gives Malory's narrative its characteristic power (Mann 1991: 2). She argues further that within this process Malory's own characters are distanced from their own past (or future) history, which impinges on them "out of the blue," and "stands in an utterly contradictory relation" to the present action in which they are participating (Mann 1991: 6–7). "Distance," says Mann, including the distance of history, is "an experience apprehended by the actors in the narrative and thus by its readers," as well as a feature of the *Morte*'s narrative mode (Mann 1991: 19). Her formulation stresses the collectivity of interest between textual characters and worshipful readers, and heightens a sense of their common predicament, each struggling to stabilize the sudden events of romance adventure within a frame of historical succession. In the starkest form, says Mann, an agent like the doomed Balin, or even Arthur or Lancelot, suffers "alienation from self," is "marginalised in relation to . . . [his] own story" (Mann 1991: 20), because his history is apprehended by him experientially in a series of separate episodic revelations, not as a conceptual whole, or not, at least, until too late. Yet for Malory's readers, Mann says, events have "the simplicity and finality of destiny" (Mann 1991: 32), partly because, to quote Field, "the simple past tense of the verbs puts the story firmly in a distant and unalterable past" (cited in Mann 1991: 37n). The destiny – tragic or heroic – that characters like Balin only intuit from within their unfolding adventures, the sense of "distance" from the story, readers find instantiated in the preterite form of the text.

All such judgments on a very long work like *Le Morte Darthur* depend strongly on the selection of examples and the critical emphases. The adventurous situations of participants within the narrative might also potentially model other relations between present and past, and present and future, and engage readers in a more flexible and positive experience of "history." For one thing, nearly half the text is in speech, and in speech Malory's characters use an energetic mixture of tenses and moods, taking readers imaginatively into the time of utterance to see events from their perspective. Here is an example from the moment when young Arthur learns his parentage:

> Thenne Arthur made grete doole when he understood that syre Ector was not his fader.
>
> "Sir," said Ector unto Arthur, "woll ye be my good and gracious lord when ye are kyng?"
>
> "Els were I to blame," said Arthur, "for ye are the man in the world that I am most beholdyng to, and my good lady and moder your wyf that as wel as her owne hath fostred me and kepte. And yf ever hit be Goddes will that I be kynge as ye say, ye shall desyre of me what I may doo and I shalle not faille yow. God forbede I shold faille yow."
>
> "Sir," seyde sir Ector, "I will aske no more of yow but that ye wille make my sone, your foster broder syre Kay, seneceall of alle your landes."
>
> "That shall be done," said Arthyr, "and more, by the feith of my body, that never man shalle have that office but he whyle he and I lyve." (Vinaver 1990: 15)

The episode provides a good example of a "distant" history striking a participant "out of the blue," but unless we force a prior knowledge of subsequent events into ironies – young Arthur will be old and sad one day; Kay will make more trouble than he is worth – then it gives a very positive view of human resilience through time and change. Arthur converts the sadness of sudden distancing, of "losing" his blood family, into affirmation of them as his foster family. Then with the dawning realization of his power as king, he makes his present will into a statement of future action, one which history will verify. He shows the magnanimity and openness to others' virtues that will make him a great leader later on. Arthur cannot command destiny – Malory never suggests anyone can, even Merlin, perhaps even God – but he can command the *feith of his body*. When everything at Camelot is falling apart in the last book, even opponents still affirm that *there was never yet man that ever coude preve kynge Arthure untrew of hys promyse* (1173). This is a kind of integrity that is never taken away from Arthur's story. Its sharing with readers over the course of the narrative binds them closely to the Arthurian world and implies their surviving recognition of its values. Even in the "dolorous" last battle, we see Arthur's intent fulfilled and verified. Mordred is Arthur's punishment for sin, as Merlin said long before (44), but Arthur's killing of Mordred is also presented as a willed human deed, a right action, and part of the *worshipfull dethe* Merlin has prophesied for the king. In the horror of familial killing, like an extreme intensification of the civil carnage that has engulfed the scene and is taking the Arthurian world from us, an active sense of "making" history, of a completed virtuous projection from past to future, is also validated, though under such great stress that it may be very hard to accept as such.

Malory's narrative treatment of history limits the power that the past should exercise over the present. Merlin not only insists that one cannot guard against future misadventure (125), he also warns against caring too much about things that cannot be helped: *thou art a foole to take thought for hit that woll nat amende thee* (43). Merlin's proverbial wisdom does not imply a narrow limit on sensibility, or a reductive fatalism, but an extension toward the past of the same willingness to accept unforeseen and unwelcome outcomes that leads to adventure in the first place. In the case to which Merlin refers, young Arthur is downcast because the pursuit of an adventure has been denied him by birth – to chase the Questing Beast is for King Pellinore's family only – but what can he possibly do about that? As Merlin goes on to reveal, Arthur's birth (on the father's side) has also made him king, and (on the mother's side) has meant that his sexual relationship with Morgawse was incest. Not all the potential outcomes from one set of circumstances are likely to be desirable.

Just as tenses in Malory are varied, the reader's sense of the anterior "distance" of the historical narrative is a relative, variable factor. The sense of historical fragmentation and separation of readers from the past arises partly because of a normative tendency to present past history as if it were familiar and close. The norm of closeness is implied when the narrative feels compelled to step in occasionally to explain differences, avoid misunderstandings, and make sly critiques of "nowadays": that *the custom was at that time that all manner of shamefull deth was called treson* (1050); that *in tho dayes . . . for favoure, love, nother affinité there sholde be none other but ryghtuous jugemente"* (1055); that hermits *in thos dayes* were former *men of worship and prouesse*, who *hylde grete householdis* (1076); that Launcelot and Guenevere may not have been in bed together because *love that tyme was nat as love ys nowadayes* (1165). These moments of unlikeness are evident because in its priorities and preoccupations the present is represented as fundamentally like the past. Because Malory believes in the matter of the Arthurian story as accessible and explicable in the terms of the present, the characteristic fear of the nostalgic subject that the desired past is really "absent" and "inauthentic," quite remote from "lived experience" (Stewart 1993: 23) is muted. The *Morte* is retrospective, and finally centered on loss, but not truly "nostalgic" in temperament, because its method disallows the full sense of present difference and deficiency on which nostalgia depends. The great past never seems archaic and largely forgotten to Malory, as it does to a writer like Tolkien. For every critique of "nowadays," Malory is just as likely to interpolate a "wit you well" or a proverb, endorsing the contemporary "gentle" audience's ability to appreciate what is happening from their common stock of wisdom and experience.

Death is the source of Malory's narrative endings, as Mann says, and many of the Winchester manuscript's marginalia point to deaths, but death is also necessarily an imperfect marker of historical distance, because, read thematically, it is a force for continuity, common to all histories. While in linear narrative death divides characters from each other, and from the readers' present, as a theme it also unites readers in sympathy with characters, and bridges past, present, and potential lives. It takes the great figures away, leaving a diminished "us" of "nowadays" behind, but it leaves the significance of their human natures exemplary and memorable, and so ideologically persistent. Ector's famous lament at Lancelot's death, cited by Mann as a locus of division, also provides a precise check-list of the knightly qualities appreciated by Malory's fifteenth-century contemporaries: *the curtest knyght that ever bare shelde; the truest frende to thy lovar that ever bestrade hors; the kyndest man that ever strake wyth swerde; the mekest man and the jentyllest that ever ete in halle emonge ladyes* (1259). Readers, as they lament Lancelot with Ector, are invited to identify closely with the "gentle" values of an author who "assumed that the social distinctions of his time would last until the Day of Judgement" (Field 1993: 37).

While the *Morte*'s third-person narrative is past tense and retrospective (not in itself a very distinctive feature), its events continue to move forward, especially in those parts usually judged the saddest. The final scenes of Arthur's life go forward at great pace. Left with limited time for reflection, Arthur models for the reader, as for Bedivere, a fine balance between emotion and pragmatism, and shows the need to get on with things:

> "Now leve thys mournynge and wepyng, jantyll knyght," seyde the kyng, "for all thys woll nat avayle me. For wyte thou well, and I myght lyve myselff, the dethe of sir Lucan wolde greve me evermore. But my tyme hyeth faste," seyde the kynge. "Therefore," seyde kynge Arthur unto sir Bedwere, "take thou here Excaliber." (Vinaver 1990: 1238)
>
> . . .
>
> "A, my lorde Arthur, what shall becom of me, now ye go frome me and leve me here alone amonge myne enemyes?"
>
> "Comfort thyselff," seyde the kynge, "and do as well as thou mayste, for in me ys no truste for to truste in. For I wyl into the vale of Avylyon to hele me of my grevous wound." (Vinaver 1990: 1240)

The Winchester manuscript has *I muste into the vale*. . . . Caxton, followed by recent editors, has *I wyl*. . . . Something untranslatable between the two seems right: Arthur is going because he has to, and it is time, but nevertheless he is purposefully going, as the best thing he can do in the circumstances. He gives the moment a drive to action, demanding a continuing attachment to the temporal rather than the frustrated regression of nostalgia.

Nostalgia and Trauma

Le Morte Darthur has been called nostalgic for many reasons: because the author was romantically cast as a man born too late, self-consciously looking back from the "autumn" of the romance tradition; because it is assumed on a reflectionist model of literature that the text must be recoiling from the horror of civil war in his own times;

or because, on a more sophisticated model of literary ideology, the text is taken to be repressing the trauma of its own times by turning to the past. It is true that Malory's knightly attitudes sometimes take his story in opposing directions: for instance, he registers great sadness as *the noble knyghtes . . .* [are] *layde to the colde erthe* (1236), but also wants to say that Arthur has *won the fylde* (1236–7), when only four men are left alive! Nevertheless, Malory was not under compulsion either to tell or hide the true nature of war or of the English fifteenth century, as modern readers understand them. His narrative is ideologically produced and generically selective, limited by its exclusion of other contemporary factors – such as towns, trade, and money – so that many areas of historical discontinuity between his own world and the world of the romances he tells are hidden or downplayed. It would be naïve to assume that under a nostalgic textual surface the trauma of England's recent loss of France and current civil war lie repressed in the *Morte* as unconscious "truths," just waiting to be outed in the end. Malory's sadness about the end of Arthur and the Round Table includes some specific aspersions on English fickleness, but is not a wholesale indictment of his age, or of the project of chivalry, however much we may think it should be. He is sad because he thinks chivalry is still such a good thing, and Arthur's reign gave the best example ever.

In medieval terms, the *Morte*'s drive to action distinguishes its sadness from ungenerative and static "melancholy." Nor is its condition "melancholia" in Freudian terms, because within it loss of the loved Arthurian world does not result in a narcissistic self-critique and loss of the ability to love (Freud 1953). Rather, memory of the lost love object – Camelot – involves some function of self-critique, but also excites continued attachment to the practices and values of an implied audience still in continuity with the past: *all jantyllmen that beryth olde armys ought of ryght to honoure sir Tristrams* (375); *there was never worshypfull man nor worshypfull woman but they loved one bettir than anothir; and worshyp in armys may never be foyled* (1119). Certainly, the past may reproach the modern world, especially in the area of love, a theme as old as Chrétien de Troyes, but memory of the past is still a source of enthusiasm for love and arms and a revelation of their continuing importance. Memory is itself a narrative theme linking past and present. Remembering and "calling to mind" are key activities that worshipful personages within the fiction share with the implied audience. The famous passage in which Malory castigates *love nowadayes* as hasty heat which is soon cold concludes with an appeal to contemporary lovers to *calle unto your remembraunce the monethe of May, lyke as ded quene Gwenyver* (1120).

There is *wepyng and dolour out of mesure* (1259) in Malory's last book, but he repeatedly follows his major characters' deaths with the comforting rituals of late medieval mourning. Arthur's stark, lonely, and uncertain departure is most unlike the end of a mighty contemporary monarch, yet Bedivere, after one moment of terror at his abandonment, offers many years' obedience in his little chantry to Arthur's last command: "pray for my soul." The long monastic careers of Lancelot and Guenevere convert their earthly worship into heavenly reward, displaying their surpassing quality still. Malory insists that Bors and his French kin were not stranded in England after

Lancelot's death – *that was but favour of makers* ("that was only made up by writers") – but went to France to stabilize the lands Lancelot had granted them, and then to the Holy Land where they *dyd many batayles* (1260). These figures turn from "the world," but in ways that remain purposive and "worshipful," and which fit well with fifteenth-century notions of a good end. There were notable fifteenth-century crusaders, among them the tournament star and humanist Anthony Woodville, Earl Rivers. In short, loss and death are the end of Arthur's story, but we do not need to read them as if the text or the fifteenth century found no ways of coping. The final book is full of references to English funeral customs – lyke-wake, vespers, Mass, matins, dole, and month mind – as if the deaths of close contemporaries were being mourned for and commemorated in familiar ways (Cherewatuk, in press).

To conclude, *Le Morte Darthur* is a fictional "history" of Arthur and his knights, whom it treats as real. It is not a history of its own times, except in a few incidental references, but it is a very revealing document about contemporary attitudes, behaviors, and mentality, especially among the landed, "gentle" classes. Like most medieval histories, it ends sadly, but it does not represent the present as a helpless condition of absence, alienation, and utter division from the past. The narrative and its exemplary agents model for readers another reaction to loss and death – one of grief, memory, and continuity.

PRIMARY SOURCES

Kingsford, C. L. (ed.) (1919). *The Stonor letters and papers, 1290–1483*, 2 vols. London: Royal Historical Society.

Kirby, J. (ed.) (1996). *The Plumpton letters and papers*. London: Cambridge University Press, for the Royal Historical Society.

Ricks, C. (ed.) (1969). *The poems of Tennyson*. London: Longman.

Spisak, J. W. (ed.) (1983). *Caxton's Malory*. Berkeley, CA: University of California Press.

Vinaver, E. (ed.) (1990). *Malory. Works*, 3rd rev. edn (ed. P. J. C. Field), 3 vols. Oxford: Clarendon Press.

REFERENCES AND FURTHER READING

Batt, C. (2002). *Malory's* Morte Darthur*: Remaking Arthurian tradition*. New York: Palgrave Macmillan.

Benson, L. D. (1976). *Malory's Morte Darthur*. Cambridge, MA: Harvard University Press.

Chambers, E. K. (1945). *English literature at the close of the Middle Ages*, Oxford History of English Literature, vol. 2, part 2. Oxford: Clarendon Press.

Cherewatuk, K. (2000). Sir Thomas Malory's "Grete Booke." In D. T. Hanks, Jr & J. G. Brogdon (eds), *The social and literary contexts of Malory's Morte Darthur*. Cambridge: Brewer, pp. 42–67.

Cherewatuk, K. (2006). *Marriage, adultery and inheritance in Malory's* Morte Darthur. Cambridge: Brewer.

Cherewatuk, K. (in press). Christian rituals in Malory: The evidence of funerals. In J. Jesmok

& D. T. Hanks, Jr (eds), *Malory and Christianity*. Kalamazoo, MI: Medieval Institute.

Crofts, T. H. (2006). *Malory's contemporary audience*. Cambridge: Brewer.

Edwards, A. S. G. & Archibald. E. (eds) (1996). *A companion to Malory*. Cambridge: Brewer.

Field, P. J. C. (1971). *Romance and chronicle: A study of Malory's prose style*. London: Barrie & Jenkins.

Field, P. J. C. (1993). *The life and times of Sir Thomas Malory*. Cambridge: Brewer.

Field, P. J. C. (1996). The Malory life-records. In A. S. G. Edwards & E. Archibald (eds), *A companion to Malory*. Cambridge: Brewer, pp. 115–30.

Field, P. J. C. (2000). Malory and the Battle of Towton. In D. T. Hanks, Jr & J. G. Brogdon (eds), *The social and literary contexts of Malory's Morte Darthur*. Cambridge: Brewer, pp. 68–74.

Freud, S. (1953). Mourning and melancholia. In J. Strachey (ed.), *The standard edition of the complete psychological works of Sigmund Freud*, vol. 14. London: Hogarth Press, pp. 243–58.

Higham, N. J. (2002). *King Arthur: Myth-making and history*. New York: Routledge.

Horrox, R. (ed.) (1994). *Fifteenth-century attitudes: Perceptions of society in late medieval England*. Cambridge: Cambridge University Press.

Mann, J. (1991). *The narrative of distance, the distance of narrative in Malory's Morte Darthur*. London: Birkbeck College.

Radulescu, R. L. (2003). *The gentry context for Malory's* Morte Darthur. Cambridge: Brewer.

Richmond, C. (1994). Thomas Malory and the Pastons. In C. M. Meale (ed.), *Readings in medieval English romance*. Cambridge: Brewer, pp. 195–208.

Riddy, F. (1987). *Sir Thomas Malory*. Leiden: Brill.

Stewart, S. (1993). *On longing*. Durham, NC: Duke University Press.

Sutton, A. F. (2000). Malory in Newgate: A new document. *The Library*, 7th ser., 1(13), 243–62.

Wallace, D. (1997). *Chaucerian polity: Absolutist lineages and associational forms in England and Italy*. Stanford, CA: Stanford University Press.

Wallace, D. (2006). Imperium, commerce, and national crusade: The romance of Malory's *Morte. New Medieval Literatures*, 8, 45–65.

21
Malory's Lancelot and Guenevere

Elizabeth Archibald

Modern readers and viewers expect to find the story of the love of Lancelot and Guenevere as a prominent and romantic part of an Arthurian novel or film, but that expectation was by no means universal in the Middle Ages; indeed, Thomas Malory was unusual in the English tradition in making the love affair a central theme of his *Morte Darthur*. Much critical attention has been given to Malory's presentation of the affair, his characterization of the lovers, and his attitude to love. One argument is that he was forced to accept a traditional element of the story, but did so reluctantly, and spent as little time on it as possible, feeling that Lancelot's greatness was compromised by his devotion to the queen. Another, focusing on the importance of honor in the Arthurian world, is that Lancelot's greatness is in fact enhanced by the way in which he deals with the impossible conflict of loyalties with which he is faced as a result of his adultery. With regard to Guenevere, recent criticism has paid increasing attention to her as a character and not merely one point of the love triangle. In this chapter I will consider some key issues and passages relating to the love affair, focusing on the last two books of the *Morte Darthur*.

Lancelot and Guenevere in the English Arthurian Tradition

The story of Arthur's betrayal by his queen goes back at least to Geoffrey of Monmouth's seminal account of Arthur's reign in his pseudo-history *Historia Regum Britanniae* ("History of the Kings of Britain"), which was completed about 1138 and was an instant success. But in Geoffrey and the accounts derived from him, Guenevere's lover is always the usurper of Arthur's kingdom, Mordred. In the extant literature, Lancelot's first appearance is in Chrétien de Troyes' *Chevalier de la Charrette* (c. 1180). At the beginning of the poem he sets out to rescue the queen, who has been abducted; he is already devoted to her (though there is no account of how or when he fell in love), and when he reaches the castle of her abductor in the land of Gorre, he breaks the bars of her window and climbs in to spend a night with her (Malory retells these events in the "Knight of the Cart" episode in "The Book of Sir Launcelot and Queen

Guenevere," Vinaver 1990: 1119–40). It may well have been Chrétien who invented the love affair between Lancelot and Guenevere; Lancelot also appears in an almost contemporary German romance, *Lanzelet*, but though he has many lovers in this account, the queen is not among them.

Whoever first devised the story of Lancelot's and Guenevere's affair, it was widely popularized by Chrétien's poem and much expanded in France in the early thirteenth century, in the non-cyclic Prose *Lancelot* and at greater length in the group of French Arthurian prose romances known as the Vulgate Cycle or *Lancelot–Grail* Cycle. The Vulgate Cycle consists of five main sections, with Lancelot dominating the last three (see chapter 14; see also Lacy 1992–6: iii–v; Dover 2003; Burgess & Pratt 2006: 274–324). The Vulgate author(s) expanded Chrétien's account to include the first meeting of the lovers and also their first kiss, which famously inspired Dante's Paolo and Francesca to consummate their illicit and fatal passion. Love spurs Lancelot to heights of chivalric achievement and to widespread acknowledgment as the best knight in the world, but it also causes him to fail in the Grail quest, outdone by his own son, the virgin Galahad.

In the final section of the Vulgate Cycle, the *Mort Artu*, Lancelot spurns the Maid of Escalot (Malory's Astolat, Tennyson's Shalott), who dies for love of him; and the malicious outing of the lovers by Mordred and Agravaine leads first to their elopement and then to the final disastrous civil war. The later sections of the Vulgate Cycle must have been among the "Frenche books" to which Malory frequently refers as his authorities, for he draws heavily on this account. Another of his French books was the Post-Vulgate Cycle (also known as the *Roman du Graal*), a thirteenth-century French compilation based on the Vulgate Cycle but differing considerably from it in both tone and content (Lacy 1992–6: iv–v; see also Pratt & Burgess 2006: 342–52). Malory followed the first part of this cycle, the *Suite du Merlin*, closely in his opening tale, and probably also knew the Post-Vulgate versions of the Grail quest and the *Mort Artu*. The Post-Vulgate Cycle offers a less positive account of Lancelot than the Vulgate Cycle: Lancelot is not so central to the plot, and his love for the queen is treated less sympathetically (during the Grail quest he has a vision of her burning naked in hell and warning him to save his soul!).

The love affair was not nearly as popular in England as in France (for discussion of all English Arthurian texts and full bibliography, see Barron 1999). Indeed, Helen Cooper argues that it may have been almost unknown in England before Malory's time, and that those who did know it probably considered it and the story of Arthur's incestuous begetting of Mordred to be "slanderous French fictions – as indeed they were" (Cooper 2003: 153; see also Archibald 2004). French romances were certainly circulating in England in the thirteenth and fourteenth centuries, but, as Cooper shows, only the early parts of the expanded Arthurian history of the French Vulgate Cycle were adapted in Middle English versions – the history of the Grail and Arthur's accession to the throne (Cooper 2003: 151; she also notes a very brief account of Lancelot's abduction of the queen in one version of a mid-fourteenth century chronicle). In the late fourteenth-century poems *Sir Gawain and the Green Knight* and the

Alliterative *Morte Arthure*, Lancelot is mentioned briefly as one of Arthur's knights, but not as Guenevere's lover, and his role is very minor; in the Alliterative *Morte*, Guenevere actually becomes pregnant by Mordred (see Putter's comments on *Sir Launfal* in this volume, chapter 16). The fifteenth-century chronicler John Hardyng, probably another of Malory's sources, clearly knew some version of the Vulgate Cycle and does include Lancelot in the Arthurian section of his chronicle, but says nothing of the love affair; indeed in Hardyng's version Lancelot marries Elaine, the mother of Galahad. Chaucer was not an Arthurian enthusiast, it seems, for his references to the legend are all ironic; he mentions Lancelot in two of the *Canterbury Tales*, "The Squire's Tale" and "The Nun's Priest's Tale," noting in the latter that women readers are very enthusiastic about Lancelot (presumably in French narratives), a back-handed compliment. In the English Arthurian tradition, Gawain was the main hero, Arthur's right-hand man and the exemplar of chivalric valor; this is of course the point of *Sir Gawain and the Green Knight*, in which Gawain's reputation precedes him, and he has to struggle to live up to it. In Chrétien and other French writers, Lancelot and Gawain are often paired, as friends or as rivals, but this was not the case in England. In both romance and chronicle, Lancelot is a very minor character, if mentioned at all (for references see Barron 1999; Archibald 2004).

In view of this lack of English interest in Lancelot, and the "deep British disquiet with adultery" that critics detect in medieval narratives of love and adventure written in English (Cooper 2003: 155), it is striking that around 1400 an unknown poet produced a Middle English version of the Vulgate *Mort Artu*, known to modern scholars as the Stanzaic *Morte Arthur*. Malory drew heavily on this poem for his last two books, though it was probably not widely known in England. From its opening the poem assumes the audience's foreknowledge of the love of Lancelot and Guenevere, which is presented as a long-established affair; Lancelot is central to the plot, and the poem ends with his death, as in the *Morte Darthur*. So Malory was not unique among English writers in turning the spotlight on Lancelot, though it was an unusual choice, as was his interweaving of episodes and themes from multiple sources, French and English, romance and chronicle. Those of Malory's readers who knew French probably expected to find some account of Lancelot and his love affair in the *Morte Darthur*, but may have been surprised by how much he left out; on the other hand, the strong focus on Lancelot may have come as a shock to non-Francophones. Caxton claimed in the preface to his printed edition of Malory that he was responding to pressure from English gentlemen who wanted an account of the national hero in English; if this is true, and not just sales talk, his readers may not have bargained for a version in which Lancelot, the cuckolder of the king, plays such a central role, and which ends with his death and glorification, rather than Arthur's.

"The Olde Love"

As the inheritor of a long and varied tradition, Malory had to make a number of decisions about how to treat Lancelot and Guenevere, which sources to follow, how to order them, and what original material to add. The Vulgate Cycle covers the history of the Grail and then Arthur's whole life, from birth to death, but Arthur is overshadowed there by Lancelot, whose exploits dominate the last three sections. Arthur rarely goes on quests and adventures, and does little fighting until the final wars against Lancelot, the Romans, and Mordred. It is Lancelot who acts as culture hero, ending evil customs, rescuing maidens, and dominating martial encounters; and the Vulgate Lancelot is constantly inspired by his love for the queen and hers for him. Malory acknowledges this in the opening lines of the third section of the *Morte Darthur*, "The Noble Tale of Sir Launcelot du Lake," where the symbiotic relationship of love and prowess so characteristic of medieval romance is made very clear:

> *So* this sir Launcelot encresed so mervaylously in worship and honoure; *therefore* he is the fyrste knyght that the Freynsh booke makyth mencion of aftir kynge Arthure com frome Rome. *Wherefore* quene Gwenyvere had hym in grete favoure aboven all other knyghtis, *and so* he loved the quene agayne aboven all other ladyes dayes of his lyff, and for hir he dud many dedys of armys and saved her frome the fyre thorow his noble chevalry. (253.12–19, my italics)

Before this tale, Lancelot has figured only very briefly in the *Morte Darthur*, in Merlin's warning to Arthur that marriage to Guenevere will be problematic, and in the account of the Roman war. Now Lancelot suddenly takes center stage, fully formed. We hear nothing of his childhood (in the Vulgate he is raised by a fairy in an underwater palace, hence his sobriquet du Lac), or of his arrival at court, and most crucially nothing of his growing love for the queen, and her response.

Many critics have noted that where the French authors make it clear that Lancelot and the queen are in a sexual relationship, Malory shies away from explicit acknowledgment; indeed, one critic has gone so far as to argue that the lovers do not consummate their passion until a late stage in the story (Kennedy 1997, rebutted by Fries 1997; Sturges 1997). This seems implausible. When Lancelot is twice tricked by magic into sleeping with Elaine, who conceives Galahad, on each occasion he thinks he is being summoned to the queen's bedroom, and responds with alacrity (794.11–795.23 and 804.4–7, 23–35). In neither scene are we given the impression that a great passion is about to be consummated for the first time. Later, in the "Knight of the Cart" episode, it is explicitly stated that *sir Launcelot wente to bedde wyth the quene*, after Lancelot has broken the window bars to join Guenevere, who had been held hostage in Meleagaunt's castle. We are told that *he toke hys plesaunce and hys lykynge untyll hit was the dawnyng of the day; for wyte you well he slept nat, but wacched* (1131.30–2). This sounds coyly suggestive (and also one-sided: there is no reference to Guenevere's pleasure or lack of sleep). When the lovers are caught together in the final book, Malory refuses to comment on their activities:

> For, as the Freynshe booke seyth, the quene and sir Launcelot were togydirs. And whether they were abed other at other maner of disportis, me lyste nat thereof make no mencion, for love that tyme was nat as love ys nowadayes. (1165.10–13)

Both the Vulgate *Mort Artu* and the Stanzaic *Morte Arthur* include this scene, and make it clear that the lovers were in bed (Lacy 1992–6: iv.121; Stanzaic *Morte Arthur*, lines 1800–8). Malory's prevarication seems to be disingenuous, drawing attention to the issue unnecessarily, though Sturges argues that "his deliberate choice of ignorance" is a way of "asserting his own readerly power over his sources . . . and of empowering his own readers in turn" (Sturges 1997: 60).

The old-fashioned love that Malory mentions here is praised just before this episode in the much-discussed digression, apparently original, which he inserted between the episodes of the "Great Tournament" and the "Knight of the Cart" (1119.1–1120.13). This may have been intended to continue the theme of loyalty raised at the end of the "Great Tournament" when Gareth explains to Arthur why he has chosen to fight against his own kin (see Batt 2002: xiv), and/or to justify the adultery which is about to take place in the episode of the "Knight of the Cart." It is most unusual for Malory to make such digressions, to use similes and metaphors, and to discuss the nature of love. The parallels he draws with nature and the seasons indicate that he regards romantic love as natural and good:

> Therefore, lyke as May moneth flowryth and floryshyth in every mannes gardyne, so in lyke wyse lat every man of worshyp florysh hys herte in thys worlde: first unto God, and nexte unto the joy of them that he promysed hys feythe unto; for there was never worshypfull man nor worshypfull woman but they loved one bettir than anothir; and worshyp in armys may never be foyled. But firste reserve the honoure to God, and secundely thy quarell muste com of thy lady. And such love I calle vertuouse love. (1119.22–30)

As Catherine Batt has pointed out, this passage assumes a male audience and a male lover (Batt 2002: xiii–xvi); it does not comment on women's behavior. Malory goes on to praise long-term devotion in a passage that some critics have taken as a recommendation of platonic love. He complains that nowadays love is

> sone hote, sone colde. Thys ys no stabylyté. But the olde love was nat so. For men and women coude love togyddirs seven yerys, and no lycoures lustis was betwyxte them, and than was love trouthe and faythefulnes. And so in lyke wyse was used such love in kynge Arthurs dayes. (1120.2–6)

The end of this passage is very surprising: Malory praises Guenevere, *for whom I make here a lytyll mencion, that whyle she lyved she was a trew lover, and therefor she had a good ende* (1120.11–13).

"A Trew Lover"

Recent criticism has paid increasing attention to Guenevere as a complex and sympathetic character, who does more than merely fulfill a necessary function as one point of the love triangle (see for instance Fenster 1996; Wheeler & Tolhurst 2001; Cherewatuk 2006). Meale sees her as an example of an interest in female subjectivity new in fifteenth-century writing (Meale 2006); for Tolhurst, the queen is more complex and human in Malory's work than in any other version, medieval or modern (Tolhurst 1998: 308).

Malory's description of Guenevere as *a trew lover* comes as a surprise because she is not seen or heard very often in Malory, and when she appears, she is frequently quarreling with Lancelot and making him suffer, or else repenting her earlier harsh treatment of him. Her anger is not unreasonable when she hears that Elaine of Corbenic has borne him a son (Galahad): *she gaff many rebukes to sir Launcelot and called hym false knyght*, though she excuses him when she hears that he was deceived into this infidelity by magic, which made Elaine look like the queen (802.18–21). But when Elaine comes to court and Lancelot is tricked into sleeping with her again, in the room next to the queen's, Guenevere is so furious that she sends Lancelot away from the court; he goes mad for several years, but is healed by the Grail. When he eventually returns to court, we hear Arthur welcome him with delight, but of Guenevere we are told merely that she *wepte as she shulde have dyed*, and then *made hym grete chere* (832.28–9). We are not allowed to hear what she says, either publicly or privately. In the last two books, however, when we are finally able to eavesdrop on the lovers as their affair comes nearer and nearer to being discovered, she is repeatedly unjust to Lancelot, and he lets her know it.

On his return from the Grail quest, we are told that Lancelot is not sufficiently chastened by his experiences to give up his lover, but deliberately champions other damsels in distress as a smokescreen for his affair (1045.18–29). This enrages the queen, who sends him away. Almost immediately she is falsely accused of poisoning a knight at a dinner party (in "The Poisoned Apple"). In Lancelot's absence, no one will defend her: the other knights tell Bors that they consider her *a destroyer of good knyghtes* (1054.4), a very serious charge in the world of chivalry. Eventually, of course, Lancelot arrives in the nick of time to save her, and the Lady of the Lake reveals the true culprit. Again we do not hear Guenevere's apology to her knight, but she does acknowledge her own ingratitude: *And evermore the quene behylde sir Launcelot, and wepte so tendirly that she sanke allmoste to the grownde for sorow that he had done to her so grete kyndenes where she shewed hym grete unkyndenesse* (1058.36–1059.2).

This is a humiliating episode for Guenevere; it is the first time that she faces the prospect of being burned at the stake, on this occasion for a crime of which she is entirely innocent. In Malory's major sources, the Vulgate *Mort Artu* and the Stanzaic *Morte Arthur*, Lancelot is not banished because of the queen's jealousy, and so there is no need for her contrition when he saves her. Malory has added this twist, and it is troubling, for it suggests that Guenevere capriciously causes serious problems for her lover, and that their affair brings him more pain than pleasure. Lancelot explicitly says this at the end of the following episode, the sad story of the Fair Maid of Astolat. Once again, Lancelot is away from the court after a quarrel with Guenevere. When Lancelot makes it clear to Elaine of Astolat that he can never love her, the young woman turns her face to the wall and dies, leaving orders that her body is to be transported to Camelot on a boat. In the hand of the corpse is a letter which is read to the court: it explains that she has died for love of Lancelot, but explicitly exonerates him (whereas in the sources she blames him): *And a clene mayden I dyed, I take God to wytnesse. And pray for my soule, sir Launcelot, as thou art pereles* (1096.33–5).

In the sources, Lancelot is not present when Elaine's waterborne corpse appears. But Lancelot is present in Malory's version, and Guenevere takes the opportunity to criticize him publicly: *"Sir," seyde the quene, "ye myght have shewed hir som bownté and jantilnes whych myght have preserved hir lyff"* (1097.14–15). Lancelot is stung by this unfair attack, since he had gone out of his way to be as kind as possible to Elaine, short of returning her love: *"I love nat to be constrayned to love, for love muste only aryse out of the harte selff, and nat by none constraynte,"* he replies, and Arthur chimes in to agree (a comment of unconscious irony). Later Guenevere apologizes to Lancelot in private *for why that she had ben wrothe with hym causeles*, and he makes another bitter reply:

> "Thys ys nat the firste tyme," seyde sir Launcelot, "that ye have ben displese with me causeles. But, madame, ever I muste suffer you, but what sorow that I endure, ye take no forse." (1098.5–8)

We do not hear her apology directly, and he has the last word here. The repetition of *causeles* and the emphasis on her cruelty create a very negative impression of their relationship.

These scenes of quarrels and apologies are surprising: in Malory's sources, they tend to be described indirectly, and the earlier Lancelots do not talk back so wearily about their suffering. This is not what we expect of one of the two most famous pairs of lovers in the world; Tristram and Isolde, the other pair, are not presented as constantly bickering and unhappy, but spend much of their time trying to arrange trysts. Lancelot's clan clearly feel that the queen treats him very badly; their criticism of her as "a destroyer of good knights" presumably applies to his unjust banishment as well as to the poisoning of Sir Patryse. Lancelot's own words reinforce the impression that he suffers from ongoing domestic abuse, in modern terms. Derek Brewer has described Malory's Guenevere as "passionate, loving, selfish, cool and entirely convincing – here, as elsewhere, the most fascinating, exasperating, and human of all medieval heroines" (Brewer 1968: 19). Cherewatuk argues that Guenevere's "shrewishness" represents "a burden of culpability for her relationship with Lancelot" (Cherewatuk 2006: 53). But is Lancelot not equally responsible for the affair? He is only sharp with her when she provokes him beyond bearing. However, Walters sees Malory's depiction of Guenevere as mostly positive: "For the most part, her relationship with Launcelot is stable, with sexual attraction taking a second place to devoted affection" (Walters 1996: xxx). This characterization would be more convincing if we saw more of the lovers together; in fact we hardly ever see them when they are not quarreling or in crisis.

There are a few scenes in which we see them being unconditionally loving, rather than jealous or accusing. When Lancelot arrives to rescue Guenevere in "The Knight of the Cart," he comes to her window at night; they talk, regretting their separation, *and than sir Launcelot wysshed that he myght have comyn in to her* (1131.12–13). Their speech is direct and very clear, and there are no misunderstandings:

"Wyte you well," seyde the quene, "I wolde as fayne as ye that ye myght com in to me."

"Wolde ye so, madame," seyde sir Launcelot, "wyth youre harte that I were wyth you?"

"Ye, truly", seyde the quene.

"Than shall I prove my myght," seyde sir Launcelot, "for youre love." (1131.14–20)

He breaks the bars at the window, and gets no sleep that night. The Vulgate version of this episode (Malory would not have known Chrétien's) occurs much earlier in the cycle of Lancelot's adventures, and is certainly not the first time that the lovers have slept together. The point in Malory's "Knight of the Cart" episode, it seems to me, is Lancelot's utter devotion to the queen, and hers to him, the *stabylyté* of their love, which is about to be severely tested.

This happens in the only other passage in Malory where the lovers are alone and probably in bed together, the fatal evening when Lancelot is trapped in the queen's chamber by Mordred and Agravaine and their cronies. Determined to avoid shame by fighting his way out, even if the result is his death, Launcelot *toke the quene in hys armys and kyssed her*; he makes a long speech expressing his devotion to her as *my speciall good lady*, and his conviction that his clan will rescue her if he is killed. Her response is that she certainly will not outlive him for long: *But and ye be slayne I woll take my dethe as mekely as ever ded marter take hys dethe for Jesu Crystes sake* (1166.11 and 26–8). He replies that he is a thousand times *more hevyar for you than for myselff*! Here, surely, we see what Malory thinks of admiringly as *the olde love* of Arthur's days, when *was love trouthe and faythfulnes* (1120.2–3, 5).

Indeed, the faith of true lovers is raised here to the level of the faith of Christian martyrs, a singular compliment, and again Malory goes well beyond his sources. In the Vulgate *Mort Artu*, the queen laments that Lancelot's death "would be a much greater tragedy than mine," and then expresses her certainty that he will rescue her if he survives (Lacy 1992–6: iv.121). There is no kiss, and Lancelot makes no reply or declaration to her, but speaks to his enemies outside the door. In the Stanzaic *Morte Arthur*, the queen regrets that *The love that hathe us bene betwene, / To suche endyng that it sholde go*, and blames the enmity of Agravaine (lines 1818–21); Lancelot does reply, but only to ask if she has any armor to hand (lines 1824–7). In Malory's account the request for armor comes before the embrace and the speeches which almost constitute an exchange of vows. After the attackers have fled, Lancelot kisses the queen again and they exchange rings before parting (1169.1–3); there is no parallel for this in the sources. The two kisses which frame Lancelot's fight here are the significant kisses in Malory's version, set between the absent kiss of their early love, and the denied kiss of their final parting. The exchange of rings seems to represent the wedding that cannot happen. It is striking that Malory chooses this moment of crisis to insist on the deep bond between the lovers, and to allow Guenevere to express her total commitment to Lancelot. It is the first and last time that we hear such declarations of love between them. This is partly because the lovers are rarely seen and heard in private together (on the interplay of public and private in Malory, see McCarthy 1988).

Lancelot's main role is to epitomize the honorable knight in a society in which *worship* (that is, reputation, honor) is of paramount importance (Brewer 1968: 23–35). Much of the *Morte Darthur* is concerned with his adventures, which prove his martial prowess; but the later books focus on the moral dilemmas and conflicts of loyalty which arise from his love for the queen, making the maintenance of his *worship* extremely complicated.

Although romantic love plays an important part in the Arthurian legend and in Malory's version of it, male fellowship is just as important, perhaps more so: "fellowship" is a key word in Malory (Archibald 1992). When Bors alone of the three successful Grail knights returns to court to tell his tale, the French *Queste* ends with the recording of his story in writing. It is characteristic of Malory that he adds a conversation in direct speech between Bors and Lancelot which emphasizes their mutual devotion:

> "And wete ye well, gentyl cousyn sir Bors, ye and I shall never departe in sundir whylis our lyvys may laste."
>
> "Sir," seyde he, "as ye woll, so woll I." (1037.4–7)

This "till death us do part" declaration of fellowship is particularly striking here at the end of the Grail quest, which has emphasized spiritual values rather than earthly ones. After long and dangerous adventures Lancelot has just returned to the court and to the queen, who was so anxious on his departure; yet his final words are not to her but to his cousin and comrade, Bors. In "The Book of Sir Tristram," Segwarydes tells Tristram, who has been dallying with his wife, that *I woll never hate a noble knyght for a lyght lady* (442.7–8). Arthur does not hate Lancelot either; we are told that the king *had a demyng* of the affair, but did not want it discussed because of his gratitude and love for Lancelot (1163.20–5). When he is brought the news that Lancelot has inadvertently killed Gareth and Gaheris during his rescue of the queen from the stake, he laments the end of his great fellowship in a passage original to Malory and much quoted for its apparent misogyny: *And much more am I soryar for my good knyghtes losse than for the lossse of my fayre quene; for quenys I myght have inow, but such a felyshyp of good knyghtes shall never be togydirs in no company* (1184.1–4). This may remind us that though Arthur married Guenevere for love, against Merlin's advice, the celebration of their wedding was dominated by her dowry, the Round Table with a hundred knights (98.14–31; see Cherewatuk 2006: 32–6).

Though the abduction of Guenevere is a central part of the Arthurian tradition, she is only abducted once in Malory's text, by Meleagaunt in "The Knight of the Cart" episode. Lancelot, however, is abducted several times and frequently propositioned; his reputation as the queen's lover seems to precede him everywhere, and spurs a number of women to try to win him away from his devotion to Guenevere. In "The Tale of Sir Lancelot," where his love for her is rapidly summarized in the opening passage (discussed above), he is captured by four queens who order him to choose one of their number as his paramour (256–9), in "a parodic invocation of the judgment of Paris" (Cherewatuk 2006: xviii). Having escaped from them, he encounters a damsel who criticizes his status as *a knyght wyveles*; she says that Guenevere is rumored to have enchanted Lancelot so that he cannot love anyone else, *wherfore there be many in this londe, of hyghe astate and lowe, that make grete sorow* (270.18–27). Lancelot manages to evade a direct answer about the queen, but declares that being married restricts a knight's proper activities: *But for to be a weddyd man, I thynke nat, for than I muste couche with hir and leve armys and tournamentis, batellys and adventures* (270.29–32). The structure of the adventure story requires an unmarried hero who can be the object of female desire, even if he has a secret lover.

Lancelot's appeal is unisex, and often affects his admirers at first sight. Elaine of Astolat fails to win his love, inevitably, but her luckier brother Sir Lavayne accompanies him to tournaments, equally smitten. He understands his dying sister's predicament, as he tells his father: *she doth as I do, for sythen I saw first my lorde sir Launcelot I cowde never departe frome hym, nother nought I woll, and I may folow hym* (1091.12–15). When Sir Urry is brought to Camelot in search of healing for his wound, Lancelot is not at court. As soon as he arrives, both Urry and his sister respond to his presence:

"Brothir, here ys com a knyght that my harte gyveth gretly unto."

"Fayre syster," seyde sir Urré, "so doth my harte lyghte gretly ayenste hym, and my harte gyvith me more unto hym than to all thes that hath serched hym." (1151.12–16)

It is hardly surprising that Sir Urry's sister marries Elaine's brother Lavayne, since both are paid-up members of the Lancelot fan club, which is extensive. We are told that Lancelot is sought out by *ladyes and damesels which dayly resorted unto hym, that besoughte hym to be their champion* (1045.23–4). No wonder Guenevere becomes so jealous that she banishes him.

"A Good Ende"

The *good ende* that Malory claims for Guenevere is presumably her retreat to a nunnery, which is part of the tradition from Geoffrey of Monmouth onwards. In some versions she flees in fear of whoever wins in the final battle, Arthur or Mordred; but in Malory's account she already knows that Arthur is dead (1243.1–10). The Vulgate *Mort Artu* describes the deaths of both Lancelot and Guenevere, but they do not meet again after he has been exiled, except in one variant manuscript (the passage is printed in Lacy 1992–6: iv.158, n. 2; see also Frappier 1936; Kennedy 2001). In the English Stanzaic *Morte Arthur*, the tone of the final interview between Lancelot and Guenevere is much fiercer and more emotionally powerful than that of the French *Mort Artu*: Guenevere denounces her own sin and guilt and Lancelot's too, and sends him away for ever (Stanzaic *Morte Arthur*, lines 3622–3737).

Malory followed this English version closely, though he also made some telling changes (1251–3). In both versions, the queen confesses that she and Lancelot have caused the war and *the deth of the moste nobelest knyghtes of the worlde; for thorow oure love that we have loved togydir ys my moste noble lorde slayn* (1252.8–11). She urges Lancelot to worry about his soul, as she is doing, and orders him *that thou forsake my company* (1252.21). With a flash of her old cruelty, she tells him to get married and be happy with his new wife. Lancelot replies that since she has entered religious life, he will too – he does not express the same guilt and contrition about the effects of their love. When the queen questions his commitment to this new life, he defends himself; in Malory's version he points out bitterly that he would have achieved the Grail quest had it not been for his adulterous love. He asks for a last kiss, which Guenevere refuses. In the Stanzaic *Morte Arthure*, she tempers her refusal with encouragement for them both to focus on pleasing God, but in Malory she is brief and harsh: *"Nay," seyde the quene, "that shal I never do, but absteyne you from suche werkes"* (1253.27–8). To the last she doubts him (whether from jealousy or from suspicion of his moral weakness); there is no comfort for him here. But rejecting Lancelot's love for ever is clearly painful for her: the nuns report that on hearing that he is hurrying to her deathbed, she prays that she may never see him again (1255.29–37). Comparing Malory's account of the final interview with that in the Stanzaic *Morte Arthur*, Meale argues that Malory's scenario is unique in "present[ing] an opportunity to make further forays into [Guenevere's] interiority":

> [I]t is only in [Malory's] version of the romance that Gwenyver's recognition of moral responsibility and culpability (as she sees it) is expanded to encompass the subjectively realized agonies of self-denial and renunciation of desire. (Meale 2006: 172)

The lovers never meet again. When Malory's Guenevere dies, she leaves orders that Lancelot is to bury her in Arthur's tomb; the marital bond is reasserted, and Lancelot is excluded by the legal union, by the physical monument of the tomb. Now Lancelot too feels an overwhelming sense of guilt:

> "Also when I remembre me how by my defaute and myn orgule and my pryde that they were bothe layed ful lowe, that were pereles that ever was lyvyng of Cristen people, wyt you wel," seyde sir Launcelot, "this remembred, of their kyndenes and myn unkyndenes, sanke so to myn herte that I myght not susteyne myself." So the Frensshe book maketh mencyon. (1256.32–9)

In fact the Vulgate *Mort Artu* as we know it does not mention this scene; there Lancelot receives the news of Guenevere's death before his final battle with Mordred's sons, and nothing is said about her tomb. In the Stanzaic *Morte Arthur*, the queen dies just after Lancelot, and it is his fellow hermits who bury her with Arthur. In Malory's account, Lancelot's speech is the equivalent of Guenevere's confession to the abbess: he acknowledges responsibility, which he had failed to do in the final interview. Although he had hoped to marry the widowed queen, he speaks here of Arthur and Guenevere as a couple, accepting the status quo.

Lancelot passes his last years piously with the survivors of the Round Table fellowship (Riddy 1987; Archibald 1992). In all three versions (the French *Mort Artu*, the English Stanzaic *Morte Arthur*, and Malory's text), this is clearly intended to exonerate him of past sins, and his saintly death proves that his penitence has won him salvation (though he and Guenevere seem to exaggerate their own responsibility for the collapse of Camelot, ignoring Mordred's prophesied role and the malice of Agravaine). This creates a powerful contrast with the very bleak death of Arthur, which happens off-stage, without benefit of clergy, attended only by enchantresses; his last speech to Bedivere seems despairing, and no mention is made of contrition or penance, or of Guenevere (1240–1; Malory's tone is darker than that of his sources).

Recent critics have discussed the ways in which Malory reflects the gentry culture and piety of his own times, as well as the turmoil of the Wars of the Roses (see for instance Riddy 1987, 1996; Radulescu 2003; Cherewatuk 2006). It is not surprising that Arthurian writers include contemporary concerns and values in the retelling of the legend. What seems much more surprising is the way in which Malory focuses on Lancelot rather than Arthur, especially at the end. Kennedy argues that Malory was attracted to the Stanzaic *Morte Arthur* in part because the English poet reduced Arthur's responsibility for the tragedy and increased Lancelot's (Kennedy 1994: 102–4): how then to explain the ending that Malory gives to the *Morte Darthur*? According to Caxton's rubric, *The xxi book treateth of his* [Arthur's] *last departyng, and how syr Launcelot came to revenge his dethe, and conteyneth xiii chapytres* (Vinaver 1990: cxlvii). This seems very misleading. It is of course true that in the last section Arthur does die, and Lancelot does arrive, too late, to defeat the king's enemies: in the Vulgate *Mort Artu* he kills Mordred's sons and their forces, but in Malory, as in the Stanzaic *Morte Arthur*, he finds on arrival at Dover that everyone is already dead (1250.9–16). There is thus no possibility of revenge; instead of fighting, he sets off alone to look for Guenevere, and the unexpected consequence is that "she who had caused Lancelot's downfall now leads him to salvation" (Kennedy 2001: 42).

Just as Guenevere was eclipsed on marriage by her dowry of the Round Table with its knights, Arthur is eclipsed in death by the drama of the redemption of the lovers, which forms the conclusion of the *Morte Darthur*. He disappears mysteriously, and Malory refuses to tell us whether he is really dead or not (1242.3–20). There is no funeral or eulogy, nor any account of his achievements or praise for them in the brief inscription on his tomb (1240–2). In contrast, Guenevere and Lancelot both focus contritely on the salvation of their souls until their deaths, which are marked by visions and signs of holiness. The vision which alerts Lancelot to Guenevere's death and the nuns' subsequent report suggest that the queen does indeed make a good end, in Christian terms (1255); so does Lancelot, whose soul goes to heaven accompanied by flights of angels, witnessed by the Bishop of Canterbury in a dream (1257.35–1258.19).

Yet this holy death is not the last word on Lancelot, and his love affair is evoked once more before the end of the book (a point not pursued by Cherewatuk 1995, 2006: 127–8 in her discussion of the ending). The final passage of direct speech in the *Morte Darthur* is Ector's eulogy for Lancelot, his brother, which is not in the sources (though it is borrowed from Mordred's eulogy for Gawain in the Alliterative *Morte Arthure*). It celebrates Lancelot as an all-round hero, *hede of al Crysten knyghtes*, not as a penitent hermit: the focus here is entirely chivalric. Guenevere is not mentioned by name – that would have been improper. But there can be no doubt that she is the subtext when Lancelot is hailed as *the truest frende to thy lover, of a synful man, that ever loved woman* (1259.14–15). Benson argues that their romantic love is transformed at the end into something comparable to the devotion between chivalric comrades, and that "in their monasteries, Guenevere and Lancelot are closer than ever" (1996: 236–7). The last section of the *Morte Darthur* does not give us Lancelot's revenge for Arthur's death, except in the sense of revenge on himself; instead it enthrones him in Arthur's place as the paramount hero, and in praising Lancelot, Ector implicitly acknowledges and approves of his love for the woman who inspired his prowess.

Primary Sources

Hissiger, P. F. (ed.) (1975). *Stanzaic Morte Arthur*. The Hague: Mouton.

Lacy, N. (gen. ed.) (1992–6). *Lancelot–Grail. The Old French Arthurian Vulgate and Post-Vulgate in translation*, 5 vols. New York: Garland.

Vinaver, E. (ed.) (1990). *Malory. Works*, 3rd rev. edn (ed. P. J. C. Field), 3 vols. Oxford: Clarendon Press.

References and Further Reading

Archibald, E. (1992). Malory's ideal of fellowship. *Review of English Studies*, n.s., 43(171), 311–28.

Archibald, E. (2004). Lancelot as lover in the English tradition before Malory. In B. Wheeler (ed.), *Arthurian studies in honour of P. J. C. Field*. Cambridge: Brewer, pp. 199–216.

Archibald, E. & Edwards, A. S. G. (eds) (1996). *A companion to Malory*. Cambridge: Brewer.

Barron, W. R. J. (ed.) (1999). *The Arthur of the English: The Arthurian legend in medieval English life and literature*. Cardiff: University of Wales Press.

Batt, C. (2002). *Malory's Morte Darthur: Remaking Arthurian tradition*. Basingstoke: Palgrave Macmillan.

Benson, C. D. (1996). The ending of the *Morte Darthur*. In E. Archibald & A. S. G. Edwards (eds), *A companion to Malory*. Cambridge: Brewer, pp. 220–38.

Brewer, D. S. (ed.) (1968). *The Morte Darthur, parts seven and eight*, York Medieval Texts. London: Edward Arnold.

Brewer, D. S. (1983). The presentation of the character of Lancelot: Chrétien to Malory. In R. Barber (ed.), *Arthurian literature III*. Cambridge: Brewer, pp. 26–52. Repr. in Walters, L. (ed.) (1996). *Lancelot and Guenevere: A casebook*. New York: Garland, pp. 3–27.

Burgess, G. & Pratt, K. (eds) (2006). *The Arthur of the French*. Cardiff: University of Wales Press.

Cherewatuk, K. (1995). The saint's life of Sir Launcelot: Hagiography and the conclusion of Malory's *Morte Darthur*. *Arthuriana*, 5(1), 62–78.

Cherewatuk, K. (2006). *Marriage, adultery and inheritance in Malory's* Morte Darthur. Cambridge: Brewer.

Cooper, H. (2003). The Lancelot–Grail cycle in England: Malory and his predecessors. In C. Dover (ed.), *A companion to the Lancelot–Grail Cycle*. Cambridge: Brewer, pp. 147–62.

Dover, C. (ed.) (2003). *A companion to the Lancelot-Grail Cycle*. Cambridge: Brewer.

Fenster, T. S. (ed.) (1996). *Arthurian women: A casebook*. New York: Garland.

Frappier, J. (1936). *Étude sur La Morte le Roi Artu*. Paris: Droz.

Fries, M. (1997). Commentary: A response to the *Arthuriana* issue on adultery. *Arthuriana*, 7(4), 92–6.

Kennedy, B. (1997). Adultery in Malory's *Le Morte Darthur*. *Arthuriana*, 7(4), 63–91.

Kennedy, E. D. (1994). The Stanzaic *Morte Arthur*: The adaptation of a French romance for an English audience. In M. Shichtman, J. P. Carley, & M. L. Day (eds), *Culture and the king: The social implications of the Arthurian legend*. Albany, NY: State University of New York Press, pp. 91–112.

Kennedy, E. D. (2001). Malory's Guenevere: A woman who had grown a soul. In B. Wheeler & F. Tolhurst (eds), *On Arthurian women: Essays in memory of Maureen Fries*. Dallas, TX: Scriptorium Press, pp. 35–43.

McCarthy, T. (1988). *Le Morte Darthur* and romance. In D. S. Brewer (ed.), *Studies in medieval English romances: Some new approaches*. Cambridge: Brewer, pp. 148–75.

Meale, C. (2006). Entrapment or empowerment? Women and discourses of love and marriage in the fifteenth century. In H. Cooney (ed.), *Writings on love in the English Middle Ages*. Basingstoke: Palgrave Macmillan, pp. 163–78.

Radulescu, R. L. (2003). *The gentry context for Malory's* Morte Darthur. Cambridge: Brewer.

Riddy, F. (1987). *Sir Thomas Malory*. Leiden: Brill.

Riddy, F. (1996). Contextualizing the *Morte Darthur*: Empire and civil war. In E. Archibald & A. S. G. Edwards (eds), *A companion to Malory*. Cambridge: Brewer, pp. 55–73.

Sturges, R. S. (1997). Epistemology of the bedchamber: Textuality, knowledge, and the representation of adultery in Malory and the *Prose Lancelot*. *Arthuriana*, 7(4), 47–62.

Tolhurst, F. (1998). The once and future queen: The development of Guenevere from Geoffrey of Monmouth to Malory. *Bibliographical Bulletin of the International Arthurian Society*, 50, 272–308.

Walters, L. (ed.) (1996). *Lancelot and Guenevere: A casebook*. New York: Garland.

Wheeler, B. & Tolhurst, F. (eds) (2001). *On Arthurian women: Essays in memory of Maureen Fries*. Dallas, TX: Scriptorium Press.

22

Malory and the Quest for the Holy Grail

Raluca L. Radulescu

In 1964 Charles Moorman stated that Malory "wished to omit all unnecessary detail, be it religious or secular" from his source, the *Queste del Saint Graal* from the French Vulgate Cycle (Moorman 1964: 189). Over four decades later, critics continue to debate the complexities of the "Tale of the Sankgreal," Malory's closest translation and adaptation of an original French romance. The importance of this section of the *Morte Darthur* cannot be overestimated, as Malory recontextualizes the Grail quest to fit into his worldly Arthuriad; in the process, he alters not only some of the narrative links, but also the portrayal of the Grail knights, and Lancelot in particular.

These changes present a sharp contrast with the French author's view that chivalry is in decline as a result of the knights' neglect of Christian duty and their failure to pursue personal salvation. In choosing to identify the Grail with the holy vessel used by Christ at the Last Supper, and in which Joseph of Arimathea collected Christ's blood at the crucifixion, Malory also departs from earlier versions of the Grail story, like that of Chrétien de Troyes, and instead follows the *Queste* (Mann 1996; see chapter 14 in this volume). This development has puzzled critics for decades, since it goes against evidence that Malory favored worldly chivalry in earlier tales. The Grail itself is for Malory the symbol of God's grace, to be obtained in the Holy Communion, the loss of which brings people to despair. However, while the French Grail was a reminder for knights in real life of the salvation which lay at hand if they abandoned their corrupt ways and repented, in Malory the "Sankgreal" is one special experience among other earthly adventures embarked upon by the knights of the Round Table.

Twenty years ago an influential analysis of the "Sankgreal" placed Malory's writing firmly in the context of fifteenth-century gentry piety, the practice of the sacrament of penance, and Corpus Christi celebrations in late-medieval England (Riddy 1987). Other important work has shed light on Malory's political use of the Grail myth and its implications for the national and international scene, including his possible access to John Hardyng's chronicle (Kennedy 1981; Riddy 2000; Shichtman 1994; Hodges

2005). More recently, Jill Mann has argued that the role of the Grail quest in the history of the Round Table becomes apparent when metaphors about wounds and healing, the individual and the fellowship, and in particular Galahad's destiny are analyzed in detail (Mann 1996). Challenging new approaches to the "Sankgreal" have included gender (Shichtman 1999; Armstrong 2003), alongside fatherhood and community, seen as overarching metaphors for an understanding of Malory's Grail narrative (Batt 2005). Nevertheless, any reassessment of Malory's "Sankgreal" needs to take into account the original links he creates between those tales that precede and follow the Grail quest, links that are particularly evident in his treatment of Lancelot and Galahad.

In the "Sankgreal" the pre-eminence of Malory's favorite knight, Lancelot, in chivalric matters is extended to the field of penance, despite his failure to achieve a complete vision of the Grail. Some of the connections between the early and later history of the Round Table are fulfilled in the person of Galahad, in an original departure from the *Queste*. However, Malory reserves to Lancelot the privilege of recounting the adventures of the quest to the court, and, more importantly, the exceptional post-Grail miracle of healing a wounded knight, Sir Urry. This chapter will address this fundamental shift of emphasis from Galahad's and the elect knights' adventures to Lancelot's, in order to identify continuities between the Grail quest and the larger context of the *Morte*, and, ultimately, Malory's view of worldly chivalry. Lancelot will be regarded as the quintessential fallible knight, yet a more compelling model of repentant sinner than Galahad, and an example that Malory's first readers could follow.

The variety of new approaches to Malory's "Sankgreal" is matched by similar shifts in the interpretation of his source, the French *Queste*. Contrary to early views, new research attests to the *Queste* being a combination of Cistercian values and other, more widespread, religious practices (Pratt 1995). Thus what appeared to earlier criticism to be Malory's impatience with the monastic overtones in his source may now be regarded as merely his "reaction against too explicit a literary mode" (Riddy 1987: 113–14). Indeed, Malory tones down the French author's inflexible advocacy for the knights' return to the authority of the church and its sacraments, administered by priests. He leaves unchanged the French emphasis on the knights' forgetfulness of God's ways, resulting in the necessity to recognize and embark on a journey of penance, but he shifts the focus from the saint-like Galahad to the sinful Lancelot. The agency of the hermits and priests in acting as spiritual guides to the questing knights is maintained, but the biblical references and theological expositions found in the *Queste* are significantly reduced in length. As a result, Malory's orthodox view of religion becomes apparent, in that religious figures have an indispensable role to administer the sacraments. However, by casting aside both elaborate explanations and theological debate, he cuts down on mystery and material extraneous to the knights' adventures. In doing this, he redirects the readers' attention from each knight's pursuit of individual salvation to Lancelot's role in the quest. In other words, Malory subordinates religious values to chivalric ones so that a great proportion of the Grail events are inevitably seen through (and measured against) a worldly, chivalric perspective (Radulescu 2004).

Despite extensive abridgements, the plot inherited from the French source remains almost unchanged; Malory's nuances influence our reading of Lancelot's place in the Grail quest, not by contrast with his son's (as in the *Queste*), but rather alongside him. Malory's Galahad emerges as an even more remote character than he already is in the *Queste*, hence less of an example that the other knights may try to emulate. Some critics have identified in Malory's account an emphasis on Galahad's nobility over his saint-like status (Evans 1985: 37–8), yet the destiny of this pre-eminent, elect knight could hardly function as a model either for the Arthurian knights in the *Morte* or for Malory's readers. Galahad is a flat, "stained glass" character, whose nobility and purity are beyond question (and, to some extent, even temptation), and whose unique achievement of the Grail distances him from the entire fellowship of questing knights. As a result, two tendencies become apparent in the *Morte*: on the one hand, the distancing of Galahad indicates Malory's impatience with sophisticated theological discourse; on the other it points to his intention to raise Lancelot's profile in the quest. Indeed, on close examination we see that Malory's Lancelot, unlike his French counterpart, initiates his own penance and is thus rewarded with a partial experience of the Grail. This has implications for the whole fellowship of the Round Table: his worldliness brings him closer to the knights who fail in the quest, and his peerless nobility confirms that the title of "best knight of the world" remains justified even when the "Sankgreal" adventures are over.

To start with, Lancelot's prominent role as best sinful knight in "Sankgreal" is far removed from the stark contrast between a sinful Lancelot and a pure Galahad found in the *Queste*. Unsurprisingly, Malory's characters are less guided by church representatives in their actions than their French counterparts. An example is provided at the very beginning of the narrative, where in both versions a damsel's arrival at the court signals a new adventure for Lancelot, who accompanies her to a monastery. There Lancelot meets his cousins Bors and Lionel; Lancelot's presence is required so that the young Galahad, who had spent his youth with the nuns, can be knighted. The French author presents Lancelot and Galahad in relatively passive roles as they follow the nuns' guidance in all respects. In the *Queste* the exchange between father and son is conducted exclusively through the nuns (2.25–3.19), which reveals a submissive relationship between the knights and the religious figures. By contrast, Malory's economical use of the plot (Vinaver 1990: 854.14–33) diminishes the role of church representatives (priests, hermits, nuns) in the knights' lives so that the religious figures serve the interests of the chivalric order rather than exerting authority over it (Radulescu 2004). Galahad's assertiveness in both versions functions as a sign of his unique status as elect knight (860.16–861.3 versus *Queste* 7.25–8); Malory, in addition, extends this feature to Lancelot, who appears self-assured and thus less dependent on the guidance of religious figures. This episode marks a start in Malory's reworking of Lancelot's role in the quest: by conferring more authority and independence on his favorite character, Malory rejects the French author's view that a sinful and proud

Lancelot needs to learn humility and undertake penance following repeated rebukes from God and church figures.

Malory's "Englishing" of the Grail story is another significant change that has attracted critical attention in recent years. From the beginning of the quest, Galahad's role in completing the fellowship is asserted when he takes his predestined place at the Round Table. However, the traditional story of Galahad's descent and noble ancestry from Lancelot is given special attention; theirs is a lineage that goes as far back as Joseph of Arimathea, the mythical founder of Christianity in Britain. In the episode following Galahad's knighting, and the knights' departure for King Arthur's court, the French source contains a private conversation between Bors and Lionel about Galahad's family resemblance to Lancelot, which anticipates a link (and later contrast) between father and son. Malory omits the dialogue altogether; the resulting sense of restraint is consistent with his tendency to omit direct speech in other parts of the *Morte* where he translates or adapts known sources. As Julie Nelson Couch has pointed out, his achievement lies in producing "a sleek line of action" in comparison with the French sources, rapidly switching "from a regressive, anticlimactic movement to a forward, motivated movement," and "from a chatty, scandalous, disrespectful court to a reserved, respectful one" (Nelson Couch 1992: 64). The absence of the exchange between Bors and Lionel accounts for an increased emphasis later on Lancelot's lineage; moreover, Malory reserves the privilege of revealing Galahad's lineage for Guenevere, and for a public occasion. This shift of emphasis casts light on the queen's place in the story as a repository of information about Galahad's ancestry and the Christian mission he is called to embark on:

> "Ye, forsothe," seyde the quene, "for he ys of all partyes comyn of the beste knyghtes of the worlde and of the hyghest lynage: for sir Launcelot ys com but of the eyghth degré frome oure Lord Jesu Cryst, and thys sir Galahad ys th[e] nyneth degré frome oure Lorde Jesu Cryst. Therefore I dare sey they be the grettist jantillmen of the worlde." (865.7–12)

In the *Queste* the queen merely comments that Galahad comes from a noble lineage (14.33–15.2); by contrast, Malory's version of the story clearly states Galahad's and Lancelot's spiritual lineage at the crucial point when Galahad is introduced to the court as *a yonge knight the whych ys of kynges lynage and of the kynrede of Joseph of Aramathy* (859.12–13). Thus Lancelot, known as a French knight and a king in his own right, is openly associated with Galahad, and both are descendants of Joseph of Arimathea, who was credited with bringing the Holy Grail to Britain, and whose son, Josephes, was said to be one of the first Christian bishops. The link between the Grail, Joseph of Arimathea, and the Arthurian story would not have passed unnoticed by fifteenth-century readers of the *Morte*. As Riddy has pointed out, the myth was used for political ends to great effect in the later Middle Ages in England; it not only provided "an egregious spiritual parallel to the secular account of Brutus' settlement of Britain," but also imagined two British "prodigious genealogies: its kings go back to Troy and its bishops to Christ" (Riddy 1987: 114). There is evidence that in the fifteenth century the English prelates claimed precedence over Continental powers on the basis of Joseph's story (Riddy 1987; Hodges 2005: 112–17). Seen against the contemporary cultural appropriation of this myth, it is clear that Malory's story of spiritual ancestry would have appealed to his contemporaries in more ways than one: on the one hand, it returns the Arthurian story to an ancient past, and a typology that may be claimed only by kings and sons of kings; on the other it shows that Lancelot's transformation at the end of the *Morte* (by becoming a hermit and a priest) can be seen as a continuation of the spiritual leadership entrusted to his bloodline.

Malory further increases Lancelot's role in the Grail story by attributing to him a foreknowledge of events equal to that possessed by Galahad, religious figures, and Merlin. In the episode when Galahad achieves his sword from a floating stone, both he and Lancelot talk about the history of the sword and the negative consequences for those who wrongly attempt to handle it. As Stephen Atkinson has noted, Malory's Lancelot "speaks with authority on the subject of the Grail" in a more direct way than he does in the French source (Atkinson 1981: 132). Although he follows the *Queste* closely, Malory gives Lancelot a status commensurate with that of Galahad, the elect knight:

> Sir, hit ys nat my swerde; also, I have no hardines to sette my honde thereto, for hit longith nat to hange be my syde. Also, who that assayth to take hit and faylith of that swerde, he shall resseyve a wounde by that swerde that he shall nat be longe hole afftir. And I woll that ye weyte that thys same day shall the adventure of the Sankgreall begynne, that ys called the holy vessell. (856.21–27)

Through privileged knowledge, Lancelot links the wound that he does not wish to receive and that *shall nat be longe hole afftir* with the beginning of the Grail adventure, which is a metaphoric wound to the Round Table. Malory's change presents a contrast with the *Queste*, where Lancelot's reluctance is linked to his concern for his good name, although he similarly displays prior knowledge of the adventures (5.28–6.6). In both versions Lancelot tells Gawain that his obedience to the king's order to handle the sword is foolish; Gawain answers that he could not disobey such an order and he refers to his *unclis wyll* (in the *Queste*, he refers to his *seignor*, that is, his lord and king). The added reciprocity in the family exchange is Malory's, and a contrast to the source. The tensions between chivalric duty and blood ties, so strikingly dramatized in the final book of the *Morte*, are anticipated in this episode, and Gawain's emphasis on family duty may be linked to Malory's own preference for personal choice in political matters rather than the automatic respect for the king (Field 1978: 33–9). Lancelot refuses to handle the sword, though Arthur urges several knights to do so, because Lancelot knows it would wound the unworthy; in addition, he predicts the wounds Galahad and Perceval will receive and warns against unquestioning approval of the king's order to these knights to handle the sword.

Moreover, Galahad mentions that the sword belonged to Balin, the unfortunate "knight with the two swords" at the beginning of the *Morte*, who unwittingly killed his own brother using it. Galahad also states his eminent place in the adventure, since Balin was responsible for the *dolerous stroke* he gave to King Pelles, *the whych ys nat yett hole, nor naught shall be tyll that I* [Galahad] *hele hym* (863.7–9). In the *Queste* Galahad does not say anything about the past history of the sword (12.12–23), nor is the link with Balin mentioned. The implications of this change, alongside Malory's careful merging of Galahad's two swords into one (the one he is given at his knighting ceremony and the one he acquires from the floating stone) are complex, and guide the reader's attention to wider connections among characters in the *Morte* and Malory's overall vision of the Arthuriad (Evans 1985).

The wound-wholeness-healing motif in the "Sankgreal" has been explored through a variety of approaches (Kelly 1985; Mann 1996; Batt 2005). Both Mann and Riddy have commented on the importance of the phrase *holé togirdis* used to describe the fellowship of knights in Arthur's lament at the beginning of the Grail quest, as well as the subsequent one in which he deplores the end of the fellowship, caused by Mordred's and Aggravayne's *evill wyll* (Riddy 1987: 116–17; Mann 1996: 210–11). Furthermore, Mann discusses the "temporary wholeness" of the fellowship achieved through Galahad's arrival, followed by dispersal through departure for the Grail quest, and then wholeness again, gained through seeing the Grail elsewhere, hence far from the court as a center of Arthurian chivalry. She notes that the "the wound opened by Balin is closed, healed by Galahad," thus closing the narrative, and that Lancelot achieves wholeness by acknowledging opening (therefore later closing) the gap between his outward reputation and the fragmentation of his inner self and also through his union with Galahad (Mann 1996: 210, 212, 217). The implications of this discussion for an understanding of the *Morte* are evident in the post-Grail adventures (Riddy 1987), though not fully exploited in Lancelot's miraculous healing of Sir Urry beyond a link with personal devotion to Christ's wounds (Batt 2005).

The return to wounds in the "Sankgreal" also reminds the reader of Malory's equation of the Holy Grail with the holy vessel containing the blood of Christ, the object whose keeper was Lancelot's ancestor, Joseph of Arimathea. As Malory's Grail is the object with healing properties, such as had already been mentioned in the Lancelot section of the "Tale of Sir Tristram de Lyones," its presence in the *Morte*, in the knights' lives, and in particular in Lancelot's, is cyclical. In the Tristram tale Lancelot's arrival at the Castle of Corbenic and subsequent vision of the Grail is followed by his begetting of Galahad on Elaine, which leads to his spell of madness, only to be healed by the Grail (824.25–7). In the above-mentioned speech about the sword, Lancelot equates the Holy Grail with the holy vessel of the Eucharist; thus the reader anticipates that the Grail will play a significant role in Lancelot's life once again, and that Lancelot will be given a special place in the quest alongside his son Galahad.

The link with the Grail adventures becomes more evident as the subtle wound to Lancelot's purity, his old sin, prevents him from receiving a complete vision of the holy vessel and Christ in the Eucharist. Lancelot's awareness of sin is Malory's change, by contrast with the French portrayal of a proud Lancelot, oblivious to his state of mortal sin, and deserving to be humbled through human and divine interventions. When a damsel rebukes Lancelot, revealing that he can no longer hold on to his title as the best knight of the world, Malory uses the occasion to turn the reader's attention to Lancelot's humble acknowledgment of his changed status:

> "Sir, I say you sothe," seyde the damesell, "for ye were thys day in the morne the best knyght of the worlde. But who sholde sey so now, he sholde be a lyer, for there ys now one bettir than ye be, and well hit ys preved by the adventure of the swerde whereto ye durst nat sette to your honde. And that ys the change of youre name and levynge. Wherefore I make unto you a remembraunce that ye shall nat wene frome hensforthe that ye be the best knyght of the worlde."
>
> "As towchyng unto that," seyde sir Launcelot, "I know well I was never none of the beste."
>
> "Yes," seyde the damesell, "that were ye, and ar yet, of ony synfull man of the worlde." (863.20–31)

In the *Queste*, by contrast, the damsel shames him openly, revealing he is no longer the best knight (12.30–13.8); while the French Lancelot is willing to protect his reputation, Malory's knows he is unworthy. The subtle shift of emphasis in this episode has led to long debates over the decades. Benson has argued that Malory persistently removes any negative nuances in Lancelot's presentation from the *Queste* in an effort to maintain and protect his favorite knight's reputation (Benson 1976: 218). By contrast, Atkinson has interpreted Lancelot's acknowledgment that he was never the best as proof of his understanding of "the new demands of the Grail adventures" and a sign that Malory "makes no consistent attempt, here or elsewhere, to eliminate evidence of Lancelot's failure or soften the blow to his prestige" (Atkinson 1985: 132). Malory is less consistent in his treatment of Lancelot than modern readers would expect; in addition, one can agree that, by leaving Lancelot's failures unaltered, Malory would draw his reader's attention to his favorite knight's persistence in repentance.

Some evidence that Lancelot already possesses qualities that would enable him to seek penance (rather than having to be persuaded to undertake it by hermits) is available in the episode when he is not allowed to enter the chapel in which a sick knight is being healed by the Grail. Here Lancelot misses the opportunity to see the Grail and loses his arms and horse to the knight; as a result, he interprets the event negatively, mainly in relation to his reputation, yet his profound inner turmoil leads to a desire to find out more:

> And whan sir Launcelot herde thys he was passyng hevy and wyst nat what to do. And so departed sore wepynge and cursed the tyme that he was bore, for than he demed never to have worship more. For tho wordis wente to hys herte, tylle that he knew wherefore he was called so. (895.29–33)

Although Lancelot's response displays some of his old chivalric pride, there are signs he provides "good material" for a penitent: his heart is moved by the event, which is an important sign of the change he is to undergo in his repentance (Radulescu 2004). Thus the episode marks Lancelot's first step on the path to humility, a path which will continue in the post-Grail story, "The Healing of Sir Urry", and later, in the final years of his life as a hermit. Lancelot's response to the loss of arms (his knightly insignia) leads him to review his past life and then blame himself for seeking *worldly adventures for worldely desyres* (a link to Malory's original Round Table oath, 120.23–4). He shows an awareness of the conflict between his former lifestyle and his sworn oath to Arthur and the fellowship; he also contrasts the worldliness of his previous pursuits with the new adventure; he is determined *to seke of holy thynges, now I se and undirstonde that myne olde synne hyndryth me and shamyth me, that I had no power to stirre nother speke whan the holy bloode appered before me* (896.6–9). Absent in the equivalent passage in the French *Queste* (61.28–62.7), the references to both Lancelot's past chivalric deeds and his recognition of the Grail as the vessel containing Christ's blood reveal Malory's continued efforts to direct attention to his favorite knight's qualities and knowledgeable position.

In this context, it is not surprising that Lancelot's special status is repeatedly stated in the "Sankgreal," even in episodes when humility and penance are (almost) enforced on him. When Lancelot meets a hermit, the encounter provides an opportunity to discuss chivalric rules and religious demands on them. In an original translation, the French author's characterization of Lancelot as *li hons du monde de qui len disoit plus de bien* (63.10–11; "the worldly man of whom people speak so well") is changed by Malory into a positive assessment of Lancelot as the man who possesses "worldly worship." As Lambert noted, Malory's unusual translation marks a new understanding of Lancelot's position, as "worship becomes not the reason for the holy man's astonishment, but the first of the things for which Lancelot should thank God" (Lambert 1975: 186). In the *Queste* the hermit tells Lancelot never to keep the company of the queen, whereas in the "Sankgreal" he seems to take into account the rigors of chivalric life, as he recommends that Lancelot should *no more com in that quenys felyship as much as [he] may forbere* (897.25–6). Noteworthy is the emphasis on giving thanks to God, as the primary source for Lancelot's worship, and turning away from earthly achievements. In a persuasive study, Mahoney has concluded that "the French Lancelot erred in thinking the source of his valour was the Queen, Malory's Lancelot errs in believing that the source of his valour is himself; both Lancelots have to learn that the true source is God," and that Lancelot's wars were wrong "because of their motivation by personal pride rather than the desire to serve God" (Mahoney 1985: 120). It may be argued, though, that Malory's Lancelot is not "as good a knight as he should be" in all respects, either religious or chivalric (Hynes-Berry 1977: 245), since Malory consistently subordinates religious values to the chivalric ones (Radulescu 2004).

Lancelot's different treatment from the expected image of the proud knight (which makes him resemble Gawain and other knights who fail in the quest) is evident in that he has no doubt concerning the nature of his sin. In the *Queste* he is more explicit and blames himself for the sin of lust and indulging in it (*car tout adés ai habité en luxure et en la vilté de cest monde* [62]; "for more than any other I have given myself to lust and to the depravity of this world"), while in the "Sankgreal" he blames himself for his lack of stability in the service of God. Atkinson noted that, "Malory stresses the importance of the individual decision to repent . . . [and] leaves it to the knights themselves to seek out confession and penance" (Atkinson 1985: 151). Indeed, Lancelot is the one who asks the hermit to hear his confession (896.14–26). By shifting the initiative concerning confession from the hermit to Lancelot (versus the *Queste* 62.24–63.6), Malory changes focus from the image of Lancelot as a proud knight who deserves punishment to a humble penitent who is seeking confession and is prepared to put into practice the penance the hermit will give him. Lancelot appears more respectable to the reader if he knows his sin and initiates his own repentance and does not merely follow the hermit's guidance. His negative presentation in the *Queste* is a consequence of its hermits' explicit rebukes, which move Lancelot to repent, whereas Malory not only suggests that Lancelot is aware of his sin, but it is a sin which he blames on his forgetfulness of the Round Table oath: *for whan I sought worldly adventures for worldely desyres I ever encheved them and had the bettir in every place, and never was I discomfite in no quarell, were hit ryght were hit wronge* (896.2–5). Furthermore, Malory foreshadows the revelation of the true nature of Lancelot's sin later when his favorite knight states that *my olde synne hyndryth me and shamyth me* (896.7); thus Malory leaves space for the hermit to enlarge and explain more about this sin, in a way that justifies the presence of the spiritual guide. By contrast, in the *Queste* hermits are only a conventional part of the frame, and it is their rebukes that trigger feelings of remorse in the knights' consciences.

Interestingly, Lancelot stands apart from other knights who have engaged on the Grail quest because he knows when to ask for forgiveness. Perceval and Bors know their way instinctively, they blame themselves for their sins, and know how to mortify themselves, while Galahad is left out of the comparison altogether, given his purity. Lancelot knows his sins, not how to expiate them; he only knows that he needs the guidance of the monks and hermits, who can explain to him the deeper significance of his adventures. To this extent Malory's orthodox view of religious practice is reinforced in the "Sankgreal" and no ambiguity is left concerning the need for intermediaries between the sinner and God. The change in the direction of the exchange from Lancelot to the hermit also accounts for Malory's cutting down on the explanation of the gifts Lancelot has been given, an explanation which takes up significantly more space in the *Queste* than in the "Sankgreal." In the *Queste* this explanation is an opportunity for the author to introduce more biblical references, and the whole speech is based on the parable of the five talents. Malory's hermit, by contrast, merely praises Lancelot for his virtues and gifts; this speech reveals Malory's desire to favor the chivalric achievement of the best earthly knight over the sinfulness of the French Lancelot (Radulescu 2004).

Lancelot's position as best knight among the sinful ones is commented on throughout the Grail quest, although he is reminded of his failure to perform penance on several occasions, and in unequivocal terms. As one hermit tells him, Lancelot's great gifts from God call for even greater penance: *ye ought to thanke God more than ony knyght lyvynge, for He hath caused you to have more worldly worship than ony knyght that ys now lyvynge* (896.29–31). Another time he needs to remember that he is *more abeler than ony man lyvynge* (927.15–16), and therefore should give praise to God. His achievement at the Castle of Corbenic is foretold by a damsel: *and yet shall ye se hit* [the Grail] *more opynly than ever ye dud, and that shall ye undirstonde in shorte tyme* (928.5–7). When he arrives at a cross, he *made his prayers unto the crosse that he never falle in dedely synne agayne* (928.16–17). However, the reader understands that Lancelot's change, and his practice of religion, remain superficial, since during the night he has a vision of seven kings and two knights in heaven and a divine voice tells him that he is banished from their company because he had *ruled ayenste* [God] *as a warryoure and used wronge warris with vayneglory for the pleasure of the worlde more than to please* [God], *therefore thou shalt be confounded* (928.35–929.1). The idea of *wronge warris* undertaken for pride, the chief sin of the Arthurian knights, is revisited here, in order to reinforce Lancelot's sin of never thinking of God. Stress falls again on religion as part of the chivalric code, rather than ruling with authority over it, and the earthly knights' path to salvation can only be long and painful.

As the repentance process is described, Lancelot attempts to learn humility, the virtue which seems to be the key to his partial vision, as well as his success in the post-Grail episode, "The Healing of Sir Urry." Humility is manifest in the physical penance Lancelot undertakes: his decision to wear a hair shirt is a sign that the path to salvation is hard (*the heyre prycked faste sir Launcelots skynne and greved hym sore*), yet his response to pain is appropriately humble (*but he toke hit mekely and suffirde the payne*, 931.8–10). His determination is visible, but the results are not immediate; this is apparent in the many episodes when he is put to the test and fails. However, he shows he is capable of displaying heartfelt humility, something Gawain is not; this openness to change may be a key to understanding his position later, in the "Healing" episode, when he is singled out among the Round Table knights, and during the last years of his life in a hermitage (Radulescu 2008).

Overall Lancelot's progress through the quest would appear to fifteenth-century readers as that of a man long steeped in sin and a beginner in penance; in the words of a hermit, Lancelot is *feble of evyll truste and good beleve* (934.3). Thus the "Sankgreal" preserves Malory's design to remind Lancelot (and the reader) that he might be excused for his frailty if he is determined to persevere in his new life and forget his knightly pride:

> Now have I warned the of thy vayneglory and of thy pryde, that thou haste many tyme arred ayenste thy Maker. Beware of everlastynge payne, for of all erthly knyghtes I have moste pité of the, for I know well thou haste nat thy pere of ony erthly synfull man. (934.19–23)

Here Lancelot's pre-eminence is stated again as one more reason for him to seek true repentance, going beyond the superficial performance of rituals. His position in the chivalric world stands as proof that he has won favor with God, and is thus all the more called upon to give thanks for God's gifts and to repay God's generosity in granting him so many earthly victories and fame. Throughout the "Sankgreal," however, Lancelot will remain on the same level, that of an inexperienced beginner in religious ways, which leads to his feeling of weariness in the episode when he spends privileged time with his son Galahad (Kennedy 1985: 265). Malory's version of the Grail quest shows Lancelot to be willing to expiate his sins, so his downfall appears to be caused not so much by his love for Guenevere, as by his instability in God's ways and forgetful neglect of thanksgiving, itself seen as a failure in chivalric conduct:

> "For I dare sey, as synfull as ever sir Laucelot hath byn, sith that he wente into the queste of the Sankgreal he slew never man nother nought shall, tylle that he com to Camelot agayne; for he hath takyn [upon] hym to forsake synne. And ne were that he ys nat stable, but by hys thoughte he he ys lyckly to turne agayne, he sholde be nexte to enchev[e] hit sauff sir Galahad, hys sonne; but Got knowith hys thought and hys unstablenesse. And yett he shall dye ryght an holy man, and no doute he hath no felow of none erthly synfull man lyvyng." (948.20–9)

The passage shows two positive sides of Lancelot's nature which Malory considers relevant in his behavior during the "Sankgreal": his refraining from murder and his forsaking sin. However, he is unstable and this remains his flaw or weakness throughout the last books in the *Morte*. Nevertheless, it is this flaw that draws him closer to the sympathetic reader. The resulting image is that outside the "Sankgreal" emphasis is placed more on the social implications of his faults (disloyalty to his lord, breaking the Round Table code) than on the moral or spiritual ones. Within the Arthurian world Malory recreates, the rule of the chivalric order should come before personal interests (Radulescu 2004).

From this perspective, Lancelot's place in Malory's new hierarchy of Grail knights becomes clearer if viewed in relation to the privileged position of Galahad, who is granted exceptional powers of healing, miracles, and visions. Although Malory inherits Galahad's traditional exemplarity, he makes no effort to guide the readers' attention to him, and to display him as a model to be followed. Indeed, neither Malory nor the French author presents any other knight as a witness to Galahad's miracles, and thus no one is (or could be) converted by them. Even though his adventures are described at length, the other knights do not have access to the same adventures and Galahad's special status means he cannot function as an example of Christian behavior. Malory maintains a conspicuous silence over Galahad's humanity, in that he is not tempted the way Lancelot and other knights are; he simply does not have to fight human weaknesses, from which he is exempt. Similarly, Perceval, the other Grail knight, is tempted, but knows how to recognize temptation and punish his weakness, thus showing a higher awareness of what is required of him in the quest. His decision not to pursue the knightly vocation after the "Sankgreal," but to devote his life to prayer, in a monastery, where he dies, further enhances his own exceptional status, alongside Galahad's. Thus Perceval may be said to act more as an example to Lancelot and Bors, the only other knights who are members of the elect. Bors is the only one who is both granted the Grail revelation and returns to the court, where he resumes his subordinate position to Lancelot. Bors' lack of conversion to a religious life up to the end, when Arthur has died and Lancelot has become a hermit, is surprising. Equally unusual is Malory's silence over his changed personal conduct following the Grail quest, especially as Bors returns to the court but is not present in the episode of "The Healing of Sir Urry" (for an analysis of this development, see Radulescu 2008).

The three elect knights, Galahad, Perceval, and Bors, do not have to work as hard as Lancelot in order to gain full sight of the Grail. The return to the world involves a return to social hierarchies, but also means that Lancelot will resume a place of responsibility as "best knight of the world," now with the meaning changed as a result of the Grail quest. While the Arthurian court lives on, unaware of the implications of the quest, it is perhaps Malory's intention to show the role of humility in understanding Lancelot's pre-eminent place as the "best knight of the world" in "The Healing of Sir Urry" (Radulescu 2008).

Furthermore, the "Sankgreal" omits the connections which the *Queste* established between the Last Supper table on which the Holy Grail appears and the Round Table. Malory focuses on the Round Table as the moral center of the knights' lives, and the moral of the fellowship includes Christian morality (Hynes-Berry 1977: 246). Thus Lancelot's glimpse of the Grail has wider implications than on the personal level because it signals to the other knights the limits of what might be granted to the sinful ones among them should they follow the path of penance. This optimistic view is supported by the description of Lancelot's trance. There Lancelot is clearly satisfied with the revelations he has been given, and certainly thinks that a good life and his repentance form the reason why he has achieved so much, despite his impatience and inexperience in religious life: *no man in thys worlde have lyved bettir than I have done to enchyeve that I have done* (1018.5–6). When, upon their return to the court, Bors passes on Galahad's message to his father, *remembir of this worlde unstable* (1035.11–12), repeated in Bors' speech (*unsyker worlde*; 1036.28), the reader is encouraged to meditate on the implications of the quest, and ponder on matters of sinfulness, lack of confession, and penance.

The pledge of friendship Bors and Lancelot take at the end of the quest also highlights the necessity to keep companionship in future adventures, whether chivalric or religious, or both. Many critics have noticed Bors' subordinate place to Lancelot at the end of the quest, when Lancelot is invested with responsibility for recounting the adventures and having them written in *grete bookes* (1036.21). This may be interpreted as a return to the hierarchies of this world, but also as a sign that even religious achievement can be viewed in a number of ways, depending on its value for the fellowship. It is Lancelot, not Bors, who will be called upon to heal Sir Urry in the post-Grail adventures, irrespective of the hierarchies established in the quest. Finally,

Malory's most original change to his source remains that of incorporating the Grail story into his *Morte* through his treatment of Lancelot, whose fascinating trajectory from sinful knight to successful healer and saintly hermit is subsequently traced in the last books of the *Morte*.

PRIMARY SOURCES

Field, P. J. C. (ed.) (1978). *Sir Thomas Malory. Le Morte Darthur: The seventh and eighth tales.* Bangor: Hodder & Stoughton.

Matarasso, P. M. (trans.) (1969). *The quest of the Holy Grail.* Harmondsworth: Penguin.

Pauphilet, A. (ed.) (1967). *La Queste del Saint Graal.* Paris: Champion.

Vinaver, E. (ed.) (1990). *Malory. Works*, 3rd rev. edn (ed. P. J. C. Field), 3 vols. Oxford: Clarendon Press.

REFERENCES AND FURTHER READING

Armstrong, D. (2003). *Gender and the chivalric community in Malory's Morte Darthur.* Gainesville, FL: University Press of Florida.

Atkinson, S. C. B. (1981). Malory's "Healing of Sir Urry": Lancelot, the earthly fellowship and the world of the Grail. *Studies in Philology*, 79, 341–52.

Atkinson, S. C. B. (1985). Malory's Lancelot and the Quest of the Grail. In J. W. Spisak (ed.), *Studies in Malory.* Kalamazoo, MI: Medieval Institute.

Batt, C. (2005). *Malory's* Morte Darthur: *Remaking Arthurian tradition.* New York: Palgrave Macmillan.

Benson, L. D. (1976). *Malory's Morte Darthur.* Cambridge, MA: Harvard University Press.

Evans, M. J. (1985). *Ordinatio* and narrative links: The impact of Malory's tales as a "hoole book." In J. W. Spisak (ed.), *Studies in Malory.* Kalamazoo, MI: Western Michigan University, pp. 29–52.

Hynes-Berry, M. (1977). Malory's translation of meaning: *The tale of the Sankgreal. Studies in Philology*, 74, 243–57.

Hodges, K. (2005). *Forging chivalric communities in Malory's* Le Morte Darthur. New York: Palgrave Macmillan.

Kelly, R. L. (1985). Wounds, healing and knighthood in Malory's Tale of Lancelot and Guenevere. In J. W. Spisak (ed.), *Studies in Malory.*

Kalamazoo, MI: Western Michigan University, pp. 173–97.

Kennedy, B. (1985). *Knighthood in the Morte Darthur.* Cambridge: Brewer.

Kennedy, E. D. (1981). Malory and his English sources. In T. Takamiya & D. S. Brewer (eds), *Aspects of Malory.* Cambridge: Brewer, pp. 28–42.

Lambert, M. (1975). *Style and vision in Malory's Morte Darthur.* New Haven, CT: Yale University Press.

Mahoney, D. B. (1985). The truest and holiest tale: Malory's transformation of *La Queste del Saint Graal.* In J. W. Spisak (ed.), *Studies in Malory.* Kalamazoo, MI: Western Michigan University, pp. 109–28.

Mann, J. (1996). Malory and the Grail legend. In E. Archibald & A. S. G. Edwards (eds), *A companion to Malory.* Cambridge: Brewer, pp. 203–20.

Moorman, C. (1964). "The tale of the Sankgreall": Human frailty. In R. M. Lumiansky (ed.), *Malory's originality: A critical study of Le Morte Darthur.* Baltimore, MD: John Hopkins Press, pp. 184–204.

Nelson Couch, J. (1992). With due respect: The royal court in Malory's "The Poisoned Apple" and "The Fair Maid of Astolat." In T. Hanks, Jr (ed.), *Sir Thomas Malory: Views and re-views.* New York: AMS Press, pp. 63–77.

Pratt, K. (1995). The Cistercians and the *Queste del Saint Graal*. *Reading Medieval Studies*, 21, 69–96.

Radulescu, R. L. (2004). "Now I take uppon me the adventures to seke of holy thynges": Lancelot and the crisis of Arthurian knighthood. In B. Wheeler (ed.), *Textual traditions of mediaeval Arthurian literature: Essays in honour of P. J. C. Field*. Cambridge: Brewer, pp. 285–95.

Radulescu, R. L. (2008). Malory's Lancelot and the key to salvation. *Arthurian Literature*, 25, 93–118.

Riddy, F. (1987). *Sir Thomas Malory*. Leiden: Brill.

Riddy, F. (2000). Chivalric nationalism and the Holy Grail in John Hardyng's *Chronicle*. In D. B. Mahoney (ed.), *The Grail: A casebook*. New York: Garland, pp. 397–414.

Shichtman, M. B. (1994). Politicizing the ineffable: *The Queste del Saint Graal* and Malory's "Tale of the Sankgreal." In M. B. Shichtman, J. P. Carley, & M. L. Day (eds), *Culture and the king: The social implications of the Arthurian legend*. Albany, NY: State University of New York Press, pp. 163–79.

Shichtman, M. B. (1999). Percival's sister: Genealogy, virginity, and blood. *Arthuriana*, 9(2), 11–20.

23
The Arthurian Legend in the Sixteenth to Eighteenth Centuries

Alan Lupack

It is commonly accepted that the high points of the Arthurian legend are the late Middle Ages, the Victorian age, and the twentieth century. The period between the Middle Ages and the Victorian revival, and especially between the 1634 and 1816 editions of Malory – a virtual long Arthurian eighteenth century – has generally, though not universally, been thought of as an Arthurian nadir. In 1925, Elise van der Ven-Ten Bensel referred to the seventeenth and eighteenth centuries as the "long barren period" of Arthurian literature (Ven-Ten Bensel 1925: 170). While it is true that no new edition of Malory was printed during this time and that there was an absence of the familiar Malorian tales, Arthurian matter of a different sort continued to play an important role. An ongoing chronicle tradition, romances, plays, ballads, topographical and other poems, prophecies, satires, almanacs, antiquarian exploration – all kept the Arthurian legends alive and provided a significant body of transitional material between the late Middle Ages and the Victorian age.

The Historicity of Arthur after the Middle Ages

The ultimate source of most of the post-medieval material up to the eighteenth century is Geoffrey of Monmouth's *Historia Regum Britanniae* ("History of the Kings of Britain"). The issue of whether or not Geoffrey's account of British history was true had serious political implications, which gave to Geoffrey's story of Arthur and other aspects of the legendary history he codified an urgency and a relevance that persisted throughout the sixteenth and seventeenth centuries and even into the eighteenth. Renaissance England, concerned as it was with questions of kingship and succession, turned primarily to chronicles for its Arthurian subject matter and sometimes used this material for political purposes. Henry VII, the first of the Tudor monarchs, traced his lineage and his claim to the throne back to Arthur and reinterpreted the legend so that not Arthur himself but his descendant, in the person of Henry VII, was said to have returned at a time of need (the Wars of the Roses) to restore stability to Britain. This Tudor myth was fostered initially by Henry VII, who named his first son Arthur, and then by Henry's successors.

In his history of England, Polydore Vergil (c. 1470–1555) challenged the authority of Geoffrey of Monmouth by claiming that Britain was not founded by Brutus but that *allmoste, even fro the beginninge of the worlde, the Ilond hathe ben inhabited, and that, according to other contries after Noes fludd it receaved inhabitants, which Cæsar calleth the natives or people bredd in the soyle wherin Gildas agreeth with mee.* Despite his rejection of the story of Brutus and his contention that the traditional histories of Britain contain "infinite" errors (Ellis 1846: 32), Vergil records the line of British kings as traditionally given by Geoffrey, beginning with Brutus and his sons. In his discussion of Arthurian pre-history, Vergil acknowledges that Aurelius Ambrosius did great deeds. But he compares the stories about Uther's son Arthur to those that the Italians tell about Roland; and he says that the common people are *soe affectioned, that with wondrous admiration they extol Arthure unto the heavens*, alleging that he performed a series of heroic acts, including the slaying of giants. He goes on to say that Arthur was reported to have returned suddenly from his Continental expedition because of *demesticall contention* and Mordred's usurpation (121–2). It is striking that whereas Geoffrey devoted nearly a fifth of his long chronicle to Arthur, Vergil gives him one page, and that the deeds recounted there are undercut with words and phrases suggesting exaggeration or embellishment.

Vergil's challenge to the Galfridian version of British history led to a sharp reaction. The fact that Vergil was Italian and Catholic was surely a factor in the negative responses that his history elicited. John Leland was one of those who felt the need to respond harshly to Vergil's account. In his travels throughout Britain gathering information on its past, Leland found the evidence he needed to refute Vergil's charges. Leland's *Assertio inclytissimi Arturii Regis Britanniae* ("Assertion of the Moste Renowned King Arthur of Britain"), published in 1544 and translated into English by Richard Robinson in 1582 during the reign of Elizabeth I (Robinson 1925), offered among other proofs of Arthur's historicity a detailed description of Arthur's seal, a transcription of the legend on the cross found at Arthur's grave site, and reports of local lore associating Cadbury with Camelot. Leland also cites an impressive number of historians, from Gildas and Nennius to writers of his own day. Astute enough both as historian and as rhetorician to recognize that some of the marvels referred to in the medieval chronicles are beyond belief, Leland drew a distinction between the fantastic and the factual, and concluded that while the excesses of some earlier writers were regrettable, the weight of the evidence supported the historicity of Arthur.

English chroniclers in the sixteenth and seventeenth centuries continued to record the reign of Arthur, though the claims about him were tempered by scholarly skepticism. In his *Chronicles of England*, John Stow announces his intention to "follow the authoritie of the receiued Brytish Historie, which *Geffrey* Archdeacon of *Monmouth* translated out of the Brytishe tong about 400 yeares since" (Stow 1580: 15, original italics). Stow gives Arthur a place in the line of British kings but criticizes "fabulous reports" about him since he is worthy to be remembered in "true Histories" as "the only proppe and vpholder of this his Countrey" (81). Similarly, Raphael Holinshed, in his *Chronicles of England, Scotland and Ireland* of 1577, famous as a source for Shakespeare and Marlowe, again records Arthur's victories against the Saxons, his continental expedition against Lucius, and his return to fight the usurper Mordred. But Holinshed, like Stow, criticizes the "fables" created by the British "to aduance more than reason would, this Arthuir their noble champion" (Ellis 1807: I.576).

Even into the seventeenth and eighteenth centuries, some chroniclers and writers were still repeating the traditional account of early British history. The poet John Milton (1608–74), famous for *not* having written an epic about Arthur, asserts in his *History of Britain*, written over a period of many years and first published in 1670, that it "cannot be thought without too strict an incredulity" that "those old and inborn names of successive Kings, never any to have bin real persons, or don in thir lives at least som part of what so long hath bin remember'd" (Fogle 1971: 8–9). Milton is, however, less certain about the historicity of Arthur: "Who Arthur was, and whether ever any such reign'd in Britain, hath bin doubted heertofore, and may again with good reason" (164). On the other hand, David Hume in his *History of England* (1754–62) states that when Cerdic "laid siege to Mount Badon, or Banesdowne, near Bathe, whither the most discomfited Britons had retired," then "the southern Britons, in this extremity, applied for assistance to Arthur, Prince of the Silures, whose heroic valor now sustained the declining fate of his country." He goes on to acknowledge that Arthur's "military achievements have been blended with so many fables as even to give occasion for entertaining a doubt of his real existence," but he seems to have had no doubts that Arthur was an authentic military leader who "discomfited" the Saxons in a great battle at Badon (Hume 1850: 45–6). Some time later, antiquarian Joseph Ritson (1752–1803) acknowledged that some writers considered Arthur to have been greater than Julius Caesar or Alexander the Great but that "his very existence has, by others, been, positively and absolutely, denied" (Ritson 1825: i). Ritson's study, published posthumously in 1825, was called *The life of King Arthur*, the very title suggesting acceptance of historicity, whatever skepticism he may have expressed about details contained in early chronicles.

One indication of the importance of Geoffrey of Monmouth in these years is that the first modern English translation of Geoffrey's *Historia* appeared in 1718. The translator, Aaron Thompson, included a long preface in which he defends Geoffrey as a historian. While Thompson does not believe that everything Geoffrey wrote was historically accurate, he is anxious to establish his general credibility. In his preface, Thompson says that though Geoffrey's Latin is "barbarous" and often obscure, yet his book "is a pleasant, and in many Places a true History of a very brave People" (Thompson 1718: iii). Thompson finds in Geoffrey's book "Traces of venerable Antiquity" sometimes mixed with fable "as are all the profane Histories of those ancient Times." But he argues that "where we want sufficient Light to distinguish Truth from Fiction, the Reverence due to one should make us bear with the other, and it can be no warrantable Zeal that would destroy both together" (ix). Whatever one might think of

Thompson's judgment about historical matters, his translation reintroduced Geoffrey's version of British legendary history to the English reading public.

Scottish Chronicles

Another issue raised by the chronicle interpretation of early British history was the relationship between the kings of England and Scotland. Some sixteenth-century Scottish histories are quite chauvinistic in their chronicling of events relating to the founding of Britain and the story of Arthur. Writing in the same tradition as the fourteenth-century Scottish chronicler John of Fordun, who might be seen as the Scottish Geoffrey, sixteenth-century Scottish chronicler Hector Boece (c. 1465–1536) presented an origin myth for Scotland which predated the founding of Britain by Brutus. Boece's Latin prose chronicle, *Scotorum historia*, published in 1527, was translated twice into Middle Scots at the command of James V of Scotland: into prose by John Bellenden as *The Chronicles of Scotland* (?1540), and into verse by William Stewart as *The Buik of the Croniclis of Scotland* (1535). Through these vernacular adaptations of Boece, in which "it is the Scots who distinguish themselves and the Britons who are cowardly and treacherous" (Fletcher & Loomis 1966: 245), the Arthurian material was reinterpreted in a manner sympathetic to the Scots and to Scottish independence.

In Bellenden's account, Uther is presented as degenerate and shameful in his lust, and Mordred (Modred in the Scottish texts) as a man with a reasonable grievance against Arthur. Mordred's rebellion comes only after Arthur names Constantine as his successor, in violation of his agreement that no one should succeed to the throne of Britain after his death except the sons of Lot and Anna and their heirs. Mordred writes to Arthur and the British nobles that it is not seemly for princes to violate their pledges without some legal cause and warns him that naming Constantine to succeed him violates the laws of God and of man (Chambers & Batho 1938: 378). Nor is Mordred's legal and moral position tainted by stealing Arthur's wife, as it is in some accounts. His cause is presented as just since he claims only what has been promised by the king.

Stewart is even stronger than Bellenden in his justification of Mordred's rebellion. He recognizes Arthur's great fame and military accomplishments but observes that he was *gottin in adulterie* and that Uther had *no lauchfull sone* (Turnbull 1858: 203–4). He also describes at some length Arthur's promise that Lot's heirs should rule after Arthur's death. But Arthur is persuaded by the British nobles to break the oath. Mordred is shown to act reasonably in petitioning Arthur to keep his word. It is only when Arthur resorts to sophistry, asserting that since the oath was made to Lot, it is not binding after his death, that Mordred is obliged to mount a rebellion to claim what is rightfully his. Stewart, who like Bellenden does not depict Arthur as the conqueror of Europe or as an emperor, suggests that Arthur is like Finn MacCool and Robin Hood, in that many lies are told about him and that anyone who claims more for Arthur than he has recorded is deceived or deceiving (Turnbull 1858: 261–2). Stewart is clearly referring to Geoffrey and those who get their information from him.

In his *Historia Majoris Britanniae* ("History of Greater Britain," 1521), John Major (b. 1469 or 1470) also raises questions about Arthur's right to rule. He notes that Arthur was a "bastard" and that Anna "bore in lawful marriage" with Loth the illustrious Valvanus and Mordred; and therefore, Major asserts, "by the right of succession, the kingdom of the Britons should have fallen to Modred" (Constable 1892: 82). Another Scottish historian, George Buchanan (1506–82), who wrote his history of the Scots, *Rerum Scoticarum Historia* ("History of Scottish Affairs") in 1582, also considers Merlin to be Uther's "procurer" (Aikman 1827: 234) because he assisted Uther as he "overcame her [Igerne's] modesty" and then helped concoct a "fable" about the transformation of Uther into the shape of Gorlois in order to "dignify the misconduct of his wife" (236). For Buchanan, there is no doubt that Arthur was conceived as a result of adultery; and he claims that Gawain and Mordred "had been defrauded of the crown, and a spurious and adulterous bastard preferred before them" (237). When Arthur names Constantine, son of Cador, as his successor in violation of the treaty he had made guaranteeing that Lot's sons would succeed him, Mordred rebels and claims the throne for "the preservation of his dignity" (243). Despite the indignities to the Scottish line, Buchanan, like Major, has much that is good to say about Arthur, who was brave, loved his country, and restored the true religion to Britain. Buchanan rejects, however, Geoffrey's tales of Arthur's conquests on the Continent and claims that the "fabulous accounts" of his exploits bring into doubt even those deeds that are true. In the Scottish tradition of history, then, Arthur's historicity becomes more certain while his moral character is presented as more dubious than that of the mythic figure in medieval British tradition.

Arthurian Topography

As Leland had done, William Camden traveled through Britain recording information for his *Britannia*, a topographical survey of Britain which was first published in 1586 and was reprinted and expanded in a number of editions before it was translated into English in 1610. By recording that "Tindagel" is where Arthur was born; that on a steep hill called Camalet, the remains of a "decayed castle" which the local people call King Arthur's Palace can be found; and that Camelford is Kamblan, where Arthur fought Mordred, Camden gives a geographic reality to the story of Arthur. In addition, Camden depicts and transcribes the cross on the tomb of Arthur at Glastonbury, thus providing eyewitness and documentary evidence for Arthur's existence. Even into the eighteenth century, local histories often included references to Arthur and Arthurian sites. John Whitaker's (1735–1808) *History of Manchester* (1771–5), for example, not only tried to locate a number of Arthur's battles listed by Nennius near Manchester but also, as a consequence, entered the debate over Arthur's historicity by arguing for a middle ground between those who would accept the most obvious absurdities about Arthur and those who would not accept his very existence. Whitaker offers both an account of Arthur's deeds and topographical evidence that he existed by noting that six or seven hundred places "are still distinguished by his name" (Whitaker 1771–5: 2, 32).

The interest in the Arthurian associations of numerous places in Britain as noted by Leland and Camden was also reflected in verse that commemorated British sites associated with Arthur. Thomas Churchyard (?1520–1604) dedicated his largely topographical poem *The Worthines of Wales* (1587) to Elizabeth I, who, according to Churchyard, was descended from Arthur. He has harsh words for writers like Polydore Vergil who attack Arthur's historicity, which he contrasts with the fictional jest of Robin Hood; and he argues that Caerleon, the site of Arthur's court, should be as famous as Troy and Athens.

Michael Drayton (1563–1631) includes in his *Poly-Olbion* (part I, 1612; part II, 1622) elements of Arthurian topography, descending ultimately from Nennius and Geoffrey. In the Fourth Song of the *Poly-Olbion*, Drayton recounts Arthur's twelve battles culminating in his victory at Badon, his conquests on the Continent, and Mordred's treachery; and he talks of Merlin bringing Stonehenge to Britain and his being enclosed by an "Elfe" in a cave that she sealed "with an inchanted stone" (Hebel 1933: 75–8). He writes elsewhere in the text of such places as Glastonbury, famed for being the site of Arthur's tomb, and of the thorn trees that bloom in the winter, and Carmarden, known as the place where Merlin was born (56, 101). This interest in Arthurian topography persists into the eighteenth century and can be seen in poems such as "Written at Stonehenge," "The Grave of King Arthur," and "On King Arthur's Round Table at Winchester" by Thomas Warton (1728–90), and "The Cave of Merlin" and "The Shrine of King Arthur" by Cæsar Morgan (?1750–1812).

Another place, a different cave of Merlin from the one Morgan writes about, inspired much political satire, dramatic presentation, and verse. The structure known as Merlin's Cave was, in fact, "a thatched 'Gothic' cottage" built by William Kent (1685–1748) in 1735 for Queen Caroline, the wife of George II. Tended by poet Stephen Duck and his wife, the Cave contained statues of Merlin and other figures from British history and literature and implied that Caroline "was the latest heiress in a single royal line leading ultimately back to Arthur" (Colton 1976: 5, 10–15). The structure inspired satire and verse from the laudatory to the erotic.

Arthur on Stage

Like the antiquarian, historical, and topographical literature that spoke of Arthur and related matters, Arthurian plays show the influence of the chronicle tradition and sometimes the political concerns that kept the Arthurian story current, even as they reflect the changing dramatic conventions of their times. In addition to some plays whose text does not survive – such as *Chinone of England*, probably a version of the same story told in the romance *Chinon of England* discussed below, *Uter Pendragon*, and *Arthur, King of England* (cf. Michelsson 1999: 116–17) – Arthurian plays of various types were written for diverse purposes. In 1587, Elizabethan playwright Thomas Hughes (fl. 1571–1623), a member of Gray's Inn, wrote a tragedy called *The Misfortunes of Arthur*. In his dramatization of Arthur's downfall, Hughes recounts Gueneuora's betrayal of Arthur with Mordred, Mordred's usurpation, Arthur's return from his wars on the Continent, and the final battle against Mordred. The play employs many of the conventions of the Senecan revenge tragedy as it moves from a ghost calling for revenge – in this case, the ghost of Gorlois, first husband of Igerna, seeking revenge on the house of Uther Pendragon – to the killing of Mordred and the fatal wounding of Arthur.

Ben Jonson's (1572–1637) masque *The Speeches at Prince Henries Barriers* was written for the celebration in honor of the investiture of Henry, eldest son of James I, as Prince of Wales in 1610. As James Merriman observed:

> Like the Tudors before him, James I was quick to see the usefulness of Arthur in bolstering his throne. Through both the Tudor and the Stuart lines, he was able to trace himself to Arthur's blood, and by his relinquishment of separate titles to the two realms of Scotland and England and his taking instead the title of King of Great Britain, James made possible the assertion by his supporters that his accession fulfilled Merlin's prophecy that under the name of Brutus England and Scotland would be united once more as they had been under Arthur. (Merriman 1973: 49)

In the masque, the Lady of the Lake and Merlin instruct James's son as he becomes Prince of Wales. The Lady of the Lake presents a shield to Meliadus (who represents Henry) and then calls on Merlin to explain its images. Merlin's reading of the shield is in effect a prediction of the glories of Arthurian and English history, including the accomplishments of the Tudor and Stuart monarchs and a final prophecy about the glory of James and his line.

A much younger Merlin figures in one of the most interesting of the Renaissance Arthurian plays to use chronicle material, *The Birth of Merlin* (c. 1620), attributed in its first printed edition of 1662 to William Rowley (?1585–?1642) and William Shakespeare (1564–1616), although now it is generally accepted that Shakespeare did not collaborate in its writing. As in some of Shakespeare's history plays, a comic sub-plot comments on the main action. The sub-plot involves the birth of Merlin to a simple woman called Joan Goe-too't, who has too willingly slept with the devil and become pregnant and who now searches for the father, whose features she hardly remembers. Uter, who berates Joan because of her sin and her unfounded accusation that he might be the father, is initially unable to perceive that the woman he loves, Artesia, sister of the Saxon general Ostorius, is far more wicked and dangerous. Just as Joan was deceived by the Devil, so the devilish Artesia deceives Uter, temporarily, and King Aurelius, whom she has poisoned, fatally.

Later in the seventeenth century, John Dryden (1631–1700) who, like Milton, considered and rejected the idea of writing an Arthurian epic, wrote a "dramatic opera" called *King Arthur*, the music for which was composed by Henry Purcell (1659–95). Originally written in 1684 during the reign of Charles II (1660–85), the play was, according to Dryden's preface, revised radically for its publication in 1691 and first performance in January of 1692 to reflect a new political situation, the reign of William and Mary. The play is set in the context of the Saxon invasions. Guinevere is replaced as the object of Arthur's love by Emmeline, the blind daughter of Arthur's ally Conon, Duke of Cornwall. She is loved, in turn, by both the Saxon leader Oswald and his magician Osmond. The play builds on the chronicle tradition of Arthur's battles with the Saxons, but – unlike *The Misfortunes of Arthur* and other Renaissance plays dealing with the chronicle material – Dryden's work is a heroic Restoration play that is more interested in the amorous struggle of Arthur and Oswald, whom James Merriman has called "nothing but a pair of Restoration beaux" (Merriman 1973: 63), than dynastic conflict. Both conflicts culminate in a single combat in which Arthur is the victor. The commercial viability of the play is evident in the fact that it was adapted by David Garrick in 1770 with Purcell's music and additional music by Thomas Arne.

The eighteenth century, too, produced historical Arthurian drama. *Arthur, Monarch of the Britons* (1759; first published in 1776) by British poet William Hilton depicts Mordred's usurpation while Arthur fights in Armorica to free its oppressed people. Arthur returns to slay Mordred, forgive his queen, and remind his successor Constantine that the British people must always be free. Arthurian pre-history figures in another play, a notorious forgery by William Ireland (1777–1835), who adapts material from Holinshed's *Chronicles of England, Scotland, and Ireland* to create the historical play *Vortigern* (written in 1795 and performed in 1796). Ireland initially claimed that the play, which enacts the history and fate of Vortigern, was written by Shakespeare. Although Ireland imitates some of the devices and motifs used by Shakespeare, his play is rather plodding and uninspired.

In 1730, Henry Fielding (1707–54) wrote his burlesque play *Tom Thumb*, which satirized and criticized everything from politics, doctors, and lawyers to printing practices and the heroic and romantic conventions of the drama of his day. Fielding's hero is the miniscule Tom Thumb, a character in chapbooks and ballads such as the prose *History of Tom Thumbe* (1621) by Richard Johnson (1573–?1659). Tom was traditionally begotten by a previously childless couple with the help of Merlin. Fielding's Tom wins fame by his valor in Arthur's wars. Fielding expanded his original play in 1731 as *The Tragedy of Tragedies*, which introduced Merlin, who did not appear in the earlier version but who in the revised version explains his role in Tom's birth by quoting from the ballad "The Life and Death of Tom Thumb."

Merlin and Prophecy

In the eighteenth century, Merlin figured in satires, burlesques, masques, and popular entertainments as a type of the magician or wizard, with little connection to traditional Arthurian material. Lewis Theobald's (1688–1744) *Merlin or The Devil of*

Stone-Henge, an entertainment with dances and music by John Galliard (?1687–1749), for example, portrays Merlin as demon-born and therefore an agent of the devil in beguiling humans, including Faust. The fact that Merlin is responsible for building Stonehenge echoes the chronicle tradition, though in the play he is said to build it as a monument to his mother. The popularity of Merlin in plays of the period is indicative of a wider interest in the prophetic tradition which has its roots in Geoffrey's *Historia* and which, like much of the Arthurian material derived from Geoffrey, often has political implications. The ongoing interest in Merlin as a prophet, suggested by Jonson's masque and other works, is seen again in *The Life of Merlin* (1641) by Thomas Heywood (?1574–1641), which used purported prophecies of Merlin as the basis for a history of England up to the beginning of the reign of Charles I. Because of Merlin's reputation as a prophet, his name was also frequently taken as a pseudonym by astrologers and writers of almanacs in the seventeenth century. In 1644, William Lilly (1602–81) began publishing almanacs under the names of Merlinus Anglicus Junior, later Merlinus Anglicus; and in the late seventeenth and early eighteenth centuries, John Partridge (1644–1715) produced an almanac under the names of Merlinus Liberatus and Merlinus Redivivus. Jonathan Swift (1667–1745) mocked the abuse of prophecies attributed to Merlin in "A Famous Prediction of Merlin, the British Wizard, Written above a Thousand Years Ago and Relating to the Present Year 1709," in which he created a prophecy with the obscure language and animal imagery typical of the genre and twisted its language so that he could wring from it any meaning he wanted by proclaiming that such obscurity is "after the usual manner of old astrological predictions" (Swift 1992: 82).

Merlin as a prophet and advisor to the king figured in Richard Hole's (1746–1803) "Poetical Romance" called *Arthur or the Northern Enchantment* (1789). Typically pre-Romantic, the poem contains long passages of natural description, depictions of peasants leading an idyllic rustic life, conflicts in which emotion overcomes reason, images borrowed from Ossian, and references to Celtic and Germanic mythology and antiquities. In its plot and its melodrama, *Arthur or the Northern Enchantment* resembles Dryden's *King Arthur* in that it involves Arthur's love for a woman, in this case Merlin's daughter Imogen, who is also loved by his Saxon rival Hengist.

Spenser's *Faerie Queene* and Arthurian Romance and Epic

While most of the literature of the sixteenth to eighteenth centuries devoted to Arthur derives from the chronicle tradition, the influence of romance is not entirely absent. The most important and the best work in the romance tradition is *The Faerie Queene* by Edmund Spenser (1552–99). Influenced by the Italian epics of Boiardo and Ariosto as well as by English medieval romance, *The Faerie Queene* carries the spirit of medieval romance into the English Renaissance. Just as Ariosto used his epic to praise the Estes, so Spenser used his to glorify Elizabeth and her Tudor heritage. Begun in the 1570s, the poem was little more than half finished when Spenser died in 1599. Of the twelve books that traditionally comprise an epic, he completed six and part of a seventh, each of which dealt with a particular virtue (holiness, temperance, chastity, etc.). Spenser's poem is an allegory, with each of the main characters representing a virtue or vice or some abstract quality. A key figure in Spenser's scheme, Arthur represents magnificence, or the quality of being great souled, which contains within it all the other virtues. After having had a vision of the Fairy Queen (Gloriana, who represents "Glory" but also stands for Queen Elizabeth), Arthur as a knight errant rides in search of her in the allegorical world Spenser created. He plays a crucial role both in the literal, heroic action of the poem and in its religious and political allegory. In Book I, Arthur slays the giant Orgoglio and frees the Red Cross Knight from his prison. Similarly, he must save Sir Guyon in Book II, in which Arthur also defeats Maleger, the leader of the vices attacking the castle of Alma, which represents the soul. Arthur also slays Corflambo, who represents the burning of lust. And he saves Belge, signifying the Low Countries, from the tyrant Gerioneo, signifying Spain, and destroys the monster, representing Roman Catholicism, under the idol set up by Gerioneo in a church. Had the poem been completed, Arthur no doubt would have had equally important adventures assisting other knights and damsels in distress before ultimately being united with Gloriana. Their union would have alluded to the Tudor myth of descent from Arthur and suggested that Elizabeth had brought back to England the glory of her famous ancestor.

At a time when the traditional medieval romances were considered old-fashioned and therefore no longer a viable form, Spenser revitalized the Arthurian material by structuring it around the largely Aristotelian concepts of virtue and thus appealing to the classical interests of his age. But even in this supreme romance, the age's interest in chronicle is apparent: in Canto 10 of Book II, Arthur and Guyon discover in the castle of Alma two books, a history of Fairyland and another called *Briton Moniments*, in which Arthur reads an account of the kings of Britain from its founding by Brutus up to Uther Pendragon. At this point, the chronicle breaks off abruptly, obviously because Arthur, the next king, has not yet ascended to the throne. Later, in Book III, Canto 3, when Britomart visits the cave where Merlin has been imprisoned by the Lady of the Lake, Merlin continues the account of the British kings from Artegall to Cadwallader. Spenser's remarkable *Brut* links his romance to the historical and political texts and concerns of the time. In addition to the adventures of Arthur and the predictions of Merlin, Arthurian elements in the poem include a young Tristram (in Book 6) and a quest for the Blatant Beast, modeled on the Questing Beast of Arthurian romance; and other Arthurian figures might have played a role if the romance had been completed.

Besides *The Faerie Queene*, several other popular romances were written, printed, and reprinted from the sixteenth to the eighteenth century. These often blend a few traditional characters, events, and episodes with original elements constructed to meet the needs of the narrative. There is in these tales less of a sense of an authorized narrative that restrains or shapes the authors' choices than one finds, for example, in nineteenth-century Arthurian poems or twentieth-century novels. *The Famous Historie of Chinon of England* (1597) by Christopher Middleton is the story of Chinon, son of Cador, Duke of Cornwall. After a foolish and misspent youth, Chinon is inspired to change his ways by the valor of Lancelot, who defeats the son of the Sultan of Babylon and thus wins the beautiful maiden Celestina for Sir Triamore. Employing Latinate sentence structures side by side with a heavily alliterated prose, *Chinon of England* draws on medieval romance, classical literature, Christian belief, and folklore, all filtered – or rather unfiltered – by the author's imagination. The jumble of motifs can be exemplified by a scene in which Oboram, king of the fairies, leads Chinon to a sword, originally made for Julius Caesar but destined by God for another use when Caesar is killed in the Senate. The sword is stuck in a rock from which Lancelot, Tristram, and Triamore are unable to draw it; but Chinon does so easily. The romance may be based on the play about Chinon recorded in Philip Henslowe's *Diary* as having been performed in 1595 and 1596.

The Most Pleasant History of Tom a Lincolne, a romance by Richard Johnson (?1573–?1659), was published in two parts, the first of which was printed in 1599, the second in 1607 – though the earliest surviving edition is the sixth, printed in 1631 (Hirsch 1978). A popular tale, it went through at least thirteen editions by 1704. Like *Chinon of England*, *Tom a Lincolne* overlays onto the Arthurian world numerous romance motifs. Tom is the illegitimate son of King Arthur and Angellica, daughter of the Earl of London. Arthur leaves him to be raised by a shepherd from Lincoln named Antonio. To exercise his martial skills, Tom forms an outlaw band that, reminiscent of Robin Hood and his greenwood followers, lives on Barnesdale Heath by robbing travelers. Tom visits Fayrie-land, journeys to the realm of Prester John, marries his daughter Anglitora, is later killed by her, and is avenged by his son, who has been made aware of the murder by Tom's ghost.

Another prose romance to treat Arthur is *The Famous History of That Most Renowned Christian Worthy Arthur King of the Britaines, and His Famous Knights of the Round Table*. Written by Martin Parker (d. ?1656), who was known as a writer of ballads, *The Famous History* was published posthumously in 1660. The romance briefly recounts Arthur's birth, Merlin's tutoring, Arthur's ascension to the throne, his defeat of the Saxons, his foreign victories, and his founding of the Round Table. Parker names all one hundred and fifty knights who sat at the table, only some of whom are traditional members of Arthur's court. In the final movement of the tale, Arthur leads his knights to Palestine and achieves "the total rout of the whole Pagan host" (Parker 1660: 18). Hearing of Mordred's treachery, Arthur must return to Britain, where both he and Mordred are slain in the final battle.

Brittains Glory (1684), a prose romance attributed to John Shirley (fl. 1680–1702), presents itself as history and asserts the historicity of Arthur, even though, as the address "To the Reader" declares, "some envious Aliens have endeavoured to prove there never was such a man." It also tells the story of Arthur by blending conventional and non-conventional elements. It begins with Merlin's assistance in his conception; recounts Arthur's defeating the Saxons, conquering Norway, Denmark, and France; marrying Geneura, daughter of the king of Denmark, who bears him a son; and then mounting a crusade in which he takes Joppa and conquers Jerusalem. The author makes the point that this is "the first time" Jerusalem was "taken by the Christians" (Shirley 1684: 20), thus ascribing to Arthur a feat usually credited to another of the Nine Worthies, Godfrey of Bouillon. Arthur must return to fight in Britain once again because, having heard rumors of Arthur's death, the Saxons broke their word and even forced Arthur's queen and son to flee to Wales. He subdues them and then pursues good works, such as building monasteries, visiting the sick, and founding schools and colleges, as well as studying the "Seven Liberal Sciences" (23) until his death.

As is seen in *The Faerie Queene* and a number of other works discussed above, there are often political implications to the Arthurian work of the period. "The sixteenth century had seen the use of the Arthurian myth for 'nationalistic' purposes by the Tudors, and the seventeenth by the Stuarts. It had underpinned the ruling dynasties, serving as a model for the monarch as a defender of England and of Protestantism, and as a model of chivalry for the aristocracy" (Ortenberg 2006: 147). Even the much-maligned epic poems by Sir Richard Blackmore (d. 1729), *Prince Arthur* (1695) and *King Arthur* (1697), present in Arthur a model of the monarch. The earlier epic presents Arthur's coming to power as a thinly veiled allegory of the triumph of William of Orange. In the later, Arthur's conquest in Gaul represents the defeat of Louis XIV by William. Blackmore blends content and formal elements from Geoffrey of Monmouth, Vergil, and Milton to create his poems, which are artistically inelegant but which are interesting as chauvinistic comments on contemporary events.

Ballads

The antiquarian impulse of the eighteenth century included a renewed interest in folk ballads and medieval romances. The most influential collection of ballads was *Reliques of Ancient English Poetry* compiled in 1765 by Bishop Thomas Percy (1729–1811). Percy's collection contained a wide range of material from the Middle Ages and the Renaissance, including Thomas Deloney's Arthurian ballad, here called "Sir Lancelot du Lake" (but elsewhere titled "The Noble Acts of King Arthur and the Knights of the Round Table, with the Valiant Atchievements of Sir Lancelot du Lake"), "King Ryence's Challenge," "King Arthur's Death," "The Legend of King Arthur" (a synopsis of the chronicle version of the story of Arthur), "The Marriage of Sir Gawaine," and "The Boy and the Mantle." These and other ballads and romances in Percy's popular anthology reintroduced the reading public to a variety of medieval themes. In addition, Percy defended medieval "romance" (a term he used almost interchangeably with "ballad") in his introduction to the third volume. Summarizing the Arthurian romance *Libius Disconius* (*Libeaus Desconus*) to show the courage and nobility of Gawain's son, he concluded that the romance is "as regular in its conduct, as any of the finest poems of classical antiquity" (Percy 1765: 3.xvi). Percy contended that though medieval romances are "full of the exploded fictions of Chivalry," they "exhibit no mean attempts at Epic Poetry" (3.xii). This linking of the romances, which often contain the "rich ore of an Ariosto or a Tasso" buried "among the rubbish and dross of barbarous times" (3.ix), with the epic suggests that eighteenth-century literary and moral concerns can be satisfied by the medieval texts.

Some works responding to Percy's *Reliques* were less than accepting of the merits of medieval literature. The burlesque opera *The Marriage of Sir Gawaine* (1782) by John Seally (1741/2–1795), for example, was dedicated "to those who love antiquity for its nonsense more than for its sense." But more significant was the imprimatur that Percy's collection and judgments gave to the publishing of medieval literature. He thus paved the way for the antiquarian/scholarly activity of the early nineteenth century that led to the publication of collections such as Joseph Ritson's *Ancient Engleish Metrical Romanceës* (1802), which included *Libeaus Desconus*, the romance that Percy praised, as well as *Ywain and Gawain* and *Sir Launfal*; and George Ellis's (1753–1815) *Specimens of Early English Metrical Romances* (1805), which offered summaries of, and quotations of passages from, such works as *Of Arthour and of Merlin* and the Stanzaic *Morte Arthur*. This interest in early Arthurian literature also resulted in the publication of Walter Scott's edition of *Sir Tristrem* (1804), which set the model for scholarly editions of medieval works in the nineteenth century.

Conclusion

The reintroduction of ballad and romance material led ultimately to a new interest in the romance tradition and the publication in 1816 and 1817 of three new editions of Malory, which became the source for the vast majority of the Arthurian literature produced in England and America from the nineteenth century to the present. The sixteenth to the eighteenth centuries did not share this emphasis on Malory, but they did preserve a chronicle tradition, which was widespread and often controversial, largely because of the use of the legend for political and propagandistic purposes. The name of Arthur and some of his deeds remained current through topographical works. Drama and popular culture also kept Arthur and Merlin in the public consciousness. An examination of Arthurian literature in the sixteenth to eighteenth centuries thus confirms that this was not a period of decline but rather a period when the chronicle rather than the romance tradition was dominant, when Arthur was frequently associated with political concerns, and when Arthurian matter was treated, albeit in ways less familiar to contemporary audiences than reworkings of Malory, by a wide range of authors.

PRIMARY SOURCES

Aikman, J. (trans.) (1827). *The history of Scotland, translated from the Latin of George Buchanan; with notes, and a continuation to the Union in the reign of Queen Anne*. Glasgow: Blackie, Fullarton & Co.

Anon. (1630). *Tom Thumbe, his life and death*. London: For John Wright.

Blackmore, R. (1695). *Prince Arthur: An heroick poem in ten books*. London: Awnsham & John Churchill.

Blackmore, R. (1697). *King Arthur: An heroick poem in twelve books*. London: Awnsham & John Churchil.

Camden, W. (1594). *Britannia*. London: Georg Bishop. (Original work published 1586.)

Chambers, R. W. & Batho, E. C. (eds) (1938, 1941). *John Bellenden. The chronicles of Scotland compiled by Hector Boece*, 2 vols. STS 3rd ser., nos. 10 & 15. Edinburgh: William Blackwood.

Churchill, W. (1675). *Divi Britannici: Being a remark upon the lives of all the kings of this isle from the year of the world 2855, unto the year of grace 1660*. London: Thomas Roycroft.

Churchyard, T. (1587). *The worthines of Wales*. London: G. Robinson. Repr. New York: Burt Franklin, 1967.

Constable, A. (trans.) (1892). *John Major. A history of Greater Britain as well England as Scotland*. Scottish History Society, vol. 10. Edinburgh: T. & A. Constable, for the Scottish History Society.

Dearing, V. A. (ed.) (1996). *King Arthur or The British Worthy*. In *The works of John Dryden*, vol. 16. Berkeley, CA: University of California Press, pp. 1–69.

Ellis, G. (ed.) (1805). *Specimens of early English metrical romances, chiefly written during the early part of the fourteenth century; to which is prefixed an historical introduction, intended to illustrate the rise and progress of romantic composition in France and England*, 3 vols. London: Longman, Hurst, Rees, & Orme.

Ellis, H. (ed.) (1807). *Holinshed's chronicles of England, Scotland, and Ireland*, 6 vols. London: Printed for J. Johnson et al.

Ellis, H. (ed.) (1846). *Polydore Vergil's English History, Vol. I., containing the first eight books, comprising the period prior to the Norman Conquest*. Camden Society vol. 46. London: J. B. Nichols & Son.

Fogle, F. (ed.) (1971). *The history of Britain*. In *Complete prose works of John Milton*, vol. 5, part 1. New Haven, CT: Yale University Press.

Garrick, D. (1770). *King Arthur or The British Worthy*. London: W. Strahan.

Hebel, J. W. (ed.) (1933). *Michael Drayton. Works*, vol. 4. Oxford: Basil Blackwell.

Herford, C. H., Simpson, P., & Simpson, E. (eds) (1952). *The speeches at Prince Henries barriers*. In *The works of Ben Jonson*, vol. 7. Oxford: Clarendon Press, pp. 323–36.

Heywood, T. (1641). *The life of Merlin, surnamed Ambrosius; his prophecies and predictions interpreted, and their truth made good by our English annals: Being a chronological history of all the kings and memorable passages of this kingdom, from Brute to the reign of King Charles*. London: J. Okes.

Hilton, W. (1776). *Arthur, monarch of the Britons: A tragedy*. In *Poetical works*, vol. 2. Newcastle upon Tyne: T. Saint.

Hirsch, R. S. M. (ed.) (1978). *Richard Johnson. The most pleasant history of Tom a Lincolne*. Columbia, SC: for the Newberry Library.

Hole, R. (1789). *Arthur or the northern enchantment: A poetical romance in seven books*. London: G. G. J. & J. Robinson.

Hughes, T. (1912). *The misfortunes of Arthur*. In J. W. Cunliffe (ed.), *Early English classical tragedies*. Oxford: Clarendon Press, pp. 217–96.

Hume, D. (1850). *The history of England from the invasion of Julius Cæsar to the revolution in 1688*, vol. 1 (of 6). New York: Harper & Brothers.

Ireland, W. H. (1832). *Vortigern: An historical drama*. London: Joseph Thomas.

Mead, W. E. (ed.) (1925). *Christopher Middleton. The famous historie of Chinon of England*. EETS o. s. 165. London: Humphrey Milford, Oxford University Press, for the Early English Text Society.

Morgan, C. (1783). *Poems*. Cambridge: J. Archdeacon.

Morrissey, L. J. (ed.) (1970). *Henry Fielding. Tom Thumb and the tragedy of tragedies*. Berkeley, CA: University of California Press.

P[arker], M[artin] (1660). *The famous history of that most renowned Christian worthy Arthur King of the Britaines, and his famous Knights of the Round Table*. London: Francis Coles.

Percy, T. (compiler) (1765). *Reliques of ancient English poetry*, 3 vols. London: J. Dodsley.

Phillips, E. (1736). *A new dramatic entertainment called the royal chace or Merlin's Cave*. London: T. Wood.

Ritson, J. (1802). *Ancient Engleish metrical romanceës*. London: G. & W. Nicol.

Ritson, J. (1825). *The life of King Arthur: From ancient historians and authentic documents*. London: Payne & Foss.

Robinson, R. (trans.) (1925). *John Leland. Assertio Inclytissimi Arturii* ["The Assertion of King Arthur"]. In *The famous historie of Chinon of England together with the Assertion of King Arthure*.

EETS o. s. 165. London: Humphrey Milford, for the Early English Text Society.

Roche, T. P. Jr (ed.), with the assistance of O'Donnell, C. P. Jr (1981). *Edmund Spenser. The Faerie Queene.* New Haven, CT: Yale University Press.

Rowley, W. (1662). *The birth of Merlin, or, The childe hath found his father as it hath been several times acted with great applause. Written by William Shakespear and William Rowley.* London: Printed by Tho. Johnson for Francis Kirkman & Henry Marsh.

Seally, J. (May 1782; July 1782). *The marriage of Sir Gawaine. The European Magazine*, 320–24; 18–21.

S[hirley], J[ohn] (1684). *Brittains glory: or, The history of the life and death of K. Arthur, and the adventures of the Knights of the Round Table: Giving a relation of their heroick exploits and victories in many lands.* London: Printed by H. B. for J. Wright, J. Clark, W. Thackeray, & T. Passinger.

Skene, W. F. (ed.) & Skene, F. J. H. (trans.) (1993). *John of Fordun's Chronicle of the Scottish nation*, 2 vols. Lampeter: Llanerch. (Original work published 1872.)

Stow, J. (1580). *The chronicles of England from Brute vnto this present yeare of Christ 1580.* London: By Henry Bynneman for Ralphe Newberie.

Swift, J. (1992). A famous prediction of Merlin, the British Wizard, written above a thousand years ago, and relating to the year 1709. In A. Lupack (ed.), *Modern Arthurian literature.* New York: Garland, pp. 81–4.

Theobald, L. (1734). *The vocal parts of an entertainment call'd Merlin, or, The devil of Stone-Henge.* London: John Watts.

Thompson, A. (trans.) (1718). *Geoffrey of Monmouth. The British history, translated into English from the Latin of Jeffrey of Monmouth. With a large preface concerning the authority of the history.* London: J. Bowyer.

Turnbull, W. B. (ed.) (1858). *William Stewart. The buik of the croniclis of Scotland or A metrical version of the history of Hector Boece.* Rolls ser. 6, part 2 (of 3). London: Longman, Brown, Green, Longmans, & Roberts.

Warton, T. (1777). *Poems: A new edition.* London: T. Becket.

Whitaker, J. (1771–5). *The history of Manchester*, 2 vols. London: Joseph Johnson.

REFERENCES AND FURTHER READING

Brinkley, R. F. (1970). *Arthurian legend in the seventeenth century.* New York: Octagon. (Original work published 1932.)

Colton, J. (1976). Merlin's Cave and Queen Caroline: Garden art as political propaganda. *Eighteenth-Century Studies*, 10, 1–20.

Fletcher, R. H. & Loomis, R. S. (1966). *The Arthurian material in the chronicles: Especially those in Great Britain and France.* New York: Burt Franklin.

Jones, E. (1944). *Geoffrey of Monmouth 1640–1800.* Berkeley, CA: University of California Press.

Merriman, J. D. (1973). *The flower of kings: A study of the Arthurian legend in England between 1485 and 1835.* Lawrence, KS: University Press of Kansas.

Michelsson, E. (1999). *Appropriating King Arthur: The Arthurian legend in English drama and entertainments 1485–1625.* Uppsala: Uppsala University.

Millican, C. B. (1932). *Spenser and the Table Round: A study in the contemporaneous background for Spenser's use of the Arthurian legend.* Cambridge, MA: Harvard University Press.

Ortenberg, V. (2006). *In search of the Holy Grail: The quest for the Middle Ages.* Hambledon: Continuum.

Ven-Ten Bensel, E. F. W. M. van der (1925). *The character of King Arthur in English literature.* Amsterdam: H. J. Paris.

24

Scholarship and Popular Culture in the Nineteenth Century

David Matthews

As we saw in the previous chapter, the fortunes of King Arthur fell to a low point in the later seventeenth century and in the eighteenth. Although, as Alan Lupack has explained (chapter 23), the Arthurian chronicle tradition remained visible in the eighteenth century, Arthurian romance was barely known after the Renaissance. Along with much else in vernacular medieval literature, the Arthurian cycle was generally regarded as lightweight and was belittled – literally so, in the case of Henry Fielding's mock-heroic play, *Tom Thumb* (1730). As a legendary character, Arthur was often ranked with such folk heroes as Bevis of Hampton and Guy of Warwick, their fabulous exploits retold in condensed versions in ballads or cheap chapbooks adorned with woodcuts. Most of the medieval Arthurian verse romances, such as *Sir Gawain and the Green Knight*, were completely unknown at this time, while the central English prose work, that of Thomas Malory, was printed by William Stansby in 1634 but then not again until the early nineteenth century. By 1800, it must have been difficult for readers of ordinary means to get hold of a copy of Malory. The poet Robert Southey – whose family was not well off – recalled that as a schoolboy, he "possessed a wretchedly imperfect copy" (Parins 1988: 99).

There was a rising interest in romances in the last third of the eighteenth century, however, so that by 1802 several shorter Arthurian romances had been printed for the first time. The publication of these verse texts was followed in 1816 by two fresh editions of Malory's prose work: one in the Walker's British Classics series with the title *The History of the Renowned Prince Arthur*, the other *La Mort D'Arthur*, probably edited by an antiquarian named Joseph Haslewood. Both of these were in the small duodecimo format and relatively cheap; the following year a more lavish production in a two-volume quarto edition appeared, *The Byrth, Lyf, and Actes of Kyng Arthur*, with an introduction by Southey. As readers in 1817 could have remarked, you wait nearly two centuries for an edition of Malory and then three come all at once.

In the next two decades, numerous Arthurian verse romances were discovered and published. In addition, non-English Arthurian material produced in Britain began to appear: Nennius' Latin *Historia Brittonum*, the earliest Arthurian source, published with a translation in 1819; Béroul's Anglo-Norman *Tristan* (marginally Arthurian), published in 1823; further versions of *Tristan* edited by Francisque Michel in 1835, and the most important source of all, Geoffrey of Monmouth's Latin chronicle *Historia Regum Britanniae*, published by J. A. Giles in 1842. In 1849, Lady Charlotte Guest completed her translation of the Welsh *Mabinogion*, which contains some Arthurian material. A minority interest at the beginning of the nineteenth century, by its end King Arthur was one of the most famous figures in all of British legend, his story retold in countless fresh forms, the images of his knights represented again and again, his exploits restaged from the meanest circus to the writing of the greatest poet of the age, Alfred Tennyson.

How this happened – how the generally ridiculed figure of the late eighteenth century became the famous paragon of British history by the end of the century – is the subject of this chapter and the next. Inga Bryden's chapter (25) looks at this process in the literature of the nineteenth century. The present chapter looks at the new Arthurian scholarship. At the same time, this chapter considers some aspects of the popular appropriation of Arthur. These two things might seem to be far apart. As I aim to show, scholarly and popular Arthurianism are not so easy to disentangle.

The Antiquarian Rediscovery of Romance

Barely known in 1800, by the end of the nineteenth century Thomas Malory's *Morte Darthur* (as it was then generally known) was without doubt the central English Arthurian text. Malory's version was *the* version and Alfred Tennyson's *Idylls of the King*, largely based on Malory, was *the* modernization.

As far back as 1754, writing his *Observations on the Faerie Queene*, Thomas Warton realized that Edmund Spenser was deeply indebted to the *Morte Darthur* as printed by Caxton and had provided a description of Malory's "fabulous history." But for most scholars at the time *poetry* was the highest form of literary art, so romance in *prose* was of less interest to them. It was Warton's later work, his *History of English Poetry* (1774–81), which had the more immediate impact on Arthurian studies. In it, Warton unearthed dozens of unread medieval romances. These texts, largely disregarded by authoritative critics, were taken up after Warton by the antiquarians Thomas Percy, John Pinkerton, and Joseph Ritson, who all produced anthologies of ballads and romances in which they included Arthurian material.

These anthologies are not easily defined. They were not popular in the sense that the chapbooks were: cheap booklets and printed pamphlets aimed at an uneducated market. Neither were they scholarly in the modern sense. They were an amalgam: aimed at, and in some cases achieving, wide distribution, at the same time as they made a claim on scholarship. Though Warton was a professor at Oxford University, most of the antiquarians were not scholars in secure positions but men seeking patronage. While classical literature remained central to education at the time, such men as Percy and Ritson delved into medieval writing, hoping to find something new. Alan Lupack has already discussed the inclusion by Thomas Percy of six Arthurian pieces in his famous and influential ballad anthology, *The Reliques of Ancient English Poetry* (1765). Along with Warton's work the success of the *Reliques* sparked off a quest for other Arthurian writings that might be lying in the manuscript repositories in the universities and the British Museum, which scholars were only just beginning to tackle. Hence in 1792 the Scottish poet and antiquarian John Pinkerton printed the northern alliterative Arthurian poems *The Awntyrs off Arthure* (under the title "Sir Gawan and Sir Galaron of Galloway") and *Gawan and Gologras* in his *Scotish Poems, Reprinted from Scarce Editions*. In 1802, partly as an attempt to better Percy's *Reliques*, the eccentric scholar Joseph Ritson produced his *Ancient Engleish Metrical Romanceës*, an elegant anthology which included the metrical Arthurian romances of *Ywain and Gawain*, *Launfal*, and *Libeaus Desconus* as well as some passages from Arthurian chronicle. Around the same time, Walter Scott edited the romance of *Sir Tristrem* from the famous Auchinleck manuscript (now National Library of Scotland Advocates 19.2.1). This appeared in 1804 and, as Lupack has already remarked, "set the model for scholarly editions of medieval works."

All of this material was completely unknown until these scholars brought it to light, so the appearance of such works constituted a new scholarly phenomenon. Nevertheless, while these fresh editions certainly had an influence, their impact was very specific. Percy's *Reliques* was a popular success which went through many editions. But most of the other works were not widely read, even Scott's edition of *Sir Tristrem* (Scott's career as wildly popular poet and novelist lay ahead of him). At the beginning of the nineteenth century, there were few people who could read Middle English verse with any facility and probably even fewer who appreciated it (always excepting Chaucer). Consequently the readership was principally among a small group of antiquarians. Percy, in later life, distanced himself from the *Reliques*; Ritson never achieved popular success. Scott, having produced his scholarly edition and before that, his antiquarian anthology *Minstrelsy of the Scottish Border* (1802), found it much more rewarding to write pseudo-antique poetry and fiction set in the Middle Ages and the seventeenth century.

The antiquarians promoted the genre of romance partly in reaction against the dominant neo-classicism of the eighteenth century. Warton, the greatest champion of romance of the age before Walter Scott, conceded that most good taste and criticism flowed from neo-classicism and its emphasis on realism. But, he suggested, something had been lost with the rejection of medieval culture, for all its superstitions. "We have parted with extravagancies that are above propriety," he wrote, "with incredibilities that are more acceptable than truth, and with fictions that are more valuable than reality" (Warton 1774–81: 2.463). Romance, more than any other genre, embodied the spirit of these fictions.

The genre was, as a result, usually viewed as "other" to everything that was known and familiar. Where the novel tended to be urban, bourgeois, contemporary, and realistic, romance offered wilderness, aristocracy, past times, and fancy. There was much emphasis at this time on the derivation of romances from the north of England and Scotland – far from the increasingly industrialized urban centers in which most of the antiquarians lived. Scott himself argued strongly that the romance of *Sir Tristrem* (in fact a northern English work) was a Scottish composition. For Scott this was partly a question of national honor: he thought (wrongly) that *Tristrem* was the earliest version of the story written in English and he wanted to claim it for Scotland. But it was not that alone that motivated him. His argument that *Tristrem* was a border composition was typical of the view of romance as a literary form in the margins, from the edge of the cultured world. This is an idea that much Arthurian romance itself plays with, of course, by depicting knights going out from the cultured world of the court at Camelot into dangerous forested otherworlds. The idea that romances preserved a vision of a wilder pre-industrial Britain was a pervasive one in the era of the rise of mechanized labor and factories.

By 1816–17, then, and the reappearance of Thomas Malory, there was already a scholarly tradition of half a century's standing. It was, however, a tradition that had most influence when its findings were exploited *outside* scholarship, in poetry and fiction.

Arthur in Scholarship, History, and Popular Culture to 1850

The second decade of the nineteenth century was a time of particularly intense bibliophilia, and early interest in Malory came not so much from a concern with literature as from a bibliographical concern with the book itself. "Of all the productions of Caxton's press," wrote the bibliographer Thomas Dibdin in 1810, the Malory edition "is probably the most curious, amusing, and scarce" (Parins 1988: 84). Literary appreciation of Malory's prose work was a little slower to develop. George Ellis, in his retold versions of romance published as *Specimens of Early English Metrical Romances* in 1805, referred to Malory's work as "a mere compilation" (Ellis 1805: 1.308). It is significant that once Malory was established, a great deal of activity was devoted to turning his work into poetry – to the approval of many. "No one who has taken the trouble to compare the old prose with the modern verse," wrote Samuel Cheetham, comparing Malory with Tennyson's *Idylls of the King* in the *Contemporary Review*, "can fail to admire the skill with which the somewhat crude originals have been transformed by the brilliant word-painting of the poet" (Parins 1988: 172–3).

At the beginning of the century, Malory's critical reputation – insofar as he had one – was low. Perhaps the best-known judgment on him was that of Roger Ascham, who in *The Scholemaster* (1570) condemned the work as consisting of "open mans slaughter, and bold bawdrye" (Parins 1988: 57). But the appearance of the Malory editions of 1816–17 – particularly the two duodecimos of 1816 – did allow a new appreciation. As memories of the Napoleonic wars faded, there was perhaps a greater receptiveness to warfare reimagined as a highly codified, chivalric pursuit. Certainly by the beginning of the Victorian period these publications were beginning to have a popular impact. The famous Eglinton Tournament of 1839, in which gentlemen and aristocrats staged a full-scale medieval event over three days, owed more to an understanding of the Middle Ages as derived from Walter Scott's (non-Arthurian) *Ivanhoe* than from the actual reading of medieval texts. Nevertheless, the extravagant event made it clear that there was a developing taste for the spectacles of jousting and medieval feasting.

In turn, those who were alarmed at the spread of capitalism and the prospect of an increasingly mechanized Britain would frequently turn to a more romantic past. Thomas Carlyle valued medieval feudalism in which the aristocracy had a role of leadership, warning that "with the supreme triumph of Cash, a changed time has entered; there must a changed Aristocracy enter" (Carlyle 1971: 194). John Ruskin, advocating thirteenth-century architecture as the supreme English style, argued that there was as much "mechanical ingenuity required to build a cathedral as to cut a tunnel or contrive a locomotive" (1907: 217). With the Middle Ages revalued in this way, it was possible for readers to look past the killing and adultery in the Arthurian story to the code of chivalry that, however much it is broken, still serves as a guide for behavior. Robert Southey, introducing the 1817 edition of Malory, admitted that "the ferocious spirit of the times" often showed through in the *Morte Darthur*, but he noted that medieval Europe was "full of cruelties" and hence "it must be considered as a great merit in the romance writers, that they have not introduced them more frequently; that they have sometimes reprehended them, and that in their ideal heroes they held up for imitation fairer models of heroic virtue than were to be found in real life" (Parins 1988: 100).

The idea of *imitation* is important. In medieval romance as well as in medieval architecture or society, there were imitable lessons. The idea that one might imitate Arthurian heroes was a key theme in an important Victorian phenomenon: the notion that Arthurian chivalry should inform modern behavior (Girouard 1981). In 1822, for example, a young man named Kenelm Henry Digby, steeped in medieval romance of all kinds, published *The Broad Stone of Honour: Or, Rules for the Gentlemen of England*. A second edition appeared a year later and further expanded editions, now subtitled "The True Sense and Practice of Chivalry," appeared after Digby's conversion to Catholicism in 1825.

Such works as these could be enormously influential. They depended on the actual medieval romances themselves, but far outstripped those romances in popularity. The scholarly production of Arthurian romances remains then somewhat in the background — essential, but not always well regarded. As the Arthurian metrical romances continued to be discovered and published, there was a growing split between the scholarly and the popular. Many of the romances were published by the book clubs that sprang up in the first half of the nineteenth century. In 1819, Thomas Ponton edited the Stanzaic *Morte Arthur* for the first of these clubs, the Roxburghe. The Scottish antiquarian David Laing reprinted *The Awntyrs off Arthure* in 1822; another Scot, William Turnbull, edited *Arthour and Merlin* for the Abbotsford Club (named in honor of Walter Scott and his home) in 1838. The following year Joseph Stevenson edited *Lancelot of the Laik* for the Maitland Club and Frederic Madden, then Assistant Keeper of the Manuscripts in the British Museum, produced the first edition of what would become the most celebrated English romance, *Sir Gawain and the Green Knight*, along with other Gawain material. In 1842 – when Tennyson published his *Morte D'Arthur*, forerunner of the *Idylls* – editions of *The Avowynge of King Arthur*, *Sir Perceval of Galles*, and *Sir Degrevant* all appeared. Important non-Anglophone material published at this period has already been mentioned: the *Historia Brittonum* attributed to Nennius, Béroul's *Tristan*, Geoffrey of Monmouth's *Historia Regum Britanniae*.

It is notable that in the romance publications listed here Scottish editors and Scottish book clubs (the Maitland, Abbotsford, and Bannatyne Clubs, for example) were influential. The *Historia Brittonum*, Béroul's *Tristan*, and the *Mabinogion* also concern British, rather than English, literature. For many, Arthurian literature was still attractive because of the way it (supposedly) came from the margins of Britain. It is interesting that an old tradition maintained that Thomas Malory was a Welshman; this was adopted for some time in the nineteenth century until disproven. It is also intriguing that Frederic Madden, one of the best scholars of the period, insisted that *Sir Gawain and the Green Knight* (in fact composed in the northwest of England) was a Scottish poem. He might have done this rather cynically, keen to make the poem appeal to Walter Scott and his Bannatyne Club. But he might genuinely have thought that even if the poem as we have it was English, its strange language suggested an earlier origin north of the border.

It is hardly surprising that Arthur should not have a particularly English appeal at this point. There was, of course, nothing English about him. The historical Arthur, if he existed, actually fought *against* the ancestors of the English. This was something that was quite well understood at the time. As Inga Bryden has noted in an earlier publication, in the eighteenth century interest in Arthur suffered as more was learned about the real history of the Anglo-Saxon period (Bryden 2005: 16). But the numerous histories of Anglo-Saxon England that began to appear in the nineteenth century were generally prepared to accept a historical Arthur, while doing away with his romance exploits. "The authentic actions of Arthur have been so disfigured by the gorgeous additions of the minstrels and of Jeffry," wrote Sharon Turner in his *History of the Anglo-Saxons*, "that many writers have denied that he ever lived." Turner attempted to distinguish "the Arthur of tradition from the Arthur of history," believing that "when all the fictions are removed and those incidents only are retained which the sober criticism of history sanctions with its approbation, a fame ample enough to interest the judicious, and to perpetuate his honourable memory, will still continue to bloom" (Turner 1799–1805: 1.228, vii). Francis Palgrave, in his *Rise and Progress of the English Commonwealth* (1832), stated that "[w]e can neither doubt the existence of this Chieftain, nor believe in the achievements which have been ascribed to him" (quoted in Bryden 2005: 26). In 1825, a posthumous work, *The Life of King Arthur*, by the anthologist Ritson attempted (without great success) to trace a "true" life of Arthur, separating it from the fables produced by Geoffrey of Monmouth. Overall there was a general understanding that the later medieval writings about Arthur were fictions, albeit fictions from which – as Digby's subtitles seem to forecast – a central truth about chivalric behavior could be derived.

The underlying acknowledgment that Arthur was in truth a Romano-Celtic figure might have hampered acceptance of him as an English hero. Publications of this period are not overtly concerned with national pride or with locating the Arthurian heritage in patriotic terms. Even as British imperialism was expanding, Arthur was upheld as representing something from a simpler and perhaps more authentic time – but not particularly as an English icon. An "Englished" Arthur, however, was not far away. By the time his edition of *Sir Gawain* appeared, Madden was already engaged on editing the two texts of Layamon's *Brut*, which contains the earliest English version of the Arthur story. This massive undertaking eventually saw publication in 1847 by the Society of Antiquaries. The publication is an interesting moment in Arthurian studies and medieval studies more widely. It was thoroughly scholarly and clearly not destined for popular reception. Because of its relatively difficult language and alien verse forms, Layamon's *Brut* has never been widely read, though it could be regarded as equal in importance to Malory (and equally interesting to read, if more difficult). At the time of its appearance, Tennyson was already embarked on his Arthurian poem cycle, influenced chiefly by the *Morte Darthur*. By mid-century, there was a widening split. The scholars had to share Arthur with the poets, novelists, and painters.

Arthurian Expansion in the Later Nineteenth Century

One summer day in 1839, a young woman in London went along with a friend to watch knights tilting – an entertainment she clearly did not regard as particularly unusual. "It was a ridiculous failure," she recorded.

> They almost invariably missed one another, and looked extremely clumsy in their heavy armour. For fear of accidents, which were not very likely to happen, they had their lances sawn across that they might break at a slight shock, and so absurdly particular had they been in this respect that some of the lances broke with their own weight and fell to pieces to the no small amusement of the bystanders. (Bessborough 1950: 93)

These words and the reaction recorded remind us that not everyone took passionately to medieval re-enactments in Victorian England. But the writer, Lady Charlotte Guest, was highly influential in introducing English readers to a slice of the medieval world, through her translation of the Welsh *Mabinogion*. In 1839, she had recently commenced the work, and would complete it ten years later. The tales of the *Mabinogion* are only partly Arthurian (see chapter 9), but they were another influence on Tennyson, alongside Malory. In the middle of the century, Guest's lavish three-volume production took its place alongside the by now substantial available Arthuriana.

By 1850, then, there were various different Arthurs on offer. There were editions of Malory (though, interestingly, there had been no new ones since 1817). There was the Celtic Arthur of the *Mabinogion*; there was the more equivocally British Arthur of Layamon's *Brut*. There was Arthur the *roi fainéant* (the "do-nothing king") of various romances in Middle English. There was also the historical Arthur, about whom, most historians conceded, little could reliably be said.

The second half of the nineteenth century saw the expansion of interest in medieval literature of all kinds. At the same time as the public at large became more aware of it, however, medieval literature was also being slowly professionalized and by the century's end had been brought under the influence of academe. A great deal has now been written about Frederick Furnivall, the founder of the Early English Text Society (EETS) in 1864, which continues publishing Middle English texts to this day. Furnivall, not himself an academic, was a wildly energetic man who combined some basic expertise in medieval English literature and a strong patriotic sense that England ought to be investing more in that literature, with boundless energy for creating subscription publishing societies (the EETS was only the first of many). Furnivall's interest in the medieval past was originally prompted by Arthurian literature, and he became interested in that first through Tennyson's 1842 poem *Morte D'Arthur* and then by his own investigation into the medieval originals (Matthews 1999: 142). Furnivall is an early example of someone led by Tennyson's poetry back to the real Middle Ages (and hence of the intimate connections between scholarly and non-scholarly Arthurianisms). He was also a great believer in the spread of (British) civilization, which he saw as firmly founded in the medieval past.

Furnivall founded the EETS in 1864 with the design of publishing two things: medieval English Arthurian literature and works illustrating the state of the dialects of medieval English. These two interests suggest that, just as the late-eighteenth-century antiquarians had been, Furnivall was initially interested in medieval literature as otherworldly, fantastic, and as coming from the margins of England. But his concerns were in fact far broader than that and the EETS quickly lost its original narrow focus to become a general medieval publishing society. Furnivall himself became no less obsessed with Chaucer, and soon founded a Chaucer Society.

In order to bring previously hidden works to a larger public, Furnivall appealed to English patriotism. In 1870, not long after the founding of EETS and the Chaucer Society, the Franco-Prussian war began. As the war came to an end early the following year, Furnivall was writing one of his annual reports to members of the EETS. He noted that the interest provoked by the war had caused the Society to slow down its work. In what could seem a slightly callous reference to the war (which had just ended disastrously for the French in the siege of Paris), Furnivall invokes "the love of Fatherland that was shown so strikingly by the German nation at the outbreak of the war, and has been called forth from the French during its continuance" to exhort Englishmen to similar levels of patriotism. He was asking them not to go to war, but to edit and read medieval texts (Furnivall 1871: 1).

Setting to work on Arthurian publications, Furnivall edited *Arthur* (1864), the short fifteenth-century verse chronicle found in Longleat MS 55, and later tackled the much bigger job of Henry Lovelich's *History of the Holy Grail* in several volumes between 1874 and 1905. These both appeared in EETS volumes, and were accompanied by the work of others: the Alliterative *Morte Arthure* (1865), edited by Edmund Brock; Lovelich's *Merlin* (1865–99), by Henry Wheatley. Despite Furnivall's own belief in the wide appeal of this material, however, most of it was destined for a very small scholarly readership. Even the Alliterative *Morte* has had to wait until recent times for an appreciative audience. The EETS was a leader in establishing Arthurian literary scholarship, but it was fresh editions of Malory in the second half of the century that had the greatest impact in spreading knowledge of Arthur among a readership at large. Malory's time had clearly come by the 1860s. It was by then no longer a disadvantage that the *Morte Darthur* was prose rather than poetry, given the ascendancy of the novel in the Victorian period. The connection was an obvious one: Sidney Lanier argued that Malory could "be said to have written the first English novel." At the very least – as Ernest Rhys put it in 1886 – "In the history of prose it [the *Morte Darthur*] is most valuable indeed" (Parins 1988: 209, 229). And if poetry was wanted, there was always Tennyson's *Idylls*.

The three Malory editions of 1816–17 seem to have covered the market for a time as it was not until 1858 that the next edition, based on Stansby's 1634 text, appeared, edited by the prolific antiquarian editor Thomas Wright. This text was issued in new editions in 1866 and 1889, while in 1868 Caxton's text was issued under the editorship of Sir Edward Strachey by the influential publishing house Macmillan. A major scholarly edition then appeared in three volumes in 1889–91, edited by the German Oskar Sommer. Numerous republications, based directly either on Caxton or on Sommer's edition, followed in the 1890s and early twentieth century. In 1900 Macmillan again published the *Morte Darthur*, now as part of its Library of English Classics, suggesting canonical status for Malory. At this time, the beginning of the new century, anyone who wanted to could read Malory and, with only a little more effort and expense, the less well-known Arthurian texts as well.

Republication slackened in the twentieth century – interestingly, there was an edition in 1913 but then nothing new for another twenty years. In the 1930s and 1940s, of course, a new cycle of interest was sparked off by the discovery of the Winchester manuscript of Malory's work in 1934 (see chapter 20). The apparent lessening of interest after 1913 could suggest that World War I cured readers' appetites for chivalric sacrifice and endless combat. But of course by then an enormous number of copies of Malory were in circulation and no doubt still being read. The drop in publication fits with a larger pattern for the reception of Middle English texts, in which there was unparalleled interest in the late nineteenth century and the early twentieth, followed by a period of retreat.

It is the case, however, that scholarship and popular reception go, if not hand in hand, then on similar paths in this period. Oskar Sommer's text established much that was new about Malory's sources and was clearly aimed at scholars. It was soon reused, however, by those putting out more popular texts. The distinction between scholarly and popular, though much firmer than in Scott's or Ritson's time, was still not entirely settled. Israel Gollancz, for example, reused Sommer's text for a four-volume edition he published in J. M. Dent's Temple Classics in 1897. Gollancz had been appointed lecturer in English (the first to have the post) at Cambridge the year before, and would become in 1903 professor of English Language and Literature at King's College London. He was a professional academic medievalist, the first in the literary sphere in Britain. But he was clearly comfortable inheriting the popular mission from his mentor, Furnivall. The Temple Classics series was aimed at a general readership, and the publisher, Dent, would later consolidate a hold on the market for popular classics with the establishment of the famous Everyman's Library in 1906. The *Morte Darthur* was re-released as one of the first books in the series; so too was Guest's *Mabinogion*.

This rise in readerly interest which saw the Malorian version of Arthur safely entrenched as English literature by the early twentieth century was linked to shifts that took place in the education system in Britain after the passing of the second Reform Bill in 1867. A growing concern to educate the newly enfranchised classes led to the Education Act of 1870, which created a national, governmentally supervised elementary schooling system, though even before then literacy was on the rise. One outcome was an explosion in children's literature. This was accompanied by anxieties about the effects of literature on the minds of those who previously would have received little or no education. Children's versions of the Arthur story were created at the same time as new editions of the *Morte Darthur* were appearing. One of the best known was *The Boy's King Arthur* produced by the American poet Sidney Lanier in 1880, aimed at boys on both sides of the Atlantic. Even when they were for adults, Malory editions were generally modernized and often abridged. From there it was a short step to the kind of expurgation deemed necessary to make Malory suitable for the young.

Malory's promoters at this period had not followed Furnivall's patriotic line. The Franco-Prussian war, which had so animated Furnivall, was a forerunner of the great twentieth-century conflicts between European nations. In World War I in particular, ideas of chivalry drawn from the nineteenth-century understanding of romance would be prevalent. But Arthurian studies in their development after 1870 were less concerned with patriotism than with the ethical character of Arthurian literature. Whether they were producing their work for children or adults, most editors of Malory at the end of the nineteenth century were concerned less with Arthur's potential as nationalist icon than with the overall text's attitude to sin. This had been, of course, the concern of the very first publisher. Caxton, perhaps already with one eye on the nascent book-buying public, instructed: "Do after the good and leave the evil" (Parins 1988: 49). As we have seen, in the sixteenth century Roger Ascham saw only the evil; late-nineteenth-century publishers and editors were deeply concerned to find the good. The "moral atmosphere" of the work clearly troubled Edward R. Russell in his pamphlet *The Book of King Arthur* (1889):

To what extent the moral atmosphere of *Morte D'Arthur* was that of Sir Thomas Malory's time – the time of Edward the Fourth; to what extent it was merely the moral atmosphere attributed to mythical times and scenes in earlier and cruder romances – to what extent it accurately represented the moral atmosphere of chivalry, when chivalry actually existed – each must decide for himself. (Parins 1988: 241)

Russell did not hesitate to give his own decision, which was that Malory did not come up to the moral level of the Greek or Roman classics. Medieval literature was a regrettable falling away: "Regarded seriously the Book of King Arthur is very much as if men had descended to become interesting dumb animals" (Parins 1988: 250). There was little to be gained from it by imitation: "If the Nineteenth Century has any perplexities which can be solved by the problems of Camelot, it must be in a very babyish condition" (Parins 1988: 250).

This was not the majority view, however. Frederick Ryland, writing about Malory in the *English Illustrated Magazine* in 1888–9, dismissed both Ascham's condemnation and the relevance of classical taste, arguing that "although not absolutely perfect, the ethical theory of the Arthurian epos is a distinctly high one; and the practice does not fall short of the theory in a greater degree than we see among ourselves." There were "conspicuous virtues" in Malory, Ryland argued: "courage, love of justice and hatred of injustice, loyalty, fidelity to promises and to the unspoken obligations implied by friendship and brotherhood, self-control, and disregard of mere bodily ease" (Parins 1988: 265). There were, as Russell's words suggest, many reservations about medieval literature at the time. But most critics were happy to say that standards of morality had to be relative and that not too much could be expected from a medieval work. Such attitudes did not slow the production of modernized and expurgated versions at the century's end, for adult and child readers like.

In the years after 1906 and the Everyman's Library versions of the *Morte Darthur* and *Mabinogion*, even as production of new editions slowed down, the stories of King Arthur and his Knights of the Round Table were already simply part of the British cultural context, likely to form the basic reading of any child (or boy, at least) growing up in the Edwardian period. Anyone who studied English language and literature at university could read Malory and other Arthurian texts in the original, which would not have been possible in the nineteenth century. Such readers might then pass the taste on to their own children. Even the modernist reaction of the 1920s against Victorian medievalism disguises a debt (as such reactions often do) to what overtly it spurns. In its title alone, for example, such a central modernist work as T. S. Eliot's *The Waste Land* (1922) gestures to the Grail story. Eliot himself attributed his interest in the Grail to a reading of Jessie L. Weston's influential *From Ritual to Romance* (1920), a work which is in part an attempt to understand the Arthurian story.

Everyone today knows what a "holy grail" is. Achieving a grail usually involves a quest, and there will probably be some jousting (even if only verbal) along the way. Arthurian metaphors today are pervasive. If we sit down to discuss such metaphors at a conference, we might well do so at a round table. The two final sections of this

Companion examine this pervasive Arthurian popular culture in the later twentieth century, particularly as it is found in novels, films, and games. Such texts obviously depend on the medieval originals of the Arthur story. But they also, crucially, grow out of and are reactions to the nineteenth-century explosion of interest in Arthur. It is true that in recent modernity Arthurian popular culture evidently owes a great deal to medieval texts: such films as MGM's *Knights of the Round Table* (1954) and John Boorman's *Excalibur* (1981) are based on Malory, for example. At the same time, however, recent film, television, and other aspects of popular culture are deeply indebted to the nineteenth century. Ideas of the medieval in current popular culture are filtered through nineteenth-century understanding. The very idea of restaging medieval battles is commonplace today and regarded as a legitimate aspect of scholarship. At the same time, though, as scholars work hard for accuracy in detail in such displays, the actual *idea* of a staged tournament is a thoroughly Victorian one based on popular entertainment going back to Scott's *Ivanhoe*. Even today, then, scholarly and popular retrievals of an imagined Arthurian past remain difficult to disentangle.

PRIMARY SOURCES

Ellis, G. (ed.) (1805). *Specimens of early English metrical romances, chiefly written during the early part of the fourteenth century; to which is prefixed an historical introduction, intended to illustrate the rise and progress of romantic composition in France and England*, 3 vols. London: Longman, Hurst, Rees, & Orme.

Madden, Sir F. (1847). *Layamons Brut, or Chronicle of Britain*. London: Society of Antiquaries.

Percy, T. (ed.) (1996). *Reliques of ancient English poetry* (ed. N. Groom). Facsimile of 1st edn, 1765. London: Routledge/Thoemmes Press.

Ritson, J. (1802). *Ancient Engleish metrical romanceës*, 3 vols. London: G. & W. Nicol.

Ruskin, J. (1907). *Seven lamps of architecture*, 2nd edn. London: Dent.

Scott, W. (1804). *Sir Tristrem: A metrical romance of the thirteenth century*. Edinburgh: Archibald Constable.

REFERENCES AND FURTHER READING

Bessborough, the Earl of (ed.) (1950). *Lady Charlotte Guest: Extracts from her journal 1833–1852*. London: John Murray.

Bryden, I. (2005). *Reinventing King Arthur: The Arthurian legends in Victorian culture*. Aldershot: Ashgate.

Carlyle, T. (1971). Chartism. In A. Shelston (ed.), *Thomas Carlyle: Selected writings*. Harmondsworth: Penguin, pp. 187–96.

Furnivall, F. (1871). *Early English Text Society: Seventh Report of the Committee, February, 1871*. London: Early English Text Society.

Gaines, B. (1974). The editions of Malory in the early nineteenth century. *Papers of the Bibliographical Society of America*, 68, 1–17.

Gaines, B. (1990). *Sir Thomas Malory: An anecdotal bibliography of editions, 1485–1985*. New York: AMS.

Girouard, M. (1981). *The return to Camelot: Chivalry and the English gentleman*. New Haven, CT: Yale University Press.

Groom, N. (1999). *The making of Percy's Reliques*. Oxford: Oxford University Press.

Johnston, A. (1964). *Enchanted ground: The study of medieval romance in the eighteenth century*. London: Athlone.

Mancoff, D. (1995). *The return of King Arthur: The legend through Victorian eyes*. London: Pavilion.

Matthews, D. (1999). *The making of Middle English, 1765–1910*. Minneapolis, MN: University of Minnesota Press.

Merriman, J. D. (1973). *The flower of kings: A study of the Arthurian legend in England between 1485 and 1835*. Lawrence, KS: University Press of Kansas.

Oergel, M. (1998). *The return of King Arthur and the Nibelungen: National myth in nineteenth-century English and German literature*. Berlin: Walter de Gruyter.

Parins, M. J. (1988). *Malory: The critical heritage*. London: Routledge.

Taylor, B. & Brewer, E. (1983). *The return of King Arthur: British and American Arthurian literature since 1800*. Cambridge: Brewer.

Turner, S. (1799–1805). *The history of the Anglo-Saxons*. London: T. Cadell & W. Davies.

Warton, T. (1754). *Observations on the Faerie Queene of Spenser*. London.

Warton, T. (1774–81). *The history of English poetry*. London & Oxford.

25
Arthur in Victorian Poetry

Inga Bryden

The Arthurian revival in Victorian Britain, part of a broader interest in medievalism, was both a literary and a cultural phenomenon. Arthurian themes were appropriated and reinvented in the areas of the visual arts, socio-political commentary, interior decoration, and war memorials, for example. In a literary context, a diverse group of writers resurrected King Arthur: besides key poetic works by Alfred Tennyson, William Morris, Matthew Arnold, and Algernon Swinburne, texts include the novelist and politician Edward Bulwer-Lytton's eclectic epic poem *King Arthur* (1848); Dinah Mulock's (later Mrs Craik) imaginative *Avillion and Other Tales* (1853); the Reverend Robert Hawker's idiosyncratic *The Quest of the Sangraal* (1864); and Sebastian Evans' (journalist, politician, artist) Arthurian poems published under the title *In the Studio: A Decade of Poems* (1875).

Arthurian subject matter (the matter of Britain) was utilized across genres, although far more Arthurian poetry than Arthurian prose fiction was produced. This was partly due to the subject's association with the tradition of writing epic poems; the literary establishment sought to express nationalist sentiment in epic form, which was deemed more appropriate than the newer form of the novel. A constant stream of minor allusions to Arthurian legend in poetry, drama, and prose fiction is evident from 1800, but in the 1830s significant reworkings, such as Tennyson's first Arthurian poems *The Epic: Morte d'Arthur* and *Sir Launcelot and Queen Guinevere: A Fragment*, appeared. By the early 1830s, then, the legends had achieved a "widespread currency" (Simpson 1990: 221). The 1880s were also a significant decade in the history of Arthurian literature as it witnessed the publication of Tennyson's *Poetical Works* (1886) in which the monumental *Idylls of the King* found its final form, besides Swinburne's *Tristram of Lyonesse* (1882), which counterbalanced Tennyson's moral Arthurianism.

Modern critical analysis has focused on Tennyson's *Idylls of the King* and the Pre-Raphaelite group of artists and poets, although discussion of a wider range of Arthurian poetry in the context of Victorian cultural concerns is evident in Roger Simpson's *Camelot Regained* (1990) and Inga Bryden's *Reinventing King Arthur* (2005).

Nineteenth-century British and American Arthurian literature is discussed in Beverly Taylor and Elisabeth Brewer's *The Return of King Arthur* (1983). Additionally, Victorian Arthurian literature is referred to in studies of Arthur in Victorian art (Mancoff 1995; Poulson 1999) or in chapters in edited books (Baswell & Sharpe 1988; Lagorio & Day 1990; Cronin et al. 2002).

Although Arthur had fallen "out of literary fashion" (Curry 1990: 149) in the first half of the eighteenth century (see chapters 23 and 24), and attempts by the poets John Milton and John Dryden to write an Arthurian epic had not come to fruition, the desire to glorify the nation in epic form remained. The nineteenth-century British cultural fascination with Arthur has its roots in a late-eighteenth- and early nineteenth-century literary and antiquarian context. Moreover, medieval Arthurian literature was reinvented as part of a new historicism, which acknowledged that history was to an extent fictional; consequently, Arthurian material need not be rejected out of hand as fantastical. Thomas Gray, in his poem "The Bard" (1757), highlights the notion that "Britannia's Issue" refers to a literary tradition, as well as a dynasty: "No more our long-lost Arthur we bewail / All hail, ye genuine Kings, Britannia's Issue, hail!" (Weinbrot 1993: 14).

Notable contributions to the revival and spread of interest in Arthur included Walter Scott's edition of *Sir Tristrem* (1804), Joseph Ritson's *Ancient Engleish Metrical Romanceës* (1802), George Ellis's *Specimens of Early English Metrical Romances* (1805), and John Dunlop's *History of Fiction* (1814). During the 1840s, Ellis's modernized Arthurian tales were available in a reasonably priced edition, together with a translation of Geoffrey of Monmouth's *History of the Kings of Britain* (c. 1138). The most popular version of the legends was Thomas Malory's *Morte Darthur* (1485), with its overarching theme of the knightly ideal – a group of cheap editions published in 1816 and 1817 helped create a wider readership. Ballad sheets and chapbooks in popular culture also featured Arthur, linking the Arthurian romances with childhood nostalgia. The latter aspect was a factor in William Wordsworth's casting aside of the legend of Arthur, mentioned as a possible theme for *The Prelude* (1850). Thomas Percy's *Reliques of Ancient English Poetry* (1765), which included six Arthurian ballads, and Thomas Warton's *History of English Poetry* (1774–81) revalorized the Arthurian legends as historical artifacts: stories which encompassed both the chronicle tradition and the imagined world of Fairy Land allegory. Nineteenth-century British culture's interest in fairies and in a "mythopoeic, poetic, pre-rational stage of human culture" (Simpson 1990: 154) was itself a form of nationalism.

The Arthurian past was also one among a whole array of pasts that the Victorians reinvented, and the critical literature on Victorian historicism is extensive. Indeed, the issue of Arthur's paradoxical status as a historical and mythical figure was at the core of historiography's growth as a discipline. How were Victorian poets to lay claim to him? In *The Epic: Morte d'Arthur* (1842), Tennyson has the poet Everard Hall ask, "Why take the style of those heroic times . . . why should any man / Remodel models?" (Ricks 1987: 147). Similarly, nineteenth-century historians wondered how to appropriate the legendary king, with the "doubtful" lineage referred to in Tennyson's idyll

"The Last Tournament" (Ricks 1987: 939), into a suitable history for an industrializing nation. Tennyson's epic cycle *Idylls of the King* draws attention to the difficulties of accounting for Arthur's existence in linear terms, since Merlin stresses that Arthur goes "From the great deep to the great deep" (Ricks 1987: 690). The mysterious nature of Arthur's coming and passing – "he will not die / But pass, again to come" (Ricks 1987: 690) – is articulated in many nineteenth-century Arthurian literary texts as a play of form, or shape-shifting, exemplified in Tennyson's city of Camelot: "it is enchanted, son / For there is nothing in it as it seems / Saving the King; tho' some there be that hold / The King a shadow, and the city real" (Ricks 1987: 701).

Yet in spite of this, Arthur was viewed as having direct social relevance for contemporary Britain. Tennyson's *Idylls of the King* is both an epic cycle and a domestic social narrative, in its form and content stressing the interrelatedness of the "condition of England" (symbolized in its landscape and built environment) and Arthur's domestic situation. Englishness, and relatedly the nature of Britishness, continues to be a live cultural issue. One of the most powerful myths of the origin of English national identity is Anglo-Saxonism, also known as Teutonism or Gothicism. The figure of Arthur (Christian Worthy, Once and Future King) came to embody manliness, honor, heroic leadership, and liberty – characteristics of Teutonism. Nineteenth-century Arthurians refashioned the Caucasian Arthur as a social model for the young knights of the nation and a Darwinian type of "modern gentleman," specifically referred to in Tennyson's *The Epic: Morte d'Arthur*.

However, as Stephanie Barczewski has pointed out, in the second half of the nineteenth century writers grappled with reconciling Arthur's role as a national hero with both a contemporary pride in Anglo-Saxonism and a tradition of anti-Celtic feeling. The pre-eminent response was to promote the idea of racial unity between Celts and Saxons (Barczewski 1997: 193) and this is evident in Edward Bulwer-Lytton's twelve-book poem *King Arthur* (1848), the first published Victorian Arthurian epic. The poem eschews the traditional matter of the Arthurian cycle and, although the narrative structure seems unwieldy in places, its overall effect is to produce a montage of cultures, races, and dynasties. Arthur defends the Cymrians against the Saxons, although Bulwer-Lytton sees the groups subsumed under the banner of the chivalric, patriotic "northernness" of the romance tradition. As befitting the hero of a literary epic, Arthur completes a series of tasks and is eventually victorious at the Siege of Carduel. The resulting dynasty and empire prophesied by Merlin can be read as an allegory of the creation of Queen Victoria's empire, albeit a sanitized version. Arthur will:

> . . . live from age to age,
> A thought of beauty and a type of fame; –
> Not the faint memory of some mouldering page,
> But by the hearths of men a household name:
> Theme to all song, and marvel to all youth –
> Beloved as Fable, yet believed as Truth.
> (Bulwer-Lytton 1853: 2.37)

The popular radical causes at the heart of the "condition of England" debate are alluded to: the people appear, according to Simpson, as "the gloomy, pauperised, and famished creatures of the hungry 1840s" (Simpson 1990: 48). Crucially, Bulwer-Lytton suggests "racial unity as a solution to social disunity" (Bryden 2005: 37), echoing Thomas Carlyle in his 1843 essay *Past and Present*. Arthur (and the reader) learns from the different races and social models he encounters on his journey. Indeed, the evolutionary model is privileged in various ways in Bulwer-Lytton's *King Arthur*: the origins of the physical world pepper the fictional landscape in the form of "lurid skeletons of vanished races" and "earliest reptile spectra" (Bulwer-Lytton 1853: 3.12), the British state is represented as a procession of monarchs, and Bulwer-Lytton self-consciously places his poem in the epic tradition, referring in the preface to Milton's unfulfilled plan for an Arthurian epic poem.

Bulwer-Lytton reinvents a mythical past to validate the present, simultaneously critiquing contemporary politics via an allegorical subplot. The Vandal court is Louis Philippe's and selected Cymric knights represent British parliamentary figures of the 1830s: Geraint is the Duke of Wellington and Cadwr (Cornwall's chief) is Hardinge of Lahore, a Waterloo veteran. Earlier Arthurian poems had anticipated *King Arthur*'s invoking of a procession of monarchs and intertwining of military and literary triumphs as part of a myth of national origin. Whereas John Walker Ord's *England: A Historical Poem* (1834–5) had lamented the decline of the English (an expression of Tory regret at the 1832 Reform Bill and the influence of radical politics), Bulwer-Lytton's *King Arthur* celebrates the nation's progress and an emerging ideology of symbolic monarchy. Unsurprisingly, Tennyson, as poet laureate, modeled Prince Albert as Arthur: "Ideal manhood closed in real man" (Ricks 1987: 974).

In Bulwer-Lytton's epic Arthur undertakes a form of secular quest. Characteristically, Victorian poets interpreted the Arthurian quest for the Holy Grail as destructive of the Round Table, and therefore of the moral and social values underpinning it. Contrastingly, the Grail itself came to symbolize unity, the implication being that achieving the "Grail" would restore faith and social cohesion to Britain. Social unity formed the ideological basis of medievalism, at least, the feudalistic branch of medievalism, according to Alice Chandler (1971). As Christine Poulson (1999) has observed, in the 1830s readers were likely to view the Grail as otherworldly. The popularization of the legend was to a large degree due to Tennyson's portrayal of Galahad as a type of moral virtue in the 1842 collection of poems (Simpson 1990: 225). The 1869 "Holy Grail" idyll further secularizes the quest, subduing the miraculous aspect of the Grail.

The figure of the Christian Arthur was appropriated by writers in the context of social and religious debate about how an ancient, now-fragmented faith might be modernized, reinvigorated, and made whole. Henry Alford's (later Dean of Canterbury) poem *The Ballad of Glastonbury* (1835) is framed by an account of the magnificent past and ruinous present state of Glastonbury Abbey. Arthur's funeral procession is one in a series of significant events in Glastonbury's history, and his burial at Glastonbury (identified as Avalon) is topographically linked with the arrival of Joseph of Arimathea and the founding of the Anglican Church. The placing of Arthur in the context of an evolutionary history, as with Bulwer-Lytton's poem, is characteristic of 1830s and 1840s Arthurian literature. The "fast perishing" towers of Glastonbury Abbey in *The Ballad of Glastonbury* seem to enact what Alford believes to be the state of modern religious faith. Appropriating Arthurian legend allows the poet to entreat "England's sons" to revive the faith of the nation specifically by restoring the ruined towers of her ancient monuments.

The quest proved a useful narrative structuring device, particularly for poets in the 1850s who focused on the story of Lancelot and Guinevere and explored the tensions between religious devotion and secular passion. Moreover, the quest represented an individual's journey of self-discovery and, as such, could articulate the anxieties surrounding class, social status, and heroism within a secular culture. For example, Galahad, the hero of William Morris's monologue *Sir Galahad: A Christmas Mystery* (1858), questions the social worth of the Grail quest, while chivalric love is viewed as a distraction contributing to its failure. Galahad and the Grail legend were also the most popular Arthurian subjects in visual art of the 1850s.

Contrastingly, the Reverend Robert Stephen Hawker's unfinished poem *The Quest of the Sangraal* (1864) can be viewed as belonging to the broader socio-cultural mission to revive religious fervor, in tandem with national identity. The eclectic symbolism of the poem is striking, as are the references to muscular Christianity: King Arthur and the four knight-questers are "soldiers of the cross" and implicitly, at a time of colonial expansion, missionaries. Unusually among Victorian Arthurian poets, Hawker sees the quest as glorifying the Arthurian state (compare Thomas Westwood's blank verse *The Quest of the Sancgreall* [1868], which depicts social fragmentation as a result of the quest for spiritual cohesion) and the Grail is identified specifically with a Cornish regional identity. The "warning to the nation" takes the form, as in other Arthurian poems, of a succession of visions, showing the restoration and subsequent loss of the Grail. Yet according to Hawker, the visions also invoked contemporary "myths" of gas, steam, and the electric telegraph.

The figuring of Arthur as a savior-hero in Victorian Arthurian poetry can be read in relation to Thomas Carlyle's notion of heroism as expressed in *On Heroes, Hero-Worship and the Heroic in History* (1841) and the broader cult of hero-worship. Arthur was peculiarly adaptable as a hero and, importantly, took his place among other medieval heroes as a progenitor of national character and a focus of patriotic attention (Barczewski 1997: 179). As Simpson comments, "paradoxically, as belief in the historical Arthur waned, it became increasingly possible to predict metaphorically an Arthurian Second Coming" (1990: 52). The legendary king provided appropriate patterns of social behavior for men to follow in everyday life. In a sense the return of Arthur to Victorian Britain, as a modern gentleman, had already occurred – in epic literary tradition. This is the conundrum of Tennyson's poem *The Epic: Morte d'Arthur*, in which the poet Everard Hall (who has destroyed nearly all of his epic *King Arthur*) questions the contemporary relevance of Arthur and epic poetry. Tennyson answers this question in the Dedication (1862) of *Idylls of the King* to Prince Albert and the Epilogue "To the Queen" (1873), drawing attention to his own meshing of the old and new in a reworked tale.

Malory's Knights of the Round Table were popular role models for young readers in an industrial society since "they combined distinctiveness of class and an ideal of public service with . . . protectiveness towards women, and loyalty to a monarch" (Whitaker 1990: 265). Poems such as Andrew Lang's ballad-like *Sir Launcelot* (1863) and Thomas Westwood's blank verse *The Sword of Kingship: A Legend of the "Mort d'Arthure"* (1868) display the influence of Malory's *Morte Darthur*. Lang uses archaic language in recounting Launcelot's quest for the Grail. Interestingly, the narrative moment when the knight is excluded from the Grail chapel, left in a desolate, darkened landscape, is visually represented later in the century in Edward Burne-Jones's painting *The Dream of Sir Lancelot at the Chapel of the Holy Grail* (1896). In Westwood's text the legend of Arthur is woven with the legend of the Nativity, Westwood adopting the parallel between Arthur and Christ.

Rather than reconstruct a medievalized past, other poems wove Arthurian legend and heroism with political concerns, notably in the 1830s and 1840s. The Duke of Wellington (Arthur Wellesley) was linked with King Arthur; for example, the second volume of John Walker Ord's *England: A Historical Poem* (1834–5) is dedicated to Wellington, whose military and manly deeds have shaped "the chivalry of modern times." In George Darley's "Merlin's Last Prophecy" (1838) Victoria is initiated into her new role as queen. Lang's poem "The White Pacha" (1892) connects the mystery surrounding Arthur's death and burial with the uncertainties about the details of General Charles Gordon's death. After Waterloo, military heroism was often associated with sport; from the 1850s, it was a component of the depiction of Christian heroism. In Arthurian literature particularly, the chivalric gentleman was seen to be so by dint of social and public achievements (Girouard 1981). The chivalric ethos was, however, critiqued by Tennyson among others: in "Gareth and Lynette" it is implied that the knightly vows Arthur insists on are too binding, "as is a shame / A man should not be bound by, yet the which / No man can keep" (Ricks 1987: 701).

Nostalgia for a romanticized, chivalric past is, arguably, the dominant preoccupation of Arthurian literature and art produced from the 1850s onwards, epitomized in the knights and damsels of Pre-Raphaelite texts. The term "Pre-Raphaelite" derived from visual art, but was "adopted and modified" to apply to literature (Smith 1995: 117). Poets such as "Owen Meredith" (Robert Lytton, Edward Bulwer-Lytton's son), William Morris, Matthew Arnold, and Algernon Swinburne focused on the domestic ideologies underpinning Arthur's kingdom, exploring the tensions between state-legitimated marriage and romantic love, between purity and adultery. Their poetry addressed the contemporary ideals and dilemmas of "modern love," also articulated in George Meredith's *Modern Love* (1862) and the poetry of Coventry Patmore, most notably *The Angel in the House* (1854–6). These texts share features such as a focus on individual characters, particular dramatic moments and moral situations, pictorial settings, color-symbolism, and experimental narrative techniques, all characteristics of Pre-Raphaelite Arthurian texts.

In this context, how to deal with Arthurian women proved tricky; Guinevere and Iseult embodied moral ambiguity and a wider cultural unease, entangled in debate about the social function of modern courtly love and attitudes toward the regulation of female sexuality. Marion Wynne-Davies points out that whereas Walter Scott could, in *The Bridal of Triermain* (1813), have Guinevere condone adultery, "a female writer such as [Charlotte] Guest was constrained to omit all sexual references even from a translation" (Wynne-Davies 1996: 117–18). Mark Girouard draws attention to the fact that "the only women on pedestals in the *Idylls of the King* are there as warnings, not for admiration, and they do not stay on them" (Girouard 1981: 199). The passion between Lancelot and Guinevere, as opposed to the impossible ideal of Arthur's purity, is central to the tragedy of Tennyson's *Idylls*. That said, the queen is not always blamed in Arthurian poetry for the collapse of Arthur's empire: in George Simcox's "The Farewell of Ganore" (1869), the social context is held to be responsible.

In Owen Meredith's "Queen Guenevere" (1855), the queen is transformed into an idol of religious and courtly love through the eyes of the unnamed narrator. In "The Parting of Launcelot and Guenevere: A Fragment" it is Launcelot who worships the queen, in spite of doubts about love's "changing hue," and as the lovers embrace, a narrative voice interjects to distance and freeze the moment. The lovers, described with an intensity of detail and color, are rendered art objects, suspended beyond time. Such an ending is characteristic of Arthurian poetry focusing on the lovers; an endorsement of romantic discourse and a "love which knows no bounds." Just as Meredith's Launcelot and Guenevere find reconciliation in a final embrace, Swinburne's Tristram and Iseult, at the end of *Tristram of Lyonesse*, find a peace beyond death.

As with Meredith's Guenevere, the namesake of William Morris's poem "The Defence of Guenevere" (1858) is eroticized and, to a degree, depicted in isolation from society – the reinvention of Arthurian legend in this way allows the protagonists' psychological tensions to be exposed as memories or projected onto external surroundings. Morris's *Defence of Guenevere* (1858) was the first volume of poetry to be associated with the Pre-Raphaelite Brotherhood (Armstrong 1993: 232). Indeed, four of the poems were inspired by Dante Gabriel Rossetti's watercolors of Arthurian subjects, in keeping with the themed pairs of poems and paintings produced by the Pre-Raphaelites (Pearce 1991). The title poem is distinctive among the Victorian Arthurian corpus in that Morris refuses to judge Launcelot and Guenevere and because the queen verbalizes her own "defense" against the charge of adultery. The sensuous, physical description of Guenevere, though, seems to undermine the text's assertion of her as a religious icon to be worshipped. Morris's Arthurian poem "King Arthur's Tomb" weaves the story of Guenevere and Launcelot with King Arthur's life and death, building multifaceted character portraits through use of characters' memories and conversations. The dramatic moment of the meeting between the former lovers, at King Arthur's tomb, is prefigured in Rossetti's watercolor *Arthur's Tomb: The Last*

Meeting of Launcelot and Guinevere (1855). Ultimately, Morris's Arthurian poems are concerned with the impossibility of imagining the past, their radical aesthetics presenting a challenge to the conservative view of Arthur as a pillar of the establishment (Armstrong 1993: 232, 236).

Like Morris and Tennyson, the poet Matthew Arnold uses Arthurian legend as a means of comparing past with present and relating poetic technique to industrial society. The role of the imaginative artist in the context of "the dislocation between past and present that cultural medievalism was premised upon and sought to repair" (Bryden 2005: 108) is thus reassessed. Arnold's three-part poem "Tristram and Iseult" (1852) explores this relation through experimental narrative techniques such as flashbacks. In part one, for instance, the dying Tristram is nursed by his wife, Iseult of Brittany, but recalls his past with Iseult of Ireland. The introduction of Iseult of Brittany as wife and mother also contributed to the domestication of Arthurian legend. Significantly, the dying lovers Tristram and Iseult of Ireland are transformed in part two of the poem: distanced and framed by the narrator's comments, they become the matter of art yet simultaneously represent the illusion of fully restoring the past in the present. Cleverly, Arnold then has the widowed Iseult of Brittany tell her children the story of Merlin and Vivian (which she heard as a child): oral and literary traditions are validated. Such endorsement allows the narrator-poet to observe that creativity, or the people's spirit, is being destroyed by industrialization.

As an antidote to Arnold and Tennyson's tempering of romantic passion and legitimating of an Arthurian moral system, Swinburne's nine-section poem *Tristram of Lyonesse* (1882) revels in the transformation of Tristram and Iseult when they drink the love potion. The innocent lovers are free from society's blame in a celebration of adulterous passion; thus Swinburne's form of medievalism was theologically and socially subversive. In the epilogue to Swinburne's "species of epic" (Harrison 1988: 99), King Mark builds a chapel to house the lovers' tomb, but this, and memory of it, is eventually wiped out by the sea. Paradoxically, at the point when Arthurian legend "disappears" it is immortalized in poetry; Swinburne's poem becomes a memorial to the lovers. The poet seems to be suggesting that by submitting to love as a universal force, lovers such as Tristram and Iseult will gain immortality "through the resurrection of their story by future generations" (Lambdin & Lambdin 2000: 132).

The death and memorialization of Arthur was one of the most popular aspects of the legend in Victorian Britain, unsurprisingly perhaps, given the social concern about provision of public burial sites and the visibility of rituals surrounding death; the cult of commemoration. The legend of Arthur's Second Coming was also pertinent in the context of theological debate about the nature of immortality. Indeed, the story "Avillion, or, The Happy Isles: A Fireside Fancy," published in the popular collection by Dinah Mulock, *Avillion and Other Tales* (1853), reworks Arthurian legend partly as an attempt to understand what form life after death might take.

The dominant perception of Arthur's death, which was informed by literary, topographical, and archaeological traditions, had a contradiction at its heart. This tension is best represented in Tennyson's description of Avalon:

"But now farewell. I am going a long way
With these thou seëst – if indeed I go –
(For all my mind is clouded with a doubt)
To the island-valley of Avilion;
Where falls not hail, or rain, or any snow,
Nor ever wind blows loudly; but it lies
Deep-meadowed, happy, fair with orchard-lawns
And bowery hollows crowned with summer sea,
Where I will heal me of my grievous wound."
(Ricks 1987: 163)

The "island-valley of Avilion" where Arthur will go to be "healed" is both specific (rooted in an identifiable, English landscape) and non-specific (static, otherworldly), drawing attention to the uncertainty surrounding Arthur's death coupled with the desire for him to return at a time of need. Thomas Warton had earlier, in "The Grave of King Arthur" (1777), distinguished between the historico-chronicle tradition, which focused on Christian Glastonbury as the site of Arthur's burial, and the romance tradition, which favored the notion of the grave as an "otherworldly" island, the latter highlighted in Edward Burne-Jones's monumental, unfinished painting *The Last Sleep of Arthur in Avalon* (1881–98). Tennyson's *Morte d'Arthur*, from which the dying Arthur's speech is taken, was written after the death of the poet's close friend, Arthur Hallam, and later incorporated in the last idyll, "The Passing of Arthur" (1869). It highlights the extent to which *Idylls of the King* – and myth itself – is about cycles of change.

In Victorian Britain, quests to identify Avalon – for example, trips to "Arthurian" relics and burial sites undertaken by county historians, travel writers, and antiquarians – were reflected in topographical attitudes toward Arthur's death expressed in written texts. The indices to the *Journal of the British Archaeological Association* (1875), the *Archaeological Journal* (1878), and the *Archaeologia* (1889) are evidence of the process of excavating Arthur: they include summaries of visits Victorians made to Arthurian sites in Britain as possible locations of Arthur's grave, as well as inventories and accounts of the objects found there. Early nineteenth-century travel writers and poets used Arthurian references to color their descriptions of local monuments, features, and landscapes: Celtic regions in particular were defined by Arthurian legend. Indeed, faith in the power of the imagination meant that, even though the existence of a historical Arthur was uncertain, he was invoked as a symbol of poetic imagination "which can, through association with certain scenery or buildings, establish a connection with the past, and then re-create that past anew" (Simpson 1990: 72). The link between the subject of Arthur's death and a cultural interest in travel and place is evident in Coventry Patmore's "Arthur and his Knights of the Round Table," published in the *Edinburgh Magazine* (May 1846), which combines a critique of Malory's *Morte Darthur* with a topographical approach.

With regard to speculation about Arthur's burial, an important text in the Victorian literary and historical inheritance was William Camden's *Remaines of a*

Greater Work concerning Britaine (1605), which contained a description of the supposed exhumation of Arthur and Guinevere at Glastonbury. Also in this context, Taliesin, a Welsh bard writing during the late fifth and early sixth centuries, seems to have had resonance for the Victorians (see chapter 6). The martial poem attributed to Taliesin, "The Stanzas of the Graves," also known as "The Graves of the Warriors," was of particular interest since it subscribed to the idea of Arthur's grave as a mystery. The comparative mythologist Algernon Herbert uses the poem in *Britannia after the Romans* (1836) to discount both Christian and pagan arguments about memorials (gravestones and cairns). Herbert's text includes an account of the discovery of Arthur's and Guinevere's remains at Glastonbury, as well as discussion of possible links between sites called Avalon and fables about Avalon.

The figure of Taliesin, then, allowed Victorian poets to connect an Arthurian past with the present. Alaric A. Watts's poem "The Home of Taliessin," published in *Lyrics of the Heart* (1851), focuses on the remains of a dwelling supposed to have been inhabited by Taliesin and thus intact at the time of the legendary Arthur's reign. Crucially, the regional landscape is mythologized via the poetic imagination contemplating specific, material evidence. The assertion of national identity through connecting a regional landscape with Arthurian legend (particularly surrounding Arthur's grave) is evident in John Jenkins's *Poetry of Wales* (1873). In the introduction to the collection, which includes both poems on Taliesin and poems attributed to him, Jenkins points out that poetry is an imaginative expression of a nation's language, apt for Victorian Britain's forging of itself as a progressive, historically-self-conscious civilization.

Yet Arthur's death also came to symbolize pressing cultural concerns: with the efficacy of muscular Christian manliness as a heroic model and the reach of empire. Sebastian Evans's long poem "The Eve of Morte Arthur" (1875) can be read in the context of increasing secularization and a sense of cultural decline, post the great agrarian depression. The poem's narrator compares memories of a (courtly) Arthurian past with contemporary society, implying that quests for heroic glory are futile in both contexts. "The Eve of Morte Arthur," in common with other poems of the time, is nostalgic for empire, although it is distinctive in linking Arthur's death to the disintegration of Britain's empire. When Arthur ruled, the poet had cultural status in that he ensured Arthur's fame through storytelling. By contrast, modern industrial Britain does not value the "knightly words" of the poet, who then struggles to find a role, an appropriate language, and an assurance that Arthur will live on in verse.

Arthurian writing of the late nineteenth century reveals a contemporary preoccupation with the notion of transience, focused on the city. In reinventing Arthurian legend to connect Arthur's death with the loss of a civilization, writers were articulating broader fears about British cultural identity. Victorian medievalism was in one sense an attempt to reform industrial capitalist society and the "rebuilding" of the mythical Camelot in Victorian poetry was informed by contemporary debate about the nature of cities. An extended description of the nature of Camelot can be found in "Gareth and Lynette" in the final version of the *Idylls* (1889). The city appears and disappears in the mist, is both substantial and insubstantial and in a continual state of becoming; in other words, it is a constructed illusion like Arthur himself. This can be interpreted as a comment on the process of myth making; in "The Holy Grail" Camelot's destruction occurs due to the desire to attain a spiritual ideal. Twentieth-century critical interpretation of the *Idylls* is concerned with the construction of Tennyson's epic as myth making, a process which is then critiqued in the poem's self-reflexivity.

As Matthew Campbell has suggested, boundaries of one kind or another (land, language, perception) are in process in the *Idylls*. Even the "landscape of the Great Battle of the West seems almost to fall off the Atlantic edges of Europe" (Campbell 2002: 439). The Celtic fringes are implicated in the history of the aspiration and destruction of the newish state of the United Kingdom. Literary depictions, such as Tennyson's, of the battle in which Arthur receives his fatal wound can be read as prophetic of the horrors of the World War I, as recognized by Wilfred Owen in "Hospital Barge at Cerisy" (1917).

According to legend, Arthur passes but does not die. He is, however, culturally reconstructed and appropriated in the cause of a range of ideological stances. Victorian poets employed Arthurian legend to convey a particular moral view or "to expose societal conflicts and to promote human change" (Lambdin & Lambdin 2000: 143). In doing so, they explored cycles of renewal and the tension between permanence and instability. This process drives both Arthur and folklore (Lindahl 1998: 15). Above all, Victorian Arthurian poets attempted to understand the paradoxical nature of Arthur's passing and of their own resurrection of the past. Arthur, like the Romantic poet Thomas Chatterton whose early death was immortalized in Henry Wallis's painting *The Death of Chatterton* (1856), "exist[s] on the interstices of the invented and the authentic" (Ackroyd 2002: 430). Despite debate earlier in nineteenth-century Britain about the "death" of poetry, Victorian epic poetry ultimately proved to be a "surprisingly vigorous anachronism" (Tucker 2002: 25).

PRIMARY SOURCES

Alford, H. (1835). *The school of the heart and other poems*, 2 vols. London: Longman & Co.

Allott, M. (ed.) (1979). *Matthew Arnold. Poems.* New York: Longman.

Bulwer-Lytton, E. (1853). *Poetical and dramatic works*, 5 vols. London: Chapman & Hall.

Cowen, J. (ed.) (1987). *Sir Thomas Malory. Le Morte d'Arthur*, 2 vols. Harmondsworth: Penguin.

Craik, D. M. (1853). *Avillion and other tales*, 3 vols. London: Smith, Elder & Co.

Ellis, G. (ed.) (1805). *Specimens of early English metrical romances, chiefly written during the early part of the fourteenth century; to which is prefixed an historical introduction, intended to illustrate the rise and progress of romantic composition in France and England*, 3 vols. London: Longman, Hurst, Rees, & Orme.

Evans, S. (1875). *In the studio: A decade of poems.* London: Macmillan.

Hawker, R. S. (1864). *The quest of the Sangraal.* Exeter.

"Meredith, O." (1855). *Clytemnestra, The earl's return, The artist and other poems.* London: Chapman & Hall.

Morris, W. (1858). *The defence of Guenevere and other poems*. London: Bell & Daldy.

Ord, J. W. (1834–5). *England: A historical poem*, 2 vols. London: Simpkin & Marshall, Baldwin & Cradock.

Ricks, C. (ed.) (1987). *Alfred Tennyson. Poems*, 3 vols. Harlow: Longman.

Ritson, J. (1802). *Ancient Engleish metrical romanceës*, 3 vols. London: G. & W. Nicol.

Scott, W. (1804). *Sir Tristrem: A metrical romance of the thirteenth century*. Edinburgh: Archibald Constable.

Swinburne, A. (1882). *Tristram of Lyonesse and other poems*. London: Chatto & Windus.

Thorpe, L. (trans.) (1987). *Geoffrey of Monmouth. History of the kings of Britain*. Harmondsworth: Penguin.

Watts, A. A. (1851). *Lyrics of the heart: With other poems*. London: Longman.

Westwood, T. (1868). *The quest of the Sancgreall, The Sword of Kingship and other poems*. London: J. R. Smith.

REFERENCES AND FURTHER READING

Ackroyd, P. (2002). *Albion: The origins of the English imagination*. London: Chatto & Windus.

Armstrong, I. (1993). *Victorian poetry: Poetry, poetics and politics*. London: Routledge.

Barczewski, S. (1997). "Nations make their own gods and heroes": Robin Hood, King Arthur and the development of racialism in nineteenth-century Britain. *Journal of Victorian Culture*, 2, 179–207.

Baswell, C. & Sharpe, W. (eds) (1988). *The passing of Arthur: New essays in Arthurian tradition*. London: Garland.

Boos, F. (1996). William Morris, Robert Bulwer-Lytton, and the Arthurian poetry of the 1850s. *Arthuriana*, 6, 31–53.

Bryden, I. (2005). *Reinventing King Arthur: The Arthurian legends in Victorian culture*. Aldershot: Ashgate.

Campbell, M. (2002). Poetry in the four nations. In R. Cronin, A. H. Harrison, & A. Chapman (eds), *A companion to Victorian poetry*. Oxford: Blackwell, pp. 438–56.

Chandler, A. (1971). *A dream of order: The medieval ideal in nineteenth-century literature*. London: Routledge & Kegan Paul.

Cronin, R., Harrison, A. H., & Chapman, A. (eds) (2002). *A companion to Victorian poetry*. Oxford: Blackwell.

Curry, J. L. (1990). Children's reading and the Arthurian tales. In V. Lagorio & M. L. Day (eds), *King Arthur through the ages*, vol. 2. London: Garland, pp. 149–64.

Dunlop, J. (1814). *The history of fiction*, 3 vols. London: Longman, Hurst.

Girouard, M. (1981). *The return to Camelot: Chivalry and the English gentleman*. New Haven, CT: Yale University Press.

Graham, C. (1998). *Ideologies of epic: Nation, empire and Victorian epic poetry*. Manchester: Manchester University Press.

Harrison, A. H. (1988). *Swinburne's medievalism: A study in Victorian love poetry*. Baton Rouge, LA: Louisiana State University Press.

Jenkins, J. (ed.) (1873). *The poetry of Wales*. London: Houlston & Sons.

Lagorio, V. & Day, M. L. (eds) (1990). *King Arthur through the ages*, 2 vols. London: Garland.

Lambdin, L. C. & Lambdin, R. T. (2000). *Camelot in the nineteenth century: Arthurian characters in the poems of Tennyson, Arnold, Morris and Swinburne*. Westport, CT: Greenwood Press.

Lindahl, C. (1998). Three ways of coming back: Folkloric perspectives on Arthur's return. In D. N. Mancoff (ed.), *King Arthur's modern return*. New York: Garland, pp. 13–29.

Machann, C. (2000). Tennyson's King Arthur and the violence of manliness. *Victorian Poetry*, 38, 199–226.

Mancoff, D. (1995). *The return of King Arthur: The legend through Victorian eyes*. London: Pavilion.

Nastali, D. (2006). Modern literature in English. In N. J. Lacy (ed), *A history of Arthurian scholarship*. Cambridge: Brewer, pp. 233–51.

Pearce, L. (1991). *Woman, image, text: Readings in Pre-Raphaelite art and literature*. Hemel Hempstead: Harvester Wheatsheaf.

Poulson, C. (1999). *The quest for the Grail: Arthurian legend in British art, 1840–1920.* Manchester: Manchester University Press.

Simpson, R. (1990). *Camelot regained: The Arthurian revival and Tennyson, 1800–1849.* Cambridge: Brewer.

Smith, L. (1995). *Victorian photography, painting and poetry: The enigma of visibility in Ruskin, Morris and the Pre-Raphaelites.* Cambridge: Cambridge University Press.

Taylor, B. & Brewer, E. (1983). *The return of King Arthur: British and American Arthurian literature since 1800.* Cambridge: Brewer.

Tucker, H. F. (2002). Epic. In R. Cronin, A. H. Harrison, & A. Chapman (eds), *A companion to Victorian poetry.* Oxford: Blackwell, pp. 25–41.

Warton, T. (1774–81). *The history of English poetry.* London & Oxford.

Weinbrot, H. (1993). *Britannia's issue: The rise of British literature from Dryden to Ossian.* Cambridge: Cambridge University Press.

Whitaker, M. (1990). *The legends of King Arthur in art.* Cambridge: Brewer.

Wynne-Davies, M. (1996). *Women and Arthurian literature: Seizing the sword.* London: Macmillan.

26
King Arthur in Art

Jeanne Fox-Friedman

The Arthurian tradition's visual imagery can seem an unwieldy lot, displaying a prodigious variety of media. Although often times coinciding with the chronological
record of Arthurian literature, and at times even pre-dating the written texts, these
visual retellings of King Arthur's legend in fact proscribe a unique path of interpretation from their textual cousins. Not merely illustrative of the written word, images
of the Arthurian legend employ the materiality of their form and function to convey
meaning and engender specific receptions. Such formal properties aid the viewer in
receiving and understanding Arthurian stories as specific reflections of and influences
on the particular cultures in which they were created.

Medieval Arthurian Imagery and the Church

What survives of medieval visual images, including those depicting the Arthurian
legend, is a mere fraction of what must surely have been produced. Our task then is
to construct a history of Arthurian visual imagery from the precious fragments that
remain. Some of the earliest depictions of Arthur's legend can be found from the
twelfth century attached to churches in the form of sculpture. This so-called secular
imagery shared the architectural spaces with the more valorized images of sacred
history. Modern notions of a stark opposition between secular and sacred were unthink-
able in this period; the church saw all aspects of life, and indeed all aspects of cosmic
existence, as their domain. Public in their display, architectural sculpture on church
façades allowed for a particularly compelling setting for the church to present its story
of sacred history. Within these public presentations the church employed secular
images such as King Arthur and his knights as potent moral exemplars woven into
the church's cosmic view. Their appearance on these church façades points as well to
the popularity of Arthurian legends in this period, as the narratives shown implied a

familiarity with the stories, whether known to the audience through oral or textual record.

An enigmatic pier carving in the Romanesque church of St Efflam at Perros, in Brittany, dated to c. 1100, has been traditionally interpreted as an Arthurian scene from the local legend of St Efflam, the patron saint of this church. The story tells of St Efflam, an Irish prince who settled in Brittany, and his encounter with King Arthur. As in the early Latin saints' lives that refer to the legendary king, Arthur is not the hero of this tale but is forced to acknowledge the greater power of the church (see chapter 2). According to the legend, Efflam, coming upon a dragon, calls on King Arthur to slay the beast. The battle that ensues between Arthur and the dragon ends indecisively with Arthur exhausted, asking the holy man for water to quench his thirst. Efflam prays and, making the sign of the cross, produces water by striking a rock with his crosier, a clear Christological sign. Arthur falls on his knees in gratitude to the saint. Efflam prays to Christ to rid the land of the dragon after which with great tumult the dragon disappears. Arthur appears here not as an exemplar of the hero but rather as the foil for the true hero, Christ. The church, ever mindful of its need to assert its greater authority over a community still deeply influenced by its pagan past, hoped to prove through this simple image the greater power of Christian culture.

In contrast to this use of Arthur at Perros as part of a local saint's legend, another interior church carving, a double capital in the nave of the church of St Pierre in Caen, Normandy, displays two images that have their origins in Arthurian romance. Dated to c. 1350–1400, the capitals show the following four stories: Lancelot on the Sword Bridge and Gawain on the Perilous Bed, both originally derived from Chrétien de Troyes' romances; and the Virgin and the Unicorn and Phyllis astride Aristotle. The designs of the stories have been attributed to the influence of French ivories of the earlier part of the fourteenth century. Christological readings of Arthurian imagery may have been relevant in the placement of these romance images within the nave of the church. Even more compelling is the placement of Lancelot's and Gawain's stories besides those of the Unicorn and the Virgin and Aristotle and Phyllis. While acknowledging our present-day amnesia as to the original purpose of these images at Caen, one wonders if the uses of images generally associated with courtly romance were meant as warnings of moral negligence on the part of the medieval viewer.

One of the best-known depictions of the Arthurian legend in an ecclesiastical setting is the archivolt of the Porta della Pescheria, the northern side doorway of Modena Cathedral in northern Italy. The sculpture has been dated to c. 1120–30 (Lejeune & Stiennon 1963) and is generally accepted to pre-date Geoffrey of Monmouth's *Historia Regum Britanniae*. The presence of Arthur's story in Italy at this time attests to the strength of an ongoing oral tradition. Breton and French *jongleurs* must have been key transmitters of the legend, especially as Modena was on the Via Emilia, an important pathway for pilgrims and crusaders in the twelfth century. The Porta della Pescheria consists of a single doorway, decorated with an inhabited vine scroll border and the labors of the month on the outer and inner doorposts, respectively.

The doorway is surmounted by an archivolt, the center of which depicts a scene from Arthurian legend. The names of all but one of the figures depicted in the tale are clearly inscribed along the top edge of the arch: Artus de Bretania (Arthur of Britain), Isdernus (Yder), Galvagnus (Gawain), Galvariun (Gauvarien), Burmaltus (Burmald), and Che (Cei or Kay) are shown as mounted knights riding to the rescue of Winlogee (Guinevere), held captive in a tower by Mardoc. Most scholars have agreed on the interpretation of the story as a depiction of Arthur's rescue of Guinevere from her abduction by a king who appears in other versions of the legend as Melwas (in Caradoc's *Vita Sancti Gildae*, "Life of Gildas," c. 1130, the earliest known version of the story) or Meleagant (Chrétien's *Le Chevalier de la Charrette*).

One means of understanding Arthur's appearance at Modena is to reflect upon the internal formal relationships within the architectural site. The Porta della Pescheria on the northern flank of the building and the Porta dei Principi on its southern flank show an extraordinary formal similarity to one another. Like the northern doorway, the Porta dei Principi has an inhabited vine scroll decoration along its outer doorposts, here with figures depicting the labors of the months and zodiacal signs. However, the narrative imagery appears not on the archivolt, as it does on the Arthurian northern doorway, but rather on the lintel, depicting a portion of the life of the patron saint of Modena, San Geminiano. The images relate the story of the saint's temptation by the devil, who in retribution for S. Geminiano's rejection, journeys to the Eastern Empire, capturing the Emperor's only daughter. The Emperor subsequently pleads with San Geminiano to come and rescue her. The saint leaves for the east, rescues the daughter from the devil, is rewarded with gifts, and returns to Modena.

On a simple narrative level, both doorways concern the rescue of a lady in distress. The Porta dei Principi, on the southern flank of the cathedral, faced the bishop's residence, comprising the more official, ecclesiastical entryway to the church. The Porta della Pescheria was the commune's entrance. Arthur's rescue of Guinevere and San Geminiano's rescue of the Emperor's daughter are thus the same basic story directed to two particular audiences, lay and ecclesiastical. Yet interpretation here goes beyond the mere retelling of one story by another. Chronicles of the First Crusade explaining human history as an ever-expanding sacred reality in which past and present co-existed tell of eyewitness accounts of seeing the chivalric hero St George just prior to battle. Within this medieval construct of history, the rescues of Guinevere and the Emperor's daughter in the visual narratives of Arthur and San Geminiano can be read as symbolic markers of the crusaders' rescue of Jerusalem, each story conforming to a cosmic history in which the central figures possess both sacred and heroic meaning.

Mosaic floors were another favored site in twelfth-century Italy for operatic displays of the church's universal history. The Norman cathedral of Otranto in Apulia contains an impressive mosaic floor in its nave and side aisles. Inscriptions tell us that Archbishop Jonathan commissioned the priest Pantaleone to create the mosaic in 1165. The floor reveals a universal history as it unfolds within a giant inhabited vine, with images that include Old Testament scenes, the legend of Alexander, zodiacal signs, labors of the month, and fantastical beasts. Between the image of the Expulsion from

Paradise and the sacrifice of Abel is a crowned figure labeled "Rex Arturus." He holds a club in one hand and rides a strange figure often identified as a goat-like creature. Just below him is an image of a large cat-like animal seen attacking a man. This mysterious image of King Arthur has engendered much speculation. Many have identified the story told with that of the tale of Arthur and the great cat of Lausanne, the Capalus, known in Welsh folklore as the Cath Palug (Sims-Williams 1991: 45). But few investigators have offered reasons for Arthur's appearance at Otranto, though a recent dissertation connects the depictions at Modena and Otranto as symbolizing the cosmic order of the seasons (Agozzino 2006). Rita Lejeune finds connections between Otranto's Arthur and images on Modena's campanile, La Ghirlandina (Lejeune & Stiennon 1963).

The British Isles produced some extraordinary Arthurian imagery. Little remains of Chertsey Abbey in the Thames valley near Windsor, the foundation having been dissolved and reduced to ruins under Henry VIII in 1537. The abbey, which dates from the seventh-century Saxon period, reached the high point of its influence in the thirteenth century after the rebuilding of a large Norman-style church in c. 1110. Henry III (1216–72) was a patron of the abbey and is thought to have commissioned a large ceramic tile pavement for the foundation. The tiles were rediscovered in the post-medieval period. Decorated floor tiles, such as the two-color decorated tiles seen at Chertsey, were a popular form of English medieval floor decoration. The Chertsey tiles are the best known of English tiles, partly due to their high degree of craftsman-ship, yet they are only one example of a larger and fairly widespread group. Although the Chertsey tiles are unique in being the only set of extant English tiles with Arthu-rian imagery, they are related both stylistically and technically to tiles found at both Halesowen Abbey in Worcestershire and Hailes Abbey in Gloucestershire. Eames (1985) dates the Chertsey tiles between the 1250s and 1290s.

Created in pairs or quartets of roundels surrounded by circular borders and flowery vines, the Chertsey tiles tell the stories of Tristan and Isolde and the battle between Richard the Lionheart and Saladin. Similar to other Arthurian imagery associated with church foundations, the tiles blend images of contemporary history and Arthurian legend. Monks at Chertsey Abbey, living lives of seclusion and forbidden any active participation in the crusades, might well have recreated in the Chertsey tiles symbolic feats of chivalric honor, allowing them metaphorical access to the wider world beyond the confines of the cloister's walls.[1]

Another example of Arthurian imagery found in the interior of churches is that of the wooden misericords, hinged seats in the choir stalls of medieval churches that afforded the clergy a physical respite from standing during the long hours of church service. The undersides of these seats were carved with scenes from all aspects of daily life. Although placed in the most sacred portion of the church, they rarely displayed sacred imagery as churchmen were perhaps loath to place their posteriors on images of Christ and the saints. Misericords date from the mid-thirteenth century through to the sixteenth century and appear in churches in both Continental Europe, mainly France, and the British Isles.

Figure 26.1 Tristan and Isolde, the "Tryst under the Tree." Misericord, Chester Cathedral. By permission of the Chapter of Chester Cathedral.

Arthurian tales and romances provide only a small fraction of the overall iconography of misericords, which is generally drawn from activities of domestic life, various medieval occupations, relations between the sexes, and scenes from bestiaries. Found mainly in Britain, the two most popular Arthurian images are the Tryst under the Tree from the romance of Tristan and Isolde, to be found at Chester cathedral (c. 1390; see figure 26.1) and Lincoln Minster (late fourteenth century), and Ywain's rush through the castle gate as the portcullis bisects his horse, seen at Chester (figure 26.2), St Mary's Enville in Staffordshire (late fifteenth century), Lincoln Minster, St Botolph's Boston in Lincolnshire (c. 1390), and the chapel at New College, Oxford (late fourteenth century).

The possible reasons for the popular and often ribald imagery of the misericords have fascinated scholars. Some have tried to see these images, including those of the Arthurian legend, as warnings of moral laxity. Many researchers see the imagery of misericords as evidence of the greater freedom given to medieval carvers as they created these more marginal images in church interiors. Michael Camille reads the popular imagery on misericords as representing one social group, the church elite, literally sitting upon, or as Camille states "obliterating," the lower classes, as the images and subject matter on these choir stalls would have been visible only to the more privileged group of clergy (Camille 1992: 93–97). Ultimately, placement of Arthurian images within the greater corpus of popular imagery of the misericords tells us less about the particular Arthurian stories chosen and their possible moral implications than the extent of popularity of the Arthur legend as it was perceived and appreciated in the medieval period.

Figure 26.2 Ywain's horse protruding from the portcullis. Misericord, Chester Cathedral. By permission of the Chapter of Chester Cathedral.

Stories of the Arthurian legend appear in a group of ecclesiastical embroideries produced in German nunneries in the fourteenth century. Among the extant examples are the stories of Tristan, Gawain, and Ywain. Three different embroideries were produced at the Cistercian convent of Wienhausen in Hanover, the earliest dating from c. 1310. Composed in rows of continuous narrative, the images include four rows of heraldic shields alternating with three rows containing stories from the romance of Tristan and Isolde. These linen panels were quite large: Wienhausen I measures 13 feet 3 inches by 7 feet 8 inches. Among other examples showing the romance of Tristan is a fragment of an early fourteenth-century embroidery done on white linen with white, green, and yellow thread, now at the Victoria and Albert Museum, London; and a 14 by 3 feet linen tablecloth from the Benedictine convent at Würzburg, dated c. 1370–5, now in the treasury of the cathedral at Erfurt.

Many of the nunneries of this period, including those mentioned above, were aristocratic institutions, often founded for the daughters of royal and noble families. It is not surprising that these embroideries were produced in female monasteries, as embroidery was one of the daily occupations of medieval women. Although we can imagine that the stories of romance from the Arthurian legend chosen by these female artists were meant as warnings against unacceptable behavior, it may also be that they were produced by these women as a means to bridge the distance between their enclosed lives and the wider world beyond.

In contrast to the embroideries made in cloistered settings in Germany, examples of quilted embroidery from Sicily cannot be connected to monastic manufacture, and appeared to have served a more secular purpose. The heraldic devices found on two examples, one now in the Victoria and Albert Museum and the other in the Bargello in Florence, seem to have been made as a wedding gift for Piero di Luigi Guicciardini and Laodamia Acciaiuoli in 1395. The embroidery represents imagery from the story of Tristan and Isolde, who, in the centuries before Shakespeare's Romeo and Juliet, symbolized devoted love. These secular examples demonstrate a new and important use of Arthurian imagery that came into vogue in the later Middle Ages, as the world of King Arthur came to signify the opulence, luxury, and power of the late medieval court and the aspirations of the ever-more influential and powerful merchant class.

Late Medieval Arthurian Art: Images of Magnificence

By far the largest category of Arthurian art to have come down to us from the Middle Ages is that of the decorative arts, objects such as illuminated manuscripts, wall paintings, and ivory and metal carvings that were meant to adorn the living spaces, public and private, of both the elite classes of royalty and nobility and the rapidly growing mercantile class – the *nouveaux riches* of the late Middle Ages. From the late thirteenth century to the end of the fifteenth century changing economic and social dynamics impressed upon these groups an ever-growing pressure to justify their power by presenting themselves as true inheritors of the valorized past. In a world where men celebrated their power by jousting not as a required prelude to war but as an entertainment, individuals felt a greater need to associate themselves with the ancient heroes of the past. King Arthur and his knights served just such a purpose. No longer heroic models of the church's *milites Christi* ("soldiers of Christ"), Arthur and his knights transformed themselves in this late medieval period into figures of magnificence; for in the Middle Ages magnificence equaled power.

Illuminated manuscripts make up one of the richest sources of medieval Arthurian imagery. They begin to appear with greater frequency from the thirteenth century, when the types of manuscripts produced and their mode of manufacture were changing. An increasingly literate culture expanded the demand for books, and this broader-based readership led to an increase in vernacular texts, such as those of Arthurian romance. In a change from earlier medieval practice, book production shifted from monks to lay craftsmen, whether traveling artisans or members of city workshops. Paris, as the site of a sophisticated royal court and a large university, was the early center for many lay ateliers. Surprisingly, we have relatively few remaining illustrated texts of Chrétien de Troyes: only 10 of the surviving 44 manuscripts of his work are illuminated. Rather, the most popular Arthurian text to be illustrated was the prose Vulgate Cycle. An early example is a Parisian manuscript, Rennes, Bibliothèque Municipale 225, dated to c. 1225, with 57 historiated initials.

Toward the end of the thirteenth century the center of vernacular book production in France moved north to the region of Picardy, which was responsible for some outstanding illustrated copies of the Vulgate Cycle. The sumptuous manuscripts dating from this period include three Lancelot cycles – London, British Museum Add. MS 10292–4, dated after 1316; Bonn, Universitätbibliotek MS 526, dated 1286; New York, Morgan MS 805, dated c. 1315 – and a compilation of the *Estoire de Saint Graal*, *Queste de Saint Graal*, and *Morte d'Artu* in London, British Library MS Royal 14 E III, dated c. 1316. The Arthurian court displayed its power on these pages through the magnificence of its attire and surroundings. Often set within the most up-to-date Gothic architecture, these graceful, swaying figures, balanced ever so delicately on the margins of the page, must have delighted the wealthy patrons of these books as they presented to the reader reflections on the idealized world of chivalric privilege.

Most discussions of Arthurian illuminated manuscripts follow the example of Loomis and Loomis (1938) of dividing the genre into two distinct periods – manuscripts created before and after 1340. Roughly straddling the catastrophes of the Hundred Years' War and the Black Death, these two periods do indeed reflect a change in patronage and style. It was in the later period that the great Valois and Burgundian courts set a new standard of opulence and magnificence that was often transmitted through chivalric images such as those of King Arthur and his knights. One of the Valois princes, Jean, Duke of Berry, a famous bibliophile, was reported to have owned three hundred manuscripts of which approximately one half were illuminated. We know of three surviving Arthurian manuscripts belonging to Jean – a Lancelot cycle (Paris, BN Fr. 117–120), a chronicle of England, *Le Brut d'Angleterre* (Paris, BN Fr. 1454), and a Tristan (Vienna, Osterreichischen Nationalbibliotek 2537). Jean's brother Charles V had an even larger collection; his royal library contained 1,200 manuscripts, including three King Arthurs, five Lancelots, eight Tristans, four Merlins, and three verse Percevals. Another Valois prince, Philip le Bon (1396–1467), the grandson of Philip the Bold and grand-nephew of Charles V, was an enthusiastic admirer of all things chivalric. Philip's desire to revive the ideal of the chivalric knight led to his founding of the Order of the Golden Fleece, a knightly association that embodied the chivalric camaraderie of Arthur's Round Table. An important bibliophile in his own right, Philip updated many Arthurian romances by having them recopied into contemporary French.

These late-medieval manuscripts employed various strategies to equate the courtly life of contemporary society with Arthur's world of idealized chivalry. Details of costume and the accurate depiction of courtly life were among the maneuvers employed. The remaining full-page illuminated folios of the romance of *Guiron le Courtois* (Oxford, Bodleian Library, Douce 383), dating to c. 1475–1500, employ just such strategies. Folio 1 presents the aging King Arthur seated in his banqueting hall beneath a richly decorated canopy as he greets a lady newly arrived at court. The scene is replete with accurate details of late-medieval court life – including the attendants at table, the serving of the meal via the porter's window, and the presence of the ubiquitous hunting dogs, here represented by a greyhound in the foreground. The aged king appears again in a tourney scene with its accurately depicted tiered galleries filled with members of the court as they intently view the jousting of the two mounted chevaliers in the center of the scene. The patron of this manuscript was a member of

Philip le Bon's Order of the Fleece as the member's coat of arms is prominently displayed on two of the remaining folios. Indeed, the appearance of coats of arms in late luxury manuscripts was yet another method by which patrons were able to elide the distance between the courtly world of the late Middle Ages and the valorized chivalric world of Arthur's legendary court.

One group of richly decorated consumer goods that employed manuscript illuminations as models were the ivory combs, mirror backs, and caskets, or boxes, that were exchanged either at New Year celebrations or as wedding gifts. Created in workshops in Paris, Cologne, and Venice, these luxury goods seemed to have had their greatest popularity during the fourteenth century. Clearly meant to appeal to the tastes of noblewomen, the relatively limited choices of Arthurian stories displayed on these objects – Lancelot crossing the Sword Bridge, Galahad in the Castle of Maidens, Gawain on the Perilous Bed, the Tryst beneath the Tree of Tristan and Isolde, all stories of dangerous liaisons between knights and ladies – attest to the glamour of the Arthurian world and its ambivalent values. A beautiful example of such a decorated item is a fourteenth-century French ivory casket now in the Metropolitan Museum of Art in New York. Like the Caen double capital discussed earlier, the French casket depicts images from the story of the Virgin and the Unicorn and Aristotle and Phyllis, as well as Arthurian references. Although we can infer a more light-hearted motive for this iconography on the ivory casket, the transference of such imagery to church decoration attests to the ubiquity and acceptance of Arthurian romance images in the Gothic period.

King Arthur appears together with other luminaries of the past and present in the images of the Nine Worthies, a theme first presented by Jacques de Longuyon in 1310. Reflecting the popular medieval schematism of threes, the poet presented these military heroes – the three honest heathens, Hector, Alexander, and Caesar; the three Hebrews, Joshua, David, and Judas Maccabeus; and the three Christian heroes, Arthur, Charlemagne, and Godfrey of Bouillon – as paragons of masculine perfection. The Worthies were wildly popular in the later Middle Ages, their images appearing in pageantry, literature, free-standing sculpture, tapestries, and wall paintings. Indeed, they were so popular that images of the Nine Worthy women were introduced as well, although no Arthurian woman was among the elect.

Often meant for civic spaces and commissioned by wealthy merchants, Arthur and the Worthies stand as exemplars of good government, a fortuitous means by which the new moneyed class could legitimize itself through association with these ancient celebrities. Painted stone statues of Arthur and Charlemagne are part of an early Worthies group in the Hall of the Hanseatic League, in the Rathaus in Cologne (c. 1325). A complete set of statues in Lüneberg's Rathaus, commissioned by the German merchant, Albert von Soest in the 1580s, attests to the enduring popularity of this subject. Emperors and kings employed the image of the Nine Worthies as well. The Hapsburg emperor Maximilian I (1459–1519), who referred to himself as "the last of the knights," was a great enthusiast for all things Arthurian. Eager to connect himself dynastically with King Arthur, indeed with many ancient luminaries,

Maximilian commissioned the well-known bronze caster Peter Vischer to create two free-standing life-size figures of King Arthur and Theodoric, another claimed ancestor, for his tomb in the Hofkirche at Innsbruck.

A remarkable surviving example of the Nine Worthies are fragments of a great set of Flemish tapestries now in the Cloisters Museum in New York. Most probably made for Jean, Duke of Berry, as his coat of arms appears along with the royal *fleur-de-lys* throughout the tapestries, they are yet another visual testament to the Valois' uses of chivalric imagery. The tapestry showing Arthur survives along with tapestries of his companions Hector, Alexander, Joshua, and David. Dated to c. 1385, the opulently dressed Worthies are seated within lush architectural settings, both of palace and church, vivid reminders of the connections between these ancient paragons of power and the fourteenth-century ducal court of the Valois.

Two examples of mural paintings of the Nine Worthies demonstrate the various mechanisms by which such chivalric stories were construed in this period. A large late Gothic church, dated c. 1520, in Dronninglund, Denmark, has an extensive series of wall paintings in the sanctuary. The fragmentary paintings that survive are presented in three rows. The top register shows Christological images and prophecies of the coming of Christ; the story of St Ursula and the 10,000 Virgins fills the second level; and on the lower level are the Nine Worthies, in paired sets, as mounted figures facing one another. A crowned King Arthur, mounted on a camel, confronts Alexander sitting astride an elephant. In the second example, the Nine Worthies appear in a secular setting, in a palazzo in La Manta, in northern Italy. Dated to c. 1430, the paintings cover a wall of the great hall. Done for one Valerano, son of the Duke of Saluzzo, and his wife Clemensia, the portraits depict the couple themselves in the guise of Hector and Penthesilea (Loomis & Loomis 1938).

Other extant domestic wall paintings containing Arthurian stories decorate the interiors of castles and homes. Much has been lost as rooms were painted over, reused for other purposes, or merely destroyed. We know, for example, that contemporary documents concerned with Dover Castle refer to "Arthur's Hall" and "Guinevere's Chamber." The oldest surviving painted Arthurian cycle, dated to c. 1140, showing the romance of Ywain, is in Rodenegg Castle near Balzano in the Italian Tyrol. Other Arthurian murals appear throughout Europe, such as at the ruined castle of St Floret in the Auvergne, dated to c. 1380, and ceiling paintings in Chiaramonte Palazzo in Palermo, dated to 1377–80. Schloss Runkelstein in the Italian Alps near Balzano is one of the richest sources of Arthurian imagery. In 1385 the house was bought by the wealthy Tyrolean bankers Niklas and Franz Vintler. Niklas had a series of murals executed on the walls of the older buildings and those of the newly built summer-house. Besides images of Tristan and Isolde and the Knights of the Round Table, Runkelstein's murals include not only the Nine Worthies but other triads inspired by them – the three greatest lovers, the three greatest swordsmen, the three strongest giants, and the three greatest giantesses.

A series of unfinished murals with images from the Tristan legend appear in the ducal palace in Mantua, one of the many northern Italian city states that came to be ruled by powerful *condottieres* – mercenaries – in the fourteenth and fifteenth centuries. Mantua's ruling family was the Gonzagas. By the time of Gianfrancesco Gonzaga the city had become a great center of humanistic culture, attracting to its court a wealth of important writers and artists. It was in this period that Antonio Pisano (Pisanello), appointed as court painter in 1424, was commissioned in 1447 to paint a series of murals in the Corte Vecchia in the Palazzo Ducale depicting the chivalric exploits of Arthur's court. The paintings were never completed and, after the roof's collapse in that portion of the palace, they disappeared from our knowledge until rediscovered in 1969. Showing scenes of Arthurian knights done in the new Italian style of linear perspective, the frescoes attest to Gianfrancesco's desire to legitimize his position, hoping to downplay his *nouveau riche* status – the Gonzagas had begun as peasants in the twelfth century – by equating the magnificence of his court with that of Arthur's. Indeed, by the late Middle Ages the frequency with which images from the Arthurian legend appeared in the decoration of homes, public spaces, and consumer goods demonstrates the degree to which Arthur's world and the elegant world of the late-medieval court had become one and the same.

Images of Arthur in the Post-Medieval World

By the mid-fifteenth century advances in printing technology allowed the story of King Arthur a wider audience. The earliest extant printed Arthurian romance is a Tristan poem printed in 1484 by Anton Sorg in Augsburg, containing 59 small woodcut illustrations. In the wide-open market that was early publishing, Antoine Vérard, an important printer of secular texts, who freely appropriated imagery from earlier sources, published several illustrated Arthurian romances in the late fifteenth and early sixteenth centuries. The first illustrated copy of Malory was published in 1498 by Wynkyn de Worde. Using Caxton's version, Wynkyn illustrated the text with small woodcut illustrations at the heads of each chapter.

The sixteenth century saw a decline in interest in the Arthurian legend, as the more humanistic ideas of the Renaissance sparked a greater interest in classical taste (see chapter 23). However, in Britain such humanistic preferences were held at bay as King Arthur's tale served the purposes of royal propaganda. The Plantagenet ruler Edward I (1272–1307), an Arthurian enthusiast who ordered the opening of the purported tomb of Arthur and Guinevere at Glastonbury Abbey in 1278, was most probably the patron of the famous Round Table at Winchester Castle. Not truly a table, but rather a table top, it is enormous at 18 feet in diameter, weighing over one ton. The table was most likely made for the popular festival of the Round Table, a celebration of music and jousting in which nobles took on the names of Arthurian knights. Although the table dates to the thirteenth century, the image on the table is later, commissioned by Henry VIII in 1522. Painted in twenty-four green and white segments, one for each of the Arthurian knights whose names appear at its far edge, it shows a large image of a seated King Arthur, crowned and bearded. A large Tudor

Figure 26.3 The Round Table in the Great Hall, Winchester Castle, dating from the reign of Edward I with painting commissioned by Henry VIII. Photograph © Hampshire County Council, used by permission of Hampshire County Council, 2008.

rose sits in the center of the table. Although it was repainted in 1798, X-rays have shown the original face on the table to resemble that of Henry (figure 26.3).

Arthur continued to be associated with English royalty during the reign of Elizabeth I (1533–1603). George Clifford, the third Earl of Cumberland, a squanderer of his inherited wealth who nevertheless was a favorite in Elizabeth's court, was immortalized by the famous miniaturist Nicholas Hilliard as Queen's champion wearing the costume of the Knight of the Pendragon for the Accession Day pageant of 1580. The later Stuart court continued the monarchy's love affair with King Arthur, especially under the patronage of Henry, Prince of Wales. The masque *Speeches at Prince Henries Barriers*, written by Ben Jonson, with set and costume design by the architect Inigo Jones, was performed at Whitehall in 1610. In the masque, Arthur appears as a star overlooking the play from above (perhaps representing King James). Prince Henry played Meliadus, Lord of the Isles. When Henry died in 1612 the popularity of Arthur's legend seemed to die with him, not to be fully revitalized until the nineteenth century.

After a fire in 1834 destroyed much of Westminster a new palace was built in the Gothic style rather than what was seen at the time as the foreign – read American

Figure 26.4 William Dyce, *Hospitality: The Admission of Sir Tristram to the Fellowship of the Round Table* (1848). From the Palace of Westminster Collection, used with permission.

and republican – Classical style. In 1848 the painter William Dyce was commissioned to decorate the Queen's Robing Room in the new palace with a series of frescoes. The Fine Arts commission, headed by Queen Victoria's husband Prince Albert, charged Dyce with creating a series of paintings based on Malory's *Morte Darthur*. Malory's story of King Arthur, written in the fifteenth century and out of print for centuries, had appeared again in the nineteenth century with new editions in 1816 and 1817 (see chapter 24). It was to form the nexus for a new national mythology in which King Arthur and his knights came to represent the nineteenth-century's vision of a vigorous and moral Middle Ages, one meant to fuel the modern British nation. Employing the academic concepts of history painting, Dyce pictured the individuals of Arthur's court as personifications of timeless British virtues, with frescoes such as *Piety: The Knights of the Round Table Departing on the Quest for the Holy Grail* and *Hospitality: The Admission of Sir Tristram to the Fellowship of the Round Table* (figure 26.4). Dyce's frescoes, although much talked about in the 1850s, were rarely seen as Dyce refused to allow an open viewing of the work. Nevertheless in the public space Dyce's work was perceived as an important expression of the Victorian Arthuriad.

The Pre-Raphaelites and Arthurian Art

At the same time that Dyce was creating his frescoes, Alfred Tennyson began publishing his Arthurian poetry (see chapter 25). His earliest poems such as "Sir Galahad"

(1842) evinced the same type of didactic moralism as the Westminster frescoes. Tennyson and Dyce, the two major Victorian interpreters of Arthurian legend, exerted a powerful influence on a group of young artists who were to make their own mark on the visual expression of Arthur's story in the nineteenth century. In 1848 a group of seven idealistic young artists formed the Pre-Raphaelite Brotherhood. These young artists – Dante Gabriel Rossetti, William Holman Hunt, John Everett Millais, Thomas Woolner, Frederick G. Stephens, James Collinson, and William Michael Rossetti – pledged to purify art by rejecting the aesthetic standards of the Academy. Discarding the sentimentality they saw prevalent in academic painting, they turned to what they believed to be the more truthful art of the *quattrocentro* in Italy, the art before Raphael. This search for a more primitive, truthful art led them to embrace the Arthurian legend, seeing it as an exemplar of the more vigorous Middle Ages of the Victorian imagination. Rather than images of heroic valor, Arthur and his knights were for the Pre-Raphaelites paradigms of romantic love. Presented to us in a unique style devoid of academic clarity, the Pre-Raphaelites' vision of eroticized love was to be an enduring legacy of modern Arthuriana.

Probably the most forceful voice for the Pre-Raphaelites' romantic vision of King Arthur was that of Dante Gabriel Rossetti. Rather than illustrating Tennyson's vision, Rossetti often invented his own Arthurian stories, such as *Arthur's Tomb* (1860, Tate Gallery, London), where Rossetti's focus was on the passion of Lancelot as he begs for a last kiss from Guinevere (figure 26.5). This more romantic exploitation of Arthur's legend, promoted by Rossetti and the Pre-Raphaelites, stood in opposition to the "official" didactic expression of Dyce's frescoes. The difference is seen not only in the subject matter chosen but in the different styles presented. The crowded and dense Pre-Raphaelite paintings, in which the figures and composition are presented within a wealth of iconographic detail, stand in stark opposition to Dyce's classical and academic formulas.

Although the Pre-Raphaelite Brotherhood was formally dissolved in 1853, the artists involved, especially Rossetti, continued to produce important Arthurian imagery. In 1855 the publisher Edward Moxon planned to publish an illustrated collection of Tennyson's early poems. Tennyson was asked to choose the artists. Only 6 of the 55 poems illustrated were Arthurian. The illustrations included works by the academic artist Daniel Maclise, "Arthur Obtains Excalibur" and "Arthur in the Death Barge"; William Holman Hunt's and Rossetti's interpretation of the "Lady of Shallot"; and Rossetti's "Sir Galahad" and "The Palace of Love." Although it was not a financial success, Moxon's Tennyson was nevertheless to become a significant influence on later nineteenth-century book illustration.

In 1857, Rossetti organized a group of artists, including Arthur Hughes, Edward Burne-Jones, and William Morris, to decorate the upper galleries of the new debating hall at the Oxford Union. Conceiving the project as a direct challenge to Dyce's frescoes at Westminster, Rossetti chose Arthurian subjects from Malory. The project began in August 1857, but was soon almost completely disbanded. Rossetti left in November and all the others except Burne-Jones followed. Only Morris completed

Figure 26.5 Dante Gabriel Rossetti, *Arthur's Tomb* (1860). Photograph © Tate, London, 2006.

his mural, *The Jealousy of Sir Palomedes*. *The Death of Merlin* by Burne-Jones was finished the following spring. Technically, as well, the project was a disaster. Unfamiliar with fresco technique, the artists painted on dampened bricks prepared only with white-wash, while the bright illumination caused by the large windows in the upper gallery made viewing the murals almost impossible. Nevertheless, they stand as important markers in the Pre-Raphaelites' romantic vision of Arthur's legend.

As Arthur's legend grew in popularity during the nineteenth century, artists continued to create their own visual interpretations. Sir Galahad, the paragon of both manly virtues and boyish innocence, was a favorite subject, with depictions by George Frederick Watts (1870), Arthur Hughes (1870), Edward Burne-Jones (1858), and Joseph Noel Patton (1884–6). Tennyson's women, especially Elaine and the Lady of Shallot, were frequent subjects for Victorian artists. In Victorian culture the physical weakness of women was thought to reveal their purity as the fairer sex. In this aesthetic, in which love, eroticism, and death were powerfully linked, images of Elaine and the Lady of Shallot presented the beauty of women at their weakest, most passive, and thus most beautiful moment, that of death. Examples include paintings by Henry Wallis (*Elaine*, 1861), Arthur Hughes (*The Lady of Shallot*, 1870), John William Waterhouse (*The Lady of Shallot*, 1888), Sophia Anderson (*Elaine*, 1870), and William

A. Breakspeare (*The Lady of Shallot*, undated). Women not only died beautiful in Victorian paintings, but bad women caused the deaths of others. Portrayals of the legend's bad girls, Vivien and Morgan le Fay, were yet another popular theme for artists, including examples by Frederick Sandys of *Vivien* (1863) and *Morgan-le-Fay* (1864), and *The Beguiling of Merlin* painted by Burne-Jones (1874–6).

Edward Burne-Jones, who worked on the Oxford mural project with Rossetti, was one of a handful of artists who maintained interest in the Arthurian legend throughout his career. First introduced to Tennyson's poetry and the work of Malory by his friend William Morris, Burne-Jones, with his elegant, romantic compositions filled with figures that seemed to exist in a dream world devoid of earthly concerns, became an influential model for many later Victorian artists and illustrators. Some of his most important Arthuriana was done in collaboration with William Morris, as the designer of the various tapestries, stained glass, and other decorative arts produced in Morris's factories. Morris used his concept of medieval workshops to form his various companies, Morris, Marshall and Faulkner (1861), Morris and Co. (1875), and The Merton Abbey Tapestry Works (1881), as artists' collectives. These decorative projects were part of the larger nineteenth-century artistic and cultural moment known as the Arts and Crafts movement, which viewed the medieval world as the symbol of a more integrated, robust, and thus truthful society where art, craftsmanship, and nature were seamlessly interwoven. True to the medieval fondness for decorative luxury, Morris's companies employed the Arthurian legend to create rich and luxurious adornments for the Victorians' private domestic spaces.

No recreation of the medieval world would be complete without modern versions of medieval illuminated manuscripts. The Kelmscott Press, a late project of William Morris, established in 1891, reflected Morris's love of what he considered the most beautiful books ever created – the illuminated French manuscripts of the late Middle Ages. Morris had planned an edition of Malory's *Morte Darthur* with illustrations by Burne-Jones, but the death of Morris in 1896 precluded its publication. However, the Arthurian romances of *Syr Percyvelle of Gales* and *Sire Degrevaunt* were published in 1895 and 1896, respectively. Each included a full-page woodcut illustration and border decorations designed by Burne-Jones.

As a demonstration of the great influence of the Kelmscott Press, a two-volume edition of Malory's text was published by John M. Dent in 1893–4. Dent meant his books to be an economical alternative to the luxury editions published by the Kelmscott Press. The books were illustrated by a young, unknown, nineteen-year-old, Aubrey Beardsley. With over four hundred images, including full-page images, decorative borders, and chapter headings, the style of Beardsley's drawings reflected the late nineteenth-century's darker, more decadent interpretation of the medieval world of King Arthur. Another interpretation was that of Julia Margaret Cameron, whose two-volume edition of Tennyson's *Idylls of the King* constitutes a unique form of illustrated Arthurian book. In 1874 Tennyson asked his good friend, the early photographer Julia Margaret Cameron, to create illustrated vignettes for his *Idylls*. What resulted was Cameron's large folio private publication, presented as a gift to Tennyson.

Figure 26.6 Morris & Co. stained glass panel (1880–90), designed by Edward Burne-Jones, *How Galahad Sought the Sangreal*. The inscription reads: "How Galahad sought the Sangreal and found it because his heart was single so he followed it to Sarras the city of the spirit." Photograph © Victoria and Albert Museum, London.

Imitating the popular *tableaux vivants* of polite nineteenth-century society, and casting members of her own circle as Arthurian characters, Cameron employed a suffused light to deliberately blur her images, thus allowing the viewer greater access to the inner emotions of the scenes portrayed.

Walter Dunlop, a wealthy merchant and art collector greatly influenced by the nineteenth-century taste for the Middle Ages, commissioned William Morris's company in 1862 to create a series of thirteen stained-glass windows for his new home, Hardon Grange near Bingley, Yorkshire (now in City Art Gallery, Bradford). Morris, given full artistic control over the project, chose Malory's story of Tristram and Iseult as the narrative theme for the windows. Artists included Arthur Hughes, Rossetti, Ford Maddox Brown, Valentine Pinsep, Edward Burne-Jones, and Morris himself. The images' delicate and refined style presented to Mr Dunlop and his guests a vision of King Arthur's Middle Ages as an idealized world of elegance and grace. A second set of stained-glass windows with an Arthurian theme were produced by Morris and Co. in 1886 for the home of Edward Burne-Jones (Victoria and Albert Museum, London; see figure 26.6). A series of four panels designed for the upstairs landing, they tell the story of the Quest for the Holy Grail, a theme that was to become dominant in the later collaborations of Morris and Burne-Jones.

Late in both their careers, William Morris, a great enthusiast for medieval tapestries, produced along with Burne-Jones a series of six panels that told the story of the Quest for the Holy Grail in spare and moral tableaux (collection of the Duke of Westminster). Designed in 1891 for the wealthy Australian mining magnate William Knox D'Arcy for his dining room at Stanmore Hall, Middlesex, they were executed at Morris's Merton Abbey and completed in 1894. Five tapestries told the story of the quest, with scenes titled *The Knights of the Table Summoned to the Quest by a Strange Damsel*, *The Arming and Departure of the Knights*, *The Failure of Sir Lancelot*, *The Failure of Sir Gawain*, and *The Achievement of Sir Galahad Accompanied by Sir Percival and Sir Bors*. A sixth narrower panel showed a masted ship, symbolic of the knights' journey and quest. Decorative verdure tapestries hung below the narrative panels, with inscriptions describing the scenes above. Completed only a few years before the deaths of Morris and Burne-Jones, two of the giants of the nineteenth-century Arthurian revival, the Stanmore Hall tapestries' mixture of aesthetic luxury and moral vision stands as an exceptional example of late Victorian art and as a final coda to the role the Arthurian knights played in the cultural landscape of nineteenth-century Britain.

NOTE

1   This use of imagery has been discussed in reference to other medieval monuments. See for example Rosenwein (1971).

REFERENCES AND FURTHER READING

Agozzino, M. T. (2006). Divining King Arthur: The calendric significance of twelfth century cathedral depictions in Italy. PhD dissertation. Berkeley, CA: University of California.

Anderson, M. D. (1954). *Misericords: Medieval life in English woodcarving*. Harmondsworth: Penguin.

Biddle, M. (2000). *King Arthur's Round Table: An archaeological investigation*. Woodbridge: Boydell.

Boase, T. S. R. (1954). The decoration of the New Palace of Westminster, 1841–1863. *Journal of the Warburg and Courtauld Institutes*, 17(3/4), 319–58.

Camille, M. (1992). *Images on the edge: The margins of medieval art*. Cambridge, MA: Harvard University Press.

Christian, J. (1981). *The Oxford Union murals*. Chicago, IL: University of Chicago Press.

Eames, E. (1985). *English medieval tiles*. Cambridge, MA: Harvard University Press.

Fox-Friedman, J. (1994). Messianic visions: Modena Cathedral and the crusades. *Res: Anthropology and Aesthetics*, 25, 77–95.

Gasté, A. (1887). *Un capiteau de l'église St. Pierre de Caen, étude archéologique et littéraire*. Caen: Henri Delesques.

Gianfreda, G. (1998). *Il mosaico di Otranto: biblioteca medioevale in immagini*, 6th rev. edn. Lecce: Edizioni del Grifo.

Haug, W., Heinzle, J., Huschenbett, D., & Ott, N. H. (1982). *Runkelstein. Die Wandmalereien des Sommerhauses*. Wiesbaden: Reichert.

Hind, A. M. (1935). *An introduction to a history of woodcut, with a detailed survey of work done in the fifteenth century*. London: Constable.

Hindman, S. (1994). *Sealed in parchment: Rereadings of knighthood in the illuminated manuscripts of Chrétien de Troyes*. Chicago, IL: Chicago University Press.

Koechlin, R. (1924). *Les ivoires gothiques français*. Paris: Picard.

Kraus, D. & Kraus, H. (1975). *The hidden world of misericords*. New York: G. Braziller.

Lacy, N. J. (ed.) (1996). *The new Arthurian encyclopedia*. New York: Garland.

Lacy, N. J. & Ashe, G. with Mancoff, D. N. (1997). *The Arthurian handbook*, 2nd edn. New York: Garland.

Lejeune, R. & Stiennon, J. (1963). La légende arthurienne dans la sculpture de la cathédrale de Modène. *Cahiers de Civilisation Médiévale*, 6, 281–96.

Lethaby, W. R. (1912–13). The romance tiles of Chertsey Abbey. *Walpole Society Annual*, 2, 69–80.

Loomis, R. S. & Loomis, L. H. (1938). *Arthurian legend in medieval art*. New York: Modern Language Association.

Mancoff, D. N. (1990). *The Arthurian revival in Victorian art*. New York: Garland.

Perry, L. (ed.) (1996). *William Morris*. London: Philip Wilson in association with The Victoria and Albert Museum.

Poulson, C. (1999). *The quest for the Grail: Arthurian legend in British art, 1840–1920*. Manchester: Manchester University Press.

Rosenwein, B. H. (1971). Feudal war and monastic peace: Cluniac liturgy as ritual aggression. *Viator*, 2, 129–57.

Scherer, M. R. (1945). *About the Round Table*. New York: Metropolitan Museum of Art.

Schroeder, H. (1971). *Der Topos Der Nine Worthies In Literatur Und Bildenderkunst*. Göttingen: Vandenhoeck & Ruprecht.

Schuette, M. & Müller-Christensen, S. (1964). *The art of embroidery* (trans. D. King). London: Thames & Hudson.

Sims-Williams, P. (1991). The early Welsh Arthurian poems. In R. Bromwich, A. O. H. Jarman, & B. F. Roberts (eds), *The Arthur of the Welsh*. Cardiff: University of Wales Press, pp. 33–71.

Stones, A. (1976). Secular manuscript illumination in France. In C. Kleinhenz (ed.), *Medieval manuscripts and textual criticism*. Chapel Hill, NC: University of North Carolina Department of Romance Languages, pp. 83–106.

Weiss, J. (ed. trans.) (1999). *Wace's Roman de Brut: A history of the British*. Exeter: University of Exeter Press.

Whitaker, M. (1990). *The legends of King Arthur in art*. Cambridge: Brewer.

Wildman, S. & Christian, J. (1998). *Edward Burne-Jones. Victorian artist-dreamer*. New York: Metropolitan Museum of Art.

Willemsen, C. A. (1980). *Enigma di Otranto. Il mosaico pavimente del prebitero Pantoleone nella Cathedrale*. Galantina: Congedo.

Woods-Marden, J. (1988). *The Gonzaga of Mantua and Pisanello's Arthurian frescoes*. Princeton, NJ: Princeton University Press.

Part VI
Arthur in the Modern Age

27

A Postmodern Subject in Camelot: Mark Twain's (Re)Vision of Malory's *Morte Darthur* in *A Connecticut Yankee in King Arthur's Court*

Robert Paul Lamb

During the last third of the nineteenth century, the United States experienced a vast social and economic upheaval. Westward migration, internal improvements, railroad building, mining, capital investment, industrialization, technological advances, increased economies of scale, monopolies, national advertising and distribution of goods, *laissez-faire* government policies, immigration, and rapid urbanization transformed a loosely knit country of diverse regions and local economies into a modern nation-state and emerging global power. Industrial and agricultural production skyrocketed, but there arose huge disparities of wealth, hardened class divisions, and mass poverty, especially among former slaves, rural whites, and the over ten million immigrants from non-Anglophone cultures who streamed into the nation. These changes caused a high degree of disorientation and alienation in the national psyche, as previous fundamental assumptions – about the nature of the self, citizenship, government, religion, and morality – seemed increasingly untenable.

Confronted by this fragmented and heterogeneous society, upper- and middle-class whites felt beleaguered. Anglo-American institutions seemed, to them, threatened by "unassimilable" elements: four million ex-slaves, an urban working class of immigrants from Asia and southern and eastern Europe, radical ideologies, labor wars, political scandals, city slums, ward politics, and economic panics. To native-born whites, such developments appeared incompatible with a century-old Jeffersonian vision of an ethnically homogeneous nation of yeoman farmers and republican citizens. With the Civil War receding into memory, a pervasive belief spread that although industrialization and consumerism had produced material comforts, they had also brought "moral complacency, triumphant secularism, and an uneasy sense of artificiality" (Shi 1995: 214). Bourgeois white men felt enfeebled by over-civilization – anemic, feminized, and increasingly vulnerable. There existed a general feeling of "hovering soul-sickness," a belief that modern life had "grown dry and passionless," and that culture needed "to regenerate a lost intensity of feeling" (Lears 1981: 142). As America headed toward modernization and modernity, a culture of character, in which one's sense of self derived from who one was and what one produced, was being replaced by a culture of personality, in which that self arose from how one was viewed by others and what one purchased.

The need for middle-class white males to assert their masculinity, to view themselves as autonomous and empowered subjects, engendered a spirit of martial ardor. This mood nourished a "cult of strenuosity" that included national manias for hiking, bicycling, hunting, fishing, vacations at cowboy "dude" ranches, weightlifting, wrestling, boxing, and football. It also led to the expansion of the YMCA, the city playground movement, physical education classes in schools, and the new popularity of intercollegiate athletics. Among intellectuals in this age of Indian extermination in the west, immigration on the coasts, and incipient American imperialism abroad, the cult of strenuosity was used "to buttress doctrines of racial superiority, military adventure, and territorial expansion"; war itself was viewed as "a therapeutic alternative for a society suffering from social unrest and the anemia of modernity" (Shi 1995: 216–18).

Seeking to restore their feelings of autonomous manhood, white males also sought to construct a usable genealogy in which to anchor themselves. Medievalism had been a pronounced feature of American culture since the 1830s Gothic Revival in architecture. After the Civil War, a new interest in medieval literature emerged, hastened by American translations of medieval French, Italian, and Middle English texts, translations of the writings of medieval mystics, popular biographies of saints and of chivalric knights, and popular adaptations of medieval romances, often written for children (Moreland 1996: 3–4). In his classic study of anti-modernism in American culture during this period, *No Place of Grace*, T. J. Jackson Lears explores the reasons for medievalism's strong appeal, here nicely summarized by Kim Moreland:

> the fragmented nature of capitalist society, the upper-class fear of class degeneration, the increase in neurasthenia due to the luxury of urban life, the lack of an arena for physical and moral testing, the dissolution of rigorous Protestantism and its replacement by indiscriminate toleration, the emphasis on rationality to the exclusion of powerful emotions, the stifling effect of social and sexual propriety, and the fragmentation of the integral self. (1996: 8)

Toward the end of a century of science, technology, pragmatism, and a teleological faith in secular progress, then, many Americans looked back longingly at a medieval period that they curiously claimed as their own birthright, one they felt was characterized by "[p]ale innocence, fierce conviction, physical and emotional vitality, playfulness and spontaneity, an ability to cultivate fantastic or dreamlike states of awareness, [and] an intense otherworldly asceticism" (Lears 1981: 142).

Mark Twain and American Medievalism

America's greatest writer, Samuel Langhorne Clemens (1835–1910), was born to impoverished would-be gentry and raised in the slave culture of the antebellum South, but by the mid-1880s he had transformed himself into the world-renowned author Mark Twain: a self-taught, widely read, well-traveled, multilingual, Anglophile intellectual who now resided in Hartford, Connecticut among the New England custodians of culture. As a boy, he had been enchanted by Walter Scott and other romancers widely popular in southern culture, but although deeply nostalgic, he was also a child of the post-Enlightenment and Jeffersonian egalitarian democracy, a spokesman for nineteenth-century America's faith in moral progress who viewed technological advances as the material manifestation of that progress. To him, the medieval revival "in the midst of the refinement and dignity of a carefully-developed modern civilization" was incongruous. Attending a medieval tournament held in Brooklyn, New York in 1870, he wrote the "doings of the so-called 'chivalry' of the Middle Ages were absurd enough, even when they were brutally and bloodily in earnest," but this new "mock pageantry" was little more than "absurdity gone crazy." Tongue-in-cheek, he exhorted, "for next exhibition, let us have a fine representation of one of those chivalrous wholesale butcheries and burnings of Jewish women and children, which the crusading heroes of romance used to indulge in in their European homes, just before starting to the Holy Land, to seize and take to their protection the Sepulchre and defend it from 'pollution'" (Budd 1992: 420).

Twain's personal journey from antebellum southern chauvinist to cosmopolitan champion of human equality, along with his valuation of realist aesthetics, pragmatism, and vernacular ideology in opposition to, respectively, romanticism, devotion to ideality, and genteel literary tastes, had altered his feelings toward Scott, whom he now saw as having promulgated an insidiously anti-democratic imitative culture upon the South of his birth. Returning to the Mississippi River in 1882 after a 21-year absence, he pulled no punches in satirizing his region's enchantment with the Middle Ages. Twain held Scott "responsible for the Capitol building" in Baton Rouge, Louisiana, a "little sham castle . . . with turrets and things – materials all ungenuine within and without" and an "architectural falsehood." Half a century later, "[t]he South has not yet recovered from the debilitating influence of [Scott's] books. Admiration of his fantastic heroes and their grotesque 'chivalry' doings and romantic juvenilities still survives here" (Twain 1883/1984: 285). Among the southern grotesqueries identified by Twain were its bombastic oratory, outmoded codes of honor, love of class and hierarchy (including chattel slavery), backwoods-styled duels and feuds, and such insipid phrases as "the beauty and chivalry" (Twain 1883/1984: 322) used ad nauseam to describe such curiosities as the men and women of New Orleans attending a mule race.

What Twain most hated about southern medievalism was its undoing of the benefits wrought by the French Revolution, which had sundered "the chains of the *ancien régime* and of the Church," creating meritocracy and serving the causes of "liberty, humanity, and progress":

> Then comes Sir Walter Scott with his enchantments, and by his single might checks this wave of progress, and even turns it back; sets the world in love with dreams and phantoms; with decayed and swinish forms of religion; with decayed and degraded systems of government; with the sillinesses and emptinesses, sham grandeurs, sham gauds, and sham chivalries of a brainless and worthless long-vanished society. . . . [In the South] the genuine and wholesome civilization of the nineteenth century is curiously confused and commingled with the Walter Scott Middle-Age sham civilization and so you have practical, common-sense, progressive ideas, and progressive works; mixed up with the duel, the inflated speech, and the jejune romanticism of an absurd past that is dead, and out of charity ought to be buried. . . . It was Sir Walter that made every gentleman in the South a Major or a Colonel, or a General or a Judge, before the war; and it was he, also, that made these gentlemen value these bogus decorations. For it was he that created rank and caste down there, and also reverence for rank and caste, and pride and pleasure in them. (Twain 1883/1984: 327–8)

He concludes by juxtaposing Scott's *Ivanhoe* with *Don Quixote*, his own favorite novel. Cervantes "swept the world's admiration for the mediæval chivalry-silliness out of existence; and the other restored it." In the South, "the good work done by Cervantes is pretty nearly a dead letter, so effectually has Scott's pernicious work undermined it" (Twain 1883/1984: 328–9).

Twain's Camelot

Twain may have been contemptuous of contemporary medievalism but he was well-versed in British and Continental history and literature. Despite being closely identified with American subjects and vernacular characters like Tom Sawyer, Huck Finn, Jim, and a host of autobiographical fictional personae, the Middle Ages were, second only to the Missouri of his youth, a touchstone of his later authorial career, forming the setting of four novels, a play, and numerous stories and essays, including *1601* (1880), *The Prince and the Pauper* (1881), *Personal Recollections of Joan of Arc* (1896), and four versions of his final novel, *No. 44, The Mysterious Stranger* (posthumous 1969).

A Connecticut Yankee in King Arthur's Court (1889) – in which a conflated medieval period from the sixth to the fifteenth centuries serves as the fabula – is a novel rich in interpretive terrain. To genre critics, it is a pioneering work in time-travel science fiction, an early example of American literary naturalism, a satire of Horatio Alger's popular "rags-to-riches" formula fictions, a dystopia written in the heyday of utopian novels, and a novel that invents the postmodern subject. To cultural critics, it is an anatomy of imperialism (influencing Conrad's *Heart of Darkness* and Kipling's short story "The Man Who Would Be King"), a study in ethnicity and the dynamics of assimilation, a critique of the nineteenth-century's teleological faith in moral and technological progress, and a literary death blow to the Frontier Myth that had long dominated American ideology. To rhetoricians and political scientists, it is a study of the mindsets of oral versus written cultures, contrasting their respective views on language, narrative, ontology, epistemology, the individual and communal society, the self and state. To historians, it is a critique of the nineteenth-century's medieval revival, an allegory on the "rise" of western civilization, and a preternaturally predictive book anticipating the nature of such twentieth-century phenomena as modern total warfare, the rise of secular dictators (the protagonist's title – "The Boss" – is revealingly translated as "Der Fuhrer" and "Il Duce" in German and Italian editions), the uses of propaganda and disinformation by the state in the age of mass communication, and modern campaigns of genocide. Even the name that "The Boss" gives to his program for a democratic republic is predictive, appropriated by Franklin Roosevelt as "The New Deal."

For those unacquainted with the novel, a brief synopsis will be necessary. Hank Morgan – "a Yankee of Yankees" (Twain 1889/1983: 4), practical, unsentimental, trained in machine and armaments making, and head superintendent at the Colt firearms factory – gets knocked unconscious in an industrial dispute and wakes up in sixth-century England, where he is "captured" by Sir Kay the Seneschal, taken to Arthur's court, hears endless monologues about improbable adventures, is described by Kay as a "taloned man-devouring ogre" (31), and is condemned to be burned at the stake. Aided by an anachronistically modern-minded page named Clarence, he uses the solar eclipse of 528 to demonstrate his magical powers, and forces Arthur to appoint him perpetual minister and give him one percent of all additional revenue he creates for the state. With Merlin plotting against him, and needing another "miracle" to convince the people of his power, he blows up the tower of his rival magician and becomes "The Boss."

Over the next seven years Hank brings modern civilization to Camelot, keeping it mostly from public view. During this time, he introduces steel and iron, and hat and textile manufacturing (heavy and light industry); an efficient and equitable tax system (redistributing income to create a home market); free trade (acquiring foreign markets); an insurance industry and stock exchange (capital accumulation and investment); a patent office (encouraging research and development); a national mint (stabilizing currency); a teaching academy and public schools (literacy); military and naval academies (defense); "man factories" (paramilitary units); Protestant denominations (separation of church and state); newspapers, the telegraph, telephone lines, and advertising (mass communication); steamboats and railroads (mass transportation); meritocracy in public and military service (undermining hereditary privilege); public hygiene and a fire department (public safety); and phonographs, typewriters, sewing machines, and baseball (consumer items and entertainment).

Encouraged by Arthur to seek adventures, Hank sets off with Demoiselle Alisande la Carteloise, whom he calls Sandy, in search of a castle where four-armed, one-eyed giants are holding her mistress and forty-four young princesses captive. This sequence – in which he meets commoners and learns of their oppressions, defeats seven knights awed by his pipe smoke, views Morgan le Fay's cruelty, discovers that the ogres are actually swineherds and the princesses hogs, and again tops Merlin by fixing a Holy Fountain through ostensibly superior magic – gives Twain an opportunity to satirize and contrast the two civilizations. In the next long sequence, Hank and Arthur travel the country incognito. Hank dynamites knights who attack Arthur; the king demonstrates his true nobility by braving smallpox to aid a woman; they observe the aftermath of the murder of a lord and are betrayed, sold into slavery, and view first-hand the barbaric treatment of the poor. In London, condemned to be hanged, they are saved when Launcelot and five hundred knights ride to their rescue on bicycles.

In the final sequences, Hank's joust with Sagramour, backed by Merlin, turns deadly after he unseats him with a lasso, and he uses a revolver to kill Sagramour and other knights who charge him. With knight errantry broken, Hank reveals his secret civilization to a gadding world and lays plans for undermining the church. He marries Sandy, moves temporarily to the French coast for their child's health, and, upon returning, discovers all in ruins. Launcelot, in charge of the stock exchange (formerly the Round Table), has engaged in insider trading, causing Agravaine and Mordred to inform Arthur of Launcelot's affair with Guenever. This leads to civil war, the deaths of Mordred and Arthur, and a church interdict on the country until Hank is dead. With the church in control, Hank retreats to a fortified cave with Clarence and fifty-two trained boys, declares the end of monarchy, nobility, and the established church, and proclaims his republic. His final modern achievement is genocide as Hank uses electrified fences and Gatling guns to slaughter the entire knighthood of England, turning twenty-five thousand men into "homogeneous protoplasm, with alloys of iron and buttons" (Twain 1889/1983: 432). With the fifty-four-man army trapped in their cave and dying from the poisonous fumes of the corpses, a disguised Merlin puts Hank into a thirteen-century sleep and is then grotesquely electrocuted when he backs into the fence.

The inspiration for *Connecticut Yankee* was Twain's first encounter with Malory's *Le Morte Darthur* in late 1884 (Strachey's Caxton-based Globe Edition). Initially enchanted, he scribbled a notebook entry:

> Dream of being a knight errant in armor in the middle ages. Have the notions & habits of thought of the present day mixed with the necessities of that. No pockets in the armor. No way to manage certain requirements of nature. Can't scratch. Cold in the head – can't blow – can't get at handkerchief, can't use iron sleeve. . . . Fall down, can't get up. (Browning et al. 1979: 78)

A subsequent entry envisaged "a battle between a modern army, with gatling guns – (automatic) 600 shots a minute" and medieval crusaders. A year later, an 1886 entry had the novel titled "The Lost Land." The time-traveling narrator, back in the nineteenth century, visits England "but it is all changed & become old, so old! – & it was so fresh & new, so virgin before"; he grieves his sixth-century sweetheart, loses interest in life, and commits suicide (Browning et al. 1979: 86, 216). Together, these early plans point to, respectively, a humorous contrast, a violent confrontation between modern and "third-world" military technology, and a sentimental love story – but little plot. As late as November 1886, Twain still had in mind not "a satire peculiarly," but "a *contrast*," claiming "I shall leave unsmirched & unbelittled the great & beautiful characters drawn by the master hand of old Malory" (Wecter 1949: 257–58). In the three chapters already written, the sixth-century characters, except for a buffoonish Merlin, were favorably portrayed. The narrator opines: "there was something very engaging about these great simple-hearted creatures, something attractive and lovable"; a "noble benignity and purity reposed" in Sir Galahad and the king; and "there was majesty and greatness in the giant frame and high bearing of Sir Launcelot" (Twain 1889/1983: 22–3).

All versions of Arthurian legend are dialogical texts, the originary fabula (about which we know little) complexly shaped by socio-historical contexts of the narrating present. As Derek Pearsall notes, Arthurian literature "has provided a medium through which different cultures" can "express their deepest hopes and aspirations and contain and circumscribe their deepest fears and anxieties" (2003: vii). This dynamic is especially foregrounded in Twain's version because the first-person narrator brings the present and past into direct contact. But although the original idea of a contrast would remain, when Twain returned to the novel, in summer 1887, the intended innocuous romance changed into a comprehensive and devastating satire, one aimed at the culture and institutions of medieval Britain and their perpetuation in late nineteenth-century Britain, then at turn-of-the-century America, and ultimately at the entire history of western civilization.

Twain, Republicanism, and Contemporary Britain

What turned this bland romance into one of the culturally richest and most complex novels of the past two centuries? First, Twain finally read all of *Morte Darthur* and found it at odds with his earlier readings of Scott, Tennyson, and Sidney Lanier's bowdlerized version of Malory. Far from being the Golden Age of honor proclaimed by medievalists, it was a world in which Arthur and his knights lie, cheat, steal, break solemn vows, betray friends, and casually slaughter men, women, and children (Bowden 2000: 180–81, 196–7). In addition, events of the previous eighteen months had intervened. As he resumed writing the novel in summer 1887, Twain told William Dean Howells, "When I finished Carlyle's French Revolution in 1871, I was a Girondin; every time I have read it since, I have read it differently – being influenced & changed, little by little, by life & environment." Now, he declared: "I am a Sansculotte! – And not a pale, characterless Sansculotte, but a Marat. Carlyle teaches no such gospel: so the change is in *me* – in my vision of the evidences" (Smith & Gibson 1960: 595, original italics).

Twain possessed a Whig view of history as the secular story of mankind's evolution from tyranny to liberty. In politics he was ideologically aligned with progressive

Republicans at home and the reform wing of the British Liberal Party abroad, several
of whose members were his personal friends. In an unpublished manuscript from the
late 1880s, he listed the stages by which British civilization had progressed. As Roger
Salomon observes, these read like a "check list of Whig-Liberal legislation": destruction of serfage and slavery, weakening of the church, representative government and
extension of suffrage, penal reform, army reform through meritocracy, stripping of
privilege from the aristocracy (1961: 27). But during the years when *Connecticut Yankee*
was germinating, the road to progress in Britain seemed impassable. In spring 1885,
Gladstone's ministry fell, with many enfranchised by the Liberal Party's Reform Act
of 1885 voting Conservative. Enforced tithing led to riots in Wales, and attempts to
disestablish the Anglican Church were proving futile. Despite some reforms, anti-
poaching laws and penalties remained strong, as did the judicial prerogatives of the
squirearchy. In 1887, a public education bill was defeated, and class status still determined military commissions. During this time, Twain was pouring through the works
of Carlyle, Lecky, Taine, Saint-Simon, and Dickens. He also became friends with
George Standring, the radical London printer and recent author of *The People's History
of the English Aristocracy*. Standring's book called for replacing the British monarchy
with a republic; documented how the ill-gotten wealth of the aristocracy enabled it
to control Lords, Commons, manufacturing, the professions, and the military; critiqued the slavish devotion of the British people to royalty; and exposed the crimes
and decadence – historical and current – of the nobility (Baetzhold 1970: 102–30
passim).

      With his characteristically American conviction that privilege and the concentra-
tion of power were insurmountable obstacles to progress, Twain contemplated with
disgust Queen Victoria's Golden Jubilee, attended by the crowned heads of Europe
who were her kin, at the same time as he bridled under Matthew Arnold's most recent
disparagement of America's democratic culture. He filled his notebooks with increasing fury. To Arnold's criticism of the American press's irreverence and America's
predilection for "funny men" like Twain, he wrote, "Irreverence is the champion of
liberty, & its only sure defense." On the English reverence for royalty, he jotted,
"Yours is the civilization of slave-making ants" and "How superbly brave is the
Eng[lishman] in the presence of the awfulest forms of danger & death; & how abject
in the presence of any & all forms of hereditary rank." His sharpest barbs were reserved
for royalty itself: "The kingly office is entitled to no respect; it was originally procured
by the highwayman's methods; it remains a perpetuated crime"; "if you cross a king
with a prostitute, the resulting mongrel perfectly satisfies the Eng[lish] idea of
'nobility'"; "The institution of royalty, in any form, is an insult to the human race"
(Browning et al. 1979: 392, 398–401, 424).

      Connecticut Yankee is informed by these views and critical of pernicious medieval
customs that Twain believed had continued into the present. But his critique is not
of Malory's book, passages of which he considered unequalled in eloquence until
Lincoln's Gettysburg Address, and part of which – Sir Ector's eulogy of Launcelot – he
quoted at length in his own eulogy of his close friend, General Ulysses S. Grant

"BROTHER!—TO DIRT   "BROTHER!—TO DIRT   "BROTHER!—TO DIRT
   LIKE THAT?"   LIKE THAT?"   LIKE THAT?"

Figure 27.1 Triptych by Dan Beard, from the first edition of Mark Twain's *A Connecticut Yankee in King Arthur's Court* (1889: 363).

(Browning et al. 1979: 159, n. 112). Rather, Twain set his fabula in the distant past in order to address the time of narration. This was a strategy he often employed. For example, the last fifth of *Adventures of Huckleberry Finn* (1884) takes place in the mid-1840s era of slavery but is really a parody on Reconstruction and its aftermath. Likewise, *Pudd'nhead Wilson* (1894) takes place from 1830 to 1853, but is actually a critique of racism and the color line in the 1890s.

Many of the abuses Twain exposes arise from his hatred of privilege, class hierarchy, and tyranny. The contemporaneousness of these issues is often underscored by the 221 illustrations that appeared in the original 1889 American edition of the book, published in New York by Charles L. Webster. The illustrations were by Dan Beard, the gifted socialist artist whose work the author enthusiastically endorsed. For example, when traveling incognito, Hank advises Arthur to address a commoner as "friend" or "brother" rather than "varlet." Arthur replies, "Brother! – to dirt like that?" Beard's illustration is a triptych, with Arthur's reply written under each pane (figure 27.1). The first shows a king speaking to a peasant, the second an antebellum slaveholder and an African American slave, and the third an industrialist and a factory worker. Under these illustrations respectively are a sword, a law book, and a bag of money with the word "oppressor" written on each (Twain 1889/1983: 275–7).

Or, as Hank himself puts it, "a privileged class, an aristocracy, is but a band of slaveholders under another name" (239). Sometimes, Beard modeled characters on contemporary personages. When Hank realizes that the "maidens" he has rescued are literally swine, a full-page illustration depicts a popular portrait of Queen Victoria with the face of a hog, the caption reading, "the troublesomest old Sow of the lot" (figure 27.2).

When Arthur raises an army and ignores the merits of Hank's West Pointers in favor of unqualified officers of noble birth, another full-page illustration identifies

Figure 27.2 "The troublesomest old Sow . . .," *Connecticut Yankee* (1889: 237).

these "chuckleheads" as the Prince of Wales (later Edward VII), his son Prince Albert, and another of Victoria's grandchildren, Kaiser Wilhelm II (225). Other figures so "honored" include the corrupt American railroad magnate Jay Gould as a satanic slavedriver and Tennyson as a thoroughly ridiculous Merlin (figure 27.3; 359, 21, 211).

Hank Morgan often speaks for Twain. Both locate sovereignty in the people and are committed to representative government. Both believe in equality of opportunity and fear concentrations of power. Both share the ideology of republicanism: that power is inherently aggressive and must be restrained by constitutional government in order to protect liberty, and that citizens must be virtuous and civic-minded, joined together in a spirit of mutual responsibility. Hank proudly states:

> I was from Connecticut, whose Constitution declares "that all political power is inherent in the people, and all free governments are founded on their authority and instituted for their benefit; and that they have *at all times* an undeniable and indefeasible right to *alter their form of government* in such a manner as they may think expedient." (Twain 1889/1983: 113, original italics)

"HE UNLIMBERED HIS TONGUE AND CURSED LIKE A BISHOP."

Figure 27.3 Portrait of Tennyson as Merlin, *Connecticut Yankee* (1889: 279).

Hank insists a change in government must issue from the people and not from the enlightened few: "I knew that the Jack Cade or Wat Tyler who tries such a thing without first educating his materials up to revolution-grade is almost absolutely certain to get left" (114). But to do this, he must rid the people of slavish habits of mind they have inherited, most especially "the idea that all men without title and a long pedigree" are "so many animals, bugs, insects" (65). Although "Arthur's people were of course poor material for a republic, because they had been debased so long by monarchy" (242), Hank believes that "a man is at bottom a man, after all, even if it doesn't show on the outside" (297) and he has faith that all nations are "capable of self-government" because "in all ages" the greatest minds "have sprung" from "the mass of the nation" and "not from its privileged classes" (242). Thus, his public schools, teaching academies, man-factories, and newspapers are intended to enlighten the masses and prepare them for self-government. His overall plan is: "First, a modified monarchy, till Arthur's days were done, then the destruction of the throne, nobility abolished, every member of it bound out to some useful trade, universal suffrage instituted, and the whole government placed in the hands of the men and women of the nation" (300).

First-Person Polyphony: Hank Morgan as Postmodern Subject

Although Hank often represents Twain's point of view, he is no mere authorial persona. Mixed in with his subject positions of egalitarian democrat, advocate of republican government, nineteenth-century liberal, and social reformer are other, less benevolent ideologies. Although he sets up a "variety of Protestant congregations" rather than making "everybody a Presbyterian" (his own sect) because an established church "makes a mighty power" and "means death to human liberty" (Twain 1889/1983: 81), he is aware that democracy is messy and despotism efficient. He admits: "unlimited power *is* the ideal thing – when it is in safe hands. The despotism of heaven is the one absolutely perfect government." An earthly despotism, he adds, would be perfect too, but only if the despot and his successors were themselves perfect, an impossibility (81–2).

Power, as republican ideology preaches, corrupts, and Hank proves as corruptible as anyone. Relatively early on, he gives way to ominously imperial and sinister language. "My works showed what a despot could do, with the resources of a kingdom at his command." He compares his budding civilization to a "volcano, standing innocent with its smokeless summit in the blue sky and giving no sign of the rising hell in its bowels." Referring to "[m]y schools and churches," "my little shops," "my military academy," "my naval academy," and Clarence as "my head executive," he issues a statement chilling to post-Hiroshima readers: "I stood with my finger on the button, so to speak, ready to press it and flood the midnight world with intolerable light at any moment" (Twain 1889/1983: 82–3). Contemplating his "revolution without bloodshed" after defeating knight errantry at the joust, he confesses, "I was beginning to have a base hankering to be its first President myself. Yes, there was more or less human nature in me; I found that out" (399).

Hank's dilemma is fourfold. First, he does not comprehend the difference between authority and power, roughly analogous to hegemony and coercion. Second, his power is based on his superior technological knowledge. If he educates the people – and can no longer pass off solar eclipses, firearms, and dynamite as personal magic – his power must necessarily vanish. Third, his political ideology locates sovereignty in the people but he cannot bring himself to respect *these* people, which creates a disjunction between ideology and inclination. Fourth, he is himself an unstable subject, reflecting in his contradictory thoughts and actions the fragmentation of the late-nineteenth-century American national self. He is both humanist and nihilist; essentialist and existentialist; realist and sentimentalist; utilitarian pragmatist and idealist; nineteenth-century liberal and proto-Marxist economist; egalitarian suffragist and totalitarian dictator; advocate of fair trade and free trade; social reformer and genocidal imperialist. A site upon which incompatible ideologies from his own time and place contend, increasingly absorbed into the ethos of the new world he has entered, and continually acquiring and maintaining his sense of self through performance, Hank

– literature's first postmodern subject – possesses no stable set of beliefs upon which to build his program (Lamb 2005: 486–7).

The distinction between power and authority was first recognized by the ancient Mesopotamians in the *Enuma Elish* (c. 1800–1200 BC), which is both a cosmogonic myth and a kingship epic. The universe's original elements of chaos seek to destroy the gods of order they have created but, in the first encounter, Ea-Enki defeats his adversary with a spell. Significantly, "this first great victory of the gods over the powers of chaos," as Thorkild Jacobsen observes, is "won through authority and not through physical force" (1974: 189). But in a second encounter, authority is not enough, and the gods turn to Marduk, a young god possessed of great strength but lacking "influence" (authority). The older gods grant him authority commensurate with theirs and, for the first time in mythopoeic thought, authority and force are united in kingship:

> We gave thee kingship, power over all things.
> Take thy seat in the council, may thy word prevail. . . .
> The gods, his fathers, seeing (the power of) his word,
> Rejoiced, paid homage: "Marduk is king."
> (Jacobsen 1974: 193)

In Twain's Camelot, the king and his knights possess power. Arthur also combines this with authority through the divine right of kings and his connection with Merlin, who represents through his spells and magic the unexplained residue of dark authority beyond the ken of Christianity (when Merlin begins an incantation to protect his tower from Hank, the people "fell back and began to cross themselves and get uncomfortable" [Twain 1889/1983: 58]). The church, of course, is the ultimate authority in this text, and the main source of Arthur's. This bifurcation of power and authority is nicely captured in Beard's illustration of Hugo on the rack in Morgan le Fay's dungeon, where over his tortured body stand a priest holding a cross and a guard with a spear (154). Hank himself notes: "To be vested with enormous authority is a fine thing; but to have the on-looking world consent to it is a finer. The tower-episode solidified my power, and made it impregnable" (62). Here he links authority with consent (the sovereignty of the people) while properly distinguishing it from power. But he then goes on to call the church a "power" stronger than Arthur's and his together (63), ignoring the authority that Arthur derives from the church and Merlin, and mistaking the church's authority for power. Although, in his opinion, he is "a giant among pygmies" because "a master intelligence among intellectual moles," nevertheless he acknowledges that the people merely "admire" and "fear" him as they would an elephant, but without "reverence mixed with it" (65–7). He could gain this reverence, this portion of authority to go along with his power, were he to accept the title Arthur offers him, but in his eyes it would be illegitimate – because not coming from the people – and so he prefers to win a title through "honest and honorable endeavor" (68). Moreover, he will discover that an aristocracy of "merit is still an aristocracy – an order dependent on political and cultural privilege" in which "the maintenance of social order is still dependent on force" (Slotkin 1985: 530). He ends up caught between the Scylla of having power without authority in a feudal state and the Charybdis of having nothing in a democratic one.

Democracy is also precluded by his perspective toward these people he theoretically considers sovereign. He begins by calling them "childlike," "white Indians," "animals," and "modified savages"; in the end, when they fail to embrace his program because, for all his power, he has failed to win their hearts and minds and gain authority, he calls them "human muck" (Twain 1889/1983: 20, 40, 108, 427). From there to "homogeneous protoplasm" (432) is but a short step.

Hank's failure to see their humanity, as Thomas Zlatic observes, derives from "the confrontation of a literate mentality with a predominately oral mind-set" (1991: 454 and *passim*). Oral culture is conservative and communal, with mental energy employed to preserve, through stories of heroic figures in set situations, what is already known. New facts are assimilated to these formulaic stories, with redundancy (*copia*) the norm so that stories can be remembered and passed along. Such discourse is non-abstract, non-analytical, and non-contextual, and their narrators are un-self-conscious, non-reflective, and matter-of-fact, recognizing no distinction between the ideal and the actual. Hank's culture, however, with knowledge and stories preserved in writing, prizes individualism, creativity, accuracy, specificity, variety, credibility, and innovative departures from what is known. Narrators like Hank are self-conscious and deeply ironic because they see the discrepancy between the real and the ideal (as when Kay describes a naked Hank as a "horrible sky-towering monster" [Twain 1889/1983: 31]).

Twain understood both oral and written culture. He grew up in the worlds of southwestern humor, African American folklore, western anecdotes, jokes and tall tales, memorized public lecture tours, and piloting, but he was also a prodigious reader in several languages, a professional journalist, and an accomplished printer. Unlike Twain, however, Hank has no appreciation of the communal elements of oral culture; in fact, he views these negatively as a lack of individualism. When Sandy relates the story of Gawaine, Uwaine, and Marhaus (extracted verbatim from Malory's *Morte Darthur*, IV, xvi–xix, xxiv–xxv in the Caxton edition), he continually interrupts to mock her, advising her on how to spice up the tale (Twain 1889/1983: 126–34). Viewing her discourse as automatic, he consequently images Sandy as a machine: her unceasing "clack" could "grind, and pump, and churn and buzz" but with no more ideas "than a fog has" (103). Others are similarly imaged as automata. For example, when he encounters St Stylite on a pillar bowing and praying, he concocts a plan "to apply a system of elastic cords to him and run a sewing machine with it" (214). He does gradually develop a mysterious "reverence" for Sandy and sentimentally reconceptualizes her in the image of a nineteenth-century wife and mother, and he makes exceptions for the king whenever Arthur's innate nobility overcomes his social conditioning, as when he gently carries a girl dying of smallpox to her mother: "the king's bearing was as serenely brave as it had always been in those cheaper contests where knight meets knight in equal fight and clothed in protecting steel. He was great, now; sublimely great" (286). At moments like this, Hank glimpses value in Arthurian Britain, but mainly he views it as a "dead nation" (74).

The "Triumph" of Technology

The Battle of the Sand-Belt at the end of *Connecticut Yankee* seems inevitable and anticipates the fighting of the Great War that would commence twenty-five years after the novel's publication, a war of immobility, trenches, poison gas, machine guns, and anonymous men mechanically turned into corpses, in which the death count arose from a technology that had outstripped both conventional military strategies and moral progress. But the twenty-five thousand knights killed wholesale at the Sand-Belt curiously resemble a culture much like the one Twain critiqued in his attack on the South in *Life on the Mississippi*, an incongruous mix of the progressive and the medieval, nicely characterized by the traveling-salesmen knights who canvass the countryside dressed in sandwich-board advertisements spreading Hank's civilization at the point of sword and lance, or by Launcelot and his fellow knights on bicycles. The technology that transforms Camelot was, in real life, transforming the North into an industrial giant and America into a global power. But by 1889 Twain had grown disenchanted with technology and suspicious of man's capacity for moral growth; his personal investment in the fated Paige typesetter was ruining him financially (Kaplan 1966: 280–311) and technology was undermining both republican values and democratic ideals. If contemporary Britain seemed to him a perpetuation of outmoded feudal institutions, modernizing America seemed increasingly a nightmare. More complexly than the American medievalists who felt a cultural weightlessness and turned to the past for renewal, Twain discovered his nostalgia and progressivism in conflict, and imagined a nearly demonic Hank gleefully demolishing the pillars of the house he has created, damning the past and present with equal force. The symmetry of Merlin defeating Hank with a spell (authority) and then being electrocuted by Hank's fence (power), as well as Merlin's grotesque "petrified laugh" (Twain 1899/1983: 443), are fit symbols of the nihilistic conclusion of *Connecticut Yankee*, an apt fable for the end of a century of progress and a caution to us at the commencement of a century of global ideological strife accompanied by even greater technologies of mass destruction.

Connecticut Yankee concludes with a dying Hank, now "a stranger" in his own time, yearning for his lost Camelot and bemoaning the "abyss of thirteen centuries yawning between . . . me and my home and my friends! between me and all that is dear to me, all that could make life worth the living!" (Twain 1889/1983: 447). Twain's own unsentimental, bitter postscript would come in a letter to Howells:

Well, my book is written – let it go. But if it were only to write over again there wouldn't be so many things left out. They burn in me; & they keep multiplying & multiplying; but now they can't ever be said. And besides, they would require a library – & a pen warmed up in hell. (Smith & Gibson 1960: 613)

In his final two decades, Twain would increasingly view human beings as little more than machines and wonder if life were, after all, but a walking shadow. These twin visions of despair pervade *Connecticut Yankee*, with its soulless technocrat narrator and complex dream structure. For Mark Twain, the path to progress would lead, in the end, to an apocalyptic vision and an existential *cul-de-sac*.

Primary Sources

Browning, R. P., Frank, M. B., & Salamo, L. (eds) (1979). *Mark Twain's notebooks and journals*, vol. 3: *1883–1891*. Berkeley, CA: University of California Press.

Budd, L. J. (ed.) (1992). *Mark Twain: Collected tales, sketches, speeches, and essays, 1952–1890*. New York: Library of America.

Fishkin, S. F. (ed.) (1996). *The Oxford Mark Twain*, 29 vols. Oxford: Oxford University Press.

Smith, H. N. & Gibson, W. M. (eds) (1960). *Mark Twain–Howells letters: The correspondence of Samuel L. Clemens and William D. Howells, 1872–1910*, 2 vols. Cambridge, MA: Harvard University Press.

Strachey, E. (ed.) (1925). *Thomas Malory. Le Morte Darthur* (The Globe Edition). London: Macmillan. (Originally published 1868.)

Twain, M. (1983). *A Connecticut Yankee in King Arthur's court*. Berkeley, CA: University of California Press. (Originally published 1889.)

Twain, M. (1984). *Life on the Mississippi*. New York: Penguin. (Originally published 1883.)

Wecter, D. (ed.) (1949). *Mark Twain to Mrs Fairbanks*. San Marino, CA: Huntington Library.

References and Further Reading

Baetzhold, H. G. (1970). *Mark Twain and John Bull: The British connection*. Bloomington, IN: Indiana University Press.

Bowden, B. (2000). Gloom and doom in Mark Twain's *Connecticut Yankee*, from Thomas Malory's *Morte Darthur*. *Studies in American Fiction*, 28(2), 179–202.

Budd, L. J. (1962). *Mark Twain: Social philosopher*. Bloomington, IN: Indiana University Press.

Camfield, G. (2003). *The Oxford companion to Mark Twain*. New York: Oxford University Press.

Jacobsen, T. (1974). Mesopotamia. In H. Frankfort, H. A. Groenewegen-Frankfort, J. A. Wilson, & T. Jacobsen, *Before philosophy: The intellectual adventure of ancient man*. New York: Penguin, pp. 135–234.

Kaplan, J. (1966). *Mr Clemens and Mark Twain: A biography*. New York: Simon & Schuster.

Kasson, J. F. (1976). *Civilizing the machine: Technology and republican values in America, 1776–1900*. New York: Penguin.

Kordecki, L. C. (1986). Twain's critique of Malory's romance: *Forma tractandi* and *A Connecticut Yankee*. *Nineteenth-Century Literature*, 41(3), 329–48.

Lamb, R. P. (2005). "America can break your heart": On the significance of Mark Twain. In R. P. Lamb & G. R. Thompson (eds), *A companion to American fiction, 1865–1914*. Oxford: Blackwell, pp. 468–98.

Lears, T. J. J. (1981). *No place of grace: Antimodernism and the transformation of American culture, 1880–1920*. New York: Pantheon.

Moreland, K. (1996). *The medievalist impulse in American literature: Twain, Adams, Fitzgerald, and Hemingway*. Charlottesville, VA: University of Virginia Press.

Pearsall, D. (2003). *Arthurian romance: A short introduction*. Oxford: Blackwell.

Powers, R. (2005). *Mark Twain: A life*. New York: Free Press.

Salomon, R. B. (1961). *Twain and the image of history*. New Haven, CT: Yale University Press.

Shi, D. (1995). *Facing facts: Realism in American thought and culture, 1850–1920*. New York: Oxford University Press.

Slotkin, R. (1985). *The fatal environment: The myth of the frontier in the age of industrialization, 1800–1890*. New York: Atheneum.

Zlatic, T. D. (1991). Language technologies in *A Connecticut Yankee*. *Nineteenth-Century Literature*, 45(4), 453–77.

28

T. H. White's *The Once and Future King*

Andrew Hadfield

In the first chapter of the second book of *The Once and Future King*, Queen Morgause boils a cat, half-heartedly planning to cast a spell of sorts. The description of the cat's agonizing death, and the stark contrast of this paragraph to the next one, outlining the insouciant complacency of its killer, is characteristic of the themes and structure of White's complex tetralogy:

> In the boiling water, the cat gave some horrible convulsions and a dreadful cry. Its wet fur bobbed in the steam, gleaming like the side of a speared whale, as it tried to leap or swim with its bound feet. Its mouth opened hideously, showing the whole of its pink gullet, and the sharp, white cat-teeth, like thorns. After the first shriek it was not able to articulate, but only to stretch its jaws. Later it was dead.
>
> Queen Morgause of Lothian and Orkney sat beside the cauldron and waited. Occasionally she stirred the cat with a wooden spoon. The stench of boiling fur began to fill the room. A watcher would have seen, in the flattering peat light, what an exquisite creature she was tonight: her deep, big eyes, her hair glinting with dark lustre, her full body, and her faint air of watchfulness as she listened for the whispering in the room above. (White 1958: 221)

For those readers familiar with White's story only through the saccharine Walt Disney film of *The Sword in the Stone* (1963), this passage might come as something of a shock. The episode marks the transition from the relative innocence of the Wart's boyhood described in that opening book – even if there are many significant pointers toward the harsh nature of the world outside the Forest Sauvage in his wide range of experiences – to the savagery of the adult world outside. The reader is forced to confront the problem of cruelty, the concept that holds the book together and which gives White's retelling of the Arthurian legends a distinctive identity. Is Morgause acting unnaturally in destroying another creature so wantonly (she later loses interest in her experiment and simply abandons the remains of the dead cat)? Or showing how dreadful and terrifying nature untamed by civilization can be?

There is a contrast between animal and human, which would imply the former, but then we also have to remember that the incident takes place in the most remote area of Arthur's empire, the Scottish islands, those least tamed by Arthur's centralizing efforts to unite his dominions. Morgause does all she can to exploit the festering resentment of her children and turn them against Arthur because of his father's seduction of Igraine, their grandmother: "They considered the enormous English wickedness in silence, overwhelmed by its *dénouement*. It was their mother's favourite story, on the rare occasions when she troubled to tell them one, and they had learned it by heart" (White 1958: 220). We have a pointed contrast between the rich, life-enhancing education that Merlyn gives to Arthur in *The Sword in the Stone* and the neglect practiced by Morgause, allied to her obvious hypocrisy in pointing out the supposed cruelty of others while she is so blind to her own.

White's portrayal of Morgause began as a savage attack on the failings of his own mother, as early readers of the book recognized, persuading White to revise the manuscript a number of times, and to transform the book itself from its first incarnation as *The Witch in the Wood* (1939) to *The Queen of Air and Darkness* in *The Once and Future King* (Warner 1967: 130; Gallix 1982: 124). More importantly, the representation of the vicious queen of the Orkneys is a significant element in White's exploration of the nature of violence and the problem of cruelty written against the background of World War II. White had been a pacifist in the 1930s, and had struggled with his decision to go into exile in Ireland, eventually offering his services to the forces and, when these were declined, seeing his novels as a part of the war effort (Brewer 1993: 11; Hadfield 1996: 209).

The series of novels explores the problem of how violence occurs and whether anything can be done to stop it. Arthur's weak response to the attacks of the Orkney family, who seek to undo his efforts at establishing stability, is to excuse their failings, arguing like a good liberal. When Lancelot, new to the court, asks what is the problem with the Orkney faction, Arthur responds that "The real matter with them is Morgause, their mother. She brought them up with so little love or security that they find it difficult to understand warm-hearted people themselves. They are suspicious and frightened . . . It's not their fault" (White 1958: 345). Clearly, such responses, whatever their truth-value, are unlikely to halt determined and wicked resistance to civilized values and show the limitations of Arthur's abilities as a ruler.

Lancelot, the ugly and lonely ill-made knight, has a very different encounter with cruelty, one that complicates the plot still further, and helps to destroy the kingdom, but brings about his own personal redemption. Lancelot and Guenever go out hawking. Having miscalculated the falcon's food the night before, Lancelot is in a terrible mood, which makes Guenever nervous and clumsy, and she winds up the twine that controls the bird badly. When Lancelot snatches it from her he realizes that "he had hurt a real person of his own age" (White 1958: 348), a revelation that causes him to fall in love with her. Lancelot's nature and education have made him into a controlled and cruel creature who enjoys hurting others, which is why he now feels such an explosion of emotion. Lancelot's self-knowledge and attempt to control his feelings, in effect to civilize himself, are simultaneously noble and disastrous, just like Arthur's liberal decency. White's narrator comments at length, drawing our attention to the importance of this seemingly insignificant episode:

> It is the bad people who need to have principles to restrain them. For one thing, he [Lancelot] liked to hurt people. It was for the strange reason that he was cruel, that the poor fellow never killed a man who asked for mercy, or committed a cruel action which he could have prevented. One reason why he fell in love with Guenever was because the first thing he had done was to hurt her. He might never have noticed her as a person, if he had not seen the pain in her eyes. (White 1958: 353)

The civilized Lancelot stands in contrast to the uncontrolled nature of Morgause. However, they both contribute to the destruction of the Arthurian world.

One reason why it is so hard to attribute an overall design and purpose to *The Once and Future King* is because it is a complex work of art that resists easy categorization and does not settle for straightforward answers to difficult questions, as the above analysis indicates. Nevertheless, we should also bear in mind how long the work took White to write, his frequent frustrations with the plans he adopted at various points, and the inevitable changes of mind that took place during the period of composition. *The Sword in the Stone* was published in 1938, *The Witch in the Wood* in 1939, after extensive rewriting at the request of his publishers, Collins, and *The Ill-Made Knight* in 1940. White then worked on the conclusion to the sequence, initially planning to add two more novels, *The Candle in the Wind* and *The Book of Merlyn*, completed in 1941. His publishers refused, disconcerted by the length of the text (and possibly by the aggressively stated anti-war message of *The Book of Merlyn*), and the final text, *The Once and Future King*, appeared in 1958, with the second book now rewritten as *The Queen of Air and Darkness*. *The Book of Merlyn* was finally published posthumously in 1977 with a preface by the author's biographer, Sylvia Townsend Warner, who points out that White's "attempt to find an antidote to war, had become a war casualty" (White 1977: 22). Elements of this final novel were incorporated into the published tetralogy, including the Wart's experiences as a bird flying over the territories below in *The Sword in the Stone* (other passages were omitted in this novel, such as Merlyn's battle with Madam Mim, which was retained in the Disney film; Brewer 1993: chs 2–7).

White's final message in the *Book of Merlyn* would appear to undermine the complex and sophisticated nature of the fictional sequence in its simplistic pacifist message, as well as repeating much of what is already in the published version of *The Candle in the Wind*. On the eve of Arthur's final battle with Mordred, Merlyn returns to help him by reminding him of the lessons he learned as a child among the animals. Arthur is transformed once again into an ant and a goose before Merlyn assembles all the animals and delivers his last message. The enemy of mankind is nationalism, "the claims of small communities to parts of the indifferent earth as communal property." The practical solution to the problem is remarkably straightforward:

The simplest and easiest solution . . . [is to] . . . abolish such things as tariff barriers, passports and immigration laws, converting mankind into a federation of individuals. In fact, you must abolish nations, and not only nations but states also; indeed, you must tolerate no unit larger than the family . . . the main thing is that we must make it possible for a man living at Stonehenge to pack up his traps overnight and to seek his fortune without hindrance in Timbuktu. (White 1977: 135)

Arthur has to choose between the way of the geese and the way of the ants: "There are no states in nature, except among monstrosities like the ants. It seems to me that people who go creating states, as Mordred is trying to do with his Thrashers, must tend to become involved in them, and so unable to escape" (163). Arthur does the right thing and compromises at any cost to end the war, calling a truce with Mordred, ceding half the kingdom "for the sake of peace. To tell the truth, he was prepared to yield it all if necessary" (167). The moral is far too easily directed, and would seem to be a rather self-regarding vindication of White's own peripatetic and solitary lifestyle. It also avoids the challenging educational message of *The Sword in the Stone*, which placed great stress on the need for a child to learn actively, to become self-reliant and independent – White was undoubtedly aware of the educational experiment of Summerhill School, founded by A. S. Neill (1883–1973) in 1921, as he worked as a teacher for six years (1930–36) (Warner 1967: chs 2–3). Neill believed that children required freedom to develop their desire to learn and made lessons voluntary, arguing that children would choose to learn if not forced to do so and follow a traditional curriculum (Neill 1998). There are clear analogies between Neill's radical ideas and the ways in which the Wart is educated by Merlyn, against the grain of the prevailing ideology. Indeed, *The Sword in the Stone* opens with a description of a traditional aristocratic education based on hunting and chivalry. However, in *The Book of Merlyn*, Merlyn simply tells Arthur the right answers.

Even without the final volume, the cyclical structure of the text was always a part of White's plans, as the title indicates, and Arthur reverts to his childhood in his tent on the eve of the final battle. Arthur is given a chance to see the future and realizes that the ideal of Camelot must be kept alive. He achieves this by telling a young page called Thomas of Newbold Revell to avoid the last battle and so preserve their story. In doing so, White returns the story to its own origins in Malory's *Morte Darthur*, a work he first read as a schoolboy at Cheltenham College (Brewer 1993: 2), another neat cyclical pattern.

The Sword in the Stone, conceived as a preface to Malory dealing with Arthur's growth to maturity (Brewer 1993: 18), begins with Sir Ector, an amiable and rather limited rural aristocrat, attempting to find a tutor for his legitimate son, the talentless and arrogant Kay, and his timorous adopted charge, the Wart (Arthur). When out chasing a falcon in the Forest Sauvage, the Wart stumbles across Merlyn's cottage. Merlyn, who lives his life backwards and so has been expecting him, agrees to become the Wart's tutor. Merlyn teaches Arthur by transforming him into a range of animals and letting him learn what he can from the experience of each new form, and from engaging with new and unfamiliar creatures and surroundings. Arthur becomes a perch, an ant, a merlin, and a badger. He also meets Robin Wood (sic), Marian, and Little John, and is taken to a jousting tournament, when the news that King Uther Pendragon has died is announced and that the new king will be whoever can pull the sword from the anvil in London. Sir Ector, Kay, and the Wart travel to London, where they will attend another tournament. When Kay leaves his sword behind in the castle in which they are staying, the Wart, acting as his squire, is sent to retrieve it. Finding the door locked, the Wart looks for a sword elsewhere, finds the anvil and pulls out the sword, thinking nothing of his feat. Kay recognizes the sword, tries to pretend that he pulled it free, but eventually confesses, and all bow to the new king, who promptly bursts into tears.

The Queen of Air and Darkness, the shortest book in the sequence but perhaps the most artistically successful, contrasts the attempts of Arthur to unify his lands and develop a civilized kingdom with the anarchic and disturbing world at the boundaries of his kingdom, the Orkneys, ruled by Queen Morgause, Arthur's half-sister. The powerful opening chapter, already referred to above, shows the four children, Gawaine, Agravaine, Gaheris, and Gareth, repeating versions of the story of Uther Pendragon's rape of their grandmother, Igraine. We learn that this is the principal basis of their education, delivered by their negligent mother. She is more concerned with half-heart-edly practicing her spells and plotting revenge on Arthur, against whom her husband, King Lot, is fighting. The children are also taught by the tedious and unimaginative tutor, St Toirdelbach, who tells them long, bellicose stories from Irish history which have no clear purpose other than to glorify violence, a pointed contrast to Merlyn's ways of educating his young charge. In the second chapter we witness the developing relationship between Arthur and Merlyn, with the wizard still trying to lead Arthur toward the path of good government, and the young king now more resistant and eager to try things out for himself. Arthur, in his boyish enthusiasm, finds war fun, while Merlyn reminds him of its terrible cost, especially for those of lower rank. Arthur gradually starts to learn that might is not right.

Meanwhile, King Pellinore, a comic figure hunting the Questing Beast, lands in the Orkneys, astonishing the locals. Morgause flirts with his knights and persuades them to go out hunting with her for a unicorn. They fail because the hunt requires a virgin to attract the beast (although her sons think she can play this role). The boys decide to catch one for her, and, after consulting St Toirdelbach, they capture one, using their maid, Meg, in whose lap it lays its head. Agravaine brutally kills the animal, showing yet again that the boys' lives are dominated by the malign influence of their mother: "This girl is my mother. He put his head in her lap. He had to die" (White 1958: 266). White is highlighting the cruelty of uneducated and directionless youth. Killing a unicorn, the most elusive and wonderful of all beasts, was an especially brutal and senseless crime, as White knew from his work on bestiaries (White 1954: 20–21). Summoned by the presence of a virgin, the unicorn was a symbol of Christ. The boys try to follow proper hunting procedure and perform a "gralloch," removing the guts of the beast so that every part of the animal can be used (White probably has the hunting scenes in *Sir Gawain and the Green Knight* in mind, as these describe the proper procedures in close detail [Tolkien & Gordon 1979: lines 1,319–64]). However, their incompetence means that they perforate the intestines and the lovely creature is transformed into a disgusting object: "Everything had begun to be horrible, and the once beautiful animal was spoiled and repulsive" (White 1958: 268). The unicorn inspires a particularly perverse form of devotion in the boys, a product of their warped childhoods, and a warning of what they will be capable of as adults:

> All three of them [Agravaine, Gaheris, and Gawaine] loved the unicorn in their various ways, Agravaine in the most twisted one, and, in proportion as they became responsible for spoiling its beauty, so they began to hate it for their guilt. Gawaine particularly began to hate the body. He hated it for being dead, for having been beautiful, for making him feel a beast. He had loved it and helped to trap it, so now there was nothing to be done except to vent his shame and hatred of himself upon the corpse. He hacked and cut and felt like crying too. (White 1958: 268)

Twisted love leads to violence, as love and cruelty are never far apart. Lancelot controls and uses his understanding of this, but the Orkney boys are traveling down a much darker path, one that White is exploring in the series of novels as his contribution to the understanding of Nazism. Morgause is unconcerned when her children return in a shambolic state, their clothes ruined. But she has them whipped when she learns that they have succeeded where she failed.

Arthur is making plans on the eve of the battle of Bedegraine and he announces his plans for a Round Table, the ideal of equality of all knights, established in conversation with Merlyn and Kay. Arthur also tells Merlyn that he has finally discovered a justification for fighting a good war, which is simply to have a good reason and to impose on people what is good for them against their wishes. Merlyn informs him that he is aware of such experiments and that when he was young "an Austrian . . . invented a new way of life and convinced himself that he was the chap to make it work, and plunged the civilized world into misery and chaos." When Kay reminds us that Arthur is fighting "to impose his ideas on King Lot" (274), we realize that we are being asked to think of Arthur in terms of Hitler. The gap between the fanatical nationalism of the Orkney faction and the civilizing efforts of Arthur, just like the gap between love and hate or cruelty, may actually be an overlap (Crane 1974: 91–2).

In Orkney the elderly knights run into yet more difficulties with the Questing Beast, with Sir Palomides and Sir Grunmore deciding to distract King Pellinore from a failing love suit by dressing up as the Questing Beast, only to encounter the real one, which chases them up a steep cliff. The Orkney boys quarrel over their mother's behavior, Agravaine determined to send their father a letter informing him of their mother's infidelity. In a heated quarrel with Gawaine, Agravaine produces a knife, and the stronger Gawaine gives him a savage, almost fatal, beating. The episode prefigures the last days of the Arthurian court and the split over Guenever's infidelity, and we are warned that Gawaine is a fatally damaged creature: "when he was in one of these black passions he seemed to pass out of human life. In later days he even

killed women, when he had been worked into such a state – though he regretted it
bitterly afterwards" (White 1958: 283). In medieval romance, killing other knights
was a sign of sin. Gawain, an enthusiast for the quest for the Holy Grail in the French
prose cycle, is a notable killer, his actions doing far more harm than good and
contributing significantly to the destruction of the fellowship of the Round Table
(Matarasso 1969: 76–80).

Merlyn tells Arthur that he will have to leave soon and that he cannot escape his
fate of being locked up for a thousand years, a reference to the medieval French Merlin
tradition. He warns the king to beware of Guenever and Lancelot but his words fall
on deaf ears. The comic plot is harmoniously resolved with King Pellinore rescuing
Palomides and Grunmore, and being then reunited with his lady, Piggy. Palomides
takes over from Pellinore as the hunter of the Questing Beast. Arthur wins the battle
of Bedegraine, fighting "the twelfth-century equivalent of what later came to be called
a Total War" (White 1958: 306), defeating Lot in a night ambush. Lot returns home
and Morgause travels to England in order to be reconciled with the new regime. Pellinore marries Piggy, and then, through the use of a spancel (a piece of human skin
taken from a dead body which traces the outline of the deceased, which if thrown
over a sleeping man and tied with a bow, would make him fall in love with the
plotter), Morgause seduces Arthur and conceives Mordred, who will bring about the
destruction of the kingdom.

The Ill-Made Knight, the longest novel in the sequence, explores Lancelot's affair
with Guenever, but also other forms of love, including Arthur's close bond with
Gawaine, Agravaine's devotion to his mother, and Elaine's doomed love for Lancelot.
The novel is based far more closely on Malory than either of the previous two works.
Lancelot, the Chevalier Mal Fet (literally, the "ill-made knight"), an ugly and obsessive boy, travels to Arthur's court because he is in love with the king, whom he met
when his father helped quell the recent rebellion of King Lot. His devotion to rigorous training in the art of chivalry has made Lancelot the best knight in the world,
and he is jealous of Arthur's regard for Gawaine, and even more so of his love for his
wife. Arthur defeats the Romans and Lancelot completes a number of quests as a
knight errant, before he falls in love with Guenever. Having slept with Elaine earlier
and produced Galahad, Lancelot reasons that he will already be compromised as the
best knight in the world, and so may as well pursue his desire for the queen. Lancelot
is also tormented, as he is in Malory and the French prose cycle, by feelings of guilt
at his neglect of his Christian vows and the stain on his purity that limits him as a
Christian knight. Arthur realizes what is going on – unconsciously, at least – but is
too well brought up to take any action:

> The effect of such an education was that he had grown up without any of the useful
> accomplishments for living – without malice, vanity, suspicion, cruelty, and the com-
> moner forms of selfishness. Jealousy seemed to him the most ignoble of vices. He was
> sadly unfitted for hating his best friend or for torturing his wife. He had been given too
> much love and trust to be good at these things. (White 1958: 406)

In representing Arthur as too noble and too refined, White further complicates our understanding of childhood. Better education will solve a host of evils, but may be a limitation in a flawed and violent world more suited to the violent anger of Gawaine.

Guenever, when she learns of Lancelot's relationship with Elaine, banishes them both from court. It is a matter of some conjecture whether White's portrayal of Guenever is a strength or weakness of the book. White was candid about his ignorance of women, asking Mary Potts, the wife of his former tutor at Cambridge, J. H. Potts, and, like her husband, a close friend of the author's, how women like Guenever might behave:

> If either you or Mary have heard anything about what love feels like at 50, or about whether a man of 50 can go on loving a mistress of the same age, with whom he has been sleeping for 30 years, I should be glad to hear it? And what about love-making during the change of life? Has Mary some famous book on this, or will she write me a brief monograph on the subject (and will it get past the censor)? (Gallix: 1982: 116; Brewer 1993: 90)

The letter is familiar and humorous, of course, as the Potts were devoted to each other, but the tone betrays a nervous embarrassment, even though White had argued earlier in the same letter (April 9, 1940), with self-conscious exaggeration, that "Guenever is terrific . . . one of the realest *women* in literature" (Gallix 1982: 115, italics original). Many readers will probably not agree. While the cruel and obsessive passions of the male characters are explored with considerable depth and insight, Guenever appears as a rather empty vessel, either pretty and remote, or unable to contain her emotions, although some critics have found White's representation persuasive (Brewer 1993: 87–93). White was, of course, working with the material he had, adapting the portrait of Guenever in Malory, with his famous defense of her character, and the first serious representation of her in Chrétien's *Le Chevalier de la Charrete* (Malory 1969: II.425–6; Kibler & Carroll 1991). But it is hard to see how some of the dialogue really adds to a sophisticated understanding of Guenever's character, given that "she is seen almost entirely from the outside . . . Her actual thoughts are very seldom revealed" (Brewer 1993: 90):

> Elaine said calmly: "Sir Lancelot was in my room last night. My woman Brisen brought him in the dark."
>
> The Queen began pointing at the door. She made stabbing movements at it with her finger, and, in her trembling, her hair began to come down. She looked hideous.
>
> "Get out! Get out! And you go too, you animal! How dare you speak so in my castle? How dare you admit it to me? Take your fancy man and go!" (White 1958: 413–4)

Guenever's "central tragedy" is that she has no children (498), and so lavishes affection and sexual love on two men in return for their companionship.

The plot continues to follow Malory closely. Elaine is banished but Lancelot remains at court, growing old and gray with Guenever and Arthur. The peoples of England – Saxons and Normans alike – start to imagine themselves as English and knights come to the court because of Arthur's reputation. These knights include Gareth and Mordred and the past returns to haunt the king. Gareth tells Arthur that Agravaine has murdered Morgause, cutting her head off, a killing that replicates that of the unicorn (451). Arthur searches for ways to distract the knights from their tendency for violence, and, realizing that tournaments are failing to contain their blood lust, suggests that they all hunt for the Holy Grail. We see the knights returning in succession, having witnessed Galahad's success. As in the French prose cycle's *Quest for the Holy Grail*, Galahad's achievements are limited because he is not subject to the temptations and torment of ordinary humanity (Matarasso 1969: ch. 15). As Lionel comments, "it may be all very well to be holy and invincible, and I don't hold it against Galahad for being a virgin, but don't you think that people might be a little human?" (White 1958: 476). Lancelot, by contrast, is unable to enter the holiest of places because of his sins, a revelation that pushes him further toward a conviction that the spiritual life is superior to the secular path of knighthood. Guenever eventually realizes that Lancelot must leave, which, along with the deaths caused by the quest for the Grail (the best half of the knights have perished), paves the way for the increasing dominance of Agravaine and Mordred, who are waiting for Guenever to make a mistake. Aware of the hostility of the Orkney faction, she throws a dinner party for Gawaine with copious amounts of Gawaine's beloved fruit. When Sir Pinel poisons an apple, the Irish knight, Patrick, eats it instead of Gawaine and the queen gets the blame. Lancelot saves the queen's honor when he defeats Sir Mador. Arthur arranges a tournament to celebrate at Corbin, where Elaine lives, and, after Lancelot is wounded, she nurses him, committing suicide when he returns to court and so fatally wounding his relationship with Guenever. The disgruntled Meliagrance kidnaps Guenever; Lancelot pursues them and sleeps with the queen, cutting his hand on the bars on the window of her room and so staining the sheets. Once again, the queen is accused of treachery and Lancelot defeats Meliagrance to defend her honor, the book ending with the conclusion of the "Indian summer" of chivalry.

The final book, *The Candle in the Wind*, also follows Malory closely but expands and develops the characterization and implicit themes of the late-medieval version of the story. The focus returns to Arthur. The book opens with Mordred and Agravaine plotting the downfall of Arthur, insisting on right in a perverse and self-interested manner that undermines Arthur's noble efforts to move from a world dominated by force to one in which justice reigns. White represents his hero as quintessentially English, and his son and enemy as "everything which Arthur was not – the irreconcilable opposite of the Englishman," possessing "the savagery and feral wit of the Pict . . . expelled by the volcano of history into the far quarters of the globe, where, with a venomous sense of grievance and inferiority, they even nowadays proclaim their ancient megalomania" (548). It is perhaps not entirely surprising that White aroused the ire of many Irish readers when he depicted his hosts during the Second World War as uncivilized inhabitants of an "Irish stinkhole" in *The Elephant and the Kangaroo* (1947) (Gallix 1982: 196–8). White not only compares the plot of Agravaine and Mordred to that of the Irish Republican Army, he has them adopt the swastika as their symbol, gathering together England's principal foes as one mass. Later they become the Thrashers, a fascist gang aiming for "Gaelic autonomy and a massacre of the Jews as well" (628), and Mordred clearly symbolizes Hitler when the queen's maid, Agnes, observes that his behavior is becoming increasing deranged: "all these speeches about Gaels and Saxons and Jews, and all the shouting and hysterics" (645). The headstrong Gawaine, in contrast, has started to turn English through his long sojourn at court. Although he "still kept his outland accent in defiance of the mere English . . . he had ceased to think in Gaelic" (554), a description that replicates the assumptions made centuries earlier when it was argued that Irish speech "made the man Irishe" (Hadfield & McVeagh 1994: 41).

However, White complicates this apparently stark contrast when Arthur admits that he tried to have all babies murdered by letting them drift out to sea in unmanned boats in an attempt to rid himself of Mordred, as the Orkney faction are all too well aware. Arthur may be quintessentially English, but the gap between English decency and foreign treachery is somewhat elastic (Crane 1974: 79, 108–10; Manlove 1977: 74–7). Arthur is now crippled with guilt and compensates for his earlier crime by leaving Mordred alone, compounding the problems he is creating for his regime. When Agravaine and Mordred confront Arthur with the evidence of Lancelot and Guenever's treachery, they are able to undercut his attempts to avoid murderous conflict:

> "Very well, Agravaine: you are a keen lawyer, and you are determined to have the law. I suppose it is no good reminding you that there is such a thing as mercy?"
> "The kind of mercy," asked Mordred, "which used to set those babies adrift, in boats?"
> "Thank you, Mordred. I was forgetting."
> "We do not want mercy," said Agravaine, "we want justice."
> "I understand the situation." (White 1958: 590)

Arthur is, as Agravaine exultantly exclaims, "hoist with his own petard" (589). Lancelot kills Agravaine when he tries to surprise him in Guenever's room, and then rescues the queen before she can be burnt at the stake and they retreat to Joyous Gard, where Arthur besieges them. Lancelot returns Guenever and affirms her innocence, but Mordred insists that Arthur continue his campaign in the name of justice, giving him the chance to abduct Guenever. On the eve of the final battle Arthur reflects on his achievements and the impossibility of establishing true justice in the face of such concerted attacks by determined and ruthless enemies, concluding, but in a slightly more subtle way than the Merlyn of *The Book of Merlyn*, that nations cause wars by overwhelming the efforts of individuals: "wars were not calamities into which amiable innocents were led by evil men. They were national movements, deeper, more subtle in origin" (668). The brief triumph of the Round Table was a candle that flickered in the wind (674). Realizing that geography is to blame and that humanity will be free of ideological chains, Arthur walks out to his fate.

White's political musings are probably less impressive for a modern reader than his representation of childhood and the development of the individual's personality. White was certainly a close reader of Freud, and it is also likely that he read Jung and, perhaps, Wilhelm Reich, as well as educational treatises such as A. S. Neill's *Summerhill School*. It is undoubtedly no accident that White is best known for his representation of childhood in *The Sword in the Stone*, most importantly, the Wart's relationship with Merlyn and his numerous metamorphoses. The Wart receives a brutal and blunt first lesson when transformed into a roach when he encounters the King of the Moat, the pike, Mr P. The future king encounters an "old despot," whose "face had been ravaged by all the passions of an absolute monarch – by cruelty, sorrow, age, pride, selfishness, loneliness and thoughts too strong for individual brains," a clear warning of what is to be Arthur's lot in the near future. Mr P. is "remorseless, disillusioned, logical, predatory, fierce and pitiless," (47), a piling up of significant adjectives that indicates to the reader that this is the first important encounter in the book. Mr P. gives the Wart the benefit of his experience, a reminder of what can happen to kings who grow old, refuse to learn anything new, and so let power corrupt them absolutely:

> "There is nothing," said the monarch, "except the power which you pretend to seek: power to grind and power to digest, power to seek and power to find, power to await and power to claim, all power and pitilessness springing from the nape of the neck."
>
> "Thank you."
>
> "Love is a trick played on us by the forces of evolution. Pleasure is the bait laid down by the same. There is only power. Power is of the individual mind, but the mind's power is not enough. Power of the body decides everything in the end, and only Might is Right." (White 1958: 47–8)

The Wart is shown a terrifying vision of what will happen to him if he does not think carefully enough about the use and abuse of the power he will inherit, and we know that some of the malign effects on the personality of Mr P. will inevitably visit the adult Arthur, however successful he is as a ruler. This episode is particularly well integrated into the thematic structure of the novel sequence. Mr P. is described as cruel, which links him to Lancelot in *The Ill-Made Knight*. Whereas Lancelot controls his cruelty and so uses a serious flaw to make himself more noble, Mr P. has surrendered to his baser instincts and become a despot. Moreover, Mr P.'s conclusion that "Might is Right" is echoed throughout the next three novels as Arthur debates this difficult issue and tries to establish the rule of law in the face of overwhelming opposition.

Mr P.'s clear, precise, and repetitive style establishes a desolate and terrifying universe devoid of sympathy and constructive purpose. There is a reductive truth in what he states and, if we simply see the overthrow of the Arthurian ideal as the final conclusion, then he is right. But what Arthur absorbs from Merlyn's teaching is to resist such inevitabilities and not to allow others to obliterate the bigger picture, a lesson that the Orkney faction never learn as they use good and bad arguments to further their dark goals. White shows that Arthur is flawed and weak in many ways but he never loses sight of the good, even when he is wrong. *The Once and Future King* interprets Malory to mean that it would have been better for everyone if a blind eye had been turned to the unstable love triangle at the heart of the kingdom. It is a generous and very human message, one that recognizes the complexity of real life, opposes rigid codes of conduct, and argues that a good heart is more important than abstract reasoning. Put another way, we might see White's work informed by a heady mixture of Dickens and the radical educational theories of the 1930s (Brewer 1993: 148, 175–6).

The deadening logic of Mr P. is manifested in an even more disturbing form when the Wart is transformed into an ant (a key episode for White, originally establishing a direct contrast to the freedom enjoyed by the pacific geese in *The Book of Merlyn*, but when that was not published White transferred it to *The Sword in the Stone*). The ants exist in a Nazi society, dominated by the worst excesses of social Darwinism (their national anthem is "*Antland, Antland Over All*" [127]). Their minds are deadened by monotonous music which prevents creative thought and their language is constructed as a series of stark opposites that inhibit expression: "the Wart discovered that there were only two qualifications in the language, Done and Not-Done – which applied to all questions of value" (124). The logic is reminiscent of Newspeak in George Orwell's futuristic novel *1984*, and the slogans that the ants employ – "EVERYTHING NOT FORBIDDEN IS COMPULSORY" (121) – recall those in Orwell's *Animal Farm*.

The most significant detail is the ants' use and abuse of logic, which looks forward to that of Mordred and Agravaine as they turn the tables on Arthur's quest for justice. The Wart listens to the endless broadcasts that the ants receive in their antennae, which increase in intensity once it is discovered that a neighboring ant's nest has an impressive hoard of seeds. White outlines for the reader the logical outline of the ants' justification for aggression. The first takes the form of a syllogism:

A. We are so numerous that we are starving.
B. Therefore we must encourage still larger families so as to become yet more numerous and starving.
C. When we are so numerous and starving as all that, obviously we shall have a right to take other's people's stores of seed. Besides, we shall by then have a numerous and starving army. (White 1958: 127–8)

The circular logic justifies an aggressive and expansionist policy and the ants are so used to imagining that their reasoning is beyond thought that no one challenges the terrifying outcome. The second broadcast is more openly contradictory, with every statement reinforced by its opposite:

A. We are more numerous than they are, therefore we have a right to their mash.
B. They are more numerous than we are, therefore they are wickedly trying to steal our mash.
C. We are a mighty race and have a natural right to subjugate their puny one.
D. They are a mighty race and are unnaturally trying to subjugate our inoffensive one.
E. We must attack them in self-defence.
F. They are attacking us by defending themselves.
G. If we do not attack them today, they will attack us tomorrow.
H. In any case we are not attacking them at all. We are offering them incalculable benefits. (White 1958: 128)

White is imitating the inspirational rants of Hitler and showing that the appearance of logical thought can lead in terrible directions. The ants and the Orkney faction are all part of the same spectrum, damaged individuals and species whose education has warped rather than nurtured their hearts and imaginations. It is not that logical thought is mistaken in itself, but that an undue reliance on its value is an illogical belief, leading to further unreason, as the direction of these two broadcasts demonstrates. At the end of *The Candle in the Wind*, Arthur thinks he hears Merlyn returning to help him and he thinks about his education: "He remembered the aged necromancer who had educated him – who had educated him with animals. There were, he remembered, something like half a million different species of animal, of which mankind was only one" (675–6). Considering the relative insignificance of mankind places his own fate in perspective and points to different ways of negotiating the future. It also reveals White's central message that only by retaining a childish desire to learn can we become properly human.

Primary Sources

Gallix, F. (ed.) (1982). *T. H. White. Letters to a friend*. New York: Putnam's.

Kibler, W. W. & Carroll, C. W. (trans.) (1991). *Chrétien de Troyes. Arthurian romances*. Harmondsworth: Penguin.

Lawlor, J. (ed.) (1969). *Thomas Malory. Le Morte Darthur*. Harmondsworth: Penguin.

Matarasso, P. M. (trans.) (1969). *The quest of the Holy Grail*. Harmondsworth: Penguin.

Tolkien, J. R. R. & Gordon, E. V. (eds) (1979). *Sir Gawain and the Green Knight*, 2nd edn (ed. N. Davis). Oxford: Oxford University Press.

White, T. H. (1954). *The bestiary: A book of beasts*. New York: Putnam's.

White, T. H. (1958). *The once and future king*. London: Collins.

White, T. H. (1977). *The book of Merlyn*. London: Collins.

References and Further Reading

Brewer, E. (1993). *T. H. White's* The Once and Future King. Woodbridge: Boydell & Brewer.

Crane, J. K. (1974). *T. H. White*. Boston. MA: Twayne.

Hadfield, A. (1996). T. H. White, pacifism and violence: The once and future nation. *Connotations*, 6, 207–26.

Hadfield, A. & McVeagh, J. (eds) (1994). *Strangers to that land: British perceptions of Ireland from the Reformation to the famine*. Gerrards Cross: Colin Smythe.

Manlove, C. N. (1977). Flight to Aleppo: T. H. White's *The Once and Future King*. *Mosaic*, 10, 65–83.

Neill, A. S. (1998). *Summerhill School*. New York: St Martin's Press.

Warner, S. T. (1967). *T. H. White: A biography*. London: Cape.

29

Modernist Arthur:
The Welsh Revival

Geraint Evans

When Tennyson's *Morte d'Arthur* was published in his two-volume *Poems* of 1842, the adjective "Arthurian," in phrases such as "Arthurian legend" and "Arthurian literature," was unrecorded in English. It first appears, as late as 1853, in the phrase "Arthurian histories" in John Hill Burton's *History of Scotland*, and the usage soon becomes productive, as the *Oxford English Dictionary* records a number of other examples in the late nineteenth and early twentieth centuries. This usage arose to reflect the new ways in which the figure of Arthur was being used in literature, history, painting, and music. Many of the texts in which Arthur appears are formally and functionally quite distinct but the figure of Arthur acts as a primary source of cohesion so that the emergence of the new adjectival form marks the appearance of a new discursive field. In the twentieth century this field takes shape against a background of imperial decline, and in the literature of Wales the battle for ownership of the iconic figure of Arthur symbolizes Welsh resistance to English rule.

Welsh literature in the late nineteenth century, particularly the poetic tradition, was still recognizably linked by form and language to the earliest surviving poems of Dark Age Britain (see chapter 6). There was an unbroken tradition that was becoming more widely known through the scholarly editing of early texts, a project made possible by the appearance of a number of printed editions from the eighteenth century in which antiquarian interest had already begun to explore the manuscript record. That unbroken poetic tradition, reaching back to the *cynfeirdd* (the earliest Welsh poets whose work has survived), also contained some of the earliest references to Arthur and the Arthurian world. In the late nineteenth and early twentieth centuries Welsh scholars and writers were well placed to explore that material as part of a process of national renewal, in which the establishment of institutions such as the University of Wales and the National Library of Wales were seen as steps on the road to self-determination.

Tennyson wrote a number of long narrative poems on the subject of Arthur, some of which came to be known collectively as *The Idylls of the King*, but *Morte d'Arthur* was the first in which the main source was Malory. Thomas Malory's fifteenth-century prose romance *Morte Darthur* was the defining text of Arthurian literature for many of the important writers and artists of nineteenth-century England, including Southey, Tennyson, Burne-Jones, and William Morris, although Malory had been out of fashion throughout the eighteenth century (see chapter 23). When Malory's work was republished in London in 1816, in rival duodecimo editions by Walker and Edwards in three volumes and by Wilks in two volumes, it had been out of print for nearly two centuries (see chapter 24). The 1816 editions were the first since Stansby's black letter edition of 1634 but they sold so well that they were followed a year later by a two-volume large octavo edition with a text taken from Caxton's *editio princeps* of 1485 and notes by Robert Southey, the poet laureate. When Malory's text re-emerged into the industrial nineteenth century it served very different functions for England, by now the largest imperial power in the world, and for Wales, the source of the Arthurian tradition and the first of England's colonies.

Tennyson's Arthuriad is one of the great poetic cycles of empire in which, as Stephen Knight has argued, a deracinated Arthur is finally assimilated into an Englishness which has been implied since Malory but is completely missing in early Welsh texts such as *Culhwch ac Olwen* (Knight 1983). Even more striking is the way in which the alignment with empire in Tennyson's Arthurian poems offers a nostalgic subjectivity to a modern readership. As the empire unravels in the twentieth century, Tennyson's description of the passing of Arthur, as Bedivere stands on the bank "[r]evolving many memories," comes increasingly to be read as an image of England's fading role: "But now the whole ROUND TABLE is dissolved / Which was an image of the mighty world" (Ricks 1987: 2.17). What replaces this dying fall in the literature of Wales is the sense of a nation reborn and of a national hero reclaimed. It is no surprise that the hero sleeping in the cave is the most common image of Arthur in twentieth-century Welsh writing, in Welsh as in English, for it is this idea that captures the essence of post-colonial opposition, which is the basis of so much national literature in the twentieth century.

One of the most powerful expressions of this idea in Welsh writing in English is in David Jones's poem "The Sleeping Lord," in which the narrative voice famously wonders whether it is in fact the gigantic warrior Arthur whose features can be seen slumbering in the landscape of Wales, or whether the sleeping lord might be Wales itself:

> Does the land wait the sleeping lord
> or is the wasted land
> that very lord who sleeps?
> (Jones 1974: 96)

In much of the literature of Wales since the mid-nineteenth century, both in Welsh and in English, the figure of Arthur serves a similar function. For Welsh-language writers such as T. Gwynn Jones, as for the English-language writer David Jones, it is no longer the Island of the Mighty that has to be regained. It is not the island of Britain but the language of Wales that has now to be reclaimed and restored as the central element in the paradigm of Welshness.

The Celtic Revival and the Rediscovery of Arthur

The Celtic Revival of the eighteenth and nineteenth centuries was a revival of interest in the exotic otherness of the Celtic countries by an English-speaking center looking out toward a Celtic "fringe" that seemed to retain many of the traditions lost to the modern world. The movement itself was part of a general antiquarian nostalgia, which can be read as a response to industrialization, an impulse that was projected not only onto the Celtic world. The importance of rural life, for example, is a constant theme in English writing since the Renaissance and the perceived loss of difference and strangeness that made Celtic Revivalism possible is still there, in a different reflex, in the sense of the vanishing countryside in the work of Thomas Hardy or Edward Thomas. For the Pre-Raphaelite painters and artisan printers of the late nineteenth century, that same yearning for richness and meaning found some of its most potent expression in the rediscovery of the world of Arthur, a chivalric, pre-industrial world in which the certainties of feudal obligation could be safely imagined as an antidote to the mobility of the modern world. However, the importance of the Celtic Revival for Tennyson and the late nineteenth century is that it created a context for the assimilation of Celtic culture into the discourses of English life. The paintings of Burne-Jones and the Arthurian poetry of Tennyson found a place in English cultural life that had been prepared by the assimilation of Celticity in a variety of media. As the nineteenth century drew to an end the idea that Arthur was indeed an English hero can be seen as an expression of cultural confidence in the integrity of empire and the unity of the kingdom.

Tennyson's poems are also significant historically because they coincide with the beginnings of a new era. The popularity of Tennyson's poems, building on the reprinting of Malory in 1816, marks not just the rediscovery of a tradition, but also the beginning of Arthur in the modern world. The expansion of empire, and the exportation of English literature as an ideological tool of education, coincides with the huge growth in publishing that came with industrialization. The editions of 1816 were printed by hand but Tennyson's *Poems* of 1842 was printed by machines powered by steam. By the mid-nineteenth century, printing and binding had been mechanized and edition sizes were no longer limited by the economics of hand-press production. Distribution was also changing to cope with expanding markets and large-scale production, and the proliferation of textual formats that characterizes the cheap reprints of the railway age was already apparent. This was the prelude to a twentieth century that saw the large-scale creation of new forms and genres within global markets. The adjectival form "Arthurian" which today unites all the poems, novels, films, computer games, and literary companions was already in place by the late nineteenth century, a product of industrialization and the commodification of culture within imperial and global markets.

The literature of Wales in the twentieth century is a story of two languages, of the rise of Welsh writing in English alongside the continuation and renewal of writing in Welsh. The twentieth century produced some of the greatest Welsh-language writers, particularly in poetry, and the language movement, which was a catalyst for political self-determination, drew heavily on the inspiration of literature. Among writers in Welsh there is a strong subjectivity of survival against the odds and of the cultural value of minority and difference, whereas some Welsh writers in English are more recognizable as part of international writing in English. In looking at the range of Welsh responses to Arthur in the twentieth century, there are two writers whose work epitomizes the attempt to reclaim Arthur as a national hero for Wales, the poet T. Gwynn Jones (1871–1949), who wrote in Welsh, and the artist and writer David Jones (1895–1974), who wrote in English.

David Jones and Welsh writing in English

David Jones is the most important Welsh Arthurian writer in English in the twentieth century. Jones worked in a number of media, and despite his subsequent reputation as a writer, he thought of himself primarily as a painter. As well as the poems and essays, he painted a number of important pictures with Arthurian subjects. These include the early drawing "Merlin-land" or "Merlin Appears in the Form of a Young Child to Arthur Sleeping" (1931), which he later used as an illustration to the "Mabinog's Liturgy" section of his long poem *The Anathémata* (1952). He uses this alongside an earlier wood engraving titled "He Frees the Waters" and the juxtaposition suggests a link – a favorite theme in Jones's work – between the Arthurian characters and the mysteries of the incarnation (Jones 1952: facing pages 185, 213). Nicolette Gray has suggested that for Jones the juxtaposition might also suggest that these are the stories that Merlin is whispering to the sleeping Arthur (Gray 1989: 40). Two related pictures from a later period are "Guinever" (1940) and "The Four Queens" (1941), which were both purchased by the Tate Gallery. David Jones's "Guinever" dominates the picture, the only light figure in an otherwise dark composition. She is pictured sleeping naked, surrounded by her retinue of wounded knights, in a vaulted room that contains an altar table, while a shadowy Launcelot is entering the room through a window. The liminality of the figure of Launcelot is a device that is echoed in the figure of Tristan in Jones's late masterpiece "Tristan ac Esyllt" (1960–63), which is now in the National Museum of Wales, Cardiff. Although the lovers embrace, she is bathed in light and color while he is darker and ill defined. The sword and the potion literally stand between them in the picture but the difference in the figuration is the real signifier of the barrier to their love.

Another field in which David Jones worked was in the creation of what he called painted inscriptions, in which texts in a number of languages are free-painted onto a white ground. Some of these explore the Arthurian world, beginning with two versions of "Hic Iacet Arturus" ("Here lies Arthur") in about 1949. The text is taken from Malory and the lettering is in pencil and crayon, perhaps in imitation of the appearance of a rubbing from a medieval inscription. The most important of the large painted inscriptions to use Arthurian material is "Cloelia Cornelia" (1959), which is now in the National Library of Wales, Aberystwyth. The whole piece forms a hymn to Mary, and in a text which combines English, Welsh, and Latin there are references to Esyllt, Tristan, and Arianrhod Eigr, the mother of Arthur. The centrality of religious experience and the historical significance of Catholic Christianity to an understanding of Britain and Wales are fundamental to all Jones's work, and in the paintings, as in the writing, the figure of Arthur is often conflated with the figure of Christ. A number of critics have tended to foreground the religious elements in David Jones but the complexity in his work always pushes it toward plural readings. Jeremy Hooker, for example, in writing about David Jones's use of Arthur, finds "an essentially protective view of Wales," a view which is "protective also in the sense that the Welsh 'web of magic and imagination' holds in keeping all that he values, and provides a model for his paintings and writings on Welsh themes" (Hooker 2001: 115).

David Jones wrote a number of essays and reviews that deal with Arthurian material, including one important long essay, "The Myth of Arthur," which was written in 1942 and revised for inclusion in *Epoch and Artist* (1959). In it Jones describes the centrality of the myth of Arthur to the language and history of Britain, as he sees it, a view that he had already expressed visually in "Map of Themes in the Artist's Mind" (1943). Jones was using early Welsh material in his writing from the beginning. His earliest published work, *In Parenthesis* (1937), is a book about his experiences leading up to the Battle of the Somme, and in it he is already using the literature and history of Wales to signify the continuity of British experience over two millennia. His long poem *The Anathémata* also contains Arthurian and Welsh material, as do a number of smaller pieces that were published posthumously in *The Roman Quarry* (1981), but his most important Arthurian work was published in the final year of his life. "The Sleeping Lord" is the title poem of a volume published in 1974, in which the narrative voice explores the physicality and significance of the Arthur who sleeps in the cave. This is Arthur the national redeemer, who awakes to return as liberator of a conquered people whose identity and language is all but lost. A meditation about the location and nature of the sleeping lord frames a section in which Arthur the Brythonic warlord is imagined hearing Mass in a world unknown to us from Malory, one in which Latin and Welsh are macaronically intertwined:

> should this *candela*-bearer
>   presume so far as to argue that
> his *cannwyll* does indeed constitute
> One of the Three Primary Signa
>   of the Son of Mary

> ... *unig-anedig Fab Duw*
> > ... *ante omnia saecula*
> *lumen di lumine* ...
> > by whom all things ...
> who should blame him?
> > (Jones 1974: 77)

Arthur the Welsh warlord is located by Jones in a tradition which is pre-Germanic, Romanized, and Christian, a world which is designed to show the pre-Galfridian Welshness of an Arthur who is still imaginatively available as a symbol of national opposition to conquest or control. Later in the poem, in a section that recalls the long series of names in the earliest Welsh Arthurian tale, *Culhwch ac Olwen*, Arthur is contextualized by a sequence of sub-Roman and early medieval figures:

> Then there was the Blessed Bran of whom the tale-tellers tell
> a most wondrous tale and then the names of men more prosaic
> but more credible to him: Paternus of the Red Pexa, Cunedda
> Wledig the Conditor and, far more recent and so more green in
> the memory, the Count Ambrosius Aurelianus that men call
> Emrys Wledig ...
>
> > (Jones 1974: 84)

Jones uses this series of names to locate his sleeping lord as the Arthur of *Culhwch ac Olwen*, an Arthur who is not so much the once and future king as the *mab darogan*, the Welsh son of prophecy, the one who will restore the Island of the Mighty to its Brythonic heirs.

In his essay on "The Myth of Arthur," David Jones perfectly pinpoints the appropriation of Arthur into the mainstream of English writing by quoting William Blake: "The stories of Arthur are the acts of Albion" (Jones 1959: 212). Jones goes on to show how the elements of the tradition that are central to his own work position Arthur in a Brythonic culture which survives, for him, in the language and literature of Wales, but Blake's formulation neatly summarizes the Romantic Arthur of Albion as the precursor of the nineteenth-century hero of Tennyson and the Pre-Raphaelites. In looking at the figure of Arthur in twentieth-century Welsh writing in English, the most fundamental division is between those writers, like David Jones, whose subjectivity is close to that of writers in Welsh, and those who write within the English tradition of Malory and Tennyson. Writers in Welsh, and English-language writers like David Jones, are writing in opposition to Tennyson, reclaiming Arthur as a Welsh hero, and anticipating a post-colonial position which elides Albion – a romanticized England – from the acts of Arthur.

The versions of Arthur that begin to appear in Wales in the late nineteenth and early twentieth centuries are nevertheless indebted to the renewed popularity of Arthur in English literature and art, if only in their opposition to it. The other important factor is the beginnings of modern scholarship, which produced printed editions of Welsh Arthurian texts and manuscripts. Charlotte Guest's translation of the medieval Welsh prose tales which she called *The Mabinogion* began to appear in 1838, and J. Gwenogvryn Evans's editions of the text of the Arthurian material in *The Red Book of Hergest* made the early Welsh material more widely available at the turn of the twentieth century. In the second quarter of the century David Jones immersed himself in this new, scholarly material, but he was far from being the first to do this. When Edward Thomas wrote his *Celtic Stories* for Oxford University Press in 1911 he used medieval Welsh and Irish sources as far as possible. His retelling of early Welsh Arthurian stories, which he titled "Kilhugh and Olwen" and "The Dream of Rhonabwy," are based mainly on Charlotte Guest's work but he presents them as coming from a time when "Wales and Ireland were entirely independent of England" (Thomas 1911: 126). That idea is central to an understanding of David Jones, who was perhaps the first Welsh writer in English whose work argued that artists could not fully participate in the English-language culture of Wales if they remained ignorant of Welsh-language history and culture.

Different texts, however, use the same material in different ways. John Cowper Powys (1872–1963) uses Welsh material in early works such as *A Glastonbury Romance* (1932), *Maiden Castle* (1937), and *Morwyn* (1937) to locate Welshness as a source of magical exoticism rather than a cultural heir of Brythonic Romanity. In these early novels characters from Welsh tradition such as Urien and Pwyll add textual complexity to what are essentially English modernist novels whose focalization is never Welsh, and in this Powys is following the tradition of Celtic Revivalism. Glastonbury is itself a powerful symbol of the English appropriation of Arthur, and Powys's early romances confirm the ideology of empire by locating the assimilated remnants of Welsh culture in a modern English town. The historical romance *Owen Glendower* (1940) has a stronger Welsh focalization, and the historical novel *Porius*, which Powys called "the chief work of [my] lifetime," is located firmly in the Arthurian world of sub-Roman Britain. The book was completed in 1949 and after a series of rejections was published in a heavily abridged form in 1951. The first complete edition, reconstructed from surviving typescripts, manuscripts, and corrected proof pages, was not published until 2007. The action of the novel takes place during one week in October 499. It is set mainly around a Roman fort in north Wales and concerns the son of a Brythonic prince in the kingdom of Edeyrnion, which is under threat from the Saxons led by Colgrim. Arthur, who is called Emperor of Britain, comes to their assistance and sends ahead the magicians Myrddin Wyllt, Nineue, and Medrawd. However, while *Porius* may be Powys's "chief work" of fiction, it is also characteristic of all his work in being mainly concerned with the psychology of myth and the dynamics of personal relationship. This makes his work quite unlike the work of other Welsh writers of the period for whom the personal has become inescapably political. Although John Cowper Powys and David Jones both make use of early Welsh literature and history, the subjectivity of Jones's work locates it as functioning in the same discursive field as Welsh-language writers whose use of history has little in common with the late Romanticism of Powys.

The revival of scholarly and popular interest in Malory's Arthur which followed the discovery of the Winchester manuscript of the *Morte Darthur* in 1934 came too late to influence the first flowering of Modernism in London and Paris. The canonical referents of high culture in the work of Pound and Eliot were Greece and Rome in the heroic age, and France and Germany in the modern age. Into that textual tradition David Jones deliberately wove elements from the matter of Britain to create English Modernist texts in which the classical world is a background to Arthur's sub-Roman Britain, a world to which we remain linked by the survival of the Welsh language. Jones argues that in modern Britain it is the Welsh who are "the heirs of Romanity" and the power of a Welsh Arthur lies in the claim to nationhood that he symbolically provides by linking the modern world with a Brythonic Island of the Mighty.

T. Gwynn Jones and Writing in Welsh

While David Jones wrote in English, the most significant literary texts of national renewal in modern Wales are written in Welsh. Although Welsh writing in English became steadily more significant as a location of national identity throughout the twentieth century, writing in Welsh underwent a renaissance from the 1890s onward, and the first three-quarters of the twentieth century were a golden age of Welsh literature, despite the steady decline in the number of Welsh speakers between 1901 and 1961 (Aitchison & Carter 1994). While the number of speakers stabilized after 1961, concern for the future of the language was the key issue of Welsh intellectual life in the second half of the twentieth century and this is clearly reflected in literary and artistic production.

T. Gwynn Jones is the most important figure in the Welsh literary renaissance that began in the late nineteenth century and flowered in the early twentieth century. In a prolific writing career he wrote a number of poems with Arthurian and medieval associations, the most important being "Ymadawiad Arthur" ("The Passing of Arthur"), which first appeared in 1902, was republished in 1910, and heavily revised for the anthology of Jones's poems, *Detholiad o Ganiadau* ("Selected Songs"), which was published by the Gregynog Press in 1926. T. Gwynn Jones's 1910 collection, *Ymadawiad Arthur a Chaniadau Ereill* ("The Passing of Arthur and Other Poems") contains three substantial Arthurian poems. "Arthur Gawr" ("Arthur the Giant") is a poem of 96 lines in 24 stanzas, and "Ogof Arthur" ("Arthur's Cave") is a poem of 104 lines in 26 stanzas. Neither of these early poems was retained by T. Gwynn Jones in the major collection of his work, *Caniadau* ("Songs"), which first appeared in 1934, and in some ways they were superseded by the achievement of the longer poem "Ymadawiad Arthur."

By the 1930s Arthur was re-established as a major figure in Welsh writing. In 1934 "Ogof Arthur" was the theme for the main poetry competition for the chair at the National Eisteddfod in Neath, where the winning poem was by William Morris

(1889–1979), a Methodist minister from north Wales. Four years later an important volume of political essays was published by Saunders Lewis (1893–1985), the pre-eminent figure in Welsh literature in the mid-twentieth century and one of the founders of Plaid Cymru (the National Party of Wales). The volume was called *Canlyn Arthur* ("Following Arthur"), the title taken from a speech by Cai in the medieval prose tale *Breuddwyd Rhonabwy* ("The Dream of Rhonabwy"), part of which appears as an epigram: *Yna y cyfodes Cai ac a dywawd: pwy bynnag a fynno canlyn Arthur, bid heno yng Nghernyw gyda ef. Ac ar nis mynno, bid yn erbyn Arthur*" ("Then Cai arose and said: whoever wishes to follow Arthur let him be with him in Cornwall tonight. And whoever does not so wish, let him be against Arthur"). This was a political rallying cry and one that explicitly linked the figure of Arthur to the call for self-determination.

One of the main objectives of Welsh-language poetry at this time was to revive the use of traditional Welsh *cynghanedd* (sound ornamentation) in poetry, a practice that promoted a new sense of nationhood. Together with writers and academics such as Emrys ap Iwan (1851–1906), John Gwenogvryn Evans (1852–1930), and John Morris Jones (1864–1929), T. Gwynn Jones was one of the champions of this revival. The complex system of consonance and internal rhyme that constitutes *cynghanedd*, in poems composed in one of twenty-four traditional meters, is a defining characteristic of Welsh poetry throughout the Middle Ages, and the revival of its use was a deliberate strategy to assert the uniqueness and antiquity of the Welsh literary tradition. Indeed, the scholar and critic Thomas Parry has noted that part of the initial success of "Ymadawiad Arthur" was the richness of its language, which he ascribes largely to Jones's wide reading of medieval Welsh poetry (ap Gwilym 1982: 397). Just as Tennyson's language is informed by a rediscovery of Malory, so Jones's poem is enriched by his reading of the then fashionable *cywyddwyr* poetry of fourteenth- and fifteenth-century Wales. More importantly, applying this revival in *cynghanedd* to the newly fashionable figure of Arthur was a classic piece of post-colonial resistance. At the turn of the century England was at the height of its imperial and economic power and the Arthurian poems of Tennyson were among the most widely read poems in English. In the work of Tennyson and the Pre-Raphaelites Arthur had been reinvented as an English hero in an age of empire, but the choice of Welsh as the medium of composition allowed T. Gwynn Jones and others effortlessly to subvert the imperial ideology of Tennyson's English hero.

"Ymadawiad Arthur" is an *awdl* (a type of metrical poem) of 447 lines divided into 88 sections, which begins with the death of Medrawd (Mordred) at Camlan. Arthur and Bedwyr (Bedivere) are left alone on the field. Bedwyr carries his king to a clearing near a lake. Arthur knows he is dying:

> "Briw, Fedwyr," ebr ef "ydwyf
> Angau a lysg yn fy nghlwyf . . .
> Olaf oll o'm clwyfau yw . . ."
>
> (Jones 1934: 16)

"I am injured, Bedwyr," he said
"Death stalks my wound . . .
This is the last of all my wounds . . .

Bedwyr takes three attempts to dispose of Arthur's sword, Caledfwlch, and, finally satisfied with Bedwyr's account, Arthur is taken away by boat. The poem ends with Bedwyr turning away in sadness as Arthur disappears into the mists of Ynys Afallon (Avalon). In most modern Welsh poems about Arthur, as in "Ymadawiad Arthur," there is very little reference to the Grail quest and Lancelot is a minor figure. This is partly because, as scholarship makes available printed editions and translations of early Welsh material, Welsh writers are able to access Arthurian material from *Culhwch ac Olwen* and the Welsh *Triads* rather than from Malory and Tennyson. The other reason is that it is the "once and future king," the returning warrior-redeemer, who is of interest to Welsh writers engaged in a national struggle for self-determination, without which the survival of the Welsh language – and therefore of Wales – seems increasingly unlikely. As in many post-colonial literatures there is a general call in Wales for figures of national resistance, and the much-traveled Arthur is reinvented as a national redeemer for a Welsh-speaking Wales.

The idea of the "sleeping lord" as national redeemer, as liberator of Wales, and savior of the Welsh language is largely a modern phenomenon in the literature of Wales, and this is partly related to the fact that the motif of the sleeping lord is not a particularly common feature of the Arthurian story. Oliver Padel has pointed out that the earliest written reference to the tradition comes from Gervase of Tilbury in about 1211, who also records that Arthur had been seen, recovering from wounds inflicted by Mordred, in a palace on Mount Etna in Sicily (Padel 2000). The idea may have had a greater currency in oral tradition in the Brythonic world, a currency that may not have been translated into written record if the motif was not always associated with the figure of Arthur. As late as the twentieth century Elissa Henken was able to find considerable evidence in Wales of popular traditions about Arthur's cave even though it was often said not to be inhabited by Arthur but by one of the late-medieval rebels Owain Glyn Dŵr or Owain Lawgoch (Henken 1996). Arthur is also largely absent from the prophetic poetry of medieval Wales. He is absent from the tenth-century *Armes Prydein* ("The Prophecy of Britain") and from the prophetic poetry attributed to Myrddin (Merlin), which lists leaders who will return to lead Wales against the invaders and expel them from Britain. The traditional leaders in the early Welsh prophetic material are consistently Cadwaladr and Cynan, and later, following the rebellions of the late fourteenth and early fifteenth centuries, Owain Lawgoch, who died in 1378, and Owain Glyn Dŵr, whose death, like Arthur's, is unrecorded. There is some evidence in William of Malmesbury's twelfth-century chronicle, *Gesta Regum Anglorum* ("Deeds of the English Kings"), of pre-Galfridian traditions in Wales and Cornwall relating to Arthur's return as a defender or liberator but this is generally absent from the Welsh tradition in the later Middle Ages and early modern period, when the motif survives but the role is given to other figures.

It is striking, therefore, that Arthur reappears in this role in Wales after Tennyson's Arthur has become so popular. The Arthur of T. Gwynn Jones in "Ymadawiad Arthur" is part of what becomes a concerted attempt in Welsh writing to recover for Welsh-speaking Wales the figure of one of its oldest literary heroes, in a poem whose language, topography, and nomenclature is oppositional to the English discourse of empire.

The function of Arthur in the cave in these Welsh texts is that of liberator from long oppression, unlike the English tradition, where he is a reserve against national calamity who sleeps so long as the country is safe and powerful. In Welsh tradition the calamity has happened while he sleeps, as the land and its language have been overwhelmed by English settlement. In nineteenth- and early twentieth-century Wales there was no need for a "darkest hour" in an imaginary future. That hour had already come and the struggle, at the height of English imperial control, was for economic and political liberation. For T. Gwynn Jones and his generation, it was a struggle for the survival of the very idea of Welshness through the survival of the Welsh language. In that context what more potent symbol could there be than to take Tennyson's beloved symbol of imperial kingship – Arthur of Albion – and turn him back into a British warrior hero who will save the language of a colonized Wales from the homogenizing ravages of English imperial ambition?

Where David Jones's "Sleeping Lord" is about the nostalgic remembrance of catastrophic loss, T. Gwynn Jones's "Ymadawiad Arthur" is about return, regeneration, and hope. Written in a different language with a different subjectivity, T. Gwynn Jones's work grows out of – and itself helps to create – an early twentieth-century language movement based on a known, living tradition that is not yet overwhelmed by a sense of elegiac loss. That sense of imminent or apparent loss is a major feature of the language movement in Wales after 1961 but it is not fully apparent in the poetry of T. Gwynn Jones.

In Malory's *Morte Darthur* there is a sense of finality in Arthur's farewell to Bedevere and there is nothing of the *rex futurus* in Arthur's own words:

> "Comfort thyself" said the king "and do as well as thou mayest, for yn me is no trust for to trust in. For I will into the vale of Avylon to hele me of my grevous wound. And if thou hear never more of me, pray for my soul." (Vinaver 1990: 1240)

At the climax of T. Gwynn Jones's poem, however, Arthur is given a 28-line speech which Bedwyr hears as Arthur's message (*neges Arthur*) and which explicitly addresses the future of his country and his own eventual return:

> A o gof ein moes i gyd,
> A'n gwir, anghofir hefyd;
> Ar ein gwlad daw brad a'i bri
> Dan elyn dry'n drueni;
> Difonedd fyd a fynnir,

A gwaeth – tost geithiwed hir;
Ond o'r boen, yn ôl daw'r byd
I weiddi am ddedwyddyd,
A daw'n ôl yn ôl o hyd
I sanctaidd Oes Ieuenctyd;
A daw Y Dydd o'r diwedd,
A chân fy nghloch, yn fy nghledd
Gafaelaf, dygaf eilwaith
Glod yn ôl i'n gwlad a'n iaith.
          (T. G. Jones 1934: 32)

Our virtues will be forgotten,
And our truths also;
Treachery will fall on our country
Under an enemy it will turn to sadness;
A world without gentility,
And worse – the pain of long slavery;
But from the pain the world will return
To cry for happiness,
And we will return
To the holy Age of Youth;
And The Day will finally come,
And my bell will ring, and my sword
I will hold, I will bring again
Praise to our country and our language.

In T. Gwynn Jones's poem the figure of Arthur is not just a participant in a drama that he cannot control; he is himself the agent of change and the author of prophecy: it is not others who speak of his return, he speaks of it himself. The rhetoric of Arthur's final speech employs biblical imagery of slavery and delivery, which would have been familiar to a Welsh readership whose largely chapel-going tradition was founded on biblical literacy. Their political promised land is one that can be assimilated into the spiritual yearnings of non-conformist salvation so that the post-colonial dream of a delivery from slavery becomes a dream of youthful renewal. The "Age of Youth" is the new beginning for a country that can be reborn so long as it still has its own language. Comparing this section with the account in Tennyson is also instructive. Although Tennyson's Arthur is given a much longer final speech than in Malory, it is a speech about the end of an era rather than the king's return: "The old order changeth, yielding place to new" (Ricks 1987: 2.17). The king says farewell to Bedivere and, as in Malory, is taken by the three queens to Avilion to be healed. The inclusion of a prophecy of renewal as Arthur's final act in T. Gwynn Jones's Welsh poem is therefore all the more striking and emphasizes that it is the Arthur of the Welsh who is speaking. Like the Arthur of David Jones's "Sleeping Lord," this is a figure who offers a vision of agency as a metaphor of action. Those who sleep must arouse themselves: those who act will be free.

A Post-Colonial Welsh Hero

It is worth emphasizing that Arthur is not the most widely used heroic figure in modern Welsh writing. In the twentieth century there are two others who tower above him: Llywelyn ap Gruffydd and Owain Glyn Dŵr, the two great symbols from medieval history of, respectively, resistance to and rebellion against English control. Some of the finest Welsh poetry of the later twentieth century is explicitly concerned with the language movement that became prominent in Wales after 1961, a movement concerned not only with linguistic survival but also with the desire for self-determination. In the poetry and iconography of the language movement in Wales it is Llywelyn who appears as the most powerful symbol of lost independence. In Gerallt Lloyd Owen's poem "Fy Ngwlad" ("My Country," 1972) the narrative voice addresses Llywelyn in the opening lines, lamenting the loss of identity and the decline of resistance in a poem that is reminiscent of the famous laments written to commemorate Llywelyn's death by the poets of medieval Wales:

> Wylit, wylit Lywelyn,
> Wylit waed pe gwelit hyn . . .
>   (Owen 1972: 22)
>
> You would weep, you would weep, Llywelyn,
> You would weep blood if you could see this . . .

In another poem, "Cilmeri" (1982), which is also written in *cynghanedd*, Gerallt Lloyd Owen explores the events surrounding the death of Llywelyn at Cilmeri in south Wales in December 1282, an event with which David Jones was also very much engaged and about which he created a painted inscription, which he gave to his friend Saunders Lewis (Gray 1981: 80). However, while Llywelyn symbolizes loss of nationhood he is not a figure who is expected to return, and, despite Glyn Dŵr (and others) being assimilated into the folklore of the sleeping lord motif and being located in secret caves in many parts of Wales, it is primarily the example of resistance and rebellion in Llywelyn and Glyn Dŵr which animates the poetry of national aspiration in the later twentieth century. The importance of Arthur is that he is the great figure of Welsh independence through his sovereignty over a Romanized but pre-Anglicized Britain. For writers such as David Jones and Saunders Lewis, Arthur has the added attraction of international visibility, whose successful recovery as a symbol of Welsh nationhood immediately reinstates Wales and the Celtic world at the center of European cultural history. While Llywelyn and Glyn Dŵr are powerful figures in modern Welsh writing, Arthur has the additionally important role of representing the antiquity of the Welsh tradition and its survival as a link with Roman Britain. "We are the heirs of Romanity," proclaimed David Jones in a letter to Saunders Lewis, sensing perhaps that pre-Conquest antiquity was a safe claim to nationhood.

Modern Welsh Arthurian texts, in both languages, are mostly concerned with the idea of the national redeemer, and rarely explore the chivalric world of tournaments, quests, and courtly love. The two most common themes are the passing of Arthur and the sleeping lord who waits in a cave for the summons to return at the hour of greatest need. In modern Welsh writing the passing of Arthur is often a metonymy for the passing of Wales or of Welshness, and it is not surprising therefore that the return of Arthur, the other most popular motif, is a powerful symbol of national renewal and linguistic revival. In the twentieth century it is the language of Wales rather than the land of Britain that is the key to Welsh identity, an identity that the slumbering Arthur promises to restore. The Modernist Arthur arose against the context of Tennyson's *Idylls*, which celebrated the triumph of empire by reappropriating Arthur as an English hero. In the century that follows there is one idea above all others which unites Welsh writing with Welsh writing in English: the *rex futurus* of legend wakes up and speaks in Welsh.

Primary Texts

Jones, D. (1959). *Epoch and artist*. London: Faber.

Jones, D. (1974). *The sleeping lord and other poems*. London: Faber.

Jones, D. (1981). *The Roman quarry*. London: Agenda.

Jones, T. G. (1910). *Ymadawiad Arthur a Chaniadau Ereill* [The passing of Arthur and other poems]. Caernarfon: Cwmni y Cyhoeddwyr Cymreig.

Morris, W. (1934). Ogof Arthur. In *Ogof Arthur, Y Gorwel a'r Holl Farddoniaeth Fuddugol yn Eisteddfod Castell Nedd 1934* [Arthur's cave, The horizon and all the winning poetry in the Neath Eisteddfod 1934]. Lerpwl: Gwasg y Brython.

Powys, J. C. (2007). *Porius*. London: Duckworth.

Ricks, C. (ed.) (1987). *Alfred Tennyson. Poems*, 3 vols. Harlow: Longman.

Thomas, E. (1911). *Celtic stories*. Oxford: Clarendon Press.

Vinaver, E. (ed.) (1990). *Malory. Works*, 3 vols, 3rd rev. edn (ed. P. J. C. Field). Oxford: Clarendon Press.

References and Further Reading

Aitchison, J. & Carter, H. (1994). *A geography of the Welsh language 1961–1991*. Cardiff: University of Wales Press.

Ap Gwilym, G. (1982). *T. Gwynn Jones: Cyfres y Meistri 3*. Llandybie: Christopher Davies.

Burton, J. H. (1853). *The history of Scotland from Agricola's invasion to the extinction of the last Jacobite insurrection*. London: Longman.

Castle, G. (2001). *Modernism and the Celtic Revival*. Cambridge: Cambridge University Press.

Davies, W. B. (1970). *T. Gwynn Jones*. Cardiff: University of Wales Press.

Evans, G. (2000). Images of national renewal in David Jones's "The Sleeping Lord." In B. Humphrey & A. Price-Owen (eds), *David Jones: Diversity in unity*. Cardiff: University of Wales Press, pp. 83–90.

Gray, N. (1981). *The painted inscriptions of David Jones*. London: Gordon Fraser.

Gray, N. (1989). *The paintings of David Jones*. London: Lund Humphries & The Tate Gallery.

Henken, E. (1996). *National redeemer: Owain Glyndwr in Welsh tradition*. Cardiff: University of Wales Press.

Hooker, J. (2001). *Imagining Wales: A view of modern Welsh writing in English*. Cardiff: University of Wales Press.

Humphrey, B. (ed.) (1972). *Essays on John Cowper Powys*. Cardiff: University of Wales Press.

Knight, S. (1983). *Arthurian literature and society*. London: Macmillan.

Owen, G. Ll. (1972). *Cerddi'r Cywilydd* [Songs of shame]. Caernarfon: Gwasg Gwynedd.

Owen, G. Ll. (1991). *Cilmeri a Cherddi Eraill* [Cilmeri and other poems]. Caernarfon: Gwasg Gwynedd.

Padel, O. J. (2000). *Arthur in medieval Welsh literature*. Cardiff: University of Wales Press.

Pittock, M. (1999). *Celtic identity and the British image*. Manchester: Manchester University Press.

Thomas, M. W. (ed.) (2003). *A guide to Welsh literature*, vol. VII: *Welsh writing in English*. Cardiff: University of Wales Press.

30

Historical Fiction and the Post-Imperial Arthur

Tom Shippey

Belief in the historicity of Arthur has ebbed and flowed with the tides of fashion and circumstance. Firm medieval conviction that the legends were true was notoriously punctured by Polydore Vergil's *Anglica Historia* of 1534, and in spite of John Leland's furiously patriotic *Assertio inclytissimi Arturi Regis Britanniae* ten years later, Vergil's major point – that no contemporary European chronicler knew anything of Arthur's famed conquests – compelled assent. John Milton considered writing an epic on Arthur, but in his 1648 *History of Britain* he wrote curtly that it was open to doubt whether there had ever been an Arthur, dismissed Nennius as "a very trivial writer," and added that "he who can accept of Legends for good story, may quickly swell a volume with trash" (Fogle 1971: 165, 166).

And there the matter rested for some two hundred and fifty years. Though the Malorian story was never forgotten, and enjoyed powerful revival in the nineteenth century from Tennyson and others, Arthur remained legend, not history. J. R. Green's authoritative four-volume *History of the English People* of 1899 mentions the legends of Arthur as a twelfth-century phenomenon, but makes no attempt to fit him into chapter 1, "The English Conquest of Britain." A few years later Green conceded Arthur a footnote, and in 1910 Sir Charles Oman was rather more generous, declaring cautiously that "[I] incline to think that a real figure lurks beneath the tale of the *Historia Brittonum*. The name was undoubtedly Roman" (211). But on the whole, though nineteenth- and early twentieth-century historians were well aware of the Arthurian story, they were not persuaded of its historicity.

Modern specialist historians have reverted to that opinion, although non-specialists are significantly more credulous. In *The isles: A history* Norman Davies asserts that "Historians mostly now agree that an Arthur-like British warlord really did exist and that Gildas's account of a famous British victory at 'Mons Badonicus' is basically trustworthy" (1999: 194). In this area it would be truer to say that historians do not agree about anything, but Davies is following a not-long-outdated fashion. For perhaps forty or fifty years in the mid-twentieth century, the "historical Arthur" was widely accepted: not because of new documentary evidence, for Gildas and Nennius at least had been familiar to scholars from the time of Polydore Vergil, and only partly as a result of input from two disciplines unknown to previous eras, namely comparative philology and scientific archaeology. The main reason for the revival of belief in Arthur's historicity was that he fitted, or could be made to fit, an ominously and increasingly familiar contemporary political model, into which several authors were able to project their own life-experience.

A first indication of this is given by Rudyard Kipling. Kipling, like his contemporary J. R. Green above, had nothing to say about Arthur: the children's *History of England* which he co-authored with C. R. L. Fletcher in 1911 does not mention him. But in the first of the three "Parnesius" stories in *Puck of Pook's Hill* (1906), "A Centurion of the Thirtieth," Kipling makes a point easily understood in his own time, if now regularly missed. The two children to whom Puck appears and to whom he presents his tableaux of the past are talking to Parnesius the centurion, very obviously Roman with his "hoopy bronze armour," his red-crested helmet, and his great shield; but when he makes a disparaging remark about Romans, Una asks him cautiously, "But you're a Roman yourself, aren't you?" He replies:

> "Ye-es and no. I'm one of a good few thousand Romans who have never seen Rome except in a picture. My people have lived at Vectis for generations."

Parnesius is in fact a Romano-Briton, Roman by ethnic origin and loyalty, British by birth and long family connection, and *mutatis mutandis* exactly parallel to people like Kipling himself, who might be called (though the term is a very vexed one) Anglo-Indians. Parnesius's career follows lines very familiar to Anglo-Indians. He wants to become an officer of cavalry auxiliaries, the "Dacian Horse," just as a young Anglo-Indian might have wanted to join a smart cavalry regiment of the Indian Army, Hodson's Horse or the Bengal Lancers. But his father vetoes the idea and insists that he join "a regular Legion from Rome," corresponding to a British Army regiment of the line. Parnesius does not like the idea, because "like many of our youngsters I was not too fond of anything Roman," remarking that "Roman-born officers and magistrates looked down on us British-born." Still, he does as his father says, is commissioned into a Legion, and immediately finds himself confronted by the poor discipline which Indian Army officers often noticed in British Army other ranks.

Kipling draws the parallel out in several ways, for Parnesius is also a follower of Mithras, the Roman Army "secret society" which closely parallels the Freemasons so powerful in Anglo-India, but his basic point is very clear: the Roman Empire was just like the British Empire. Furthermore, both were under threat. Parnesius goes off to garrison Hadrian's Wall, where he operates just like a British subaltern on the Northwest Frontier of India, and finds himself increasingly without support from Rome. The Boer War had made Kipling similarly uncertain about the resolve of contemporary British politicians, and his famous poem "Recessional" (1898) shows his concern about British imperial decadence. His co-authored children's history sums up the situation with the words, "Roman Britain went to sleep behind her walls . . . What a lesson for us all to-day!" (1911: 20). Kipling, in short, opened the way for a complete reimagining of the Arthurian story, which would center not on the romance of Merlin and Lancelot and Arthur and Guinevere, but on politics and on the fall of empire, into which twentieth-century British writers increasingly felt they had special and novel insight.

Kipling's lead was followed, for instance, by Sir Arthur Conan Doyle, whose short story "The Last of the Legions" (1911) recasts the Roman abandonment of Britain as a case of ungrateful provincials demanding independence (as was increasingly the case with India), and getting much more than they bargained for. But a vital legitimation of the whole idea was offered by a serious historian, R. G. Collingwood, in the authoritative pages of the Oxford History of England. For the first volume of this, *Roman Britain and the English Settlements* (1936), Collingwood was supposed to write the Roman chapters and leave the Anglo-Saxon ones to his colleague J. N. L. Myres, but at the end of his section he went rather beyond his brief and wrote a few pages (321–4) which made an indelible mark on later Arthurian writing. What Collingwood did was to propose that maybe even Geoffrey of Monmouth's account might preserve a kernel of truth after all. He declared, firstly, that "the historicity of [Arthur] can hardly be called in question"; secondly, that "Artorius is a recognised though not very common Roman family name"; thirdly, that "[h]is place in the military organization of his age is clearly stated in the *Historia Brittonum*" (i.e. Nennius); and finally, that if Arthur was the Roman commander of a Roman field army, it would in the fifth century have been an army of mail-clad cavalry, the late Roman *equites cataphractarii*, a suggestion which saves the legendary image of "knights in armor" from the accusation of total anachronism. Collingwood sums up by declaring:

> Through the mist of legend that has surrounded the name of Arthur, it is thus possible to descry something which at least may have happened: a country sinking into barbarism, whence Roman ideas had almost vanished; and the emergence of a single man intelligent enough to understand them, and vigorous enough to put them into practice by gathering round him a group of friends and followers, armed according to the tradition of civilized warfare and proving their invincibility in a dozen campaigns. (Collingwood & Myres 1936: 324)

The campaigns had been discussed only a few years before by Collingwood's father, W. G. Collingwood (1929). But like Kipling's story, Collingwood Jr's hypothesis was a response not to the past but to the present. As he wrote in the mid-1930s there was indeed grave danger of Britain being overwhelmed by "barbarism," and about to be saved from it by a notoriously small "group of friends and followers" in the Battle of Britain. It is possible that Collingwood was thinking of tanks rather than Spitfires – hence the fascination with armored cavalry – but what he did was at once to give new life to a discredited medieval image, and to insert it into an absolutely contemporary and immediately graspable political situation. It is not surprising that writers of fiction saw the possibilities – as with Kipling, relating them to their own life-experiences.

A particularly obvious case is that of Alfred Duggan, whose life corresponds with almost allegorical exactness to the trajectory of the fall of empire (see Derbyshire 2005). Born in 1903 in Buenos Aires, he was brought to England by his mother when he was two. His mother's second husband was none other than Lord Curzon, Viceroy of India 1899–1905, and one of the grandest (if not the most efficient) to occupy that post. As an undergraduate at Oxford, Duggan was a member of the Evelyn Waugh set commemorated in *Brideshead Revisited* (1945), itself an elegy for vanished grandeur. Immensely rich and thoroughly dissipated, Duggan might well have been sent down if his stepfather had not been Chancellor of the University. But Curzon died in 1926, loaded with honors but privately considered a failure, and Duggan's mother lost the family fortune in the Depression. Duggan joined the army in World War II and saw some service, but was discharged as medically unfit, ended the war as a hand in an aircraft factory, and seemed well on the way to oblivion. In 1950, however, he published a successful historical novel about the First Crusade, *Knight with Armour*, and thereafter published fourteen more at the rate of one a year until his death in 1964. Duggan, then, was intimately associated with the success of empire, also saw its sudden dissolution, and lived on into a period of recovery. His work shows a deep interest in historical parallels, and among the clearest cases of this are his second and third novels, both published in 1951, *The Little Emperors* and *Conscience of the King*, which between them try to explain the Roman Empire's loss of Britain, the English settlements, and the Arthurian moment, in a way strongly colored by his own experiences.[1]

Kipling's Roman/British parallel is made overt in the "Historical Note" which Duggan appended to *The Little Emperors*. In this he argues that people have been misled by the scope and scale of Gibbon's massive *Decline and Fall of the Roman Empire*, which runs from before the Christian era to 1453. Awed by the size of the book, people have come to think that the fall of the Roman Empire was a long and gradual process. But in Duggan's opinion, this was not the case. The Western Empire collapsed in the seven years covered by his novel (AD 405–12). At the start of that period it seemed invincible, utterly destroying separate barbarian incursions: but seven years later Gaul had been overrun, Rome itself had been sacked, and Britain had been told to look to its own devices – a situation thought at the time to be temporary, but never rectified. He sums up: "[the destruction of the Western Empire] was as sudden and unexpected as the fall of the twentieth-century European Empires in Asia" – of which, as said above, he had personal and personally calamitous knowledge. He had reason to write two novels that between them try to explain what caused the rot.

In a phrase, the explanation offered by *The Little Emperors* for imperial collapse is "governors like Lord Curzon" – that is, just the kind of "Roman-born Roman," or English-born Englishman, whom Kipling's Parnesius found so offensive. Its central character is Caius Sempronius Felix, Praeses of Britannia Prima, or head of civil administration. Not British-born himself, Felix is completely loyal to the Empire and to the urban civilization it represents, which he tries to maintain with every resource of forced labor, harsh taxation, secret police, and torture. Nevertheless, he finds himself unwillingly caught up in a series of rebellions, as his military colleagues and the British upper classes choose and then murder one separatist emperor after another – the "little emperors" of the title. The novel's main irony is that in the end, on the run from his own secret police, Felix realizes that all his efforts to preserve civilization have been a mistake: people are better off, happier, and more honest, the further they get from Londinium. In Britain, the future belongs to the still-tribal West.

Conscience of the King opens some forty years after the events of *The Little Emperors*, and covers a much longer time span (AD 451–531). It offers an answer to two rather obvious questions about the fifth and sixth centuries in Britain, both raised by Sir Charles Oman (see above), whom Duggan expressly cites. First, how did society move from being a centralized bureaucracy to being the patchwork of kingdoms described by Gildas? Second, why is it that English and Welsh accounts of the *adventus Saxonum* do not corroborate each other? In particular, *The Anglo-Saxon Chronicle* gives a clear account of the foundation of Wessex by Cerdic, starting from a five-ship landing in Hampshire in AD 495. But if the battle of Mount Badon was won by Arthur not long after AD 500, somewhere in the southwest, surely Cerdic and Arthur must have come into contact? But the *Chronicle* never mentions Arthur, and early Welsh tradition knows nothing of Cerdic.

Cerdic is the "king" of *Conscience of the King*, and the irony is that he has no conscience. Building on the theory, mentioned once again by Oman (1910: 224), that Cerdic was not an Anglo-Saxon name, but a Saxonized form of British-Roman Coroticus, Duggan makes him a turncoat. At the start of the novel he is the third son of a Latin-speaking Sussex landowner, the kind of person Felix would have described as an *honestioris*. His father is quietly trying to turn local prominence into local dominance, building up his bodyguard into an army, grooming his second son to be a bishop and take over the church, aiming to be hailed as king and make his position hereditary. He is confident that he can defend the boundaries of his own region, between the forest and sea, with his own resources. Cerdic, however, has no place in this scheme, but does have the advantage of learning Saxon in youth, encouraged by an interpreter-grandfather (another idea mentioned by Oman, though dismissed by him as a "wild suggestion," 1910: 225), and by memories of a Germanic ancestor in Roman service (which Duggan claims as his own discovery). When Cerdic's father is forced to give some support to a last attempt, headed by Gildas's Ambrosius, to reintroduce British unity and Roman discipline, Cerdic becomes an officer of a Saxon auxiliary unit. The attempt fails, Cerdic kills his eldest brother and has to flee, masquerades as a Saxon and is instrumental in the Saxon conquest of his homeland in Sussex, well recorded by the *Anglo-Saxon Chronicle*. But he is revealed as a traitor and fratricide, has to flee again, and sets up as an independent chieftain, embarking on the conquest of Wessex just as the *Chronicle* says. Late on in this process he encounters Arthur, and loses the battle of Mount Badon, or *obsessio montis Badonici*, though not disastrously.

A feature of Duggan's novels is their dependence on archaeology. Near the end of *The Little Emperors*, Felix visits St Albans, and the description given of broken gates, depopulation, and ramshackle patching draws on the Wheelers' account of Verulamium (1936). Sections of *Conscience of the King* read like a tour of archaeological sites, including Corinium (Cirencester), Venta (Winchester), and Calleva (Silchester). Cerdic is especially struck by the latter, which he describes as "abandoned while it was still a going concern," populated only by one old woman cooking scraps over an open fire on a marble floor surrounded by frescoes. He notes that the church is in ruins, but that one building has kept its roof, within it a statue of Mars behind an altar, as if the inhabitants had reverted to paganism in despair before fleeing. Duggan worked up hints from contemporary archaeology – Silchester had been especially extensively excavated since the later nineteenth century (Clarke et al. 2001) – to create a detailed picture of what the "fall of civilization" might mean in practice. Something he stresses is increasing practical incompetence among the working classes as well as the rulers: Cerdic survives the Siege of Mount Badon by noting that the camp-followers of Arthur's army have pitched their tents higgledy-piggledy, so that when he leads the Saxons in a surprise breakout they can get into the tangle of canvas and guy-ropes, where Arthur's heavy cavalry are unable to charge.

What one sees in Collingwood, in Duggan, and in a number of mid-twentieth century writers, is at bottom an attempt to reconcile two different imaginary worlds, which one might call the post-Geoffrey of Monmouth tradition (knights in armor, Arthur and Guinevere, Lancelot and Mordred, Excalibur and the Grail), and the Fall of Empire image (deserted towns, language change, meager and unreliable records). The latter was too solidly based to be rejected, the former too well known and attractive as narrative to be discounted. There is a brief attempt to integrate them in C. S. Lewis's Merlin-centered fantasy novel *That Hideous Strength* (1945), when one of its more redundant characters, Dr Dimble, delivers a short lecture on the Arthurian tradition, and argues that "the whole thing hangs together, even in a late version like Malory's." The two sets of characters – courtly Lancelots and sinister Morgawses – are memories of a divided society, Christian Romans in the towns and druidical British up-country, with Arthur in the middle, British by birth but Roman by training, "trying to pull this society together and almost succeeding." A few years later, in the "Author's Note" to her *Sword at Sunset* (1963), Rosemary Sutcliff would say much the same thing, arguing like Collingwood that behind the "numinous mist" of legend:

> there stands the solitary figure of one great man. No knight in shining armour, no Round Table, no many-towered Camelot; but a Romano-British war-leader, to whom, when the Barbarian darkness came flooding in, the last guttering lights of civilization seemed worth fighting for.

Sword at Sunset is the fourth in a sequence of novels which, like Duggan's two but more extensively than those, span the period of Roman rule and retreat: *The Eagle of the Ninth* (1954), *The Silver Branch* (1957), *The Lantern Bearers* (1959), and *Sword at*

Sunset (1963), set respectively c. AD 140, c. AD 296, c. AD 455, and approximately AD 470–530. The events in all four novels are related to the theme of imperial weakening and withdrawal, and a dominant image is that of "guttering lights" in a growing darkness. Even more than Duggan's, Sutcliff's novels draw inspiration from contemporary archaeology (though imaginatively; see Thomson 1925). The first of them is centred on the discovery at Silchester of a wingless Roman eagle (Joyce 1881), which Sutcliff connects with the belief, since discredited, that the Ninth Legion, while in Britain, somehow disappeared from the imperial order of battle. The second draws on an Ogham stone, also found in Silchester, inscribed "Evicatos," early British for "spearman." Most remarkably, much of *Sword at Sunset* is derived from an attempt to explain the discovery at Newstead, a Roman fort north of Hadrian's Wall and rehabilitated in the post-Roman period, of the skeleton of an adult, perfectly formed, but diminutive woman, lying in a pit beneath the bones of nine horses, all buried in the center of the old parade-ground (Curle 1911). What chain of events could possibly have led to this?

Sutcliff's explanation owes a good deal to Kipling (of whom there are several other traces, and on whom she wrote a monograph in 1960). The girl is presented as one of "the old race, the Little Dark People," Kipling's "Little Folk": pre-Celtic aborigines, who in legend became the fairies, "the People of the Hills." Fearing their notorious magic, Arthur's men, establishing Newstead as the base for their wars in the north, bury her murdered body beneath their horses killed in battle, as horses are creatures of the sun and will keep her ghost from walking. But Arthur's alliance with the Little People is received doubtfully by his own men, and especially by his wife Guenhumara. The fact that he leaves her with her newborn child in their underground dwelling, the "hollow hills" of fable, causes her to believe that they have left her with a changeling and is responsible for her betrayal of him with Bedwyr (the Bedivere of legend, here replacing Lancelot as better grounded in Celtic tradition). In general, Sutcliff's novel follows the Geoffrey of Monmouth tradition as regards narrative, but the setting remains that of Collingwood, an important feature being Arthur's breeding plan for large horses capable of acting as armored cavalry chargers – Duggan's Cerdic had remarked that the Arthurian failure might have been caused by trouble over a woman, but in his opinion was more likely to have stemmed from losing all his "big foreign horses."

In the Sutcliff re-creation, furthermore, vital figures are those who can be seen as belonging to both traditions, the Roman one and the Celtic one, and in particular Ambrosius, Vortigern, and the Emperor Maximus. She describes Ambrosius as High King of Britain, descended from Maximus and a British princess, as claimed in the *Mabinogion*'s "Dream of Macsen Gwledig." Utha, or Uther Pendragon, is his brother, and Arthur is Utha's illegitimate son; he carries the seal of Maximus in his sword-hilt. Vortigern, meanwhile, is Ambrosius's cousin, descended from the same British royal house, but not from Maximus: he is accordingly pure British, not Brito-Roman, and is recognized by many as the true heir. Cerdic, finally, with his British name and Saxon allegiance, is explained as the son of Vortigern by the Jutish princess Rowen, in legend daughter of Hengest. The story has been made into one of ethnic, religious, linguistic, and cultural conflict, very much in line with twentieth-century preoccupations.

A continuing complication for Sutcliff, however, was just the fact that (most of) Britannia became England. She might heavily demonize the invading Saxons as barbarians, but she was well aware that they formed the foundation of her own language and culture, and that of her readers. Would the present world have been a better place if all of modern Britain and America spoke Welsh, or Latin? What was the point, or the effect, of the Arthurian resistance? Sutcliff's answer here is that Ambrosius, and later Arthur, were attempting only to gain time: time for ethnic mingling, for the development of personal connections and mutual respect. After Badon the Saxon chieftains negotiating surrender remind Arthur that their ancestors also fought for Rome, and manned Maximus's Second Legion. Empires, in short, may seed benefits even after they have withdrawn or been defeated.

Sutcliff, the daughter of a naval officer, continued the pattern of authors from Establishment/Service families, but this was not the case with her contemporary Henry Treece, whose many novels show markedly anti-Establishment views, and who was a founder of the now-forgotten "New Apocalypse" movement. His juvenile novel *The Eagles Have Flown* (1954) and adult novel *The Great Captains* (1956) parallel Sutcliff's *Lantern Bearers* and *Sword at Sunset* closely in date and setting, and the latter cites familiar authorities, including Collingwood and Myres (1936), and Collingwood Sr (1929); but Treece's view of the fall of (the Roman) Empire shows less concern than *Schadenfreude*. *The Great Captains* is centered on Modredus, a gutter-child adopted by Ambrosius in a display of Roman meritocracy; but as the novel opens Ambrosius is senile and defeated; Modredus murders him, changes his name to Medrawt, and goes over to the rising Celtic power of Arthur, or as Treece presents him, Artos the Bear, a knowingly incestuous savage. The story offers barbaric retakes on the familiar motifs of the Sword in the Stone and the Round Table, as well as the cavalry leader and the *dux bellorum*, and Medrawt duly betrays Artos with Gwenhwyfar. In a final scene Artos has conquered at Badon – where he faced Cerdic in a scene seemingly influenced by Duggan – has become Artorius, and seems to have re-established Empire. But he too is murdered by a crippled and insane Medrawt, and the reconquest collapses in jealousy and popular discontent.

The 1960s and 1970s marked the zenith of Arthur's newly-recovered historicity, and one may wonder whether, just as novelists drew on scholarship and archaeology, so scholars and archaeologists were affected by images from popular fiction: Hutton (2008) offers further explanations. After Sutcliff, a string of works came out in quick succession which attempted to connect Arthur with archaeological fact and to write him back into history, notably Geoffrey Ashe's collection *The Quest for Arthur's Britain* (1968), Leslie Alcock's *Arthur's Britain* (1971) and "*By South Cadbury is that Camelot . . .*" (1972), and John Morris's *The Age of Arthur* (1973). For specialist historians this initiative was ended abruptly by a 1977 review article by David Dumville, which concluded contemptuously that all Alcock and Morris had done was to recreate Geoffrey of Monmouth. Collingwood's 1936 collaborator, J. N. L. Myres, also published a much-expanded version of his own chapters in the 1980s, in which he rejected all connection with Collingwood and remarked of Arthur that "No figure on the border-line of history and mythology has wasted more of the historian's time" (1989: 16). These refutations, however, not only failed to trickle through to non-specialists, but have made almost no impact on the Internet: Arthurian websites are still dominated by variants on Ashe, Alcock, and Morris.

Another factor of increasing importance from the 1960s was what one might call "Celticity." Works like the *Mabinogion* and the *Gododdin* had been known to scholars from the nineteenth century, but became increasingly accessible during the twentieth. Rosemary Sutcliff was to write her version of the *Gododdin* in one of her few adult novels, *The Shining Company* (1990), but the most engaging fictionalization of it is John James's *Men Went to Cattraeth* (1969), each chapter of which begins with a quotation and translation from John Williams ab Ithel's edition of 1852. The novel strongly ironizes the familiar picture of post-Roman Britain. It is told by Aneirin, "Pre-Eminent Bard of the Island of Britain" but also – in his own mind and that of his fellows – "greatest Poet of Rome." James's Britons, who set out from Din Eidin or Edinburgh to re-conquer Bernicia from the Saxons, are totally convinced that they are Romans. But the Rome of their imagination is that of the marvel-world of the *Mabinogion*. When they come to Hadrian's Wall, Aneirin explains that:

> It was raised in one night, complete from sea to sea, by the Magician Vergil, at the bidding of King Hadrian. This was one of the works that Hadrian did for the pleasure of his leman Cleopatra.

The world he lives in is one of extreme poverty, where the three hundred and one armored horsemen equipped by Mynydog the Wealthy are seen as the greatest host ever assembled in the history of war; and one of deep historical ignorance, where (as in "The Dream of Macsen Gwledig" in the *Mabinogion*) it is assumed that Rome was once conquered by Britain, and where the marks of *Romanitas* include bagpipes, devotion to the Virgin (Christ is not mentioned), attachment to pastoralism and hatred of agriculture, and above all, the practice of oral poetry in Welsh, of which the prime example is the *Gododdin* itself. James takes liberties, too, with dates. Even revised theories about the poem place it later than Gildas's Mount Badon, but James presents the whole expedition as a sacrifice-play by Mynydog. He sends the whole expedition out, and also betrays it to the Saxons, simply to keep the Saxons occupied while he sends the young Arthur south from Edinburgh to his father Uther Pendragon, knowing that only Arthur, unlike the heroes of the *Gododdin*, will be able to unify the warring British kingdoms. A final irony is that the aged Aneirin telling the story is convinced that Arthur has defeated the Saxons for all time and that the Brito-Roman future is safe in the hands of his son Medraut.

A similar conversion to Celticity can be seen in Count Nikolai Tolstoy's *The Coming of the King* (1988), a work by an author in several ways comparable to Duggan. It has to be said, first that this is a work of immense learning, which draws on almost every Dark Age text surviving from northwest Europe, from the Welsh

Myrddin poems to *Beowulf* and Norse sagas, and second that it is unfinished: it was advertised as "The First Book of Merlin," but no sequel has to date appeared. Nor is it likely to, for markedly post-imperial reasons. Briefly, and cautiously, one may say that Count Nikolai, though English-born, has kept a title inherited from Czarist Russia. Just before *The Coming of the King* he published a work called *The Minister and the Massacres* (1986), which (along with other works) accused prominent British public figures of committing war crimes, by sending Russian and Yugoslav prisoners back to their home countries after World War II to be executed by their own governments as traitors. Tolstoy was sued for libel, lost, and damages were awarded against him so great that one imagines that any future book royalties would simply be swallowed up.

It is striking that in *The Coming of the King* Tolstoy inserts, into a totally Celticized world centered on the figure of Merlin, a Roman tribune called Rufinus. On internal evidence, Rufinus is the son of the sixth-century philosopher Boethius. Like Duggan's Ambrosius, he makes a valiant effort to impose Roman discipline on a ragtag Celtic army. Much of his conversation concerns Byzantine campaigns with Belisarius's *equites cataphractarii* – a motif used earlier in John Masefield's *The Badon Parchments* (1947). And in a final showdown he recreates Collingwood's "single man . . . armed according to the tradition of civilized warfare" by turning on the Saxons first a *ballista fulminalis*, second an arrow-shooting machine-gun, and third Greek fire, with which he incinerates Beowulf (in legend, killed by a dragon). He is himself mortally wounded in the battle, and dies, asking Merlin to have his lead identity tablet (modern "dog-tag") buried in his paternal home. Drawing conclusions about writers' personal motivations is notoriously improper, but it is hard not to see Count Nikolai's experience projected on to Rufinus: both exiles from an eastern empire, stranded in the far west among ignorant or ungrateful barbarians, but still keeping up their standards, and hoping still for an imperial re-conquest. Arthur himself never comes into focus in *The Coming of the King*, though he is several times mentioned, nor is the title explained: one can only guess what the overall plan of the complete work would have been.

There have of course been many other attempts to write the Arthurian story, or the Arthurian moment, as a historical novel. Raymond Thompson's survey counts more than forty up to 1985, and the rate of production has probably increased, with a particular fondness nowadays for the trilogy or longer sequence. Examples include Mary Stewart's Merlin trilogy *The Crystal Cave* (1970), *The Hollow Hills* (1973), and *The Last Enchantment* (1979); Marion Zimmer Bradley's *The Mists of Avalon* (1979) and its continuing sequels, co-authored with or written by Diana L. Paxson; Stephen Lawhead's "Pendragon Cycle," *Taliesin* (1987), *Merlin* (1988), *Arthur* (1989), *Pendragon* (1984), and *Grail* (1987); Jack Whyte's nine-book series re-marketed as "The Camulod Chronicles" and begun by *The Skystone* (1992); and Bernard Cornwell's "Warlord Chronicles," *The Winter King* (1995), *Enemy of God* (1996), and *Excalibur* (1997). All authors naturally aim at originality and offer different perspectives, or different combinations of the legendary, historicist, and mythical versions of the Arthurian story. Yet one feels that the rules of the game have become once more relatively fixed, as is suggested by the very titles. The political setting is one of warlords and petty king-doms; the theme is defeating barbarism and countering anarchy; there will be a strong and sometimes strident claim of authenticity, beneath which one usually sees the familiar Nennius/Geoffrey/Malory outline; romantic Celticism is very marked, though there is an awareness of Rome in the background; magic and Merlin are sometimes explained rationalistically (as in the Stewart sequence), sometimes given a mystical "New Age" emphasis (as in Bradley's work and its successors). All these are now estab-lished features of the Arthurian story as commonly received. Meanwhile, though the "post-imperial" concerns of Duggan or Sutcliff or Tolstoy no longer have much reso-nance, especially for American audiences, similar projections have come in to take their place – as one can see most clearly, now, from Hollywood movies.

The best of these remains John Boorman's *Excalibur* (1981), which sticks to the familiar Malorian story, with strong influence from T. H. White. Much more politi-cized are Jerry Zucker's *First Knight* (1995) and Antoine Fuqua's *King Arthur* (2004). The first retells a very old part of the Arthurian legend – the abduction of Guinevere by (in the movie) Malagant, and her rescue by Lancelot – but makes the story primar-ily one of power politics and only secondarily romantic. Malagant's real aim is to take over Guinevere's queendom of Lyonesse. She agrees to marry an ageing Arthur in exchange for his protection, and Malagant kidnaps her so as to gain her country by forced marriage. Her rescue by the much younger Lancelot leads to an abortive romance, which, fortunately for "family values," goes no further than a kiss. In the end a major rewriting of the traditional story is imposed, with Arthur conveniently dead in battle, also conveniently leaving no heirs, and the way cleared for Guinevere and Lancelot to succeed him and live happily ever after.

There are, however, striking parallels with the First Iraq War of 1992, with Lyonesse as Kuwait, Malagant as Saddam Hussein, and Arthur as George Bush Sr, and it has been pointed out (Haydock 2002) that in one critical scene an attempt is made to justify foreign interventions. Malagant, speaking to Arthur and the Round Table, challenges them by asking, in effect, what is the difference between their takeover of Lyonesse and his own: "Or is the law of Camelot to rule the entire world?" Arthur (here played by Sean Connery) replies, with a strong and surely deliberate echo of the US Pledge of Allegiance:

> There are laws that enslave men and laws that set them free. Either what we hold to be right and good and true, is right and good and true for all mankind, under God, or we're just another robber tribe.

But that, one might well say, is just the question. How can one tell that "what we hold to be right" is right "for all mankind"? And using the phrase "under God" only makes one wonder what would happen if Malagant replied with an appeal to Allah. If the writers discussed above can be seen as "post-imperial," one might well see Zucker's movie as nervously "pre-imperial": it is using the legendary Arthur to offer a retrospective justification for a new stage in American foreign policy.

Antoine Fuqua's 2004 movie *King Arthur*, by contrast, once again rejects the Malorian version and takes up a reinforced version of Collingwood. His idea of the cata-
phracts of Artorius had been revived in a book by C. Scott Littleton and Linda A.
Malcor, *From Scythia to Camelot* (1994/2000), which follows Malone (1925) in noting
that a Sarmatian cavalry unit had been based in the north of Britain in the second
century, commanded by Artorius Castus, and goes on to argue that these scale-armored
Sarmatians were the originals of the knights of the Round Table (see chapter 35). The
main weakness of the theory is the gap between the second and fifth or sixth centuries,
shown as bridged by continuous fresh drafts of conscripts from the far steppes, but the
movie makes the usual if especially strident claims to historical truth, finding the real
people behind the legend, etc. The opening credits begin with the telltale phrase (see
Davies above) "Historians agree. . . ." What this means in practice is that the Sarmatians, here given familiar Arthurian names, including Lancelot, Gawain, Bors, etc., add
one more ethnic element to the familiar mix of Romans, Britons, and Saxons. In
Fuqua's version the Saxons, led by Cerdic, are the usual repulsive and now racist barbarians; the Romans are effete, decadent slave-owners, about to cut their losses in Britain
and withdraw; and the Britons, or "Woads," are attractively druidical and incipiently
feminist (for their leaders are Merlin and his warlike daughter Guinevere), but kept
down by the Romans – and by their Sarmatian janissaries. I have argued elsewhere
(Shippey 2007) that this is a post-Vietnam movie, in which the Sarmatian heroes stand
for American soldiers, forced by a faraway government set on withdrawal to oppress
people with whom they would rather make common cause, but in which the Sarma-
tians/Americans are in the end victorious. The turning point of the movie comes when
the Sarmatians, having received their discharge papers and now free to return home,
come back to support their Brito-Roman commander Arthur and the Woads against
the Saxons, at the Battle of Mount Badon; this time they are fighting voluntarily, not
under compulsion, and have become liberators rather than oppressors.

One can only say that on many levels this is a "feel-good" movie, which eliminates
the historical Anglo-Saxon success, further reduces the traditional adultery of Lancelot
and Guinevere to no more than smoldering glances, and engineers a particularly
incongruous happy ending, with Arthur and Guinevere married by Merlin and usher-
ing in a new era of freedom, unity, and lasting peace. Several commentators, however,
made a connection with the Second Iraq War of 2003, and though this was denied
by the scriptwriter, who brought up the Vietnam parallel instead (see Matthews
2004), it carries some conviction. *King Arthur* follows the familiar Hollywood "liberation" narrative, which projects political problems on to external oppressors – as in
Mel Gibson's *Braveheart* (1995) or Roland Emmerich's *The Patriot* (2000) – and
assumes that military victory over the oppressors is all that is needed. The connection
with recent American/British foreign policy is all too easily made. In this respect the
King Arthur movie functions as an apologia for a nascent empire, rather than a warning
to or commentary on a declining one.

It is tempting, and sometimes inevitable, to see authors projecting their own circumstances into their fictions, and the fictions changing with the circumstances.

Kipling surely saw his schoolfellows from *Stalky & Co* (1900) as so many young Parnesiuses gallantly guarding an ungrateful homeland. Duggan perhaps saw himself in the old woman of Silchester cooking scraps among the relics of past wealth. Sutcliff less pessimistically held out for honorable burial of the past and a brighter future, while Tolstoy kept up hopes of *revanche* and return. American writers and moviemakers seem to be moving round the circle to an image of a successful Arthur, without the legendary stains of adultery and incest, or the historical reality of racial and linguistic defeat.[2]

As remarked at the start of this essay, the idea of a "historical" Arthur is effectively dead among specialist historians, and indeed provokes general embarrassment (see Hutton 2004). But as Professor Hutton also points out, the appetite of the general public for such an idea, including the educated public, has never been stronger. For this there are no doubt many reasons, but one is that the past century has taught many melancholy lessons about overstretched empires, ethnic cleansing, movements of population, imperial complacency, and imperial loss of nerve, often applicable (however dubious the phrase) to "the age of Arthur." In "King Arthur" we continue to recognize ourselves.

NOTES

1 Self-reference is even clearer in Duggan's first novel. The hero of this is Roger de Bodeham, whose knightly career during the First Crusade is one of virtually unrelieved failure: Duggan himself lived at Bodiam Manor, saved from the wreck of the family fortune (Derbyshire 2005). Particularly ironic is the fact that Roger, humiliated and cuckolded, is nevertheless the man responsible for the final successful scaling of the walls of Jerusalem. But he is killed in the moment of victory, and no one notices.

2 The writer of the novel based on the movie, Frank Thompson (*King Arthur*, 2004), is under the impression that the Battle of Mount Badon was so successful that the Saxons never returned to Britain; in which case he would presumably have written his novel in Welsh, or Latin. Hollywood does not do failure, however heroic.

REFERENCES AND FURTHER READING

(Fictional works mentioned are not listed here: titles and dates of first publication are given in the text.)

Alcock, L. (1971). *Arthur's Britain. History and archaeology AD 367–634*. New York: St Martin's Press.

Alcock, L. (1972). *"By South Cadbury is that Camelot . . .": The excavation of Cadbury Castle 1966–1970*. London: Thames & Hudson.

Ashe, G. (ed.) (1968). *The quest for Arthur's Britain*. New York: Praeger.

Clarke, A., Fulford, M., Rains, M , & Shaffrey, R. (2001). The Victorian excavations of 1893. Silchester Roman Town – The Insula IX Town Life Project. At www.silchester.reading.ac.uk/victorians, accessed February 2008.

Collingwood, R. G. & Myres, J. N. L. (1936). *Roman Britain and the English settlements*. Oxford: Clarendon Press.

Collingwood, W. G. (1929). Arthur's battles. *Antiquity*, 3(11), 292–8.

Curle, J. (1911). *A Roman frontier post and its people: The Fort of Newstead in the Parish of Melrose.* Glasgow: J. Maclehose & Sons.

Davies, N. (1999). *The isles: A history.* London: Oxford University Press.

Derbyshire, J. (2005). Alfred Duggan's past. *New Criterion*, 23(Feb.), 28–33.

Dumville, D. N. (1977). Sub-Roman Britain: History and legend. *History*, 62, 173–92. Repr. with original pagination in D. N. Dumville (1990). *Histories and pseudo-histories of the insular Middle Ages.* Aldershot: Variorum.

Fogle, F. (ed.) (1971). The history of Britain. In *Complete prose works of John Milton*, vol. 5, part 1. New Haven, CT: Yale University Press.

Green, J. R. (1899). *History of the English people*, 4 vols. New York: Harper & Bros.

Haydock, N. (2002). Arthurian melodrama, Chaucerian spectacle, and the waywardness of cinematic pastiche in *First Knight* and *A Knight's Tale*. In T. Shippey & M. Arnold (eds), *Film and fiction: Reviewing the Middle Ages.* Cambridge: Brewer, pp. 5–38.

Hutton, R. (2003). Arthur and the academics. In R. Hutton (ed.), *Witches, druids and King Arthur: Studies in paganism, myth and magic.* London: Hambledon, pp. 39–58.

Hutton, R. (2008). The early Arthur: History and myth. In E. Archibald & A. Putter (eds), *The Cambridge companion to Arthurian legend.* Cambridge: Cambridge University Press.

Joyce, J. G. (1881). Third account of excavations at Silchester. *Archaeologia*, 46, 344–65.

Kipling, R. & Fletcher, C. R. L. (1911). *A history of England.* Garden City, NY: Doubleday Page.

Littleton, C. S. & Malcor, L. A. (2000). *From Scythia to Camelot: A radical reassessment of the legends of King Arthur, the Knights of the Round Table, and the Holy Grail.* New York: Garland (originally published 1994).

Malone, K. (1925). Artorius. *Modern Philology*, 22(4), 367–74.

Matthews, J. (2004). An interview with David Franzoni. *Arthuriana*, 14(3), 115–22.

Morris, J. (1973). *The age of Arthur: A history of the British Isles from 350 to 650.* New York: Scribner.

Myres, J. N. L. (1989). *The English settlements.* Oxford: Clarendon Press.

Oman, C. (1910). *A history of England*, vol 1: *England before the Norman Conquest.* London: Methuen.

Shippey, T. (2007). Fuqua's *King Arthur*: More mythmaking in America. *Exemplaria*, 19(2), 310–26.

Thompson, R. H. (1985). *The return from Avalon: A study of the Arthurian legend in modern fiction.* Westport, CT: Greenwood Press.

Thomson, J. C. (1925). *A great free city: The book of Silchester.* London: Simpkin Marshall Hamilton Kent.

Wheeler, R. E. M. & Wheeler, T. V. (1936). *Verulamium: A Belgic and two Roman cities.* Oxford: Oxford University Press.

31
Feminism and the Fantasy Tradition: *The Mists of Avalon*

Jan Shaw

The second half of the twentieth century saw the emergence of women writers as key contributors to contemporary Arthurian literature. The Arthurian myth – the "matter of Britain" – is a key myth of origin in British culture. Revisioning this myth from the point of view of women, at this time, reflects the emergence of women as significant cultural voices who had gone unheard, mostly unspoken, from at least the legendary time of Arthur himself.

Marion Zimmer Bradley's *The Mists of Avalon* first appeared in 1983. It has been an enormous popular success and is still in print. Critically its reception has been mixed. Most problematic has been whether or not the text contributes to the feminist project in its broadest terms – to alleviate the subordination of women – or whether it in fact reinscribes the mechanisms and privileges of patriarchal structures. A work of such length inevitably has its problems, and a complete revisioning of social structures seems an impossible task. As a result, most critics find that the text presents opportunities in some dimensions but fails in others. Lee Ann Tobin argues that "the tendency for contradictory political messages" is characteristic of women's popular fiction, but that this should not undercut the subversion that is effected (Tobin 1993: 154).

This chapter considers the operation of fantasy in *The Mists of Avalon*. Fantasy is construed here as multifaceted. While it includes the fantasy elements in the narrative – the magic, the spells, and the privileged knowledge of the Sight – these are not the primary concern of this chapter. The text is self-evidently a fantasy in these terms. This chapter instead considers fantasy as a discourse of repressed desires vicariously fulfilled: the fantasy of feminine learning, autonomy, and agency that is Avalon. It also considers fantasy as structural break and disjunction, of that moment of hesitation, or even a lingering uncertainty left after a compete reading. I will begin by offering definitions of fantasy, followed by some considerations of the interaction between feminism and contemporary Arthurian fantasy by women, before discussing *The Mists of Avalon* in some detail in the second half of the chapter.

The Fantasy Tradition

Traditional definitions of fantasy focus primarily on epistemological concerns: on dichotomies of truth/untruth, possibility/impossibility, reality/imaginary. The reader must accept, as truth, a logic of impossibility and irrationality, of dreams and magic. Gary Wolfe offers this definition of fantasy as "the most commonly cited": "FANTASY. A fictional narrative describing events that the reader believes to be impossible" (Wolfe 1986: 38). In addition to his own definition, Wolfe offers a survey of a further twenty definitions from mid-twentieth-century critics and writers. A dominant concern throughout is the "impossible" in direct and definitional opposition to the "mimetic." In terms of this opposition, fantasy is primarily extra- or intertextual: it refers outward to the "real" world or textual representations of it. It is therefore irrevocably intertwined with what is possible and "real," and is highly culturally specific. Less oppositional are references to "the supernatural" and "magic." Rather than an absence of reality, these terms tend to suggest the presence of another kind of agency. Further definitions gesture toward an alterity which is irreducible to the self: "apparent arbitrariness," "arresting strangeness," and "wonder." These terms suggest inexplicability and tend to indicate qualities or impressions, referring to the atmosphere of the text or the response of the reader. These terms describe neither absence nor any concrete presence; they go beyond the absence/presence dichotomy.

What we find here is that epistemological definitions exhibit an interplay between sameness and difference. They can be anywhere on the spectrum of otherness: from the other as the absence of the one, the definitional "not me," through the other as the presence of another kind of agency, to the other as a state of affairs out there, not quantifiable in terms of me. One could say, then, that a significant feature of fantasy is an exploration of the terms of existence, of the tension between sameness and difference.

Another influential definition of the mode of fantasy is psychoanalytic. Rosemary Jackson, in her important work *Fantasy: The Literature of Subversion*, argues that fantasy is "a literature of desire, which seeks that which is experienced as absence and loss" (Jackson 1981: 3). For Jackson fantasy opens up the cultural order to moments of disorder and "illegality." Dominant value systems are usurped, and that which is papered over by cultural operations is revealed: "the fantastic traces the unsaid and the unseen of culture: that which has been silenced, made invisible, covered over and made 'absent'" (4). Fantasy opens up a space for the exploration of forbidden and repressed desires, allowing for their vicarious fulfillment though expression.

Jackson borrows from Freud's notion of the "uncanny," that is, the breaking through of an unconscious repression. Freud argues that there are two types of uncanny. The first is associated with an individual repression, the second with a cultural repression. The strongest of all cultural repressions are taboos: they are disruptive to culture, and their repression is required to ensure smooth cultural continuity.

Fantasy literature – Jackson's "Romantic" and "faery" literature – provides a privileged space for the articulation of the repressed without the confrontation of the uncanny. Forbidden desires can be articulated, explored, vicariously enjoyed, all within the safe confines of an otherworldly tale. In order to avoid the discomfort of the uncanny, this experience must remain within an imaginary world. Allowing such a moment to enter into realist fiction is tantamount to allowing it to move into the world of "common reality," and therefore the uncanny re-emerges. In this instance – what Jackson calls the "modern fantastic" – the uncanny is deeply subversive of the reality in which it is contextualized. Containing the experience in fantasy forecloses any possibility of realization of forbidden desires within the "real" world, and the subversive potential of fantasy can thereby be circumvented.

For Jackson, then, fantasy is grounded in its individual and social context. It comes from within; within the individual, within the culture. It is not a gesture toward alterity or the sublime; it does not transcend common existence. On the contrary, it is a critique of what has been, or is, or might be in the future; but its resolution is not possible, now, in the real world. Fantasy is, therefore, deeply enmeshed in the cultural context in which it is produced.

Fantasy and Feminism

Defined as a space for the articulation of repressed desire, fantasy open up avenues for feminist enquiry. Fantasy can allow the terms of existence to be explored, dominant ideological paradigms to be disrupted, and the forbidden and repressed to be explicated. Fantasy provides a space where the unspeakable can be spoken, and for some considerable historical time the feminine voice was largely unspoken.

One fundamental point of connection between feminism and contemporary Arthurian fantasy by women is the challenge to the terms of existence of magical women. Certainly magic, as a self-evident break in realism, has always been a part of fantasy, and the feminine has long been associated with the practice of that magic. Geraldine Heng argues that Arthurian literature used the concept of magic (as an indefinable external agency) to contain and dehumanize proscribed feminine agency (Heng 1991: 254). Contemporary responses by women writers to this process of othering include the legitimization of magic through religious ritual, or through naturalization by reworking magic as privileged knowledge and skill rather than sorcery. The adoption of pre-Christian religions (usually Celtic paganism) is noted by Charlotte Spivack as a "recurring feature" in fantasy writing by women (Spivack 1987: 9). It is certainly used to great effect in *The Mists of Avalon*. In Mary Stewart's *The Crystal Cave*, *The Hollow Hills*, and *The Last Enchantment*, magic is reworked as skilled engineering through the figure of Merlin and later Nimue. The break in realism that fantasy provides can be turned in upon itself to legitimize a different kind of agency.

Fantasy can also make space for the destabilization of ideological imperatives through structural disjunction. Undercutting the expectations of narrative logic is a way of upsetting the order of things. This draws attention to structural elements that generally go unscrutinized. Destabilizing structure is a way of indicating that the existing order is not "natural" and could be different. A range of structural elements have been noted as popular with women writers of fantasy. Spivack lists as the most commonly used devices the de-stereotyping of gendered characterizations, the shifting of focalization to a female point of view, and the breaking down of teleological expectations of plot. Spivack also offers as less common, but more subversive, the renunciation of power, the vindication of mortality and the depolarization of values (Spivack 1987: 8–15).

All of these strategies can be found throughout Arthurian fantasy written by women. For example, the good versus evil polarity is strategically foregrounded in both Gillian Bradshaw's series (*Hawk of May*, *Kingdom of Summer*, *In Winter's Shadow*) and Fay Sampson's *Daughter of Tintagel* series. In these texts the binary metaphors are so structurally overt (for example they both use Light versus Dark) that they are available for critique by characters within the text. Another example of destabilization is the use of shifting focalizations. Women writers often position female protagonists as narrator/focalizer, but at times a further shift takes place. Ann F. Howey explores focalization which moves between different female characters/narrators in Sampson's series, in which each book has a different narrator, and in *The Mists of Avalon*, where the narrative voice shifts from one character to another (Howey 2001: 91–8). This shift functions as a structural decentering strategy. In the later discussion I will return to examine facets of focalization in *The Mists of Avalon*. This structural element, I will argue, is a key construct in the development of the ideological position in a text. It is, therefore, a particularly useful tool for feminism.

Fantasy provides a rich space for the working through of cultural repressions. Traditionally, Arthurian literature foregrounds the masculine ideology of chivalry. Heng posits that the masculine thereby "inhabits" the textual consciousness. The feminine register, on the other hand, can be found in the repressions of the text; in the "alternative discourses" or "competing voices and claims" which, if not contained – papered over, smoothed out, filled in – would threaten the stability and unity of the text. The feminine register therefore traditionally inhabits the textual unconscious (Heng 1991: 253). In contemporary Arthurian fantasy by women, as the feminine moves from the textual unconscious to "inhabit" the textual consciousness, texts play out the cultural repression of feminine agency and autonomy. This can be done through the explicit delineation of repressions, or through the exploration of alternative socio-cultural possibilities. An example of the first can be found in Bradshaw's figure of Gwynhwyfar. She is educated and resourceful; she makes an excellent administrator and is honored as such by her court. This is, however, a highly singular and privileged position. When she finds herself out of context, in the court of another, she loses her privileged status and, like any other woman, is reduced to an object of exchange between men: "the trophy of war," a "stolen woman" (Bradshaw 1993: 195). A spirited breaking through of repressions is offered by Vera Chapman in her *Three*

Damosels trilogy. In *The King's Damosel* the female character of Lynette breaks the stereotype of the dependent and passive woman. She is outspoken, courageous, resourceful, and daring. She is finally rewarded as the chosen one who achieves the Grail (Spivack 1987: 127–37). However, women who work outside traditional feminine roles do so at their own risk and cost. While Lynette goes on various adventures she is, at various times, raped, tortured, and thrown into a dungeon. Thus the mechanisms of repression, while they are made explicit, nevertheless continue.

The broadest exploration of socio-cultural alternatives is offered in *The Mists of Avalon*. This text offers the construction of another social order, a feminine social order, an order of agency and autonomy outside masculine understanding and control. It provides women with a different way of knowing the world and operating within it, while also providing women with a refuge, a community constructed by women on their own terms, where women can live independently without the help, protection, or oppression of men.

Marion Zimmer Bradley: *The Mists of Avalon*

The Mists of Avalon tells the story of a struggle between oppression and freedom. It is a gendered struggle in which the Goddess religion is fighting for survival against the relentless march of a misogynist Christianity. The Goddess religion is a fantasy of feminine autonomy, and is aligned with mysticism and privileged knowledge. It is centered on the isle of Avalon, the magical other of Glastonbury. Christianity is located in the real world – the world of men and kings, where there is no magic, only horses, swords, and battles with the Saxons.

My reading of the text is as a fantasy that explicates repressed feminine desires, and explores alternative feminine knowledges and social formations. It elevates women to the status of independent agents and knowing subjects. A close reading of the Prologue is offered, which examines the focalization of Morgaine at both psychological and ideological levels. The ideological paradigm established here dominates the rest of the narrative. The character of Gwenhwyfar is considered, as a demonstration of the repressed feminine, and this is contrasted with the socio-cultural opportunities offered to women on Avalon. Ultimately, however, this ideological position – this fantasy – is shown to be unsustainable, and an extraordinary reversal takes place in the Epilogue. In the Epilogue the struggle ends. The ideological structure the text apparently sought to overcome is reinscribed. The desire for feminine autonomy is expelled from the text and from the world. It is contained in Avalon, already lost in the mists.

Focalization: Establishing alternative ideological paradigms

The term focalization, as used here, refers to point of view, or perspective, including not only the spatio-temporal perspective from which things are "seen," but also the viewpoint from which events are experienced psychologically (cognitively and emotionally), and how they are positioned ideologically (Toolan 2001: 60).[1] Of the three main facets of focalization – spatio-temporal, psychological, and ideological – the following argument focuses on the final two. A consideration of psychological focalization can allow the reader access into the machinations of characters, the wishes and desires of characters, and how they experience the world, which might not be evident through their actions alone. It is focalization through the psychological perspective of the character. An examination of ideological focalization reveals something quite different. Instead of considering what insights we might gain into the interior workings of a character, ideological perspective focuses on how the text encourages the reader to evaluate characters and events.

The Mists of Avalon is written mostly in the third person with the main focalizer as Morgaine, and also Gwenhwyfar as a significant contributor. Viviane, Igraine, and Morgause are occasional points of focus. Morgaine is established as the main focalizer of the text as a whole in the Prologue. She says, "This is my truth; I who am Morgaine tell you these things" (xi). The Prologue is one of a number of first-person narratives of Morgaine, signaled by the heading *Morgaine speaks*. These sections sometimes run for some pages, and italics are used as they are throughout the text to mark private thoughts. These sections of text often represent a compression of narrative time, a narrative summary of events between main episodes. They can also be interpretative comments from Morgaine, reaffirming her position as primary focalizer. Thus Morgaine's consciousness slips in and out of the foreground, allowing her figure to be sustained as primary focalizer, notably as ideological focalizer, but also allowing for other voices and points of view to be explored, particularly on a psychological level.

The Prologue establishes the primary ideological focalization of the text. Through the first-person voice of Morgaine it sets up a dichotomy between Christianity and the Goddess. Christianity is described as being of the "now" and its power extends over language, thought, and history. Morgaine predicts that the future, and thereby the past, will be in the hands of the priests, they will "tell the last tale." In the "now" of the Prologue – the world after the narrative has ended, the immediate future of the narrative itself – the priests have already disallowed historical difference; they have "created the world once and for all as unchanging" (ix). This is in direct contrast to the "great secret" of Avalon: "that by what men think, we create the world around us, daily new" (ix). In the past this "wisdom" was widely known, but the priests cleverly "safeguard" their new unchanging world with the sound of church bells, which have the effect of "driving away all thoughts of another world" (ix). Thus the text foregrounds the construction of history as retrospective, and of social reality itself as subjective and ideologically based. Morgaine claims that "the truth is like the old road to Avalon; it depends on your own will, and your own thoughts, whither the road will take you" (xi).

Morgaine describes the Goddess as having been linguistically contained as the dichotomous feminine: either evil, as "a demon" or "Satan," or conversely she is construed as the Virgin Mary. The reconfiguration of the Goddess as Mary is in the continual present: "they *clothe* her in the blue robe of the Lady of Nazareth," suggesting that the repression is endlessly re-enacted (ix, my italics). Christian transformation as a timelessly recurring external or superficial veiling is again evident in the description of Avalon, which the priests "came *to cover* . . . with their saints and legends" (ix, my italics). The final opposition set up in the Prologue is the "One God and One Truth" against religious pluralism and the "many faces" of a personal and subjective truth. This is the culmination of a passage that sets up Christianity as intolerant and controlling, and the Goddess religion as tolerant and accepting.

The closing lines of the Prologue claim it, and the tale that follows, as Morgaine's own truth, foregrounding it as Morgaine's psychological focalization. But the die has been cast. The Prologue gestures toward Alistair Minnis's sense of the intrinsic prologue of medieval scholarly texts, whose function is to provide an explication of the art or science of reading to be enacted upon a particular text (Minnis 1984: 30). In this logic the Prologue is ideologically privileged. Further, the temporal location of the Prologue, being later than that of the tale which follows, and its being spoken in the first person by Morgaine, the text's main character, lends first-person experiential authority to the events described in the later text. The Prologue also authorizes Morgaine as omniscient by noting her giftedness in the Sight. The text is thus positioned as an authoritative but subjective account, with objections to inaccuracy strategically discounted in the opening pages. Therefore, while the Prologue is unashamedly psychologically focalized through Morgaine, its privilege as a prologue is to cast an ideological veil over the reading of the rest of the text.

This ideological veil is reinforced by a consistent maintenance of ideological focalization for much of the text. Throughout the novel priests are portrayed as self-righteous, judgmental, and misogynist. Father Columba at Tintagel is small-minded, ignorant, and vicious. Igraine muses that he had become a priest because "no college of Druids would have had a man so stupid" (5), and she openly defies him when he threatens to beat Morgaine (90). Father Patricius is harsher still, and more accomplished, coming to Arthur's court after cleansing Ireland of "the evil magicians" and intending to do the same in Britain (300). As the Archbishop of Arthur's court he is Gwenhwyfar's personal priest and he assiduously cultivates in her that self-loathing which drives her to new heights of religious hysteria, finally causing Arthur to break his oath to Avalon. The nuns are carefully excluded from such censure, paving the way for the parallels drawn between the nuns of Inis Witrin and the priestesses of Avalon in the Epilogue. It should be noted, however, that Gwenhwyfar, repressed to the point of agoraphobia, a "canting fool" for Christianity, was raised by the nuns of that convent.

Desire: Repression and realization

As noted above, the text plays out the cultural repression of feminine agency and autonomy through the explication of those repressions and the exploration of alternative socio-cultural possibilities. In the character of Gwenhwyfar, patriarchal and religious oppressions are explicated, from their beginnings to a final release, which can only be achieved by divine grace. Alternative socio-cultural possibilities for women are explored through the character of Morgaine as priestess of Avalon.

Gwenhwyfar is at the extremity of Christian and patriarchal repression.[2] The operation of this repression is made clear from the second time she appears in the text. Gwenhwyfar's psychological focalization shows that her conscious efforts to please as a child resulted in her consciously repressing first her voice, then her will, and through great effort on her part as an adult she must continually repress her resentment. We are told that Gwenhwyfar was a delicate and sensitive child, raised by a series of stepmothers who did not understand her. She quickly learned that her "shouting" father did not approve of her speaking out, so she stifles her opinions and uses her "shyest little voice" whenever she speaks to him (293). This behavior has been reinforced by her convent learning: "she must obey her father's will as if it were the will of God" (309). Despite the appearance of reticence and timidity, the adult Gwenhwyfar is seething with anger and rebellion. She resents being treated like a fool at home, where her father calls her "My pretty little featherhead" (293, 295). And when she is lying in the litter being carried off to her wedding with Arthur she resents being married off without her consent:

> She was merely part of the furniture . . . She was only a bride . . . She was not herself, there was nothing for herself, she was only some property of a High King . . . She was another mare, a brood mare . . . Gwenhwyfar thought she would smother with the rage that was choking her. (309)

Unfortunately, however, Gwenhwyfar cannot escape the overwhelming and impeccable logic of the ideology which oppresses her.

> But no, she must not be angry . . . Women had to be especially careful to do the will of God because it was through a woman that mankind had fallen into Original Sin, and every woman must be aware that it was her work to atone for that Original Sin in Eden. No woman could ever be really good except for Mary the Mother of Christ; all other women were evil, they had never had any chance to be anything but evil. This was her punishment for being like Eve, sinful, filled with rage and rebellion against the will of God. (309)

Through this psychological focalization we can see that Gwenhwyfar measures herself as a failure by the standards of her religion. However, the ideological focalization positions this standard as misogynist. The extreme language, the sweeping generalizations, the impossible standard of goodness, and the perfect logic in which even Gwenhwyfar's resistance is anticipated and countered, are overtly contrived to oppress, and they oppress Gwenhwyfar on every level. Throughout the text repeated psychological focalizations reveal that Gwenhwyfar suffers the same inner conflict, which she cannot resolve within such a religious framework.

The force of will Gwenhwyfar must enact upon herself to repress her mixed emotions plays itself out in the physical symptoms of agoraphobia. The "panic" rising in her as she lies in the litter is rage. Later, when Arthur effectively gives her permission to take Lancelet as a secret lover she is at first appalled. Then she is overwhelmed with anger and fear at the choice before her: "she would never dare to go out of doors again for fear of what she might choose to do" (387). The open air represents a freedom which is wildly tempting but which is forbidden to her, and her desire for it fills her with shame and fear: "How could she ever bear to go out of doors again, or to leave the safe, protected space of this very room and this very bed?" (388). It is this psychological focalization which gives the reader an insight into Gwenhwyfar's character which is lost from almost every other character in the text. What she is afraid of is not "out there" at all; what she is afraid of is herself.

In contrast to Gwenhwyfar and the repressions of a patriarchal Christianity, the socio-cultural possibilities of a matriarchy, including the independent woman, are explored through the character of Morgaine and the society of Avalon. Avalon presents an exploration of possibilities that are forbidden to women within the strict Christian framework played out in the character of Gwenhwyfar. Avalon represents access to an extensive education, most particularly to privileged knowledges, and it inculcates independence of mind and body and encourages informed choice. Gwenhwyfar's upbringing denies her all of these, and even denies her the wish for them.

Avalon is portrayed as a community of women independent of men. It was built and is sustained by women. The priestesses of Avalon can fend for themselves – their initiation rite casts them out of Avalon, and they must find their own way back alone (158). Throughout the text, Viviane and Morgaine travel widely across Britain. Morgaine often travels unaccompanied. Alone and pregnant, she finds her way even to northern Orkney. Later, she travels to and from north Wales, Avalon, Tintagel, and Camelot, sometimes escorted and sometimes not. It seems that priestesses from Avalon are quietly present everywhere, as Gwenhwyfar notes with some annoyance: "Why is it that we, a Christian court, must always have here one of those damsels of the Lady of the Lake?" (958).

Avalon is also a school. It provides a high level of formal education for girls. Throughout the text psychological focalizations of women trained in Avalon reveal a deep awareness of their learning as far superior not only to that of women in general, but also to that of the most educated of men, the Christian priests. In the opening pages of the text Igraine muses on her superior learning, which enables her to read, write, and speak Latin better than her husband's priest: "Igraine did not think of herself as well educated . . . nevertheless . . . she could pass among the Romanized barbarians as a well-educated lady" (5). The training of a priestess is described by Morgaine in a first-person, italicized, *Morgaine speaks* section. While this marks the description as a highly subjective psychological focalization, Morgaine has already been established in the text as an intelligent, determined, and unusually wise and gifted child, who is reflective and measured in her judgments. Her description of the training includes the development of practical skills and higher learning. Experience in woodwork, food preparation, herb lore, and healing are coupled with knowledge of oral literatures and histories, music, and reading and writing. The two most highly valued attributes are the Sight (the gift of access to privileged knowledge of other times and places) and wisdom. Disciplining the mind is a key part of the training of a priestess: "forcing the mind first to walk in unaccustomed paths" (158).

This juxtaposition between a knowledgeable Avalonian tradition and a Christianity that requires passivity in women, with guilt as the price for any independent thought or action, continues for most of the text. Gwenhwyfar's childlessness feeds her guilt, but also promotes her religious doubt, and the increasing inner conflict manifests itself externally as an escalation in piety. The pressure Gwenhwyfar inflicts on Arthur directly leads to his betrayal of Avalon and the wholesale Christianization of Camelot. Consequently Avalon finds itself drifting further into the mists. The fantasy of feminine independence and autonomy is fading, and the growing desperation of this privileged community fuels the narrative imperative for the second half of the text.

Reading the text from the perspective of the repression and realization of feminine desire brings us to a disturbing conclusion. Repression is more effective than realization. Gwenhwyfar, as the agent of her own repression, has an ever-expanding range of influence. Morgaine, as the exemplar of the independent woman, despite living for years in Camelot, has no instructive effect on any character in the text. Rather than realization being an irreversible breaking-through of repression, realization is only a moment that is vulnerable to the powerful self-corrective effects of repression.

Fantasy: Resolution and normalization

Fantasy can provide a space for the vicarious fulfillment of forbidden desires. It is, however, also a space of containment. The fulfillment it offers, as vicarious, is outside of the "real" world, located in some other place, safely containing the urge to transgress within that other place (Jackson 1981: 72). In *The Mists of Avalon*, Avalon provides such a place, and part of the fantasy of the text is the exploration of the extension of those possibilities out into the "real" world; the extension of feminine autonomy and agency into the outside world. In the end, the real world cannot sustain this fantasy, "reality" is reasserted, and the fantasy of feminine autonomy is nicely contained in an ever-fading Avalon. By the end of the main text all hope of a reconciliation between Avalon and Camelot have ended. Avalon has moved so far into the mists that only Morgaine can move between the worlds. The House of Maidens is almost empty; young women no longer come to Avalon to be educated into independent and productive lives. Camelot is thoroughly Christian, to such a degree that Mordred can use it even against Arthur. By the end of the narrative the shrine to the Goddess on Dragon Island has been cast down, the land is at war, and Mordred, Avalon's last hope gone wrong, lies dead. Arthur, wounded by Mordred, dies in Morgaine's arms as they approach the shores of Avalon.

Such a gloomy end, however, is not sustained, and the Epilogue introduces new hope at the close of the text. Morgaine and Christianity are reconciled, and while Avalon fades into the mists, Glastonbury becomes the place of the future. The Epilogue is focalized through Morgaine, but the third-person narrative presentation contributes to a constructed objectivity. This combination draws the reader to identify with Morgaine's positive reading of Glastonbury and the Christianity she finds there.

Glastonbury is in a state of change. It is alive with growth, people, and light. From the moment Morgaine steps ashore she is surprised: "the trees were different, and the paths, and she stopped, bewildered, at the foot of a little hill – surely there was nothing like this on Avalon?" (1003). Unlike the declining Avalon, where Morgaine is accompanied by the shadows of the faery people, Glastonbury seems filled with people. Morgaine meets a "procession of robed monks" (1003), nuns, a gardener, the mother abbess, and a number of novices. The "veil" which separates Avalon from Glastonbury is like a shroud on Avalon: "mist lay thick on Avalon" (1001). Glastonbury, on the other hand, is in the "sunlight" (1002) and the "daylight" (1008). It is more real than Avalon, it is "in the world" (1009). The Epilogue describes Glastonbury as a bright, new version of what Avalon once was.

The reflections of Avalonian practices and values in the Glastonbury community position this community as a legitimate custodian of universal religious beliefs. The nuns on Glastonbury are surprisingly like the priestesses of Avalon. They are visually indistinguishable. Morgaine describes "a woman in a dark robe not unlike her own" (1004), the nun becomes "[t]he woman in black" just like a priestess (1005), and the novice becomes "the young girl, robed in black" (1005). The novices mistake Morgaine for a visiting nun. They all call her "sister" (1004) and "mother" (1006, 1007), and she calls the novice "daughter" (1006, 1007). Like the priestesses of Avalon, the nuns of Glastonbury drink water only from the Sacred Well: "We drink only the water of the chalice well – it is a holy place, you know," and Morgaine remembers Viviane telling her that "*{t}he priestesses drink only the water of the Sacred Well*" (1005). Morgaine muses: "Never did I think I would stand side by side with one of these Christian nuns, joining her in prayer" (1004).

Indeed, the rehabilitation of Christianity in the Epilogue is quite extraordinary when considered in the context of the text at large. Morgaine had expected the nuns to be "sad and doleful, ever conscious of what the priests said about the sinfulness of being born women" (1006). Instead the young novices are "innocent and merry as robins." It is not mentioned in the Epilogue, but it was here, at the convent of Inis Witrin, where Gwenhwyfar was educated. Gwenhwyfar *was* ever conscious of the sinfulness of being born a woman: all women other than Mary "were evil, they had never had any chance to be anything but evil" (309). What was cast as a grave injustice earlier in the text is reduced here to a "thought," a memory, or perhaps a mistake or misinterpretation which is now shown to be incorrect. Another surprising discovery is that the novices here are well educated, having been taught Latin in the convent. Again the stark contrast to Gwenhwyfar, who could barely write her own name, goes unnoted. Morgaine finds the young novices irresistible: "the girl was so much like one of her own young priestesses" (1007). And they are surprisingly confident and assertive, claiming that "there are ignorant priests and ignorant people, who are all too ready to cry sorcery if a woman is only a little wiser than *they* are!" (1006). Despite this bold claim, the priests still control the production of knowledge. When Lionors calls Avalon "unholy," Morgaine attacks the source of knowledge, retorting that, "unholy it is not, whatever the priests say" (1005).

The most significant mirroring of Avalon on Glastonbury is in the location of the churches. As the differences between the two places become blurred so does the difference between the Goddess religion and Christianity. In the Lady's chapel of the church on Glastonbury, Morgaine experiences an epiphany. Morgaine recognizes the small statue of St Brigid as "the Goddess as she is worshipped in Ireland" (1008). Morgaine sees here the survival of Goddess worship in the world outside Avalon: "Exile her as they may, she will prevail. The Goddess will never withdraw herself from mankind" (1008). Morgaine's revelation is complete when she sees the Holy Thorn outside the church door. The Holy Thorn of Avalon is the bush that sprouted when Joseph of Arimathea struck his staff into the ground just outside the chapel. Despite its status as a Christian icon, every time a traveler comes to the chapel at Avalon Morgaine gives them a cutting of this plant to take into the world. Morgaine makes this special trip to Glastonbury to bring a cutting of the Holy Thorn to plant at Viviane's grave. When Morgaine finds that the Holy Thorn is already in Glastonbury, in the same location as it is in Avalon, she concludes: "The holy thing had brought itself from Avalon, moving, as the hallows were withdrawn from Avalon, into the world of men where it was most needed" (1008). Morgaine is satisfied: "No, we did not fail . . . I did the Mother's work in Avalon until at last those who came after us might bring her into this world" (1009). Glastonbury and its Christian community have overtaken Avalon as the religious center of the text.

Throughout the text Morgaine is a powerful and knowing priestess of the Goddess. For 1,000 pages the text has sustained a dichotomous split between a harsh and narrow Christianity and a tolerant and forgiving Goddess. And yet, in the Epilogue, Morgaine's "knowledge" of Glastonbury, of its religious community, is revealed to be imperfect. Morgaine has been to Glastonbury only twice in her long life – once when the child Gwenhwyfar was lost and again for Arthur's crowning (1002) – but still she thinks she knows this place. What Morgaine finds is difference where she expects sameness, and sameness where she expects difference. Morgaine's certainty thus undercut, her life-long campaign for the Goddess is put into question. Despite these textual preparations for a revelation, however, the most problematic shift in ideological focalization is when Morgaine is satisfied by the statue of St Brigid. Morgaine is completely satisfied by a representation of the Goddess in the "real world," but it is a representation that casts the Goddess out of the divine. Moreover, it is a representation that strips her of agency, allowing only the power of intercession. Thus the text comes to normalize the position of women as being satisfied: they should remain happy but retiring, and not meddling with the ways of the world. Avalon, which championed women's education and knowledge, capability, and independence, which sought to defend its people by influencing state politics and deposing a king, is safely contained in the mists. The fantasy of women's agency and independence has been worked through and the status quo is resumed.

Conclusion

In *The Mists of Avalon* fantasy operates as a way of ultimately re-establishing the dominant order. The text argues that the fantasy of feminine autonomy can function, but in another time and place. It is not workable in the "real" world of the text, nor, by extension, in the world of common reality. The text, allowing imaginary satisfaction, provides a compensation for this social lack. As Jackson argues, fantasy is not necessarily subversive. It can work just as well to rework, rewrite, and recover subversive elements to serve the dominant ideology (Jackson 1981: 175). The Epilogue serves to rewrite Morgaine's life-long project.

That being said, there is one final point to consider. If the Prologue is recalled at this point, a striking contrast is apparent. I have argued above that in the Prologue there is no ambiguity about the polarity between Christianity and the Goddess religion. In the Prologue Christianity contains the feminine, covers the land, and rewrites history in its own terms. The Prologue sets up a tension, a dichotomy between the feminine and the masculine, in which no quarter is given, even to the "slave nuns" of Christianity. In the Epilogue it is these nuns who hold the future of the Goddess in their unknowing hands. Further, while the Epilogue appears at the end of the text, and the Prologue at the beginning, this does not reflect the temporal relationship between the two. The Epilogue takes place one year after the death of Arthur, but the Prologue, while spoken in the voice of Morgaine, is external to the narrative events of the text. The Prologue is, therefore, implicitly located after the Epilogue. Therefore, while the fantasy of the text finally works to contain the subversion of feminine autonomy, even to the point of Morgaine's apparent acceptance and satisfaction, the structural frame of the text – the Prologue and the Epilogue – work together to usurp narrative certainty. Which is the final word, after all? The Prologue itself provides for different truths: "there is no such thing as a true tale. Truth has many faces" (x–xi). Of course the location of the Epilogue at the end lends it interpretive privilege, and most readers would not remember or revisit the Prologue, but the ambiguity nevertheless remains. After a complete reading we are left with this moment of hesitation, this structural break, which leaves hanging the question: if closure is forestalled before it begins, can the fantasy of the text ever finally be contained? Such a textual and temporal inconsistency should not be papered over, but allowed to stand as the rupture that it is. It is in these places, where the seamlessness of the text is broken, where the fantasy refuses containment, that the real potential lies.

NOTES

1 My usage of the term focalization, following Toolan, varies from that of Hildebrand and Howey. While both make insightful and useful contributions, they do not consider the various facets of focalization delineated here.

2   The reception of Gwenhwyfar has been generally sympathetic, but this is tempered with
critiques of weakness. She is "blamed" for the
Christianization of Camelot (Noble 1997:
148), Howey finds her momentarily proud and
willful (Howey 2001: 38), and Hildebrand critiques her as narrow-minded (Hildebrand
2001: 100). The reading closest to my own is
perhaps that of Gordon-Wise (1991).

Primary Sources

Bradley, M. Z.. (1993). *The mists of Avalon*. Harmondsworth: Penguin. (Originally published
by Michael Joseph, London, 1983.)

Bradshaw, G. (1992a). *Hawk of May*. New York:
Bantam. (Originally published by Simon &
Schuster, New York, 1980.)

Bradshaw, G. (1992b). *Kingdom of summer*. New
York: Bantam. (Originally published by Eyre
Methuen, London, 1981.)

Bradshaw, G. (1993). *In winter's shadow*. New York:
Bantam. (Originally published by Methuen,
London, 1982.)

Chapman, V. (1975). *The green knight*. London:
Collings.

Chapman, V. (1976a). *The king's damosel*. London:
Collings.

Chapman, V. (1976b). *King Arthur's daughter*.
London: Collings.

Sampson, F. (1989a). *White nun's telling*. London:
Headline.

Sampson, F. (1989b). *Wise woman's telling*. London:
Headline.

Sampson, F. (1990). *Black smith's telling*. London:
Headline.

Sampson, F. (1991). *Taliesin's telling*. London:
Headline.

Sampson, F. (1992a). *Daughter of Tintagel*. London:
Headline.

Sampson, F. (1992b). *Herself*. London: Headline.

Stewart, M. (1970). *The crystal cave*. London:
Hodder & Stoughton.

Stewart, M. (1973). *The hollow hills*. London:
Hodder & Stoughton.

Stewart, M. (1979). *The last enchantment*. London:
Hodder & Stoughton.

References and Further Reading

Aichele, G. (1997). Postmodern fantasy, ideology,
and the uncanny. *Paradoxa*, 3(3/4), 498–514.

Clute, J. (1977). Fantasy. In J. Clute & J. Grant
(eds), *The encyclopedia of fantasy*. New York: St
Martin's Press.

Fuog, K. E. C. (1991). Imprisoned in the phallic
oak: Marion Zimmer Bradley and Merlin's
seductress. *Quondam et Futurus: A Journal of
Arthurian Interpretations*, 1(1), 73–88.

Gordon-Wise, B. A. (1991). *The reclamation of a
queen: Guinevere in modern fantasy*. New York:
Greenwood Press.

Heng, G. (1991). A map of her desire: Reading the
feminism in Arthurian romance. In E. Thumboo
(ed.), *Perceiving other worlds*. Singapore: Times
Academic Press, pp. 250–60.

Hildebrand, K. (2001). *The female reader at the
Round Table: Religion and women in three
contemporary Arthurian texts*. Uppsala: Uppsala
University.

Howey, A. F. (2001). *Rewriting the women of Camelot*.
Westport, CT: Greenwood Press.

Jackson, R. (1981). *Fantasy: The literature of subversion*. London: Methuen.

Minnis, A. (1984). *Medieval theory of authorship:
Scholastic literary attitudes in the later Middle Ages*.
London: Scolar.

Noble, J. (1997). *The mists of Avalon*: A confused
assault on patriarchy. In M. Alamichel & D.
Brewer (eds), *The Middle Ages after the Middle
Ages in the English speaking world*. Rochester, NY:
Brewer, pp. 145–52.

Sandner, D. (2004). *Fantastic literature: A critical reader*. Westport, CT: Praeger.

Spivack, C. (1987). *Merlin's daughters: Contemporary women writers of fantasy*. New York: Greenwood Press.

Tobin, L. A. (1993). Why change the Arthur story? Marion Zimmer Bradley's *The mists of Avalon. Extrapolation*, 24(2), 147–57.

Todorov, T. (1973). *The fantastic: A structural approach to a literary genre* (trans. R. Howard). Cleveland, OH: Case Western Reserve University Press. (Original work published 1970.)

Toolan, M. (2001). *Narrative: A critical linguistic introduction*, 2nd edn. Routledge: London.

Wolfe, G. (1986). *Critical terms for science fiction and fantasy*. New York: Greenwood Press.

Part VII
Arthur on Film

32
Remediating Arthur

Laurie A. Finke and Martin B. Shichtman

One of the most memorable set pieces in *Monty Python and the Holy Grail* (1975) is the Black Knight sequence. Its hilarious parody of cinematic violence signals simultaneously Arthur's comic failure as a political leader and the persistence of his reputation for orchestrating lavish spectacles of violence. As the Python troupe recognized, Arthur's legendary status as "King of the Britons" has always depended upon his ability to harness violence as a mechanism for achieving political legitimacy. The exaggerated comic violence of the sequence, with Arthur hacking away at the defiant Black Knight's limbs until he is reduced to a sputtering torso, depends upon the medium's ability to represent spurting blood and gore as simultaneously realistic and stylized.

At the end of a decade when directors were breaking away from the constraints against violence imposed by censorship, the Python parody exposed the extent to which audiences' viewing of "realistic" cinematic violence depended less upon their own experience of blood and gore than upon their prior viewing habits (Sam Peckinpah's [1971] *Straw Dogs* provides the relevant intertext, already parodied in the Monty Python television series season three "Salad Days" skit). The Black Knight gag, however, transported word for word to the stage thirty years later in *Spamalot*, Eric Idle's 2005 Broadway musical adaptation of *Holy Grail*, falls flat on its face. Reduced to a Penn and Teller magic trick, complete with red streamers pouring out of hacked off limbs, the sequence has been silently buried in the second act. It makes at best a perfunctory and unmemorable appearance most likely to appease the film's fans, who can probably recite the lines from memory. One YouTube reviewer, ZackyV68, describes the Vegas version of the scene:

> it's really funny in the play version I saw at Wynn, here at Las Vegas. The Black Knight gets pegged on the wall and Arthur uses the swords to slash his legs off (looking like nothing was hit) and the Black Knight was like "haha you missed!!" then the Knight's legs fell off lol [laugh out loud].

Why, we might well ask, does a sequence that has become a classic comedy routine fail so miserably (YouTube reviewers notwithstanding) when transported to a new medium? This, in essence, is the question we pose in this essay. What role do the media that transmit the legend have in shaping it?

That the Arthurian legend has been retold innumerable times since the twelfth century, when Geoffrey of Monmouth's *Historia Regum Britanniae* created a stir among the Norman aristocracy, has become a commonplace ritualistically rehearsed in scholarly works on the subject. That these legends have taken shape in a variety of different media is perhaps as frequently remarked. Arthurian legends have been the subject of countless written texts (poems, romances, histories, novels), but they have also appeared in other media, in paintings, operas, musicals, films, and more recently rock songs, comic books, and video games. While previous studies have explored adaptations of Arthurian stories in particular media – for example, Richard Barber's collection on Arthurian music (2002), a whole spate of recent books on Arthurian film, or Elizabeth Sklar and Donald Hoffman's collection on King Arthur in popular culture (2002) – there is little scholarship that examines the effects that media themselves have on adaptations of the material.

This chapter, rather than offering a synoptic survey of Arthurian legends in different media, articulates a theory and method for investigating the mediating role of media in perpetuating and adapting Arthurian narrative. We explore the relevance for the Arthurian legend of recent work in media studies, particularly Jay Bolter's and Richard Grusin's concept of "remediation," paying attention not only to the "formal logic by which new media refashion prior media" and their contents (1999: 273), but also the ways in which that refashioning causes us to revisit older media, asking of them new kinds of questions. We investigate the mechanisms through which the cinematic apparatus mediates (and indeed remediates) our experience of medievalism, complicating the reception of the original medieval text, the intermedial intertexts, and the films themselves. Drawing upon Joshua Logan's *Camelot* (1967) and Hans-Jürgen Syberberg's *Parsifal* (1982), we explicate the work of adaptation that makes film a unique site for the synthesis of multiple media – literary, theatrical, musical, cinematic, political. We end by demonstrating the ongoing nature of this remediation by considering how our reception of films (like John Boorman's [1981] *Excalibur* or *Monty Python and the Holy Grail*) may be further shaped by emerging media – DVD formatting and internet sites like YouTube – into which they have recently been adapted.

What is a medium? We might be tempted to think of media, as *The Oxford English Dictionary* does, simply as the material or technological apparatuses – film, television, radio, newspapers, and more recently, the internet – through which we view (and note the metaphor of transparency) our world, focusing only on the channel of communication. Bolter and Grusin, however, argue that our ability to recognize these technologies as media "comes not only from the way in which each of the technologies functions in itself, but also from the way in which each relates to other media. Each participates in a network of technical, social, and economic contexts; this network constitutes the medium as a technology" (1999: 65). We must understand all media not simply as neutral carriers of content, but as a complex hybrid network of material, technological, social, political, cultural, economic, and signifying practices. Bolter and Grusin define media as "the formal, social and material network of practices that generate a logic by which additional instances are repeated or remediated, such as photography, film, or television" (1999: 273). This definition makes a good starting point for a consideration of film as a medium; it has the advantage of pointing out the ways in which media bring together material and technological and semiotic practices. For our purposes, then, film must be understood as a form of contemporary mass media, not distinct from all the others but thoroughly integrated into a network of visual and aural communication that makes claims both to immediacy and hyper-mediacy, transparency and opacity.

Bolter and Grusin use the term "remediation" to describe "the process by which new media technologies improve upon or remedy prior media forms" (1999: 273). Newer media, they argue, "refashion prior media" through a doubled logic that mul-tiplies media at the same time it tries to erase all traces of mediation (1999: 5). A new medium oscillates between claims to "immediacy" and what they call "hyperme-diacy," which they define as the tendency of media to call attention to their status as media: "Although each medium promises to reform its predecessors by offering a more immediate or more authentic experience, this promise of reform inevitably leads us to become aware of the new medium as a medium" (1999: 19). This process, they argue, has "expressed itself repeatedly in the genealogy of Western representation" (1999: 56).

Although film, which has been around for more than a century, does not offer the same kind of novelty as the so-called "new media" (to which we will return at the end of this chapter), it does illustrate quite handily this double logic of remediation. Let us consider figure 32.1, a single shot from Joshua Logan's (1967) film *Camelot*, itself a remediation of the Lerner and Loewe musical, which remediated T. H. White's novel, *The Once and Future King*. This is the final shot of Act I; as the music swells, the knights begin to assemble around the Round Table Arthur has just invented. The shot is meant to thrill the viewer with its monumental scope. By way of contrast, in book two of *The Once and Future King*, *The Queen of Air and Darkness*, as Arthur is supposed to be preparing to go to war to establish his legitimacy as ruler through violence, he, Sir Ector, and Kay sit in his pavilion debating the details of Arthur's dream of democracy, of a Round Table "with no top," capable of seating a hundred and fifty knights. Kay, with a plodding pragmatism, insists that this is mathemati-cally impossible.

"Say it was fifty yards across. . . . Think of all the space in the middle. It would be an ocean of wood with a thin rim of humanity. You couldn't keep the food in the middle even, because nobody would be able to reach it."

Figure 32.1 Camelot (1967), directed by Joshua Logan.

"Then we can have a circular table, not a round one. I don't know what the proper word is. I mean we could have a table shaped like the rim of a cart-wheel, and the servants could walk about in the empty space, where the spokes would be. We could call them Knights of the Round Table." (White 1987: 265)

What White considers a subject of amusement, the physical impossibility of a round table that would hold – as Sir Thomas Malory had it – one hundred and fifty knights, Logan embraces as an opportunity to imagine the grandeur of the Arthurian court. But even as he endeavors to reproduce a moment that never happened, the gathering of Arthur's knights around a colossal table – one considerably larger than the supposedly "real" Round Table on display in Winchester's Great Hall – Logan primarily succeeds in calling attention to the medium in which he is working. Logan's Round Table is, perhaps, more than anything else a product of the economics of the Hollywood blockbuster. As lavish as the Broadway production of *Camelot* might have been – written by Lerner and Loewe, the team behind *My Fair Lady*, and starring Richard Burton and Julie Andrews, *Camelot* was, by any standard, a major Broadway musical – it was nevertheless limited in scale by the size of the theatre, the size and shape of the stage, and the difficulty a crew would encounter in having to move an enormous prop on and off stage, night after night. Logan, on the other hand, could construct his Round Table in a massive Hollywood soundstage where it could serve to create one breathtaking shot and then be disassembled, never to be used again.

For Logan, size matters. His Round Table fills the cinemascope screen. Cinemascope, with its flattened horizontal space, provides the perfect medium for recreating the inflated romantic aspirations of the Arthurian legend, which fantasizes a king so open, so noble, so popular that nobles would flock from throughout Christendom to serve him, a king so wealthy and powerful that he could provide appropriate accommodation for this onslaught of aristocrats and control their violent tendencies. Logan's Round Table repudiates and remediates White's bemused mockery of the overblown ambitions of medieval romance, constructing the spectacle that Malory could only have imagined. This single shot of Arthur assembling his knights around his newly installed Round Table, filmed from above as a crane shot, offers its viewers a sense of immediacy that neither book nor stage could achieve. In its epic scope the shot is an example of what Tom Gunning has described as the "cinema of attractions." It is pure visual spectacle, demonstrating the way in which the logic of hypermediacy can insinuate itself even into the logic of immediacy (Bolter & Grusin 1999: 155). Audiences are invited to marvel at the ability of film to create authentic illusions, to make fantasies seem *almost* real, even when we know them to be fictions. In Logan's hands, the cinema of attraction becomes a mechanism for connecting the fantasies of medieval romance to the romantic self-fashionings of America in the late 1960s, where middle-class suburbanites continued to believe in the efficacy of might for right, the expansion of the American imperium – even to the moon – and the need for larger movie theatres with even larger, more spectacular screens to display the limitlessness of their own potential.

Hans-Jürgen Syberberg's Arthurian vision may even be more expansive than Logan's. It is certainly more overtly hypermediated. Unlike Logan, Syberberg is completely uninterested in creating illusions of reality; for him, cinema is quintessentially hypermedia; it should call attention to its own artifice. His 1982 version of Wagner's *Parsifal* posits film-making itself as the Holy Grail – a blender through which all media are remediated. The film provides a space in which high art – the music dramas of Richard Wagner, for instance – can co-habit with the detritus of western civilization, where hundreds of years of genius and junk can be brought together in the service of a fantasy that is simultaneously bound by the past that has produced it and also capable of resisting the limitations of history. Let us look at one simple shot from the extraordinarily complex opening sequence of the film (figure 32.2).

Filmed in front of an enormous death mask of Richard Wagner that serves as a set for the film, this shot depicts a woman, a queen as indicated by the crown on her lap. She is reclining on a couch, holding a book – an illuminated manuscript – in which we can just make out a picture of King Arthur and his Round Table, one of the few references to the matter of Britain in the film. The presence of the book in the shot indicates the extent to which Syberberg's remediation of Wagner's opera is also a remediation of earlier German texts such as Wolfram von Eschenbach's *Parzival*. As such, it both embraces and rejects the discourses of Germany's many pasts; it both accepts the narratives offered by medieval poetry and nineteenth-century musical drama and seeks to transcend them. The medium of the book, however, denies the

Figure 32.2 Parsifal (1982), directed by Hans-Jürgen Syberberg.

image both the immediacy and the grandeur Logan's shot gives to the Round Table. It reduces the Round Table to a story, a fairy tale. Syberberg takes all the pomp and ceremony of the matter of Britain suggested by Logan's Round Table and reduces it to a tiny picture in a book, which can then be closed and put away, freeing both Wagner and Syberberg to create their own remediations of the legend.

Syberberg's struggles with the many media that gave form to the German version of the Grail story are evident in the opening sequence, which remediates Wagner's overture. In an opera or musical drama, the overture is instrumental music designed to signal the audience to take their seats, that it is time for the show to begin. As such it marks an artificial transition in the physical space of the theatre, equivalent to dimming the house lights. The overture is conventionally performed with the theatre curtain down so there is nothing for the audience to look at while they listen to the music. In remediating this theatrical experience, a film must provide some visual entertainment to accompany the music, ensuring its immediacy – the immediacy promised by the medium of film. Syberberg's complex overture sequence, however, creates a hypermediated experience that does not just occupy viewers as they listen to the overture; it overwhelms them. Syberberg multiplies media, filling the screen and bombarding the audience with the visual detritus of Western media culture, not only with music, but with photographs, stages, models of stages, puppet shows, books, and props for the opera. Syberberg's remediation of Wagner's opera will be a history of the media that have served to transmit the legend of Parsifal. Before beginning the opera's narrative – which will play out in his 4-hour 25-minute film – Syberberg, with astonishing brevity, at least to anyone familiar with either Wolfram von Eschenbach's thirteenth-century medieval poem or with Wagner's nineteenth-century music drama, prefigures the Grail catastrophes – the onset of the waste land and the initial failures to locate redemption – through the medium of photography. The film opens as the camera pans across a series of pictures of ruins as the overture to *Parsifal* plays. These photographs are scattered like so much rubbish on a table, along with a dead swan, its bloody body pierced by an arrow.

As if this initial representation of the Grail waste land as the detritus of media events was insufficient to remind viewers of the opera's plot, however, or simply not long enough to cover the overture, Syberberg proceeds to remediate the story yet again, this time miming all of the events of the story that lead up to the opening of Act I through the medium of the puppet show, an art form popular in the middle ages, the nineteenth century, and among the twentieth-century German avant-garde. The puppet show is watched simultaneously by the film's audience and by child actor David Luther – soon to be identified as the movie's eponymous hero, and, perhaps, as he is dressed in pseudo-medieval garb, already filling that role. This telescoping of time, along with its compression of audiences, past and present, suggests Syberberg's consciousness of his role in the remediation process, his understanding that this film is but one instance of the media procession hypermediating the Grail text, but by encompassing all media, it can perhaps be the last.

As the puppet show and Wagner's overture approach their conclusion, Syberberg leaves his audience one final image, the shot reproduced in figure 32.2 – the fulfillment of the overture montage. Just before the film segues into the first act of Wagner's music drama, Syberberg's camera locates the actress Edith Clever, who plays both Parsifal's mother – she has already had a brief, maternal scene with David Luther, during which she presents him with a bow and arrow and attempts to kiss him – and Kundry, the wandering, disturbing, tragic, erotic presence that haunts Wagner's Grail community. Here she seems to be miming her role as Parsifal's dead, or soon-to-be dead, mother who has lost her son to the chivalric order represented by the Round Table pictured in the manuscript illumination on her lap. Here, the marginalized other, the woman through whose abject difference the Grail community constructs its chivalric identity, seems in the final moments of her life to cast an omniscient glance at the medium through which that chivalry is transmitted – the book – just as, at the film's end, Clever, as Kundry, the exotic Semitic outsider, will cast an omniscient glance over the entirety of the Wagnerian opus, when she is pictured staring down on a snow globe that contains a model of Wagner's Bayreuth opera house.

Figure 32.3 Parsifal (1982), detail.

As the camera zooms in to focus on the manuscript page with its picture of the Round Table, Syberberg leaves his viewer perplexed and, perhaps, perturbed with this self-conscious remediation of the written word (figure 32.3). We stare over the director's shoulder as he stares over the shoulder of his actress/character(s) reading, or perhaps just holding, a book that is barely identifiable; is it a manuscript, some remnant of the "real" Middle Ages? The shot calls attention to the medium of cinema as it embraces all of these possibilities, reimagines, and supersedes both the medieval text and Wagner's musical reimagining of it. But even more striking is the probability that Syberberg believes that once his film has been viewed through the many intermediary spaces he has created, all imaginings of both the Middle Ages and Wagner will be shifted, the past will be transcended. Arriving last in a long line of remediations, he seems to argue that his film will stand, at least for a while, as the apotheosis of Wagnerian drama, appropriating all previous media forms to itself and initiating a reassessment of everything that has preceded it.

But even as it argues for cinema's primacy among all other media, Syberberg's film reaches something of a dead end, a suffocating space of incessant self-referentiality. If

Logan's shot of the Round Table strives for immediacy and Syberberg's for hypermediacy, we must remember that remediation works through a logic that involves both. To illustrate this, we must turn our attention to newer forms of "hypermedia," recent applications "that present multiple media (text, graphics, animation, video) using a hypertextual organization" (Bolter & Grusin 1999: 272). DVDs are a good example of this newer digital hypermedia. As larger television screens and high-definition formatting make watching a DVD feel increasingly like a movie theatre experience, cineastes, once disdainful of any form of home viewing, have been drawn to this technology. But DVDs offer more than just an opportunity to watch a film in the comfort of one's home. They remediate the process of film viewing, providing viewers with "extras" that frequently vie with the main feature for our attention: trailers, missing scenes, alternative endings, documentaries, video games, cast biographies, historical "footnotes," and audio commentary.

While *Camelot* and *Parsifal* are both available on DVD, neither of these films takes full advantage of the technology's promise. The audio commentary that accompanies John Boorman's (1981) film *Excalibur*, however, offers a starting point for an analysis of the medium's potential for remediating Arthurian narrative. Elvis Mitchell (2003) considers how the process of adding commentary to DVDs "was perfected by Criterion, a company that took as its mission eliciting lengthy interviews with directors and boiling them down into thoughtful, and often staggeringly intense, conversations about filmmaking." Mitchell suggests that DVD audio commentary tantalizes with the potentiality of access to origin. It offers the prospect that analysis by screenwriters, directors, and actors could render all further interpretation superfluous, granting viewers immediacy through access to the film-makers themselves, who seem to be sitting with us in our living rooms discussing their work. "For a time," he argues, "it seemed that Criterion's output might eliminate the need for film schools altogether, since their essential components, access to films and information about them, were packaged in two-disc sets . . . The Criterion Collection's laser disc presentations were so deluxe that the filmmakers themselves literally signed off on them: the cases included a somber black label with the director's signature and the legend Director Approved Special Edition."

Robert Hanning, in his analysis of medieval textual glossing, suggests that "[a]s an explanatory technique, glossing belonged primarily to the schools and the pulpit, but as a concept it achieved a much broader cultural currency, functioning as a metaphor for all kinds of textual manipulation, even what might be called textual harassment, that is, the forcible imposition of special meanings on single words or entire verbal structures" (Hanning 1987: 27). In so many ways, DVD audio commentary functions as a high-tech textual gloss. Like the medieval textual gloss, the audio commentary stands simultaneously both in counterpoint to the text it analyses and as its supplement. Proximity endows the gloss with an authority that overshadows all other possible commentaries, so much so that the gloss even threatens to overwhelm the text it analyses. But ultimately the bonds that tie text and gloss together slip, as do the connections between a film and its DVD audio commentary. They become destabilized, susceptible to interpretations that require reassessments of their relationships.

For the DVD of *Excalibur*, John Boorman's audio overlay hints, at times, at a thoughtful, careful reappraisal of his film. But with one striking sequence, culminating in the rape of Igrayne, Boorman's commentary devolves into an uncomfortable – though fascinating – discussion about reimagining sexual violence in Arthurian romance. Boorman's stuttering, stammering narrative of why he chose his daughter to play Igrayne calls into question the immediacy of audio commentary. It holds out the hope of immediate access to authorial interpretation while simultaneously withholding that meaning, calling attention to the process of mediation itself. Although *Excalibur* offers moments of gratuitous nudity, arguably for the sake of authenticity, Boorman seems somewhat reluctant to talk about how, in his film, bodies – primarily female bodies – are constructed as objects of desire, sites for a multiplicity of gazes, each with its own set of social, political, and sexual agendas. In his DVD audio commentary, Boorman steps back and looks admiringly, for the most part, on his cinematic creation. But he only hesitatingly reflects on his rendering of gendered identity in the homosocial world of the Arthurian legend. Even as he fills the screen with sexually charged images, Boorman seems intent on discussing nearly anything else.

In Malory's *Morte Darthur*, Uther Pendragon's desire for Igrayne coalesces with his determination to take all that belongs to Gorlois, the Duke of Cornwall, including his wife. Igrayne, however, rebuffs the king's advances: *she was a passing good woman and wold not assente unto the kynge* (Vinaver 1990: I.7). Boorman's remediation of this scene complicates the sexual politics of the situation. Having made claim to Excalibur, "the sword of power," Uther celebrates with those who have sworn fealty to him. At a dinner celebration, Uther and Gorlois bind themselves to one another, cutting their arms and intermixing their blood. Gorlois then taunts his newly made blood brother: "My wife will dance for us. Igrayne, dance! You may be king, Uther, but no queen of yours will ever match her." Igrayne's body becomes a site both of bonding – she is after all displaying herself for Uther and his men – and contestation. Boorman's Uther might have been satisfied simply to possess property – hence the refrain, "one land, one king." But Gorlois cannot leave well enough alone, and Igrayne's dance prompts a hypermasculine response from Uther, as sexual desire becomes entangled with homosocial one-upmanship.

While this sequence plays itself out, John Boorman's commentary is heading in an altogether different direction. He addresses why he chose actor Gabriel Byrne to play Uther, lingering on Byrne's heavy Dublin accent and the various problems it caused. When Gorlois introduces Igrayne, Boorman discloses, almost as an aside: "That's my daughter, Katrine, playing the unfortunate creature [long pause] Igrayne, who gives birth to Arthur." Boorman then shifts topics again, apparently unable to address effectively his casting choice, unable to watch and comment on his daughter's sexualized exhibition, even as his cinematic knights are banging their flagons on the table to cheer on Igrayne's ecstatic dance. The juxtaposition of the onscreen action with the director's audio commentary is astonishing. Katrine Boorman/Igrayne is dancing her way to orgasm as John Boorman nervously – his discourse filled with long pauses and stumblings – turns his attention to the significance of the matter of Britain: "The legend, you know, it's always, the Grail legend, the Arthurian legend, it has always obsessed me. It seems to be central to the English-speaking nations. The power of it is that it's really in three parts: there is the early part which is the birth of Arthur, or Uther, his father Uther, this kind of brutal period where man seems to be emerging from the swamp . . . then there is Camelot, which is the rise of Arthur and civilization. Then there is the collapse of civilization and the waste land, which is to represent the past, the present, and the future of humanity." Boorman's commentary is interesting for its inarticulate evasions, for what it cannot say. Having turned his daughter into an object of the male gaze, he averts his eyes; he cannot bring himself to look. The obsession that is playing itself out on the screen is one he cannot bear to discuss. The obsession that he does discuss is academic. The commentary, far from rendering the scene transparent, hypermediates it, filling Boorman's silence before his daughter's sexuality with distracting noise.

Malory spends little time detailing Uther's rape of Igrayne. Malory's squeamishness about sexual detail is more than made up for in Boorman's film, which gives Uther's rape of Igrayne a sadomasochistic edginess, complete with paraphernalia of bondage and domination. Uther, in the guise of Gorlois, walks into Igrayne's bedchamber, roughly kisses her, rips off her nightdress, and proceeds, while still fully armored, to rape her. The scene is disturbing, even more so because of the varied witnesses to the sexual violence, including Gorlois' daughter, the child Morgana, and, it is hinted, perhaps Gorlois himself, since Borman intercuts Gorlois' dying moments with Uther and Igrayne's sexual climax, suggesting that Gorlois must witnesses the submission of his wife as he breathes his last breath. The problematic role of the film's director in vividly expanding what Malory only hints at is not entirely lost on Boorman, but he is uncomfortable talking about it. Can Boorman possibly have avoided, for more than twenty years, inquiries about casting his own daughter as the victim of a graphically depicted sexual violation? Still, his discussion of the scene is halting and troubled. He says: "In this scene we see the death of Cornwall, with Uther, as it were, raping his wife, but, of course, it is in the guise of Cornwall, because Merlin has transposed him. That's the young Morgana, of course. And, uh, so people, a lot of people ask me, well, what, how do you feel about directing your daughter being raped. Well, she wasn't being raped, of course, it was, uh, it was just a scene. She didn't mind, nor did I."

Boorman protests not nearly enough. His film offers rape as performance, and its multiple levels of voyeuristic opportunity serve, in part, to eroticize what would otherwise be little more than an act of brute aggression. Morgana, the film-makers, and the cinematic audience all know that a rape is occurring. Igrayne, on the other hand, does not, and the line between rape and rough sex is blurred by the movie. Igrayne believes that it is her husband, returned from battle, who takes her forcibly in front of their child. She is surprised by the violence of the sexuality, but also responsive, her participation signaled by her placing her left leg over her lover – actually over his armor – as he pounds away at her. Boorman's camera collaborates in confusing violence with sex, in shielding the offender – keeping him armored, protected in his impermeable masculinity – while opening the victim to any number of desiring gazes. The camera and Uther become one, violating Igrayne/Katrine.

Again, Boorman tries to discuss the scene in question, but allows himself to become distracted, this time with technical issues. He begins not by talking about the action on the screen but rather about the set: "This is a marvelous set done by Tony Pratt, who has done a lot of my pictures, uh, and, in fact, in this heavy monumental kind of gothic, not gothic exactly, but, uh, Germanic kind of style, was very successful, perhaps more successful than the later Camelot, which was a kind of goldy, gold and silver, which I was, um, was my fault really, because I wanted it, Tony did it, but it wasn't as effective as this. I think the most difficult thing for Katrine in this scene was the proximity of the fire. We wanted to get the flames rising around them, so when we intercut with her husband dying, you had, uh, also the flames." Although Boorman insists that his daughter was only playing a role – "She didn't mind, nor did I" – he confuses the actress with her character throughout his audio commentary. His focus on the technical obscures, but not much, his own conflicted position concerning what he has produced. John Boorman's DVD audio commentary veers away from a discussion of his film just when discussion of the project becomes too personal and too disturbing. In every sense we learn more from what Boorman doesn't tell us, what he can't bring himself to tell us, than from the superficial overview he tries to provide. Even as the authoritativeness of the DVD audio commentary proves insufficient, opening spaces for interpretation rather than closing them, the DVD's special features – including the audio commentary – remediate not only Boorman's film, but the Arthurian legend itself.

DVD extras, like commentary, only begin to uncover the impact of new media on Arthurian narrative. We would like to close by returning to the Black Knight sequence from *Monty Python and the Holy Grail* with which we began, this time as it is remediated on the internet at YouTube (2006), the popular web site where users can upload, view, and share video clips, both homemade and commercial, a site that is currently being hailed as "the future of media" (Garfield 2006: 3). The site, which has become a cultural phenomenon in its own right, boasts more than 65,000 new video uploads every day. On YouTube homemade videos of piano-playing cats jostle with classic TV commercials, popular music videos, and even professional entertainment "stolen from or surrendered by Hollywood" (Garfield 2006: 3). All of our previous discussion has assumed a situation in which video entertainment is produced and distributed by Hollywood or other national film industries that more or less limit the ways in which viewers interact with the content. YouTube changes that situation, creating a new locus whose very emptiness (the site designers provide only a template into which users dump whatever content they choose) allows for an almost infinite variety of uses and remediations (that much of this content – both video and verbal – is inane may even be beside the point). On YouTube, the Black Knight sequence is detached from its place in *Monty Python and the Holy Grail* and uploaded in much

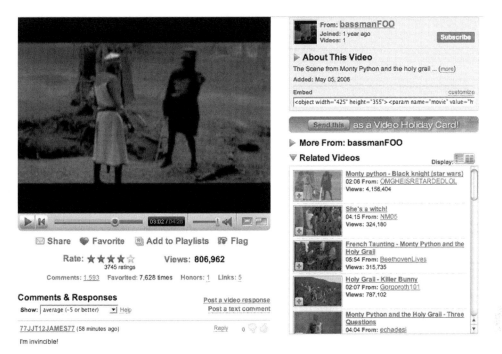

Figure 32.4 YouTube Black Knight sequence.

the same way that the designers of medieval books broke apart works like, say, *The Canterbury Tales*, circulating the stories independently in new contexts, paired with new content. The clip circulates independently of the film, creating new meanings as it is juxtaposed with other media. Like most websites, YouTube is hypermedia; it is a chaotic mélange of different media – graphics, multiple videos, text, sound, photographs, and animation in multiple panes and windows – all jumbled together, all simultaneously competing for our attention (see figure 32.4). Everywhere is the ubiquitous link that allows users to jump willy-nilly from one window to another, from one bit of information to whatever proximate bit catches their attention. YouTube simply cannot be passively viewed, like a film. It requires active manipulation on the part of the viewer, who must constantly choose – what links to click, what videos to watch, what responses to make.

The clip from Monty Python is displayed in a small window roughly 3 × 4 inches (which can be expanded to a full-screen view). To the right is a box with information about the poster, in this instance BassmanFOO. Also to the right are thumbnail pictures of other clips from the film that have been uploaded to the site, as well as a series of unrelated "Promoted Videos," including a film on "How to Balance Two Forks on a Toothpick." Below the clip are a seemingly endless stream of "Comments and Responses" from users who have viewed the clip. These consist almost exclusively of quotations from this and other scenes in the film ("what are you going to do, bleed on me?"), followed by the enigmatic "initialese" favored by inveterate "texters" – lol (laugh out loud), rofl (rolling on the floor laughing). Taken as a whole (an almost impossible task), the experience of viewing the Black Knight skit on YouTube seems to imitate (or remediate) what it would be like for a group of friends to sit around a room, perhaps sharing a few beers or getting stoned, and watch the movie, yelling out the lines in unison. The recitation becomes less commentary than a form of social bonding. In other words, uploads to the site do not convey content so much as they become a mechanism for forging new kinds of imagined friendship networks that extend far beyond the confines of any party space (in this they are like social network-ing sites like MySpace or Facebook, internet phenomena that developed at almost exactly the same moment as YouTube). Our Monty Python clip links some 2,184 individuals (as of March 2, 2008) who have responded to it, frequently with little more than an assertion that they like it as much as the next guy. In 1967, the same year Joshua Logan released his film version of *Camelot*, the French situationist Guy Debord wrote in *Society of the Spectacle*, that "The spectacle is not a collection of images; it is a social relation between people that is mediated by images" (Debord 1992). YouTube seems perfectly to realize that vision, though whether as nightmare or utopia is still an open question.

As our analysis above suggests, the Arthurian legend cannot be understood without also thinking about the various media that have served as its hosts. We have tried to suggest that those media must be explored simultaneously as objects, as social rela-tionships, and as formal structures. They reconfigure the way we conceive of reception and how we locate ourselves in interpretive communities. The story of Arthur has really changed little since the Middle Ages. However, the technologies that have reproduced it during the twentieth century – in theatres, at home on DVD, or online at a computer – have fundamentally altered our relationship with it.

Primary Sources

Vinaver, E. (ed.) (1990). *Malory. Works*, 3 vols, 3rd rev. edn (ed. P. J. C. Field). Oxford: Clarendon Press.

White, T. H. (1987). *The once and future king*. New York: Ace Books.

References And Further Reading

Barber, R. (ed.) (2002). *King Arthur in music*. Woodbridge: Brewer.

Bolter, J. D. & Grusin, R. (1999). *Remediation: Understanding new media*. Cambridge, MA: MIT Press.

Debord, G. (1992) *The society of the spectacle* (trans. K. Knabb). London: Rebel Press. (Originally published as *La société du spectacle*, Buchet/Chastel, Paris, 1967.)

Garfield, R. (2006). YouTube vs. boob tube. *Wired*, 14. At www.wired.com/wired/archive/14.12/youtube.html. Accessed March 2, 2008.

Hanning, R. (1987). "I shal finde it in a maner glose": Versions of textual harassment in medieval literature. In L. A. Finke & M. B. Shichtman (eds), *Medieval texts and contemporary readers*. Ithaca, NY: Cornell University Press, pp. 27–50.

Gunning, T. (1990). The cinema of attractions: Early film, its spectator and the avant-garde. In T. Elsaesser & A. Barker (eds), *Early film: Space, frame, narrative*. London: British Film Institute, pp. 95–103.

Mitchell, E. (2003). Everyone's a film geek now. *New York Times*, August 7, 2003.

Sklar, E. S. & Hoffman, D. L. (eds) (2002). *King Arthur in popular culture*. Jefferson, NC: McFarland & Co.

YouTube (2006). Monty Python and the Holy Grail – The Black Knight. At www.youtube.com/watch?v=2eMkth8FWno&feature=PlayList&p=83C4001CC5B518F4&index=3, accessed March 2, 2008.

FILMOGRAPHY

Camelot (1967). Dir. Joshua Logan. DVD Special Edition Warner Home Video, 1998.

Excalibur (1981). Dir. John Boorman. DVD Warner Home Video, 1999.

Monty Python and the Holy Grail (1975). Dir. Terry Gilliam & Terry Jones. DVD Special Edition Sony Pictures, 2001.

Parsifal (1982). Dir. Hans-Jürgen Syberberg. Film Munchen. DVD Imagine Entertainment, 1999.

33
Arthur's American Round Table: The Hollywood Tradition

Susan Aronstein

At the end of T. H. White's *The Book of Merlyn*, King Arthur foresees his narrative future: "Then there were people . . . in an undiscovered hemisphere who still pretended that Arthur and Merlyn were the natural fathers of themselves in pictures which moved." Arthur's vision predicts the translation of Malory's "definitive" text from page to screen, from Britain to Hollywood – a shift in which America will appropriate Britain's greatest king and claim Arthur and Merlin as its "natural fathers." White, writing in 1941, offers here a surprisingly accurate glimpse into the Arthurian legend's tomorrow: Hollywood films have replaced Malory, Tennyson, and White himself to become the twentieth and twenty-first centuries' most widely disseminated Arthurian texts. Since these films have taught most Americans most of what they think they know about King Arthur, the Knights of the Round Table, Camelot, and the Holy Grail, they merit the attention of Arthurian scholars.

Study of what Kevin J. Harty dubbed "Cinema Arthuriana" began with his 1987 filmography; in 1991, he edited *Cinema Arthuriana*, a collection of articles on Arthurian film. Harty followed with other collections: *King Arthur on Film* (1999a), a special issue of *Arthuriana* (co-edited with Norris Lacy, 2000), and a revised and expanded edition of *Cinema Arthuriana* (2002). In addition to Harty's collections, the 1990s saw the publication of individual essays in *Studies in Medievalism*, *Arthuriana*, and *Cinema Journal*. In 1996, Rebecca and Samuel Umland published *The Use of Arthurian Legend in Hollywood Film*. These initial discussions of Arthurian film introduced several approaches to the subject: the translation of source to film, modernization, feminism, Arthurian legend, and film genre. More recent works – Susan Aronstein's *Hollywood Knights* (2005), Martha Driver and Sid Ray's *Medieval Hero on Screen* (2004), and Lynn Ramey and Tison Pugh's *Race, Class, and Gender in Medieval Film* (2007) – build on these earlier discussions to focus more intently on Arthurian films as medievalisms, reconstructions of the medieval past that address contemporary issues and anxieties.

This focus on the films as reflections of the cultures that produced them provides the principle of selection for this chapter, which briefly surveys representative examples of Hollywood Arthuriana's four sub-genres – contemporary Grail films, Connecticut Yankee tales, chivalric romances, and cinematic retellings of "Malory" – in the context of myths about America and its place in the world. This survey traces a history of national anxieties, from questions of immigration, ethnicity, and class in the early twentieth century, through post-World War II and Cold War uneasiness about both communism and the nuclear age, to the crises of the 1960s, the attempts – centered around Ronald Reagan and his administration – to revalorize old myths and values in the 1980s and 1990s (and the simultaneous critiques of those attempts), and finally to post-9/11 anxieties about America's role in the "war on terror." In each of these periods, Arthurian legend provides a space in which to valorize or interrogate a mythic America – its manifest destiny as the New Jerusalem with the millennial potential to usher in God's kingdom on earth, its promise of democratic possibility, its Yankee ingenuity capable of bringing light to the Dark Ages.

"Is the Grail in New York City?": Class, Civic Virtue, and National Identity

When White predicted that Americans would render the *Morte d'Arthur* in "pictures which moved," he imagined a relatively straightforward translation of print to screen; and, indeed, in 1915, D. W. Griffith announced his plan to direct such a film. Griffith, however, never made this film and American Arthurian cinema begins not with a Malory-style chronicle but with three Grail narratives set in contemporary times: William Worthington's *The Grail* (1915), James Austin Wilder's *The Knights of the Square Table* (1917), and Clarence Brown's *The Light in the Dark* (1922, re-released in 1923 as *The Light of Faith*). These early Grail films address anxieties about class in America's cultural melting pot at the same time that their relocation of the Grail to American soil presents the nation as the new Promised Land. In *The Grail*, the hapless fiancé of the daughter of an embezzling banker rescues his lady and her father "in a series of scenes," that Harty observes, "draw clear parallels to Galahad's quest for the Holy Grail" (2002: 9). This quest valorizes traditional "American" virtues – honesty, perseverance, and hard work – and argues that anyone can find "the Grail" – and achieve domestic and economic success – through adherence to these values.

While *The Grail* addresses anxieties about upper-class misconduct, Wilder's (1917) *Knights of the Square Table* counters critiques of the nation's split between the haves and the have nots while ameliorating concerns about the threat posed to "America" by lower-class immigrant groups. Its narrative begins with "Pug's" formation of an anti-chivalric gang to fight what he claims is an unjust order, epitomized by Detective Boyle, who has killed his thieving father. The film follows the adventures of Pug's gang of delinquents and, after a sequence of convoluted plot moves, Pug is seriously injured; Boyle offers him a drink from a junk-store glass that magically transforms into the "Grail": the Grail heals the boy and the film ends with the repentant Wharf

Rats recognizing their need for benevolent authority, rejecting their criminal roots, and becoming Boy Scouts – members of the new American Round Table.

Brown's (1922) *Light in the Dark* also addresses issues of class and national identity by relocating the Grail to American soil. The film begins as Elaine, estranged from her wealthy fiancé, Warburton Ashe, takes up residence in a working-class boarding house. Elaine suffers a breakdown and Tony, one of her fellow boarders, cares for her. The film cross-cuts Elaine's tale with Warburton's discovery of a chalice while on a hunting trip in England and his arrival back in America amid speculation that he carries the Holy Grail. When Elaine sees the newspaper headline – "Is the Holy Grail in New York City?" – she tells Tony, who, as a working-class immigrant has not had access to Tennyson, the story of the Grail. In Elaine's version, Galahad, inspired by his lady's faith, finds the Holy Grail "so all the world will be healed"; her tale inspires Tony to "borrow" Warburton's chalice for Elaine. She, "doubting, yet lifted on the wings of another's faith," touches the Grail and miraculously recovers. The film concludes with a vision of America that unites the classes in a new democratic chivalry. Tony is hauled off to court and – just when things look grim – the Grail performs another set of miracles, causing Warburton to forgive Tony and reuniting the lovers.

Taken together, these three films establish the narrative trajectory of Hollywood Arthuriana's Grail tradition: adherence to the values of a modern chivalry of honesty, faith, hard work, and charity achieves a literal or metaphorical Grail, heals socio-economic wounds, and reaffirms America's status as the promised land of democratic possibility. As such, they are very much films of the early industry, teaching their immigrant audiences how to be good Americans. When the sub-genre re-emerged during the Reagan–Bush years with Barry Levinson's adaptation of Bernard Malamud's *The Natural* (1984) and Terry Gilliam's *The Fisher King* (1991), however, it did so in the context of a different America; while the early films could rely on a culture of consensus that subscribed to their basic myths about the nation, these later films played to an audience reeling from the events of the late 1960s and 1970s – Vietnam, Watergate, the Iran hostage crisis, corporate corruption, and economic recession – and questioning those same myths. Thus, in these films, the Grail serves not to affirm an existing American promised land but to call a national waste land back to forgotten truths and discarded myths.

The Natural figures America's waste land as a dusty baseball diamond and a long, dry season, splitting the Grail legend's wounded king into two characters, the team's manager, Pop Fisher, and Roy Hobbs. In Malamud's novel, this transformation of Arthurian themes to American baseball works to deconstruct the myths of American exceptionalism and democratic possibility; Levinson's film, however, rewrites the novel to tell an uncomplicated tale of remembering and restoration, in which Hobbs stands in for the disillusioned Vietnam/Watergate generation. The film begins with a montage that provides the novel's rootless Hobbs with a mythic American past – spent playing ball with his father in a golden-lit wheat field – and introduces both the film's Arthurian subtext and its concern with America's millennial potential; Hobbs "draws" a glowing core of wood from a lightening-split tree and shapes it into the bat "Wonderboy," an American Excalibur, a sign of divine election that symbolizes Hobbs's destiny to carry on his father's American values. However, he – like America in the 1960s – loses his way; he is shot by Harriet Bird, a woman who insists that there must be "something more" than those values – a critique that wounds the king and precipitates the waste land. The film then cuts to Knights' Field and Pop Fisher's opening speech, "I should have been a farmer." These words encapsulate *The Natural*'s core values, the truth that America has forgotten: it is the loss of those rural values – hard work, family, connection to the land – associated with the farms of Hobbs's youth that has led to the waste land of Knights' Field, the non-functioning drinking fountains, and the long, dry season. When Hobbs finds his way back to the game and these values, he revives this waste land; the rain pours down and the Knights embark on a winning streak. The film ends with a radical revision of the novel's dark conclusion. This Hobbs does not throw the pennant game; he hits the ball into the lights, setting off a veritable Fourth of July's worth of spectacular fireworks.

The Natural's firework extravaganza, with its evocation of America's "birthday," celebrates a revitalized nation, one in which cultural authority and privileged destiny have been restored. In its tale of remembering and restoration, this film insists – as did the Reagan administration – that the nation must go forward into the past. At the end of the Reagan–Bush era, however, Terry Gilliam returned to the Grail legend to address the waste land of the haves and the have-nots that Reaganomics had wrought. *The Fisher King* begins with an unlikely Grail knight, Jack Lucas, a radio talk-show host isolated behind the smoked glass windows of limos and penthouses, indifferent to the plight of the less privileged. This indifference prompts him to exploit Edwin, "a lonely man (who) reached out to the world . . . through the radio . . . and found only pain," precipitating a massacre at a popular bar and plunging Jack from the penthouses of privilege to the streets of New York, where he becomes part of what he once so despised, "the expendable masses." He tries to commit suicide and is rescued by Parry, a homeless man trapped in the madness brought on by his wife's death in Edwin's massacre, and his Grail quest begins. Parry believes that the Grail rests in a millionaire's apartment on the Upper West Side and that Jack is God's chosen Grail knight. Judged by the standards of Jack's world, Parry is delusional. However, the film argues that if the land and the Fisher King are to be healed, both Jack and its audience must adopt Parry's values. They must learn to read society's trash as wonderful, redefine New York's disempowered from "expendable masses" to an essential community, and define "power" as not privilege but responsibility. When Jack finally learns the truth of the Grail – that others are "thirsty" – he saves the suicidal millionaire, heals both Parry and himself, and transforms the waste land of New York City – and, by extension, the nation – into a fantasia of fireworks.

Bringing Camelot Up-to-Date: Hollywood Yankees in King Arthur's Court

While Hollywood Arthuriana's Grail films present a seamless continuity between the Arthurian past and the American present, in which the Grail represents American values as universal and timeless (if occasionally forgotten), its Connecticut Yankee films typically debunk a superstitious, hierarchical, and barbaric past and valorize a rational, democratic, and technological present, arguing that Arthur needed a little American intervention to realize Camelot's utopia. Hollywood's Connecticut Yankee tradition begins with Fox's 1921 silent film, which establishes both the bits it will take from Twain – time-travel, the use of technology to escape execution, the modernization of Camelot, the Yankee's unconventional style of jousting, the critique of an aristocratic class system and the introduction of democracy, the rescue of Sandy, and knights in shining armor on modern vehicles – and its decidedly non-Twain celebratory tone and message. Wealthy Martin Cavendish, whose mother disapproves of his romance with a secretary, is knocked out by a burglar and awakens to find himself in Arthurian times. After escaping death by "predicting" a solar eclipse, he proceeds to modernize Camelot, convince King Arthur that "all this nobility stuff is bunk," and save the kingdom by providing Arthur's knights with the latest in modern gadgetry. Cavendish awakens, applies his assertions about class to his own situation, and elopes, affirming America's self-definition as a democratic and classless society.

In 1931, as America moved deeper into the Depression, Fox remade the film, casting Will Rogers in the title role as Hank Martin. His adventures begin when he delivers a battery to a decaying gothic mansion; here he finds a host obsessed with the Arthurian past and determined to tune his radio into the court of King Arthur. Hank, unimpressed, announces his intention to go "home and get Amos and Andy," but before he can do so, a blow to the head lands him in Camelot, a kingdom ruled by superstition and aristocratic elitism. Hank dismisses both. "I'm not a magician," he insists, "I'm a democrat," and modernizes the kingdom, establishing factories to produce all the comforts of modern life. When Morgan le Fay kidnaps Arthur's daughter, Hank lectures the king on Yankee self-sufficiency and convinces him to shed his crown for common garb and come along on the rescue mission. Morgan captures them all, but fortunately Hank's factories have produced plenty of modern weapons. All are rescued, Camelot is saved, and the page and the princess ride a helicopter into the sunset.

While Will Roger's Yankee assures his audience that, just as Hank wormed his way out of his Arthurian predicaments, they – through Yankee ingenuity – can overcome hard times, Bing Crosby's 1949 Yankee offers post-War America an optimistic fantasy about love, technology, and Anglo-American alliances. This version of the tale, set at the turn of the twentieth century, portrays its hero as the archetypal can-do American, a blacksmith turned auto-mechanic who dreams of a bright future filled with technological miracles. Like earlier Hollywood Yankees, Hank escapes the stake through technology and embarks on a modernization of Camelot, teaching the court's musicians to become "four beat" men, introducing the ideals of romantic love and suburban domestic bliss ("Instead of going out slaying dragons, I'd be sitting around home watering the lawn"), and attending to the king's political education. The film ends with Hank and a modern-day Sandy reunited in a world made possible by Hank's adventures in Camelot; because he convinced Arthur to change England from a world of aristocratic privilege to one of democratic possibility, England and America become natural political and romantic allies – a state of affairs that sets the stage, the film implies, for the Allied victory in World War II.

Although the 1950s, 1960s, and 1970s saw the broadcast of a handful of unremarkable *Connecticut Yankees* – many of them vehicles for popular cartoon characters – it was 1979 before the tale hit the wide screen again in Disney's space-age version of Twain, *Unidentified Flying Oddball* (reissued as *A Spaceman in King Arthur's Court*). *Oddball* rehashes standard Disney myths about America, extolling the national character, reaffirming America's technological, military, and moral superiority, and reinstating its global position. A fortuitous lightning bolt sends NASA employee Tom Trimble back to the Middle Ages, where he escapes fire through technology (his space suit is heat-resistant), unexpectedly triumphs in single-combat (sending his look-alike robot in his stead), and employs modern weaponry (robots, lunar rovers, and rocket engines) to defeat Arthur's enemies. To this standard Connecticut Yankee formula, *Oddball* adds an emphasis on America as a political and military institution. While earlier Connecticut Yankees embody the American spirit, Tom explicitly represents the nation, singing the *Star-Spangled Banner* as a weapon in his battle against Merlin and planting the American flag on Arthurian soil as he blasts off to the tune of *Yankee Doodle Dandy*. By arguing that Arthur's kingdom needs America to save it, the film reminds its audience of America's role in World War II – a time when its mission was clear and its destiny as a global "city on the hill" (the definition of America as a divinely sanctioned and privileged example for "all eyes" that dates back to John Winthrop's 1630 sermon, and had recently been revived in the campaign rhetoric of Ronald Reagan) unquestioned, a time that an already-campaigning Reagan repeatedly invoked as he urged the nation to go forward into the past.

A decade later, a television version of the tale cast Keshia Knight Pullman as the time-traveling Yankee. A pleasing if dull froth of a film, it adds little to the tradition, give or take its heroine's teaching Feminism 101 to Guinevere and her ladies. The Disney Channel's 1998 telecast, *A Knight in Camelot*, starring Whoopi Goldberg as scientist Vivien Morgan, also retells the tale for an after-school audience. However, in this film, technology takes second place to ideology; in fact, Vivien's attempt to modernize Camelot with a steam-powered mill fails because it both reproduces the inhumane conditions of slavery and sacrifices safety to increased production. Merlin has called her to Camelot for her ideas, not her science. The casting of Whoopi Goldberg in the central role highlights the issue of slavery and allows the film to nod to America's own blighted past at the same time that it identifies the nation as a democratic promised land and Vivien as the source of Camelot's proto-American utopia.

In its attempt to reinstate an unproblematic vision of an American "city on the hill," *A Knight in Camelot* participates in a post-Reagan shift in Hollywood's use of the Connecticut Yankee narrative, one in which Yankee ingenuity and democratic spunk have, like the truth of the Grail, been lost. In fact, Disney's 1995 feature film, *A Kid in King Arthur's Court*, explicitly connects the Connecticut Yankee and Grail traditions, chronicling the healing of two wounded "kings." It begins as Merlin calls into the future for a knight "who can take up the sword Excalibur and save Camelot." Camelot is indeed in trouble: Arthur, mourning Guinevere, has allowed an evil knight too much control, his oldest daughter is in love with a lower-class man, and the court lives in fear of the Black Knight. However, the "knight" from the future – teenage Calvin, who plays baseball for the Knights – is also in trouble: convinced that he is a "dweeb," he is afraid to dream of being a hero. Both Calvin and Arthur need to remember essential truths that they have forgotten: Calvin, that local boys can make good, and Arthur (who was a stable-boy when he drew Excalibur) that all men are equal. When Calvin recovers his American can-do heritage and Arthur remembers his democratic roots, boy and king work together to save Camelot; the film ends as Calvin returns to his baseball game, transformed from a ball-fearing dweeb into a home-run-hitting Disney hero.

Black Knight (2001), starring Martin Lawrence, also recasts the Connecticut Yankee tale as a Grail narrative. Unlike *A Kid in King Arthur's Court*, however, this film critiques, rather than valorizes, the "American" values promulgated in the earlier Connecticut Yankee films; as such, it comes the closest to the spirit of Twain's novel. The film begins with Medieval World, the locally run, down-at-heel South Central Los Angeles amusement park, where its Yankee worker, Jamal, is facing financial ruin at the hands of the soon-to-be-opened corporate behemoth, Castle World. Jamal plans to bail out – to go to Castle World and a better salary – and advises his boss also to "forget about the community" and take the money and run. On his way out of the door, Jamal falls into the "moat" and emerges in the medieval realm of King Leo, a tyrant who has usurped the throne from the true queen.

Jamal's initial experiences in this realm follow the standard Connecticut Yankee trajectory; however, when he, like his cinematic predecessors, is granted a position of authority – "Chief of Security" – Jamal proceeds to become a purveyor not of progressive and democratic ideologies but of crass commodities – frappacinos, Skywalker clothing, and Jamal in the Box. In fact, he rejects the role of the "Black Knight," hero of a rebellion that will restore the true queen to the throne and liberty to the people. Jamal's rejection of this role shifts the focus of this Connecticut Yankee film; instead of relating a tale about the conversion of a medieval king from feudalism to democracy, this narrative chronicles Jamal's conversion from capitalism to community. Jamal finally accepts his responsibility to both medieval and modern communities, leading a successful uprising against Leo and then returning to the modern day, where he puts the lessons he learned in the past to work in the present, revitalizing Medieval World and bringing hope to the waste land of modern America.

The latest in the long line of Hollywood Connecticut Yankees, SpongeBob SquarePants, brings the narrative back to its roots in American optimism. In *Lost in Time* (2006), America's new favorite local boy and his sidekick Patrick knock each other out in a medieval theme park joust. They awaken in the real Middle Ages to find that they must defeat the evil Sir Plankton, slay the jellyfish dragon, and free the Princess. It is fitting that SpongeBob should find himself in the role of Hollywood Yankee: he is, however ironically, the direct descendent of the can-do American, a dreamer and a doer, a hardworking local boy who always makes good.

Defending Arthur: American Chivalric Romance

The Hollywood Connecticut Yankee tradition transports American optimism, technological know-how, and democratic ideals to the medieval past; its Yankees serve as midwives at the birth of a proto-American utopia. Hollywood's chivalric romances, on the other hand, follow the coming-of-age adventures of a would-be knight to present Yankee values as timeless. The heroes of these films, often themselves outsiders – lowborn or new to the court – embody proto-American values as they save Camelot from itself. These cinematic Arthurian romances originate in the popular 1949 serial, *The Adventures of Sir Galahad*, starring George Reeves, a cliffhanger that uses Sir Galahad's successful adventures to ameliorate anxieties brought on by the end of World War II, the advent of the nuclear age, and the beginning of the Cold War. A nameless knight arrives at Camelot and handily defeats the court's champions (Bors and Mordred); he reveals his identity (Galahad) and begs Arthur for a place at the Round Table. Arthur promises that, as soon as Galahad performs the necessary initiation rite (standing vigil over Excalibur), he will be inducted into knighthood. Kay recounts the sword's history: it is an invincible weapon, given to Arthur by the Lady of the Lake, to serve "both king and people" – a sword that "allowed him to defeat the Saxons" and assures peace "as long as we guard Excalibur."

Kay's description of Excalibur as an invincible weapon that brought peace to the land invokes the atom bomb that had so recently ended World War II; the rest of the narrative both makes this equation more explicit and attempts to assuage anxieties raised by the existence of such a weapon. Galahad fails; the sword is stolen. While Arthur and his knights prepare for war, Galahad desperately seeks to recover Excalibur and return it and its invincible powers – accompanied by a glowing metallic hum – to Arthur. After several hours of lurking knights, plots and counterplots, swelling music, and galloping horses, Galahad confronts the Lady of the Lake, who has taken the sword "from those who seek to use its power for evil purposes," concluding that "it would be better if the sword were destroyed forever." Galahad protests, "Arthur is a good and righteous king; deny him Excalibur and he will lose his kingdom." Conceding to Galahad's wisdom, the Lady entrusts Excalibur to Arthur's keeping and the series ends in Arthurian triumph: the invading Saxons are conquered, the "unknown Betrayer" revealed, and Galahad assumes his well-earned place at the Round Table.

The Adventures of Sir Galahad translated post-War concerns about the nuclear era to the medieval past, assuring its audience that the "Excalibur" of nuclear power was safe, necessary, and God- (or Lady-) given. This series also provided the narrative and thematic structure for the rest of the Arthurian romances Hollywood produced during the Cold War. These romances, as did *Sir Galahad*, drew on the Western, the swash-buckler, and the spy film to tell tales of young knights, outsiders to Arthur's court, who with gauche optimism, democratic principles, ingenuity, and natural talent – and against all odds – save a smug court from the "enemy within." Filmed at the height of McCarthyism and in the shadow of Hollywood's black list, these films warned Americans to stick to their guns and beware the traitor in their midst. 1954 saw the release of both *The Black Knight* and *Prince Valiant*; both of these films follow *The Adventures of Sir Galahad*'s narrative format – outsiders, skeptical courts, internal trai-tors, marauding Saxons, and the final triumph and revalorization of Arthur's utopia. Furthermore, *Valiant*, which revolves around the Saxons' theft of the "Singing Sword" of power, a sword that rightfully belongs in Christian and Arthurian hands, explicitly references *Sir Galahad* and its fable of nuclear power.

The 1956–7 television series *The Adventures of Sir Lancelot* owes a clear debt to these earlier examples of Hollywood Arthurian romances. Its main characters – Lancelot, the novice knight, and Brian, the kitchen boy, whom he adopts as his squire – recover stolen artifacts (Excalibur, a ruby with weapons potential), defend the kingdom from invaders, insist on worth rather than birth, unmask traitors, unite lovers, and gener-ally assure peace and prosperity in Arthur's kingdom. Once this series went off the air, Hollywood's fascination with medieval Western/swashbucklers waned; *The Siege of the Saxons* (1963), which rehashes many of the Cold War films' themes, marks the end of this iteration of the genre. When Arthurian romance returned to Hollywood in the late 1970s and early 1980s, its "knights" were a farm boy and a space-pilot from a galaxy far, far away (*Star Wars*) and an archaeologist-adventurer from the 1930s (*Indiana Jones*). In order for these resurrections of post-World War II genres – the cliffhanger serial, the chivalric romance, and the action adventure film – to work, however, they needed to reinscribe the myths about America's privileged destiny at the heart of these genres. George Lucas and Steven Spielberg accomplish this reinscrip-tion by reversing Hollywood Arthurian romance's original narrative trajectory. While post-World War II examples of the genre rehearse and reaffirm American values as they narrate tales of clueless courts that need to save themselves by converting to the hero's "American" point of view, the *Star Wars* and *Indiana Jones* movies, addressing an audience that has rejected that point of view, tell stories in which the "court's" survival depends upon the conversion of cynical "knights" to its abandoned values.

The conversion narratives offered by these film trilogies provide a model for a disil-lusioned, post-1960s American audience, arguing, Reagan-like, that a return to the past will carry it into the future. As Luke Skywalker, Han Solo, and Indiana Jones turn to the values of the past – belief, hope, hard work, commitment – they demon-strate the means by which America itself can reclaim its millennial promise. In its story of Luke Skywalker and his struggle to free the galaxy and redeem his father, the original *Star Wars* trilogy chronicles a Perceval-type tale of the making of a Jedi Knight: the conversion of a boy who feels that he can do nothing about the Empire into the savior of the Republic. As Luke turns to the Force, rejects the ways of his father and the Emperor (modeled on Richard Nixon), and embraces his destiny – and with it the values of Obi Wan and Yoda (a mixture of World War II militarism and 1960s religious counter-culture) – he becomes a galactic Arthur, the boy who pulls the sword (or light saber) from the stone and uses it to wage peace. Luke's story is aimed at a young audience, who came of age in the 1970s and early 1980s; to an older audience, disillusioned by the events of the 1960s, the films offer the tale of Han Solo, the mercenary suspicious of "hokey religions" who converts to a true believer. The conversion of Luke and Han to abandoned values saves a great Republic that, like America, has lost its way, putting it back on track to realize its privileged destiny and become a galactic Camelot.

In many ways the *Star Wars* saga, with its tale of a boy who, with the help of an aged wizard, finds his father's sword and brings peace and democracy to the galaxy, is the more obviously Arthurian of the two trilogies. However, Indiana Jones ends his career (at least thus far) with a Grail quest, a narrative turn that explicitly identifies the roots of all three films in Arthurian romance. Like Han Solo, Indiana Jones is a cynic, a loner in need of a court and the values that court can bestow. From the very first film, Indiana must learn both to abandon his cynicism and embrace belief – in the Ark, the Ankara stones, the Grail – and to accept his role as an American knight, guardian and defender of the weak. As he does so, he reasserts America's destiny as both New Jerusalem and Camelot, returning the Ark of the Covenant to American soil and becoming the last in a long line of Grail knights.

Camelot, America, and the New Jerusalem: Arthurian Chronicles

The *Indiana Jones* trilogy's implicit conflation of the Ark and the Grail makes explicit the typological connections between Israel, Camelot, and America that are repeatedly played out in Hollywood Arthurian chronicles. The first of these chronicles, *The Knights of the Round Table* (1953), establishes the outline for Hollywood's take on the rise and fall of Camelot: Arthur's deliverance of the land from chaos, his establishment of a democratic, proto-American utopia, and the fall of both king and kingdom. The film begins with a voice-over describing a land in chaos, "for every overlord held rule in his own tower and fought with fire and sword against his own fellow"; Arthur opposes this chaos of individualism with a political and social order based on "natural law": "we are not many people; we are one people," founding a political utopia on an American 1950s ideal of a pluralist society. *Knights* then turns to an exploration of how to protect Camelot's (and America's) utopia: a Cold War vigilance against the enemy, the willingness to use defensive violence, and the subjection of individual desire to community duty. Camelot, in this film, falls for two reasons: Arthur is too soft – determined to "begin his reign in peace" he pardons the rebels, including Mordred – and Guinevere places her private desire for Lancelot over her public duty to the nation. These flaws allow Mordred to betray the kingdom, precipitating the final battle, Arthur's death, and the return of chaos. *Knights*, however, ends not with the shattering of the Round Table but with the passing of the Grail. In the film's final sequence, Lancelot and Galahad return to the destroyed court; the Holy Grail appears and God's voice assures the audience that if "faith in what is eternal is restored, of fellowship and honor, naught is lost," ending on a high note, as the audience recognizes America – a pluralist, democratic utopia, a nation under God – as the natural heir to Camelot.

Disney's 1963 animated version of Arthur's childhood, *The Sword in the Stone* (based on the first part of T. H. White's *The Once and Future King*), reinforces *Knights'* equation between Arthur, Camelot, and America; in it Merlin, constantly muttering about England's "medieval mess," educates Wart, a "local boy" with "wit and imagination," in the ways of democracy and technology. When, at the end of the film, Wart pulls the sword from the stone, the audience is assured that, as in the Connecticut Yankee films, this King Arthur will transform the elitist superstitious medieval world of Ector and Kay into a democratic and modern utopia. Hollywood's next Arthurian chronicle, *Camelot* (1967), based on Lerner and Loewe's 1963 musical, picks up where *The Sword in the Stone* leaves off, chronicling, as does *Knights*, the rise and fall of Camelot. However, while *Knights*, in keeping with its Cold War politics, emphasizes internal vigilance and carefully patrolled borders and *Sword*, as a Disney film, valorizes the alliance between individual dreamers and technology, *Camelot*, in keeping with America's 1960s vision of its world mission as policeman and disseminator of democracy, offers a more global vision. Arthur believes that everyone will want to join his democratic Round Table in which knights will use their "might for right" – that a little might, joined with a lot of ideology, will bring peace to the kingdom. And so it does; the knights can soon turn their attention to tournaments and May Day picnics, and mayors can hand over unneeded city keys to the king. Camelot, however, as it is in *Knights*, is fated to fall and the seeds of its ultimate doom in this film are, like its utopic vision, rooted in the 1960s. Guinevere and Lancelot are a mere sidebar; the real villain is the cynical younger generation, embodied in the leather-wearing, hippie-like Mordred, which is unwilling to look past the admitted flaws of their fathers to the values they attempt to uphold. Because Arthur cannot make Mordred his ideological son, Camelot falls and war looms; however, as the ending of the film suggests, Arthur's utopia can be restored by good sons who believe in and pass on the tales of Camelot – an appeal to its audience for a return to the dreams and values of America's past.

While *Camelot* valorized old tales, the most popular Arthurian movie of the period, *Monty Python and the Holy Grail* (1975), merrily debunked them and the troupe's send-up of the legend precluded any serious cinematic treatment of Arthuriana for nearly a decade. It was 1981 before the Arthurian chronicle – riding on the coat tails of *Star Wars'* success – hit the big screen with John Boorman's *Excalibur*. In this film,

Boorman, heavily influenced by Jungian philosophy, rewrites Arthur's tale as an archetypal battle between true kingship and poisoned patriarchy, radically transforming its ideological message. While earlier Hollywood chronicles valorize a political utopia founded on proto-American ideals of a pluralist democracy, *Excalibur* argues that such a utopia is possible only when "the king and the land are one." In this film, Camelot's doom comes when its privileged knights and ladies lock themselves into their golden city, ignoring the plight of those outside their walls, precipitating a waste land and scattering Arthur's knights on a quest for the Grail. Too late, Arthur remembers the "Truth" on which his kingdom was founded; he rises from his sickbed only to fall in the final battle, and the film ends not with the passing of the Grail and Arthurian authority to America but with the vague hope that someday a king will come again. *Excalibur*'s depiction of a corrupt and privileged court uses Hollywood's traditional equation between America and Camelot to critique rather than valorize the nation: if America is the natural heir to Arthur's "utopia," then it is responsible for a national waste land and America must reassess its values and reinstate forgotten truth before it is too late.

Hollywood's next wide-screen Arthurian chronicle, *First Knight*, re-establishes the connection between Camelot and America as a positive one. *First Knight* re-presents Camelot as the "city on the hill" – sanctioned by divine election to spread democracy to the world. In it, Arthur argues, "There are laws that enslave men and laws that set them free. Either what we hold to be right and good and true, is right and good and true for all mankind, under God, or we're just another robber tribe." As it tells the Indiana-Jones-like tale of Lancelot's transformation from loner mercenary to Arthur's best knight, it encourages its audience also to abandon critique and re-subscribe to the nation's post-World War II myths about itself. In fact, in this version of the legend, Lancelot and Guinevere's belief in "Camelot" and what it stands for averts Arthurian tragedy; Arthur may die, but not before he hands over queen, kingdom, and sword to Lancelot, assuring the continuity of what is "good and right."

First Knight was the only wide-screen Arthurian chronicle released between *Excalibur* and *King Arthur* (2004). These years, however, produced three made-for-television versions: an adaptation of Persia Woolsey's "feminist" retelling of the Arthurian legend, *Guinevere* (1994), *Merlin* (1998), and a mini-series based on Marion Zimmer Bradley's best-selling novel *The Mists of Avalon* (2001). None of these offerings is interested in the proto-American political subtext of the cinematic genre; instead, they all nod to *Excalibur* as they situate Arthur at the transition between the mystical past and the rational present. Each of them also – in spite of their purported feminist take on the legend – attribute Arthur's fall to the powerful women of the old religion, women too proud to accede to the coming of a new Christian and male order. As such, they, however unwittingly, participate in what Susan Faludi identified as American popular culture's larger "backlash" against women (1991), rehearsing and exorcising anxieties about female power and the threat it poses to masculine dreams of order and utopia.

While Antoine Fuqua's *King Arthur* (2004), which advertised itself as "the truth behind the myth," returned the cinematic Arthurian chronicle to its political roots, it, like *Excalibur*, presented a critique of the national status quo, equating "America" not with Arthur's future Camelot, but with the corrupt and imperialist Rome that he must abandon. Instead of telling the tale of the rise and fall of Camelot, the film chronicles Arthur's dawning realization that he serves an order that has abandoned the true tenets of democracy in its quest for power and lands, and his eventual siding with the Woads – men "who want their country back" – against both Rome and the invading Saxons. The film ends where most Hollywood chronicles truly begin, with the wedding of Arthur and Guinevere and the unrealized promise of a new utopia, founded in values that America – the film strongly suggests – has abandoned.

King Arthur's attempt to wrest the Arthurian legend from its Hollywood tradition by transporting it from its high medieval setting to tell – supposedly – the legend's pre-history, suggests what is at stake in Hollywood's long Arthurian tradition. Because the good old days of Camelot and King Arthur signify an ideal past to which we aspire to return, Hollywood versions of the legend use their tales to inscribe a politics of nostalgia, arguing that the nation should go forward into the past. In their depictions of Camelot, the Grail, and the ideal knight, these films both show us America as it should be and identify what will destroy us. As such, Hollywood Arthuriana is an ideologically loaded, contested genre. Its history – from the Grail tales' constructions of proper citizens, through the Connecticut Yankee tradition's exploration of American technology and ingenuity, and the chivalric romances' proto-American heroes, to the chronicles' equation of America and Camelot – calls us to heed Umberto Eco's warning about the dangers of our fascination with the medieval past: "Since the Middle Ages have always been messed up" it is critical that we ask "what Middle Ages" (or what Arthur) "we are dreaming of" (1986: 68).

PRIMARY SOURCE

White, T. H. (1977). *The book of Merlyn: The unpublished conclusion to the once and future king*. Austin, TX: University of Texas Press.

REFERENCES AND FURTHER READING

Aronstein, S. (2005). *Hollywood knights: Arthurian cinema and the politics of nostalgia*. New York: Palgrave.

Eco, U. (1986). The return of the Middle Ages. In *Travels in Hyperreality* (trans. W. Weaver). New York: Harcourt Brace Jovanovich, pp. 59–86.

Faludi, S. (1991). *Backlash: The undeclared war against American women*. New York: Doubleday.

Fraser, J. (1982). *America and the patterns of chivalry*. Cambridge: Cambridge University Press.

Gorgievski, S. (1997). The Arthurian legend in cinema: Myth or history? In M. F. Alamichel & D. Brewer (eds), *The Middle Ages after the Middle Age*. Cambridge: Brewer, pp. 153–66.

Harty, K. J. (1987). Cinema Arthuriana: A filmography. *Quondam et Futurus: Newsletter for Arthurian Studies*, 7(3), 5–8.

Harty, K. J. (1991). *Cinema Arthuriana: Essays on Arthurian film*. New York: Garland.

Harty, K. J. (1994). *The knights of the square table*: The Boy Scouts and Thomas Edison make an Arthurian film. *Arthuriana*, 4, 313–23.

Harty, K. J. (ed.) (1999a). *King Arthur on film: New essays on Arthurian cinema*. Jefferson, NC: McFarland.

Harty, K. J. (ed.) (1999b). *The reel Middle Ages: Films about medieval Europe*. Jefferson, NC: McFarland.

Harty, K. J. (ed.) (2002). *Cinema Arthuriana: Twenty essays*, rev. edn. Jefferson, NC: McFarland.

Harty, K. J. & Lacy, N. (eds) (2000). Screening Camelot: Further studies of Arthurian cinema. *Arthuriana*, 10(4), special issue.

Lacy, N. (1989). Arthurian film and the tyranny of tradition. *Arthurian Interpretations*, 4, 75–85.

Lupack, A. & Lupack, B. T. (1999). *King Arthur in America*. Cambridge: Brewer.

May, L. (1980). *Screening out the past: The birth of mass culture and the motion picture industry*. Oxford: Oxford University Press.

May, L. (2000). *The big tomorrow: Hollywood and the politics of the American way*. Chicago, IL: Chicago University Press.

Ramey, L. & Pugh, T. (eds) (2007). *Race, class, and gender in "medieval" film*. New York: Palgrave.

Ray, S. & Driver, M. (eds) (2004). *The medieval hero on screen*. Jefferson, NC: McFarland Press.

Ryan, M. & Kellner, D. (1988). *Camera politica: The politics and ideology of contemporary Hollywood film*. Bloomington, IN: University of Indiana Press.

Shichtman, M. B. (1984). Hollywood's new Weston: The Grail myth in Francis Ford Coppola's *Apocalypse Now* and John Boorman's *Excalibur*. *Post Script: Essays in Film and the Humanities*, 4(1), 35–48.

Umland, R. & Umland, S. (1996). *The use of Arthurian legend in Hollywood film*. Westport, CT: Greenwood Press.

Wakefield, R. (1988). *Excalibur*: Film reception and political distance. In B. Bjorklund & M. E. Cory (eds), *Politics in German literature*. Columbia, SC: Camden House, pp. 166–76.

Wood, R. (1986). *Hollywood: From Vietnam to Reagan*. New York: Columbia University Press.

FILMOGRAPHY

The Adventures of Sir Galahad (1949–50). Dir. Spencer G. Bennet. Columbia Pictures Serials.

The Adventures of Sir Lancelot (1956–7). Dir. Bernard Knowles & Anthony Squire. Incorporated Television Company.

The Black Knight (1954). Dir. Tay Garnett. Warwick-Columbia Pictures.

Black Knight (2001). Dir. Gil Junger. Twentieth-Century Fox Film Corporation.

Camelot (1967). Dir. Joshua Logan. Warner Brothers Studio.

A Connecticut Yankee (1931). Dir. David Butler. Fox Film Corporation.

A Connecticut Yankee in King Arthur's Court (1921). Dir. Emmett J. Flynn. Fox Film Corporation.

A Connecticut Yankee in King Arthur's Court (1949). Dir. Tay Garnett. Paramount Pictures.

A Connecticut Yankee in King Arthur's Court (1989). Dir. Mel Damski. Schaeffer Karpf Productions in Association with NBC.

The Empire Strikes Back (1980). Dir. Irvin Kershner. Lucasfilm.

Excalibur (1981). Dir. John Boorman. Orion Pictures.

First Knight (1995). Dir. Jerry Zucker. Columbia Pictures Corporation.

The Fisher King (1991). Dir. Terry Gilliam. Tri-Star Pictures.

The Grail (1915). Dir. William Worthington. Laemmle Films.

Guinevere (1994). Dir. Jud Taylor. Alexander/Enright and Associates.

Indiana Jones and the Last Crusade (1989). Dir. Steven Spielberg. Paramount Pictures.

Indiana Jones and The Temple of Doom (1984). Dir. Steven Spielberg. Paramount Pictures.

A Kid in King Arthur's Court (1995). Dir. Michael Gottlieb. Walt Disney Pictures.

King Arthur (2004). Dir. Antoine Fuqua. Touchstone Pictures.

A Knight in Camlelot (1998). Dir. Roger Young. Walt Disney Television.

The Knights of the Round Table (1953). Dir. Richard Thorpe. MGM Studios.

Knights of the Square Table (1917). Dir. Alan Crosland. Edison Films.

The Light in the Dark (1922). Dir. Clarence Brown. Associated First National Pictures.

Merlin (1998). Dir. Steve Barron. Hallmark Entertainment.

Mists of Avalon (2001). Dir. Uli Edel. Constantin Film Produktion.

Monty Python and the Holy Grail (1975). Dir. Terry Gilliam & Terry Jones. Michael White Productions.

The Natural (1984). Dir. Barry Levinson. Columbia Tri-Star Productions.

Prince Valiant (1954). Dir. Henry Hathaway. 20th Century-Fox.

Raiders of the Lost Ark (1981). Dir. Steven Spielberg. Paramount Pictures.

The Return of the Jedi (1983). Dir. Richard Marquand. Lucasfilm.

The Siege of The Saxons (1963). Dir. Nathan Juran. Columbia Pictures.

SpongeBob SquarePants: Lost in Time (2006). Dir. Vincent Waller. Nickelodeon, Paramount Home Entertainment.

Star Wars (1977). Dir. George Lucas. Lucasfilm.

The Sword in the Stone (1963). Dir. Wolfgang Reitherman. Walt Disney Productions.

Unidentified Flying Oddball (1979). Dir. Russ Mayberry. Walt Disney Productions.

34

The Art of Arthurian Cinema

Lesley Coote

Perceptio *and* inventio, *"seeing" and "discovering"*

In the Middle Ages, *inventio* was the process whereby a narrative was recreated by the author of a text (visual or literary) for transmission to an audience. The author discovered the meanings inherent in his material – story, narrative, rhetorical techniques – and then re-presented it according to his own vision and the requirements of his audience. When a director and his team recreate a text, they have to attempt an understanding of how the original source text was created, and why. In the process of this recreation, therefore, some of the qualities of the original will remain present in the cinematic text. The director, like the medieval author, "discovers" (in the senses of "finding" and of "uncovering") the text. Three films in which this is the case are *Lancelot du Lac* (Robert Bresson, 1974), *Perceval le Gallois* (Eric Rohmer, 1978), and *Excalibur* (John Boorman, 1981).

Lancelot du Lac

Mirrors were potent symbols in medieval culture. The view in the mirror represented truth, but was also associated with death. Death itself was a mirror, in which the sinner sees his/her true self before the Judgment. In *Lancelot du Lac*, Queen Guenièvre holds up a mirror, the symbol of a truth and an impending tragedy that only she can see.

Perception, seeing, and not seeing are centrally important to the understanding of Bresson's *Lancelot*. The film itself is full of eyes – not human eyes, but the eyes of horses. In a film about knighthood and chivalry, horses are key characters; after all, it is they who put the *cheval* in *chevalier*. Bresson's horses appear throughout the film, and their sounds – hooves, breath, neighing, and whinnying – punctuate the soundtrack. The horses watch the human characters knowingly, and in the end they suffer the same fate: Lancelot's horse falls with its master, an arrow in its head. Their eyes, unlike those of the human characters, stare straight out of the frame, directly at the viewer. They challenge us to look harder, not only to see but to perceive. They encourage not only observation, but a moral response. The audience are encouraged to relate to the characters in the filmic text (as in *La Mort le Roi Artu*, Bresson's thirteenth-century source text), and to realize that their own perception, like their view, is equally partial and sometimes obscured.

This effect is reinforced by Bresson's use of camera angles and the composition of his shots. The camera angles, especially in action and transitional scenes, are frequently unusual, with shots from below and above, at different angles from their subjects, edited together in discordant ways. Many shots feature the body in part only, usually the legs and lower body, of humans or of horses. The effect of this is to dissolve the individuals into a single jellied mass, a corporate body of "knighthood," implying a common code, a common ethos, a common purpose – although this also reinforces the irony that these knights are not united, have abandoned or betrayed their common code, and have no purpose left after the failure of the Grail quest. Their corporate anonymity is further reinforced by the effects of the full plate armor which they wear; their individual identity is lost when their visors are lowered, an action which Bresson stresses by continual close-ups of visor raising and lowering, accompanied by the sound of the hinges and the clash of metal on metal.

Guenièvre is one of the most far-sighted characters in *Lancelot du Lac*. The age of prophecy is dead, a fact to which she draws attention by her reference to Merlin's prophecy of doom. Bresson represents the prophetic presence from his source text in terms of a *souciant* nature. He uses horses and other animals, especially birds, in this way (for example, the jackdaw which caws with ill omen when Mordred approaches the outbuilding where Lancelot and Guenièvre are having an illicit tryst). Gauvain watches the clouds for omens, such as the cataclysmic storm that accompanies the tournament, instilling an uncontrollable fear in Guenièvre, portending Lancelot's wounding, Mordred's treason, and the deaths of them all. Bresson emphasizes this with a shot of Lancelot's pennant, the means of his identification, ripped from the apex of his tent by the storm, lying unnoticed in a puddle.

Gauvain achieves prophetic vision at the point of death. Christ-like, wrapped in his bloodstained bandages after being accidentally dealt a mortal wound by Lancelot, Gauvain warns Artus of the fatal consequences of attacking his killer. Bresson has changed the character of Gauvain from the source text, where he is much older and very prone to human weaknesses, to make him a *naïf* young man for whom Lancelot is an example and a hero. Gauvain's youth adds pathos to Lancelot's betrayal of his chivalric reputation.

Bresson makes Guenièvre a girl-queen, trapped in her marriage to an older man who appears to treat her with cool harshness. She is the archetypal "damsel," imprisoned in a tower (a common medieval trope), rescued by Lancelot, then forced by circumstances to return to her husband. Guenièvre is better able than her lover to see and to understand her predicament, but she is powerless to prevent the outcome; it is men (on horses) who make history. Guenièvre points out the tension at the heart of the chivalric code, in which she and Lancelot, indeed the whole of Camelot's society, are trapped, the tension between the "masculine" qualities of loyalty, strength, courage, and hardihood, based on knightly violence, and the more "feminine" qualities of courtly love, based on relationships with women. This tension is central to medieval Arthurian narrative.

Bresson sets up this conflict at the film's violent opening, with heads being lopped off, decomposing corpses hanging in the trees, and armor being pierced, blood flowing. This is the first of three episodes of violence that make a framework for the narrative. Alongside these, there are three instances of the taking (or not) of hands in gestures of *amicitia*, which in medieval terms can mean either warm friendship or erotic love. This follows Bresson's source: medieval writers and theologians loved to arrange their work in "threes." On his return to the Round Table, Lancelot goes to a room over a barn (an ironic "upper room" in biblical terms) to meet his lover. After "worshipping" her by kissing the hem of her skirt (the courtly lover as Virgin Mary), Guenièvre expects Lancelot to take her hand and to make his *aveu* (avowal) of love for her, as courtly love requires. Instead, he tells her that their affair must end. Guenièvre is so desperate that she goes as far as to ask, or demand, what should be hers by right. She rejects his moral argument, and the moral/religious basis of the Grail quest, in defense of the supremacy of love over violence.

The tournament scene at the center of the film corresponds with another failed taking of hands. Lancelot goes to Mordred's tent, offering his hand in a gesture of reconciliation. He believes at this point that Mordred can only guess about his adultery with the queen, which Mordred has been plotting to expose, and couches his gesture in the political discourse of public concern. Again, Lancelot's perception is faulty; he does not see the woman's scarf that Mordred is hiding in a dark corner, away from the lantern's light. Mordred stands imperiously in the harsh golden light, refusing to respond. When Lancelot sees the scarf, he realizes that it is Guenièvre's, and that their adultery has been exposed. Lancelot is subsequently reunited with Guenièvre, but he is still torn between the two extremes of the chivalric code. He puts off sexual activity until after he has won honor by fighting in the tournament at Escalot. Instead of being impressed, Guenièvre realizes that "honor" is directed toward men rather than toward her.

Bresson's tournament sequence is the film's *tour de force*, a brilliantly realized filmic example of *amplificatio*, or the exploration of a single trope from as many viewpoints as possible. The camera looks from different angles at the same subjects, from a variety of focal lengths   a knight's knees, a flagpole with small pennants being raised, each one slightly different in color, if not in shape. As this happens, similar (traditional Breton) music is played. This is edited together with shots of the legs and feet of knights, with the legs and bellies of their horses, mounting and running against one another. There is the "ooh" of the crowd, the crash of bodies falling. There are shots of the sandy earth of the tournament field, onto which broken lances are tossed. Each time, we see similar (but never the same) shots of Artus and Gauvain in the stands, their heads moving from side to side as the knights charge. A gradual realization dawns that the anonymous knight with the plain shield is Lancelot. On the way to the tournament, Artus has already refused to surrender his willful blindness to Lancelot's adultery with his wife. The honor and the thrill of partaking in Lancelot's tournament victories is his vindication.

The final battle is the working out of the violence and betrayal that was implicit in the Grail quest with which the narrative began. It is preceded by another gesture of hands, as Lancelot returns Guenièvre to Artus, at her own insistence, in order to heal the rift between them. As Lancelot leads her to the meeting with Artus, Guenièvre holds onto Lancelot's arm just above the wrist. As she leaves him, her hand passes over his very closely, but they do not touch. Guenièvre's mirror is revealed to be a portent; love must wait for death. The promised night of passion never happened. As she tells Lancelot, it is the promise, the potential of their love which will survive, a hope seemingly fulfilled in the bird that flies away from the heap of dead bodies (a familiar ending to medieval battles).

Frequently what we see in the film is empty spaces. "My hands are empty," says Lancelot to Artus on his return from the Grail quest, and so they prove to be, both physically and morally. He has nothing to offer Guenièvre but excuses based on false religiosity, only false hope for Artus, an example based on a lie for Gauvain, and a reconciliation based on guilt and fear for Mordred. Lancelot cannot even save himself. The empty spaces convey a sense of failure, wasted potential, and lack. This is evident at the beginning, when Artus shows Lancelot the room containing the now empty Round Table. Artus begins by indicating the seats of individual knights, giving the dead occupant's name, but he moves from "here sat [name]" to simply "there . . . and there . . ."; the memory, and the sense of loss, are too painful to articulate. Like Guenièvre's bed without Lancelot, almost everything in the film is empty: chivalry without honor, knighthood without brotherhood or purpose, the Round Table without its occupants, a society without hope and without a future.

In this Bresson is echoing his source, although his simplified narrative, selection of material, and stripped-down style enable him to emphasize this more strongly. The temporal limitations of the film impose their own imperatives; the film demands singularity of vision in a way that the "epic" written narrative does not. Within this story of failure, Bresson's Artus is a failed king. He is unable to tell his knights what to do or to provide comfort and purpose for them, unable to provide the impetus for reconciliation and communal healing, which they need after the Grail quest, unable to gain the love or respect of his young wife, unable to make up his own mind. When Gauvain challenges him to give advice on what the knights can do to help themselves, Artus responds, "pray, perfect yourselves," an answer for which Gauvain has obvious contempt. Guenièvre reveals that she hates and despises Artus. Artus, like Lancelot, cannot "see."

Again, Bresson is following his source. The medieval Artu of *La Mort* is a pathetic figure, reactive rather than proactive. He does not want to know the truth about Guenièvre and Lancelot, although "everyone" knows and talks about it behind his back, and the only time in which he acts positively is in vindictive anger after he learns of the adulterous affair. Artu (not Mordred) arranges Agravain's attempt to catch the lovers together, then picks a quarrel with Lancelot, and arranges for the queen to be burned.

Bresson's Lancelot, like his Camelot, has been symbolically dead since the Grail quest. When symbolic death has occurred, actual physical death is secondary. Both are gradually drained of meaning through the film. However, it is the promise, the potential of both Lancelot and Guenièvre's love and of the Arthurian legend, which will survive. It is this, not their initial failure, which really matters.

Perceval le Gallois

The original source text for *Perceval le Gallois* is the unfinished romance of *Perceval*, or *Le Conte du Graal*, composed in the 1180s and left unfinished by Chrétien de Troyes (see chapter 14). The story was resumed after Chrétien's death by at least four different continuators, but Eric Rohmer, who had taught Old French, used only Chrétien's text, rather than using the continuations to provide an "ending." Rohmer knew and followed Chrétien's narrative closely, using his own modern French translation as the film script. He took Chrétien's text, "dis-covered" its contents, then added his own vision and cinematic rhetoric, re-presenting it as a film. This is his, very medieval, claim to moral and intellectual *auctoritas*. Rohmer has been criticized for adding his own ending to Chrétien's narrative, but in the light of this claim, he becomes simply Chrétien's latest continuator.

Rohmer follows Chrétien's text closely. He has extracted what he considers to be the most critical parts of each section, in order to preserve the essence of Chrétien's style and narrative, while excising enough to allow, as Bresson does, the visual images to "speak" for themselves. Instead of a closely woven tripartite structure such as that of Bresson or Boorman, Rohmer adopts the episodic structure of his source text, retaining almost all of Chrétien's episodes in their original order. Each episode is bridged by a "journey" scene or sequence, in which a character, usually Perceval, moves from one side of the (semicircular) set to the other, following a twisting course through the same arrangement of painted metal trees. This movement is usually accompanied by spoken or sung narrative. In this way Rohmer creates an impression of movement through the narrative, which parallels Perceval's physical and psychological journey and yet manages at the same time, by the use of the same visual clues, to unify his episodic narrative. The camera sometimes moves, and sometimes pans, around the space. In the context of the film as a whole, panning (the camera follows the action while fixed to a single spot) is used in order to surprise. At the film's opening, the camera pans away from the singing chorus to reveal "birdsong" being created artificially by other chorus members. Later, Perceval's surprise at the appearance of a rider is conveyed by a swish (fast) pan. Special effects are reserved for supranatural events, such as the appearance of the Fisher King's castle, the arrival of the

mysterious girl, and the (cartoon) goose. The cut is used to convey synchronicity.
When Perceval sends his vanquished opponents to the court of King Arthur, their
appearance before the king is revealed by editing, while Perceval's narrative continues
in another location.

In his presentation of *Perceval*, Rohmer has achieved a fusion of romance epic narrative, medieval mystery play, and, most interestingly, the medieval practice of performing Old French lyric poetry. The chorus is presented as a group of traveling
minstrels (*trouvères*) who present the narrative, sometimes spoken but mostly sung. In
the medieval tradition, they frequently perform as a soloist and complementary voices,
accompanying themselves on reconstructed medieval instruments. The pitch, tone,
and tempo of voices and instruments work together to produce the soundtrack. An
important, and widespread, practice across Europe in the Middle Ages was the "dance-
play," in which actor/dancers would perform all or part of a sung narrative, miming
the actions while speaking or singing part of the musical accompaniment. In this type
of performance, the actors would be joined by members of the chorus, who were also
the singers and players of musical instruments. Rohmer has reproduced this on film,
with the singers of the chorus joining the actors to perform the story – for example,
when chorus members become the laughing girl and the fool, or when they become
courtiers and serving men and women, while still singing the narrative, and commenting upon it. The characters, especially Perceval and Blanchefleur, frequently pick
up the narrative from the chorus in the third person ("the knight said . . ."), blurring
the lines between narration and performed narrative. The whole weaves together into
an inextricable, unified, multidisciplinary, very medieval, work of art in a twentieth-
century medium.

Rohmer said that he wished to convey the strangeness, the otherness, of the medieval world to a modern audience. He achieves this not only by his method of performance, but by his sets, costumes, and manner of performance. The sets are based upon
medieval manuscript illuminations, although Rohmer himself made the point that,
due to an absence of contemporary manuscript illustrations, these are not so much
representative of twelfth-century *art romain* as of later, thirteenth-century, images. In
accord with the medieval images, Rohmer has not attempted to make the relationship
between his sets and his human characters in any way proportional; as he himself
commented, the idea of perspective did not exist in the Middle Ages. He also follows
medieval manuscript images in the architectural framing of many of his sets. Marty
(1985) has noted his use of the Romanesque arch as a unifying factor, comparing this
to the use of similar arches in twelfth-century architecture, while Williams (1983)
has compared Rohmer's use of these settings within a semicircular set as similar to
the curve of medieval illustrations, in which a circular course is used to draw the eye
around a series of images, indicating the passing of time.

Gesture was part of rhetoric in the Middle Ages, and Rohmer's characters frequently imitate the exaggerated gestures of characters in medieval art. These are
stylized, and are indicative of either emotion (as when Perceval's mother literally
throws up her arms and falls in an exaggerated swoon), or of ritualized situations such

as greeting, eating, courting, taking leave, and even fighting. The images in medieval art are representational, reflections of the "real." What matters is not the naturalism of the image, but what is signified. The stylized gesture reminds the viewer of the signified emotion in the natural, the "real," world, and this is what the viewer "reads." In a similar way, the modern viewer interprets the non-natural images of comic books, cartoons, and video games.

Rohmer does seem to realize that, while this certainly adds to the strangeness of his film, he needs to make the whole accessible and understandable to his modern audience. Unlike Bresson's untrained *modèles*, he utilizes trained actors, who inject "naturalistic" meaning and emotion into their characters' performances. It is possible to be attracted to the *naïf* and well-intentioned Perceval, or to feel the tiredness of Arthur, or the desperation of the beautiful but abused Blanchefleur, while still being disconcerted at the stylized and "strange" nature of their gestures and settings. The sets and costumes also include authentic-looking medieval armor and dress, and authentic reproductions of medieval *realia* such as tableware, furnishings, chessboards, lamps, and the extravagantly pleated white tablecloths that were symbolic of wealth in the Middle Ages. The metal trees and metallic-looking castles add a more modern, surrealist tone.

At the beginning of the film, Perceval is living at his mother's home in Wales, regarded as the margin of the civilized world. His understanding of the world has been engineered by his mother, after the deaths of his father and brothers in battle, in order to keep him from leaving home to become a knight. He is associated with women and peasants, and other marginalized people (he kisses serving girls). Perceval's first appearance reveals his marginalized position: he takes up his own narrative, describing in the third person how he throws his javelins, at the same time miming the actions, by himself. His aloneness is emphasized as he fails to interact with the knight to whom he speaks. He responds to the knight's question by asking questions of his own which have no relation to the knight's attempts at dialogue. Following his meeting with the five knights, whom he mistakes at first for devils, then for angels, then God, Perceval, like the author/director, undertakes a journey of *inventio*, both discovering and dis-covering the values of the social world, as he is gradually integrated into chivalric, aristocratic society.

Perceval's journey is closely related to the emergence of the code of chivalry at the end of the eleventh century. His development as a man has been arrested by the failure of his mother to release her control over him, although the knightly qualities that he has inherited from his father are visible to others with the aristocratic sensibility to be able to see them, such as King Arthur, Gorneman de Gorhaut, and Gauvain. Perceval demonstrates inherent strength, hardihood, and generosity, but he learns about courtly manners, skill, loyalty, courtly love, the care of the helpless, and the spiritual love of Christ. He, and his audience, must learn the difference between seeming and being, between appearance and substance.

Gorneman de Gorhaut, King Arthur, and Blanchefleur are what they seem to be, as is Sir Gauvain, but others are not, and as such their function is to draw attention to what they *should* be. The Knight of the Heath appears to be a courtly lover, but mistrusts and maltreats his lady; the Red Knight appears to be a powerful knight, but he is disloyal and abusive to his lord, King Arthur, and is easily overcome by the country boy's skill in throwing a javelin into his eye. The Older Sister appears to be a courtly lady, but she mistreats her knightly lover by making unreasonable demands of him – but Sir Gauvain, while deliberately appearing to be a coward, is in reality a true knight.

Perceval's inability to see the difference between appearance and reality leads him into comic irony (he thinks a pavilion is a church, then steals kisses and a ring from the lady inside, ignoring her obvious distress while thanking her for her hospitality and "gifts"). It also prevents him from asking questions about the Grail and the Bleeding Lance, which would have enabled the healing of the Fisher King. As he learns to be a knight, Perceval also learns to know himself, and to relate to others within society. He reaches a turning point in his personal development after his visit to the Fisher King. Up to this point it is Perceval who has been asking all the questions, but the mysterious girl begins to ask questions of *him*. He has been referred to constantly and impersonally as *le valet* ("the servant"), but now she asks his name. Chrétien says that he has to guess, but he guesses correctly, "Perceval." Later, when asked by the hermit, he announces boldly that he is "Perceval le Gallois."

Perceval leaves the female world to enter the world of the male. It is only when he has rejected the female by no longer submitting to his mother's tutelage that he is able to enter into a heterosexual love relationship with Blanchefleur. His love for her reminds him of the love of his mother – in medieval understanding, a reflection of the love of the Virgin Mary for Christ and for all sinners – and causes him to set off in search of his mother. In medieval romance, secular love both mirrors and leads to spiritual love; this is implicit in the image of the three drops of blood left in the snow by the bleeding goose. As Perceval contemplates the drops of blood, a symbol of Christ's passion, he thinks he sees the face of his beloved Blanchefleur. This leads him, after five years in which he has forgotten God, to the hermit (who is his uncle), who will lead him to a full realization not only of human love as sacrifice, but also of the sacrificial love of Christ.

This is played out in the final scene, a version of the Passion narrative enacted in the form of a medieval mystery play. The chorus sings the Passion narrative (secular and spiritual singing were very closely related in medieval art and performance), while actors from the film take on the roles of characters from the Passion. Fabrice Lucini, who plays Perceval, is now also Christ. At the climax of the play, he is wounded by the Bleeding Lance, recalling its appearance in the Fisher King's hall. It is Good Friday, and Perceval has achieved an emotional and spiritual understanding of who he is within society, and of who he is in relation to God. The film ends with the young knight continuing on his quest. Everything appears the same, but all has changed. Perceval now has the physical, personal, and spiritual attributes that will enable him, outside the time frame of both Chrétien and the film, to successfully complete his Grail quest.

Excalibur

John Boorman's ultimate source is Sir Thomas Malory's *Le Morte Darthur*, although it has been very strongly suggested, and with reason, that this is filtered through the views of modern commentators, in particular the "Celtic" interpretations of Jessie Weston. Malory's text is an epic production – a reworking and translation of the whole of the Old French Vulgate cycle – as is the film, which follows Arthur's story, albeit selectively, from beginning to end. The power of Boorman's work lies in his visual artistry. Whereas Bresson uses minimalist settings and costumes, which have both "authentic" medievalist and modern elements, and Rohmer bases his sets and costumes on medieval manuscript illustrations, Boorman's settings and costumes relate to the works of nineteenth-century Pre-Raphaelite painters, which are better suited to his "romantic" treatment of the legend. The whole is strongly interwoven with a strand of New Age Celticism. In *Excalibur*, the supernatural, the magic, and the prophetic overwhelm the chivalric element of Malory's text.

In Malory's text the supernatural is accessed by prophecy, which punctuates the narrative throughout. It is the duty, sometimes the misfortune, of human agents to make possible prophecy's fulfillment, for good or evil. In text and film Arthur marries Guinevere despite Merlin's warnings, while the film ends as the barge with the three noblewomen bears the dying Arthur away to Avalon, having relocated Lancelot's career as a hermit before the final battle and having him die, as in Bresson, with the rest of the remaining Round Table knights. As a prophecy well known in Malory's England put it, "his end will be mysterious."

In *Excalibur*, nature dominates and envelops the human beings who populate it, indicative of powerful forces of supernature by which their affairs are shaped. The sword is lifted from the lake in the mists of morning, and descends back into it after Arthur's death, in the interval between twilight and darkness, symbolizing the birth and death of the Arthurian dream. *Excalibur* has a tripartite structure similar to that of *Lancelot du Lac*, in that it begins and ends with the violence of internecine battles and the bloody deaths of knights, with a joust at its center. Bresson's violence, however, signifies violent death, the loss of life, and the corruption of knightly ideals. The violence at the beginning and end of *Excalibur* is eroticized and charged with spiritual significance. In the beginning, Merlin hands Uther the (phallic) sword of power, after which Uther rapes Cornwall's wife Ygraine, a violent sexual act which resembles combat. Uther ejaculates in time to Cornwall's death gasps, emphasized by a thumping musical score. In Malory, these events cannot be synchronous, as Merlin uses the two-hour gap between Cornwall's death and Arthur's conception to "prove" that Arthur must be Uther's son. At the film's end, Mordred deals Arthur a mortal blow with his (phallic) spear while Arthur drives Excalibur into his son's neck, and Mordred says, "Let us embrace."

The joust at the film's center is not, as in Bresson, "play," but a trial by battle to establish the innocence or guilt of Guinevere, condemned to burn for adultery and treason. The accuser is Gawain, here taking up the role allotted in Malory to Sir Mador, who accuses Guinevere of killing Sir Patrice with a poisoned apple. Lancelot and Gawain do take part in single combat in the *Morte Darthur*, but this is later in the narrative, resulting from Lancelot's killing of Gawain's brothers. Boorman's aim is to show the negative forces of rumor and jealousy which have entered the society of the Round Table, not through defeat, losses, and the failure of the Grail quest, as in *Lancelot*, but through luxury and indolence brought on by success.

Boorman reproduces Malory's method of paralleling themes and events with examples later in the narrative. As Uther rapes Ygraine in disguise, so Morgana seduces Arthur, leading to the birth of a child. Mordred is thus, in the context of the film, the mirror of his father, the son who displays his father's negative qualities. Arthur, on the other hand, displays Uther's *positive* qualities. As Uther drives Excalibur into the rock to prevent anyone else from exercising his power, so Arthur repeats the action in his hurt and anger at Guinevere's adultery and Lancelot's betrayal. While Uther receives the sword and has to be told to "give," Arthur hands Excalibur, of his own volition, to his worst enemy to be made a knight and therefore a king. Igrayne's dance is paralleled by Guinevere's. Arthur's discovery of his real "self" in the first part of the film is paralleled by his rediscovery of this after the administration of the Grail by Perceval, while Morgana is a perverted image of her own mother, Igrayne.

Women are a largely negative presence in *Excalibur*. The theme of the Fall is woven intimately into the narrative. Uther is morally unhinged by watching Igrayne dance, and Guinevere is seen as enchanting Arthur by giving him a strange cake. Guinevere goes to her meeting with Lancelot on a horse, emphasizing her control of masculinity. Lancelot, surrounded by the wild nature associated with the female, attempts to back away from her, positioning Guinevere as the sexual aggressor. They are viewed from Merlin's cave in juxtaposition with an iconographic image of Adam and Eve. Guinevere's becoming a nun is brought forward, so it becomes a result of post-lapsarian guilt, rather than atonement for the collapse of Camelot and the death of its knights, as in Malory. Before his death, Lancelot admits to Arthur that his love for Guinevere, "the old wound," will never heal, linking the woman to the ultimate debacle and the fall of civilization. This failure is ultimately Eve's fault.

In the film, as in the *Morte Darthur*, there are good and bad practitioners of magic. By eliding three of Malory's female characters (Morgan, Morgause, and Nineve) to make Morgana, Boorman is able to create a character who is driven by the desire for revenge on the son for Uther's rape of her mother. Nothing in *Excalibur* "just happens," as it does frequently in medieval Arthurian romance. This gives the film a very modern aspect. Boorman's twentieth-century audience requires villains to have credible motivation. Morgana's shape-shifting powers, by which she seduces her brother and bears his child, Mordred, are derived from her Celtic past as a *fay*, or fairy, not from Malory or his French originals, in which Morgan simply sleeps with

Arthur by mutual consent when she visits his court without her husband. Morgana's resourcefulness and sheer ability to gain and use power are undermined by her use of it to keep herself beautiful, implying that she is, as Woman, weak and vain after all. The ultimate destruction of Morgana is thus the triumph of the masculine, although it is something of a Pyrrhic victory, in which almost all die. The dying king is entrusted to the ministry of women. The idea of Woman as nature/nurture and the earth as Mother, and yet the agent of temptation and destruction, is maintained throughout and is a strong theme of the film.

The power of pagan Celtic spirituality is contained in Boorman's conception of "the dragon," connecting as it does to Geoffrey of Monmouth's "Prophecy of Merlin," in which the British and the invading Saxons are represented by a red and a white dragon. The dragon as a prophetic symbol is relatively common in medieval English (and Welsh) "Arthurian" prophecies. The film is dominated by lush, green land-scapes, offering a loose connection with the Celtic association of supernatural, divine powers with natural phenomena such as rocks, streams, and lakes. Merlin is associated with the elements, with plants and animals, with "wild" nature, and with the female. His position in relation to Arthur's court, and to the world of humans in general, is liminal. Although his presence at Camelot is not secret, he moves in the shadows, he converses with Morgana at the back of the room, and does not seem to move as freely as she does within the company of knights. Merlin's wild, ragged, and hermit-like clothing emphasizes his liminality, while his "hard edge" is denoted by his metal skullcap. He serves his own prophetic agenda, with little sympathy for mortals; he ignores Igrayne's anguished cries as he takes away her baby. In character and performance, Nicol Williamson's Merlin in the film has many echoes of Malory's.

Whereas the Grail is a very "present" absence in Bresson, and a luminous physical presence in Rohmer, the Grail episode in *Excalibur* seems incongruous and clumsily handled. If the film is based on Malory, why should the Grail knight be Perceval, rather than Galahad? One of the reasons for this may be the pre-existence of Rohmer's film. Boorman's Perceval is pieced together from the adventures of other characters in Malory. He is Malory's Gareth, put to work in the kitchens by Sir Kay because his noble origins are unknown. He is Sir Bors, offering to fight for Guinevere in case Sir Lancelot does not appear in the lists. He is the Perceval of Chrétien's continuators. Finally he is Sir Bedevere, unwillingly throwing Arthur's sword back in to the lake as his lord lies dying. Instead of being used to heal the Fisher King, the Grail is administered to Arthur himself, as Boorman has elided Arthur with the Fisher King. Like the Fisher King, Arthur and his kingdom revive, offering Boorman the chance for a moment of creative, medievalist bravado. Arthur and his knights ride to defend the land against Mordred and his mother, as the earth springs into life in a flourish of buds, green leaves, and falling blossoms, as in the "spring" sequences of medieval lyrics, to the accompaniment of Carl Orff's (modern treatment of the medieval) *Carmina Burana* – an echo of Malory's "May" passage.

Another reason for the absence of Lancelot's son Galahad may be the director's desire to keep Arthur at the foreground of the film. For this reason, Lancelot's adventures are mentioned but not shown. Arthur is ever-present, even in his physical absence from the screen. He is the chief object of desire, even for Guinevere, who, it is implied, only turns to Lancelot because she cannot fully possess Arthur. As he says to her, he must live for his legend, and cannot be a mere "man." In the context of his Grail story, Boorman makes a very important point about the medieval perception of kingship, "the king is the land, and the land is the king." This echoes medieval political theology, in which the king is *christus*, God's anointed representative on earth. Boorman's use of cinematic technology presents this in vivid form, with the visual elision of Arthur and Christ in Perceval's Grail vision. The idea that a weak or depraved king would affect the physical well-being of his country was common in medieval England. Arthur is the guarantee of peace, safety for the weak (women and naked young children play outside the castle), promoter of arts and sciences (inside the castle, all manner of learning, entertainment and scientific development is under way), of plenty (the Round Table is awash with food and drink), and of justice (Arthur places this before his love for his wife). For Merlin, as for many medieval English people, Arthur is "the One"; he embodies the Celtic and the Christian, the old and the new, chivalry and kingship. He is the inspirational force behind the Round Table (which he, with the blessing of Merlin, founds, rather than it being Guinevere's dowry as in the source texts) and Camelot. His kingship is received from God by the pulling of the sword from the stone, although his personal qualities must maintain it. His development in wisdom and maturity is made visible by Boorman in his physical development and costume, from the beardless page to the bearded man in armor, to the graying patriarch giving his life for his realm. As the king and the land are one, so are Arthur and Excalibur. He is the ultimate priest and king, wielder of both the spiritual and secular swords.

Literature and Culture

There is no such thing as "historical accuracy" in legend, which can only be true to itself. A filmed text can only be true (or not) to its written source. Each of these films seeks to discover, in the medieval sense, its source. The difference between them is contextual. *Lancelot du Lac* and *Perceval* were made in a cinematic context that stresses the legend as literature, but in *Excalibur*'s Anglo-American (Hollywood) context – on which Boorman relied for funding – Arthur has become part of popular culture. Boorman's audience expects to see certain aspects of the legend in any film about Arthur (sword, Grail, joust, battle, adultery, wizards), and this is what he selects. Although he is less "accurate" than Bresson or Rohmer, he has less freedom to be so. In the light of this, Boorman's achievement of medievalist *inventio* is considerable, and his film deserves, alongside *Lancelot du Lac* and *Perceval*, to be considered "art."

References and Further Reading

Baby, Y. (1985). Metal makes sounds: An interview with Robert Bresson (trans. N. Jacobson). *Field of Vision*, 13, 4–5.

Bartone, R. (1992). Variations on Arthurian legend in *Lancelot du Lac* and *Excalibur*. In S. Slocum (ed.), *Popular Arthurian traditions*. Bowling Green, OH: Bowling Green State University Popular Press, pp. 144–55.

Beatie, B. A. (1988). Arthurian films and Arthurian texts: Problems of reception and comprehension. *Arthurian Interpretations*, 2(2), 65–78.

Callaghan, L. (1999). *Perceval le Gallois*: Eric Rohmer's vision of the Middle Ages. *Film and History*, 29, 46–53.

Codell, J. (1992). Decapitation and deconstruction: The body of the hero in Robert Bresson's *Lancelot du Lac*. In D. Mancoff (ed.), *The Arthurian revival: Essays on form, tradition and transformation*. New York: Garland, pp. 266–82.

Coote, L. A. & Levy, B. J. (2006). The subversion of medievalism in *Lancelot du Lac* and *Monty Python and the Holy Grail*. *Studies in Medievalism*, 13, 99–126.

Denery, D. G. (2005). *Seeing and being seen in the later medieval world: Optics, theology and the religious life*. Cambridge: Cambridge University Press.

Dronke, P. (1996). *The medieval lyric*. Woodbridge: Boydell & Brewer.

Fieschi, J. (1979). Une innocence mortelle. *L'Avant-Scène du Cinéma*, 221, 4–6.

Foury, M.-H. (2001). *Excalibur* de J. Boorman: quête originelle d'un imaginaire contemporain. *Cahiers de Conques*, 3, 239–60.

Frappier, J. (2000). Perceval or *Le conte du graal* (trans. R. Cormier). In D. Mahoney (ed.), *The Grail: A casebook*. New York: Garland, pp. 175–200.

Goetinck, G. W. (2000). The quest for origins. In D. Mahoney (ed.), *The Grail: A casebook*. New York: Garland, pp. 117–48.

Harty, K. J. (2002). Parsifal and Perceval on film: The reel life of a Grail knight. In A. Groos & N. Lacy (eds), *Perceval/Parzival: A casebook*. New York: Routledge, pp. 301–12.

Hindman, S. (1994). *Sealed in parchment: Rereadings of knighthood in the illuminated manuscripts of Chrétien de Troyes*. Chicago, IL: Chicago University Press.

Hoffman, D. L. & Sklar, E. S. (eds) (2002). *King Arthur in popular culture*. Jefferson, NC: McFarland.

Lacy, N. J. (2002). Mythopoeia in *Excalibur*. In K. Harty (ed.), *Cinema Arthuriana: Twenty essays*, rev. edn. London: McFarland, pp. 121–34.

Marty, J. (1985). *Perceval le Gallois* d'Eric Rohmer: un intinéraire Roman. *Cahiers de la Cinematheque*, 43, 125–32.

Nickel, H. (2002). Arms and armor in Arthurian films. In K. Harty (ed.), *Cinema Arthuriana: Twenty essays*, rev. edn. London: McFarland, pp. 235–4.

Paquette, J.-M. (1985). La dernière métamorphose de Lancelot: Robert Bresson. In D. Buschinger (ed.), *Lancelot*. Göppingen: Kümmerle, pp. 139–48.

Pruitt, J. (1985). Robert Bresson's *Lancelot du Lac*. *Field of Vision*, 13, 5–9.

Quandt, J. (ed.) (1998). *Robert Bresson*. Toronto: Toronto International Film Festival Group.

Reader, K. (2000). *Robert Bresson*. Manchester: Manchester University Press.

Rider, J., Hull, R., Smith, C., with Carnes, M., Foppiano, S., & Hesslein, A. (2002). The Arthurian legend in French cinema: Robert Bresson's *Lancelot du Lac* and Eric Rohmer's *Perceval le Gallois*. In K. Harty (ed.), *Cinema Arthuriana: Twenty essays*, rev. edn. London: McFarland, pp. 149–62.

Rohmer, E. (1979). Note sur la traduction et sur la mise en scène de *Perceval*. *L'Avant-Scène du Cinéma*, 221, 6–7.

Rosenbaum, J. (1997). The rattle of armour, the softness of flesh: Bresson's *Lancelot du Lac*. In *Movies as Politics*. Berkeley, CA: University of California Press, pp. 201–9.

Teisch-Savage, N. (1978). Rehearsing the Middle Ages. *Film Comment*, 14, 50–56.

Thompson, K. (1998). The sheen of armour, the whinnies of horses: Sparse parametric style in *Lancelot du Lac*. In J. Quandt (ed.), *Robert Bresson*. Toronto: Toronto International Film Festival Group, pp. 338–71.

Whitaker, M. (2002). Fire, water, rock: Elements of setting in John Boorman's *Excalibur* and Steve Barron's *Merlin*. In K. Harty (ed.), *Cinema Arthuriana: Twenty essays*, rev. edn. London: McFarland, pp. 44–53.

Williams, L. (1983). Eric Rohmer and the Holy Grail. *Literature Film Quarterly*, 11, 71–82.

FILMOGRAPHY

Excalibur (1981) Dir. John Boorman. Orion Pictures.

Lancelot du Lac (1974). Dir. Robert Bresson. Compagnie Française de Distribution Cinématographique.

Perceval le Gallois (1979). Dir. Eric Rohmer. Les Films du Losange.

35

Digital Divagations in a Hyperreal Camelot: Antoine Fuqua's *King Arthur*

Nickolas Haydock

"I am Arthur!" shouted one of the children, a bucket sitting on his head like a helmet.

"No!" shouted another small boy. "You are a Woad! I am Arthur!" (Frank Thompson, *King Arthur*, 2004)

HIC IACET ARTURUS, REX QUONDAM REXQUE FUTURUS. In the Bergsonian theory of Giles Deleuze, *quondam* and *futurus* are virtual moments that can only be actualized in the present (Deleuze 1986, 1989). Cinema screens the scandal of history, so that it is thoroughly presentist, like memory itself. Parsing the sources of the English imagination, Peter Ackroyd says that Arthur represents "the great national fount of myth and symbol," "a legend of origin combined with a legend of revival" whose endurance stems at least in part from a seemingly limitless adaptability (Ackroyd 2002: 124, 118). The Arthur created by desires for origins and revivals has little to do with the *dux bellorum* who won the day – but not the war – against the Saxons at the Nennian battle of Badon Hill. That piece of the real only becomes significant because of the legends that accrue to it, from the earliest chronicles through the romances of the high Middle Ages and down to what Kevin Harty has dubbed "cinema Arthuriana" (Harty 2002; Higham 2002; Finke & Shichtman 2004). These Arthurs originate and stage periodic returns from a parallel universe that the myth itself calls the Isle of Avalon, but which I denote by the more prosaic title: the medieval imaginary (Haydock 2002, 2007, 2008). This chapter is concerned primarily with the ways in which Antoine Fuqua's *King Arthur* (2004) and its companion video game actualize this virtual Arthur.

The realist aesthetic of Siegfried Kracauer (2004) and his suspicion of both fantasy and historical cinema, which were for him much the same thing (1960: 77–91), represent one arm of my pincer approach to Arthurian cinémedievalism and digitization. With Kracauer, I view mass entertainment as the distilled expression of collective desires, which serve not merely to reflect but also to intensify ideals such as patriotism, nostalgia for charismatic leadership, or a belief in the historical destiny of nations. A central tenet of post-Lacanian psychoanalysis maintains that desire constructs its objects, not the reverse. As one of the West's few remaining master myths, Arthur is capable of incarnating almost any desire – romantic, rationalist, or racist; nationalistic, nostalgic, or new age; fundamentalist, fascist, or futuristic; post-colonial, post-ideological, or even post-Twin Towers. Indeed, it is possible to take the temperature of almost any western age or society simply by attending to what it makes of Arthur's story. Yet whether we seek him in the tomb like Henry II, and thereby seek to fix and control his influence, or lose ourselves within the *selva oscura* of hyperspace and multimedia, Arthur's ability to survive repeated incarnations is a sure sign of his immortality.

The second pincer of my approach is what Baudrillard has called the "procession of simulacra" into the realm of hyperreality, where both reference and history are fatally attenuated in spasms of reproduction (1994: 1–42). The apparent contradiction in Baudrillard's theory of the hyperreal rests in his insistence upon the erosion of reference to any reality whatsoever and, simultaneously, the postmodern obsession with technologies of its accurate representation. Many recent cinematic historical fantasies like *King Arthur* lavish money and attention on material details and egregiously veri-similar effects (like the kilometer-long Hadrian's Wall built for the film and its computer-generated imagery [CGI] extensions) while treating the historical record with nothing like the same care. As Baudrillard maintained: "Concurrently with this effort toward an absolute correspondence with the real, cinema also approaches an absolute correspondence with itself . . . *the cinema is fascinated by itself as a lost object as much as it (and we) are fascinated by the real as a lost referent*" (1994: 47, original italics). The reflexivity of Arthurian cinémedievalism is a theme in what follows, but so too is its specular ideology whereby we establish the reality of the present by fashioning its source in the past. If our desire for origins provokes us to seek him in the tomb, our desire for renewal proves that Arthur has always been a regent of the virtual.

The Desire for Origins: The Seven Sarmatians

Medievalists who analyze the products of cinémedievalism have often been reluctant to abandon the real/reel distinction in their rush to stake a claim in the realm of popular culture. This means that their use of sources can sometimes pander to popular appetites for knowing what "really" happened as a basis for the analysis and evaluation of historical films. In his discussion of *King Arthur*, Tom Shippey trenchantly remarks, "perhaps the least truthful part of the Fuqua film comes in the first two words of the opening credits, 'Historians agree. . . .' On this subject, historians do not agree about anything" (Lupack 2004: 123; Shippey 2007: 314). Many critics find the ubiquitous appeals in such films to new evidence or to uncovering the truth behind the legend attractive, and perhaps justly so. Shippey certainly does not fall into this trap and, along with other critics of the film, such as Kevin J. Harty (2004), Alan Lupack

(2004), Susan Aronstein (2005), and Caroline Jewers (2007), rightly identifies *From Scythia to Camelot* by C. Scott Littleton and Linda A. Malcor (1994/2000) as the basis of the film's depiction of Arthur's knights as a band of Sarmatian cavalry. Yet despite its openly hypothetical stance, this work is also touted as the scholarly, albeit controversial, "source" to which the film's director, screenwriter, producer, actors, and its paid historical consultant John Matthews unanimously refer in marketing the film. The film's screenwriter David Franzioni (rather disingenuously, as will be demonstrated below) closes his interview with Matthews thus: "I'm so tired of seeing movies about movies." He urges people not "to default to the images" but rather to "default to their experiences" (Franzioni 2004: 120). As we will see, Arthur may be "just a guy," but he is a virtual guy made from other movies in nearly every detail. Franzioni's affected, hyperspace vocabulary, urging audiences to "default to their own experiences," also hints – perhaps unwittingly – at the fact that many traits of Arthur and his Sarmatian "knights" are ready-made elements designed to ease the marketing convergence of the film and its video game, where we are all invited to "play the legend."

The chief source of *King Arthur*'s plot, characterization, and even its "ideology" has very little to do with Arthur, historical or legendary. It is based quite closely on Akira Kurosawa's film *Seven Samurai* (1954) and the reinscription of that classic *jidai-geki* in a franchise of American westerns, beginning with Preston Sturges' *The Magnificent Seven* (1960). What we have in Fuqua's film, then, is yet another in a long line of medievalized westerns, issuing from a genealogy that includes the masterpiece of a widely recognized auteur and its commercially successful formula. It is this genealogy, not the putative Sarmatian ancestry of Arthur's knights, that most influences what happens in the film. To recall the earlier citation of Baudrillard, the postmodern desire for origins is commonly doubled in film, calqued by cinema's nostalgia for its own past. In addition, the film's focus on ethnicity, explored thoughtfully by Shippey (2007), Jewers (2007), and Aronstein (2005), takes on a slightly different coloring when viewed through the prism of Sergei Eisenstein's *Alexander Nevsky* (1938), which provides not only the source for an important scene but also the model for the film's erotic, Manichean nationalism. In short, the Littleton–Malcor hypothesis is a pretext in both senses of the word, one that allows Franzioni and Fuqua to cloak their Russian samurai cowboys in plausibly historical garb.

What seems to have taken place here is a by turns intriguing and absurd synthesis that rather nicely demonstrates how historical film and film history become entangled. Whatever one thinks of the Littleton–Malcor hypothesis of the breadth and influence of Ossetian culture, one cannot but be astonished by the ways in which *King Arthur* adapts it. According to Littleton and Malcor, some half million contemporary Ossetians living in southern Russia and on the steppes represent the survivors of a nomadic culture whose influence is said to have been vast. The western boundary of their ancient influence was supposedly Britain, where Sarmatian cavalry perhaps fought for the Roman leader Lucius Artorius Castus in the second century AD against the Picts and Scots. It is from this Sarmatian culture that Littleton and Malcor believe many

elements of the Arthurian legends derive. In an idea taken up more popularly by
Harold Reid in *Arthur the Dragon King* (2001: 223–6), Littleton has also traced the
Sarmatian influence eastward from the steppes all the way to Japan, where he has
found Arthur's double in the hero Yamoto-Takeru (1983, 1995). For Littleton, both
Arthur and Yamoto-Takeru derive from a "heroic tradition [that] has managed to
span the Eurasian landmass from one end to the other" (1995, 259). Both are thought
to have descended from the Sarmatian hero Batraz, whose adventures loom large in
the Ossetian Nart Sagas. In attempting to do justice to the breadth of territory
encompassed by the legendary descendants of Batraz, the film-makers seem to have
wanted their own recuperation of this monomyth to be equally expansive. They
include large-scale elements drawn from Japan and Russia in a syncretic version of
the Arthur story, yet these elements are drawn not from medieval folk tales but rather
from the films of the Japanese director Akira Kurosawa and the Soviet Sergei
Eisenstein.

Kurosawa's influence, both direct and filtered through the screen of Hollywood
westerns, is ubiquitous and sometimes profound. In the first action sequence of *King
Arthur*, Arthur and his knights ride down to the rescue in the V-formation that was
the trademark shot of the *Magnificent Seven* franchise, which the screenplay's novelization cutely dubs "the dragon formation" (Thompson 2004: 30). Throughout the film
the knights crowd the cinemascope screen, pulled into close proximity by the use
of a telephoto lens. Their horses are positively frenetic, shifting and snorting their
way through every sequence. These features of the cinematography are trademarks
of Kurosawa's *jidai-geki*. But rather than pile up disconnected references, let us look
first of all at an extended sequence that rather pointedly confirms the pastiche nature
of the film's Campbellesque monomyth. The extended tour of duty forced upon
Arthur and his knights surely sets up resonances with the extended and repeated
tours of American soldiers serving in Afghanistan and Iraq, who were also being
hounded by determined guerilla warfare (Aronstein 2005: 205–13). And as Tom
Shippey reminds us, the "final mission" topos has been a staple of post-Vietnam
film-making for some time (2007: 316–26). The unexpected placing of Marius's
Roman villa in the north of Britain beyond Hadrian's Wall has troubled many
reviewers but is explicable in terms of the film's hybrid historical and filmic antecedents. In their journey into southern Scotland, Arthur and his knights, located in
the Sarmatian second century, are attacked by the Woads (Picts), directed by Merlin.
One engagement that, according to medieval battle lists, did take place above the
Wall was the Battle of Celidon Wood, which Geoffrey of Monmouth lists as the
seventh of Arthur's battles and which Littleton and Malcor, following Jackson (1953:
48), place in the moorlands near the upper Clyde and Tweed valleys (2000: 330,
n.10). Unlike the earlier chronicler Nennius, Geoffrey makes the northern Picts and
Scots Arthur's adversaries in a number of engagements, and Littleton–Malcor read
back from this "evidence" to postulate that all twelve of their second-century hero's
battles were against the Picts and Scots in the north of Britain, the tenth occurring
in Celidon Wood.

In the film, as in Geoffrey's account, an entrapment is orchestrated by fencing off exits from the wood, and just as in Geoffrey the result is not a slaughter but rather a benign gesture of allowing the trapped soldiers to escape. Geoffrey claims that Merlin's mountain in Scotland was "encircled by hazels and thick thorns" (*precinctus corulis densisque frutectis*), making access difficult. This detail perhaps inspired the strategy of Merlin's ambush in the film, which entraps the knights within a labyrinth of barbed ropes that cut off their retreat. The Scottish location and the Pictish foes are certainly indebted to the Littleton–Malcor hypothesis, but most of the details are drawn not from "new evidence" but directly from that much-maligned source, Geoffrey of Monmouth.

In fact, both histories — medieval and modern — are really only raw materials contributing to a scene that owes less to the constructed career of Lucius Artorius Castus than to Kurosawa's version of Macbeth. The sequence restages a justly famous scene from Shakespeare's "Scottish tragedy," as reinterpreted by Kurosawa. In *Throne of Blood* (alternative title, *Spider Web Castle*, 1957) the Japanese reflexes of Macbeth and Banquo dash with increasing fear and frustration back and forth through "Spider Web Forest," only to come upon dead ends that appear out of thin air. In *King Arthur* the spider webs are fashioned from rope studded with Geoffrey of Monmouth's thorns, which the Woads shoot across the paths of the knights, weaving a web to trap their prey like so many spiders. In both films the riders finally conclude that they are trapped by supernatural forces: "Evil spirits," says Kurosawa's Washiro; "Inish, devil ghosts," says Fuqua's Dagonet.

More important for the film's imaginary convergence of feudal Japan with Dark Age Britain is its uncanny structuration of identity, class, and ethnicity in terms of Kurosawa's *Seven Samurai*. Upon their release from indentured servitude in the Roman legion, the Sarmatians become in effect masterless samurai, like Kurosawa's *ronin*, free to do as they like but alienated by their long service from home and family. *Pace* Tom Cruise, almost every great *chambara* is about "the last samurai." Initially Arthur's knights treat the Woads with the same contempt that Kurosawa's samurai at first display for the farmers who "hunt" them. In *Seven Samurai* the scene that brings class conflict to the fore and for a time allays it comes when the samurai discover a cache of weapons and armor hidden in the village that the farmers have despoiled from ambushed warriors. The seventh samurai, Kikuchiyo, himself a hybrid mixture of samurai and farmer, gives the *ronin* a lesson in class resentment:

> Farmers are stingy, foxy, blubbering, mean, stupid, and murderous! God damn! That's what they are! But then, who made them such beasts? You did! The samurai did it! You burn their villages, destroy their farms, steal their food, force them to labor, take their women! And kill them if they resist. So what should the farmers do? Damn . . . Damn! (Kurosawa, *Seven Samurai*)

Like Kurosawa's *ronin*, the Sarmatian knights were to begin as the scourge of the people they come to defend. When they arrive at Marius's villa they discover with disgust the reality of exploitation that their military service to Rome has supported, a colonial regime of forced labor, stolen food and women, murder, and torture.

The recurrent scenes of grave mounds with swords plunged into them would seem to allude to the "Sarmatian hypothesis" but again visually at least these scenes descend directly from Kurosawa. Both the screenplay and its novelization, in line with Sarmatian archaeology, call for the swords to be plunged to the hilt into the earth, leaving what would appear to be a small cross as a kind of headstone. The film, however, embeds the sword in the tumuli only a few inches, creating a marked citation of Kurosawa's film. In both films, after the first of the deaths, we are shown scenes in a graveyard on the outskirts of a village where Arthur/Kikuchiyo sit mourning a death for which they deem themselves responsible and where wine/sake is spilled onto a tumulus. These graves become an iconic marker in both films, an image to which the films repeatedly return. As Caroline Jewers remarks, these "echo the *ubi sunt* topos so beloved of epic" (2007), but this particular visualization of the topos is distinctly Kurosawan. In fact Fuqua's original cut – minus the happy ending – ended in more elegiac register similar to that of *Seven Samurai*, contrasting the grave mounds and their sword markers with the solemn survivors.

In *Seven Samurai* all four dead heroes are killed by matchlock rifles, weapons that Kurosawa typically puts in the hands of his villains. In *King Arthur* this rather anti-heroic imbalance is served by arming the Saxons with armor-piercing crossbows that take the lives of Dagonet and Lancelot. Tristan, like the sword-master in Kurosawa's film, goes on a scouting mission and brings back an example of this questionable technology as a trophy. Ultimately he is killed not by a crossbow but by a seax in a duel with Cerdic. Yet as in Kurosawa's film, these characteristic weapons of the enemy (crossbows and seax) are used to stigmatize their fighting styles as both figuratively and literally underhanded. Likewise, Arthur's knights are associated with their horses in a proleptic nod to the etymology of chivalry (Old French *cheval*, "horse") but with a nod as well toward the reincarnation and animism of Shinto Buddhism.

The notorious battle of Mount Badon, wherever it took place, was almost certainly not a siege but a pitched battle on an open plain. Franzioni's decision to site the battle in a fortified town on Hadrian's Wall allows the detailed imitation of Kurosawa to be completed. The opening of the sequence shows the Sarmatian knights abandoning the town to its fate in order to take the freedom that has been given them. The scene is based closely on Sturges' *The Magnificent Seven*, where the gunfighters leave the town before the final battle, though slowly change their minds as they again strap on their side-arms – an act which seems to recall them to their noble natures. The scene in *King Arthur* is vastly superior: there is no talking or debate, only confusion followed by stiffening resolve as they finally submit to their horses' unwillingness to continue along this rather selfish path. When they line up alongside Arthur on the hill over-looking the battlefield, Fuqua cannot resist another cinematic citation: in *Robin Hood, Prince of Thieves*, Kevin Costner's Robin and his Saracen friend (Morgan Freeman) converse beneath a tree in the Sycamore Gap, known locally as "Robin Hood's Tree," one of the sites offered on marketed tours of Hadrian's Wall. The Saxon spy is commanded by Cerdic to climb the tree for a better vantage point from which to view the slaughter of his own people. From an impossible distance hundreds of yards away and from within the fort, Tristan draws first blood in the battle by killing the traitor with a miraculous display of marksmanship worthy of Robin himself.

As the battle begins in earnest, it is clear that Arthur owes his art of war to Kurosawa's Kambei. One would expect that the officer of a Roman legion, whatever his name, would be reluctant to open a fortified position to the enemy. Cerdic realizes early on that "he's got a plan, this Roman." Indeed he has, as *Seven Samurai*'s Kambei puts it: "We'll let them in, not all of them at once. As soon as they enter, we shut the rest off and trap them. They'll be helpless. . . . They must be lured in." Though Fuqua's film employs more pyrotechnics and many more extras, Arthur's plan proceeds in exactly the same fashion. He allows the first wave through the gate and then has it closed behind them, only to open it again once they have been dispatched. Here as in Kurosawa's film the battle plan relies upon the coordination of different groups to attack the enemy from all directions at once. Even the now (in)famous shot showing Guinevere and a group of women taking down a wounded man has its source in Kurosawa, though Fuqua's version also nods in the direction of Boudicca, valkyries, and vampires.

Where Fuqua's film does finally diverge from Kurosawa's, particularly in the PG-rated version generally released, is in its happy ending. Like Kurosawa's samurai or Sturges' gunslingers, Fuqua's Sarmatians begin the film on the cusp of a social change that obviates their place in society. This identity crisis is momentarily bridged in all three films as the samurai/cowboys/Sarmatians heroically accept their role as protectors of the weak. In Kurosawa's version, however, this sense of belonging is cruelly foreshortened when, after the battle, the remaining samurai realize that only the farmers have really won anything and the three survivors leave the village just as they had entered it: alone, feared, and without a home. The Western remake of the film retains this sense of a rootless, vanishing breed in the two gunslingers but cushions the blow for audiences by allowing the Mexican ephebe to turn from the hired guns and to marry a native of the village. After an unsuccessful trial screening Fuqua was pressured into giving his film a softer ending, which ultimately concludes, like *The Magnificent Seven*, with a marriage, but also with a triumphant celebration of ethnogenesis.

Seven Samurai Meets *Alexander Nevsky*

While *Seven Samurai* certainly provides a key to Arthur's hybrid identity in Fuqua's film, the conflicts both internal and external in Kurosawa's work are based on class and the economic realities that underlie them. *The Magnificent Seven* goes some way toward recasting these conflicts in terms of ethnicity, wherein white gunslingers from the north aided by their own hybrid figure – a young Mexican wannabe gunslinger –

intervene in a conflict between bandits and villagers south of the border. However, neither in Kurosawa's film nor even in his epigones is the moral nature of the conflict so clearly a matter of right versus wrong, of good versus evil, as it is in Fuqua's *King Arthur*.

Earlier I invoked Siegfried Kracauer's notion that "collective desires" are manifested and indeed encouraged by historical fantasies. This is perhaps nowhere more evident than in *King Arthur*'s imaginary reconstruction of Dark Age ethnicity in the Manichean binary of Sergei Eisenstein's *Alexander Nevsky*. Perhaps the greatest propaganda film ever made, Eisenstein's masterpiece pits a nation uniting under a charismatic leader against a Teutonic invasion in league with a cynical and opportunistic Catholic Church. Sound familiar? Eisenstein's Manichean fantasy certainly deserves our respect: it is a superb film made in the shadow of Nazi Germany's rise to the status of an international menace, while Eisenstein's next work, *Ivan the Terrible*, devastatingly undermines the authoritarian streak of the earlier film in its evocation of Tsarist cruelty and paranoid suspicion. But *King Arthur*'s deployment of Eisenstein's *Nevsky* represents what I see as a dangerous trend in contemporary cinémedievalism, which might be dubbed Manichean nostalgia. With no disrespect to critics who have seen the film's ideology as reflecting current or more recent wars such as those in Vietnam (Jewers 2007; Shippey 2007) or the Persian Gulf (Aronstein 2005), I see the film as profoundly nostalgic for the ethical clarities of World War II. Such nostalgia for Manichean clarity is also evident in the recent film versions of the post-War fiction of J. R. R. Tolkien and C. S. Lewis.

Eisenstein's film was originally entitled *Rus!* – the rallying cry of the Russian forces in his film. The same cry is adopted by the Sarmatian knights in *King Arthur* to express solidarity with the ancient Ossetian culture from which they putatively derive. The cry echoes throughout *King Arthur*, particularly from the character Bors, who typically makes the connection explicit by screaming "Artorius!" and then "Rus!" After the marriage of Arthur and Guinevere has united the Sarmatians with the native peoples of Britain, Bors again bellows "Artorius!" and then sheepishly omits the "Rus!" as no longer appropriate. His silence signals a recognition of the difference this marriage makes, the imaginary unification of Britain under a single leader. Against this in both films are posed the mute synecdoches of a proto-Nazi salute: open, extended hands adorn the helmets of the Teutonic hordes in *Nevsky*, while the Roman Marius in *King Arthur* receives a Nazi salute from a soldier whose body remains outside the frame. The twentieth century is proleptically signified as that which gave body and voice to these truncated gestures of unquestioned obedience.

The extended sequence in the colonial villa of the aristocratic Marius is a devastating depiction of a monster realized as a Roman Catholic. The episode, I would argue, is a euhemerized interpretation of the monstrous "saint" of Mont-Saint-Michel in the Alliterative *Morte Arthure* and the fifth book of Thomas Malory's *Morte Darthur*, inspired by the equally barbarous slaughter of the innocents in *Nevsky*. Euhemerism is a common tactic in postmodern movie medievalism, activated to offer rational explanations for medieval myths. Fuqua's Marius is not the giant cannibal of medieval legend, merely a fat, petty despot who thinks himself a "saint" and who starves the native populace to death in order to enrich himself. Like the monster of Mont-Saint-Michel, Marius signifies the inhumanity of Rome's boundless acquisitiveness. His colonial villa has, like Malory's Lucius, *an egle displayed on loffte* (Shepherd 2004: 126). But like the giant of Mont-Saint-Michel, the dark secret of his perversity can be discovered by following one's nose "to the source of the reek" of rotting flesh (Alliterative *Morte Arthure*, line 1041). If the giant is a grotesque parody of the Catholic Eucharist, Marius parodies the devotion of anchorites by entombing the disobedient in an anchorhold and slowly starving them to death, while his monks chant masses for their souls. The alleged complicity of the Roman Catholic Church in the Nazi "final solution" thus gains an imagined analogue in Dark Age Britain, inspired by a Stalinist reading of thirteenth-century Russian history.

The eroticization of nationalism is an important theme in *Nevsky*, and Fuqua's film assiduously follows suit. Lancelot loses the contest of smoldering glances to Arthur simply because the latter is the more selfless defender of Britain. The love triangle is resolved in different ways in the two films, but crucial to each is the introduction of the Bolshevik idea of the woman warrior. Like Eisenstein's Vasalisy and Besson's Joan of Arc, Guinevere goes to war less as a gender warrior than as an embodiment of nationalism itself. Rather disappointingly for many, including Caroline Jewers (2007) and myself (though perhaps for different reasons), the Bacchic exploits of Guinevere (played by Keira Knightley) are soon complete. She discards her leather-thong bikini and paint-on tattoos for a white wedding gown. Having played her part as the Arthurian counterpart of the woman warrior Vasalisy, she humbly assumes a role equivalent to the more docile Olga, a prize that goes to her nation's staunchest defender.

The "battle on the ice" of Lake Chudskoe is rightly regarded as one of Eisenstein's most accomplished set pieces and the homage to it in *King Arthur* is a more than adept stylization. Like the "Odessa Steps" sequence in *Battleship Potemkin*, the ice battle has become a cinematic *tour de force*. Fuqua here rises to the challenge by producing some remarkable shots, like the camera tracking the cracking ice or the *memento mori* shot of the Saxon Cynric, who sees the face of a drowned comrade beneath the ice. The sequence was shot in a green valley in County Kildare, Ireland, seeded with gravel and fake snow, employing dozens of cameras. The snow-capped mountains and gray sky were added later by CGI and the footage intercut with shots filmed in studio water tanks (figure 35.1). While the result achieved never quite lives up to Eisenstein, who was working with a much smaller toolbox, it too is a splendid set piece. We will take up below the virtual nature of cinémedievalism and how its production of immediacy and realism relies upon the ever more complicated pastiche of multiple simulations.

Here though I want rather to focus on the elemental nature of the battle itself as an example of what Frantz Fanon (1991) dubbed "Manichean delirium" to denote the paroxysms of binary thinking that are a stubborn inheritance of colonialism. Arthur, his mounted Sarmatian knights, and a long caravan of serfs and wagons travel along

Figure 35.1 King Arthur (2004). The battle on the ice, before and after CGI.

the ice, eliciting little more than a few ominous creaking sounds. Their combined
weight would be many times that of the small force of foot-soldiers led by Cynric
which finally catches up to them on the frozen river. Since neither of the opposing
leaders thinks to hug the shoreline, the two armies face off and prepare for battle on
(relatively) thin ice. The first clue that we have entered an imaginary world of moral
physics comes when Cynric's archer fires an arrow that skids to a stop a hundred feet
or so before reaching its target. Tristan and Gawain respond in kind, the former
shooting three arrows at once, all of which find their marks in Saxon chests with such
force that they are knocked over backwards. There is no wind in the scene; the success
of the Sarmatians clearly points to an abundant superiority, but of what kind exactly?
As the Saxons advance, Arthur instructs his archers to "make them cluster," employing, *mutatis mutandis*, the pincer tactics of Eisenstein's Alexander. When the ice refuses
to break, Dagonet runs into the breach and chops a hole in the ice, which does not
fracture radially but rather beats a direct path for the Saxons and explodes into large
fragments. There are accomplished shots of Saxons sliding down vertical planes of ice
into the cold water, shots that directly imitate those of Eisenstein. The cracking ice
takes some time to turn back in the other direction and threaten the Sarmatians, but

none falls through the ice except for Dagonet, who is already dead before he hits the water. The ice weighs in balance the fates of the two sides and evil is plunged into the depths. Only when most of the Saxons have already fallen into the water does the balance shift and the miraculous crack turn in the opposite direction. This strange physical world is only explicable in Manichean terms. The Sarmatians' arrows fly further and their feet tread more softly than those of the Saxons: the spirit riseth up and the flesh presseth down.

Romancing Genetics

There is a better chance that the Saxon leader Cerdic was actually the historical Arthur than that he and his son Cynric were killed at the battle of Mount Badon. Cerdic went on to found the West Saxon dynasty, which his son continued. He is certainly the prototype of the salt-of-the-earth Cedric the Saxon in Walter Scott's *Ivanhoe*. In *King Arthur*, the character of Cerdic despotically enforces genetic purity among his soldiers: the brief *witena gemot* on the rights of victors to the spoils of war ends abruptly when he executes a soldier attempting to rape a native – and then shocks the grateful damsel in distress by ordering her death as well. "Don't touch their women. We don't mix with these people. What kind of offspring do you think that would yield? Weak people, half people. I will not have our Saxon blood watered down by mixing with them." Cerdic's anti-miscegenation policy in many ways takes its clue from the now discredited Anglo-Saxonism or Aryanism of the nineteenth and earlier twentieth centuries, which judged the British Isles overwhelmingly Germanic once the native inhabitants had been geographically marginalized, exterminated, or bred nearly out of existence. A number of recent books trace the rise and obsolescence of what Hugh A. MacDougall calls "racial myth in English history," which conceived Germanic peoples as marked by their unmixed heredity and the English as the especially favored descendants of these tribes, pioneers of personal liberty and political freedoms (MacDougall 1982; Frantzen 1990; Geary 2002; Higham 2002). Now the pendulum has swung in the opposite direction and connections are routinely drawn between Anglo-Saxonism and Victorian imperialism. The rise of historical linguistics in the nineteenth century eventually challenged underlying assumptions about connections between race and language. And the advent of Nazi Germany demonstrated the horrors that grow not simply from racism itself but from attempts to connect race and nationality.

From the perspective of contemporary advances in genetic mapping, such as the work of Brian Sykes (2006), Cerdic's quest for Saxon purity has been dealt a mortal blow. Sykes puts the total genetic inheritance of Germanic peoples in the British Isles at no more than 30 percent and attributes the lion's share of that to the later Viking/ Norman incursions. For our purposes, what most fascinates in Sykes' approach are his meditations on how gender differences are expressed in the gene pool of Britain. He expresses a clear preference for mitochondrial DNA, which records the female line, and a more ambivalent attitude toward the weak and unstable Y-chromosome, which leads men toward violence:

> The first conclusion, blindingly obvious now I can see it, is that we have in front of us two completely different histories. The maternal and the paternal origins of the Isles are different. . . . On our (i.e., British) maternal side, almost all of us are Celts. (Sykes 2006: 279–81)

In Eisenstein's *Alexander Nevsky* the Teutonic warlord orders a holocaust: "Wipe them off the face of the earth." Cerdic in *King Arthur* is equally unequivocal: "Burn it all. Never leave behind you a man, woman or child that can ever bear a sword." Indeed, like the German commander in *Alexander Nevsky*, Cerdic is a Nazi calque. The novelization of the screenplay has him exclaim, "We must cleanse the earth!" (Thompson 2004: 97). Later, he recalls the clansmen of Griffith's *Birth of a Nation* (1915) when he raises a burning cross in front of Hadrian's Wall: "The massive flame cracked and roared. No one had encountered such a thing before, but they all knew what it meant. The Saxons were promising total defeat, absolute annihilation" (Thompson 2004: 258). Not surprisingly, this needlessly provocative image was left out of the film.

On the other hand, Fuqua's Guinevere represents the Celtic bedrock, a daughter of one of Sykes' seven daughters of Eve, probably Jasmine, whose descendants appear to have migrated after the Great Ice Age over the course of many generations from the Near East through Portugal and Spain to settle eventually in "Cornwall, Wales and the west of Scotland" (Sykes 2001: 209). Early on in *King Arthur*, Guinevere tells Arthur, "I belong to this land," and then goes on to equate Arthur's father having chosen a native Briton as his wife with an affection for Britain itself in an erotically charged piece of dialogue. The ethnic components of Arthur's identity are parsed; she detests his Roman side and appeals both sexually and politically to his Celtic side. Arthur's hybridity highlights the structure of what Jeffrey Jerome Cohen (2000) has dubbed "the postcolonial Middle Ages" quite distinctly. Guinevere chips away at his collaboration with the Roman oppressors of a people he will belatedly accept as his own. In the rationalist euhemerism of the film, Arthur as a child pulls Excalibur from the ground in a failed attempt to save the life of his Celtic mother. As Merlin tells him: "It was love of your mother, Arthur, not hatred of me that freed that sword." The pulling of the sword from the earth, then, signifies that Arthur's legitimacy to rule comes not from Rome but from his "feminine," Celtic side. Personal liberties and political freedoms are shown to descend not from ancient "democracies" or the "English Constitution" so touted by traditional classicism or Anglo-Saxonism, but rather from the oppressed, blue-faced but red-blooded Celtic fringe of *Braveheart*. Even the reincarnation central to the Arthurian myth of a once and future king is given a politically correct twist. Boudicca-like, Guinevere is entombed by the Romans but revived by Arthur to lead her people in their time of need against a new enemy, the Saxons (figure 35.2).

Figure 35.2 King Arthur (2004). Keira Knightley as Guinevere, woad warrior queen.

Playing (with) the Legend

One thing that perhaps helps to account for our frustration with the fantasy history of cinémedievalism is the promise that the medium once held out to many to have the capacity to deliver faithful representations of reality. Discussing Andre Bazin's comment on the advance of cinema technologies that "every new development must, paradoxically, take it nearer and nearer to its origins," Robert Burgoyne (2003: 234) remarks that this has in fact come true, though in a very different sense from that which Bazin anticipated. Although Bazin may have meant that cinema would eventually arrive at a perfect replication of the real, CGI in fact pushes cinema's origins back beyond the nineteenth- and twentieth-century dream of the mechanical or electronic reproduction of reality, all the way to pre-modernity, to medieval or mythic times when the lines between fantasy, fact, and speculation were not yet clearly drawn. We are now just at the outset of a technology that, like the recent *300* (Snyder 2006), can represent history and legend almost exclusively by computer-generated animation.

These are issues too large to unpack in any further detail here, but instead I want to focus briefly in the conclusion of this chapter on how the reality effects of film serve to anchor further excursions into the virtual space of video games through the cinematic device *par excellence*, montage. My argument is that virtual representations are often posed as hidden or spiritual realities beneath, behind, or beside the world as we have been led to know it. This spiritual reality is animated like the classical moving picture itself by rendering continuity through an erasure of the boundaries between discrete images. In the video game *Lara Croft, Tomb Raider: Legend* (2006), in Glastonbury, the city of glass, Lara Croft watches through a glass darkly as her mother in a parallel universe makes the fatal mistake of pulling the sword from the stone, urged on by a doltish Eve-figure, Amanda, ensuring that the past is repeated. In the made-for-TV mini-series *Mists of Avalon*, Morgaine learns to part the mists of Glastonbury to gain access to the hidden world of Avalon, which also seems to exist in a parallel space–time continuum. These games and films actualize virtual spaces that one could argue are present in the legend from the outset, the spaces of an imaginary archaeology, typically gendered feminine, which invite descendants to participate in their recovery while exposing them to the dangers of compulsive repetitions.

Ideally, video games made to accompany digital cinema would be crystalline images of the worlds they supplement, allowing players to deterritorialize films, to actualize what is only virtual in them, to render the opaque transparent. Recent franchises like *The Matrix*, *Stars Wars*, and *Harry Potter* spread their stories across a series of media, encouraging the audience to participate in what Henry Jenkins (2006) calls "transmedia storytelling." Certainly the economic motivations of such a marketing strategy are paramount, creating multiple points of access to a franchise and encouraging brand loyalty by the dispersal of information across old and new media. Saturation marketing invites audience participation as nominal co-creators of a franchise through a "fan culture" of merchandising, internet chat, fan fiction, and even fan cinema. *King Arthur* in many ways represents a much less successful attempt to capitalize on this "culture of convergence." Yet its strategies of convergence do represent a trend with which critics of movie medievalism will increasingly be forced to reckon.

The *King Arthur* video game itself begins with an extended "cut scene" which reproduces the opening of the film up to the point when the *kagemusha* "bishop" looks out of the window at the invading Picts and three bolts smack the carriage next to his head. Here a match cut takes us to this same shot in virtual reality, easing our integration from film to game world. In fact the cut scenes in their low-density resolution closely resemble the pixelation of the game's virtual world. Interestingly, the transition between film and game takes place at a window, the metaphor *par excellence* for hyperspace: part screen, mirror, and window (Friedberg 2006). Like the mists of Avalon and the glass of Glastonbury in the examples discussed above, the window in the film/game is the threshold that marks an ontological cut, a window within a window whose *mise-en-abyme* is charged with a titillating hint of scopophobia.

Unfortunately, things through the looking glass are pretty much the same. The goal of the game interspersed with cut scenes is to reproduce precisely what happens in the film. Failure to do so results in death and an invitation to restart the challenge. The game maps the film as a quest along a circular path through the English midlands and the north of Britain, punctuated by six rabbit holes into virtual space, proceeding roughly due north and returning on a parallel road south. Killing sufficient numbers of the enemy endows one with a shining aura that, as in the Homeric *aristeia*, invests the warrior with superhuman powers. Passing through the various levels, one earns tokens such as increasing strength or experience until, fully charged with all available powers, one meets Cerdic in a final showdown at Mount Badon. Indeed, to reach the level of this duel one has to have killed something very close to the nine hundred and sixty enemies Arthur himself is credited with killing in the early histories.

The synergy between film and game begins in fact to look like part of an original strategy rather than something added *post hoc*. One would expect a Roman legion to fight with spears and gladii and to dress in the same uniform, but in both film and game each of Arthur's Sarmatian knights is distinguished by his weaponry, dress, and movements. For instance, Tristan wears what appears to be a Sarmatian pointed cap and sports a Saracen sword and re-curved bow; Gawain's weapon of choice is a giserne; Lancelot is the knight of two swords; and Bors wields a ninja-like configuration of brass knuckles and forearm blades. All this paraphernalia can be a bit distracting in the film, but along with the individuated fighting styles of different characters the details seem to stem from a planned convergence with the world of the video game where such means of individualized characterization are a staple of game programming, encouraging players to identify with separate characters and to be able distinguish one from another. Thus in both film and game Arthur's "signature moves" include a slashing pirouette and a kill-shot performed with the sword held overhand below shoulder level, Lancelot turns his two swords into a pair of scissors to cut off the heads of his victims, and Tristan has a rapid-fire feature allowing him to loose three arrows in machine-gun-like succession. Conversely (and absurdly) the ice battle sequence in the game recalls an arcade game where sheets of ice stand on end and one must shoot through the gaps to kill the Saxons on the other side. Albeit rarely, one does get to walk through doors the film does not open, as in figure 35.3 within the walls of Marius's palace. The game and the film seem part of a single overall design where both convergence and divergence are deliberately planned to compose variegated worlds.

Finally, from my discussion of *King Arthur*, it is possible to draw at least three generally applicable lessons for the study of contemporary cinémedievalism. First, while medievalists will always be tempted to compare these films to medieval sources or academic scholarship, cinema too has a history through which it interprets and reconstructs the past. This particular film's convergence of speculative scholarship with auteur cinema is remarkable, but the phenomenon of such mixtures is not. Second, we must be attuned not simply to the risible rhetoric of "the truth behind the legend" but also to the popular science that underwrites this endless production of a more "authentic" past. Lastly, and perhaps most importantly, we must not re-erect the wall that used to separate film and written documents between film and newer media. The texts that increasingly engage students of cinémedievalism are perhaps best described by Jenkins' term "world-making," which includes not only the imaginary ontology of such texts but also their desire to produce a sustainable and multivalent media franchise, coherent in itself but remaining open to future development.

Figure 35.3 Inside Marius's villa in the *King Arthur* video game.

Increasingly, these franchises and not simply the films in isolation will become objects of study. All three lessons fit neatly under a single rubric: convergence. But of course convergence has been the defining if not enabling trait of medievalism as well as Arthurianism all along, at least since the moment Caxton decided to merge Malory's tales into a printed book and thereby created the single most successful franchise in storytelling history.

Primary Sources

Benson, L. D. (ed.) (1994). *King Arthur's death: The Middle English Stanzaic Morte Arthur and Alliterative Morte Arthure*, rev. edn (ed. E. D. Forster). Kalamazoo, MI: Medieval Institute Publications.

Franzioni, D., with Matthews, J. (2004). Interview with David Franzioni. *Arthuriana*, 14(3), 115–20.

Shepherd, S. H. A. (ed.) (2004). *Malory. Le Morte Darthur*. New York: Norton.

Thompson, F. (2004). *King Arthur* (novelization of David Franzioni's screenplay). New York: Hyperion.

Thorpe, L. (trans.) (1966). *Geoffrey of Monmouth. History of the kings of Britain*. New York: Penguin.

References and Further Reading

Aberth, J. (2003). *A knight at the movies: Medieval history on film*. New York: Routledge.

Ackroyd, P. (2002). *Albion: The origins of the English imagination*. New York: Anchor.

Aronstein, S. (2005). *Hollywood knights: Arthurian cinema and the politics of nostalgia*. New York: Palgrave.

Baudrillard, J. (1994). *Simulacra and simulation* (trans. S. F. Glaser). Ann Arbor, MI: University of Michigan Press.

Burgoyne, R. (2003). Memory, history and digital imagery in contemporary film. In P. Grainge (ed.), *Memory and popular film*. Manchester: Manchester University Press, pp. 220–36.

Cohen, J. J. (ed.) (2000). *The postcolonial Middle Ages*. New York: Palgrave.

Deleuze, G. (1986). *Cinema 1: The movement-image* (trans H. Tomlinson & B. Habberjam). Minneapolis, MN: University of Minnesota Press.

Deleuze, G. (1989). *Cinema 2: The time-image* (trans H. Tomlinson & R. Galeta). Minneapolis, MN: University of Minnesota Press.

Fanon, F. (1991). *Black skin, white masks* (trans. C. Farrington). New York: Grove Press.

Finke, L. A. & Shichtman, M. B. (2004). *King Arthur and the myth of history*. Gainesville, FL: University Press of Florida.

Frantzen, A. J. (1990). *Desire for origins: New language, Old English and teaching the tradition*. New Brunswick, NJ: Rutgers University Press.

Friedberg, A. (2006). *The virtual window: From Alberti to Microsoft*. Cambridge, MA: MIT Press.

Geary, P. J. (2002). *The myth of nations: The medieval origins of Europe*. Princeton, NJ: Princeton University Press.

Harty, K. J. (ed.) (2002). *Cinema Arthuriana: Twenty essays*. Jefferson, NC: McFarland.

Harty, K. J. (2004). Review of *King Arthur*. *Arthuriana*, 14(3), 121–3.

Haydock, N. (2002). Arthurian melodrama, Chaucerian spectacle, and the waywardness of cinematic pastiche in *First Knight* and *A Knight's Tale*. In T. Shippey & M. Arnold (eds), *Film and fiction: Reviewing the Middle Ages*. Cambridge: Brewer, pp. 5–38.

Haydock, N. (2007). Shooting the messenger: Luc Besson at war with Joan of Arc. *Exemplaria*, 19, 243–69.

Haydock, N. (2008). *Movie medievalism: The imaginary Middle Ages*. Jefferson, NC: McFarland.

Higham, N. J. (2002). *King Arthur: Myth-making and history*. London: Routledge.

Jackson, K. H. (1953). *Language and history in early Britain*. Edinburgh: Edinburgh University Press.

Jenkins, H. (2006). *Convergence culture: Where old and new media collide*. New York: New York University Press.

Jewers, C. (2007). Mission historical, or "[T]here were a hell of a lot of knights": Ethnicity and alterity in Jerry Bruckheimer's *King Arthur*. In L. T. Ramey & T. Pugh (eds), *Race, class, and gender in "medieval" cinema*. New York: Palgrave, pp. 91–106.

Kracauer, S. (1960). *Theory of film: The redemption of physical reality*. London: Oxford University Press.

Kracauer, S. (2004). *From Caligari to Hitler: A psychological history of the German film*. Princeton, NJ: Princeton University Press. (Originally published 1947.)

Landy, M. (1996). *Cinematic uses of the past*. Minneapolis, MN: University of Minnesota Press.

Landy, M. (ed.) (2001). *The historical film: History and memory in media*. New Brunswick, NJ: Rutgers University Press.

Littleton, C. S. (1983). Some possible Arthurian themes in Japanese mythology and folklore. *Journal of Folklore Research*, 20, 67–82.

Littleton, C. S. (1995). Yamoto-Takeru: An "Arthurian" hero in Japanese tradition. *Asian Folklore Studies*, 54, 259–74.

Littleton, C. S. & Malcor, L. A. (2000). *From Scythia to Camelot: A radical reassessment of the legends of King Arthur, the Knights of the Round Table, and the Holy Grail*. New York: Garland (originally published 1994).

Lupack, A. (2004). Review of *King Arthur*. *Arthuriana*, 14(3), 123–5.

MacDougall, H. A. (1982). *Racial myth in English history: Trojans, Teutons, and Anglo-Saxons*. Hanover, NH: University Press of New England.

Reid, H. (2001). *Arthur the dragon king: The barbaric roots of Britain's greatest legend*. London: Headline.

Rosenstone, R. A. (2006). *History on film/film on history*. New York: Pearson Longman.

Shippey, T. (2007). Fuqua's *King Arthur*: More mythmaking in America. *Exemplaria*, 19(2), 310–26.

Sykes, B. (2001). *The seven daughters of Eve: The science that reveals our genetic ancestry*. New York: Norton.

Sykes, B. (2006). *Saxons, Vikings, and Celts: The genetic roots of Britain and Ireland*. New York: Norton.

FILMOGRAPHY

300 (2006). Dir. Zack Snyder. Warner Bros Pictures.

Alexander Nevsky (1938). Dir. Sergei Eisenstein. Mosfilm.

Battleship Potemkin (1925). Dir. Sergei Eisenstein. Goskino.

The Birth of a Nation (alternative title *The Clansman*) (1915). Dir. D. W. Griffith. David W. Griffith Corp.

Braveheart (1995). Dir. Mel Gibson. Icon Productions.

Ivan the Terrible, Part One (1944). Dir. Sergei Eisenstein. Alma Ata Studio.

Ivan the Terrible, Part Two (1958). Dir. Sergei Eisenstein. Alma Ata Studio.

King Arthur (2004). Dir. Antoine Fuqua. Touchstone Pictures.

King Arthur video game (2004). Krome Studios.

Lara Croft, Tomb Raider: Legend video game (2006). Eidos Interactive.

The Last Samurai (2003). Dir. Edward Zwick. Warner Bros Pictures.

The Magnificent Seven (1960). Dir. Preston Sturges. Mirisch Corporation.

Robin Hood, Prince of Thieves (1991). Dir. Kevin Reynolds. Warner Bros Pictures.

Seven Samurai (1954). Dir. Akira Kurosawa. Toho Company.

Throne of Blood (alternative title *Spider Web Castle*) (1957). Dir. Akira Kurosawa. Toho Company.

Index

Printed and bound by CPI Group (UK) Ltd, Croydon, CR0 4YY